SOUTHERN STORM

SOUTHERN STORM

Sherman's March to the Sea

NOAH ANDRE TRUDEAU

HARPER

An Imprint of HarperCollins*Publishers*
www.harpercollins.com

HarperCollins books may be purchased for educational, business,
or sales promotional use. For information, please write:
Special Markets Department, HarperCollins Publishers,
10 East 53rd Street, New York, NY 10022.

All photographs courtesy of the Library of Congress.
All drawings first appeared in *Harper's Weekly* magazine, 1861–1862.

Designed by Kara Strubel

Library of Congress Cataloging-in-Publication Data

Trudeau, Noah Andre
Southern storm : Sherman's march to the sea /
Noah Andre Trudeau—1st ed.
p cm.
Includes bibliographical references and index.
ISBN: 978-0-06-059867-9
1. Georgia—History—Civil War, 1861–1865—Campaigns. 2. Sherman,
William T. (William Tecumseh), 1820–1891. I. Title.
E476.69.T78 2008
973'.378—dc22   2007041326

08 09 10 11 12 DIX/RRD 10 9 8 7 6 5 4 3 2

Dedicated to the memory of Burke Davis (1913–2006).

First on the ground to Appomattox
and first with Sherman to the sea.

Contents

Preface   ix
Author's Note   xiii
List of Maps   xv

PART ONE: *Preparation*

1 A Gathering of Eagles   3
2 Captive Audiences   14
3 The Stormbringer   23
4 The Plan   33
5 "Paradise of Fools"   59

PART TWO: *Atlanta to Milledgeville, November 15–24*

6 "Dies Irae Filled the Air"   75
7 "Lurid Flames Lit Up the Heavens"   89
8 "Forage of All Kinds Abounds"   105
9 "Arise for the Defense of Your Native Soil!"   122
10 "Whites Look Sour & Sad"   138
11 "Ugly Weather"   152
12 "But Bless God, He Died Free!"   169
13 "We 'Shot Low and to Kill' "   182
14 "The First Act Is Well Played"   216

PART THREE: *Milledgeville to Millen,*
                    November 25–December 4

15 "We Went for Them on the Run"   241
16 "Poor Foolish Simpletons"   255
17 "I Never Was So Frightened in All My Life"   268
18 "Give Those Fellows a Start"   307

Contents

PART FOUR: *Millen to Savannah,*
December 5–10

19   "Splendid Sight to See Cotton Gins Burn"   347

PART FIVE: *Savannah,*
December 11–January 21

20   "I Was Soon Covered with Blood
     from Head to Foot"   405
21   "I Beg to Present You as a Christmas Gift
     the City of Savannah"   459
22   "But What Next?"   509

PART SIX: *Finale*

23   "The Blow Was Struck at the Right Moment
     and in the Right Direction"   525

Union Forces Roster   549
Confederate Forces Roster   559
Chapter Notes   565
Bibliography   613
Acknowledgments   653
Index   657

Preface

On December 21, 1864, two young men—hardened for military campaigning and always ready for adventure—crossed paths in the main office of the *New York Herald*. Each was an experienced reporter just returned from a major campaign. John Edward Parker ("Jep") Doyle had marched with Sherman from Atlanta to the sea. David Power Conyngham had been at Nashville when George H. Thomas had wrecked John B. Hood's Rebel army. Both had vivid stories to tell, stories that would soon be conveyed in the *Herald*'s tightly packed columns for days to come. As was common practice in that day, small-market papers clipped and pasted the coverage in their own sheets, so these accounts would circulate well beyond the New York area. By then Conyngham and Doyle had returned to the front (both now with Sherman) to pick up the story and carry it through to the end.

Even before the dramatic year 1865 was over, a book would appear that offered a striking narrative of Sherman's campaign across Georgia, one that was rich with detail and well supplied with lively anecdotes and character sketches. The book almost immediately became the template for all subsequent accounts of this operation, with a staying power that is impressive. One distinguished scholar, writing just after the United States marked its Civil War centennial, proclaimed it an "indispensable volume for anyone studying Sherman's famous campaign," and it has appeared in Sherman biographical bibliographies extending into the twenty-first century. Its author was David Power Conyngham.

Make no mistake, Conyngham did his homework. He drew from accounts penned by fellow correspondents who had been with the march, and he used his personal contacts among the army's officer corps to fill in the spaces. Save for the fact that he was not actually present for the scenes he so vividly describes as a firsthand participant, Conyngham's account had sufficient truth about it that generations of later writers turned to it as the real thing.

Thus, from the very beginning, the story of Sherman's March to the Sea was once removed from primary sources and subject to the dramatic sculpting of a skilled adapter. From that first subtly false step, the saga of the March to the Sea was catapulted into the realm of myth and legend.

Everyone knows Sherman's March. Just to say the words is to select from a list of mental images of destructiveness, raw power, civil terror, and youthful adventure whose choice depends a great deal on where one encountered Civil War 101. Many of the memoirs of actual military participants compound the problem rather than resolve it. The most successful compress events into a narrative that is often generalized as to time or place, and which often combines several incidents into one. The most enduring memoirs of Sherman's March represent a personal condensation, simplification, and intensification of what was actually experienced. It is on this ever so slightly distorted foundation of reality that the widely understood story of Sherman's March rests.

In the pages that follow I have attempted to compensate for that distortion. I have relied heavily on actual diaries and period letters from participants military and civilian. Taken individually, most of these diaries are unremarkable, some downright boring. Cumulatively, however, a wealth of little details emerge that helped me sharpen the viewfinder. I quickly realized that some of the official reports, especially those for the cavalry operations on both sides, were not to be taken at face value. Throughout my treatment of these movements and actions, I relied on available diaries and letters to keep things honest, to which I added healthy doses of what I hoped was common sense.

Sherman, too, despite an outspokenness that often passes for frankness, needed to be handled with care. Here, fortunately, I had the invaluable journals of Henry Hitchcock, George Nichols, and others on the General's staff to balance things. The fine selection of contemporary dispatches written in the field that are found in the official records further helped me determine what Sherman knew and when he knew it. The standard story has the General fixed on his objective from the moment his legions departed Atlanta; in reality, he kept his options open until he finally had to commit himself in early December. Instead of an exercise of predestination, I approached this as any other military campaign, subject to all the uncertainties and improvisations that such implies.

One source you will see indirectly acknowledged in the bibliography is the network of narrative historical markers erected over the years along the various routes of Sherman's operation. Graced by texts and research provided by two able Georgia historians—Wilbur G. Kurtz Sr. and Allen P. Julian—they contain countless little details regarding roads taken or residences visited. Sadly, many were missing when I passed through, others had been relocated, but the texts for all have been preserved. Even as I write this, the state of Georgia is constructing a new series of markers as part of a heritage trail. From the preliminary materials I have seen, it promises to be a significant addition to our understanding of the March to the Sea.

A part of the saga that interested me very much was the weather story. The generalized narratives I encountered seemed to suggest sunshine and blue skies for the entire journey. Yet daily logs kept by participants told a very different story. In the process of trying to make sense out of those entries, I found that even the most mundane diary of Sherman's March usually had some things to say about the weather on a given day. When I indexed these together and compiled them chronologically, I realized that on any given twenty-four-hour period I had a dozen or more weather observations. To be sure, the data were subjective ("cold," "warm," "cool," or "hot" for temperature, for instance), but when they were taken as a group, a consensus of weather conditions emerged and became part of my story. Based on the information in those diaries, I calculated the temperature ranges you will see for each day of the march.

A fair number of diary entries for soldiers taking part in this campaign are best summarized with the phrase: "Nothing of interest to report." Yet when one takes into account the totality of the fifty or so diaries with entries for a particular day, I never found that to be the case. I was continually amazed at the rich variety of small, personal stories that emerged. It is part of my hope that by following the march from day to day, and fitting these stories into the fabric of the whole, a more truthful narrative of events will emerge. I hope too that it is a more compelling one.

Author's Note

A basic understanding of Civil War military organization, tactics, and weapons is assumed in the text that follows, so a brief primer may not be out of place here. For the most part, the military forces of each side were organized along the same hierarchy: in descending order of size, corps, divisions, brigades, regiments, and companies. The Union forces engaged in the Savannah Campaign were organized along traditional lines. Like their cobelligerents in the east, those in the west tended to follow a numbering system (e.g., Seventeenth Corps, First Division, Second Brigade) and when I am referring to those units with the names of their commanders I have not capitalized the result (e.g., Geary's division, Carmen's brigade). Regiments are always referred to by their number and state, such as the 4th Minnesota. The Confederate organization in this campaign was much more problematical. It represented an ad hoc mix of "regular" Confederate States units (mostly belonging to Wheeler's cavalry corps) and Georgia state units, which were themselves of various kinds. The Confederate roster at the end of this book does not reflect an actual table of organization at any part of the campaign, but is simply a means of visually organizing the disparate commands that at one time or another and in one way or another, between November 15 and December 21, 1864, got in Sherman's path.

The two essential unit formations, at least as far as this book is concerned, are column and line. Column is a marching formation; usually three or four abreast, a column packed a regiment into as compact a space as practicable for rapid movement along a road or across open ground. Once engaged in combat, columns transformed into lines of battle, usually at least two, sometimes three with the third a reserve. The ends of a line were its flanks; the process of bending back a segment of the line so that the men stood at an angle to their original orientation was called refusing the flank.

The standard combat formation relied on a massing of rifles and the resultant firepower for its effect. Often positioned in advance of the compact lines of battle were more widely dispersed and irregular detachments known as skirmish lines. Most references to the soldiers involved in this duty are as skirmishers; sometimes I employ the word *voltigeurs*—a French equivalent. During periods of rest, Civil War military units were usually surrounded by a ring of armed outposts called a picket line. The function of these small detachments was to provide security to the encampment and serve as a tripwire against any enemy effort to surprise the main body. These soldiers are chiefly referred to pickets, though sometimes I use the term *videttes*.

Directional references in the text are always from the point of view of the side under discussion. When it comes to spelling from original, especially manuscript, sources, I have used my variable rule to eliminate the qualifier *sic* from the text. Where I feel a particular spelling conveys a vivid sense of character, I have preserved the original; otherwise I have exercised some judicious editorial cleaning up of manuscript passages.

Maps

Options 36

Hood and Sherman: September–November 1864 39

Tuesday, November 15, 1864 76

Wednesday, November 16, 1864 90

Thursday, November 17, 1864 106

Pontoon Bridge 121

Friday, November 18, 1864 123

Saturday, November 19, 1864 139

Sunday, November 20, 1864 153

Dunlap's Hill: November 20, 1864 167

Monday, November 21, 1864 170

Tuesday, November 22, 1864 183

Macon-Griswoldville 194

Griswoldville: 2:30 P.M. 207

Griswoldville: 5:00–6:00 P.M. 211

Wednesday/Thursday,
November 23/November 24, 1864 217

Friday, November 25, 1864 242

Saturday, November 26, 1864   256

Sunday, November 27, 1864   269

Monday, November 28, 1864   279

Tuesday, November 29, 1864   290

Wednesday, November 30, 1864   301

Thursday, December 1, 1864   308

Friday, December 2, 1864   315

Saturday, December 3, 1864   321

Sunday, December 4, 1864   329

Waynesboro: December 4, 1864   337

Monday, December 5, 1864   348

Tuesday, December 6, 1864   354

Wednesday, December 7, 1864   361

Thursday, December 8, 1864   369

Friday, December 9, 1864   376

Savannah Lines   413

Right Wing, December 13, 1864   421

Fort McAllister: December 13, 1864   433

December 16, 1864   464

PART ONE

Preparation

CHAPTER 1

A Gathering of Eagles

The Central of Georgia Railroad station platform was empty when Confederate president Jefferson Davis arrived in Macon, Georgia, at 4:00 A.M., September 24, 1864. It had been an arduous, roundabout trip for Davis and his aides, involving at least three train changes and innumerable delays. Nothing had been communicated in advance of the president's arrival, so as the busy city roused itself to face another day, it did so ignorant that the most powerful individual of the world's youngest nation was in its midst.

The presidential party, departing the hushed station without a fuss, went to the home of Howell Cobb. A former U.S. congressman and secretary of the treasury (for James Buchanan), as well as a general who fought under Robert E. Lee in the east, Cobb was presently commanding Georgia's "minute man" reserve. It was a time of crisis for the Confederacy, which had suffered the loss of Atlanta—an important manufacturing center and transportation hub—just twenty-three days earlier. Now Davis had journeyed from Richmond, Virginia, as he later recollected, with a "view to judging the situation better and then determining after personal inspection the course which should seem best to pursue."

Likely during his Macon visit, Davis and Cobb (whom he considered a "pure patriot") discussed what to do about the man they both viewed as the main obstacle to Confederate success in Georgia, the state's governor, Joseph E. Brown. An outspoken and popular figure, Brown had come to represent an extreme position in the ongoing conflict between the imperative needs of a centralized government and the rights of its constituent states.

Even as a nascent Confederacy struggled to maintain its military resources to survive, Brown was equally active protecting what he termed the "sovereignty of the State against usurpation." Whether it was reclassifying Georgia government jobs to immunize them from the national draft, or requisitioning military supplies slated for export, Brown was a constant irritant to the Davis administration. While Cobb did not agree with many Davis policies, he understood that the defeat of Confederate aspirations meant an end to Georgia's sovereignty as well, and his frustration with Brown's obstructions led him to denounce the governor as "a traitor, a Tory." Cobb's anger had a special urgency, for unless there was a dramatic change in the war situation, he knew that his state's future would be too terrible to contemplate.

Davis had been settled at Cobb's only a few hours when an ad hoc committee of local notables invited him to speak that very morning at a mass meeting previously scheduled to raise money for Atlanta refugees. Davis agreed. The crowd gathered at the Baptist church greeted the fifty-six-year-old Confederate symbol with what a reporter present termed "prolonged applause." Those close to the front of the room saw a proud, determined man worn down by having to carry too much on his slim shoulders. The words of a woman who saw him just a few days earlier likely found variations in the thoughts of those present: "poor man he pays for *his* honors." But when Davis spoke, there was no softening of his steely defiance or iron resolve.

Fully aware of all the recent reverses suffered by the Confederacy, Davis assured the crowd, "Our cause is not lost." While an enemy force may have captured Atlanta, it was also now isolated deep within the South, wholly dependent upon a single rail line to Chattanooga to keep it supplied. Once the moment arrived when the Yankee army had to abandon Atlanta—and it would—Southern "cavalry and our people will harass and destroy it." In a purposely ambiguous reference, Davis mocked an unnamed individual who had accused the Confederate president of abandoning "Georgia to her fate." This person, Davis declared, "was not a man to save our country." Then came some plain talk: Georgia could expect little if any help from outside the state in the present crisis. What was needed at this critical time was for Southern women to endure their privations with stoic courage, and for every patriotic male to flock to the colors. "If one-half the men now absent [from the army] without leave will return to duty, we can defeat the enemy," Davis assured those present. "Let no one despond," he finished. "Let none distrust, and remember that if genius is the beautiful, hope is the reality."

The next day Davis traveled to Palmetto, some twenty-five miles southwest of enemy-occupied Atlanta; headquarters for General John B. Hood, commanding the Confederate Army of Tennessee. Hood was a wounded lion if ever there was one. Once a vigorous, vital man, he had been cruelly whittled down by the war, his left arm crippled while leading troops at Gettysburg in July 1863, and his right leg amputated below the thigh from fighting at Chickamauga the following September. A society matron who met him around that time thought he had "the [sad] face of an old crusader who believed in his cause, his cross and his crown." It was during Hood's painful recuperation spent in Richmond that he had visited often with Davis. The two found common ground and established a rapport.

In time Davis promoted Hood to lieutenant general* and assigned him to lead a corps in the Army of Tennessee, then commanded by General Joseph E. Johnston. Hood's appointment came in time for the bitter spring campaign of 1864, which began in May. By July Davis was thoroughly fed up with Johnston, who had slowed but not stopped or significantly damaged a much larger Union army pushing south from Chattanooga. Johnston, whose management of the campaign would spawn a rancorous postwar controversy, declined to keep Davis informed of his circumstances or intentions, even as he deftly backpedaled his soldiers to the gates of Atlanta. When Johnston intimated he was prepared to abandon the city to preserve the army's freedom of movement, Davis acted. He removed Johnston from command and— to the surprise of many—promoted John Bell Hood to replace him.

Thrust into a high place because he was a fighting general, Hood quickly undertook a series of fierce offensive strikes at the Union forces enfolding Atlanta. None succeeded in halting the Yankee juggernaut, and on the night of September 1 Hood pulled the Army of Tennessee

---

* Davis much preferred West Point graduates for high-level military appointments.

out of the Gate City, which immediately fell to Union forces, accompanied by much fanfare in the North. Hood reassembled what remained of his army at Lovejoy's Station, then shifted it to Palmetto, while the Federals rested easy in their freshest conquest. What was to happen next topped the Davis agenda.

The Confederate president had expended considerable political capital in appointing Hood, and the reverses suffered by the Army of Tennessee had become a rallying point for antiadministration factions. In the wake of Atlanta's fall there were even calls for Johnston's reinstatement, something that Davis refused to consider. Others suggested one of the Confederacy's underemployed heroes, General Pierre Gustave Toutant Beauregard, another on the president's blacklist. The odds that Davis had come all this way to replace Hood with Beauregard were slim, but the politically canny Confederate leader believed he could exploit the out-of-favor general's prestige without entrusting him with an army.

Hood had a ready explanation for his failure to hold the Gate City. It was, he stated, due to fumbling by some of his key subordinates and a lack of nerve on the part of his soldiers. Just a few weeks before their face-to-face Hood had written Davis that according "to all human calculations we should have saved Atlanta had the officers and men . . . done what was expected of them." Hood singled out one of his corps commanders for most of the blame: Lieutenant General William J. Hardee. Some sixteen years Hood's senior, Hardee possessed impeccable military bona fides, even if his manner was annoyingly distant, patrician, and judgmental. Hardee had already played a significant offstage role in undermining the man who had preceded Johnston in command of the Army of Tennessee, General Braxton Bragg. Yet when Bragg had been reassigned and the position offered to Hardee, he had declined, leaving Davis only the distasteful option of summoning Johnston.

Hardee was no friend of Hood. While he did not question that officer's experience or courage, he had serious doubts regarding his ability to effectively manage such an important enterprise. Hood, in turn, suspected that Hardee was deliberately undermining his authority and reveling in his failures. Any ground for compromise had long since eroded, leaving Hood adamant that Hardee had to go. It was into this poisonous atmosphere that Jefferson Davis arrived at 3:30 P.M., September 25. Fittingly, it was raining.

Davis was too good a politician to prematurely reveal his hand. While Hood doubtless used their meeting to continue his tirade against Hardee, Davis made no commitment. What most interested the Confederate president was knowing what Hood intended to do next. The general did have a plan; one that, considering his situation, was about as good as possible. As he was outnumbered by the Union forces in Atlanta by better than two to one, Hood's best chance to do any real damage was to march around to the city's north side to disrupt the enemy's attenuated supply line. This would inevitably draw the Federals away from the city to protect the vital rail link with supply depots in Tennessee. Hood would keep his small army just out of reach to seek opportunities to strike at exposed portions of the enemy's force, but only when the odds favored him. Even if he could not maneuver the Yankees into such a position, the fact that all the attention was on him meant that the rest of Georgia would be left alone.

Jefferson Davis liked what he heard. Hood's plan offered the glittering (albeit remote) prospect of saving Georgia, protecting the Gulf States, and maintaining the vital supply lines that carried produce and materiel from the Deep South to Virginia. If he succeeded, Hood would blight the fruits of the enemy's spring campaign in Georgia, turn Atlanta's capture into a hollow victory, and maybe—just maybe—force the Union army back toward Tennessee.

Should the enemy forces not play along and instead attempt to thrust forward through Georgia, Hood would be close enough to attack their rear. Add to this their familiarity with the Georgia countryside, the prospect of a general rising of guerrilla forces, and an active Confederate cavalry, and Davis had a "not unreasonable hope that retributive justice might overtake the ruthless invader." Hood also offered his resignation, but Davis was sold enough on the plan's potential that no change at the top was further considered.

That night the president was serenaded by the 20th Louisiana band, then visited by a crowd of soldiers to whom he made a short but spirited speech, which was well received. The next day, as Hood later recollected, he and Davis "rode forth together to the front, with the object of making an informal review of the troops. Some brigades received the president with enthusiasm; others were seemingly dissatisfied and inclined to cry out, 'Give us General Johnston.' " Davis also met with the Army of Tennessee's principal subordinates, none of whom offered any endorsement for Hood, though only one, Hardee, said a change was needed.

Hardee's position came as no surprise to Davis, since he and the punctilious senior officer had already exchanged messages on the subject. It was a source of continuing frustration to Davis that so many of his most experienced leaders would not suppress their self-interest for the good of the cause. "I now ask is this a time to weigh professional or personal pride against the needs of the country?" Davis pressed Hardee at one point. Hardee never budged from his position that it was necessary for Davis to choose one or the other to lead the Army of Tennessee.

Jefferson Davis left Palmetto on September 27 after authorizing Hood to proceed with his plan unless otherwise instructed, but without a final decision on the Hardee matter. His next destination was the Confederacy's first capital, Montgomery, Alabama. The journey gave him time to mull over the problem. He made up his mind when the train reached West Point, where he sent a telegram to Hood reassigning Hardee to take charge of the Department of South Carolina, Georgia and Florida.

By the time he reached the next stop, Opelika, Davis had composed a personal message for Hood. During their face-to-face Davis had reflected on the need to better coordinate the various military assets in the region by appointing someone to oversee operations. Davis, now inclined to proceed with that appointment, was considering General Beauregard for the job. He invited Hood to express his opinion, though he knew from their conversations that the officer would not object.

Davis arrived in Montgomery early on the morning of September 28. This time the citizens had been forewarned so he was formally welcomed and taken to the state capitol, where he addressed the Assembly. "The time for action is now at hand," Davis told them. He reiterated the theme that every able-bodied man was needed at the front. He scoffed at any in the crowd who thought it was proper to open negotiations with the North regarding a possible reunification of the states. "Victory in the field is the surest element of strength to a peace party," Davis proclaimed. Anyone who felt otherwise, he warned, "is on the wrong side of the line of battle."

That night Davis met with another of the key figures responsible for defending the southern Confederacy, Lieutenant General Richard Taylor, who commanded the Department of Alabama, Mississippi and East Louisiana. He was the son of the twelfth U.S. president (Zachary Taylor) and Davis's brother-in-law through the president's first marriage. The officer was a cold-eyed realist. When the president opened their meeting by citing the excellent reports he'd received about the improving morale in Hood's army, the general's reply was blunt. "I . . . warned him of the danger of listening to narrators who were more disposed to tell him what was agreeable than what was true," Taylor stated.

When Davis spoke of Hood's plan to operate on the Union communication and supply lines in hopes of actually drawing the enemy out of Georgia, Taylor was skeptical. The Federal commander, he noted, had enough troops in his Chattanooga and Nashville garrisons to check any northward movement Hood might undertake, leaving him at Atlanta free to "march where he liked." Davis wanted to know how much help Taylor could supply from his department to assist in central Georgia's defense. "None," Taylor replied. He explained that beside the logistical nightmare of trying to move large bodies of men across the Union-controlled Mississippi River, the fact was that few troops serving on its west side would willingly come east. Taylor did allow that bringing a popular figure like Beauregard into the picture would "awaken a certain enthusiasm."

The optimism Davis had allowed himself after meeting with Hood positively wilted under the officer's sour barrage. Davis said "he was distressed to hear such gloomy sentiments from me," but Taylor saw it as his duty "to express my opinions frankly to him." They conferred a while longer before Davis left the next morning on a circuitous rail journey to his next stop, Augusta, Georgia. Taylor saw the president off without any bitterness about the deteriorating situation. "I had cut into this game with eyes wide open," he reflected, "and felt that in staking life, fortune, and the future of my children, the chances were against success."

The train routing to Augusta brought Davis back through Macon, where General Hardee, now reassigned, boarded on his way to Charleston, South Carolina. There was no enmity between the two, for Davis's decision had brought solace to both men. "I can say with certainty that

General Hardee was not relieved because of any depreciation of his capacity, his zeal or fidelity," Davis later testified. Hardee, for his part, opined that Hood's plan was the "best which can be done, if that does not succeed no other will."

In Augusta, on October 3, Davis met with General Beauregard. The Louisiana-born officer arrived from an inspection tour of South Carolina with a sense that time was running out on his opportunities for redemption. As the commanding officer at Charleston in 1861, he ordered the batteries to fire on Fort Sumter, and later he was the commander in the field for the first Confederate victory at Manassas. Buoyed by the popular acclaim and political support he received, Beauregard publicly attacked the Davis government for its lack of war preparations, an action that resulted in his banishment to a western subcommand.

It was at the battle of Shiloh in April 1862, when the officer leading the Southern forces was killed, that Beauregard took the reins of an operation he had opposed, and withdrew his men from the battlefield. His subsequent abandonment of the strategically important transportation and supply hub at Corinth further tarnished his reputation. ("There are those who can only walk a log when it is near the ground," Jefferson Davis scoffed when he learned of Beauregard's action, "and I fear he has been placed too high for his mental strength.") There followed a series of appointments to military backwaters, culminating in June and July 1864, when he found himself sharing the defense of Petersburg, Virginia, with General Robert E. Lee. Although equal in rank, Lee had the full confidence of Jefferson Davis as well as direct control over most of the troops on the field, leaving Beauregard to play an increasingly unhappy second fiddle. His summons to meet with Davis promised the chance to command in the field with the fate of the Confederacy at stake. Such a destiny mated well with Beauregard's romantic soul.

Beauregard opened the meeting by proposing a sweeping reorganization of the South Carolina defensive system, part of which involved promoting a favorite aide two steps in rank to lead it. Davis patiently heard him out before tabling the matter* and moving on to his agenda.

---

*   Davis later agreed to promote the officer one step in rank, but before the order could be implemented the officer in question died of yellow fever.

He started with an overview of Hood's plan. Davis's enthusiasm for the intended course of action was obvious to Beauregard, who approved the scheme, pronouncing it "perfectly feasible, . . . according to the principles of war." Davis now got down to the main point of their meeting. He proposed to create a new military command jurisdiction, to be called the Division of the West, encompassing five states and including the commands of John B. Hood and Richard Taylor (the South Carolina coastal defenses would be added later). He wanted Beauregard to take charge.

Beauregard, who had hoped for command of an army, realized at once that what Davis was offering was essentially an administrative and advisory posting, but he would be on his own stage instead of sharing space with others. He understood that much of the appointment was more symbolic than substantial since, as he later stated, "he would be without troops directly under him, with very scanty resources to count upon, and—far worse than all—with a marked feeling of discouragement and distrust growing among the people." Without making any effort to negotiate terms, Beauregard accepted the new position. He recollected that besides promising him the cooperation of the War Department, Davis suggested that his first official act be to meet with Generals Hood and Taylor. However, before Beauregard left to carry out his new duties, Davis needed him for one more event.

Arm in arm with Beauregard and Hardee, Davis addressed a mass gathering in Augusta. He took care to praise both the officers on stage with him; Hardee, "the hero of many hard-fought fields," and Beauregard, who "goes with a single purpose . . . not to bleed but to conquer." Much of the rest of his speech inspired fear and hope alternately in the hearts of those present. "Would you see the fair daughters of the land given over to the brutality of the Yankees?" he asked. "We are fighting for existence, and by fighting alone can independence be gained. You must consult your hearts, perform more than the law can exact, yield as much as free-men can give, and all will be well," he exhorted. "Brave men have done well before against greater odds than ours, and when were men ever braver?"[*]

The return leg of Jefferson Davis's visit to the troubled front was

---

[*] Howell Cobb had to have the last word, telling the crowd that if all eligible men rallied now to the colors they would "very speedily send the Yankees back to stink and rot and go to——!"

made pleasant by a stop in Columbia, South Carolina, where he stayed with his good friends James and Mary Chesnut. James, a colonel in the Confederate army, had been on Davis's staff for a period. Mary kept an extensive diary that would, in time, become one of the principal windows into life in the South during the Civil War. As Mary remembered it, Davis arrived soon after dawn, and following a hearty breakfast the president tried to relax by sitting out on the Chesnuts' piazza. The respite was brief, for some boys recognized him as the "man . . . who looks just like Jeff Davis on a postage stamp." Before long a large crowd had gathered, forcing Davis to retreat into his room. More citizens arrived, and the pressure increased on Davis to say a few words. At 1:00 P.M. he stepped back out on the piazza, which was by now thronged by what Mary recollected as an immense crowd of men, women, and children.

Davis began by praising those present for their steadfastness in the "great struggle for the rights of the states and the liberties of the people." Once more he lambasted any talk of conciliation with the North. With an unspoken reference to his replacement of Johnston by Hood, Davis asked, "Does any man imagine that we can conquer the Yankees by retreating before them, or do you not all know that the only way to make spaniels civil is to whip them?" He returned to one of the core messages of his talks, reiterating that "now is the good and accepted time for every man to rally to the standard of his country and crush the invader upon her soil."

Davis spoke movingly of the noble Army of Tennessee's imminent return to health. He expressed his great hopes for Hood's operation, which, the president promised his audience, would soon threaten Sherman's tenuous supply link between Atlanta and Tennessee. Davis built to an upbeat finish. "I believe it is in the power of the men of the Confederacy to plant our banners on the banks of the Ohio [River]," he exclaimed, "where we shall say to the Yankee, 'be quiet, or we shall teach you another lesson.'"

Mrs. Chesnut had a mint julep waiting for the president when he finished his speech. That evening, thanks to the generosity of neighbors, a fine dinner was served, with excellent wine. Long after the guests had dispersed, the dinner settings been cleared, and the president departed to continue his journey back to Richmond, Mrs. Chesnut ruminated on her chat with Custis Lee, a Davis aide. Lee, she wrote, "spoke very candidly and told me many a hard truth about the Confederacy and the bad time which was at hand. What he said was not so impressive as the unbroken silence he maintained as to that extraordinary move by which Hood expects to entice . . . [the Federal force at Atlanta] away from us."

The slow ride from Columbia back to Richmond, requiring another three changes of train, provided Davis ample time to reflect on the steps he had taken. All that was within his power to do, he had done. Beauregard, Hood, Taylor, Hardee, Cobb—all would have important parts to play in the difficult days ahead. If those men had actually listened to his words, they understood that their salvation would not come from without but from within their region. "If every man fit to bear arms will place himself in the ranks with those who are already there," Davis had said, "we shall not battle in vain, and our achievement will be grand, final and complete." If Hood executed his plan well; if Beauregard could choreograph the resources to meet the threats when they appeared; if Taylor, Hardee, and Cobb understood the need to work together, all would be well.

Not long after he returned to Richmond, Davis reported to the Confederate Congress on the progress of the war. He predicted a new phase of the conflict during which Confederate armies would no longer be tied down defending fixed places like cities, which would free them to maneuver to advantage as Hood's plan allowed. "There are no vital points on the preservation of which the continued existence of the Confederacy depends," he told the lawmakers. "There is no military success of the enemy which can accomplish its destruction. Not the fall of Richmond, nor Wilmington [, North Carolina;] nor Charleston, nor Savannah, nor Mobile, nor all combined, can save the enemy from the constant and exhaustive drain of blood and treasure which must continue until he shall discover that no peace is attainable unless based on the recognition of our indefeasible rights."

CHAPTER 2

Captive Audiences

A web of iron links bound Atlanta to the Atlantic coast. In prewar times these connections brought prosperity and convenience to those fortunate enough to be located along the right-of-way. Since the war began, those railroad routes marked those same fortunate ones as targets, and what was once a source of pride had become cause for much anxiety. The northern leg of this route to the sea consisted of a track belonging to the Georgia Railroad. It linked Atlanta to Augusta, from which point waterways or other rail connections completed the journey. The southern leg represented two operations: the Macon and Western Railroad hooked Atlanta to Macon, from there the Central of Georgia Railroad completed the circuit through to Savannah.

One of the first stops moving east from Atlanta on the Georgia Railroad was Covington, a gracious village that serviced several nearby plantations. Young Tillie Travis loved her town but despaired over the effect the war was having on it. Because of its proximity to Atlanta, Covington had already endured visits by Union cavalrymen who burned its railroad depot and associated buildings. A number of Covington's residents had fled since Atlanta's fall, so many that Travis observed, "Our town looked deserted, indeed." As September passed through October into November, Travis and the other holdouts had grown used to the almost daily rumors that "the Yankees are coming!" Many of those still in town were in a state of denial because of the constant false alarms. Thinking about those enemy soldiers, Travis noted that "we had almost concluded that they would vex us with their presence no more."

A mile and a half from Covington was Oxford, home of one Zora M. Fair, a South Carolina refugee of considerable pluck. Determined to do more for the Confederacy than stoically enduring privations, the young lady stained her skin with walnut juice, frazzled her hair, and went into Atlanta to spy disguised as a Negro girl. Her friends were aghast when they found out about her escapade, but the determined girl returned to set down what she saw and heard in a letter that she sent off to Georgia's governor.

Some nine miles east of Covington was the sprawling plantation managed by the widow Burge. Born in Maine as Dolly Sumner Lunt (and a relative of the abolitionist U.S. senator Charles Sumner), Mrs. Burge had followed her sister from Maine to Georgia, taught school, and married a certified Southern gentleman named Thomas Burge. Mr. Burge died in the late 1850s, leaving Dolly with a daughter (Sarah, called "Sadai") and the responsibility of running the plantation on her own. She proved adept, both in adjusting her New England morality to embrace slavery and in her careful management of the busy enterprise. Already she had witnessed the sad procession of refugees from Atlanta, as well as suffering visits from Yankee raiders who rustled some of her livestock.

Dolly Burge offered no apologies for keeping slaves. "I can see nothing in the scriptures which forbids it," she said. Like many thoughtful owners, she eased any pangs of conscience through benevolent stewardship of her charges. "I have never bought or sold slaves and I have tried to make life easy and pleasant to those that have been bequeathed me," she explained. Her biggest worry was the outcome of this terrible war. "Shall we be a nation or shall we be annihilated?" she wondered.

Pushing east from Covington, the Georgia Railroad passed through the well-appointed town of Madison, where Emma High lived. The natural beauty of the town was a continuing marvel to her. "The winter was a mild one and there were roses in bloom," she recalled, "rich and beautiful and in great profusion in many of the flower gardens." Madison was, by general consensus, one of the most attractive towns in the state, an appearance that offset its more eccentric residents, such as Edmund B. Walker. Walker believed in being prepared, so he purchased a coffin built exactly to his measure, which he stored in his attic. As the years passed and his waistline expanded, Walker was known to make periodic visits to his final resting place to assure himself that he still fit.

South of the town, in Jasper County, was the Aiken Plantation, run by the owner's wife while he was away in the army. Frances B. Aiken was the youngest of the twelve children, all of whom helped their mother manage the operation and watch over the slaves. Later in her long life, Frances never forgot how her mother prepared to deal with any invaders. Her plan was not to spite them but to welcome and charm them, pitting Southern hospitality against Northern aggression. Anyone who knew her mother knew that this was no contest at all.

The Georgia Railroad terminated on the Savannah River at Augusta, one of the Confederacy's busiest arsenals. The city leaders had been slow to assess potential Yankee threats, so it wasn't until mid-August that serious work began to erect fortifications around the city. A force of some 500 slaves labored in the summer heat to dig the defensive strong points. The feeling that Georgia's fate was not being sufficiently considered in far-off Richmond was shared by many. One Augusta newspaper editorial rhetorically asked the Confederate government "whether the State of Georgia is necessary to the achievement of our independence?" By mid-September every available slave had been pressed into the job of protecting Augusta, so many in fact that when the post's military commander requested a detail to dig some soldier graves, he was told that no extra hands were available.

The course of the Macon and Western Railroad ran south and then east of Atlanta. The population of Macon, another important location for manufactures and munitions, had swelled with workers and refugees. Among the latter was a family from north Georgia. Rebeca Felton's husband had moved his dependents here early in 1864 to escape the ravages of the Union army's campaign against Atlanta, but then the capture of the Gate City had put Macon's future in doubt. "It was very astounding to remember all these reverses and yet we were constantly told we would certainly succeed," she recalled in later years, "and we clutched at every item of news that indicated a success."

North from Macon about twenty-three miles was Hillsboro, which had already felt the hard hand of war. A column of Union cavalry had paused briefly in the town on a late July raid aimed at freeing Union

POWs caged near Macon. Mrs. Tabitha Reese endured the presence of Yankee officers in her parlor, even as their men freely pillaged outside. The whole affair left Mrs. Reese's nerves frayed with what the doctors termed "nervous prostration." Her daughter, Louise, dreaded the next visitation, which seemed inevitable. "We know what terrible means," she declared. " 'Terrible as an army with banners.' "

From Macon, the Central of Georgia Railroad looped eastward toward Savannah. A spur at Gordon connected the state's capital, Milledgeville, with the circuit. Legislators from around Georgia began trouping toward Milledgeville in late October for the state assembly's annual session, scheduled to convene on November 3. The elected officials faced a wide range of issues, from finance to state defense. Included on the agenda was a bill to amend the state's ban on grain-based liquors to allow for the manufacture and consumption of lager beer. Smart money was betting that the bill would pass.

The legislative session opened with a strident message from Governor Joseph E. Brown, who excoriated the Davis administration for failing to prevent Atlanta's capture. "But the misfortunes following the misguided judgment of our rulers must not have the effect of relaxing our zeal or chilling our love for the cause," Brown proclaimed. He dropped something of a bombshell by proposing a convention of states—Southern and Northern—to consider continuing the war. "States can terminate wars by negotiation," Brown insisted.[*]

Behind all the bold words of the governor and the state legislators was the knowledge that if the Yankee army should target Milledgeville, they would all flee. There were others in the town whose sense of duty chained them to this post. One was Dr. R. J. Massey, responsible for "six different wards, something like two hundred sick, wounded and convalescents." Another was Dr. Thomas F. Green, superintendent of the Georgia Lunatic Asylum. His daughter, Anna Maria, was an honor student and a dedicated diarist. Also determined to remain was the Georgia secretary of state, Nathan C. Barnett. Among his responsibilities was the Great Seal of Georgia and all records pertaining to the current legislative session.

Milledgeville boasted more than its share of impressive houses. One

---

[*]   Brown's resolution never had a chance. Backed by a scornful rejection from Richmond, the governor's foes had little trouble killing the measure.

was the Orme house, with its distinctive Doric-columned portico. The mansion's mistress, Mrs. Richard McAllister Orme, had strong northern roots. Her father, John Adams, was president of the Phillips Academy in Andover, Massachusetts, whose graduates included at least one Union officer in Atlanta. Not far away was the Governor's Mansion, patterned after a fourteenth-century Italian villa. Its front door opened into a great hall and a rotunda topped with a gilded dome, all illuminated by crystal chandeliers. One of the state's first families preceding Governor Brown included a cat lover in its ranks, who had a pet entrance cut into one of the house's fine carved doors.

The Milledgeville spur threaded northward to terminate at Eatonton, where the war's demands had put women into the working force at the Eatonton Manufacturing Company, which produced a durable heavy cloth called osnaburg as well as pants for soldiers. Other women had formed a Ladies Aid Society whose squads of knitters were urged on with the battle cry, "a sock a day." Patriotic pride centered on the 102-foot-high flagpole, whose mastlike look was credited to the retired sea captain who had directed its construction. The captain also raised and lowered the standard each day, carefully handling the emblem that had been hand-sewn by a female resident who had attended the first Confederate Congress just to get the proper specifications.

The Central of Georgia continued its eastward wandering, passing through the town of Millen, where another spur shunted off the main trunk line, this one making possible one of the Confederacy's newest and largest prisoner enclosures. Camp Lawton, as it was called, came into being as a way of relieving the overcrowding and suffering at Camp Sumter (also known as Andersonville), south of Atlanta, which had been in operation since late February. With losses reaching toward one hundred a day from disease, starvation, and violence, a decision was made in July to build another prison. A site was found five miles north of Millen blessed with a good supply of fresh water, high ground for guard stations, and easy access to the railroad spur. Construction on Camp Lawton began in late July, and the first Union prisoners reached the stockade in mid-October as Hood's planned move forced Camp Sumter's temporary closure.

Reaction by the POWs to the new, still incomplete facility was mixed. An Ohio artilleryman swore that there was little improvement over Andersonville, while an infantryman from Illinois found the new location to be "much more pleasant" than Camp Sumter. "Disease and starvation together are decimating us daily," recorded another Federal captive, "and the average deaths are twenty to thirty-five per day." There were regular visits from Confederate officials anxious to recruit disaffected Yankees into their ranks. These "galvanized Rebels,"* as they were called, were promised better fare and treatment, benefits that a few found irresistible. "Let us not judge them too harshly," noted a captive who did not sign up, "remembering how sorely they were tempted." Confederate officials hoped that Camp Lawton was secluded enough to be secure from enemy raiders, even though the nearby railroad marked it clearly on Union maps.

Farther north along the Millen spur was Waynesboro, near which a visitor would find the Carswell house, known as Bellevue. Mrs. Carswell, the former Sarah Ann Devine, was a New Englander who loved to tend her garden. Her special pride was the rosebush that ran along the side of the house. There is no evidence that Mr. Carswell, a lawyer and judge, ever gave much thought to his wife's horticultural passion, but in the not very distant future that rosebush would come to mean life itself.

Seventeen miles outside Savannah, young Jennie Ihly was boarding with her grandparents, who lived near one of the main roads leading into the port city. Writing years later, Jennie described herself then as "a merry hearted girl, little dreaming of the realities of war, for to me it sounded like a fairy tale as I heard it discussed by the people of matured years." Lying between this household and Savannah was a belt of tidal marshes that had been cultivated for rice and sea island cotton. Working the rice fields was difficult, dangerous labor, and slave mortality was high.

The Central of Georgia Railroad terminated at Savannah, a town renowned for the public greens that checkerboarded its central district, crowned by the twenty-acre Forsyth Park. Shortly before the war Savannah played host to the English writer William Thackeray, who described it as a "tranquil old city, wide streeted, tree shrouded." Although the heaviest ground fighting in Georgia was well off to the west, Savannah's residents had constant reminders of the turbulence

---

* So called after a manufacturing process, these were soldiers whose "new" allegiance thinly coated over their original loyalties.

just over the horizon. Refugees were a common sight, as were the temporary holding pens that sprang up to accommodate transiting enemy prisoners. To one observer the Yankees, many from Andersonville, were "altogether the most squalid gathering of humanity it has ever been my lot to look upon."

Savannah was a once-bustling seaport whose business had been dramatically curtailed by a Federal naval cordon to the occasional bold blockade runner.* Among those hurt by the loss of trade was Octavus Cohen, a merchant and cotton exporter. His twenty-four-year-old daughter, Fanny, would soon be moved by events to step from the shadows of anonymity by keeping a journal of the happenings in her city. Another daughter who would leave a record of this time was Frances Thomas Howard, whose father helped man Savannah's defenses. A resident who feared the changes that were coming was Caro Lamar, who managed her household in the absence of her husband. She was especially suspicious of one of the family's slaves, William, who she worried would betray them at the first opportunity.

William became one of the few named members of a largely invisible community within the territory defined by the three railroads. Something around 150,000 African-Americans lived and labored on the plantations and in the households of the region. Theirs was a society kept in place by coercion and bound together by a diverse range of personal responses to their plight. Some slaves were docile—broken in spirit and resigned to their fate—while others actively fought their status with force and guile. In between these extremes was the majority—bound to the land because of extended family, or force of habit, or anxiety over dramatic change, or even a sense of obligation to their owners.

Some lived lives of punishment and fear. The slaves working on the Farrar farm, six miles outside Eatonton, endured a hellish existence punctuated with floggings and tortures designed to increase the pain. They reserved a special hatred for the big red hound owned by Farrar's neighbor that was used to hunt down escaped blacks. A sentiment shared but never spoken out loud was one of vengeance against the damned dog.

---

* Ironically, this encouraged some to believe that Savannah had been made more secure, since the Yankees would no longer consider it a priority target.

The touchstone for all Georgia slaves was freedom. This desperate longing was something they could never admit or show to the whites who controlled their lives, but which they would not deny among themselves. The social observer and landscape architect Frederick Law Olmsted traveled through Georgia in the years before the Civil War. Talking to a slave, Olmsted related that he had been given to understand from the whites he had met that blacks did not want to be free. "His only answer," noted Olmsted, "was a short, contemptuous laugh." According to George Womble, a slave on a plantation near Clinton, a common saying among the blacks was, "I know that some day we'll be free and if we die before that time our children will live to see it."

The outbreak of the Civil War had greatly weakened the forces controlling slave life in Georgia. While whites often thought of their slaves as childlike, they also feared them. Many of the white men who had managed the black labor force and policed the coercive laws that kept them in their places had been called up for military service, leaving wives, mothers, and elders to maintain the social order. Propaganda replaced brute force as the slaves were told tales of the ill treatment they could expect in Yankee hands. In some cases the stories were embellished to a degree that verged on absurdity. A widow living near Lithonia told her slaves that the Federals "shot, burned and drowned negroes, old and young, drove men into houses and burned them." Most blacks saw through the subterfuge. Said one, as recorded in dialect by a white Union officer, "Massa hates de Yankees, and he's no fren'ter we; so we am de Yankee bi's fren's."

This was the double edge of the slave system. On the one hand it provided a vast pool of unpaid labor to handle the crops or construct fortifications. On the other it represented an elemental force that threatened to burst free at the first provocation. A young boy living near Eatonton had experienced enough about life to recognize the fear. "The whites who were left at home knew it was in the power of the negroes to rise and in one night sweep the strength and substance of the Confederacy from the face of the earth," remembered future writer Joel Chandler Harris. "Some of the more ignorant whites lived in constant terror."

Many slaves were ready for liberation and awaited only the opportunity to manifest itself. By most measures, thirty-five-year-old Willis Bennefield was a privileged servant. He belonged to a doctor with a plantation just outside Waynesboro who used Willis to chauffeur for him on his calls. As a boy Willis had accompanied the doctor's sons to school and waited for them on the outside steps. "I got way up de alphabet by listening," he recollected many years later. Among his happier memories of those times was going to church. "We had dances, and prayers, and singing, too," he stated. "We sang a song, 'On Jordan's stormy banks I stand, and cast a wishful eye.'"

CHAPTER 3

The Stormbringer

William Tecumseh Sherman lived with a ghost. It was the spirit of his first son, William Jr., who had been the receptacle for every hope and aspiration of his inordinately proud father. "You must continue to write me and tell me everything—how tall in feet and inches—how heavy—can you ride and swim—how many feet and inches you can jump. Everything," wrote Sherman in early 1863. His desire to be with his wife and oldest boy was so powerful that he arranged for them to join him near Vicksburg during a rare slow period in the western war. Little Willy (he was just nine) showed his winning ways by becoming an honorary sergeant in one of his father's regiments. Then tragedy struck. Willy grew ill, an army surgeon diagnosed typhoid, and the failing child was rushed to Memphis, where specialists informed Sherman the case was hopeless. The beloved boy departed this world on the afternoon of October 3, 1863.

To his great friend and mentor, Ulysses S. Grant, Sherman revealed that "this is the only death I have ever had in my family and falling as it has so suddenly and unexpectedly on the one I most prised on earth has affected me more than any other misfortune could." Sherman knew who to blame. "Why, oh why, should that child be taken from us, leaving us full of trembling and reproaches? Though I know we did all human beings could do to arrest the ebbing tide of life, still I will always deplore my want of judgment in taking my family to so fatal a climate at so critical a period of life." To his wife he also confessed that "sleeping, waking, everywhere I see poor Willy. His face and form are as deeply imprinted on my memory as were deep-seated the hopes I had in his future." Yet out of this great loss was forged a grim determination. "On, on I must go till I meet a soldier's fate, or see my country rise . . . till its flag is adored by ourselves and all the powers of the earth," he vowed.

The emotional blow of Willy's death would be followed in slightly more than a year by professional triumphs that would make Sherman one of the North's most celebrated military heroes. It was typical of a life charted in great lows and grand highs, and of a serpentine personal odyssey that carried Sherman from an intense contemplation of suicide to the stern rejection of influential friends bearing presidential aspirations. While Sherman would later protest that it was the powerful flux of national events that caused him to be "forced into prominence," he nevertheless relished the spotlight. He was a private man who wielded the written word in public forums like a rapier. He dedicated his life's energies to protecting the uniquely American democracy, but his vision of this blessed society also embraced racial bias as part of the natural order of things as well as pragmatic limits to some freedoms. He was a person of profound ethical and spiritual contradictions, and possessed of many faces. Speaking to a gathering of veterans in 1866, Sherman revealed, "I am full of passion and sometimes act wildly."

William Tecumseh Sherman (the middle name was his father's homage to the Shawnee warrior chief) was born in Lancaster, Ohio, in 1820. His father died when he was nine, forcing his financially pressed mother to scatter her children out to relatives and friends for upbringing. Young William became surrogate son to Thomas Ewing, a politician with enough clout to have the boy admitted to West Point, where he graduated sixth in the class of 1840. Sherman knocked around in military assignments for thirteen years (he was posted to California during the Mexican-American War) before trying and failing in a banking career. Subsequent efforts to succeed in law and real estate went bust as well. "I would feel rejoiced to hide myself in any obscure corner," he told a friend. On another low occasion he anguished, "I look on myself as a dead cock in the pit and will take the chances as they come." At last Sherman found a job that suited his talents, that of superintendent of the Louisiana Military Seminary in Alexandria. He took the position in 1859.

Events beyond the seminary's walls cut short the superintendent's tenure. On January 26, 1861, Louisiana joined five other states in declaring itself independent of the United States. Sherman remained at his post for one more month (to collect his last paycheck) and then went north. (But not before warning his colleagues, "You are rushing into war with one of the most powerful, ingeniously mechanical and determined people on earth.") Following a brief stint as president of a Saint Louis streetcar company, he rejoined the army bearing the rank of colonel, commanding a regiment of U.S. regulars. After a good showing in a badly managed battle at Bull Run, Sherman was made second in command in Kentucky, an assignment which soon became first in command once his superior abruptly stepped down. It was a disastrous promotion.

Kentucky was a volatile border state, with passions running high on both sides. Sherman had yet to find his equipoise—the balancing point where training and personality merge into a self-confident leader. He reacted badly to the pressures, made some unwise public statements, and came near enough to a breakdown that several newspapers labeled him insane. He was bounced from Kentucky to Missouri, then sent home to rest. It seemed that his return to the army would be chalked up as another failure in his life.

His wife (Thomas Ewing's daughter) used all the family leverage she could muster to have Sherman returned to a field command. He led a division at the battle of Shiloh, where he served under U. S. Grant, a man he greatly admired. The two became an effective team through the Vicksburg and Chattanooga campaigns, victories that propelled both men into the national spotlight. When Grant was brought east in early 1864 to command all Union armies in the war effort, Sherman was given responsibility for the key operation in the west.

Outwardly, the man accepting these important new duties looked nothing like a warrior-chief. Sherman, recollected one of his soldiers, usually "wore very common looking clothes. He generally looked like some old farmer; his hat all slouched down and an old brown overcoat." Yet those with the perception to look beyond external appearances saw a man prepared to wage relentless warfare. "With his large frame, tall, gaunt form, restless hazel eyes, aquiline nose, bronzed face, and crisp beard," wrote one of Grant's aides, "he looked the picture of 'grim-visaged war.' "

Sherman was in perpetual motion. "He is a very nervous man and can't keep still a moment," a soldier observed. Even while he was continuing an unbroken discussion of the war situation with Grant's aide, Sherman constantly fidgeted. "He twice rose from his chair, and sat down again, twisted the newspaper into every conceivable shape, and from time to time drew first one foot and then the other out of its slipper and followed up the movement by shoving out his leg so that the foot could recapture the slipper and thrust itself into it again." Sherman's way of talking at such times was stream-of-consciousness. Bold ideas couched in epigrammatic phrases were rattled off with the hammering intensity of a Gatling gun. Sherman's explanation: "I'm too red-haired to be patient."

"To the casual observer, his quick and nervous manner, the flash of his eagle eye, the brusque command, might give token of hasty conclusions, of disregard of details, of eager, and impatient habits of thought," added a member of Sherman's staff. "There could be no greater error. Nothing was more characteristic of his plans, nothing more noteworthy in the general orders which outlined their execution, than the marvelous foresight, itself the fruit of patient thought, which included and took into account each probable contingency, each necessary detail, every other being brushed aside as an encumbrance."

It wasn't luck that brought Sherman to the mountaintop, though luck had played its part in his journey. Sherman's success began with a solid foundation in the military arts. "Sherman was the professional and practical soldier," wrote one admirer. "He studied topography, knew roads, mastered the details of a campaign in advance as no other general did." The smallest matters received his attention, and no aspect of a planned campaign, however trivial, escaped his attention. His men respected his thoroughness, something Sherman used to his advantage. "Without being aware of it, I seem to possess a knowledge into men & things, of rivers, roads, capacity of trains, wagons, etc., that no one near me professes to have," he noted. "All naturally & by habit come to me for orders and instructions."

By the latter part of the war Sherman exuded leadership. "Gen. Sherman is the ablest General in the United States Service I believe," declared a Pennsylvania soldier. "Every man under Sherman has the greatest confidence in him," seconded a New Yorker, "and make up their minds that when he strikes it is sure death to all rebs within his range." To this a Minnesota artilleryman added, "we felt as though Sherman could be trusted in every time of trial." Speaking with a civilian clergyman, Sherman confided his secret. "The true way to be popular with troops is not to be free and familiar with them, but to make them believe you know more than they do. My men believe I know everything; they are much mistaken, but it gives them confidence in me."

Largely because of his West Point training, Sherman (as did most of his peers) believed that order could be imposed on the chaos of war. "War is the conflict of arms between people for some real or fancied object," he wrote. "It has existed from the beginning. The Bible is full of it. Homer immortalized the siege and destruction of Troy. Grecian, Roman, and European history is chiefly made up of wars and the deeds of soldiers; out of their experience arose certain rules, certain principles, which made the 'art of war' as practiced by Alexander, by Caesar, by Gustavus Adolphus, and by Frederick the Great. These principles are as true as the multiplication table, the law of gravitation, of virtual velocities, or of any other invariable rule of natural philosophy." Late in the conflict Sherman ended a debate with a Rebel general regarding his interpretation of the "laws of war" with the exhortation: "See the books."

When the Civil War began, Sherman tried to apply the rules he had been taught. He railed against soldiers under his command who preyed on civilian populations. "No goths or vandals ever had less respect for the lives and property of friends and foes," he fumed at one point. Even in 1862 Sherman was complaining to his superiors that "too much looseness exists on the subject of foraging." By 1863 Sherman found himself forced to reexamine his convictions. He was an eminently rational being ("My idea of God is that he has given man reason, and he has no right to disregard it," he said). Too much of what Sherman had observed in the war up to that point did not fit the rules as he had learned them. Too many lines were being blurred, especially regarding civilians and the war. The labor of Southern farmers fed Southern armies, the eyes of Southern civilians informed Southern strategy, the actions of Southern civilians fighting as guerrillas made them a foe almost impossible to confront in any conventional manner.

Sherman's battlefield successes and increasing national prominence gave him the confidence to analyze the problem and provided the authority to act on his conclusions. His response was not to discard the rules of war, but to imbue them with a great elasticity. "[The] northern people have to unlearn all their experience of the past thirty years and be born again before they will see the truth," he wrote. Almost every military action Sherman took after 1862 would be justified in reference to the rules of war, but what some of his equally well-schooled opponents never understood was that these were *Sherman's* rules of war.

Sherman was an adept problem solver thanks to the way he approached matters. From the data and assumptions before him he would select those that fitted best with his sense of what was right, endow those conclusions with the qualities of absolute fact, and act upon them—seldom, if ever, reconsidering the matter. The driving and defining force behind everything he did was his personal faith, a highly individualized amalgam of patriotism and national destiny. He believed that the United States, in the years just prior to the commencement of the war, had achieved a divine balance. The nation, as Sherman later wrote, had "prospered beyond precedence," and its citizens "realized perfectly the advantages they possessed over the inhabitants of other lands." God—Sherman's, that is—intended the United States "for a long and prosperous nation[al] life, & not for destruction in the bloom of its youth."

By the tenets of his faith, the South had forfeited any consideration for a gentle application of the rules of war. "On earth, as in heaven, man must submit to an arbiter," Sherman wrote, as if penning a prayer. "He must not throw off his allegiance to his government or his God without just reason and cause. The South had no cause." Sherman's cold reasoning led him inexorably forward. "Satan and the rebellious saints of Heaven," he continued, "were allowed a continuous existence in hell merely to swell their just punishment. To such as would rebel against a Government so mild and just as ours was in peace, a punishment equally would not be unjust." Some twenty-three years after the fighting had ended, Sherman would still insist: "We veterans believe that in 1861–5 we fought a holy war, with absolute right on our side, with pure patriotism, with reasonable skill, and that we achieved a result which enabled the United States of America to resume her glorious career in the interest of all mankind, after an interruption of four years by as needless a war as ever afflicted a people."

In applying his rules of war to the rebellious South, Sherman used a number of refining corollaries. He believed very much in collective responsibility. If a band of irregulars ambushed some of his transports from the riverbank, then everyone within an area along the waterway who could have known about the action were coconspirators. His instructions in such cases were that "army commanders should order and enforce a devastation more or less relentless, according to the measure of such hostility." To take the issue to a larger scale, until the people of the South demanded that their leaders stop the war, they were a part of the equation that kept the war going. "Even yet, my heart bleeds when I see the carnage of battle, the desolation of homes, the bitter anguish of families;" Sherman wrote, "but the very moment the men of the South say that instead of appealing to war they should have appealed to reason, to our Congress, to our courts, to religion, and to the experience of history, then will I say peace, peace."

Sherman reserved a special hatred for the Southern intelligentsia who had been seduced by the hollow god of secession. Of one such man, Sherman wrote that he was "endowed with intellect, wealth, power and experience—He chose war, and for him I have no mercy. He should drink the cup of poisoned venom to its bitterest dregs." Speaking of this leadership class to his wife, Sherman was no less vengeful. "We must *Kill* those three hundred thousand I have told you of so often, and the further they run the harder for us to get them."

Another corollary was the supremacy of law as an antidote to the progressive fragmentation of civil society. "The law is or should be our king; we should obey it, not because it meets our approval but because it is the law and because obedience in some shape is necessary in every system of civilized government. For years this tendency to anarchy had gone on till now every state and county and town . . . makes and enforces the local prejudices as the law of the land. This is the real trouble, it is not slavery, it is the democratic spirit which substitutes mere opinions for law." The end game here was chaos. "If the United States submits to a division now," Sherman warned, "it will not stop, but will go on till we reap the fate of Mexico, which is eternal war."

Speaking to a trusted aide, Sherman made it plain that the "war is on our part a war *against anarchy*." God, Sherman was certain, simply wouldn't allow "this fair land and this Brave People" to slide into the abyss of social chaos. On another occasion he declared himself the sworn enemy of "mobs, vigilance Committees and all the other phases of sedition and anarchy which have threatened and still endanger the Country which our Children must inherit." Such havoc challenged the natural order of leadership that was part and parcel of Sherman's idealized society. The war, he told a clergyman in 1864, "is intensifying the greatest fault and danger in our social system. It daily increases the influences of the masses, already too great for safety. The man of intelligence and education is depressed in value far below the man of mere physical strength. These common soldiers will feel their value and seek to control affairs hereafter to the prejudice of the intelligent classes."

The great and important objects of the war that was being waged, Sherman believed, were order and peace. Those goals were so important that anything impeding their most efficient and rapid prosecution was subject to serious scrutiny and even suppression. That included the fourth estate. A "free press . . . ," Sherman snapped, "rarely comprehended the necessities of battle." He was convinced that while Southern newspapers were kept on a tight leash, those in the North operated without controls, irresponsibly providing the enemy with accurate strength estimates and often informed speculation concerning future movements.

"I say with the press unfettered as now we are defeated to the end of time," Sherman grumbled. He issued orders promising arrest as a spy for any reporter whose coverage "might reach the enemy, giving them information, aid, and comfort." When the newspapers pushed back, Sherman dug in his heels. "If the press can govern the country, let them fight the battles," he declared. "I am no enemy to freedom of thought, freedom of press and speech," he insisted, "but in all controversies there is a time when discussion must cease and action begin." Sherman was eager to use his newfound popularity to take the lead on limiting press access to events under his control. "As the press has now more power than the Congress that makes our laws . . . ," he declared, "and it is probable it will produce the result which history demonstrates in other singular cases that the people will discover that it is better to curtail the liberty of the press as well as the liberty of speech."

The fact that the future status of African-Americans had been brought to the fore by the war annoyed Sherman to no end. "I would prefer to have this a white man's war and provide for the negroes after the time has passed," he told his wife in 1863, not long after the Lincoln administration issued the Emancipation Proclamation. "With my opinion of negroes and my experience, yea prejudice, I cannot trust them yet." Sherman's bias placed him squarely at odds with his president and his superior officer on this issue, and he did everything within his power to impede efforts by Lincoln and Grant to recruit black soldiers within his command area. "I have had the question put to me often: 'Is not a negro as good as a white man to stop a bullet?' Yes; and a sand-bag is better; but can a negro . . . improvise roads, bridges, sorties, flank movements, etc., like the white man? I say no." Summing it up, he told a southerner and former acquaintance, "I care not a straw for niggers."

Sherman believed that the hard war he advocated and practiced would have no lasting repercussions. Its essence, he explained, was "which party can whip. It's as simple as the schoolboy's fight, and when one or the other party gives in, we will be the better friend." To others protesting his stern policies, Sherman promised, "When peace does come, you may call on me for any thing. Then will I share with you the last cracker, and watch with you to shield your homes and families against danger from every quarter."

Sherman was a man of destiny who was very aware of the fact. "My children and children's children will now associate my name with their Country's History," he bragged in 1863. A year later he remarked: "I do think that in the Several Great Epochs of this war my name will bear a prominent part." "If I have attained any fame it is pure and unalloyed by the taint of parasitic flattery and the result is to you and the children more agreeable," he assured his wife, "for it will go to your and their benefit more than all the surface flattery of all the newspaper men of the country." To his surviving son, Sherman said, "People write to me that I am now a Great General, and if I were to come home they would gather round me in crowds & play music and all such things. That is what people call fame & Glory."

It was Sherman's anointed task to join the great material and human resources of the North with a winning plan driven by his determination to succeed. A recurring metaphor in Sherman's writings likens war to a great storm, and while he may have had the skill and knowledge to generate the tempest, his mastery of it was far from complete. "You might as well appeal against the thunderstorm as against these terrible hardships of war," he said to the mayor of Atlanta. "We have accepted the issue [of war] and it must be fought out," he told another Southern official. "You might as well reason with a thunderstorm." Lecturing a former friend who had sided with the South and who had protested Sherman's policies, he said, "Talk it over with your neighbors, and ask yourselves if, in your trials and tribulations, you have suffered more from the Union soldiery than you would had you built your barn where the lightning was sure to burn or tear it down." "To make war," he cautioned in early 1864, "we must and will harden our hearts. Therefore when preachers clamor and sanitaries* wail don't join in, but know that war, like the thunderbolt, follows its laws and turns not aside even if the beautiful, the virtuous and charitable stand in its path."

---

* Sherman is referring to civilian organizations devoted to soldier welfare, such as the U.S. Sanitary Commission.

CHAPTER 4

The Plan

When William Tecumseh Sherman published his *Memoirs* in 1875, his recollections immediately became a focal point for the General's personal enemies and others seeking to protect the reputations of those he had disparaged. (So much so that the *New York Herald* bannered it as the "most spicy book of the day.") Controversy erupted over ownership of the idea for the March to the Sea, which even then had become a fixture of American legend and lore. Leading the pack of those who challenged Sherman's paternity was Henry Van Ness Boynton, a sometime reporter for a Cincinnati newspaper and a breveted brigadier general with an honorable wound received at Missionary Ridge. Helped with access to official records by some in the Grant administration who felt Sherman's memories had slighted their chief, Boynton cranked out a refuting book that hit the market the same year as Sherman's, earning its author the General's undying enmity.

What emerged from Boynton's tome was a prodigious assembly of quotations from Sherman's work contrasted with official records, all of which seemed to aggregate a great deal but which actually added up to very little. The paper trail of the Civil War was littered with schemes and stratagems, and more than one officer ran his finger through the center of the Confederacy and on to the coast. Even Sherman acknowledged that the idea of " 'cutting their way to the sea' " was "common talk around the campfires of the West." Nearly twenty years after the war he was still answering questions on the subject. "I have no doubt that hundreds and thousands of men thought of such a scheme," wrote Sherman in 1883, "but the truth is nobody did it till we did in 1864."

The plan came together in bits and pieces, in fits and starts, with some elements taken from past operations and some improvised by necessity. It was unfinished even at the outset of the movement, a work in progress that benefited from contributions by many of Sherman's subordinates, who added their parts—small and large—to his overall conception. The result was one of the most famous episodes of the Civil War and American history.

At the beginning of U. S. Grant's nationally coordinated Federal military offensive of 1864, Sherman, commanding nearly 100,000 men based around Chattanooga, Tennessee, confronted a Confederate force of 64,000 led by General Joseph E. Johnston, whose task was to block any Federal penetration into central Georgia. Sherman's mission, personally given him by Grant, was to "knock Jos. Johnston, and to do as much damage to the resources of the enemy as possible." (In an irony that probably wasn't lost on Sherman, he performed a great service toward Lincoln's reelection by failing in his primary objective of wrecking the Confederate army and instead turning his efforts to a more obtainable goal, the capture of the Gate City. "Atlanta is ours, and fairly won," Sherman announced on September 3. Crowed the Republican-friendly *New York Times*, "The political skies begin to brighten. The clouds that lowered over [our] . . . cause a month ago are breaking away.")

Grant was thinking about the next phase even before Sherman carried out his share of the spring operations. At this stage in his forecasting, Grant projected Sherman continuing through Atlanta to Mobile, Alabama, then an important and still active Rebel seaport. By the time Sherman had fought and maneuvered his way into the Gate City in early September, the picture had undergone a dramatic change. A month earlier, Union naval forces, which had overwhelmed the Confederate forts guarding Mobile Bay, took possession of its entrance. With this blow, the military value of Mobile dropped to almost nothing—at least as a port of entry for supplies. "Now that we have all of Mobile Bay that is valuable," Grant wrote Sherman on September 10, "I do not know . . . [what] will be the best move [for you to next make]."

Sherman was already taking steps to keep himself mobile. His first idea was to turn Atlanta into an armed camp held by relatively few troops to allow the bulk of his force freedom to operate in the open. In the clean clinical corridors of Sherman's thinking process, that meant that Atlanta's disloyal civilians would have to be evicted. On September 8 he issued orders expelling all citizens not working for his armies, a decision he justified on the basis of military necessity. This ignited a paper storm from the town representatives and General John B. Hood, who had succeeded Johnston. To city officials who pleaded for mercy, Sherman explained that his order was "not designed to meet the humanities of the case, but to prepare for the future struggles." In his reply, Sherman ticked off the facts as he understood them and concluded with the statement that war is "cruelty and you cannot refine it."

When Sherman offered to transport the evicted residents into General Hood's camp, the Confederate officer saw red, accusing the Yankee officer of "studious and ingenious cruelty." This provided Sherman with the kind of public forum that he found irresistible. In an exchange of messages that he would eventually release to the press, Sherman countered Hood with instances where Confederate leaders had removed civilians from harm's way, and, noting the property damage that had already been done to the city, insisted that "it is kindness to these families of Atlanta to remove them now." When Hood appealed in God's name, Sherman promptly waggled his finger at the Confederate general (and those leaders like him) "who, in the midst of peace and prosperity, have plunged a nation into war." Sherman terminated the dialogue after one more exchange, deciding that to continue it was pointless.

The equations Sherman applied to human beings played no favorites. Even as he and Hood were sparring over the forced civilian evacuation, they were also discussing a prisoner exchange. Hood opened the bidding on September 8 with a generic request containing no reference to numbers involved. Sherman checked to see how many Rebel POWs he held, and in his reply set the target number at 1,810. He also added an important stipulation. He was only interested in men taken from his armies who were healthy enough to immediately resume their places in the ranks. Sherman pointedly was not interested in sickly prisoners, or those belonging to eastern Union armies, or those whose

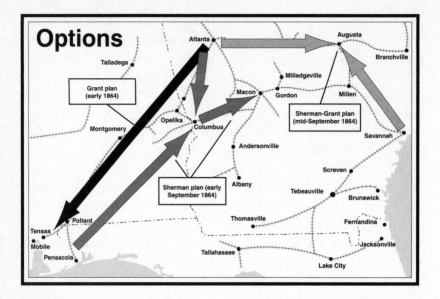

term of service had expired. After sputtering about this matter, Hood proceeded with the exchange; however, not anticipating Sherman's fine print, he had already brought some up from Andersonville who did not qualify. These were turned around almost in sight of their liberation. Said one of the embittered POWs, "this act of Sherman's will kill hundreds, as all hope of ever getting out of this is gone."

Despite his initial decision to fortify and hold Atlanta, Sherman soon realized that he had spent its propaganda value in its capture, and to continue defending it would only bring diminishing returns. Union forces in Atlanta were dependent upon a single rail line running north to Federal supply depots in Tennessee. Rebel actions to cut or interdict the railroad forced Sherman to disperse men and materiel to defend and repair it; this reduced his strength and allowed the enemy to claim the all-important initiative. As he phrased it, he had his "wedge pretty deep, and must look out that I don't get my fingers pinched." He and Grant now began some long-distance jawing about what to do.

Sherman's rapid-fire mind chewed through the possibilities. On September 4 he was thinking of a joint operation with Union forces operating out of New Orleans to capture Columbus, Georgia, a hundred miles south of Atlanta on the Chattahoochee River, site of one of the Confederacy's most productive arsenals. With Columbus, and a connection south to a supply source secured, Sherman then imagined a thrust farther into central Georgia. Six days later Grant wondered if Sherman might better move to capture Augusta, 150 miles east of Atlanta, site of the Confederate Powder Works, the South's largest propellant manufacturer. Sherman was willing but worried about logistics. He remained fixed on the need for a secure base of supply along the eastern side of Georgia before he would commit to cutting loose from Atlanta.

By September 12 Grant and Sherman were back to square one. Sherman learned that he could expect no help from New Orleans, while Grant admitted that he lacked the strength to take and hold a supply depot in eastern Georgia. The lieutenant general did feel that a small force might be detached from Virginia to close the port of Wilmington, North Carolina. Well, Sherman replied, if you had enough surplus assets to close Wilmington, you could use them instead to capture Savannah. "If once in our possession . . . ," he argued, "I would not hesitate to cross the State of Georgia with sixty thousand men, hauling some stores, and depending on the country for the balance." Sherman saw how he could threaten Macon with its busy ordnance factories so that once the enemy reinforced there, he could swing up to capture Augusta against weak opposition. "Either horn of the dilemma will be worth a battle," Sherman concluded.

(Even as he was progressively refining his strategic ideas for the military operation, Sherman was seeking political accommodations that might ease the way. His grand objective all along had been to knock Georgia out of the war. The defeat of Hood in battle and Atlanta's capture had been important steps in that direction. Hardly had Sherman settled in the Gate City than he was trying to talk the state's leaders into leaving the Confederacy. Working through a trio of prominent Georgians who were against continuing the war, Sherman sent a message to Governor Brown offering to "spare the state" from further destruction and paying for supplies requisitioned by his men. The quid pro quo was that Brown "would issue his proclamation withdrawing his State troops from the armies of the Confederacy." Brown replied with a public statement, noting that he and Sherman "would have power to bind no one by any compact we might make," and besides, the proud people of Georgia would "never treat with a conqueror upon her soil." Thus ended Sherman's first foray into high-stakes politics.)

———— *The Plan—Hood, Beauregard, and Thomas* ————

In every scenario he had imagined so far, Sherman had moved his army from one established supply base to another. He just could not conceive any operation of consequence unless Grant gained control of Savannah and its waterways. In typical Sherman fashion, his recognition of its importance to his evolving scheme elevated its significance on the national level. The Confederacy's leaders, he told Grant, "may stand the fall of Richmond, but not of all Georgia."

Suddenly, the intellectual stimulation of debate and discussion was interrupted by movements of the enemy. On September 24, a major Confederate cavalry force, led by the fearsome Nathan Bedford Forrest, challenged Union control of the Tennessee River by capturing the garrison at Athens, Alabama, in the northeast corner of the state. Forrest's move posed a direct threat to middle Tennessee. Then, on September 29, Hood (now with Jefferson Davis's blessing) began to march his army counterclockwise around Atlanta. By October 3 his infantry were wrecking the Federal depots at Acworth and Big Shanty, smack on Sherman's supply line. Two days later a division of Hood's army tried to capture the critically important Union strong point at Allatoona Pass. The effort failed, but it was a near thing.

Hood's movement forced Sherman to dance to the Confederate tune. He began transferring some of his troops into defensive positions along the rail line while directing any newly arriving units to concentrate at Chattanooga and Nashville. Sherman also sent one of his most capable officers, Major General George H. Thomas, to take charge in Tennessee. Then, leaving one corps to garrison Atlanta, Sherman set off after Hood. Even as his men began their wearisome tramp back along roads they had already traversed triumphantly in the opposite direction, Sherman was pondering what he'd rather be doing.

In a message sent to Grant on October 1, Sherman wondered aloud that if Hood quit his railroad wrecking and marched his army northward, "why will it not do to leave Tennessee to the forces which Thomas has, . . . and for me to destroy Atlanta and march across Georgia to Savannah and Charleston, breaking [rail]roads and doing irreparable damage? We cannot remain on the defensive." His thinking now made

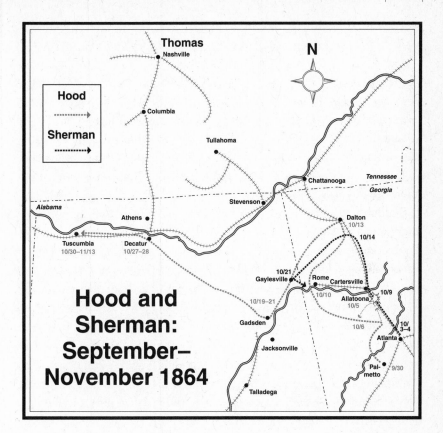

Hood and Sherman: September–November 1864

an important leap forward—he no longer required a secure supply base waiting at the end of the campaign.

As Sherman pushed his forces northward along the railroad, repairing it as he went, Hood remained nimbly out of reach. Up to this time the Confederate officer had operated solely with a cavalry force under Major General Joseph Wheeler, but Sherman could foresee the day when the formidable Forrest would be added to the current campaign. As each day of pursuit proved fruitless, Sherman became increasingly convinced that playing Hood's game accomplished nothing. "It will be a physical impossibility to protect the [rail]roads, now that Hood, Forrest and Wheeler, . . . are turned loose. . . . I propose we break up the railroad [we currently control] from Chattanooga [to Atlanta] and strike out with wagons for Milledgeville, Millen and Savannah," Sherman wired Grant on October 9. "Until we can repopulate Georgia, it is useless to occupy it, but the utter destruction of its [rail]roads, houses, and people will cripple their military resources. By attempting to hold the [rail]roads we lose 1,000 men monthly, and will gain no result. I can make the march, and make Georgia howl."

Sherman was counting on the special relationship he enjoyed with Grant to enable him to promote his plan. As he later put it, "We were as brothers—I the older man in years, but he higher in rank. We both believed in our heart of hearts that the success of the Union cause was not only necessary to the then generation of Americans, but to all future generations." On a more informal occasion, Sherman added of Grant, "He stood by me when I was crazy and I stood by him when he was drunk; and now, sir, we stand by each other always."

Grant's grand strategy had been predicated on destroying the enemy's armies. Sherman knew this and understood that it required careful and patient argument for his friend to accept the concept of turning his most powerful western armies against infrastructure rather than armed forces. ("This may not be war but rather statesmanship," he suggested to Grant.) Hearing no response from Grant to his October 9 message, Sherman made additional points with a follow-up sent two days later. "Hood may turn into Tennessee and Kentucky, but I believe he will be forced to follow me," Sherman argued, hoping to assuage Grant's principal concern. "Instead of being on the defensive, I would be on the offensive, instead of guessing at what he means to do, he would have to guess at my plans. The difference in war is full 25 percent."

Crossing Sherman's note in telegraphic transit was one from Grant that spoke both to his professional concerns and his personal regard for Sherman's particular brilliance. "If there is any way of getting at Hood's army, I would prefer that, but I must trust to your own judgment. I find I shall not be able to send a force from here to act with you at Savannah. Your movements therefore, will be independent of mine." The more Grant thought about matters, the more willing he was to be convinced by Sherman's plan. But Grant answered to a boss in Washington who was not as quick to embrace such a shift in strategy. On October 12 Grant was advised that President Lincoln "feels much solicitude in respect to General Sherman's proposed movement and hopes that it will be maturely considered. . . . [A] misstep by General Sherman might be fatal to his army." Lincoln's implication was clear; a mistake by Sherman might be fatal to the administration's reelection hopes.

Grant addressed this concern the next day, sending his message to Lincoln's chief of staff, Major General Henry W. Halleck, knowing that the president would see every word. "On mature reflection," Grant began, "I believe Sherman's proposition is the best that can be adopted." After pointing out the impossibility of keeping an Atlanta garrison supplied, he observed that by leaving a barren waste in his wake, Sherman would create a buffer zone to impede any enemy pursuit. Properly reinforced, Thomas could hold Tennessee, and even then Sherman would retain enough strength to defeat Hood if he turned on him. "Such an army as Sherman has (and with such a commander) is hard to corner or capture," Grant concluded.

Even as this exchange was occurring, Hood and Sherman continued their slow dance in northwest Georgia. As they marched, Sherman's men foraged extensively, prompting complaints from the affected civilians. "Your friends have broken our railroads, which supplied us bountifully," Sherman replied, applying his rules of war, "and you cannot suppose our soldiers will suffer when there is abundance within reach." With Sherman pressing him from the south, Hood veered to the west; by October 15 he had halted at Gaylesville, just on the Alabama side of the Georgia border. Up to now he had closely followed the script he had crafted with Jefferson Davis; although his opponent had not left himself open to any damaging blows, Hood's men had certainly filled Sherman's life with vexations. The question Hood now considered was whether or not his accomplishments (and more like them) were enough.

It was the same day that Hood arrived at Gaylesville that Sherman received the authorization he had been seeking. The message, dated two days earlier, came from Secretary of War Edwin Stanton, who acknowledged that Grant had decided to let Sherman carry out his plan. "You may count on the co-operation of this Department to the full extent of the power of the Government," the war secretary promised. Sherman had now acquired all the approvals he needed to set out on his march through Georgia. The only problem was Hood, who still posed a threat to Union interests in northern Georgia. If Hood would commit himself to a movement into Tennessee, then Sherman could retrace his steps to Atlanta without censure. Otherwise it would look as if he was backing away from Hood's challenge. Sherman let some of his anxiety show in a message to a subordinate commander written on October 16. "I want the first positive fact that Hood contemplates an invasion of Tennessee; invite him to do so," Sherman instructed. "Send him a free pass in."

Hood finally obliged Sherman on October 17 by marching his men farther west, away from the threatened Union supply line. That same day, Sherman, monitoring events from the Georgia border to be sure that Hood's column was receding, started to get affairs in order for what he was now calling his "grand movement into Georgia." Orders went out to the various Union commands to begin culling out "the most indifferent wagons and worthless mules and horses, . . . the sick and wounded, prisoners of war, surplus servants, tents, chairs, cots, and the furniture that now fill our wagons and disgrace the army."

Two days passed, and with Hood showing no signs of wavering from his westward course, Sherman could finally exhale somewhat. In a message sent to Lincoln's military chief of staff, he stated: "I now consider myself authorized to execute my plan to destroy the railroad from Chattanooga to Atlanta, . . . [and] strike out into the heart of Georgia, and make for Charleston, Savannah, or the mouth of the Appalachicola [River]."

Nevertheless, Sherman kept his forces in place until he was certain that Hood wasn't going to double back or push into Tennessee close enough to him to necessitate he act. The last thing Sherman needed was the perception that he had ignored a threat he could have parried. Sherman wanted Hood to invade Tennessee, but he needed the act to take place far enough to the west that no one would think he had been lax in his responsibilities. As the days ticked off, Sherman watched Hood and fretted that circumstances might not allow him to undertake his cherished plan. "Damn Hood!" Sherman exclaimed. "If he will go to the Ohio River I'll give him rations!"

On October 18 Sherman heard from the officer he had left in charge of the Atlanta garrison, who unknowingly proposed to steal his thunder. Major General Henry W. Slocum was not yet included among those whom Sherman believed needed to know of his plans. Slocum reported that matters were so quiet around Atlanta that he thought he might launch his own raid into Georgia with just two divisions. Sherman responded two days later, letting Slocum know that a grand march was in the works and, further, instructing Slocum to prepare "1,500,000 rations of bread, coffee, sugar, and salt, 500,000 rations of salt meat." Also, Slocum was to have the "lightest pontoon bridges and trains ready."

The same day, Sherman received a nervous message from the officer he had left in charge in Tennessee, George H. Thomas. Twenty-four hours later Sherman sought to buck up his subordinate. "If you can defend the line of the Tennessee [River] in my absence of three months, it is all I ask," Sherman said. He also made clear his intention "to sally forth and make a hole in Georgia and Alabama that will be hard to mend." On October 20 Sherman sent a long note to Thomas designed to assuage him even more. He revealed a few more details of his planned march, suggesting he might be able to destroy the military production centers of Macon and Augusta. "By this I propose to demonstrate the vulnerability of the South and make its inhabitants feel that war and individual ruin are synonymous terms. . . . I know I am right in this and shall proceed to its maturity." Sherman spelled out in no uncertain terms what he expected of Thomas. "I want you to retain command in Tennessee, and before starting I will give you delegated authority over Kentucky, Mississippi, Alabama, &c., whereby there will be unity of action behind me," Sherman wrote. "If . . . Hood turns on you, you must act defensively on the line of the Tennessee [River]."

Thomas's first response, sent October 21, did not directly address Sherman's wishes, but instead enumerated all the units then available to him, which did not match the number Sherman was crediting him with having on hand. Messaging Grant on October 22, Sherman was careful to paint an uncluttered picture. "I feel perfectly master of the situation here," he declared. "I am now perfecting arrangements to put into Tennessee a force able to hold the line of the Tennessee [River] whilst I break up the railroad [from Dalton to Atlanta] . . . and push into Georgia, and break up all its railroads and depots, capture its horses and negroes, make desolation everywhere." On October 23 Sherman made sure that Slocum in Atlanta was filling the larder. "Go on, pile up the forage, corn and potatoes, and keep your artillery horses fat," Sherman instructed him. "If Georgia can afford to break our railroads, she can afford to feed us. Please preach this doctrine to men who go forth, and are likely to spend it."

That same day Sherman continued to buttress Thomas's confidence. "All Georgia is now open to me and I do believe you are the man best qualified to manage the affairs of Tennessee and North Mississippi," he told him. Three days later Sherman sent Thomas a pair of messages. The first offered overall advice ("Minor points may be neglected, but the stronger places . . . strengthened") and proffered assurances that Sherman's plan would proceed only "provided always you can defend the line of the Tennessee [River]." In the second note Sherman seemed to forget his pledge. "I must leave it [the defense of Tennessee] to you for the present and push for the heart of Georgia." Sherman was certain that once he began his movement into the heart of the state Hood would "turn back." Writing to Lincoln's chief of staff on October 27, Sherman warranted that the troops he was forwarding to Thomas "will enable him to hold Tennessee." Thomas, Sherman added, "is well alive to the occasion, and better suited to the emergency than any man I have."

The forces Sherman had selected for his Georgia expedition began marching back toward Atlanta on October 29. His next messages to Thomas emphasized all the troops that were being redirected to assist him. Thomas's responses were more measured, most often identifying only the units that were on hand and their combat readiness. With Hood poised on the south bank of the Tennessee River, first at Decatur, then farther west at Tuscumbia, and displaying every indication of advancing into middle Tennessee, Thomas's low force inventories began to take on an urgent tone. His uneasiness was discerned by Halleck and especially Grant, who now reconsidered his appraisal of Sherman's scheme. On November 1 Grant asked Sherman, "Do you not think it advisable now that Hood has gone so far north to entirely settle him before starting on your proposed campaign?" That same day Halleck added his two cents. "I think you should concentrate all you can against Hood," he urged, reflecting Lincoln's insecurities.

Now the time delays inherent in the long communications network began to play their own games. At 9:00 A.M. November 1, even before Grant's message with its big question started west, Sherman composed a note that anticipated the last-minute objections. He ran through a generous list of troops either with or on their way to Thomas. He reiterated that if he were to reverse course now, "the work of last summer would be lost." On November 2 Sherman dispatched a direct answer to Grant's November 1 message. "Thomas will have a force strong enough to prevent [Hood's] . . . reaching any country in which we have an interest," he assured his friend and superior officer. Sherman also advanced the argument that turning toward Hood was exactly what the enemy wanted him to do or, as he stated it, "Jeff. Davis' cherished plan of making me leave Georgia."

The telegram Sherman received from Grant on November 2 answered the note he had sent before getting Grant's of November 1. Grant, after looking carefully at the information Sherman had provided, decided to set aside his own misgivings by trusting his friend's judgment. "With the force . . . you have left with Thomas, he must be able to take care of Hood and destroy him," Grant said. "I do not really see that you can withdraw from where you are to follow Hood without giving up all we have gained in territory. I say, then, go as you propose." Grant's simple approbation took a weight off Sherman's shoulders and allowed him to regain his sense of humor. Responding to a note from a subordinate, Sherman hinted at the great raid in the offing and forecast, "You may look for a great howl against the brute Sherman."

For the next ten days Sherman played a delicate balancing act as he strove to maintain the positive picture he had created for Grant and Lincoln. There was always the chance that Hood would reverse course for a dash back into Georgia that would scuttle Sherman's plans. There was also the possibility that Thomas would fret enough about the Tennessee situation that Grant would be forced by Lincoln to halt the march. Some elements Sherman could influence or control; for the others he depended on fate.

On November 9 everything threatened to unravel when a small newspaper, the *Indianapolis Journal*, printed a brief but remarkably accurate summary of Sherman's intentions. The story was picked up and amplified the next day by other papers, including the *New York Times*. The leaks came from officers Sherman had sent up to Thomas in Chattanooga. While Grant and officials in Washington fumed and threatened all sorts of arrests, Sherman (remarkably calm considering the nature of the disruption) proposed to counter information with disinformation. He suggested that the War Department release false intelligence such as "Sherman's army has been much re-enforced, . . . and he will soon move by several columns in circuit, so as to catch Hood's army," or "Sherman's destination is not Charleston, but Selma."

The suggestions were ignored, and the incident passed without seriously impeding the operation.

While his men began actively preparing for the grand movement, Sherman telegraphically held Thomas's hand. "I hope we shall be ready for him," Thomas had wired on November 2. The next day Sherman advised Henry Halleck in Washington, "I . . . feel no uneasiness as to Tennessee." Even though his preparations for the Georgia march had passed a point of no return, Sherman assured Halleck that he could still intervene in Tennessee if a crisis loomed. Nonetheless, he was not seriously considering canceling the operation. "I propose to adhere as nearly as possible to my original plan," Sherman told Halleck, knowing he would tell Lincoln.

Thomas was still hedging his bets, reporting the troop repositioning he was doing, but offering few clues into his state of mind. "I have made great exertions to prevent stampeding," he confided to Sherman on November 3, "and so far have succeeded measurably well, but I find it hard work." His messages over the next few days continued in this vein. On November 11, Sherman gave Halleck his nearly final assurances. "I have balanced all the figures well," Sherman said, "and am satisfied that General Thomas has in Tennessee a force sufficient for all probabilities." Sherman's continued solicitation toward Thomas's concerns paid its dividends on the morning of November 12 when Thomas wired Sherman: "I have no fear that Beauregard [i.e., Hood] can do us any harm now."

This message reached Sherman at Cartersville, Georgia. The army commander was resting on the porch of a nondescript wood house, watching with intense interest as one of his signal corps technicians hooked a portable telegraph key to some wires and tapped out a call for messages from Chattanooga. After several minutes of counterpointed clicking, Sherman was handed the paper with Thomas's message. Recalled Sherman: "I answered simply: 'Dispatch received—all right.' About that instant of time, some of our men burnt a bridge, which severed the telegraph-wire, and all communication with the rear ceased thenceforth."

There were no more chances for anyone to call him back. Sherman was now entirely on his own and on his way. "Free and glorious I felt when the magic telegraph was cut!" he exclaimed.

─────── *The Plan—Precedents and Orders* ───────

The basic template for Sherman's March had been forged in February 1864, when he led a force of 20,000 men on a raid due east from Vicksburg to Meridian, Mississippi, a one-way distance of some 133 miles. "The expedition is one of celerity," Sherman announced to his men, and to facilitate rapid movement he divided his force into two wings. Sherman also employed some calculated misdirection prior to setting out, designed to leave the impression that his objective was Mobile, Alabama. As the two wings moved along parallel roads, Sherman saw how hard it was for the enemy to concentrate against him, since any effort to oppose one wing could be undone through the flanking threat posed by the other.

Sherman made it a point to limit the number of wagons accompanying his columns, so his men lived off the country and did well. Once at the transportation hub of Meridian, his soldiers wrecked everything of possible value to the Confederacy. "I have no hesitation in pronouncing the work as well done," Sherman reported. Special attention was given to tearing up the railroad lines with specific instructions provided in special field orders. "The enemy cannot use these roads to our prejudice in the coming campaign," Sherman bragged in his report. There were also directives meant to limit the damage done to civilian buildings, though enforcement was not strict. "When the provisions, forage, horses, mules, wagons, &c. are used by our enemy it is clearly our duty and right to take them," Sherman argued, "because otherwise they might be used against us." He concluded that the "government of the United States has . . . any and all rights which they choose to enforce the war."

Another facet of this operation was the presence of sizable numbers of slave refugees. Sherman's columns penetrated a region not previously visited by Union raiders, so at this first appearance of the blue columns roughly five to eight thousand African-Americans stopped what they were doing to tag along to Vicksburg and freedom, some afoot, some on horseback, others riding in oxcarts. Sherman's orders and practices provided no support for these noncombatants. When the war was over, the nation could look to the issues regarding blacks; until then they only interfered with his military operations aimed at bringing about that end. Keeping them out of the way would be much on Sherman's mind as he planned his grand movement into Georgia.

The operation Sherman now conceived was the Meridian Expedition squared, perhaps even cubed. More men were involved, the distances greater, and the risks higher, since, unlike in the February raid, which returned to home base, Sherman had no intention of coming back, and this time there was no supply depot waiting for him. After much mulling he boiled the essential elements down into nine instructions, which were codified in Special Field Orders No. 120, issued at Kingston, Georgia, on November 9.

> *I. For the purpose of military operations this army is divided into two wings, viz, the Right Wing, Maj. Gen. O.O. Howard commanding, the Fifteenth and Seventeenth Corps; the Left Wing, Maj. Gen. H.W. Slocum commanding, the Fourteenth and Twentieth Corps.*[*]

Sherman's selection of generals Howard and Slocum to command the respective wings was a key decision, for upon their shoulders would rest much of the responsibility for managing day-to-day affairs. Both were West Point graduates, an accomplishment that ranked high in the way Sherman judged his officers. While he agreed that politically appointed generals could be capable, inspirational, and even courageous, he also believed that their dual nature meant they could never be focused completely on the military job. Sherman viewed the political generals as men who "looked to personal fame and glory as auxiliary and secondary to their political ambition, and not as professional soldiers." Sherman described Howard and Slocum as "both comparatively young men,[†] but educated and experienced officers, fully competent to their command." Each had served in the east in the early part of the war, and both had blemishes on their records.

Wounded twice in the right arm at Fair Oaks, Virginia, in June 1862 (resulting in the loss of the limb), the Maine-born Oliver Otis Howard recovered sufficiently to take charge of a corps at the battle of

---

[*]   The Right Wing was also referred to as the Army of the Tennessee (after the river), while the Left Wing was sometimes called the Army of Georgia.
[†]   Howard had just turned thirty-four; Slocum was thirty-seven.

Chancellorsville in May 1863. It was Howard's command that broke, exposing the vulnerable right flank of the Union army, and suffering a staggering 41 percent casualties. Two months later, at Gettysburg, Howard's corps was again manhandled. Fate thrust him into overall command of Union forces on the field for much of the first day's fight, and although he demonstrated generally ineffectual leadership, the U.S. victory that followed under Major General George Gordon Meade brought Howard an official congressional commendation.

When Howard's corps was transferred to the west in the fall of 1863, he went along to take part in operations around Chattanooga, where his performance was unexceptional. Assigned to command a different corps during Sherman's Atlanta campaign, Howard managed to be in the right place at the right time when the job of taking over the multicorps Army of the Tennessee came open. Selected by Sherman as much to eliminate unwanted candidates as for his own leadership qualities, Howard got through the campaign without any significant gaffes. A lean, brown-haired, earnest man, Howard was smart, personally courageous, and dedicated to his work. He was also so outwardly religious in his demeanor that some of his troops took to calling him "Old Prayer Book."

Sherman's other selection, Henry W. Slocum, was a New Yorker with a similar résumé (he led corps at both Chancellorsville and Gettysburg), though without Howard's stumblings. A cautious, conservative officer loath to take risks (his reluctance to order his troops to Gettysburg on the first day led one staff officer to derisively pronounce his last name in two drawn-out syllables), Slocum could also nurse a grudge. He sat out much of the Atlanta Campaign in a backwater post because he refused to serve with the officer to whom he was assigned. When that individual resigned Sherman's service over Howard's promotion to lead the Army of the Tennessee, Slocum was recalled to command a corps, which he did in a competent fashion.

Sherman desired men in charge of his two wings who were capable, not easily panicked, and without any overriding ambition or imagination. As he made clear in a similar context, he "needed commanders who were purely and technically soldiers, men who would obey orders and execute them promptly and on time." Howard and Slocum fit the bill and so were slotted into these key positions.

II. The habitual order of march will be, wherever practicable, by four roads, as near parallel as possible and converging at points hereafter to be indicated in orders. The cavalry, Brigadier General Kilpatrick commanding, will receive special orders from the commander-in-chief.

The wing formation, already road-tested during the Meridian Campaign, offered Sherman great flexibility in deployment and kept his force compact enough to be mutually supportive as it advanced, at least in theory. Also, spread out to this degree, the march order created a roughly sixty-mile-wide zone covered by the wings in their advance, providing units operating away from the main columns (principally foragers) with some degree of security.

Sherman's experience with cavalry, especially during the Atlanta Campaign, was not the kind to inspire much confidence. Time and again the mounted arm had failed to carry out its assignments, and on several occasions it suffered serious, even catastrophic defeats. So Sherman, on the verge of undertaking the greatest mobile operation of the Civil War, assigned the bulk of his most active arm to Thomas in the north, holding back just one division to provide security for the march.

The man he picked to command his cavalry, H. Judson Kilpatrick, was the kind perhaps most imagined (and reviled) by the long-suffering infantry—a flamboyant, boisterous, and pugnacious Irish-American whose deeds rarely matched his words. The officer Sherman was leaving behind in Tennessee to refit and remount most of his cavalry (after forwarding the best horses to Kilpatrick) had enough spunk to question the choice. "I know [that] Kilpatrick is a hell of a damned fool," Sherman answered, "but I want just that sort of a man to command my cavalry on this expedition." Grading Kilpatrick's performance during the Atlanta Campaign, Sherman gave him high marks for his drive and intensity. Given the disasters that had befallen the others Sherman had entrusted with the responsibility, perhaps he also believed that Kilpatrick possessed the one prerequisite for a successful cavalry officer: luck.

III. There will be no general train of supplies, but each corps will have its ammunition train and provision train distributed habitually as follows: Behind each regiment should follow one wagon and one ambu-

lance; behind each brigade should follow a due proportion of ammunition wagons, provision wagons, and ambulances. In case of danger each army corps command should change this order of march by having his advance and rear brigade unencumbered by wheels. The separate columns will start habitually at 7 a.m., and make about fifteen miles per day, unless otherwise fixed in orders.

When it came to recollecting the grand march into Georgia, Sherman and his men invariably understated the relative size and vulnerability of the five wagon trains (one for each infantry column plus one for the cavalry) that trailed the marchers. Massachusetts captain Daniel Oakey was typical when he wrote that transportation was "reduced to a minimum, and fast marching was to be the order of the day." The image that emerged from this campaign was that the Federal columns advanced into the Georgia heartland with few wagons.

In fact, the aggregate number of wagons on hand was 2,520, or roughly 40 wagons per thousand men. In contrast, when the 120,000-man Army of the Potomac had set off to confront General Robert E. Lee and the Army of Northern Virginia earlier that year, the Federals marched with 4,300 wagons, or about 35 per thousand. The wagon allotment on the Georgia march was less than Sherman had allowed during the Atlanta Campaign (52 wagons per thousand men), but he was still taking along a lot of wheeled vehicles. The fact that each column had its own wagon train meant that there would be no efficiencies that might have been gained from consolidation into one or two trains. It should also be noted that these calculations do not take into account the pack mules used by the various units, nor does it allow for extra vehicles appropriated on the way.

Providing security for these multiple trains loomed large in the planning of each day's march. It was not unusual for an entire division to be tasked with protecting the wagons, assisting in their movement, or guarding the rear of the train near the tail of the column. Thus on any given day most if not all of four infantry divisions out of thirteen total would be assigned to wagon train security, movement, and maintenance. It was a significant allocation of resources for an undertaking that would become celebrated in popular memory for having hardly existed.

(Not mentioned in Sherman's orders was the substantial cattle herd—about 5,500 head—that would accompany the wings. These cattle had to be driven along the dirt roads and, more importantly, across all watercourses and swamps encountered. By way of comparison, most of the celebrated cattle drives that ambled across the wide open western plains after the war averaged 2,000 to 3,000 head. These were usually managed by a twelve-man crew who moved the animals strung out in a line perhaps five miles long. Using this measure, and remembering that the Georgia terrain was anything but wide open, Sherman's cattle train likely stretched eight to ten miles.)

IV. The army will forage liberally on the country during the march. To this end, each brigade commander will organize a good and sufficient foraging party, under the command of one or more discreet officers, who will gather, near the route traveled, corn or forage of any kind, meat of any kind, vegetables, corn-meal, or whatever is needed by the command, aiming at all times to keep in the wagons at least ten days' provisions for the command and three days' forage. Soldiers must not enter the dwellings of the inhabitants, or commit any trespass, but during a halt or a camp they may be permitted to gather turnips, potatoes, and other vegetables, and to drive in stock in sight of their camp. To regular foraging parties must be intrusted the gathering of provisions and forage at any distance from the road traveled.

Sherman took great care to calculate how many rations he needed to bring along and what foodstuffs he could expect to find on the way. He utilized a map prepared by the Department of the Interior that displayed the Georgia counties he intended to traverse, over which he hand wrote livestock and crop production from information he found in the 1860 Census. "I had wagons enough loaded with essentials, and beef cattle enough to feed on for more than a month," he wrote, "and had the Census statistics showing the produce of every county through which I designed to pass. No military expedition was ever based on sounder or surer data."

Sherman understood exactly what the nonmilitary implications were of these orders. He realized from experience that it would be impossible to strictly enforce the limitations he had set. He knew his boys, and surmised that hardly any approached the status of sainthood. He expected them to be what he would later describe as a "little loose in foraging," and was prepared to accept that a few would do " 'some things they ought not to have done.' " After a recent addition to Sherman's staff pondered these foraging guidelines, he came to a grim conclusion. "Evidently it is a material element in this campaign to produce among the *people of Georgia* a thorough conviction of the personal misery which attends war, and of the utter helplessness and inability of their 'rulers,' State or Confederate, to protect them."

> *V. To army corps commanders alone is intrusted the power to destroy mills, houses, cotton-gins, &c., and for them this general principle is laid down: In districts and neighborhood where the army is unmolested no destruction of such property should be permitted; but should guerrillas or bushwhackers molest our march, or should the inhabitants burn bridges, obstruct roads, or otherwise manifest local hostility, then army commanders should order and enforce a devastation more or less relentless according to the measure of such hostility.*

Sherman's means of imposing some restraint upon the foragers rested on his personal example and the influence exerted on his behalf by his officers. Through past practices and inferences, as well as occasional publication of his orders and communications on the subject, Sherman believed that the thin line between a stern military policy and uncontrolled looting could be managed.

"Of course you cannot question my right to 'forage on the country,' " he lectured an enemy commander late in the conflict. "It is a war right as old as history. The manner of exercising it varies with circumstances, and if the civil authorities will supply my Requisitions, I will forbid all foraging. But I find no civil authorities who can respond to calls for forage or provisions, and therefore must collect directly of the People." Because the South was in conflict with the North, southern civilians had no basis for complaint. "There are well established principles of War & the People of the South having appealed to War are barred from appealing for protection to our Constitution which they have practically and publicly defied. They have appealed to War and must abide *its* Rules & Laws. . . . A People who will persevere in War beyond a certain limit ought to Know the consequences. Many, Many People with less pertinacity than the South has already shown have been wiped out of national Existence."

VI. As for horses, mules, wagons, &c., belonging to the inhabitants, the cavalry and artillery may appropriate freely and without limit, discriminating, however, between the rich, who are usually hostile, and the poor or industrious, usually neutral or friendly. Foraging parties may also take mules or horses to replace the jaded animals or their trains, or to serve as pack-mules for the regiments or brigades. In all foraging, of whatever kind, the parties engaged will refrain from abusive or threatening language, and may, where the officer in command thinks proper, give written certificates of the facts, but no receipts, and they will endeavor to leave with each family a reasonable portion for their maintenance.

In the war's last year, Sherman codified his thinking on this matter: "Now it is clearly our war right to subsist our army on the enemy. Napoleon always did it, but could avail himself of the civil powers he found in existence to collect forage and provisions by regular impressments. We cannot do that here, and I contend if the enemy fails to defend his country we may rightfully appropriate what we want."

VII. Negroes who are able-bodied and can be of service to the several columns may be taken along, but each army commander will bear in mind that the question of supplies is a very important one and that his first duty is to see to them who bear arms.

It is certain that Sherman had no comprehension or care to comprehend the powerful effect that the appearance of his armies had upon the slaves in his path. Twenty-plus years after the fighting ended, he could still avow that "domestic slavery at the South before the war was not cruel and inhuman." To him the matter was one of cold equations, a bloodless calculus. "The U.S. has its hands full, and must first assert its authority and maintain it as against the Armies of the Confederacy, and then it will have time to give some attention to these negroes who have been turned loose by the Planters and former owners," he reasoned in late 1863. More than a year later this outlook was unchanged by experience. "Now you Know that military success is what the nation wants, and it is risked by the crowds of helpless negroes that flock after our armies."

While most of the soldiers in Sherman's columns shared their commander's prejudices, what they encountered led some to a deeper appreciation of the matter. Long after the war, speaking to a gathering of veterans in Ohio, a Union officer who participated in the march told a likely apocryphal tale of coming upon a grinning blind black man sitting amid the ruins of his former owner's plantation, his family scattered to the winds. Asked how he could be so merry with such desolation around him, the black man replied that "bress God, freedom's come." The officer telling the story then reflected: "That was his conception of freedom; it took the place of eyesight and home and friends and children; it was every thing to him; and so I say that the war gave to us a conception of freedom that we never had before."

VIII. The organization at once of a good pioneer battalion for each army corps, composed if possible of negroes, should be attended to. This battalion should follow the advance guard, should repair roads, and double them if possible, so that the columns will not be delayed after reaching bad places. Also, army commanders should study the habit of giving the artillery and wagons the road, and marching their troops on one side, and also instruct the troops to assist wagons at steep hills or bad crossings of streams.

IX. Capt. O.M. Poe, chief engineer, will assign to each wing of the army a pontoon train, fully equipped and organized, and the commanders thereof will see to its being properly protected at all times.

The pontoon trains were Sherman's secret weapon, whose critical role in the coming campaign would be seldom recognized or acknowledged. The route that Sherman ultimately settled on pushed his columns over nine separate rivers or creeks that represented sixteen distinct crossing points (one river, the Ogeechee, would be bridged seven times before the end of the expedition). While men and horses may have splashed over a number of these, the all-important wagons could not. Without a means for prompt and efficient crossing of these obstacles, Sherman's columns faced inordinate delays that in turn degraded foraging results, since the longer the files stood in place, the harder it became to supply them from the nearby countryside. Such delays also offered time for the enemy to concentrate against their opponent's known course. Whether or not Sherman's bold scheme would succeed depended very much on maintaining celerity of movement, which in turn depended on how well the pontoniers did their job.

The man Sherman assigned to make this happen was another individual whose outstanding contributions to the war effort did not translate into postwar fame, except perhaps in the obscure lexicons of military engineers. Orlando M. Poe was a West Pointer with brains (graduating sixth in the class of 1856) whose wartime career path would have severely vexed a less patient man. Although busy in the engineering branch when the Civil War erupted, Poe (like many professionals of his caste) was soon put in charge of leading volunteers into combat.

The skills needed to wrestle nature into compliance transferred well to getting citizen soldiers into fighting shape, so by early 1863 Poe was a brigadier general in charge of a division. Congress now let him fall into administrative limbo by neglecting to confirm his volunteer rank, leaving him the unhappy choices of either resigning from the service or reverting to his lower rank in the regular army. Poe, choosing his first career, returned to the engineers, where he was demoted to captain. It was in this capacity that he entered upon the campaign.

The table of organization for Sherman's forces included three engineer units reporting directly to Poe. The men of the 58th Indiana were responsible for managing the pontoon train for the army's left wing, and to the 1st Missouri Engineers went similar duty for the right. The third engineering unit, the 1st Michigan Engineers and Mechanics, constituted Poe's emergency reserve, to be assigned at his discretion as circumstances arose.

Poe's brief included a number of other activities of importance to Sherman's operation. One was cartography. It was Poe's task to provide Sherman and his key commanders with maps sufficient to enable the four columns to advance in rough parallel with each other. ("I have enough on hand to supply one to each corps and division commander," Poe reported with pardonable pride on November 1.) Working from charts captured from Confederate sources and those compiled by the U.S. Coast Survey, Poe created and duplicated a broadly accurate master layout that showed the principal roads, water barriers, and towns, but was noticeably lacking other significant topographic features and smaller passageways. Once the march was under way, the master maps would be regularly updated by actual observation and from scouting reports, with major changes reproduced photographically for distribution.

Also in the chief engineer's portfolio was general oversight of the various pioneer details. These were construction gangs dedicated to road improvements, clearing bridge approaches, and camp preparations. Each corps was responsible for its own pioneer force (which by the end of the campaign would include a large number of blacks), but Poe represented Sherman's quality control. There was also an amount of scouting undertaken by engineer officers, and when the need arose to destroy some substantial structure or machinery, Poe could expect the call.

"I would be lost without him," Sherman later said of his chief of engineers.

*   *   *

There was one critically important piece in the mosaic of Sherman's planning that he could not control, though, characteristically, he thought he could—the weather. The prospect of heavy rains was Sherman's nightmare, for it would mire his columns as effectively as a major enemy effort. Yet accurate forecasting was much more a folk art in 1864 than a codified science. The concept that weather wasn't a purely local phenomenon but the product of a dynamic process whose origins could lie many hundreds of miles distant was only beginning to take hold. America's great generic genius Benjamin Franklin had grasped this on an intuitive level, but until it was possible to record simultaneous weather observations from stations located across the country, it remained an unproven inspired hunch. Telegraphic communication made such a reporting network technically possible, and a scientist at Washington's Smithsonian Institution named Joseph Henry was taking the first steps in that direction before the war. Henry's efforts halted abruptly when the military commandeered the whole communication infrastructure for its use.

Most of Georgia's weather in November and December was generated by systems spawned in the Colorado region, where cold Canadian air tumbled in with warmer Gulf air in a natural spin cycle. A whirling mass acquires motion with steering largely provided by strong upper-atmosphere wind currents that would remain unknown until the mid-twentieth century, when they would be named after a technology of that era—the jet stream. The irony was that had the knowledge base been there, the network of wires was in place for the military to have provided officers like Sherman with weather reporting information that could have aided their prognostications.

Lacking such a knowledge base, Sherman was left to his own understanding as he pondered the all-important question of when to set off. Politics played a part by dictating that he wait until after the election, but how long after? Some nineteen years into the future, one of Sherman's division commanders in the upcoming campaign, Brigadier General William B. Hazen, would oversee the government's publication of a national anthology of weather proverbs. In the book's preface, Lieutenant H. H. C. Dunwoody, widely recognized for his forecasting acumen, had praise for the folk wisdoms, provided they were looking only a short time ahead ("A mackerel sky, Not twenty-four hours dry"), but pure disdain for those predicting several days or weeks in advance. Yet it was upon one such augury that Sherman now timed the beginning of his march.

Sherman shared this meteorological insight with his military secretary, Major Henry M. Hitchcock, who told his wife about it in a November 10 letter. "The rains seem to have ended, —last night's storm winding up with a bracing wind from the N.W., and this morning being bright and beautiful," Hitchcock reported. "We hope this means just what the General has been desiring, —that the fall rains should come altogether, early in November, and give us fine weather for some weeks, which is what we want now." Sherman had already made this clear to his subcommanders on November 8, when he informed them: "This is the rain I have been waiting for and as soon as it is over we will be off." That same day he told the secretary of war that it "is now raining, which is favorable as the chances are, after it clears away, we will have a long spell of fine weather for marching."

He was blissfully unaware that hundreds of miles to the northwest the elements were beginning to mix and would soon organize themselves into the first of several rain-producing storms, while well overhead the prevailing steering winds were solidly in place to set the storms on a course directly across Sherman's route.

CHAPTER 5

"Paradise of Fools"

SATURDAY, NOVEMBER 12, 1864

The last "up" trains departed today from Atlanta to Chattanooga. Everything that had been deemed unnecessary for the coming operation had been shipped out: camp supplies, animals, people. "It would astonish you to see what the government is doing here in the way of rail roading," a Michigan soldier in Cartersville wrote his siblings. "As many as seventy-five or a hundred trains of cars pass here every twenty-four hours and every train loaded to its utmost capacity." A Minnesota infantryman passing through the town remembered seeing "several trains of cattle cars loaded with women, children, household goods, female slaves, etc., all piled indiscriminately together. Even the tops of the cars were covered with black faces pointed toward the North and liberty."

The forces Sherman had designated for his grand movement into Georgia were gradually converging on Atlanta. Out about sixty-five miles to the northwest were most of the Fifteenth and Fourteenth army corps. Already there were indications of what was to come as squads continued work that had begun on November 10, destroying anything of military usefulness in Rome, Kingston, Cartersville, and points in between. "The Railroad Depots[,] Foundry and every thing of value to the enemy in Rome was destroyed," noted an Ohio soldier. Other, nonmilitary buildings were torched too, "the work of rowdy soldiers." "The light of the conflagration gave the skies a brilliant effect, that was visible many miles distant," reported a correspondent for the *Cincinnati Daily Commercial*, presumably keeping a low profile. An Indiana boy recalled that his regiment "passed Cartersville and burned both it and Kingston. The rations stored in the latter place was issued out to the men and the depot fired." This soldier, who had participated in his share of bloody fighting, was glad to see a hard hand applied to southern civilians. "I think forbearance has long ago ceased to be a virtue," he said.

Closer to Atlanta the Seventeenth Corps was spread out in encampments around Marietta, while the Twentieth Corps was posted throughout the city itself. There, Sherman's chief engineer, Captain Orlando M. Poe, received the orders he had been expecting to begin destroying the city's "railroads, depots, steam machinery, &c." Poe wrote that "Sherman directed me to proceed with my work, but to be careful not to use fire, which would endanger other buildings than those set apart for destruction." A New York officer out for a ride watched a "detail of men [who] were at work tearing down the large railroad building; another squad were tearing down a large brick school building; others were tearing up railroads." A different observer, a New Jersey quartermaster, approved "knocking things to pieces generally and making the old Gate City of the South rather untenable for any Army to hold or manufacture in."

Even as buildings were being felled, amusements were still under way. An Illinois soldier working as a clerk went to one of Atlanta's theaters that evening. The show he saw "opened with a grand overture by a Brass Band followed by musical performances by the leader of the Band, upon a fiddle and drum. Then came a comic song from 'perfect used up man' who promises that whenever he gets up again he'll stay up if he can. Then a patriotic and sentimental song by a trio of soldiers, and last but not least a Pantomime entitled 'The Lovers Serenade.'" This final piece featured a mother and her two daughters whose notoriety stemmed from a scarcity of supply: they were among the last women left in Atlanta. The bored soldier's review: "Did not expect to see much and wasn't disappointed."

Other soldiers amused themselves trying to guess what was in the wind. "Perhaps I may prove to be a false prophet," ventured a Michigan man, "but everything indicates that this part of the country is to be abandoned by our forces." "It is very evident that some great movement is at hand," seconded a Wisconsin officer. "Some think we are going to one place, some to another, but we are evidently going to do something and you may rest assured that Sherman will make his mark again." The speculation was not limited to the Yankee boys. South of Atlanta several Confederate militia and cavalry regiments were monitoring events. Already reports had come in regarding Captain Poe's activities in Atlanta. The enemy juggernaut was stirring. "Events are shaping themselves," a Georgia cavalryman observed grimly.

It was around midday when the very last "up" train pulled out of Atlanta on its northward journey. Soon after it passed, soldier details swarmed over the track to dismantle it. Men and officers watched the engine and cars rattle by with mixed feelings. "I remember seeing the last train going north with a full knowledge that we would be cut off from all knowledge of the world for several weeks at least," recollected a Michigan soldier. An Illinois man felt more anxiety, but not for himself. Among the passengers on that train were "many officers who had resigned, and soldiers whose terms of service had expired," he explained. "Large sums of money were committed to them by their comrades for delivery to families or friends at home."

The passage of the final train left an indelible impression on a senior member of Major General Howard's staff. He never forgot how "slowly but majestically the great driving wheels turn over—the huffing of the engines is heard—the air is made brilliant by bright sparks—the bands play—the men shout themselves hoarse and swing frantically their hats. Good bye! good bye! is heard on every hand as the train moves slowly off. We watch with throbbing hearts and possibly with trembling lips and moistened eyes this last link that binds us to home and friends and all we hold dear. It fades away and disappears at a sharp bend in the road near by, and the whistles shriek their last farewell."

SUNDAY, NOVEMBER 13, 1864

To those around him, William Tecumseh Sherman appeared in fine fettle, a staff aide describing him as being "in good spirits and chatty." The general's bonhomie masked some serious anxieties about his family. Sherman had learned from his wife that his youngest, Charles, was very sick. Writing to his daughters Minnie and Lizzie, he expressed the hope that the infant "will live long and take poor Willy's place in our love." In a last letter to his wife Sherman made it clear that no one could ever take Willy's place. "I may be in error," he confided, "but with him died in me all real ambition and what has come to me since is unsought, unsolicited." When he composed his closing epistle to his great friend, Ulysses Grant, Sherman made light of the uncertainties ahead. "I will not attempt to send Couriers back [to report my movements,] but will trust to the Richmond papers to Keep you well advised."

In Atlanta, Captain Poe's program of destruction continued apace. "Our men under orders have, and are, destroying all public Buildings, all Mills, shops, Hospital buildings and all private buildings that can be turned into machine shops," explained a Minnesota bandsman. "They are also destroying the depots, turn tables and all other fixtures of a large Rail Road Terminus. They are also taking up the rails and ties and destroying them." Already Poe's orderly scheme was being modified by soldier arsonists. A Wisconsin officer was observing the battering down of a heavy stone railroad roundhouse when a "fire suddenly burst out in the opposite side of town somewhere on the Chattanooga Railroad." The thickening smoke drew a crowd of curious, including this officer. "It proved to be the gas works," he commented. "Some soldiers had thrown in a [fire] brand to 'see how it would burn.' " The blaze spread to several nearby foundry buildings, attracting even more spectators, including General Slocum, who simply made sure that any undamaged machinery was destroyed.

That same day the formidable railroad bridge across the Chattahoochee River was smashed. "A cable was attached to some part of the bridge," recalled an Illinois man on the scene. "A regiment pulled at the cable, giving the work a swaying motion that increased to a pendulum-like swing, until at length it began to give way; then huge beams swung loose in the air, iron rails struck fire as they fell upon the stone piers, and several spars came crashing down into the turbulent river." North of the river, the town of Acworth suffered the fate of Rome, Kingston, and Cartersville. "It is evident that our soldiers were determined to burn, plunder, and destroy everything in their way on this march," noted one horrified Federal officer.

South of Atlanta, a small man wearing general's stars and his escort rode into Jonesboro, then the headquarters for Confederate regional operations. Major General Joseph Wheeler, who stood five feet five

inches tall, was described as "very quick and alert in his movements."
He would need to be both, as he found himself the officer in charge of
all the regular Confederate cavalry units assigned to oppose the enemy
south or east of Atlanta. His mounted corps had been part of Hood's
army until Beauregard, in a rare exercise of command authority,
ordered it to maintain contact with Sherman's forces even as Hood's
main body was slipping away to the west. Hood agreed, but only
because he got Bedford Forrest's cavalry in exchange.

Wheeler was a West Pointer who graduated two years ahead of the
Yankee he would be facing, H. Judson Kilpatrick. He shared a lot of
characteristics with his classmate. Like Kilpatrick, Wheeler was at his
best when he could see his enemy and charge. Like Kilpatrick, his after-
action reports usually read more favorably than the results warranted.
Facing an immediate crisis, Wheeler was active to the point of reckless-
ness, very aggressive, and personally courageous. When he had to
manage a broader strategic operation, he was often out of his depth.

Once he arrived in Jonesboro, Wheeler was handed the first of his
new problems. The officer formerly in charge had not given sufficient
attention to intelligence gathering, so while everyone knew that the
enemy was busy burning things in Atlanta, the composition or size of
the Union forces involved was unknown. Wheeler immediately set to
work assigning scouting patrols with orders to identify the enemy
units. He set to his task with a professional determination not shared
by all those serving under him. Reflecting on these times, one Kentucky trooper recalled that he and his comrades "were convinced that
the end [of the war] was near."

William T. Sherman and his staff reached Marietta about midday.
Riding as part of his entourage was Major Henry Hitchcock, a thirty-
five-year-old Saint Louis lawyer and acquaintance who, though protected from the draft by his status and employment, wanted to see
something of the war before the fighting ended. His application to join Sherman's staff had been accepted, and Hitchcock had
caught up with his new boss on October 31. Learning Sherman's ways
was turning into a series of eye-openers for the newly minted military
secretary.

As the command party entered Marietta, Hitchcock was shocked
by the wholesale vandalism he witnessed and, even more unsettling to
him, Sherman's seeming indifference to obvious violations of his

orders. The last straw came when flames erupted from the town court-house. The aide confronted the general, pointing out that the building was doomed. When Sherman answered that there was nothing he could do, Hitchcock began to wonder if he had intended all along to destroy it.

A short time later Sherman took Hitchcock aside to point out some passing soldiers. "There are the men who do this," he explained. "Set as many guards as you please, they will slip in and set fire. . . . I never ordered burning of any dwelling—didn't order this, but can't be helped. I say *Jeff. Davis burnt them.*"

Later that afternoon, Sherman came up to Kilpatrick's cavalry division, where he received an impromptu review. An Indiana trooper present remembered that the army commander "was greeted by cheers from the men all along the line," while a Pennsylvanian in the mounted ranks recalled it as "a beautiful sight." Major Hitchcock was also caught up in the pageantry of the moment and thought the whole affair was "superb for picture." But when he raised his gaze to the horizon, the smoky columns marking Marietta lingered, making for a "terrible commentary on this display and its meaning."

The same sights provoked a very different impression from a Pennsylvania trooper. "The railroad in our rear was completely burned up," he observed. "We were isolated, and spent the night in sleep, or sitting by our fires thinking of friends at home, from whom we were now entirely separated, and [making] conjectures upon the route to be traveled, where our new base was to be, and when we would reach it. For miles around, as far as the eye could reach, great blazing fires lit up the heavens with a glow of magnificence. The work of destruction was going on."

MONDAY, NOVEMBER 14, 1864

The scouts Wheeler had dispatched returned today with much-needed information. They identified three Union Army corps—the Fifteenth, Seventeenth, and Twentieth—and Kilpatrick's cavalry division. Also noted was the railroad wrecking and the fires still burning in Atlanta.[*]

---

[*]   Since Wheeler's effort had been focused east and south of the city, his scouts missed spotting the Fourteenth Corps, which was marching in from the northwest.

What all this information meant was something else again. A flurry of messages clattered out from Wheeler's headquarters. To officials in Richmond he merely noted Yankee camp rumors that "Sherman will move forward." Reporting the same to General Hood, Wheeler allowed the possible targets as "Augusta and Savannah." His message copied to Lieutenant General Richard Taylor, whose command area lay to the south, designated the possible threats to "Mobile or Savannah." The list of those receiving Wheeler's report underscored a critical flaw in the entire Confederate defensive scheme.

The region south and east of Atlanta consisted of a number of defensive zones centered around built-up areas. From his headquarters in Charleston, Lieutenant General Hardee was responsible for Savannah and Augusta. Richard Taylor, based in Selma, Alabama, worried about a thrust toward Mobile. Macon was Howell Cobb's watch, while another officer looked after Columbus.[*] It was Jefferson Davis's hope that these officers would collaborate for their mutual interest, but in practice few were willing to risk weakening their already inadequate resources to assist a neighbor. To further complicate the situation, all the areas outside these defensive zones were someone else's problem. Beauregard had been brought in to break down these administrative barriers, and how well he did his job or failed to do it would be an important factor in the coming campaign.

For his part, Beauregard spent this day in Tuscumbia, Alabama, engaged in a frustrating effort to glean the plans Hood had for the Army of Tennessee. Ever since he had first met with Hood back on October 9, Beauregard had been trying to work in tandem with the increasingly unpredictable commander of the largest Confederate force in the west. Choosing to believe that Hood was operating with the direct sanction of Jefferson Davis, Beauregard declined to exert any peremptory authority, instead limiting himself to persuasion and suggestions. It seemed, however, that Hood was having none of it.

Beauregard's particular odyssey with Hood started at their second meeting. It was supposed to be at Blue Pond, northeast of Jacksonville, Alabama, but when Beauregard arrived he learned that Hood's headquarters were nearly thirty miles farther west. Nettled that Hood

---

[*] No one contemplated a serious defense of Georgia's capital, Milledgeville; nevertheless, Governor Brown and the state assembly expected to be kept informed.

hadn't bothered to inform his immediate superior of the change, Beau-regard finally caught up with his principal subordinate on October 21 in Gadsden. It was here that Beauregard learned that Hood was abort-ing the harassment scheme approved by Jefferson Davis, and was intending instead to invade Tennessee in order to capture Nashville.

Beauregard spent two days closeted with Hood working on the new plan, with special attention to one factor that the army commander seemed predisposed to ignore—logistics. The campaign Hood now proposed to undertake had a remote chance of succeeding, and only if "carried out fearlessly and, above all, judiciously." In almost the same thought, however, Beauregard also acknowledged that Hood "might not be able to execute it as designed." Yet despite these serious misgiv-ings, he made no effort to stop the operation from proceeding. It never entered Beauregard's mind to put his foot down in any manner. Not that Hood made it easy. The next meeting played out like the second, with Beauregard en route to the agreed-upon rendezvous only to dis-cover that Hood and his army were elsewhere. With Sherman keeping his distance, it wasn't enemy pressure that was causing these abrupt alterations of course, but rather Hood's own constantly evolving appre-ciation of the situation.

Their relationship was becoming spiked with petty spites. Deciding to exercise a little authority, Beauregard ordered one of Hood's corps to assemble in formation on November 12 for what he considered an "informal review." Hood, after promptly canceling the event, moved his headquarters to the north bank of the Tennessee River, again with-out informing his superior. Beauregard fumed while his assistant adju-tant general combed the army camps, searching for Hood. He persisted in his belief that Hood was operating with the continued approval of Jefferson Davis.

Unknown to the commander of the Division of the West, Davis had just taken Hood to task for not striking at any scattered portion of Sherman's force or, in military parlance, beating them in detail. Hood answered (directly to Davis) that Sherman had not begun dividing his force (some of it heading north, some south) until after the gap between them had widened so that a sudden blow was not possible. While promising Davis to take advantage of every opportunity that presented itself to hurt Sherman, Hood pushed ahead with his developing scheme to invade Tennessee.

In far-off Richmond the topic of the day was the confirmation received that Abraham Lincoln had been reelected for a second term, along with speculation on what impact it would have on the war. The editors of the *Richmond Examiner* had been poring over the New York papers, which were reporting Sherman's plans that Federal authorities in Virginia had tried to suppress. The prospect of a march through Georgia, the *Examiner* decided, was a "big Yankee lie." It didn't take a military genius to see that Sherman's only purpose in burning his Atlanta base was to concentrate against Hood. Even if the New York reports were true, the *Examiner* continued, a movement across Georgia without a supply base waiting would only "lead him to the Paradise of Fools."

Sherman, who reached Atlanta during the afternoon, was pleased by all the reports he received—food and forage were well in hand, and Captain Poe was hard at work wrecking legitimate military targets. The engineer's principal objectives this day were the railroad lines that in better times had pumped commerce into the city like arteries bringing blood. "We burn all stations, towns &c along the line of the R.R. leaving the country desolate," scribbled an Ohio diarist.

Another diary keeper, one of Captain Poe's men, wrote, "Today we are at work tearing up track and committing all kinds of destruction, for to[day] we have burnt up 2 large depots and a round house which was large enough to hold 50 or more engines. We also blowed up a stone depot with 700 lbs of powder." The ingenuity displayed by Captain Poe's men was impressive. The railroad depot "was a fine building some 80 ft. wide & 200 long with an arched roof with no supports resting on brick side walls in which smaller arched doorways were placed closely together," remembered a Massachusetts infantryman. "A Battering Ram was improvised out of a heavy iron rail slung by the middle from a high horse. With this a half-a-dozen men knocked away pier after pier while the roof came down a part at a time." "I saw that magnificent structure the depot fall this morning," recorded an Indiana soldier, "and the crash was terrible indeed."

As daylight yielded to evening, much of the official work paused, and the unofficial activities began. A soldier in the ranks of a late-arriving regiment, some eight miles out from the city, could plainly "see the smoke of her burning as from afar." An Illinois soldier noted, "Tremendous fires in Atlanta to-day." A Michigan surgeon stood in awe as "the flames mount up to heaven, hissing, crashing & rushing on from one [building] over to another." To a New Jersey officer the "vast waves and sheets of flames thrusting themselves heavenward, rolling and tossing in mighty billows" was a "grand but awful sight."

A precocious ten-year-old named Carrie Berry, whose father had been allowed to remain in town because he was doing Union Army work, wrote in her diary: "They came burning Atlanta to day. We all dread it because they say that they will burn the last house before they stop. We will dread it."

The experience of one Fourteenth Corps brigade marching into Atlanta represented William Tecumseh Sherman's worst nightmare. Led by a guide unfamiliar with the roads, the unit was sent in the wrong direction at an intersection. "We already had marched twenty miles when we reached the river and after marching two miles down the river an aid[e] from division headquarters came up and ordered our brigade back," remembered one footsore Minnesota soldier. "Wagons crossing delayed us so that it was eight o'clock before we reached our stopping place. The colonel was mad and the boys were mad. . . . When one thing goes wrong everything seems perverse, and we were delayed by numberless little circumstances." Were this brigade's experiences to become the norm in the days ahead, the danger to the integrity of the columns would be great. Other than lots of weary men, no damage was done in this case, save to the ego of the guide who erred. "I think that had the officer who led us astray heard all the remarks made about him, he would not have felt highly flattered," said the soldier. Added an Ohio man in the same brigade, "there was swearing enough to make the air blue."

In the hundreds of camps around Atlanta, Union soldiers completed their own preparations, mental and otherwise. This meant a thorough housecleaning in the bivouac of the 1st Battery, Minnesota Light Artillery, whose members had just learned that no personal baggage would be allowed on the cannon limbers. One gunner and his pal "overhauled our knapsacks & destroyed several shirts, pair of pantaloons & other clothing, besides both our journals." The infantry had less to discard and more time to ponder. Thinking how cut off they now were from the North, an Illinois soldier recorded "a feeling of loneliness beyond anything we have yet experienced." Another Illinois man, on guard duty this evening, marveled at the power represented by all the bivouac fires. He thought that "the earth seems like another firmament decorated with twinkling stars but it is only a Yankee camp."

Sherman set up his headquarters in the house owned by John Neal,* where he got a taste of Captain Poe's work when some fragments "came uncomfortably near" from a secret ammunition cache that exploded in a nearby burning building. All of his forces save the Fourteenth Corps were scheduled to start out tomorrow. That meant there were time-tables to check, wagon loads to secure, a cattle herd to organize, and orders to confirm. Already the vast machine that was Sherman's operation was in motion as scouting parties slipped out of town to reconnoiter the first day's routes. No one expected any serious opposition on day one, but a prudent commander took no chances. Flurries of orders issued from the various Union headquarters as final operational decisions were announced.

The Twentieth Corps, representing half of the Left Wing, would march eastward from Atlanta following the Decatur Road. Major General Henry W. Slocum, in charge of the wing, would ride with this corps. The Left Wing's other component, the late-arriving Fourteenth Corps, would spend November 15 in Atlanta, completing its resupply. The commander of the Twentieth Corps, Brigadier General Alpheus S. Williams, was especially concerned about maintaining the pace, telling his family in his last letter to them that "the prospect of bad roads is not amusing." Williams's instructions to his pioneer detachments were especially detailed. He worried too about discipline on the march. "Straggling and pillaging must be stopped by the most prompt measures," read his orders, "the safety of the corps depends upon this."

Both Right Wing corps would be marching on November 15—the Fifteenth Corps under Major General Peter J. Osterhaus† and the Seventeenth led by Major General Frank P. Blair Jr. Major General Oliver O. Howard, commanding the wing, fretted about the ammunition supply, which could not be replenished en route. His told his corps commanders that "the greatest possible economy must be observed in its use." Major General Osterhaus did not want his corps to thin out

---

* Referred to in contemporary accounts as "Judge Lyon's house" after its occupant at the time.
† The corps had been commanded during the Atlanta Campaign by Major General John A. Logan, who was on leave, politicking in Illinois, when the army departed the Gate City.

while marching and reminded the leading division not to move too fast. Frank Blair warned that "the flanks of the army will be infested to a greater or less extent with bands of guerrillas, whose principal object will be to pick up stragglers." His remedy was to institute the "most rigid measures" to keep the men in ranks.

To Kilpatrick's cavalry Sherman gave the job of clearing the way and screening Howard's right flank. For all his bravado and bluster, Kilpatrick was nervous about the upcoming operation. "Was there no enemy to oppose us?" he asked. "Yes, yes! sufficient, if concentrated in our front, to have disputed the passage of every river and delayed us days and days, which of itself would have been fatal." To a soldier-correspondent who wrote from the ranks of the 9th Pennsylvania Cavalry, the fires and destruction he witnessed on the ride into Atlanta represented the "signal that a great and hazardous move was about to be made." A trooper in the 9th Ohio Cavalry expected no easy time, since he understood that the "position of the cavalry . . . was to be at all times between the infantry and the enemy."

Throughout the "selling" of this campaign to Grant, Halleck (and through him to Lincoln), and even Thomas, Sherman had held out the prospect of his launching damaging strikes at Macon and Augusta, places containing significant strategic targets. Now, as he finalized his orders for the first phase of the operation, Sherman removed Macon from the list. His orders to General Howard, whose line of march would bring him within range of the munitions and war manufacturing center, specified a route "via McDonough and Monticello, to Gordon," bypassing Macon.

Sherman gave his reasons well after the fact. Posing a threat to Macon was more advantageous than actually assaulting its fortifications, since the enemy would have to assign scant resources to its defense, leaving the pathways north of it uncontested. This was critical, since Sherman's biggest concern was any potential "opposition at these great rivers which crossed our path, where a few thousand men well handled could have delayed us for weeks and swelled the dangers and difficulties." Also, capturing Macon could take days, and Sherman knew that he "could not then afford to lie in siege . . . even for a week, because the necessity for food compelled us to move through new fields daily." So Macon was to be spared, though Sherman planned to give every indication of intending otherwise.

Six days earlier he had issued a statement to his men, telling them just about all he wanted them to know regarding the upcoming operation. It circulated through the various regimental camps where some heard it read for the first time today:

The general commanding deems it proper at this time to inform the officers and men of the Fourteenth, Fifteenth, Seventeenth, and Twentieth Corps, that he has organized them into an army for a special purpose, well known to the War Department and to General Grant. It is sufficient for you to know that it involves a departure from our present base, and a long and difficult march to a new one. All the chances of war have been considered and provided for, as far as human sagacity can. All he asks of you is to maintain that discipline, patience, and courage, which have characterized you in the past; and he hopes, through you, to strike a blow at our enemy that will have a material effect in producing what we all so much desire, his complete overthrow. Of all things, the most important is, that the men, during marches and in camp, keep their places and do not scatter about as stragglers or foragers, to be picked up by a hostile people in detail. It is also of the utmost importance that our wagons should not be loaded with any thing but provisions and ammunition. All surplus servants, non-combatants, and refugees, should now go to the rear, and none should be encouraged to encumber us on the march. At some future time we will be able to provide for the poor whites and blacks who seek to escape the bondage under which they are now suffering. With these few simple cautions, he hopes to lead you to achievements equal in importance to those of the past.

PART TWO

Atlanta to Milledgeville

NOVEMBER 15–24

CHAPTER 6

"Dies Irae Filled the Air"

TUESDAY, NOVEMBER 15, 1864
Midnight–Noon

———— *Left Wing* ————

The camps of the Twentieth Corps began stirring well before sunrise, some as early as 3:00 A.M. Starting around 5:00 A.M., corps officers began the complicated task of herding their roughly 13,700 men into marching order along the Decatur Road. A New Jersey quartermaster marveled at the process of "waiting and working to get order out of chaos, organizing and arranging the confused array of troops, trains, artillery, ambulances and other impedimenta that had there massed."

A gunner in one of the four batteries accompanying the corps encountered a group of happy soldiers. "They had just been paid off and were playing chuckaluck," he remembered. The cannoneers were grumpy, for some had just learned that they could not store their knapsacks on the artillery wagons but would have to carry them. The "boys make up faces about it," commented the gunner. The mood was more solemn in the ranks of the First Brigade, Second Division. A soldier in the 5th Ohio, injured on November 14, died this morning. There was only time for an abbreviated graveside service and a hasty burial on the divisional campgrounds.

Atlanta

Weather:
partly cloudy
low 40s to mid-50s

Lithonia
Conyers
Apalachee
Social
Circle
Rutledge
Covington
Madison
Buckhead
Greensboro
Stockbridge
Jonesboro
Newborn
(Sandtown)
Lovejoy's Station
McDonough
Shady
Dale
Bear Creek
Station
Jackson
Eatonton
N
Griffin
Monticello
Planter's
Factory
Hillsboro
Blountsville

UNDER THE GUN
[LW] Lithonia
[RW] Stockbridge
[Cavalry] Jonesboro

Milledgeville

Forsyth
Clinton

Atlanta to Milledgeville
DAY ONE:
Tuesday, November 15, 1864

Gordon
Griswoldville
Macon
Irwinton

The First Division began marching around 7:00 A.M. The order for today's movement was the First followed by the Second and Third. Their route took them through an area that had been the scene of intense fighting in July. "Here we saw low breastworks that were made while the battle was raging, broken trees, empty ammunition boxes, parts of soldiers' equipment, canteens, and haversacks scattered in all directions," recalled a New York soldier.

The old battlefield also represented a good vantage point for viewing Atlanta. A New York infantryman was one of many this day who paused here and turned his gaze toward the Gate City. "I beheld a column of black smoke ascending to the sky," he wrote. "Then another column of smoke arose, and another, and another, until it seemed that they all merged together and the whole city was in flames." For the New Jersey quartermaster it was a "fearful sight." The heavy smoke hid most of what was happening from view, "but the crackling of the flames and crack of falling walls and buildings told the worst was going on." Recollected an Indiana boy, "as we left I had to think about Sodom and Gomorrah."

The newspaperman present for the *New York Herald* noted that the three divisions of the Twentieth Corps, "with a [supply] train of more than six hundred wagons," occupied "when stretched out on the march, nearly eight miles of road." While the advance started out at about 7:00 A.M., the trailing division and the wagons would not begin their march until nearly noon.

Atlanta

With the logistical tails of the two wings still in the process of leaving town and an entire army corps arriving, Atlanta was heavily congested this morning. A Fourteenth Corps staff officer who rode in at 9:00 A.M. "found every street so crowded with troops and wagons that it was almost impossible to get along on horseback." Somehow Captain Poe and his detachments continued their work amidst the bustle and hurry. The first part of today's program involved finishing the job already begun "battering down the walls, throwing down smokestacks, breaking up furnace arches, knocking steam machinery to pieces and punching all boilers full of holes." It was the second part of the program that most worried Poe, when fire would be set to the heaps of debris left after the wrecking was completed. The chief engineer knew from experience that once the soldiers saw his men setting controlled blazes, there would be little to stop them from undertaking their own uncontrolled retribution.

Matters were already out of hand in places. Near the camp of the 58th Indiana, a regiment specializing in bridge building, pontoon drills were interrupted by the torching of a nearby cluster of wood-frame hospitals. According to the regimental chaplain, "First, there was a hammering and banging within, as the kindling was being prepared; and soon flames began to rise from the numerous small buildings. The lumber used in the construction of the houses was pine, hence the flames spread rapidly." Instead of indignation or anger, the good chaplain felt only detached resignation. "A notion has possessed the army that Atlanta is to be burned, but I suppose the wish is father to the thought."

Destruction was also on William Tecumseh Sherman's mind this morning, though he was contemplating the kinds justified by the rules of war. His orders to Poe had been explicit; the only structures in

Atlanta liable for destruction were those "which could be converted to hostile uses." Poring over his maps this morning, Sherman realized that the route planned for the Left Wing bypassed a pair of important bridges at the Oconee River. That would not do. Off to Major General Henry Slocum went instructions to detach a sufficient force to wreck them once he reached the town of Madison.

Perhaps responding to the dour mask Major Hitchcock had sported since they had departed from Marietta, Sherman took pains at breakfast to explain why Atlanta was paying such a terrible price. By his reckoning, the great amount of munitions and material that was either produced in the city or shipped from it made Atlanta second only to Richmond as a strategic target. "We have been fighting Atlanta all the time, in the past: have been capturing guns, wagons, etc., etc., marked 'Atlanta' and made here, all the time: and now since they have been doing so much to destroy us and our Government we have to destroy them, at least enough to prevent any more of that," Sherman said.

―――― *Right Wing* ――――

The powerful Right Wing—consisting of the approximately 15,900-man Fifteenth Corps, the 11,700-strong Seventeenth Corps, and some 5,100 cavalry—roused early to begin moving at daylight. The Fifteenth Corps marched in sequential order; the First Division followed by the Second and the Third.* The Seventeenth Corps advanced Third, Fourth, First.† Since the Confederates had been always most concerned about a quick Yankee thrust toward Macon, they had posted much of their available cavalry and militia to meet just such a contingency. So, unlike the Left Wing, which passed without incident through a widely dispersed line of enemy scouts this day, the soldiers and troopers of the Right Wing had people shooting at them almost immediately.

Pressing rapidly southward in conjunction with the right flank of the Fifteenth Corps, Kilpatrick's cavalry overran a Confederate out-

---

* The corps marched today without its late-arriving Fourth Division, which would spend the next twenty-four hours resting and resupplying in Atlanta.
† The Seventeenth Corps consisted of three divisions for this campaign, its Second Division having been assigned to Major General Thomas in Nashville.

post at East Point even before the enemy realized what was happening. A young rider in the 10th Ohio Cavalry recorded it as an "Exciting time," boasting that they "ran into the Rebel Pickets, drove them into their camp, took their camp, Equipage, several prisoners and part of their wagon train." The officer commanding the brigade later counted eight POWs captured.

Spirits were generally high among the foot soldiers. "We were cheery and marching quite rapidly," said an Ohio infantryman in the Fifteenth Corps, "and the boys struck up the anthem, John Brown's soul goes marching on, and other National airs." "Started early this morning for the Southern coast, somewhere, and we don't care, so long as Sherman is leading us," exulted an Iowan in the Seventeenth Corps. Rather than Sherman, a Missouri man put his reliance "on our strength and the Providence of God."

There were problems small and large. In the ranks of the 31st Iowa the worry was over soldier James Martin, who had broken out with a fever soon after the movement got under way and who was clearly showing signs of the measles. The regiment's options were to leave him to the tender mercies of the Southerners or carry him along. The ailing soldier was put into a wagon as the column tramped southward.* In the Seventeenth Corps Brigadier General Manning F. Force was fuming. Yesterday his division commander had insisted on issuing whiskey to the soldiers. Today there were several so inebriated in one company that they could not stay in ranks. Force, determined to make an example of the unit commander, hastily composed an order reprimanding him to be read at evening camp.

Bigger problems confronted the commanders of the trailing divisions. Although the head of each corps was marching well, delays farther back along the line were considerably slowing down the supply vehicles. "It took some time for this large body of troops to move out with its great wagon train," declared a brigadier in the Fifteenth Corps. "We . . . made slow progress," added a Minnesota soldier, "ten minutes' march and twenty minutes' standstill, weight on left leg and head under wing." In an effort to get things moving, a company of the 1st

---

* Martin would make the entire journey as an invalid. A mention of him dated December 15 describes his condition as "very low."

Missouri Engineers was taken off road repair duties and assigned to assist the wagon teams.

It was late in the morning when the leading Fifteenth Corps elements encountered and dispersed a Confederate outpost near an unapologetically named station stop on the Macon and Western Railroad. "We found some Rebel pickets at Rough and Ready, who fled precipitately on the approach of our advance," crowed a soldier in the 100th Indiana. Frantic outriders carried word of the Yankee progress to one of the most experienced Confederate units posted in the area.

Organized throughout Kentucky in the first flush of Southern nationhood in 1861, the Rebel brigade from the Bluegrass State had seen action in some of the west's fiercest battles, including those of the Atlanta Campaign. Once it became clear that the unbreakable Federal grip on their home state meant they could not go home, men took to calling these Kentucky soldiers the "Orphan" Brigade. In September the Kentucky infantrymen were pulled out of the Army of Tennessee, put on horses largely confiscated from captured Federal raiders, and appended as "mounted infantry" to the defensive area south of Atlanta.

For acting major John Weller, the reassignment had provided a welcome interlude after numbingly endless periods of marching and fighting. As an added benefit, Weller had gotten to know the Stubbs family, whose house fell within his defensive zone. The young lady of the house was such a special attraction that each day Weller tried to time his inspection tours to arrive at the Stubbses' place around 10:00 A.M. Then, "if she was in good voice," Miss Stubbs "would sing the sweet songs of the day and chat so entertainingly, that, somehow, dinner would be announced before I was aware of the flight of time." Today, Weller had just assured the young lady's worried father that there would be plenty of warning should the Yankees move out of Atlanta when he was called to the front gate, where one of his troopers was waiting. "Cap.," the courier said excitedly, "they are fighting at headquarters!" With a hasty good-bye to the Stubbs family, Weller rode off toward Atlanta.

Noon–Midnight

If word of Sherman's march reached the Georgia capital of Milledge-ville this day, there was nothing on the state legislative docket to show it. A reporter present for the *Augusta Daily Chronicle & Sentinel* filed this report:

> *The session is drawing its slow length along.*
>
> *There is a tiresome amount of debate in the House. Petty issues often consume hours in running discussion, and it is a little notable that some of the poorest speakers are those who are oftenest on the floor.*
>
> *The most predominant feature of the session is the introduction of bills to change the lines between certain counties. These bills are so numerous and so apparently trifling, as to be generally regarded a nuisance and encumbrance to the calendar. A man becomes dissatisfied with some action of his county, or with the rate of local tax, and runs to the Legislature to be cut off into another county. The practice consumes much time. Several bills for changing lines were passed to day, none of which would interest your readers.*

The authorities in charge of the Confederate prison compound Camp Lawton, outside Millen, began the process of thinning out its population. According to an Illinois POW, "Nearly one thousand sick and wounded leave here to-day for Savannah to be exchanged." For those left behind, conditions remained grim. An Ohio prisoner drafted as a butcher recalled that he and his comrades "slaughtered thirty-five head of cattle per day; the animals were small and very lean, averaging about 350 pounds each; this, after deducting rations for the officers and guards, left about one-fourth of a pound per man, per diem, including the bone."

Left Wing

The region through which the Twentieth Corps marched had already been well scoured during Atlanta's two-month occupation, so prospects for grub were slim. "We have found but little forage today as the country has been foraged over before," grumbled a Wisconsin soldier.

The village of Decatur barely registered with most of the Yankee boys, though it lay square in their path. A Connecticut soldier thought it "a small and insignificant place." A New Jersey quartermaster who paused there for dinner had time for a more complete survey. Decatur, he noted in his journal, had "its Court House, a dilapidated enclosure in the square where the marketing is done, with the usual amount of stores and taverns around the square, and also a church and some 40 or 50 other buildings."*

The stop-and-go slogging pace meant idleness for portions of the Twentieth Corps column, which in turn meant time for mischief. "As our advances was slow and the night very damp, several deserted houses along our route were burned," wrote an Illinois soldier. The officer commanding the 33rd Indiana noted that after his unit passed through Decatur at dusk, "many of the buildings were wrapped in flames." The Illinoisan, who put the number at "several," opined that the incendiarism ended when "guards were stationed through the town." Further down the road, some unoccupied outbuildings of a small farm fell victim to vandals. Recalled a Connecticut soldier, "I remember one very pretty girl weeping with her family over the ruins of their stable, expressing a wish 'that you'uns were millions of miles away.' "

The head of the Twentieth Corps column went into camp late in the afternoon near an impressive natural landmark known as Stone Mountain. A very awed Ohio boy described it as "a vast body of granite rock devoid of vegetation which rises abruptly & majestically from a large plain to a towering height."† "Standing thus isolated and rising to such a height, it forms a very striking feature in the landscape," seconded a New Yorker. Another from the Empire State added that the sight excited the "surprise and wonder of our boys whose homes were in the shadows of the Adirondacks; when home, they looked at mountains every day but they never saw a mountain like this."

The Left Wing covered some thirteen to fifteen miles today. Orders for the next day projected the advance even deeper into Georgia, but as the soldiers bedded down for the night, most eyes were oriented toward Atlanta. An Illinoisan observed that "the western sky was

---

* The village had been the site of a major Union headquarters during summer operations around Atlanta.
† Actually, about 750 feet.

lighted up with a more brilliant glow than that imparted by the sun's declining rays; it was the light of burning buildings." "I suppose 'Atlanta' is one of the things that were but is not," quipped an Ohio soldier. The thoughts of an Indiana officer were apocalyptic. "Dies irae, Dies irae filled the air," he reflected, "and fell upon the hearts of the inhabitants of doomed Georgia."

Right Wing

The sots who had so infuriated Brigadier General Force were still out cold when the trailing division marched past them. "I saw 4 or 5 drunk men lying beside the road," an Iowan noted in his diary. Few in the tail end of the two columns were enjoying the day. "The wagons, being rather heavily loaded our progress as rear guard is very slow," griped one of them. His regiment, the 64th Illinois, was the end of the end, the last in line in the last brigade of the last division in today's rotation. This meant they had to drive forward all the stragglers they encountered. Another in the ranks found their job "a disagreeable task, for, in the case of a large army like ours, it must be that some, from accident, sickness or otherwise will be found far in the rear of their respective commands; in consequence, our duty necessitates us to urge them on farther than their physical strength will oftimes permit them." The fate of the drunks is unrecorded.

Sweeping south just to the west of the Fifteenth Corps, Kilpatrick's cavalry encountered enemy positions on full alert near Jonesboro. The Confederate commander, Wheeler, had been in the town as late as 2:30 P.M., when he sent off his only summary of today's movements, reporting that the Federals (units unidentified) "advanced with infantry, cavalry, artillery and wagons early this morning. Have driven our cavalry back to this place. Enemy have burned many houses in Rome, Marietta and Atlanta; they also destroyed railroad and burned railroad bridges over Chattahoochee [River]." Right after sending this, Wheeler moved his headquarters to the next line of resistance, near Griffin, leaving a rear guard covering Jonesboro.*

---

* Wheeler's strength during the opening phase of the campaign was approximately 2,500 men.

This force was engaged late in the afternoon by Kilpatrick's vanguard, consisting of the 8th Indiana Cavalry and the 5th Kentucky Cavalry. The Confederates, fighting from behind earthworks backed with some artillery, were holding the Indiana troopers at bay until the Kentucky regiment rushed in from a side road. At this point, recorded a proud Hoosier cavalryman, "We charged them and drove them back in confusion." The Rebels retreated to another prepared position just south of the town, formidable enough to deter further pursuit. "I deemed it best to retire," reported the careful Union Kentucky commander.

There was more combat to the east as first the Seventeenth and then the Fifteenth Corps pressed against the long line held by some 1,000 members of the Orphan Brigade. When the riders screening the Union infantry struck the Orphan position, the Yankees found themselves under fire and out of carbine range, as the recently mounted Confederate infantrymen had retained their rifles. The resulting fight was more noisy than deadly, though acting major Weller, up from his visit to the Stubbs farm, was certain that his boys "were hitting some one every now and then."

The two Right Wing infantry columns, which departed Atlanta by separate routes, were converging now, and even as the badly outnumbered Kentucky rebels were gamely preparing to resist the whole Seventeenth Corps, leading elements of the Fifteenth appeared suddenly on their left flank. Like the Orphans, this was another body of infantry mounted on horses. The 29th Missouri numbered about 115 men, but unlike the Orphans, they were armed with shorter-range cavalry carbines. "We made lots of noise, but didn't hurt the 'rebs' much; neither did they hurt us much," recalled a member of the unit. With the Yankees in large numbers flooding in from front and flank, discretion triumphed over valor as the Confederate combat veterans retreated toward Stockbridge.

The Orphan Brigade's withdrawal was part of a general pullback of Confederate forces south of Atlanta. Most of the Georgia militia gathered around Lovejoy's Station on the Macon and Western line. Altogether, some 2,400 soldiers made a weary night tramp toward Macon, stopping at Griffin. "We had a very hard march . . . ," one militiaman wrote his wife. "We rather skeddadled, I think."

From Griffin, Georgia major general Howell Cobb promptly forgot anything Jefferson Davis had said about not counting on outside help. Cobb shot off a brief report of affairs to Richmond, indicating that all local forces were in the process of concentrating at Macon. It was there, Cobb informed the distant Confederate officials, "where re-enforcements should be sent at once."

Also today, Major General Joseph Wheeler made it official regarding a matter that would become a controversial aspect of the coming campaign—the treatment of Georgia civilians by his men. When he had left Hood's army, Wheeler's instructions were to "destroy everything from which the enemy might derive sustenance." The cavalry commander now significantly scaled back these orders, limiting his men to wrecking factory machinery and driving off stock, but only if they were in the enemy's path. No foraging of civilian supplies or burning of buildings was authorized. However, Wheeler's directives ignored the fact that his command lacked a supply system, so his men would have to live off the land. Additionally, it was Confederate policy that cavalrymen were individually responsible for replacing animals lost in action. All this, coupled with the loose control Wheeler exerted over his far-flung units, would seriously limit his enforcement of these new guidelines.

The Right Wing columns marched through the briefly held Rebel defenses before finding sufficient water and camping space for the night; the Fifteenth Corps near the South Fork of the Cotton River, the Seventeenth on Upton Creek. As the tired men moved about their bivouacs, their gaze was drawn irresistibly northward. "The whole region for miles was lighted up with a strange and indescribable glare," recollected an Ohio soldier. "Atlanta on fire—Ah! cruel war," echoed another Buckeye, "and cruel it has become."

Atlanta

One major miscalculation this day was the assumption that the Fourteenth Corps and the Fourth Division of the Fifteenth Corps—both still in Atlanta—could be effectively resupplied. Thanks to the empty shelves reflecting the goods already shipped north or snagged by the columns now under way, plus the constantly expanding blazes, it was proving difficult for those still in town to restock. A staff officer in the

Fourteenth Corps recalled that things went relatively smoothly until after 3:00 P.M., when the spreading fires prompted frustrated supply clerks to tell the "soldiers to go in and take what they wanted before it burned up." "As we left the town the Quartermasters were throwing clothing into the streets for the boys rather than have them burned up as the flames rapidly approached," seconded an Illinois man in the Fifteenth Corps.

The members of a regiment who replaced their worn outfits with new had to perform a maneuver that wasn't in the drill book. "It must have been a weird sight to see this horde of excited men frantically trying to change clothing while on the march, the officers at the same time attempting to maintain a semblance of discipline," remembered one soldier in the ranks. "Guns at all angles, bundles under arms, one foot shod, the other with sock only, pants on backward, everything askew but all good natured."

Captain Poe's men had done their jobs to his exacting satisfaction, enabling him to report that for "military purposes the city of Atlanta has ceased to exist." Poe also derided those "lawless persons, who, by sneaking around in blind alleys, succeeded in firing many houses which it was not intended to touch." In his diary, Poe branded these unauthorized actions a "great scandal of our army." The result was what one Ohio soldier called "smoke, dust, bustle and confusion." "This has b[e]en a dreadful day," scribbled the young diarist Carrie Berry. "Things have b[e]en burning all around us." When darkness fell, the Berrys were relieved to see a provost guard assigned to their house, yet the whole family still sat up all night, fearfully watching for flying embers and other flaring debris.

Punctuating the crackling inferno was the uneven staccato of exploding munitions. Some Union soldiers thought this was dud U.S. ordnance from the brief siege and bombardment back in August, while others put the blame on hidden caches of Confederate stores. "Every instant there was the sharp report, or the smothered burning sound of exploding shells and powder concealed in the buildings, and then the sparks and flames shooting away up in the black and red roof, scattering the cinders far and wide," observed an Illinois soldier.

Which buildings survived and which were lost was sometimes a matter of luck and sometimes the result of courageous personal initiative. Thanks to the vigorous protests of Father Thomas O'Reilly, pastor of the Church of the Immaculate Conception, soldier squads were detailed to protect it and several other houses of worship as well as at least one public building. It took an inspired ruse by Dr. Peter Paul Noel D'Alvigny to preserve the Atlanta Medical College from the flames. When a Federal work party arrived to begin torching the structure, D'Alvigny showed them a ward full of patients not yet evacuated. The surprised officer in charge agreed to postpone the job until morning. D'Alvigny gambled (rightly) that his hospital would be overlooked in the hurry to leave town the next day. Only after the kindling had been extinguished and the Yankees gone did the doctor dismiss the hospital attendants he had pressed into service for his charade.

In his later years, when he had a lot to say about the incidents of his military career, William Tecumseh Sherman was tight-lipped about the burning of Atlanta. Neither his campaign report (written on New Year's Day 1865) nor his *Memoirs* (published in 1875) justifies it. His recently added staff officer, Major Henry Hitchcock, captured a fleeting vignette of Sherman watching the flames this night with the comment that the glare would be "probably . . . visible at Griffin, fifty miles off." An Ohio officer in the Fourteenth Corps added this recollection: "I saw Gen. Sherman walking about the streets of the blazing city paying no heed to the flames seemingly nothing." Concluded this officer, "I don't believe he has any mercy in his composition."

A round of especially fiery spasms erupted between 8:00 and 10:00 P.M. "The [blazing] waves rolled from house to house and from block to block like the waves of the sea," wrote a New York soldier. One of Captain Poe's detachment, watching from a good observation point, thought the scene before him "was truly superb with a touch of the terrific. Nearly the whole business part of town, where all the large buildings were, was in flames. . . . Great tongues of flame shot up fifty ft. above the roofs & constantly the walls would fall in with a crash which sent a cloud of cinders up among the stars." A Massachusetts soldier long remembered the "strange light, and the roaring of the flames that licked up everything habitable, the intermittent explosions of powder, . . . the crashing of falling buildings, and the change, as by a turn of the kaleidoscope[,] of strong walls and proud structures into heaps of desolation."

To this spectacle was added the dramatic underscore of music. The 33rd Massachusetts was one of the few regiments that still maintained a band at this late stage of the war. It came by Sherman's headquarters early in the evening for a concert that included the "Miserere" from Verdi's opera *Il Trovatore*. In future years Major Hitchcock avowed that hearing it "always will . . . carry me back to this night's scenes and sounds." A requested favorite was "John Brown's Body." Listening to the melody played by the band illuminated by the burning buildings, another member of Sherman's staff declared, "I have never heard that noble anthem when it was so grand, so solemn, so inspiring." The 33rd's band wasn't the only one in town this night. The First Brigade of the Third Division in the Fourteenth Corps boasted a group also, this led by a S. V. W. Post. As the ensemble set up for its performance, its leader joked to the audience: "Nero made music while Rome burned, why not Post make a little while Atlanta burns."

Looking at the city from the window of his small room in the Neal house, Sherman's aide Hitchcock dreaded the next day. Noticing that the fires seemed to be dying down by 11:30 P.M., he worried that the "only danger yet is from stragglers and teamsters, after the guards are withdrawn, which they must tomorrow. I see plainly how true it is [as Sherman said] that 'there are the men who do these things.' " Hitchcock's sentiments were echoed by young Miss Berry, who wrote in her diary that at times "it looked like the whole town was on fire." Marauding Union soldiers, wrote the little girl, "behaved very badly. . . . Nobody knows what we have suffered!"

CHAPTER 7

"Lurid Flames Lit Up the Heavens"

—————— *Left Wing* ——————

The Fourteenth Corps—some 14,000 strong—began marching east from Atlanta along the Decatur Road at sunrise. Behind the soldiers, the Gate City still shuddered from the last paroxysms of ruination. "The air was resonant with explosions," recalled an Illinois officer, "while flames were mounting to the sky from burning depots and factories all over the city." "The roaring of the shells when they burst sounded like a fight," recorded another Illinoisan. Sentiments of pity were in a decided minority. "Who set it afire?" wondered an Ohio man. "We knew not, and some cared less." "A last look at the city, or what once was the city of Atlanta, tells the lovers of our country that the doom of the traitor is sealed," was the grim assessment of a Wisconsin boy.

"Country sandy and water scarce," remembered an Ohio soldier of the morning's march. An Illinois officer in the Second Division observed how the "men were cheering and singing patriotic songs, and fairly revelling in the excitement and novelty of the situation." Another exuberant soldier long recalled the images of this morning: "The Corps, marching to the music of the bands, with swinging, regular step, arms

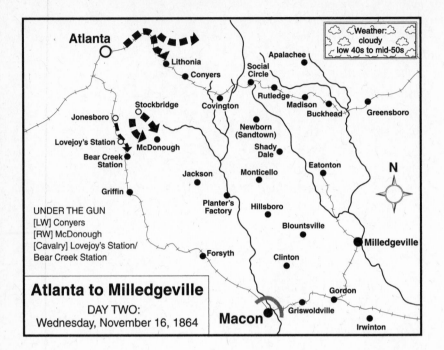

Atlanta

Weather:
cloudy
low 40s to mid-50s

Apalachee

Lithonia
Social
Conyers
Circle

Rutledge
Stockbridge
Covington
Madison
Jonesboro
Buckhead
Greensboro

Newborn
(Sandtown)
Lovejoy's Station
Shady
McDonough
Dale
Bear Creek
Eatonton
Station
Jackson
Monticello

N

Griffin

Planter's
Hillsboro
Factory

UNDER THE GUN
Blountsville
[LW] Conyers
[RW] McDonough
Milledgeville
[Cavalry] Lovejoy's Station/
Bear Creek Station
Forsyth
Clinton

Atlanta to Milledgeville
Gordon
DAY TWO:
Griswoldville
Wednesday, November 16, 1864
Macon
Irwinton

glistening in the sunlight, and colors unfurled to the balmy breezes, was as fine a picture as eyes ever saw."

While the outward mood was festive, an undercurrent of anxiety was present as well. "All believed we would meet resistance; that supplies would be destroyed, and bridges burned, and roads obstructed," an Illinois officer reflected. Even the sight of so many wagons carried a double edge. "What doubts, what hopes and fears filled our minds as we took up our line of march, to see those mighty trains as they moved along conveying all that our vast army depended upon for subsistence," added an Ohio soldier.

According to Sherman's watch—and therefore by everyone else's timepiece—the headquarters party departed Atlanta at 7:00 A.M. The General intended to accompany the Fourteenth Corps for a while. He issued no orders this day; since the campaign's opening phase was preset, his intention was to intervene only in the case of some unforeseen circumstance. Nevertheless, Sherman was reviewing all the variables he had considered to assure himself that every reasonable contingency had been anticipated. To the amazement of one of his aides, Major Hitchcock, the distracted commander blithely trotted past a drunken soldier who was volubly cursing him. "General rode quietly by him, not ten ft. off—heard all—no notice," Hitchcock wrote.

Their passage across the old battlefield momentarily shook Sherman out of his meditation. It was here that he had lost Major General James B. McPherson, a friend and protege, who had commanded one of his armies in the recent Atlanta Campaign. In Sherman's mind, McPherson symbolized all young men of character and promise struck down by the unaccountable fates of war. "Behind us lay Atlanta, smoldering and in ruins, the black smoke rising high in the air, and hanging like a pall over the ruined city," Sherman remembered in later years. Looking southward, he could see the Fourth Division of the Fifteenth Corps marching south to catch up with the rest of the Right Wing, "the gun-barrels glistening in the sun, the white-topped wagons stretching away to the south." A nearby band launched into its umpteenth rendition of "John Brown's Body," and some of the passing soldiers took up the melody. "Never before or since have I heard the chorus of 'Glory, glory, hallelujah!' done with more spirit, or in better harmony of time and place," wrote Sherman.

In the Twentieth Corps, bivouacked near Stone Mountain, the various camps were bustling well before dawn. "Felt a little sore this morning," reported a Wisconsin soldier. A Connecticut man reported that he and his comrades were "tired and sleepy as men need to be[,] for the first day or two is always much worse for the men than it is after they become accustomed to marching." Even as the soldiers milled about their morning campfires, their awareness of the danger around them took on a new urgency. When they called the rolls in the 105th Illinois, it was discovered that two were gone from its ranks. "We know not whether they Deserted or otherwise," a member of the regiment noted in his journal. A quartermaster in the First Division heard that a pair from his brigade were also missing. It was supposed they were "picked up by the enemy's cavalry while they were out foraging, one of those [is] reported killed."

The process of uncoiling from the encampments was sluggishly executed. "The marching to-day was necessarily slow, owing to the bad character of the roads and bad condition of our animals," recorded the commander of the Second Division, the first to depart. This set the tone as the other two divisions queued up to follow. "We marched in a regular funeral style," opined a Wisconsin soldier, "slowly and having to halt every little while." A Massachusetts man likened the tramp to a "train of freight cars hitching along." He also noted that "the profanity indulged in by the men . . . was something alarming."

Once it became evident that the First Division, scheduled last in today's rotation, would not be moving for quite a while, someone had the bright idea to keep the men busy tearing up the track near Stone Mountain. Most of the labor fell to the division's Third Brigade, whose members now began to repair the road, as some of them termed it. "The modus operandi is as follows," explained a Wisconsin farmer in those ranks. "We first picked up one side of a section of the road & turned it bottom side up, much after the manner of turning over a furrow of green sward. We then pry off the ties from the rails, pile them in a heap, and fire them. Across those heaps of burning ties we lay the rails, and as soon as they are heated sufficiently in the center we take them by the ends & bend them double, so as to lay a double track the boys say."

The First Division commander later reported that the Third Brigade "destroyed two miles of track." However, a Georgian who passed by Stone Mountain right after the Federals cleared out recorded that the ties were burned "only partially," and the track iron was injured "slightly." He also related that an "open car that contained [a] few heavy pieces of machinery belonging to the Atlanta [Iron] Rolling Mill is standing on a track five miles below Decatur. The water tank near the same spot is standing."

A small detachment consisting of the 2nd and 33rd Massachusetts regiments, the 111th Pennsylvania, and a portion of the 1st Michigan Engineers and Mechanics represented the last organized units to leave Atlanta today. "Piled all surplus property to be burned," noted one of the engineers. A Massachusetts soldier in the 33rd, frustrated over the wanton destruction that had taken place despite efforts to control the demolitions, proclaimed Atlanta a "perfect ruin." One of the Michigan engineers assigned to torch a structure was stopped in his tracks by a ten-year-old girl, who walked up to him and said, "Mr. Soldier, you would not burn our house would you, if you do where are we going to live?" The engineer paused, wondering if destroying one more dwelling would make any difference in the war. The girl, he later wrote, "looked into my face with such a pleading look that I could not have the heart to fire the place, so I dropped the torch and walked away."

——— *Right Wing* ———

By late morning Confederate Major General Joseph Wheeler had received sufficient information from his scouting parties to enable him to send off reports to the eight officers and officials on his distribution list. He was still charting just three of the Federal infantry corps—the Fifteenth, Seventeenth, and Twentieth—but had discerned that the Yankees were moving in two large columns. "Enemy advancing this morning," Wheeler grimly announced.

Even as the Union camps were rising for another day of marching, a few units were arriving after having spent their first day shepherding the wagons. Hardly had they settled in before Sergeant William S. Fultz of the 11th Iowa and his buddy, Jerry J. Miller, went hunting for cooking water. On their return trip they passed through the bivouac area for their division's First Brigade, where they found everyone asleep and a cooking pot steaming with fresh sweet potatoes. "The temptation was too great for hungry boys that had been up all night assisting teams to move along the . . . road," recalled Fultz. "So reaching down we got hold of the camp kettle and carried it to the company and had sweet potatoes for supper as we called the meal."

A slight scrap was waiting for the first Federal units that reached the South Fork of the Cotton River on their way to Stockbridge. A small rear guard from the Orphan Brigade was covering the only bridge and shots were exchanged as the mounted Union advance trotted into view. The Rebels had no intention of holding their ground, so while the Yankees paused to regroup, the Kentucky riders scrambled across the bridge, setting it afire as they did so. The fast-moving Federals extinguished the flames and established a security perimeter on the opposite bank, while a detachment from the 1st Missouri Engineers replaced the charred planking. Portions of the Second Division of the Fifteenth Corps idly watched the labor while the bulk of the command "enjoyed a good rest." Some forty minutes after the skirmish began, the first infantry regiments were filing across the restored bridge.

Kilpatrick's cavalrymen jangled out early from their camps about

Jonesboro and pressed along the Macon and Western Railroad. The enemy was waiting for them a short distance north of Lovejoy's Station. "The shells whistled over our heads in the rear," wrote a diarist in the 9th Pennsylvania Cavalry. The Federal troops had encountered portions of Brigade General Thomas H. Harrison's brigade, whose Arkansas, Tennessee, and Texas riders were disposed to be a little stubborn this morning. Instead of breaking contact and falling back to the next prepared position as they should have done, the Rebels stuck to their trenches.

An effort to flank them by the 8th Indiana Cavalry was blunted when the troopers discovered their "route was blocked by fallen trees and other obstructions." Kilpatrick arrived on the scene. Once he detected what he thought was smoke from burning stores, he concluded the enemy was pulling out and ordered the nearest available unit to attack. The effort by the 3rd Kentucky Cavalry (supported by portions of the 2nd Kentucky Cavalry and 9th Pennsylvania Cavalry) was successful. "We were so completely run over that we were scattered in every direction," bemoaned a defender, "those of us who were not killed or captured." In addition to some prisoners taken, two cannon were reclaimed. The guns, lost by a Union raiding party during the Atlanta Campaign, were wholeheartedly welcomed back into the fold by the Yankee horse artillery. A battery officer later bragged how the captures upgraded his unit into "a six-gun battery of steel Rodman guns."[*]

The Union riders regrouped and continued southward. No one supposed that the fighting was over for this day.

Noon–Midnight

Armchair strategists in Richmond were convinced they had cracked the secret of Sherman's whereabouts. Reports in the Yankee papers of a grand movement to the coast were simply "nonsensical," reasoned the editorial writers for the *Richmond Dispatch*. More likely and logical, they argued, was a march toward Tennessee to intercept Hood. "At last advices Sherman had reached the neighborhood of Bridgeport, which

---

[*]   In order to reduce the ordnance train size, all army batteries—which normally consisted of six guns during the Atlanta Campaign—were reduced to carrying just four.

is on the Tennessee River, between thirty and forty miles below Chattanooga," the paper reported with smug confidence. The crystal ball seemed equally clear for the editorialists writing in the *Augusta Daily Constitutionalist*. Sherman's target, the paper declared, was Macon. Doing some quick calculations, its editor determined that Sherman's movement had to be so encumbered by his supply trains "that a [Confederate] force of 10,000 determined men can make [the Yankee army] . . . a retreating and disorganized one."

In Milledgeville, most of today's legislative activity took place in sundry committees, so there was little for the correspondent of the *Augusta Daily Chronicle & Sentinel* to report. He did mention a session in the state's Supreme Court where Georgia's right to determine eligibility for Confederate service was being argued. The state's case was handled by a former U.S. Congressman and current militia officer, Robert A. Toombs. Toombs, who had served under Robert E. Lee at Antietam, denounced Richmond's claim of suzerainty "with unsparing vehemence." Almost as an afterthought, the capital reporter added, "Considerable excitement exists here on account of the movements of the enemy."

There was considerable excitement as well in newspaper offices throughout the North. In the Queen City, the *Cincinnati Daily Commercial* proclaimed Sherman's movement "one of the boldest undertakings recorded in the annals of war." Off in Philadelphia, editorial space was filled with a consideration of all Sherman's potential targets, with no preference expressed by the writers. Readers in Chicago were the beneficiaries of some astute rumor gathering. Sifting through various sources, the *Chicago Tribune* offered a correct organization of Sherman's forces along with a very accurate strength estimate. From Saint Louis, the Chicago paper reprinted this tidbit: "An officer of Sherman's staff is here, who says he had orders when his leave expires to join Sherman by way of the Atlantic coast, at Savannah. He expects Sherman to march entirely across Georgia to that place."

Forty-five miles northwest of Savannah, Union prisoners at Camp Lawton were watching over two carloads of sick comrades who had arrived during the night from Andersonville. A space had been set aside for those who were seriously ill, but it offered little in the way of treatment. According to one POW, "no shelter was provided, no blankets [were] given those who occupied it, and medicines were not issued there." Foremost on everyone's mind was the prospect of a prisoner exchange coupled with a fierce determination to survive. A reminder of what awaited those who lacked the stamina to endure could be seen each morning as some of the huddled lumps of humanity scattered about the compound no longer moved—men dead in the little holes they had dug with bare hands for meager shelter. A member of one burial party never forgot how tightly the corpses clenched clumps of earth and how they took the "torn fragments with them to the tombs."

Left Wing

The general route for the Fourteenth Corps split outside Decatur, with two divisions following the track of the Twentieth Corps while the third, accompanied by Sherman, angled southwest toward Lithonia. The region through which they were passing had been on the receiving end of a number of military operations during the Atlanta Campaign and looked it. "Old worn-out cotton fields and forests of small pines alternate," noted a Minnesota farmer. "Foragers were sent out but returned empty handed," added a Wisconsin man. "We were to[o] near Atlanta yet." The barrenness seemed somehow appropriate when the 75th Indiana halted for the night near Stone Mountain to discover a fatality in its midst, a member of Company E named John S. Shull. "No one knew he was sick until he was discovered dead," reported a shocked member of the regiment. Early the next morning a few friends "tenderly laid our comrade's body at the foot of Stone Mountain, whose monumental peaks, formed by the hand of nature, mark his grave."

As the Fourteenth Corps passed through Decatur, at least five soldiers recorded impressions of the village and none reported any recent arson, despite the recollections of Twentieth Corps men passing here yesterday. A jingoistic Minnesotan thought Decatur "a seedy Southern village, . . . [with] an air of sleepiness and senility that distinguishes all cities and villages south of the Ohio River from those north of it." According to an Ohio boy, Decatur was "a small place of old wood colored wood buildings," while a passing officer remarked on its "old, weather-beaten, unpainted appearance." The opinion was shared by a Pennsylvanian who termed the place "dilapidated and almost deserted." A more thoughtful Illinois soldier put his finger on the reality and tragedy of Decatur, "a desolate looking town, half in ruins with a few sad looking inhabitants, who showed the effects of having been robbed by friend and foe until nothing remained to them but mere existence."

As the leading elements of the Fourteenth Corps fanned out into encampments near Lithonia, a security perimeter was established and contact made with some of the 300 or so locals. "Saw good looking girl as I put out pickets," wrote an officer in the 94th Ohio. The lady proved to be a pipe smoker and an eager talker. The officer related that he "had a rattling conversation for two hours." Another Federal paid a house call to meet a family consisting of "the old man, the old woman, four marriageable but unmarried daughters, and one married daughter." The ladies all denied using snuff. "I however, took out my paper of fine cut tobacco and it was but a few moments until each one of them had a quid of it in her mouth 'just to see what it tasted like,' " recorded the bemused officer. "They pronounced it 'fust rate,' 'most as good as snuff.' "

The route followed today by the Twentieth Corps was easier in terms of distance but harder in degree of difficulty. The rough track leading east from Stone Mountain was rudimentary at best, so the units assigned to assist the wagons worked overtime. "Marched slow all day," muttered one impatient foot soldier, "and the wagons stall every mile." Added a New Jersey quartermaster: "Roads bad in places and detained from time to time by difficulties ahead; now creeping along and then getting on a trot, some bad mud holes and one or two rail bridges made."

The faster-moving head of the column reached the Yellow River shortly before midday. No enemy effort was made to interdict the passage. The crossing itself did not require engineering support, even though the pontoon train was standing by. A correspondent present recorded that the river was twenty or thirty feet wide at this point, and that the Federal columns utilized "a good bridge, which might have been easily destroyed."

There was good news and bad waiting for the soldiers who crossed. The bad news was that the terrain was worse on the far side of the river than it had been on the near. The senior officer first on the scene reported that "east of the Yellow River the road crosses a number of swampy streams and steep ridges." The good news was that the troops had finally reached a region not picked clean by details operating out of Atlanta during the past two months.

"Forage is very plentiful," wrote a satisfied Pennsylvania diarist, "sweet potatoes (or yams as they are called down here), corn, plenty of hogs and poultry." A nearby New Yorker scribbled in his diary that he "got plenty of sweet potatoes and fresh pork." A New Jersey man recollected that "the crowing of a rooster[,] the squeal of a pig, or the quack of a duck was its own signal of death, and sweet potatoes which were afterwards found in great plenty disappeared at a greater rate than a bushel per minute." Foreshadowing one problem to come, an officer complained, "I find [it] very hard work to keep my men within reasonable bounds in their foraging operations. In fact, . . . it is each man for himself, and the first fellow gets the fat turkey."

More elements that would become march routine were emerging. The bonanza enjoyed by the first units to reach the end of the day's movement was not shared by those bringing up the tail. When the 31st Wisconsin finally dragged into camp at 1:00 A.M., a weary member of the regiment noted in his diary, "I ate some hard tack and then laid down to sleep." Other facets of the march experience involved the foraging process. There was risk, for in addition to the two Indiana soldiers absent from morning roll call, diarists and letter writers took notice of at least nine other Union soldiers captured while out scrounging this day. There was also the game of wits between Yankees determined to uncover hidden loot and Southern civilians equally determined to thwart them. A quartermaster in the 13th New Jersey recorded that "some of the 3rd [Wisconsin], while hunting today for provisions or valuables dug up a new made grave under the supposition it was only made for the pretext to conceal something edible or valuable—but it proved to be the resting place of a hound buried only three days ago— and it was interred a second time."

All this foraging did not impede the primary mission of the march. A New York soldier noted that his regiment "burnt a cotton mill," while an Indiana infantryman observed that "isolated houses would mysteriously take fire, lighting up the line of march almost with the brilliancy of day." That sense of wonder expressed by the Hoosier was horror to the eyes of a Decatur resident named Martha Amada Quillin. Writing a year after the events took place, she vividly recalled how "the lurid flames of burning buildings, lit up the heavens and dissipated the darkness of night." While her frightened imagination intermingled bivouac camp fires, smoldering railroad ties, and torched structures, Miss Quillin (whose own home was spared) would be haunted in her dreams by the imagined "screams of the frightened neighbors as the fire swallowed up the labors of a life time." She remained long embittered about "this most *christian* order [of destruction] of his *most christian majesty.*"

That man at the center of the storm rode silently for hours. "Absorbed in thought," was Major Hitchcock's assessment. Sherman allowed in his *Memoirs* that some of the time he was weighing possible end points for the grand movement, and at this stage was still considering a variety of options, "either Savannah or Port Royal, South Carolina, and [I] even kept in mind the alternate of Pensacola[, Florida]."

The headquarters party stopped about six miles from Decatur to let Sherman rest. A passing file of soldiers remembered him "sitting on the porch of a log cabin, the humble abode of a Georgia 'cracker,' . . . a cigar in his mouth, while beside him sat one of the female 'poor white trash,' puffing away at her corn-cob pipe." Major Hitchcock observed that the family greeted their unexpected and unwelcome guests with "no fear or cringing." While the only man present remained silent (he was sick, Hitchcock was told), the women (three of them, with "sundry children") spoke without rancor. Both the married ones had absent husbands—one gone to parts unknown, the other dead from battlefield wounds. Hitchcock listened without comment as one of the young ladies swore that "few of the people about here were in favor of the war."

After Sherman enjoyed a short nap, the command group moved on, passing along the Fourteenth Corps column. When necessary, Sherman led the party off the road onto bordering fields to allow the foot soldiers the right-of-way. Shortly before camping for the night near Lithonia, Sherman halted at a slave cabin. A nearby soldier never forgot the sight of the great General "sitting in the passageway between the two ends of a cabin, a dozen or two negroes standing around and staring at him in wonder and awe." One of them—Major Hitchcock termed him an "intelligent fellow"—conversed with the General. He described conditions on the farm where he lived and related that he had been warned by white folks that the Yankees drove blacks ahead of them in a fight to serve as cannon fodder. "Our servants will help dispel these stories, and must," declared Sherman.

Knowing that the boss would be camping among them, the first units arriving near Lithonia went to work tearing up the railroad. "Line of fires on track for ½ mile or more visible," recorded Major Hitchcock, "striking sight, men all in high spirits." Sherman, after settling into night camp, was soon jawing with surgeon John Moore of his staff. Later he made a cryptic remark within earshot of Major Hitchcock that suggests he still fretted about a recall order reaching him, even at this late date. Said Sherman: "Three days more clear and don't care!"

Orders issued tonight for the Left Wing reflected growing concerns about the slow movement of the wagons, and the knowledge that the terrain ahead was more rugged. Sixteen regiments in the Twentieth Corps were detailed "to assist their respective trains up the hills . . . and at such other points as may be necessary on the march." To avoid keeping the column strung out when halted, "the troops and trains will always double up, and when possible the trains will park in the fields," leaving the road open. In the Fourteenth Corps it was necessary to remind the train guards that they also had an obligation to "assist the wagons over bad places, hills, &c."

Another problem not anticipated was that the prospect of forage was luring the wagon drivers away from their teams during halts, costing more time to round them up. All quartermaster officers were strictly enjoined not to let that happen. Also, all "unauthorized vehicles that retard in the least the march" were to be "put out of the trains."

————— *Right Wing* —————

The Fifteenth and the Seventeenth corps marched in tandem today, at least until near Stockbridge, where the Fifteenth (save one division) peeled away to the southwest toward a place called Lee's Mill, from which another track led back toward McDonough. The Second Division remained on the Stockbridge-McDonough road, followed by all of the Seventeenth Corps. Both the Fifteenth and the Seventeenth corps made some operational changes meant to improve the pace of the wagons. "Begin to-day marching alongside the road, leaving the road to wheels," Brigadier General Manning F. Force scribbled in his journal. At least the Seventeenth Corps had a road to leave to the wheels. Matters were tougher for most of the Fifteenth Corps, which turned onto a parallel trail where a member of the rear guard recorded finding "it very hard marching as we had to march in two ranks on each side [of] the wagon train and the road was very narrow."

Officers in several regiments now formed permanent foraging details in anticipation of soon reaching areas not previously scavenged. Once they were past Stockbridge, the supply gathering began in earnest. "The boys went out and got plenty of sweet potatoes, beans and corn and the like," reported an Ohio soldier; "we find plenty to eat thus far." "I was detailed this day to forage," added an Iowa boy, "brought in one fat porker." Exclaimed an Iowan in another regiment, "foragers got lots of hogs[,] beef & potatoes & [we] are beginning to live again."

As the main body of the Fifteenth Corps angled in to approach the town of McDonough from the west, its leading elements encountered a line of Rebel videttes, likely from the Orphan Brigade. The Confederates had no orders to hold, so as the Yankee riders deployed and fired, the Rebels withdrew. "Some skirmishing," was how a Missouri diarist summed up the encounter. A party of signal corps officers riding with the advance helped to see the Southerners off, enthusiastically reporting a charge that drove "a brigade of rebel cavalry from the town."

This cleared the way for the troops advancing down the main road from Stockbridge to pass through the village in style. "We entered the town of McDonough at noon," recorded an Ohio volunteer, "our bands playing and colors flying. This was a small place and about deserted." The 48th Indiana was assigned provost duties, and soon after General Howard arrived, "a lot of cotton was burned on his orders." A few soldiers from the 93rd Illinois rummaged through the post office, finding a "large Confederate mail . . . , but there was nothing of consequence in it, mostly love letters."

The mood was more somber in the camp of the 1st Battery of Minnesota Light Artillery. A battery mate, Davis King (the boys called him Spence), had been ill when the march began and traveled in an ambulance. At some point today he died, almost exactly three years to the day of his enlistment. "We buried him that night, poor fellow;"

reflected a comrade, and his passing "was very much regretted by the whole Company."

Overnight orders for the Right Wing, like those for the Left, reflected continuing worries about the slow clip of the wagon trains. Major General Osterhaus, commanding the Fifteenth Corps, was especially riled. "It is perfectly preposterous to think that the troops should be delayed successively for hours, and thus lose the necessary amount of rest, because a worthless wagon-master or teamster sees fit to disregard his duties," the German-born officer sputtered.

The route to be followed by the Fifteenth Corps would bring it closest to Rebel troop concentrations around Macon, a fact not lost on the officers responsible for watching over the wagons. The colonel commanding the train guard was specifically reminded of this and fully authorized to "take such steps as he may think necessary for their protection."

Some nine miles southwest of McDonough, Kilpatrick's cavalry, covering the Right Wing's western flank, encountered another line of Confederate defenses at Bear Creek Station.* The Rebel cavalry commander, Joseph Wheeler, was present when the first contingent of mounted Federals recoiled after a brief exchange with Southerners waiting in earthworks. This allowed Wheeler to claim a repulse, even as he ordered the units at Bear Creek Station to withdraw. His opposite number wasn't in a mood to wait until it was completed.

While a pair of dismounted squadrons from the 10th Ohio Cavalry feinted against the position's left flank, a mounted battalion swept in around the right end, sabers flashing. One Buckeye trooper noted that the battalion "carried through [the charge] in good style and drove the Rebels back." The commander of the 10th later reported twenty prisoners taken for a loss of four killed, seven wounded, and four lost as POWs. Kilpatrick's column pushed on for a few additional miles before camping south of the station.

As the troopers settled into their night camp, discipline went to hell. After being keyed up all day and engaging in two combat actions, the cavalrymen now found themselves in a land of abundance, filled with goods free for the taking. "Forage of all kinds plenty," noted a member of the 92nd Illinois Mounted Infantry. Hogs were especially

---

*   Modern Hampton.

numerous, so the men wasted no time putting their carbines to use. Once he learned the reason for all the gunfire, Brigadier General Kilpatrick was furious, branding it "most unmilitary, and a willful waste of ammunition." He kept his headquarters clerks busy making a dozen or more copies of an angry order to be read at all morning assemblies. "Let the men catch and kill their hogs with their sabers, a weapon that can be used equally as well to kill hogs as rebels," Kilpatrick huffed.

Another problem confronting the cavalry chief today was poor march discipline. Everywhere Kilpatrick looked, he saw that units were moving at a trot, a more rapid pace than the prescribed walk, one sure to wear out horseflesh. "All company officers who allow the men of their companies to trot their horses, without orders having been properly received to that effect, and by the bugle from the head of the column, will be dismounted, placed under arrest, and sent to march with the division train till such point is reached where a court-martial can be convened for their trial and dismissal," he warned. To make certain that the directive wasn't lost on his men and officers, Kilpatrick also commanded that this instruction be read to the troops "twice each day until further orders."

From his position with Hood's army at Tuscumbia, Alabama, General Beauregard struggled to choreograph a response to Sherman's move. At 3:00 P.M. he telegraphically advised Richmond of breaking events. He surmised that the Federal movement would be aimed toward "Augusta or Macon" with an ultimate destination of "Charleston or Savannah." Knowing full well that asking for troops from far-off departments would be a waste of time, Beauregard suggested that forces in nearby North and South Carolina be concentrated to support neighboring Augusta if the city were attacked. He also signaled his intention to send Richard Taylor to "assume command of all troops operating against Sherman."

His actual instructions to Taylor had more specificity. "You will cut and block up all dirt roads in advance of him, remove or destroy supplies of all kinds in his front," Beauregard directed. "Wheeler's cavalry," he added, "will harass his flanks and rear." Taylor was also told to proceed to Macon "with the available forces you can spare from your department." This last was written more for the historical record than for reality because Taylor, as he had made patently clear in all briefings, had no troops to spare. Nevertheless, upon receiving the message, the Confederate officer headed toward Macon. "There was nothing to be said and nothing to be done, saving to discharge one's duty to the bitter end," he later wrote.

Another Beauregard message went to Howell Cobb, who was with the Georgia militia troops at Griffin (where they had stopped after retreating from Lovejoy's Station). Cobb was advised to prepare Macon for a siege, and also to look to the "safety of prisoners at Millen." Writing to his wife in Macon, Cobb projected false bravado, avowing that he had "no serious fears now that Macon can be taken—still it will not be so comfortable to be there with a Yankee army around it."

Incredibly, with all the complicated planning for his Tennessee invasion fully under way, General Hood added his bit to the mix. He advised Wheeler: "If Sherman advances to the south or east destroy all things in his front that might be useful to him, and keep a portion of your force constantly destroying his trains." The last suggestion, had it been aggressively pursued, might have caused Sherman real problems. It turned out to be but a lone voice lost amid the clamor of sectional commanders demanding that Wheeler employ his assets as scouts so they might monitor the enemy's progress and prepare their defenses before issuing appeals for help.

CHAPTER 8

"Forage of All Kinds Abounds"

THURSDAY, NOVEMBER 17, 1864
Midnight–Noon

Scrambling ahead of the approaching Union columns, panicked civilians raced to get out of harm's way, spreading alarms everywhere. Those they warned faced some tough decisions. If there was thought to be time enough, various valuables and foodstuffs were secreted with varying degrees of guile, but almost always with the complicity of family slaves. Others shipped what goods they could to places they believed would be safe. Finally, as the portents increased in urgency, they had to decide whether to remain or flee.

The Buttrills of Sylvan Grove, outside Jackson, waited too long to effectively hide much, but with Macon not quite forty miles distant the family patriarch, Asa Buttrill, loaded two large wagons with food and valuables before setting off for the city on November 16. That night the women of the household were cheered by a visit from a half dozen teenage boys (including Asa's son, Taylor) scouting for the Macon militia. Asa's daughter, Mary, and her aunt, Emma Manley, decided to flee to Macon the next day.

Everyone was awake well before sunrise, preparing a carriage for the journey. Fortunately for the ladies, a convalescent Confederate soldier lodged with the Buttrills agreed to drive them. Once the women finished packing, the young scouts took station under cover in a nearby

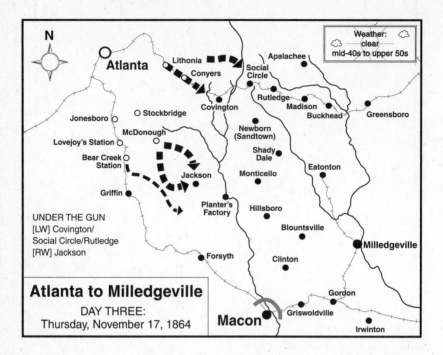

N

Weather: clear
mid-40s to upper 50s

Atlanta

Lithonia
Conyers

Apalachee
Social Circle

Jonesboro

Stockbridge

Covington

Rutledge

Madison
Buckhead

Greensboro

McDonough

Newborn
(Sandtown)

Lovejoy's Station

Bear Creek
Station

Jackson

Shady
Dale

Monticello

Eatonton

Griffin

Planter's
Factory

Hillsboro

UNDER THE GUN
[LW] Covington/
Social Circle/Rutledge
[RW] Jackson

Blo{}untsville

Milledgeville

Forsyth

Clinton

Atlanta to Milledgeville

DAY THREE:
Thursday, November 17, 1864

Gordon

Macon

Griswoldville

Irwinton

orchard, a prudent precaution, as it turned out. Suddenly a large party of armed mounted men swarmed around the house, their dust-covered uniforms presenting a mocking imitation of Confederate gray. In answer to their repeated calls for the man of the house to show himself, the family's black butler explained, "He is gone." Then Mrs. Buttrill appeared and faced the Yankee riders.

"Madam, where are Wheeler and Forrest?" one of them demanded.

"Sir, I do not know."

"Madam, don't tell me a lie."

"Sir," Mrs. Buttrill answered with some asperity, "I would have you know I am a Southern lady."

The Yankees were operating without support from the main column, gathering intelligence, not foraging, so they departed in a rush. With them went the young Rebel scouts, racing back to Macon with the news. In their haste, the Federals overlooked the family carriage hitched up and ready to go. After quick farewells, the twenty-two-year-old Mary, her aunt, two maids, and the convalescent driver drove off toward Macon.

Right Wing

The Seventeenth Corps marched First Division, Third, Fourth today, and was further subdivided when the Fourth shifted over to what one soldier called "a byroad." While a more direct route, the Fourth Division's trail crossed a large stream whose dilapidated bridge required time to repair before the wagons could proceed. Among the other two divisions, taking a more exposed course, security concerns were paramount. "Orders to be ready to resist and repel an attack that may be made on the train," scribbled a Wisconsin soldier in his diary, adding, "expect an attack from Cavalry." In the Third Division, Brigadier General Manning F. Force had to assign a full brigade "to help the wagons along."

It was payback time for a number of slaves in the area, who made sure that the Yankee officers heard all about the bloodhounds that tracked anyone trying to escape, including Union prisoners. Said one Illinois soldier: "Advance ordered to kill all bloodhounds and other valuable dogs in the country."

The Fifteenth Corps marched in one long column (Third Division, Fourth, First, Second) until about a mile past Locust Grove, when the procession split, the Third and Fourth heading east on the direct road to Jackson, while the First and Second tramped to the southeast on a longer circuit leading to Indian Springs. An Illinois man in the Fourth Division made note of the procedures for protecting the supplies: "The wagon trains are moved as far as possible on the road, preceded by a brigade, with here and there a detachment of troops marching in the road as guards, the rest moving in two ranks on either side of the train. The rear is guarded by a brigade." A soldier in the 93rd Illinois was part of another detail watching over the wagons. "We are flankers on the right side of the train," he scrawled in his diary, "the 59th [Indiana] on the other side. . . . We marched about one hundred yards from the road . . . , it was a hard place to march."

Foragers scattered out from the main column. An Illinoisan belonged to one such detail that came upon a "fine lot of Hogs of which we killed one dozin of," he recollected. The meat was piled onto a wagon that was then driven to the main road, where the soldiers waited patiently for their division to reach them so they could distribute the goods to the quartermasters. "The poor people looked surprised and begged us not to touch their scanty commissariat," stated an Ohio boy in the Third Division. He added a grim postscript: "Sherman's order was to forage liberally off the rich, and it was rigidly observed." "Now I reckon you want to know what the Yankees did for us," wrote a McDonough resident afterward. "Well, bad enough but no worse than I expected."

So far in the operation Kilpatrick's cavalry had been pressing southward along the Macon and Western Railroad, forcing the Confederates (cavalry and militia) to fall back in a general movement toward Macon. Today Kilpatrick broke the pattern by veering off the rail line in an easterly and southerly course to close up on the friendly infantry. One result of this action was that for this day at least, Yanks and Rebs were diverging instead of converging. "Country beautiful, forage in great abundance, and roads good, and very little annoyance from the enemy," related an Illinois trooper. "Have had a little skirmishing," contributed a diarist in the 8th Indiana Cavalry. "We have destroyed a large amount of cotton." Added the Illinoisan: "We begin to find a great many good mules and a few good horses which are invariably taken by Sherman's thieves, as the rebel papers call us."

Around midday the 5th Kentucky Cavalry was sent off along a side road to attack an enemy camp said to be on the Towaliga River. Instead of the brigade-sized force he had expected, the Kentucky commander found a small post of twenty men and one burned bridge. After completing his mission the relieved officer returned to the column, convinced that stupidity somewhere had sent his lone regiment on what might have easily become a suicide mission.

Left Wing

Those in Sherman's headquarters party, camped outside Lithonia, were awake at 4:00 A.M., had breakfasted by 5:20, and were on the road by 7:00. They had just reached the village when progress ground to a halt. Per orders, the 1st Michigan Engineers and Mechanics was busy destroying the railroad, using the cant hooks that Captain Poe had ordered made especially for the job of effectively twisting the heated rails. Sherman, recorded a member of his staff, "had to stop & see that it was well done." According to a passing member of the Fourteenth Corps, the General spent some time "standing on the R.R. track giving directions as to how he wanted the track torn up and destroyed." "I attached much importance to this destruction of the railroad," said Sherman, "gave it my own personal attention and made reiterated orders to others on the subject."

The destruction authorized for Lithonia was limited to the railroad line and any buildings connected with it. When the town's depot was torched, sparks and fiery debris set several neighboring structures ablaze, which the soldiers made no effort to save. According to an Illinois officer, one of the ruined places had been a "fine dwelling." By the time the Second Division passed through the village, some members of its household had salvaged what they could and sat disconsolately guarding the small pile. "The picture was a sad one and spoke volumes of War's misery," commented a soldier.

The Fourteenth Corps (again marching in the order First Division, Third, Second) began passing through the next rail stop, Conyers, around midday. Many of its 500 citizens had opted to stick it out. Conyers, reported an Ohio man, was "full of women and children. Only two or three men seen." The correspondent on hand for the *New York Herald* reported that the residents "flocked in large numbers to doors and windows to see the long expected and much feared Yankees, and listen to the music of a score of bands that gave forth their martial strains." An Ohio officer with an eye for the ladies still recalled a Miss Glenns in later years. His assessment: "Pretty foot and ankle, beautiful complexion and I should have liked to stay a while as she asked, but no use." Another soldier met up with an older woman who wearily related that this was the sixth occasion she had changed locations, starting in Kentucky, only to have the Yankees catch up with her every time. Enough was enough, and from here on, according to the soldier, "she reckoned she would let them go first."

A local character known as "Aunt" Winnie Puckett became enshrined in Conyers lore for protecting her business, Costley's Mill. According to the hallowed tale, Aunt Winnie first put all the flour she had into sacks, then hid the packets in her millpond. Only the outer layers of flour caked in each bag, protecting the core. Then, when the Yankees actually appeared, Aunt Winnie raised such a ruckus that the soldiers left her—and more importantly, her mill—alone.

Conyers was not without its divertissements. An Ohio enlisted man took advantage of an extended halt in town to read from some pilfered books, one containing Shakespeare's sonnets, another an introduction to Greek grammar. When the soldier left the town, he promised himself that someday he would undertake a serious study of the ancient language. A divisional staff officer and his friend banged on doors in town until they found a house with a piano. His companion played "The Star-Spangled Banner," followed by a rendition of "Dixie" to assuage their reluctant host. This drew the man's daughters out of hiding, and the young ladies allowed themselves to be induced to sing a Confederate song or two. A splendid time was had by all. "We left them, though, notwithstanding their elegant and patriotic songs," remembered the officer. "They, no doubt, hoping we might be shot before night."

The country around Conyers was "sandy & timber stands & scrub with an occasional pine," scribbled a Minnesota diarist. "Forage of all kinds abounds, especially sweet potatoes," wrote a Pennsylvanian. "We get sweet potatoes & one chicken. Sugar molasses abounds." "All kind of forage plenty," added a Hoosier; "Nice clothing and Dresses, Silk and . . . muslin, Thread, &c."

Before Sherman's headquarters departed Lithonia, a signal corps officer with three escorts climbed a large hill located about a mile and a half northeast of the village. They reported smoke to the north, which Sherman's staff interpreted as marking the course of Major General Slocum's column. The Twentieth Corps had left its camps near the Yellow River and turned to the southeast, moving toward the town of Social Circle. The Second Division led the way, followed by the Third and the First. "Our course may be marked by the track of smoke we leave behind," wrote a Massachusetts officer, confirming the signal officer's observations. "We passed several cotton presses & store houses all in flames. . . . Every unoccupied house is burnt & as most of the people have left there are few left untouched."

This was territory not scoured by any previous Federal operations, so there were pickings galore. Captain Frank D. Baldwin of the 19th Michigan commanded one of the more respectable scrounging operations of the entire campaign. "My duties were defined and consisted of collecting forage & other supplies that would be of use to the command," he proudly recounted. "Should any man of the detachment prove unsatisfactory in any way, I was authorized to send him back to his command to be replaced by another man. However, the command was composed of the best lot of men I ever saw; fearless & too orderly to indulge in vandalism & void of any desire for unlawful pillage & plundering."

Baldwin set a standard not often matched by others. "From the calves and hogs which we killed by a shot or by the bayonet, we ate only the hindquarters, the balance we left to rot, or for the dogs or buzzards," reported an Illinoisan. A marcher in the 22nd Wisconsin remembered being passed by a forager "carrying an armful of bedding, making for some point or command ahead. A rain of gibes and jeers greeted him as he passed forward to the head of the regiment when [Lieutenant] Colonel [Edward] Bloodgood ordered him in charge of a guard by whom he was taken to the rear." A soldier in the 149th New York reported that a regiment's pet dog was "huge on catching fowls. Have honey & sweets from a building well filled[.] Had to laugh at one boy with a bee hive & the bees flying all around[.]"

Seen from the other side, the effects of this foraging were devastating to individual planters. "[Cotton] Gin house and screw burned, stables and barn all in ashes, fencing burned and destruction all around," wrote Thomas Maguire, whose Promised Land plantation suffered a Yankee visit. "The carriage and big wagon burned up, corn and potatoes gone, horses and steers gone, sheep, chickens and geese[,] also syrup boiler damaged, one barrel of syrup burned, saddles and bridles in the same fix." In the days to come Maguire would face a threat from an unexpected quarter: "plundering neighbors who are here in droves."

Yet again the tail end of the column struggled to keep pace. "The trains moved awfully slow," recorded a Connecticut man. "Short marches & long halts for the cattle to get a mile or two ahead," complained a member of the 2nd Minnesota. Wrote one disgusted New Yorker, "Standing still in the road at 12." A Wisconsin comrade reported that they "waited till heartily tired for an order to march."

Noon–Midnight

Confederate Major General Joseph Wheeler transmitted three situation reports today. In them he finally identified the Fourteenth Corps as part of the Federal column, so for the first time Confederate authorities had a complete picture of Sherman's forces. The absence of an overall commander was beginning to rankle the heavily stressed cavalryman. "Please give me [the] wishes and intentions of [the] Government, or send some one who knows the course they desire pursued," he complained to Richmond. From the information he was getting, it seemed to Wheeler that several Yankee columns were on the "shortest road to Macon." In that city, a civil order closed all the liquor stores, while a military directive from Major General Howell Cobb summoned every able-bodied man to arms. Another Cobb order put all transportation under central control.

Cobb was caught in a seesaw of emotions. Maintaining a calm face to his wife, he joked that "we shall have lively times in the course of the next ten days." Appealing directly to Jefferson Davis, he labeled Sherman's movement "the most dangerous of the war," and argued forcefully that if the garrisons of Charleston, Savannah, and Wilmington, North Carolina, could be ordered to Macon, the chance existed to crush Sherman's advance, leading directly to "the greatest result of the war." Writing to Davis's military adviser, Cobb worried that Macon's feeble defenses could not withstand a major assault.

Governor Brown's eyes in Macon belonged to Brigadier General Robert Toombs, just arrived from Milledgeville, where he had defended Georgia's sovereignty before the state supreme court. "Things are very bad here," Toombs wired. Citing the paltry roster of units ready to defend the city, he urged the governor to "send all the troops you can. If we do not get help we must abandon this place." The public face of iron resolve was presented by the city's newspaper, the *Macon Daily Telegraph*: "Macon is to be defended to the last, and those best informed believe it can be held against any force Sherman can bring against it."

No one in the town of Madison, square in the path of the Left Wing, had any illusions of defense. Frantic residents hurried to fill a last train waiting at the depot with steam up, as a rueful Yankee described the next day, "with such things as they had time to get away with." The townspeople did such a good job that another Federal would gripe about all the empty store shelves he saw. At least Madison's residents did not have to deal with Wheeler's men, a privilege denied those farther south. Writing to Jefferson Davis about a month after the events took place, a Griffin resident named P. A. Lawson explained, "When General Sherman left Atlanta Wheeler's cavalry commenced their retreat before him, and but a handful of Sherman's men ran W[heeler's] whole command down to Griffin, and while S[herman's] army was marching through Fayette, Clayton, Henry, and Butts [counties], Wheeler's cavalry was burning up all the corn and fodder, driving off all the stock of the farmers for ten miles on each side of the railroad, all of from ten to twenty-five miles to the right and rear of Sherman's forces. Worse than all, the stock of mules and horses which General Wheeler's forces carried off, nine out of ten they have appropriated to their own use."

In the state capital, Milledgeville, Governor Brown was trying to get ahead of fast-developing events. Delivering a special message to the General Assembly, he demanded "the passage of a law . . . authorizing the Governor to make a levy *en masse*, of the whole male population, including every man able to do Military duty, during the emergency." Brown also sent off a telegraph to General Wheeler, promising to "do all I can to rally force to aid you," while also reminding that officer of the importance of his daily situation reports. Another telegram went off to General Beauregard in Alabama, in which Brown had to confess that "we have not force to stop the movements of the enemy."

Included among the litany of issues that Howell Cobb pressed on Richmond was the matter of Yankee POWs. "The prisoners should be removed from this State," Cobb insisted, anxious about Yankee raids aiming at freeing the captives. At Camp Lawton, outside Millen, then the state's largest prison compound, the inmates were taking advantage of the pleasant, even warm, days. A wood-chopping detail was organized, thirty strong. The men worked without guards, but with the knowledge that if any of them failed to return, no one in the thousand-man division to which they were assigned would be allowed to collect wood until the prodigal returned. Even though the weather was uncommonly temperate, everyone knew that colder days were coming. Right now the mortality rate was ten per day, estimated an Illinois POW. Once the weather turned bitter, however, that would change.

----------- *Right Wing* -----------

The Right Wing marched widely dispersed today, so the foraging only improved as the day wore on. A soldier in the 11th Iowa, serving as rear guard for the Fourth Division of the Seventeenth Corps, reported that despite being the very last in a long line, the men "found plenty of fresh pork and all the sweet potatoes we could carry." A happy diarist in the 4th Minnesota (Fifteenth Corps) wrote: "A plenty of chickens & potatoes." Soldier complaints were a matter of too much of a good thing. "Our men are clear discouraged with foraging," chortled an Illinois man. "They can't carry half the hogs and potatoes they find right along the road."

Amazingly, large amounts of easily movable property remained to be confiscated as well. "The men detailed for [foraging] . . . are finding lots of horses and mules," reported a Fifteenth Corps soldier. An Ohio boy was perhaps stating the obvious when he commented: "Along our route today we surprised the citizens very much[,] they were not expecting us so soon." In the Seventeenth Corps, the requisition of animals was joined to a determination not to leave anything valuable to the Rebels. "We . . . obtained a number of good horses and mules," wrote an Ohio diarist, "turned out our poorest, shot them and supplied their places with good ones." Also slated for destruction were the usual suspects. "Fire is doing its work among the cotton," related another Buckeye. "Black clouds of smoke mark well our way."

Just a short distance away from the main columns, death or capture awaited the unwary or unlucky. "[Rebel] cutthroats are following us & watching our movements," warned an Iowa diary keeper. A party from the 55th Illinois that took a wrong turn found itself several miles from the main column when the sun set. The men camped for the night, taking care to post a picket detail that reported another group bivouacked nearby. A cautious investigation revealed the neighbors as "a troop of Confederate cavalry." The wary Federals laid low, watched the enemy ride off in the morning, and eventually rejoined their column without further incident. Sometimes the danger was close at hand. Recorded a diarist in the 11th Iowa: "A couple of orderlies got drunk [this evening] . . . and one shot and killed the other."

As the Fifteenth Corps drew close to Jackson, its mounted advance encountered a hodgepodge of convalescent Rebel soldiers and local boys out to make a noise. The Confederates first fired at the Yankees some three and a half miles out of town on the McDonough Road. Then, according to a resident, "They retreated beyond the creek and made a stand this side (the Jackson side) and fired on the enemy as they came into sight on the opposite hill, and again retreated. They halted across the next creek and again exchanged shots with them and ran into Jackson." At this point, the Rebels scattered.

The first Federals to enter the town found the courthouse already smoldering, courtesy of Wheeler's departing cavalry. However, most of the county records were preserved through the quick thinking of a town official named Wiley Goodman, who packed them on a wagon and carted them into Jasper County, where he hid them in the woods until the danger had passed.

Just ahead of the Right Wing corps was the first major water barrier to be encountered, the Ocmulgee River. There were no bridges to utilize (passage here was via ferry), so the engineers would have an opportunity to display their skills. The two corps would cross the Ocmulgee near a cloth-manufacturing center called Planter's Factory.* Major General Oliver Otis Howard decided to seize the crossing point before the Rebels realized he wasn't moving directly against Macon. Orders went to Major General Osterhaus, Fifteenth Corps, to handle the matter. Osterhaus selected a small regiment of mounted infantry, the 29th Missouri Mounted Infantry, for the job.

The unit, numbering about 115 men, trotted forward as the main column closed on Jackson. The mounted riflemen galloped through the town, scared its residents into hiding, then hurried on to the river without further incident. An advance party floated across by ferry to scout the area, while the rest of the regiment foraged a bit, and waited for the heavy columns to reach them sometime next morning.

Major General Howard also sought to misdirect his opponents as to his real objectives. General Kilpatrick was told to do all that he could to make the enemy "think we are making for Macon, via Forsyth." At the same time, Confederate defenders at Griffin, realizing that the enemy had bypassed them and now threatened to cut them off from Macon, cleared out. "Great excite[ment]," said a Georgia cavalryman in the town. "Brig[ade,] corps & squads of cavalry hurrying to & fro from the front. We have a large wagon train, retreat on several roads."

The carriage carrying Mary Buttrill, her aunt, two maids, and a convalescent soldier handling the reins had reached a place about a

---

* Also known as Planter's Mill, Ocmulgee Mill, Nutling's Mill, Hunter's Mill, and Button's Factory.

mile east of the Ocmulgee River. Already on their odyssey they had overtaken Mary's father, laboring with a pair of heavily laden wagons; they next encountered Mary's brother, Taylor, and a comrade on another scout. Buttrill's party had crossed the river on a small flatboat ferry and was stopped for lunch with the family of Stephen Johnson when someone pointed behind. Already, the bank where they had crossed the Ocmulgee was dotted with Yankee soldiers.

There was no time to be lost, and the women knew they would only slow the procession down. In a flash the carriage, accompanied by the pair of scouts, was jouncing off toward Macon. "If this war ever ends, you'll see me drive up to Sylvan Grove in this rig," the convalescent called out as he whipped the team to disappear in a cloud of dust. When the ladies made a move to enter the plain house, they were turned back, Mrs. Johnson saying she feared the Yankees would burn her out if she took in refugees. A few minutes more, and a crowd of bluecoat riders filled the yard.

"Where are those damn rebels that were here with you?" demanded a trooper.

"Gone," Mary answered.

A Buttrill maid acted as if the departing scouts had taken the left fork of the road, so a few of the Federals rode off on a wild goose chase. Looking around her at a gallery of unfriendly faces, Mary at last called out: "Is there a gentleman in this vast crowd who would take us to an officer, where I could ask for protection for my Aunt, two maids, and myself?"

One of the Yankees dismounted and pushed through the others to her side. "I have a mother and sister," he said, "and I will protect you at the risk of my life." Their self-appointed guardian led them a short distance to a two-room cabin. Nearby Mary saw the two wagons her father had used in his effort to remove valuables to Macon, now captured, their contents strewn about. The obliging enemy broke open a trunk and invited the ladies to take what they wanted, adding that whatever was left would be given to the workers at a nearby factory that was being burned.

A little later the ladies came under the protection of Colonel George Spencer, commanding the 1st Alabama Cavalry (U.S.) attached to the Seventeenth Corps. This officer took a liking to them, seeing that they had a roof over their head after dark. (It took a day for the Union columns to pass by their frail sanctuary. Then they returned to Sylvan Grove to find the family house "standing alone, palings, fences, gin houses, cotton, cows, chickens, horses, mules, everything in the house, except [Mrs. Buttrill's] . . . room, destroyed.")

Overnight orders written for the Right Wing tonight displayed a serious concern regarding straggling. Surgeons were instructed to take position in the rear of their respective regiments and allow "no one to fall behind except such as are unable to march." "The practice of marching regiments stretched out to two or three times their natural length is so unsoldierlike and unnecessary that all commanding officers who take any pride in their regiments will . . . take measures to prevent it," read another directive. Finally, officers and men were reminded "that we are not warring upon women and children."

Left Wing

Today's plan had been for the Twentieth Corps to cover most if not all the distance to Social Circle, but the roads and wagons did not cooperate. "It has been a very hard days march," complained an Ohio soldier. "The country being very hilly." "Moving very slow," added an Indiana comrade, "bad roads." The officer commanding the 33rd Indiana griped that "there was but little system in the management of the immense wagon train and troops." Things went from bad to worse when the head of the First Division (last in today's rotation) bumped into the stalled rear of the Third (number two in order). From that point on, grumbled a quartermaster, "we had slow and tedious work." "Some wagon was continually breaking down or would get stuck in mud holes, thereby blocking everything behind them and causing the mule-drivers to unload their vocabulary of cuss words," recalled a New Yorker. Many units, up since dawn, did not bed down until midnight or later.

Almost from the start of the march, escaping slaves had been attracted by the passing Union columns. Today marked the first day that their presence in large numbers was becoming apparent. "The niggers flock around us and want to go with us," a New York soldier observed. Sometimes the first encounter was a one-on-one. After getting directions from a slave, a Wisconsin regiment marched only a short distance when the black caught up with it. "Massa," he said, "I'se gwine 'long with uns." His expression made it clear that the topic was not open for discussion. A Connecticut man came face-to-face with one of the dirty little secrets of the slave system. While his regiment was halted near a plantation, the soldier "got into conversation with a very pretty girl, thinking she was the daughter of a planter, from the fact she seemed so well educated. I made some inquiries about her parents when to my great surprise she told me that she was a 'nigger,' and both the slave and the daughter of the planter who was a minister."

At Conyers, some of Sherman's staff, including Major Hitchcock, spent time with a local Mrs. Scott, a widow. She readily admitted to telling her slaves that the Yankees in Atlanta had "shot, burned and drowned negroes, old and young, drove men into houses and burned them, etc.," reported Hitchcock.

An officer prowled around outside, finding several reasons to worry. He observed that the railroad track here had been recently refurbished, disputing Hitchcock's smug image of a hapless Confederacy. Also, he noticed that they were entering a region with more sand in the soil and patches of white clay, "which makes the worst mud." All would be fine as long as the rains held off. On the plus side, found copies of Augusta newspapers (dated November 13) were encouragingly silent regarding the prospect of an enemy invasion.

When Sherman's headquarters were set up for the night, about a mile from the Yellow River, the General sent for a local man to advise him on the roads and river crossings. "Don't want white man," he snapped. One of his aides, Major James McCoy, finally fetched a slave. Major Hitchcock, who thought the black man was a "very intelligent old fellow," recorded Sherman's attitude as "polite." Once the General had learned all he could about local conditions, the conversation turned to other matters. He told the patriarch that he was "free if you choose and deserve it. Go when you like, —we don't force any to be soldiers— pay wages, and will pay if you *choose to come*: but as *you* have family, better stay now and have general concert and leave hereafter." According to Major Hitchcock, Sherman was especially adamant on one point. *"But don't hurt your masters or their families,"* he said with emphasis, *"we don't want that."*

Sherman's command style during the first phase of the great march remained very much hands-off. Courier contact between the wing commanders and his headquarters was minimal, nor were signal officers tasked with maintaining more than intermittent communication between the separated columns. Sherman was counting on an initial period of confusion on the Confederate side regarding his route and objectives. He was also banking on the unimaginative steadiness of Howard and Slocum to stick to the plan.

During the "selling" of the march to Grant, Lincoln, and even Thomas, Sherman had suggested that Hood might well abandon his Tennessee schemes to chase after him. Such a possibility was never part of the daily force assignments. Everything in the disposition of Sherman's forces on the march was forward looking; there were no backward glances. This evening, Sherman's Left Wing commander took advantage of the short distance between the Twentieth and Fourteenth corps to send his boss a brief progress report. After explaining the moves he intended to make in the next few days, Major General Slocum concluded with words that must have brought a smile to Sherman's weathered face: "I have seen no enemy and everything is working well."

For many of those in the Fourteenth Corps, today was the first day of serious railroad wrecking. "We pry some of the rails loose then all get on one side of the track & turn the track entirely over," related an Ohio diarist. "When the end first started goes over the men run behind and past those who are lifting so it is kept moving like a furrow unless it breaks apart. If it does then we have to look out or we get hurt." "The ties were all burned and the rails bent," added an Illinois man. A Minnesota soldier recalled tearing and burning the line until "we arrived at the smoking embers of the work of troops in advance of us."

Along the destroyed tracks at Conyers, a squad from the 34th Illinois prowled the village, having been told that the provost guards had pulled out and that there still was plenty of food for the taking. After helping themselves, the men hauled their load to camp. "I shut my eyes not with a clear conscience," admitted one of them, "but with the clear satisfaction that an excellent breakfast would be mine in the morning."

Even as the two prongs of the Left Wing were settling into night camps, other actions were unfolding to ensure the next day's progress. The 9th Illinois Mounted Infantry, under its commander Lieutenant Colonel Samuel T. Hughes, normally employed screening the advance of the Twentieth Corps, "dashed into Social Circle before dark," reported a newsman present, "and nearly succeeded in capturing a train of cars. Failing in this, [Hughes] . . . contented himself with burning the depot and coming back to camp with a rebel surgeon and $2,700 in rebel money."

Back in the camps, the soldiers in the Second Brigade, Third Division, Fourteenth Corps were trying to sort out a strange incident. It began about midday, when the brigade stopped for dinner about four miles beyond Lithonia. Some members of the 101st Indiana caught a man in Union uniform skulking around the bivouac. According to a Minnesota soldier, the suspect (whom just about everyone thought was a spy) "attempted to sham insanity, but did not succeed in deceiving anyone but was marched under guard to brigade headquarters." Added an Ohioan: "He is dressed in our uniform and pretends to be insane." The prisoner traveled with the division to Conyers, where the Second Brigade bivouacked for the night. Another Ohio boy related that the suspect "tried to get away after dark, the guard shot at him & run his bayonet through him, but after it all he was so fast he would have gotten away had not Cap. [William Wallace] overhauled him & knocked him down with his saber reversed." The man's wounds were serious, but he appears to have survived the incident. With fine understatement, another Ohio man noted: "He still tells a confused story."*

More routine matters were under way at the point where the Fourteenth Corps expected to cross the Yellow River, just below a railroad bridge that had been destroyed in an earlier raid. While nearby infantry prepared dinner or flopped down for the night, members of the 58th Indiana toiled on their first pontoon assignment of the campaign. Illumination was provided by torches and bonfires. The river here was some 100–120 feet wide, and the plan was for the army to cross in the morning on two bridges. While pioneer troops struggled against steep banks to construct an approach to the river, the Indiana engineers brought up their wagons to unload the flat-ended pontoon boats. The craft (sturdy wood frames with reattachable canvas sides) were pushed out onto the river, then anchored stepwise from bank to bank, some six feet apart. Each of the two crossings required six boats, each end being firmly lashed to the river bank. Next a series of long beams or

---

*   His fate is not recorded.

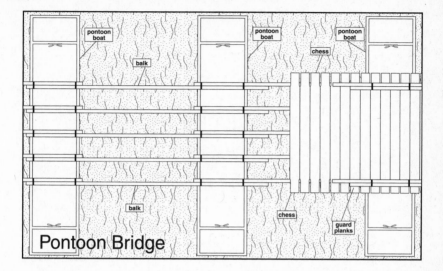

Pontoon Bridge

balks were laid across the boats, reaching from shore to shore. Perpendicular atop these came the planks or chesses, held in place with guard planks. Having trained long and hard for just such a circumstance, the Indiana engineers had the bridge ready for traffic well before dawn.

Left Wing orders written tonight addressed the slow movement of the wagons and the wasting of ammunition. "Brigade commanders should give their personal attention to the movement of the trains in their charge," admonished Brigadier General Alpheus S. Williams of the Twentieth Corps. A Fourteenth Corps directive made it clear that the "use of cartridges in killing of sheep, hogs, cattle, &c., foraged in the country is positively forbidden." Those with the authority to order buildings burned were cautioned to be mindful of the surrounding foliage and to take steps to ensure that the fires did not spread into nearby woods, where the flames could easily spread out of control.

CHAPTER 9

"Arise for the Defense of Your Native Soil!"

FRIDAY, NOVEMBER 18, 1864
Midnight–Noon

Right Wing

Major General Oliver Otis Howard was not by nature a high-strung individual. Nor was he an especially cerebral officer; however, he now faced a situation that demanded the probing thoughtfulness of a chess master. Part of his mission was to execute a believable threat against Macon, and toward that end his line of advance was taking him closer and closer to the Rebel citadel. This proximity posed a danger that Confederate authorities could not ignore, but at the same time it put Howard's Right Wing in significant peril. For the next few days his strung-out columns would be vulnerable to hit-and-run attacks launched from the armed city, and the limited road network had brought his two corps together at a water crossing without any existing bridge. It would take time for his military engineers to build one, and until they did, the bulk of his command would be stalled on the Ocmulgee River's west bank.

The first order of today's business was to protect the ferry area. A thin line of pickets from the 29th Missouri had staked Howard's claim throughout the night; now he had to up the ante to solidify his control. The call went out to the division nearest Planter's Factory, which

proved to be the Third of the Fifteenth Corps. The Federals had already secured the river craft that plied their trade here, but even with these in hand it was slow going. A member of the 93rd Illinois, the second regiment to make the passage, described his transportation as "an old fe[r]ry boat" and calculated "only 50 could get on at a time." A comrade in the 63rd Illinois put the volume at "about 30 men" in each circuit made by the "small Ferry boat." "As the enemy was known to be near," added an infantryman in the 4th Minnesota, once across "a detail threw up some light breastworks."

Through an oversight, the pontoon detail had not been staged forward at the end of yesterday's march, so valuable time was lost while the engineers and their wagons squeezed through the congestion to the riverbank. It was not until nearly 11:00 A.M. that the first pontoniers arrived, a section of thirty wagons pulled by as many mule teams, enough material to construct one floating bridge. The order was for two, but the other pontoon section was nowhere in sight. Those on hand from the 1st Missouri Engineers set to work, their efforts spurred on by the lowering clouds threatening a storm.

With the various columns halted for an indeterminate period, foragers had time to prowl. "We lived on the fat of the land today," recorded an Ohio diarist. "The Reg't had more Fresh Pork[,] Sweet Potatoes &c than they could possibly use." The sentiment was echoed by a brigade commander in the Seventeenth Corps who recorded an "abundance of sweet potatoes and fresh meat, and some meal, flour, sugar and salt besides forage for animals, and some horses and mules. We live well."

The delay also allowed the word of the Yankee presence to spread among the surrounding plantations and farms. "About a hundred Negroes came in," observed an Ohioan, "each bringing a good horse or mule." A squad from the 10th Iowa was helping itself to well water in front of a house, watched over by a black servant who gradually came to realize what was happening. According to a soldier present, "he took a frantic spill & screamed out in a most frightful strain (as he pointed off to the East): 'Our folks! Our folks! Gone! Gone! Gone!!!' " As the 63rd Illinois marched past a slave sporting a black silk hat and standing alongside three women, a soldier in the ranks called out a friendly invitation for him to come along. The black man nodded, shook hands with the women, said, "I're off," and eased into the blue ranks. The women, recalled a Illinoisan, "all put their big aprons to their face and began to cry. It was a sad parting scene, and to us a reminder of the tender chord that was touched when we said 'good bye.' "

Planter's Factory was a major object of interest for the soldiers in the area. The cloth manufacturing facility had been located where the river level dropped precipitously to provide an ample supply of water power. "There was a grist mill and a saw mill besides the factory which was four stories high, new, and in fine running order," recollected an Illinois soldier. A cannoneer noted the complex as consisting of "2 splendid buildings which the Rebels had used night & day for the man-ufacture of cloth for the army." An Indiana man eyed "lots of women & girls" in the workforce, estimated to number 150. A staff officer with General Howard, who counted seventy-five looms, spoke with the owner, who claimed he had only purchased the place a month ago. In other circumstances the view at the plant could be described as picturesque. Wrote a member of the 20th Illinois: "The most majestic scenery was seen at the mills[,] Steep high banks, rocky bottoms and deep cascades." Artistically attractive it may have been, but there was also no doubt that Planter's Factory was a legitimate target slated for destruction.

Brigadier General H. Judson Kilpatrick had his cavalrymen in the saddle soon after sunrise to execute his feint against Forsyth. Throughout the morning his troopers tramped slowly along the back roads heading south, flushing out several Rebel vidette posts as they went, almost always letting the enemy scouts escape to Forsyth with word that the Yankees were coming. By the time his advance had pushed within five or six miles of the rail station and supply depot, Kilpatrick was "convinced that the impression had been made upon the enemy that our forces were moving directly on that point." His column now swung east, then angled northward to New Market, where the troopers rested.

The feint proved everything Major General Howard had hoped for when he ordered it. Confederate field commanders remained convinced that Forsyth had been a prospective target, and only their determination to hold it prevented Sherman's riders from adding it to the list of violated towns. Besides the militia manning Forsyth's defensive positions, zealous partisans burned all the "bridges on the road from Forsyth to Indian Springs." Both generals Wheeler and Gustavus W. Smith took credit for the victory. "On the 18th, after a series of severe, but successful, engagements with Kilpatrick's Cavalry, we turned him off from his march upon Forsyth, saving that place also," read one report of Wheeler's actions. For his part, Smith crowed that his civilian-soldiers "reached Forsythe . . . just in time to repel the advance of Sherman's cavalry and save the large depot of supplies at that place."

Left Wing

The Twentieth Corps marched Second Division first today; so, "long before chicks began to squeal for life," Brigadier General John W. Geary had his soldiers moving. Behind them came the Third Division, which stopped in Social Circle long enough for the men to grab an early lunch. "Some of the 85th boys are cooking dinner," said an Indiana soldier; "others are engaged in tearing up the railroad track; some feeding their horses and mules from a corn crib near by, while others made a raid on a barrel of sorghum, went after pigs, chickens, etc." Soldiers entered the house of the George Garrett family, where they helped themselves to the larder besides giving two little girls a good fright. Before they left, one of the Yankees took the stopper from a barrel of syrup stored in the cellar, letting it gurgle onto the dirt floor. "I thought this a dirty, mean trick," recollected one of the youngsters.

"Citizens don't like the 'Yanks,'" observed an Illinois man. "One Rebel woman wishes South Carolina would sink for bringing on this war. Thinks we ought not to trouble Georgia because it was last to secede. We can't see it." A New Yorker thought Social Circle was a tidy-looking place with a fair number of "good looking girls." The ladies kept their distance, however, prompting another New York infantry-man to claim that the place was misnamed, with "no evidence of the residents being either social or cordial with us." The receptive mood wasn't improved when the railroad depot and a nearby cotton ware-house were set ablaze. However, most of the town's striking residences were spared the torch.

Outside Conyers, where the encampment of the Third Division, Fourteenth Corps, was bustling (the men marched second today, pre-ceded by the Second and followed by the First), Major James A. Con-nolly hustled to complete some unfinished business. When he arrived here yesterday, Connolly (on Brigadier General Absalom Baird's staff) had learned from slaves of a nearby plantation owner named Mr. Zachry, whose son, in the Confederate service, had sent his father a captured U.S. flag. Under Connolly's orders the plantation house was searched and its owner questioned, but no flag was found. Today Con-nolly was determined to settle the matter.

He threatened the elder, telling him that the Yankee boys knew about the hidden standard, and unless he produced it his house would be burned once the army marched away. When Zachry begged for a guard, Connolly refused, repeating his prediction that the minute the officers departed, vengeance-seeking soldiers would torch his place. Connolly could be very convincing. "In less than ten minutes the old rascal brought the flag out and delivered it up," the officer said with grim satisfaction, adding, "I don't know whether his house was burned or not."

For his part, Sherman was matching wills with the weather. Hitchcock described the morning as "cloudy and threatening rain," while Sherman believed it to be "the perfection of campaigning, such weather and such roads as this." On their way to the Yellow River, the headquarters party paused at the Reverend Gray's house, then occupied by the good minister's wife, her daughter, and grandchildren. While Hitchcock chatted, soldiers ran free around the property, helping themselves to all kinds of forage. "Evidently bitter rebel, but civil enough, and talked quietly," recorded Hitchcock. "Never saw Yankee soldiers before 'except prisoners passing.' Like a woman, that!"

Sherman and company, reaching the pontoons built overnight by the 58th Indiana, traversed the Yellow River without incident. The water at this point was about one hundred feet wide, and it ran deep, though Major Hitchcock thought it "fordable." As they were passing over, cattle were being herded across the river in two groups, one wading near the ruined railroad bridge, the other forced to swim downstream from the pontoons. "Cattle are the most trying things for pontoon bridges," Hitchcock commented, "apt to crowd and rush."

As the headquarters party drew close to Covington, word came that a deputation of local notables was waiting to greet Sherman. The General, recalled another aide, "not anxious to witness such an instance of submission, prudently avoided them by taking a back street through the town." Hardly had they turned onto the detour when a young man in Confederate uniform intercepted them. The enemy soldier, wounded in Virginia and recuperating in Covington, had been told by the provost guards to surrender to Sherman. The General promptly turned the invalid over to Colonel Charles Ewing of his staff, who wrote out a parole for the young man after learning that "there is a mighty pretty girl where he stays." Winks and nods were shared as the grateful Rebel headed back into town.

A couple of young and adventurous signal corps officers with Sherman's party, learning of his flanking maneuver against the reception party, decided that a prepared meal shouldn't be missed. Appointing each other the General's representatives, they presented themselves to the welcoming committee and were royally wined and dined. "This was all intended for Genl. Sherman," mused an aide, "but as he had declined to partake they did the best they could."

Noon–Midnight

General Beauregard's efforts to energize Confederate defenses against Sherman were set back today thanks to the worn-out transportation network. His preferred choice to take command, Lieutenant General Richard Taylor, was stuck on the road from Mobile to Macon, and exactly when he would arrive was anyone's guess. With Taylor checked, Beauregard went to the next name on his list by recommending to Richmond that Lieutenant General Hardee, then in Savannah, be given temporary authority over Macon.

Beauregard was himself stalled in transit, having only just reached Corinth, Mississippi. Since he could not be present in person at this critical time, Beauregard tried to project his presence through a ringing proclamation.

TO THE PEOPLE OF GEORGIA:

Arise for the defense of your native soil! Rally round your patriotic Governor and gallant soldiers! Obstruct and destroy all roads in Sherman's front, flank, and rear, and his army will soon starve in your midst! Be confident and resolute! Trust in an overruling Providence, and success will crown your efforts. I hasten to join you in defense of your homes and firesides.

Beauregard's wasn't the only exhortation in circulation today. From Richmond, Georgia senator B. H. Hill telegraphed his constituents:

TO THE PEOPLE OF GEORGIA:

You have now the best opportunity ever yet presented to destroy the enemy. Put everything at the disposal of our generals; remove all provisions from the path of the invader, and put all obstructions in his path. Every citizen with his gun, and every negro with his spade and axe, can do the work of a soldier. You can destroy the enemy by retarding his march. Georgians, be firm! Act promptly, and fear not!

Words were fine, but Georgia's leaders were seeking more substantial support. Today Jefferson Davis did his best to buck up his old friend Howell Cobb while, at the same time, promising nothing from outside the region.

> *In addition to troops of all kinds you should endeavor to get out every man who can render any service, even for a short period, and employ negroes in obstructing roads by every practicable means. Colonel [Gabriel] Rains, at Augusta, can furnish you with shells prepared to explode by pressure, and these will be effective to check an advance. General Hardee has, I hope, brought some re-enforcements, and General Taylor will probably join you with some further aid.* You have a difficult task, but will realize the necessity for the greatest exertion.*

The public rhetoric in Macon reflected a different picture. Readers of the *Macon Daily Telegraph* were advised "that the military authorities will do every thing in their power to stop the advance of the enemy, and we trust they will receive the cordial support of the entire community." Major General Cobb, his headquarters now in town, received reconnaissance reports indicating that the enemy was crossing the Ocmulgee in strength at Planter's Factory. Cobb's chief scout complained that it was proving difficult to locate any civilians with useful information "as all have taken [to] the forest."

Lacking any central command, Macon's various defenders were each deciding how best to deploy themselves. The militia commander, Major General Smith, then at Forsyth, determined that the best place for his citizen-soldiers was "in the fortifications at Macon, leaving the outside work to the cavalry." Major General Wheeler was also getting advice in lieu of reinforcements. "Employ your cavalry to best advantage, retarding advance of Sherman's army and destroying supplies in his front," counseled General Beauregard. From General Hood came the admonition that Wheeler "should not allow any portion of your mounted force to be shut up in a besieged city, but keep them constantly harassing the enemy, destroying his trains, and cutting off his foraging parties." Wheeler's situation report for November 18 was blunt: "Enemy pressing on rapidly."

In Milledgeville, the General Assembly set records approving a slew of measures prompted by the growing crisis. An act was passed autho-

---

*   Hardee's reinforcements consisted of 200 men; Taylor was bringing only himself.

rizing the Georgia Supreme Court to convene wherever circumstances allowed; another limited the liability for owners of cotton warehouses burned by the enemy. Governor Brown received his authority to raise a *levy en masse*, and special tax relief was extended to citizens who had property commandeered by local officials or "rendered valueless by reason of the public enemy."

Their work done, the legislature adjourned so that the elected officials could scatter to the winds. "Some members," reported an observer, "unable to get seats on railway trains [using the spur line], hired private conveyance to the Central [rail]road at Gordon and other points. I heard of two members who paid $500 each for a carriage to the Central Railway. The panic was complete."

At the Governor's Mansion, Joseph Brown was eating an unapologetic serving of crow. In previous discussions with Confederate officials, Brown had given broad assurances that in an emergency the manpower he had protected from impressment would rally to the state's defense. Sherman, however, had moved too fast; and the Georgia authorities had reacted too slow. Today Brown composed a message to Jefferson Davis that admitted the fact: "A heavy force of the enemy is advancing on Macon, laying waste the country and burning the towns. We have not sufficient force. I hope you will send us troops as re-enforcements till the exigency is passed."

This evening, a prominent citizen named William G. McAdoo called on Governor Brown. "Everything in the Executive Mansion was in the wildest uproar," he recollected. "The halls and rooms were filled with convicts arrayed in Penitentiary Stripes removing furniture and every thing valuable from the Mansion* and Mrs. Brown, pale and hurried, was every where at the same instant. The Governor's iron face was unmoved. . . . The energetic evacuation of Milledgeville was now grown frantic."

There was no panic farther east at Camp Lawton, where the processing of the sick for prisoner exchange had reached a lucrative stage. "By paying the doctor a good sum, from twenty to fifty dollars in greenbacks, he will put a person on the sick list, and thus they will get out of prison," attested a POW. Business was so good, he contended,

---

* Needing the laborers, Brown had offered amnesty to any prisoner willing to serve in the present emergency.

that "many of the sick are actually crowded out to give place to those who have bought their freedom. The doctors are making quite a speculating game out of it."

——— *Right Wing* ———

The first section of Missouri engineers completed their pontoon across the Ocmulgee River by 1:00 P.M., at which time the passage (measured at 264 feet) was open for business. The second section of boats and bridging elements did not make it through the press of wagons and men until nearly 3:00 P.M., so the additional crossing wasn't completed until two hours later. This kept things backed up, allowing even more bored soldiers opportunities to rummage around. "Here many of our boys went out foraging, and some got sweet potatoes, others turnips," recorded an Ohio soldier; "some found whiskey and those were pretty well corned."

Idlers from the 100th Indiana came upon a cache of current newspapers at Indian Springs, which, in more peaceful times, enjoyed a brisk business as a health resort. "The Confederate officials promulgated some highly inflammatory addresses to the people of Georgia, exhorting them to rise up in their might and crush out the invaders," read one bemused Hoosier. Other soldiers "entered into interesting conversation with the inhabitants of the village and those who fled from the cities and towns to this far inland resort, hoping to escape the dread coming of Sherman's army."

Among these unfortunates was a newlywed couple and friends whose celebrations had been cut short. The group (four altogether), arriving from Macon on November 17, had been detained overnight. Given permission today to return to Macon, the wedding party had not gone far before an artillery officer stopped their carriage to swap horses—their sleek pair for his dilapidated set. The exchange completed, the bridegroom tried without success to urge his new team on, his futile efforts drawing forth a chorus of jibes and jeers from passing infantry. "But the tears of the gentle women melted the hearts of the soldiers," wrote one of them, "who lent a helping hand and the party was soon beyond the lines, and on the road to home and friends."

General Howard's intention was to cross all of the Seventeenth Corps, followed by the remaining divisions of the Fifteenth Corps and Kilpatrick's cavalry. His original design had the cavalry going over first, but thanks to the diversionary movement against Forsyth, the Yankee horsemen did not reach the Planter's Factory area until well after sundown. In their stead, a small mounted party led by Captain James M. McClintock of the signal corps crossed the river to scout all the way to the village of Monticello. "Drove in the enemy's pickets at M[onticello]," McClintock wrote in his diary. "Exchanged a few shots and returned. Arrived in camp at 8 P.M."

Back along the river, as the various units were formed up and marched to the Planter's Factory bridges, they encountered an unexpected wrinkle. Before reaching the pontoons, the columns passed through checkpoints manned by provost guards and quartermasters, who confiscated all unauthorized animals. Too many units needing fresh mounts weren't getting them, while too many foot soldiers were riding. Even the gunners with artillery batteries were not exempt, and "in this way many of our cannoneers lost the nags they had picked up," groused one of them.

Additionally, large piles of foraged goods accumulated at the checkpoints, since most of the soldiers had used the horses and mules as pack animals, leaving them with loads that were more than they cared to carry. "This looked hard to some of them who had a dozen hams and a lot of chickens, or a sack of sweet potatoes, and all sorts of good things to eat," commented an observer. Slowly, the herd of broken-down animals left in the exchange began to grow.

The Ocmulgee crossing was becoming the major impediment that General Howard had feared. The lag in bringing up the pontoon train had delayed the schedule until the afternoon, and the process of weeding out all the unauthorized animals had further slowed the pace. Then it began to rain; sprinkles at first, but soon turning into a more steady downfall. "At the eastern end of the bridge the bank rose quite abruptly, making a steep hill," remembered a member of Howard's staff. "The falling rain softened the clay ground and made the crossing difficult. The wagons and artillery carriages were helped up the hill by over 1,000 men stationed along the road between the river and crest of the hill." Seconded a weary Howard, "The crossing of the Ocmulgee, with its steep and muddy banks, was hard enough for the trains." It was going to be a long night for all concerned.

———— *Left Wing* ————

Brigadier General John W. Geary's division, leading the Twentieth Corps this day, pushed rapidly along the Georgia Railroad until it reached the station stop called Rutledge. There the advance came to a temporary halt while the work of destruction commenced. A soldier in the 28th Pennsylvania recalled his unit burning "a considerable amount of public property among which was several [railroad] cars." A member of the 29th Ohio never forgot marching "along the R.R. and in many places we would stop and pile fence rails on the track and set fire to them, in other places we pried up the track and turned the road bottom side up." "Men feel a little jaded," groaned an Ohioan. "A night's rest will restore most of them."

Behind Geary's men followed the rest of the corps, some of it wrecking track, some of it foraging. Most of the Yankee boys wondered at the quantities of foodstuffs they found. "Forage abundant," wrote an amazed Indiana soldier. "Thousands of bushels of sweet potatoes passed by untouched." The officer commanding the 150th New York was so impressed that he felt he had to itemize today's gleanings in his official report. "Sent out two companies foraging," he wrote, "procured 1,530 pounds of fresh pork and 10 sheep, and 6 head of fat cattle— average weight dressed, 300 pounds a head; aggregate, 1,800 pounds— and 42 bushels of sweet potatoes, [plus] about 64 gallons of syrup."

Several incidents underscored the narrow margin between an adventure and a disaster. One occurred as the column approached Social Circle. Colonel Ezra A. Carmen, commanding the Second Brigade in the First Division, Twentieth Corps, detailed a number of foraging parties, consisting of two companies from each regiment. His instructions were explicit; the detachments were to "proceed along each side of the road, keeping within half a mile of the column, and collect what subsistence they could find for the use of the brigade." One party consisted of forty-three men from companies D and K of the 107th New York under the command of Captain George W. Reid.

Reid, whose top priority was "whiskey uppermost," according to a member of the regiment, led his men several miles from the line of march. Even worse, he allowed his command to fall beyond support distance of the rear guard. Reid and his detail did not return to camp that night. It wasn't until several days later that a few lucky survivors showed up to report that the detail had been ambushed and captured to a man.

In a way, Reid and his little command were lucky. A group of foragers from the Fourteenth Corps shot it out with a squadron of Rebel cavalry. A trooper from the 8th Texas Cavalry noted in his diary that his men scrapped with about nine foragers near Oxford. "After a run of some two miles, we killed three and wounded four," he boasted. A member of the 105th Ohio was part of a rescue operation that brought in the dead and wounded. He recorded that one of the corpses had eight bullet wounds, and added that the men "were angry & wanted to burn the town [of Oxford] but the rebels did not belong there so [we] would not."

Some ten miles southwest of Social Circle, most of the Fourteenth Corps passed through Covington. A few regiments made quite a production of it. "On the 18th we marched through the beautiful town of Covington, with our ranks closed up, bands playing and colors flying, as if we were on a holiday parade," recollected a member of the 75th Indiana. Two military hospitals had operated in the village, so the ranks of the onlookers were spotted with convalescent Rebel veterans. An infantryman in the 31st Ohio recalled seeing "a crippled Confederate soldier . . . among the few bystanders. One of the boys called to him, 'Hello, pard; what regiment?' —The fellow gave the number, '—Jawjay, sah,' and gave us the military salute."

The correspondent for the *New York Herald* was present when one of the Federal bands struck up "Dixie." "Every window and door swarmed with blooming war widows, stately matrons and shy virgins in homespun and coarse linen," he reported. Once it had everyone's attention, the band segued into "Yankee Doodle." "Oh, what a retreat," chuckled the newsman, "windows came down with a slam and doors closed very abruptly, until not a fair face was visible."

One fair face that did not disappear belonged to Tillie Travis, who sat quietly knitting as the solid masses of Union soldiery trooped past her porch while groups rummaged around for food. Her stoicism was a pose, for Tillie was not known for holding her tongue when it came to the subject of the Confederacy and her worried mother had put the fear of God into the girl to keep her silent. Tillie held her vow until a Union officer "attempted to reconstruct me by arguments to prove the sin of Secession." Tillie's swift response at last drove the Federal away, but not before he commented, "I see it is no use to argue with you." Tillie had a secret laugh on the plucky Yankee, for snug in the center of the yarn balls she was handling were gold watches, hidden in plain sight for safekeeping.

Experiences of Covington's blacks covered a broad spectrum. "Negroes all want to follow us[,] but our limited supplies prevents our taking many," wrote a diarist in the 34th Illinois. A comrade in the 105th Ohio related that he "saw several darkey women and men who wished to come. I advised the women not to come, they were anxious to come and said that they were abused by their masters shamefully." Slaves who crowded up to the ranks of the 21st Wisconsin seemed genuinely surprised that the fearsome Yankees did not sport any horns. "Some of the boys told them that, in order not to scare them we had taken them off and put them in the wagons," quipped a member of the regiment.

Another side to the story was vouched for by Tillie Travis, one of whose young female slaves came running up to the house shrieking that she was being robbed by Sherman's men. A nearby Federal wondered aloud what all the fuss was about. "Your soldiers," Tillie replied, "are carrying off everything she owns, and yet you pretend to be fighting for the negro." When the slave girl saw an officer's black servant wearing one of her hats, she went up to him to shake her fist in his face. "Oh!" she exclaimed, "if I had the power like I've got the will, I'd tear you to pieces."

Passing quickly through Covington was a section of the 58th Indiana, hurrying its pontoon train to the Alcovy River. The first elements of the Fourteenth Corps to reach there found an improvised but usable crossing via a platform built on the ruins of an original bridge. It was good enough for infantry, but wouldn't take wagons, so orders went back to the Yellow River for one of the sections to hustle forward. The new instructions arrived at 4:00 P.M. Thirty minutes later one of the two pontoons had been dismantled and packed for travel. Less than two hours after that the Indiana engineers were setting to work at the

Alcovy River, which one of them described as "a deep, sluggish stream, with almost no banks," about seventy-five feet wide. The officer in charge decided to run his bridge alongside the platform already in place, so within two hours the new pontoon was handling traffic. Sherman's secret weapon was performing to expectations.

The General's night headquarters were located about a mile and half west of the Alcovy River on the farm of Judge Harris. After asking around, the *New York Herald* reporter learned that the jurist, who hailed from Massachusetts, was not a kind master. Estimates of his slaveholdings ranged from 60 to 200, housed in what the correspondent called a "village of negro huts." A crowd of curious and excited blacks was on hand as Sherman's staff began erecting the night camp. "Glory be to de Lord, de Lincoln's hab come!" called one, while another shouted "Bress de Lord!" Major Hitchcock asked a younger member of the group (he thought him twenty-five to thirty) why he had left his owner. "I was bound to come, Sah," he answered, "good trade or bad trade, I'se bound to risk it." Hitchcock thought that the simple faith these men and women had in the Union presence was striking and touching.

Sherman had another black elder brought to him to be queried about local roads and conditions. As Sherman recollected the moment, he asked the slave if he understood what the war meant for him and his people. The patriarch "supposed that slavery was the cause, and that our success was to be his freedom." Believing that authority in the slave community was vested with the elders, Sherman patiently explained "that we wanted the slaves to remain where they were and not to load us down with useless mouths . . . , that our success was their assured freedom; but that, if they followed us in swarms . . . it would simply load us down and cripple us in our great task."

To the end of his life, Sherman was convinced that the "old man spread this message to the slaves, which was carried from mouth to mouth, to the very end of our journey, and that it in part saved us from the great danger we incurred of swelling our numbers so that famine would have attended our progress."

It was also at this place that Sherman saw firsthand how some of his orders were being implemented by the common soldiers. He encountered one "with a ham on his musket, a jug of sorghum-molasses under his arm, and a big piece of honey in his hand, from which he was eating." Catching the stern look of his commanding officer, the quick-thinking Yankee stage-whispered to a comrade: "Forage liberally on the country." Sherman said he "reproved the man, explained that foraging must be limited to the regular parties properly detailed, and that all provisions thus obtained must be delivered to the regular commissaries, to be fairly distributed to the men who kept their ranks."

Earlier in this evening, Sherman had another run-in, this witnessed by the colonel of a regiment who related it to the *New York Herald* reporter. Said the officer, "a number of soldiers . . . were filling their canteens from a molasses barrel, near Sherman's headquarters, [and] were quarreling over the division of the syrup, when Sherman passing by cooly crowded in among them, and dipping his finger in it put it to his lips, remarking, 'Don't crowd, boys, there is enough for all.' "

A sack of Rebel mail intercepted in Covington was left at Sherman's camp for Major Hitchcock to peruse. Among the missives he discovered the letter that Miss Zora M. Fair had composed in Oxford for Governor Brown, recounting her adventures as a spy in Atlanta. From others in the sack Hitchcock gathered that Miss Fair's friends did not approve of her extracurricular activities. He brought the note to Sherman's attention and was surprised when the general ordered a detail to knock on doors in Oxford to try to find the girl. "I don't mean to hurt her," Sherman explained, "but will give her a scare." When the search party reported back it was to say that Miss Zora M. Fair was not to be found. Her letter to Governor Brown would remain undelivered.[*]

A few miles outside Covington, Mrs. Dolly Sumner Lunt Burge fell asleep fully dressed, expecting Yankees at any moment. During the day she had taken steps to protect her property by sending two of her mules into hiding and secreting food in different places. She also let her black coachman drive the forty fattened hogs she owned into the swamp for safekeeping. Now her only defense was with the Lord. "Oh, how I trust I am safe!" she prayed.

---

[*]   One postwar story records her hiding in a neighbor's upstairs room, whose door was concealed by a large piece of furniture. Other accounts have her out of town at the time of Sherman's visit.

CHAPTER 10

"Whites Look Sour & Sad"

SATURDAY, NOVEMBER 19, 1864
Midnight–Noon

——— *Right Wing* ———

The combination of rain, bad roads, and congestion was turning the Right Wing's crossing of the Ocmulgee River into a protracted ordeal. "We got up this morning wet & nasty," groused an Illinoisan in the Fifteenth Corps. The "roads today are very slippery," seconded an Iowan in the Seventeenth Corps, "which as the country is so hilly, makes difficult marching." "On both sides of the stream, for many miles, the roads lay through low, flat ground, sodden with recent rains, and the heavy wagon trains soon converted them into almost bottomless abysses of mud, entailing upon the men severe labor in corduroying, and extricating artillery and wagon trains," wrote a soldier in the 32nd Illinois. A member of the 4th Minnesota observed that the men's "blankets are so wet and heavy that some of them could not be dried by fire and had to be left, being too heavy to carry, and so the boys will have to suffer and get along as best they can."

In good weather the passage over the Ocmulgee would have been a matter of hours for the Right Wing's 28,000 soldiers; instead it dragged on throughout the day, into the night, and would extend well into the next morning. Major General Howard opted to keep up the pressure

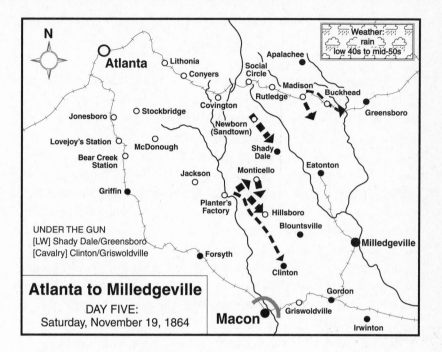

N

Atlanta to Milledgeville
DAY FIVE:
Saturday, November 19, 1864

on Macon to divert attention from his increasingly exposed wagon train, which he later described as a "source of anxiety" for him. As the first elements of the Seventeenth Corps reached the small village of Monticello, they turned south and east toward Hillsboro, on the direct road to Macon. Also in motion as part of Howard's diversionary scheme was Kilpatrick and his cavalry. This force, as Howard later reported, "as soon as over the river, again quickly turned down the first roads toward East Macon."

The cavalry's crossing of the Ocmulgee River took place before sunrise and was suitably dramatic. "Great fires were kept blazing on both banks of the river to light up the bridge," recalled a trooper. "The light was so bright that it reflected the factory, and trees upon the banks, and the crossing columns of troops in the water as clearly and distinctly as if the river had been a mirror." Getting over the broad stream was no mean feat. "The cavalry cross two by two, each trooper dismounted and leading his horse," explained one of them. "The artillery, eight horses to a gun, sink the [pontoon] boats to within a few inches of the top, the bridge rising behind the gun as it goes from boat to boat."

--------- *Left Wing* ---------

The Twentieth Corps, constituting the extreme northern flank of Sherman's grand movement, passed through Madison today. First in line was Brigadier General John W. Geary's division (the Second), which followed the railroad tracks eastward, on course for the Oconee River. "The weather is wet and disagreeable," attested a Pennsylvania diarist. "Colored people are pleased to see the Yanks," added an Ohio soldier. "Whites look sour & sad." When the 111th Pennsylvania marched through Madison, their procession was subjected to a dour inspection by a group of old-timers. "A wag in Company A, at a moment when no sound was heard except the route step of marching feet, seeing the manifest distress of these white-bearded patriarchs, swung his cap and, looking at the group, shouted at the top of his voice, 'Hurrah for *Lincoln!*' " chuckled a member of the regiment. "The old fellows nearly rolled off their chairs."

Behind Geary's men marched the Third Division, followed by the First, both of which turned south. Groups of soldiers operating ahead of the main column ran loose in the town for a while, leading an Illinois man to mutter that "our men ransacked it badly," but order was quickly established so that the Yankees who followed almost all complimented what they saw. "It is the finest village this side of Nashville," declared an Illinois man. "Yards full of the most beautiful roses and other plants." A correspondent working for the *New York Herald* thought "the town looked too pretty to think of in connection with the march of an army."

When the 102nd Illinois halted in the courthouse square, they were entertained by a band playing patriotic airs. "The men have obtained files of old papers, and are scattering them by hundreds through the different regiments," wrote a member of the regiment. As a railroad depot, Madison had its share of legitimate targets. A deputation of town notables had tried to negotiate an exemption, but Slocum was not prepared to amend Sherman's rules of war. "Cotton stored near the railroad station was fired, and the jail near the public square gave up its whips and paddles to increase the big bonfire in the public square," noted an Ohioan. "The Calaboos[e] was burnt while the Bands plaid," recorded a Wisconsin diarist. Private houses in the village were subject to soldier searches, but were otherwise left alone.

The railroad agent's wife (he was off in Savannah) pleaded with the Union boys not to burn her husband's office. "But it was of no use whatever," said a Connecticut soldier. "The windows were opened, fire thrown in and it was soon wrapped in flames. I almost always have sympathy for the women. But I did not much pity her. She was a regular secesh and spit out her spite and venom against the dirty Yanks and mudsills of the north." Missed or ignored in the random searches was Edmund B. Walker's coffin, which survived the Federal visit; many years later, young descendants would sneak into the attic to gawk at the space outlined in the dust indicating where it once rested.

Emma High's resourceful mother produced her husband's Masonic apron to back her request for help from any society member in the group of soldiers outside her home. An officer stepped forward, took charge, and posted a guard. Meanwhile, Emma watched, wide-eyed, as the young men in blue descended on her next-door neighbor's flower garden. The plants, she recalled, were "stripped of all [their] . . . bright hued roses and the soldiers wove them into garlands and decorated their arms—crossed and tied them with the garlands, singing and making great sport of the occasion."

Perhaps it was the beauty of the town that inspired Major General Slocum to indulge in a rare display of command prerogative by having a number of brigades pass before him in review. A soldier in the Third Brigade of the First Division remembered going through Madison in "fine style, colors flying[,] music playing[,] marching in column by platoon, and [being] . . . reviewed by Gen. Slocum as we passed the public square." Another infantryman (Second Brigade, Third Division) recalled marching under Slocum's gaze "with handsomely aligned ranks, precise movement and arms at right-shouldershift, the feet keeping step to the soul-stirring air of 'Dixie.' "

The Second and Third brigades of the Third Division drew most of the railroad-wrecking assignment. "We spent the whole forenoon in tearing up the track," recorded a soldier in the 85th Indiana. "It is rather interesting to see an army stack arms, step forward and take hold of the end of the ties and upset five miles of track at one lift."

A few miles south and west of Madison, the Fourteenth Corps fin-

ished passing through Covington, then turned southeast, toward a
spot on the map called Shady Dale. The Second Division led the way,
followed by the Third and the First. A *New York Herald* correspondent
wrote that "the roads were found almost impassable from the rain that
had fallen in torrents during the night." An Ohio soldier never forgot
moving "ahead in a heavy rain, the troops straggling much on account
of a bad road." The weather was making everyone grumpy. "You awake
in the morning only to find yourself as lame & sore as ever," grumbled
an Ohioan. "Every step gives pain."

The sound of rain drumming on his canvas tent fly greeted Major
Hitchcock this morning. The commander of the Fourteenth Corps,
Brevet Major General Jefferson C. Davis, stopped by to report that all
his transportation and supplies were over the Alcovy River, and his
rear guard was just getting across. This was more good news for Sherman, who outwardly remained a picture of confidence, though his
mind never ceased mulling over probabilities and possibilities. Recorded
Hitchcock, who treasured his close relationship with his boss, "the
General explained today to me of his plans in any one of several con-
tingencies."

A few of the younger members of the headquarters entourage
decided to improve their personal transportation by riding ahead of
the column to find some horses and mules. Just before reaching the
town of Newborn, the group was fired on from ambush, but their
attackers fled almost as quickly as they had appeared. None in the
party was hit, so they continued on their mission as if nothing had
happened.

Confederate Lieutenant General William J. Hardee reached Macon
this morning, endowed with Beauregard's authority to take charge of
the forces in the region. The intelligence that greeted his arrival was
grim. As he promptly reported to Richmond: "The enemy [is] on both
sides [of the] Ocmulgee River, about thirty miles from Macon. A
column is reported near Social Circle marching on Augusta." High on
his to-do list was the urgent need to accumulate sufficient weapons to
arm the militia forces gathering in Georgia and South Carolina. In a
separate message Hardee telegraphed Richmond requesting that all
"spare arms [be] sent to Charleston, S.C., subject to my orders."

There was more bad news. Hardee had alerted Savannah to prepare its land side defenses, only to learn that the earthworks were incomplete and that much labor was needed to finish them. The officer in charge, Major General Lafayette McLaws, wanted to use his troops for the task, but Hardee told him "to press negroes if you need them." On the plus side, during his train ride from Augusta to Macon, Hardee had passed over the long railroad bridge at the Oconee River and saw its strong defensive possibilities. He was now able to use his temporary authority to make certain that troops were directed to that potential choke point.

For his part, General Beauregard's biggest struggle today was with his transportation. He departed Corinth, Mississippi, heading toward Mobile, Alabama, from where he hoped to find a train that would take him to Macon. He was frustrated that General Hood, headquartered in Florence, Alabama, still had not moved his army. Beauregard had reduced Hood's options to two; he could either "divide [his force] and re-enforce Cobb [at Macon], or take the offensive [into Tennessee] immediately to relieve him." Beauregard had no clue what Hood intended to do.

Despite these travails of the high command, Southern newspapers remained upbeat. According to the *Augusta Constitutionalist*, "After a careful survey of the topography of the country lying before SHERMAN, the distance he must travel before he can strike any vital point, and the difficulties that naturally environ an incursive army of that kind, we apprehend no serious result from the movement." Editors were equally sanguine in the Confederate capital, where the writers for the *Richmond Dispatch* assured readers about Sherman that the "country cannot support him, and it is impossible he should carry more than ten or fifteen days' supplies." Looking to the illustrious leadership that was directing affairs in Georgia, the paper was positively bullish. "With such men at the head of such a force as we are informed Georgia can still furnish, it will be a very difficult job to march to Savannah, we should think."

At Camp Lawton, outside Millen, Union prisoners crawled out from under whatever shelters they had managed to erect to protect themselves from the overnight rain. A half-ration of meal received yesterday evening was supplemented today with a load of beef heads, whose stink, related one captive, "would have turned our stomachs under ordinary circumstances." Those clever enough to have hidden money from spot searches did better. "Rice, bean soup, biscuits, pies and corn dodgers were made and sold on Market Street at exorbitant prices," noted the POW.

Noon–Midnight

——————— *Left Wing* ———————

Pushing eastward along the Georgia Railroad, Brigadier General John Geary's division (Twentieth Corps) reached Buckhead, where a small party of Rebel scouts was dispersed before the infantry set to wrecking things. "Burned many cotton mills and presses," noted an Ohio diarist, "took dinner at Buckhead station[,] burned the station." Geary later supplied a bit more detail when he reported destroying "the water-tank, [a] stationary engine, and all the railroad buildings." A Pennsylvania soldier recalled burning "several thousand bushels of corn," while a New Yorker reported having "a first rate time killing hogs and getting potatoes."

Most attention was given to the tracks. A New Jersey infantryman recollected "tearing up and burning all the wood work of the road," while a brigadier reported destroying "a considerable distance of the railroad . . . by burning the ties and bending and twisting the rails." Some units were satisfied with a process that produced quantity over quality. "Our Division started out from Madison alone and proceeded to tear up the railroad for a long distance without severing the rails from the ties, like a plow turns the sod over," attested a Pennsylvania farm boy.

John Geary marched his main column as far as Blue Springs, where most of the command bivouacked on the plantation of Colonel Lee Jordan of the Rebel army. Geary sent a detachment forward from there to carry out his principal objective, the destruction of the railroad bridge across the Oconee River. It was a fine piece of engineering, some 400 yards long and rising 60 feet above the water. The strike group, Geary later reported, "thoroughly destroyed" the structure. Another detail was sent north several miles to wreck a large mill and to destroy all the ferryboats along the Apalachee River.

For all the rest of the Twentieth Corps today was a sloppy tramp southeasterly from Madison. "The roads are rather muddy and hard walking," said a New York soldier. The lousy weather and poor roads did not dissuade many slaves from liberating themselves. An Illinois soldier remembered how they joined the Federal columns "loaded down with bundles and babies." "There were old Pomps, young Pomps, She Pomps and pickannies," reflected a New York man, "and as they trudge along they form a grotesque procession and one that should be seen to be appreciated." When a squad from the 102nd Illinois reached one plantation, they found a large stash of cotton burning, watched over by an elderly black man. When someone wondered aloud who started the blaze, he answered: "You Yankees did it, and I'm glad of it—*it would never have done me no good.*"

Between the population of Madison and the surrounding home-steads, a number of encounters took place between the invaders and residents. The officer in charge of the town's provost guard recorded dining invitations for lunch and supper, a visit from a former U.S. sen-ator (Joshua Hill), and the gift of a flower bouquet. The meetings were less social for more isolated homeowners. "I don't know what in the world the people through here are going to live upon," worried one woman to a soldier, "for your army is taking everything." Another infantryman joined a group that was filling canteens from a house well. They were surprised when the house mistress came to the porch with an appeal for them not to waste the water. "Why ma'am, what's the difference to you?" asked one of the soldiers. "There's a whole corps on this road and by night there won't be any left."

For Dolly Burge, waiting apprehensively at her plantation nine miles east of Covington, this was the day she had been dreading. After a restless night and breakfast without incident, she decided to visit her nearest neighbor. Hardly had she reached him before she heard that the dreaded Yankees were close at hand. Dolly raced back to her home, yelled to her slaves to hide themselves, and in the next instant the vandals were all around her. "Like demons they run in!" she exclaimed. "My yards are full. To my smoke-house, my dairy, pantry, kitchen, and cellar, like famished wolves they come, breaking locks and whatever is in their way."

Amazingly, a guard appeared, but his authority extended only to the house itself; everything else was fair game. When Dolly protested, the young soldier shrugged. "I cannot help you, Madam; it is orders," he said. Mrs. Burge watched in silent, incendiary anger as she witnessed her livestock taken and the cabins used by her slaves plundered. When a sympathetic Union officer, who was also a distant relation, tried to console her, she burst into tears. "I saw nothing before me but starvation," she later wrote. The officer so calmed her that by the time he departed, Dolly was calling him a friend. Two guards later replaced the single one, and together with Dolly, her family and slaves spent what would be a second night without sleep for the plantation mistress from New England. "I . . . kept walking to and fro," Dolly remembered, "watching the fires in the distance and dreading the approaching day, which, I feared, as they had not all passed, would be but a continuation of horrors."

As they got through the swampy lowlands of the Alcovy River, the Fourteenth Corps made better time in its march toward Shady Dale. Once more the Yankee boys traveled through a bountiful land. "Troops have plenty to eat," wrote an Illinois man in his journal. "Plenty of corn and potatoes," said a fellow soldier. When the 21st Wisconsin reached its camp for the night, the men found a nearby hog pen filled to capacity. "There was sport for the boys," laughed a member of the regiment, "and ere long their hogships [were] given a passport for eternity."

One unexpected problem that emerged was the large number of soldier casualties resulting from undisciplined melees over poultry and fowls. "Several . . . men wounded by shooting at chickens," recorded a diarist in the 34th Illinois. Another in the 113th Ohio noted that two men in a foraging detail "were accidentally shot, or rather carelessly by their comrades, while shooting chickens." Trying to make light of the matter, an Illinoisan spoke of a soldier "accidentally wounded in the leg while a vigorous assault was being made on a flock of turkeys by the foragers." In response, wrote another member of the 34th Illinois, "Provost guards are taking up many of the boys for shooting near the column."

"Negroes by the hundred are coming into our line and we are keeping them with us[,] using them to get forage for us and we find them not bad fellows to have along," reported an Indiana man. Major James A. Connolly, who had earlier browbeaten a plantation owner into surrendering a captured U.S. flag, had to chuckle this afternoon. Most of the citizens in the area, he noticed, had tried to hide their livestock and valuables in swampy places. They had used their slaves to help them; however, "the negroes told the soldiers of these hiding places and most of these hidden valuables find their way into our camp to-night."

Sherman's headquarters party spent two hours in Newborn, mostly because the General was hugely enjoying himself conversing with a "queer old cock" (Hitchcock's words) named John W. Pitts. A soldier marching past caught sight of "Gen. Sherman sitting with his hat off[,] tracing his map and questioning an old citizen standing near." Mr. Pitts, who had founded the little village, was given the full Sherman lecture: the Southern cause was hopeless, its leaders were on the wrong course, its people deserved whatever happened to them. To all this Pitts agreed, even volunteering that the "Confederates were a great deal worse than our men, that they pillaged and plundered everybody, and the inhabitants dreaded their coming."

Finally the command group moved along, cantering another seven miles before settling in for the night. Along the route they could hear occasional shots as foragers plied their trade. It was reported that several soldiers had been killed or injured in the activity. Hitchcock thought that something needed to be done about it, but Sherman was unconcerned. "I have been three years fighting stragglers," he explained, "and they are harder to conquer than the enemy." Also, from where he sat, Sherman saw nothing wrong with taking supplies in this manner. "The country was sparsely settled, with no magistrates or civil authorities who could respond to requisitions, as is done in all the wars of Europe," he later wrote in justification, "so that this system of foraging was simply indispensable to our success."

Like many thoughtful people guided by grand theoretical abstractions, Sherman had problems when he saw the human face of people affected by his policies. Earlier this day he had been confronted by an older lady whose foodstuffs and livestock were, according to Major Hitchcock, "rapidly disappearing" at the hands of Sherman's men. Sherman refused her request for a guard, proffered some lame excuses, and foisted her onto Brevet Major General Jefferson C. Davis, who was even less likely to be conciliatory. Now Hitchcock could overhear Sherman thinking aloud. "I'll have to harden my heart to these things," he said. "That poor woman today—how could I help her? There's no help for it. The soldiers will take all she has. Jeff Davis is responsible for this."

Well after sundown, Hitchcock wandered a bit to observe with interest as several signal officers experimented with a long-distance communication. Three rockets were set up, ignited, and sent whooshing into the night sky, a prearranged signal alerting the Right Wing that the northern jaws of Sherman's movement were beginning to close on the Georgia capital. "Sherman's plans are splendid," he declared.

Right Wing

The Seventeenth Corps completed its crossing of the Ocmulgee River then marched off toward the town of Monticello, leaving the more direct roads to Hillsboro to the Fifteenth Corps (still not yet entirely over the river) and the cavalry. The extra miles tramped resulted in some compensation when the soldiers entered Monticello, which one of them described as a "beautiful town." Major General Blair sent his troops through with "colors flying." The town's young men were all gone, but left behind were "any amount of fine looking gals" for the Yankee boys to ogle. An artilleryman pronounced Monticello "a pretty little village, with some handsome women in it, a great rarity in the South."

Also making the gunners' day was their discovery of sacks of shelled corn stored in the courthouse by Rebel quartermasters. Saved the work of finding and packing the fodder, the happy cannoneers piled the bags on their caissons. After somebody mentioned that captured Union prisoners had been held in the town's jail it wasn't long before "it was reduced to ashes." From Monticello, the Seventeenth Corps columns turned south, walking along until they reached Hillsboro, where they bivouacked.

Trudging along with a small squad of Confederate prisoners was a Rebel cavalry officer whose imperious ways had won him no friends among Monticello's residents. In fact, one of them—a young lady—had revealed his hiding place to the Yankees just to rid the town of his noxious presence. Ignoring a pledge of honor, the officer tried to escape, only to be decked by one of the soldiers guarding him. A member of

Howard's staff saw the man, who looked dejected and thoroughly beaten. Continued the amused Federal, "the point of it all was the citizens deliberately turned this stupid fellow over and both the men and ladies appeared to enjoy his troubles intensely."

It was a harder passage for the Fifteenth Corps, which had to lug its wagons up the thoroughly churned east bank of the Ocmulgee. One weary soldier retained vivid images of "the men floundering through the mud and water, slipping and stumbling, causing heads to be cracked by the muskets of those prostrated in the mud." Three divisions of the Fifteenth Corps navigated the latticework of farm roads that represented a more direct course to Hillsboro, while the rear guard (Fourth Division) remained on the river's west side.

This meant that the Fifteenth Corps officers had to proceed as much by instinct and luck as by the very generalized maps they had, and not everyone guessed right. "We took the wrong road and so lost two hours," griped a Minnesota soldier, "and had some hard work in getting right again." It was especially tough on the wagon guards, who had to remain close to the lumbering, sliding vehicles. One unfortunate slipped under the wheels and broke his leg. Commented a weary comrade in the 93rd Illinois, "every man out of humor."

Major General Howard's headquarters this night were in Hillsboro, where he took dinner with the Reese family. Young Louise Caroline Reese kept one eye on her mother, still struggling with her nerves after a Yankee visitation during the summer, and the other on her uninvited guests. "Gen. Howard sat at the table and asked God's blessing," she related, "[while] the sky was red from flames of burning houses." Howard left a guard with the Reese household; after he departed several of his staff officers remained to play some sentimental numbers on the family's piano and to sing several songs. By the time they withdrew, Mrs. Reese was a basket case, unable to rise from her chair. "All night we sat with the enemy all around us," recollected Louise.

Back at Planter's Factory the program of destruction was getting under way. The grist- and sawmills were burned today while preparations were made to finish the job just before the pontoon bridge was dismantled, which was scheduled for next morning. As part of this day's events, the factory contents were "divided amongst the poor women and girls of which there was a great number." Off to the side of the crossing point itself, the crowd of broken-down animals continued to grow as healthier creatures were confiscated from soldiers not authorized to have them, to be exchanged for worn-out wagon and artillery teams.

This was another hard day for Kilpatrick's troopers. After resting a short while on the river's east bank, Kilpatrick had his men moving along the farm roads taking them south and east. They were to assume the lead position on the Right Wing by reaching the town of Clinton, some fourteen miles northeast of Macon, and a little more than that beyond the nearest friendly infantry camped around Hillsboro.

"Roads very slippery," wrote a trooper in the 92nd Illinois Mounted Infantry, while another proclaimed it "a hard day's travel." It wasn't until about 9:00 P.M. that Kilpatrick's men entered Clinton. Just outside the town the mounted vanguard encountered a Rebel outpost. Reported a *New York Herald* correspondent on the scene: "General Kilpatrick being in advance, and mistaking the rebels for his own men, narrowly escaped death from their shots." Six of the enemy scouts became prisoners.

This was an area with an ominous history for the cavalrymen. Some three months earlier, a mounted raiding force led by Major General George Stoneman had been overwhelmed near here by Confederate forces spilling out from Macon. Stoneman and many of his troopers had been captured before being packed off to Southern prison camps. With this on their mind, the troopers sent out on picket built themselves a solid rail barricade. Kilpatrick mulled over a scouting report from the 9th Pennsylvania Cavalry containing "valuable information in regard to the movements of the enemy about Macon." According to the regimental surgeon, Kilpatrick "learned that part of Wheeler's force had crossed the river near Macon, and now confronted him."

Georgia's head of state, his family, their milch cow, and the last soldiers on duty departed Milledgeville for points south. Governor Brown intended to see his family and servants as far as the town of Montezuma; from there they faced a thirty-mile trek by wagons to the governor's plantation in Dooly County, southwest Georgia. When the cars reached Gordon, about twenty miles east of Macon, the military force detrained. The small command, under Brown's state adjutant and inspector general, Major General Henry C. Wayne, was emblematic of the state's fortunes. Its 500 men consisted of cadets from the Georgia Military Institute, one artillery battery, a small company of cavalry and one of militia infantry, and a unit made up of factory and penitentiary guards, as well as another consisting of men formerly under guard—convicts doing time for minor offenses who agreed to serve in exchange for a reduced sentence.

In Macon, Lieutenant General Hardee continued to chart the progress of the enemy columns. A force of Yankee infantry was spotted in Hillsboro, while blue-coated cavalry had reached Clinton—important points north and northeast of the city. When Major General Wheeler arrived at 11:00 P.M., he and Hardee had a quick strategy session. The lieutenant general needed to know something definite about the enemy's strength and plans. Clinton, on a main road between Macon and Milledgeville, seemed the best place to start. Accordingly, Hardee "ordered Wheeler to make an attack on the enemy to-morrow at Clinton, [so] as to ascertain definitely his movements and intentions."

CHAPTER 11

"Ugly Weather"

SUNDAY, NOVEMBER 20, 1864
Midnight–Noon

——— *Right Wing* ———

A heavy fog splayed across the countryside around Clinton, blurring and obscuring the town's many trees and muffling small sounds. Added to the rain and mud, the morning was miserable for the Yankee cavalrymen, under orders to hold the place pending the arrival of friendly infantry. From his headquarters in the Richard Hutchings house near the main road, Brigadier General H. Judson Kilpatrick reacted to intelligence of Confederate mounted probes pushing out from Macon by sending forward his own detachments to harass them. Then all he could do was wait for the slow-marching foot soldiers to arrive.

——— *Left Wing* ———

The Fourteenth Corps abandoned its camps around Newborn, the Second Division in the lead with orders to "push on toward Eatonton Factory," a cloth-producing facility. Behind the Second moved the First and Third divisions, with Sherman's headquarters party tucked

N

Weather: rain
low 40s to low 50s

Atlanta
Lithonia
Conyers
Apalachee
Social Circle
Rutledge
Greensboro

Covington
Newborn (Sandtown)
Madison
Buckhead

Stockbridge

Jonesboro

Lovejoy's Station
McDonough
Shady Dale
Eatonton

Bear Creek Station

Jackson
Monticello

Griffin

UNDER THE GUN
[LW] Eatonton
[RW] Monticello/Hillsboro/
Blountsville
[Cavalry] East Macon

Planter's Factory
Hillsboro

Blountsville
Milledgeville

Forsyth
Clinton

Atlanta to Milledgeville

DAY SIX:
Sunday, November 20, 1864

Macon
Griswoldville

Gordon

Irwinton

between. Major Hitchcock pronounced it "ugly weather," with "heavy clouds, some rain, sullen mist and fog all round horizon." The grim conditions mirrored the aide's troubled thoughts. As much as he hated to admit it, Hitchcock was coming around to Sherman's point of view. "We must make war," he told himself, "and it must *be* war, it must bring destruction and desolation, it must make the innocent suffer as well as the guilty, it must involve plundering, burning, killing."

No one bothered to share these dire tidings with the slaves of Shady Dale. The place itself, recorded the *New York Herald* correspondent, was just another name for "the plantation of an old man named Matthew Whitfield, who owns nearly the whole of [the] . . . county, and an abundance of stock and crops." Most of the town consisted of ramshackle cabins for the slaves "who worked the large plantation upon which Mr. Whitfield resided." Added Major Hitchcock, "We are told he left yesterday or this morning, having collected his horses and mules and ordering the negroes to bring them along. But the darkies wouldn't follow him, and instead they remained with the stock and joined the Yanks in high glee."

"The brigade band played a quickstep tune as we went through," recalled an Ohio infantryman, "and the negroes flocked out to see us and hear the music, particularly the women, some of whom followed us for over a mile, or rather kept up with the band, dancing and keeping time to the music." One of the women told a Wisconsin soldier "that she had heard of the bluecoats for a long time and now to see us." The Midwest boy asked her if she wasn't glad to meet the Union soldiers. "She said, 'yes, I love to look at you.' " Reflected the Yankee: "You could see hope and joy in their eyes."

Off to the east, the Twentieth Corps was moving in a roughly parallel fashion in two separate columns. Farthest out, marching along the west bank of the Oconee River, was John Geary's division. The forty-four-year-old brigadier noted "the weather rainy, the roads very deep and swampy." As his columns unwound from their encampments on the Jordan plantation, the soldiers finished burning the owner's cotton and corn. Also on the list of targets was Parks Mill, which Geary's men reached by 8:00 A.M., where a small bridge had been washed away and not replaced. The crossing here was by ferry, so Geary had his men round up the boats. The mill owner's wife played the Mason card, which secured a guard for her residence, through her smokehouse was emptied by the hungry Federals.

After leaving their camps south of Madison, the two other Twentieth Corps divisions struggled to make much progress. The mud, reported a Connecticut man, "was thick and sticky," while a Michigan comrade griped about "the clayey roads." The tail end of the column had it the worst. "The roads were in a bad condition and had to be corduroyed in many places before the wagons could pass," wrote a New York diarist. "It is raining so hard all of the time the wagons worked up the mud, which made it hard marching for the men."

Behind them, Madison's residents (at least those not as resourceful as Emma High's mother) were making a doleful inventory of losses. "The Yankees left us Sunday morning without a mouthful to eat, nothing to cook and nobody to cook if we had," complained one. "The inhabitants seemed to be filled with consternation, for they never dreamed that we would penetrate such a retired and remote region of the country," said a Massachusetts soldier. "While passing an elegant mansion to-day, we observed the first manifestation of Union sentiment on the part of citizens since the march commenced," added an

Illinoisan. "A number of ladies at the mansion waved their handkerchiefs as we passed, and the men cheered heartily."

A black older couple had joined the procession accompanying the Left Wing columns. An Illinois soldier had witnessed the couple's decision to leave: the two stood outside their owner's home, ready to go, with all their personal belongings in the small bundles that they carried. Their owner tried to convince them to stay, even getting them to admit that he had never mistreated them, and reminding the elder male that they had grown up together as children. All this was true, but with tears in their eyes, the two were determined to leave. "We must go," the black man said, "freedom is as sweet to us as it is to you." Added the soldier: "And go with us they did."

Right Wing

Major General Oliver Otis Howard's overriding concern was to pass his wagons safely over the muddy Georgia roads to Gordon, where he expected to link up with the Left Wing and Sherman himself. Complicating Howard's situation were the enemy troops in Macon, who weren't cowering behind their battlements but actually striking at him. Howard's orders for today were designed to place a heavy infantry screen between Macon and his vehicles while at the same time using his cavalry to threaten the city from an unexpected quarter. Accordingly, the Seventeenth Corps was directed east from Hillsboro to Blountsville, while the Fifteenth Corps (three divisions of it) marched south from Hillsboro to Clinton, where it would take its blocking position. Once the Fifteenth reached Clinton, it would free up Kilpatrick's riders for their Macon raid.

Before the long tail of Howard's wing finally cleared the Ocmulgee River, there was some unfinished business to conduct. Planter's Factory was put to the torch and destroyed. There was also the problem of the herd of broken-down and discarded creatures that had been accumulated near the pontoon bridge. The order to dispose of the problem wriggled down the chain of command until it stopped with the bridge builders, the 1st Missouri Engineers. Daniel B. Baker, one of the engineers, would never forget what happened next.

"The animals were placed in a short bend in the river," he wrote, "not far from the bridge with a strong guard of soldiers to keep them from getting away, the soldiers forming one part of the corral and the river the other. As soon as the troops were all over the bridge, we began taking it up, and as soon as this was done the whole regiment was drawn up in a line from a point on the river bank below the bend to a point above the bend, and the order to commence firing into the poor animals began, and it was kept up as long as there was one of them left standing."

The firecracker sounds momentarily startled the rear guard of Brigadier General John M. Corse's Fourth Division (Fifteenth Corps), the last infantry to depart the Ocmulgee River. The soldiers "supposed [it] to be skirmishing, but it proved to be the Killing of worthless horses & mules at the 'crossing,' " noted an Ohio veteran. Corse's men, plus the wagons, were on course for Monticello. Their aggressive leader wasn't happy about his responsibilities, for it was clear that his command would be shepherding their charges (the pontoon train, 300 wagons belonging to Kilpatrick's men, and 3,000 cattle) until they reached Gordon.

Ahead of them, the Seventeenth Corps was passing through Hillsboro and having a grand time doing so. "A colored gal showed that she was pleased at seeing us by dancing on the porch, much to the pleasure of the boys," remembered an Ohioan. Another Yankee boy had his fun by cobbling together an effigy of Confederate president Jefferson Davis, which he then hung prominently along the town's main street. "It excited many a pun and joke among the boys, as they witnessed its exhibition in passing," chuckled a member of the 64th Illinois. Once through Hillsboro, the Seventeenth Corps angled off to the south and east.

Farther south, the remaining three divisions of the Fifteenth Corps closed on Clinton. An Iowa soldier found the passage "muddy & very foggy." "The roads were so slippery it was hard work to stand up and march," muttered an Ohioan, while a Hoosier was certain that "nearly every man on foot, both officers and soldiers, fell down, some of them a dozen times."

As the head of the Fifteenth Corps column reached murky Clinton about midday, Kilpatrick's troopers began pulling out, creating some confusion that was exploited by a band of audacious Rebel cavalrymen who rushed through the fog to snatch some prisoners, among them a man who said he was the servant of the Fifteenth Corps commander, Major General Peter J. Osterhaus.

This minor coup was one of the few bright spots for Confederate Major General Joseph Wheeler, trying to carry out General Hardee's instructions to probe the enemy positions. On his way from Macon to Clinton, Wheeler's column was harassed by some of the detachments Kilpatrick had sent forward for that very purpose, and valuable time was lost in chasing them away. Then, when the advance party came scrambling out of Clinton with their prisoners, they were closely followed by some angry Yankees, leading to a brief melee in which Wheeler afterward claimed the advantage.

Hardly had Wheeler begun to assess the meaning of finding Union infantry in the town when a courier reached the bantam general with news from Macon that an enemy force was approaching from the east, and the brigade he had posted to protect that quarter had gone to meet it, leaving a hole in the city's defenses. Macon, with its arms-producing facilities, iron foundries, and munitions works, was too important to put at risk. There was nothing he could do but meet this threat, so Wheeler turned a portion of his command around and headed back.

Still stuck in transit, General P. G. T. Beauregard stopped in West Point, Mississippi, long enough to send one hectoring telegram off to General Hood ("Push on active offense immediately") and one containing advice to Major General Wheeler. "My views are that positions should be defended only so long as not to risk safety of troops and materials required for active operations in the field," Beauregard instructed his subordinate. "Meanwhile remove to safe locality all Government property on line of enemy's march, and consume or destroy all supplies within his reach."

Beauregard's earlier public proclamation was given firm stamp of approval by the editorial writers for the *Augusta Daily Chronicle & Sentinel*. "Let not this stirring appeal go by unheeded!" they exclaimed. "Act in accordance with its burning words! Act promptly. Rally around the banner of your own chosen General, and all will be well." In distant Richmond, a well-placed War Department clerk, after reviewing all communications received, nodded approvingly at Governor Brown's call-up of Georgia's white male citizens. "I think Sherman is in danger," wrote the official.

In Camp Lawton the process of transferring the Union prisoners elsewhere was accelerated. By now the infirmary (such as it was) had been entirely evacuated, and those remaining behind the stockade walls endured a seemingly endless wait as the most important lottery in their life plucked lucky individuals from their midst.

For Sergeant Lucius W. Barber, part of Sherman's forces in the Atlanta Campaign until he was captured in early October, this was a winning day. Thanks to an acquaintance, Corporal Rollin Mallory, Barber's name was added to a list of POWs to be exchanged. The two tried without success to have their friend, Private Millen Mackey, tacked on, but there was no room. Besides, the men were told that all remaining prisoners would be transferred within a week. Then, as their names were called, an opportunity presented itself when someone failed to answer. Mackey made a move to step forward but then held back, believing it better to wait until his exchange could be official.*

Barber passed through the stockade gate on his way to the parole station. "We were free," he exulted. "The earth, the air, the very ground we trod on, seemed to echo our soul's deep gratitude." Within minutes, Barber and his companion had clambered aboard a train heading for Savannah.

Located some nine miles east of Macon at Station No. 18 on the Central of Georgia Railroad, the "thrifty little village" of Griswoldville was the by-product of Yankee grit, determination, and ingenuity. The town was laid out around a manufacturing complex created by Samuel Griswold, a transplanted Connecticut businessman and entrepreneur. Built before the war to produce cotton gins, the main factory had followed the money when war came, and by 1864 was turning out a Confederate version of the Colt Navy Revolver.

Griswoldville had been spared any serious damage from a major Union cavalry raid in late July thanks to the presence of a sizable militia force. Not four months later, the overall picture had changed. Gone

---

*   The delay would prove fatal. Mackey escaped and directly joined the regiment, while Barber and his friend were held up in the exchange process. Mackey was later captured and killed by guerrillas in North Carolina, before Barber or Mallory returned to the unit.

was the protection afforded by the citizen-soldiers, replaced by a thin screen of outposts and pickets, intended to alert Macon of any threat in time to hustle forward a reaction force to meet the danger.

The trip wires failed to perform their assigned task thanks to the resourcefulness of Captain Frederick S. Ladd, leading a raiding party drawn from three companies of the 9th Michigan Cavalry, part of the Second Brigade in Kilpatrick's division. Ordered to scout as far as Griswoldville and damage what he could, Ladd successfully detoured around the Rebel roadblocks to reach the village, undetected, not long after 10:00 A.M. Hoping to make up in boldness what he lacked in numbers (the raiding party numbered between sixty and a hundred troopers), Ladd ordered his command to charge yelling into town with pistols popping.

While civilians dashed for cover, the Michigan boys burned some of the outbuildings, then went after the pistol factory itself. According to a member of Ladd's party, "The arsenal was guarded by a body of Confederate soldiers, but they were driven off, and in a few moments the building was in flames." Then, as Colonel Smith D. Atkins (commanding the Second Brigade) later reported: "After this work was accomplished he [Ladd] captured one of the enemy, and compelled him to lead his little party out of the town on a route to avoid the enemy, who had all the roads in their possession." Two Michigan troopers left behind were captured, and a third—slightly wounded in the hip—was carried out.

Noon–Midnight

——— *Left Wing* ———

Before the Oconee River ferryboats operating at Parks Mill were destroyed, a small Yankee expedition landed on the east bank, intent on mischief or misinformation, or both. Not quite two months after the fact, Brigadier General Geary took credit for the operation, though the soldiers themselves—members of the 134th New York—declared that the action was the result of a mistaken appreciation of where the division was heading.

Whether under orders or in search of better pickings, about twenty New Yorkers crossed the Oconee, rounded up some horses, then set off for the nearest town, Greensboro. There they presented themselves as the vanguard of a mighty horde. Greensboro's mayor was told that the Federals had been "given orders to search, but that public property was all they were ordered or expected to burn." Things were moving along in a smooth fashion until several of the party liberated some liquor stocks, and soon the plundering got out of hand. "They took from Mrs. Philip Robinson one gold watch; from Mrs. William D. Davis, one watch; from Mr. John A. Miller about two hundred dollars and from Mrs. Mary Colt two hundred dollars," recorded the mayor.

Then, as abruptly as they had arrived, the Yankees were gone. They would rejoin Geary's column in a few more days, though not without losing several members as stragglers. Called to account for themselves, they explained that they had boasted to Greensboro's mayor that Sherman's command, "numbering from fifteen to fifty thousand, was . . . moving on the town." Geary liked the tale so much that he made it part of his official report, writing that the visiting band "convinced the inhabitants [of Greensboro] that the most of General Sherman's army was close by with designs upon Augusta."

The bulk of Geary's division moved south from Parks Mill, following the Oconee until Denham's Tanyard and Leather Factory was reached. The operation there had reaped the bounty of a Confederate States government contract to make footwear for the Rebel army. "The shoes were given to any one that wanted them," recorded a Pennsylvania soldier. "What leather was wanted was taken, and the remainder destroyed." Here Geary camped for the night.

The two other Twentieth Corps divisions, on a similar course approximately fifteen miles to the west, slogged along bad roads but still managed to forage supplies. "Every house along the road was visited by the men," wrote a Michigan diarist, "and molasses, sweet potatoes, poultry & pigs were confiscated without regard to quantity and quality." So plentiful were the foodstuffs that an amused Massachusetts man would note that "the reg't passed 300 bushels of sweet potatoes lying by the road-side, & that after a whole Army Corps had gone by."

There was something about this gray-visaged day that brought out sentiments of just retribution in even the least militant of soldiers. "Every cotton shed has to be purified by fire," observed the surgeon with a Michigan regiment. "The smoke ascends to the skies bearing aloft the prayers of the Yanks for success & the curses of the rebs for our defeat." Reflecting on the large quantities of food and equipment he saw destroyed today, a New Jersey quartermaster wrote: "I believe every man in the army would walk 5 miles out of his way even to set fire to a hundred fences that had been used merely for camp at night, sometimes they carry to our camps arm fulls to sleep on but they are sure to fire the same when leaving."

Union scouts, who were operating well ahead of the heavy columns, actually entered the outskirts of Georgia's capital late this day. According to Milledgeville residents who encountered them, the enemy riders asked about Confederate troop strength in the town while they cautiously poked around. Then they pulled down telegraph wires, scooped up a few horses, and departed as enigmatically as they had arrived.

By the time accounts of those sightings spread around town, they were muddled enough to be worthless. "We would hear on the road first one and then another rumor," recorded Anna Maria Green, daughter of the superintendent of the Georgia Lunatic Asylum, "and all so contradictory we could place little confidence in any." Green found time to visit with some male friends who were heading off to Gordon to join in Georgia's defense. One of them seemed positively giddy at the prospect. Even as she was bidding her acquaintances good-bye, Green could see another member of the household furtively hiding valuables. It was not a good omen.

Some twenty-seven miles northwest of the Georgia capital, the lead elements of the Fourteenth Corps were camping for the night below Eatonton Factory on one of the main roads leading to Milledgeville. The factory itself was now a ruin, thanks to the personal attention it received from Captain Orlando M. Poe. Sherman's chief engineer didn't bother to record the feat in his official report, but his diary entry for November 20 laconically notes that the "factory was burnt by Gen'l Sherman's order as well as all cotton in sight." An Ohio soldier on the sidelines wrote that it was "a large cotton factory which employed about 60 girls manufacturing clothes for the Rebel army. We burnt the factory, notwithstanding the girls could not see the use of doing it."*

---

* A nearby bridge across the Little River was torched by retreating Confederates but saved by an alert Federal lieutenant, who rounded up some foragers to secure the span. However, the bridge was not part of Sherman's plan, so the Federals would wreck it themselves.

In spite of the rain and mud, the Fourteenth Corps did a thorough job locating food. "Plenty of forage: pork, potatoes and corn meal," recorded a Wisconsin diarist. "The foragers brought in horses, mules, oxen and sheep, with plenty meal, meat, sweet potatoes and other delicacies," seconded an Ohio man. Added a Minnesotan: "We have marched through a very level and fertile country and forage is abundant. . . . If any one fails to live well it may be attributed to his own laziness."

It took until sundown for the rear of the Fourteenth Corps column to pass entirely through Shady Dale, but each segment was greeted as if it was the first to arrive. "Here the colored peoples give us our entertainment," noted an Indiana boy. A new band would appear, begin to play, and in a short time it would be surrounded by a throng of black women and children "dancing and bobbing their heads in ecstasies of delight."

When the First Division settled into camp near Shady Dale, the general commanding, William P. Carlin, was witness to a remarkable scene. One of the bands had launched into yet another performance of "John Brown's Body" when about a dozen young African-American girls came out of nearby houses, "formed into a ring around the band at the head of the column, and with a weird, plaintive wail, danced in a circle in a most solemn, dignified, and impressive manner," wrote Carlin years afterward. "What their meaning was I did not know then, nor do I now, but I, of course, interpreted it as an expressive of goodwill to our cause."

Sherman's headquarters for the night were about a mile north of the Eatonton Factory, which Major Hitchcock pointedly wrote of in the past tense. Now that the two columns of his Left Wing were converging, Sherman was anxious to avoid gridlocking the limited roads. He sent a note off to Major General Henry Slocum, riding with the Twentieth Corps, confirming that their point of concentration was to be the Georgia capital. "In moving to Milledgeville, keep your force on the east of the railroad, and General Davis will keep his west," Sherman instructed. Hoping to hear back from Slocum, Sherman decided to hold his headquarters in place until noon, November 21.

Orders written this night for the Left Wing reflected growing concern over the soldiers using their weapons to gather food. "The discharge of fire-arms by foragers and others has become an evil which must be stopped," proclaimed a Fourteenth Corps circular. In the Twentieth Corps, the "most stringent measures" were demanded by headquarters "to stop the waste of ammunition occasioned by the indiscriminate firing by foraging parties." The refugee procession trailing the Fourteenth Corps was greatly irritating its commander, Brevet Major General Jefferson C. Davis. His published orders fumed that the coffle had grown so much that it "would be suicide to a column which must be constantly stripped for battle and prepared for the utmost celerity of movement." Blacks were barred from riding in army wagons or atop horses and mules unless they were identified as officer servants.

Local blacks were telling Major Hitchcock that Southern forces would surely defend Milledgeville and that they would have a battle for the place. "I don't think the General expects them to fight there," was the aide's comment. He also noted, "Artillery was heard this evening, far to the S. and S.W.—probably Kilpatrick near Macon."

Right Wing

A band of heavy rain moved through Jones County, catching the Seventeenth Corps strung out on the road from Hillsboro to Blountsville. "It has commenced to rain again & the roads are almost impassable," noted an Illinois diarist. A weary Wisconsin soldier recollected the day's tramp as "awful for man & beast," while a journal keeper in the 20th Illinois could only manage that the "mud is deep." The weather was playing havoc with Major General Frank Blair's tactical arrangements. An Iowan marching with the rear guard observed that "the roads have become so muddy that it is impossible for the artillery to keep up with the infantry." Matters became ugly for those guarding the herd, one soldier remembering that "during the day a number of cattle mired down in a deep, boggy swamp by the roadside, when a detail was ordered out to shoot them."

Major General Blair singled out one of the few mounted regiments in his command for special censure in a message dispatched this night. Colonel George E. Spencer, 1st Alabama Cavalry, was upbraided for the "outrages committed by your command during the march" and told that unless things improved Blair was prepared to "place every officer in it under arrest." The general's tirade had the intended effect, as no other transgressions by the 1st Alabama Cavalry are noted in the official record of the campaign.

Things were somewhat better for the Fifteenth Corps, since these men had a shorter distance to march. "Lots of rain," wrote a concise Indiana diary keeper. "In the mud men wet and muddy from head to foot," recorded a Missouri officer with Scripture on his mind. "Jordan are a hard road to travel." Once the soldiers reached Clinton they found no signs of the earlier skirmish. "All quiet on our arrival," wrote a grateful Indiana soldier. Rumor, not impeded by the bad weather and roads, darted impishly among the columns. "This evening the cavalry dashed in on the part of Macon that is on the west side of the river," wrote an Illinois soldier. "They took the town."

Shortly after noon, Brigadier General Kilpatrick led his cavalry division out of Clinton, under orders from Major General Howard for "a second demonstration from the left bank [of the Ocmulgee River] against Macon." A *New York Herald* correspondent translated these instructions to mean mounting a threat against Macon, "but not sacrifice life in its capture."

The flamboyant cavalry commander had a pensive side that grasped the broader strategic implications of the role assigned to his mounted division. "There was a rebel force at Augusta," he later wrote, "another in Savannah, another at Milledgeville, and still another at Macon, along with the State Militia of Georgia and Wheeler's Cavalry, ready to strike at the first opportunity. If these forces could have been massed—if Hardee could only have known Sherman's objective point and ultimate intentions—I doubt if the march would have been a success."

Kilpatrick's troop dispositions reflect his intention to feign attack. He dropped off his First Brigade (save one regiment) to block the main road to Macon, while using his Second Brigade on a sweep to the southeast in order to approach the city from its eastern flank. A single regiment (the 3rd Kentucky Cavalry) covered a road splitting the difference between the pair. For the First Brigade, November 20 was marked by skirmishing and sharp encounters with enemy pickets. ("They made a stubborn resistance to our march," recalled a Hoosier.)

For the Second Brigade, November 20 was marked by something approaching a battle.

Closing on Macon via the Milledgeville Road, Kilpatrick's advance (92nd Illinois Mounted Infantry) struck a Rebel roadblock some four miles from the city. The men here were from Wheeler's command (part of Colonel Charles C. Crew's all-Georgia brigade) and did not panic. When a battalion of the 92nd acted to flank the barricade, Crews's troopers countercharged, only to run into a wall of gunfire laid down by two hundred fast-firing Spencer carbines. The Georgians scattered, chased for a short distance by the 10th Ohio Cavalry. Speaking at a postwar reunion, the brigade commander asked, "Do you recollect how that Rebel brigade scattered in utter confusion in every direction through the woods and fields?"

As this action was playing out along the Milledgeville Road, Kilpatrick with his headquarters escort rode south to the railroad tracks and telegraph line. Although the connection through Gordon to Augusta had been cut at Griswoldville at about 10:30 A.M., the line to Macon was intact. Kilpatrick watched as the signal corps officer on his staff tapped into the No. 1 wire and, after a few minutes of listening, handed him a message intercept. Addressed to General Beauregard, the note read: "For God's sake hurry up troops and save the bridge over the Oconee." It was signed, "Hardee." When Kilpatrick's operator tried to learn more, he was unmasked by an alert Macon telegrapher. A brief dialogue ensued:

> *Yank: Please inform Gen. Hardee that Gens. Howard and Kilpatrick will take breakfast with him in the morning.*
> *Reb: All right; we've got Stoneman's old quarters ready for them.*

Kilpatrick was enjoying himself hugely until the line went dead, cut by another Federal party carrying out the orders of destruction. Sighed Kilpatrick, "Our fun was over."

Once the roadblock manned by Crews's troopers had been dispersed, Kilpatrick continued to press toward Macon. Consciously or not, he was following a course that had been used by his unfortunate predecessor, Major General George Stoneman, during his disastrous July raid. Before long, Kilpatrick's column had reached Walnut Creek, about two miles outside Macon.

Here the ground favored the defense, with the road west of the creek climbing up a steep hill that was flanked to the north by a second rise. The Confederates had established a strong point on the high ground in an old frontier outpost, Fort Hawkins, while on the lower crest, a farm owned by Samuel S. Dunlap, there was a two-gun battery with infantry support. The defenders (numbering 1,000 to 1,200) were a mix of militia and veterans. As an indication of the South's strained resources, some of the steadiest troops were artillerymen fighting as infantry because their units lacked sufficient horses to pull the cannon.

At 3:30 P.M. Kilpatrick's advance challenged Macon's defenses. A portion of the 92nd Illinois Mounted Infantry, with its quick-shooting Spencers, pushed to the creek, while the six guns of Kilpatrick's horse artillery opened up on the hilltop positions. A few Yankee overshoots landed in the Central of Georgia Railroad's workshop area, leading to a hasty exodus by the employees who took all the functioning engines and cars into Macon. Back on Dunlap's Hill, a line of defenders in skirmish formation shook out from the earthworks to challenge the dismounted Illinois infantry.

The full Federal deployment was masked by trees along the creek's east bank, helping conceal a charging column of fours from the 10th Ohio Cavalry, which burst from cover and pounded up the hill. The Rebel gunners, who had a clear shot, were plagued by faulty friction primers, resulting in several misfires. "It was quite a descent to [Walnut Creek] . . . ," remembered one of the Ohioans, "but before the [Rebel] guns could fire the second round we were upon them with the saber."

The advantage was momentary. Even through Kilpatrick had two more cavalry regiments close on hand, none were moved forward to exploit the breach. The Ohio troopers on the hilltop began to take hits from the guns in Fort Hawkins, while in the distance they observed a well-organized line of infantry forming for a counterattack. Wrote the Buckeye commander, "Seeing that the [captured] guns could not be removed, and that there was barely time to withdraw the regiment before the rebels would be upon us, I ordered the column to retire."

While these events were unfolding along the main wagon road to Milledgeville, smaller-scale combat was taking place just to the south, where the railroad bridge traversed Walnut Creek. Here a detail from the 92nd Illinois Mounted Infantry succeeded in rushing the span and

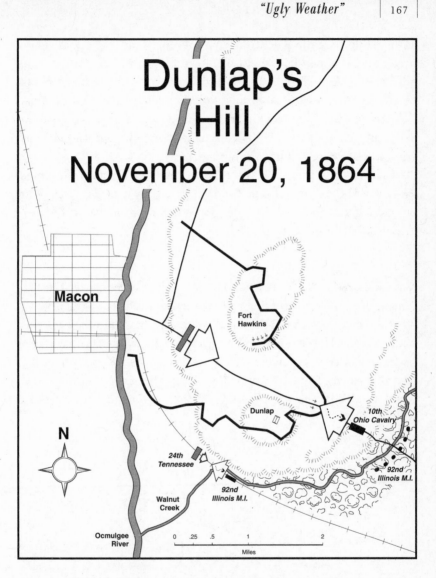

Dunlap's Hill
November 20, 1864

Macon

Fort Hawkins

Dunlap

10th Ohio Cavalry

N

24th Tennessee

92nd Illinois M.I.

92nd Illinois M.I.

Walnut Creek

Ocmulgee River

0   .25   .5   1   2

Miles

driving off its defenders, but they were almost immediately slapped back by a counterthrust. The Confederate soldiers (from the 24th Tennessee), then taking up positions covering the bridge, prevented the Federals from torching it. This proved something of a hollow victory, for just to the east details from three of Kilpatrick's regiments were busy prying up the track and burning the ties.

Losses in this fracas were light. The gunners serving the two cannon that were briefly overrun suffered one dead and two wounded. The 92nd Illinois reported two wounded, and the 10th Ohio added seven more. At no time did Kilpatrick commit more than a small portion of his force to the spearhead, choosing to employ most of his troopers for railroad wrecking. Fully a third of his troopers were kept at the task overnight. In a message sent tonight to Major General Howard, Kilpatrick promised to keep blocking the roads in his sector "until the trains are well out of the way." His command camped along the railroad, with pickets posted along Walnut Creek.

A sour coda to this affair was reported by the *Augusta Daily Chronicle & Sentinel:* "Some of our troops behaved badly in East Macon by plundering and committing other depredations after the enemy were driven off. We forbear to give details."

*   *   *

Major General Wheeler reached Dunlap's Hill not long after the 10th Ohio had withdrawn. Fearing a follow-up attack, he used the first two of his brigades to arrive to fill in the defensive line. He then checked with General Hardee, who was concerned about reports that enemy raiders had visited Griswoldville. Since Wheeler's weary riders represented the most veteran troops he had on the scene, Hardee issued orders for the officer to probe toward the manufacturing center that very night.

CHAPTER 12

"But Bless God, He Died Free!"

MONDAY, NOVEMBER 21, 1864
Midnight–Noon

Left Wing

Heavy rains delayed the morning's march schedule for John Geary's division, still operating independently from the rest of the Twentieth Corps. The rear guard, supposed to break camp at 6:00 A.M., did not actually get under way until nearly three hours later. It fell to the last departing troops to finish the destruction of Denham's Tanyard and Leather Factory. "Burned Denham's Factory, tannery, and adjacent buildings, except dwelling houses," reported one of Geary's brigade commanders. "When we left the buildings were all ablaze," wrote a New York diarist, whose colonel observed that as the regiment tramped past Denham's the structures "were burning splendidly."*

Progress today was a slow go. An Ohio soldier acknowledged that the muddy tracks were knee-deep in places. An equally weary comrade still had the energy to quip that the "roads were perfectly horrid clay soil & our boots were very heavy for t'would stick like a poor man to his friend." In his official report, Brigadier General Geary

---

* Only the 100-foot-tall brick chimney survived the factory blaze. This striking symbol of Sherman's wrath stood for more than a century afterward.

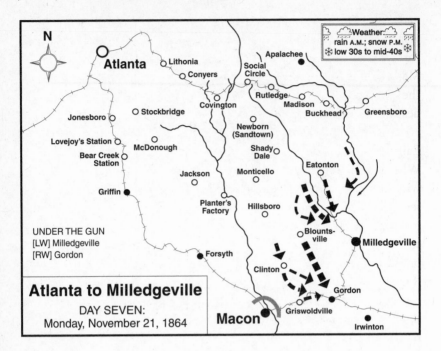

N

Weather:
rain A.M.; snow P.M.
❄ low 30s to mid-40s ❄

Atlanta
○ Lithonia
○ Conyers
Apalachee ●
Social
Circle

Rutledge ○
Madison ○
Buckhead
Greensboro

○ Stockbridge
Covington

Jonesboro ○

Lovejoy's Station ○
McDonough ○
Bear Creek
Station ○

Newborn
(Sandtown)
Shady ○
Dale

Eatonton ○

Griffin ●

Jackson ○

Monticello ○

Planter's
Factory ○
Hillsboro ○

UNDER THE GUN
[LW] Milledgeville
[RW] Gordon

Blounts- ○
ville
Milledgeville ●

Forsyth ●

Clinton ○

Atlanta to Milledgeville

DAY SEVEN:
Monday, November 21, 1864

Gordon

Macon ●
Griswoldville ○
Irwinton ●

registered that the mud was "very deep and the streams much swollen."

The route followed by Geary's column carried the men past Turnwold Plantation, then home to a fifteen-year-old named Joel Chandler Harris, who would grow up to be a writer, creator of the Uncle Remus tales. The eager teenager, perched on a rail fence, never forgot the sights and sounds of the next few hours. "The skies were heavy with clouds, and a fine, irritating mist sifted down," he recollected. "The road was more than ankle-deep in mud, and even the fields were boggy. There was nothing gay about this vast procession, with its tramping soldiers, its clattering horsemen, and its lumbering wagons, except the temper of the men. They splashed through the mud, cracked their jokes and singing snatches of songs."

Farther west, the other two Twentieth Corps divisions were having their own problems. The "morning dawned dark and lowering, with occasional gusts of rain," reported a brigade commander. "Men under difficulty managed to keep up fires to get their breakfasts," commented a New Jersey quartermaster. "Ground very soft and covered with water," scribbled an officer from Illinois. "The roads were so bad we had to help the teams up every hill," griped a Wisconsin soldier. The wagon drivers, recalled a New Jersey infantryman, "yelled [until] their throats [were] sore." The Illinois officer happened to be present when Major General Slocum came upon a vehicle that was stuck fast in the glutinous gumbo. "Genl Slocum cussed . . . and ordered wagon destroyed," he recorded.

Beginning around midmorning the Union troops entered and exited Eatonton, which, one of them observed, "looked like a very nice town." When a quartermaster from the 13th New Jersey passed through, he witnessed what he later termed "quite a ridiculous transaction—a female and a madder woman I never saw, smashing to bits a sewing machine because it was a Yankee invention, or else she determined no soldier should carry it off." Eatonton was also the terminal stop on a branch line linking it to the Central Railroad at Gordon. "Burnt 3 large Railroad Warehouses and one Depot," itemized a Wisconsin man.

Little effort was made to pry and bend the railroad tracks. The rail line, according to a *New York Herald* reporter, was "a very shammy built concern, not available for a heavy traffic. It was laid with the old fashioned strap iron,* and appeared much worn. Not so much attention was paid to its destruction, although it was cut in several places. . . . No rolling stock was found upon it."

Also targeted were a few businesses and the 102-foot flagpole, as well as all physical evidence of the South's peculiar institution. "You never saw such a complete wreck of Pa's store," related a resident. "There was not a five cents worth left in it." According to a member of the 70th Indiana, the Federal troops "passed through Eatonton [and] cut down the flag pole."† "At Eatonton the calaboose and whipping stocks were burned," added an Ohioan, "and the negroes fairly danced to see them in flames." There was a celebration too at the Farrar farm, where, after hearing the slaves complain about the neighbor's fierce tracking hound, Sherman ordered the animal shot. Major Hitchcock noted that "the darkies there were in great glee over it. No wonder."

"I never saw so many soldiers, wagons, [and] livestock at one time before," declared Miss Matt Marshall, an Eatonton resident. "It seemed

---

* This refers to a very early type of rail which consisted of a thin iron strap laid along the upper surface of a wood "stringer."
† Local lore says that the oversize flag usually displayed was safely hidden in a hollow tree.

to me that the whole Yankee army was passing through here." The little boy of the town's Methodist minister was so awestruck by the endless columns of men that when one of them asked him to show where the chickens were hidden, he proudly revealed his father's carefully constructed hiding place underneath the house. As Miss Marshall heard the sound of the Yankee bands announcing their arrival, she clenched her hands to suppress her indignation. At that moment she wanted very much to "hang every Yankee in the Confederacy."

Along Geary's route, after the procession past Joel Chandler Harris had wound out of sight, the teenager made his way back to the plantation, where he found one of the older female slaves bending over the still body of her elderly companion.

"What is the matter with him?" asked Harris.

"He dead, suh!" the woman answered. "But bless God, he died free!"

Members of the Left Wing's other half, the Fourteenth Corps, managed to find their own lighter side to the day's travails. The "soil here consisted of a sticky white Clay [and] we had to carry klumps along on the feet the size of a peck measure," commented a concise Wisconsin man. "The mud was ankle deep and as adhesive as sticking plaster," commiserated a Minnesota comrade, "and with our heavy loads we floundered through it in as cheerful frame of mind as a squad of bounty jumpers going to execution."

In an effort to pick up the pace, General Sherman forwarded to the Fourteenth Corps' commander intelligence of a byway across Murder Creek that connected with a main road leading toward Milledgeville. However, what looked doable on a map proved less so for those tasked with following the alternate course. "The difficulties of our march were much increased by the obscure roads we followed," muttered an Illinois soldier. "Every body is in a fuss," contributed another member of that regiment. "Mud knee deep. Reg'ts and Brigades all mixed up."

Sherman kept his headquarters party waiting until 11:00 A.M., still hoping to hear from Major General Slocum and the Twentieth Corps.*

---

* Although Major Hitchcock thought the two would meet either at the factory or in Eatonton, there is no evidence that such a meeting took place.

"Dismal day and steady rain," complained Major Hitchcock. Finally the party plodded off, "threading our way through and by wagons laboring along, up hill and down, or stuck fast." Sherman decided to tag along with the division crossing Murder Creek. Not long after getting over the rain-swollen stream, he and his staff spotted a house, where they stopped for lunch. The woman who greeted them was quick to explain (much to Hitchcock's skeptical bemusement) how much her family had opposed the war.

Even as Sherman and Hitchcock were chatting with the house owner, other members of the headquarters staff were talking with "a very smart negro woman," who proved remarkably well informed regarding the overall history of the war. She had borne a child fathered by her white master, likely because the mistress of the house was unable to produce her own. Consequently, her treatment at the hands of the woman was quite harsh. When the slave asked about Sherman, the aides obligingly pointed him out to her. Catching sight of the General, she exclaimed: "Dar's de man dat rules de world!"

Right Wing

Chance and circumstance presented Confederate forces around Macon with their best opportunity yet to do some serious damage to Sherman's aspirations. Thanks to the poor roads and unceasing rain, the Right Wing was stretched out for more than twenty miles, with its head just at Gordon, while its wagon-heavy tail was still slogging through Hillsboro. One consequence of the Union feint toward Macon was to concentrate Confederate military assets (Wheeler's cavalry, various militia, and detached veteran units) more effectively than if it had been ordered. So while Rebel forces in this quarter were well in hand, any Federal numerical advantage was compromised by the attenuated columns, which left Howard thin all over. A strong thrust from Macon toward Clinton held the real prospect of overwhelming a significant portion of the Right Wing's supply train, and wreaking havoc with Sherman's timetables.

It was a time for risk-taking, but the command-and-control systems put in place by Richmond and the state of Georgia were utterly unequal to the task. The two officers who might have brought the requisite leadership to Macon—P. G. T. Beauregard and Richard Taylor—were not yet on the scene thanks to the decrepit transportation network. The officer in charge, Lieutenant General William J. Hardee, understood that his primary responsibility was the security of the Georgia and South Carolina coast. His temporary assignment to Macon was for the sole purpose of defending that point. Once the direct threat had passed, Hardee's attention shifted back to his principal charge. The other experienced military man on the scene, Major General Wheeler, was too busy reacting to the Federal movements to look beyond the enemy in his immediate front.

All the remaining high-ranking individuals on the scene were state officers obsessed with protecting Macon from assault, and content to let matters lie as the danger diminished by the hour. No one was thinking about the grand scheme of things, or charged with coordinating a strategy to meet the constantly changing situation. The leadership vacuum was complete.

None of this was known to Major General Oliver Otis Howard, who rightly assumed the worst. His biggest concern was that a strong Rebel effort, launched from East Macon, "might . . . catch our long snaky trains and cut them asunder." To counter such a move, Howard ordered two Fifteenth Corps divisions to march from Clinton to the area northeast of Macon in order to block any attempt to cut the Gordon Road. A third division was shunted directly toward Gordon, while the Fourth (Corse) continued to provide close support to the slow-moving trains.

"Weather wet and roads awful bad," scrawled one of Corse's men. "The roads are in a terrible condition," agreed an Illinoisan, "and the mule teams are sticking in the mud in consequence." Added a soldier in the 50th Illinois, "mud in places, knee deep; wagons getting mired every few moments." In his postcampaign report, Brigadier General Corse recalled the exhausting period as one of "continuous wet weather and heavy roads."

Hillsboro was not even a faint memory for most of the departing Union soldiers, but for the town's occupants the Federal visitation was never to be forgotten. Louise Reese came to realize that the Union incursion into their isolated world came in waves. First was the mounted advance, closely followed by the industriously efficient foragers. "They drove off every cow, sheep, hog, yea, indeed, every living thing on the farm—took every bushel of corn and fodder, oats and wheat—every bee gum, burnt the gin house, screw, blacksmith shop, cotton &c&c," she said.

Next through the town was the main column, which included Major General Howard with his staff, who paused at the Reese household for dinner. Behind the infantry was the wagon train, then arrived the "worst of all[,] the stragglers and most to be dreaded." The guard departed with the wagons, leaving the ladies with only their wits to protect them from the vagabonds—white and black—who came prowling. Fortunately, except for some scary moments, the Reese family was left alone. "Thus passed the great Union army, composed of many nations and kinds of people," reflected Louise, "through our beloved country leaving desolation and ruin in its track."

Noon–Midnight

——— *Left Wing* ———

Even though the trails were, as one of the Twentieth Corps' soldiers put it, "in some places actually bottomless," determined Yankees managed to scrounge and destroy. "I went to a farm house and got some sweet potatoes," recorded a Michigan diarist, adding, "several hives of bees were upset & the honey taken." A fellow member of the regiment (19th Michigan) thought that they were "living bully." A soldier slithering along with John Geary's detached division scratched that they "captured thirty mules, and burned several cotton presses and two hundred bales of pressed cotton." Bad luck dogged a foraging party when one of its group was seriously injured in a riding accident. "I . . . was compelled to leave him at a plantation house," admitted the officer in charge. "God only knows if we will ever see him again."

It was an especially vexatious day for the main column's rear guard. About 1:00 P.M. all movement ground to a halt when an artillery wagon broke down, blocking the road. Then, with the column stalled, a number of Rebel cavalrymen appeared, threatening to attack the train until the 61st Ohio came hustling over to chase them off. Finally moving again, the wagons advanced in an excruciatingly slow pace that, at 9:00 P.M., became no pace at all. Investigating the problem, the rear guard's commander discovered "about sixty wagons [that] had become almost hopelessly stalled in a sort of quagmire." Infantrymen set aside their rifles to lug and push. The day's ordeal only ended around midnight, when the exhausted procession reached the assigned bivouac area.

John Geary's men camped on the plantation owned by a Dr. Nesbit. The mucky marching was exhausting as Private Oscar Wright, 5th Ohio, discovered when he was posted on picket and promptly fell asleep. The clatter of someone riding nearby woke Wright with a start. By then the interloper was gone, and despite the cold Wright was sweating as he thought about the extreme punishment meted out to sleeping sentries. "The rest of my vigil, you may be sure, was a wakeful one," he attested years afterward.

The main column, traveling off to the west, followed the railroad as far as Dennis Station. Teeth were chattering in the face of a stiff, cold wind that benumbed the columns. By now, casual vandalism was matter-of-fact. A soldier in the 102nd Illinois penned in his diary that his comrades "tore down [a] house to make coffee for dinner for kindling."

"Men are forging for potatoes, chickens, hogs, etc. and having abundance of every thing," declared a Fourteenth Corps member. "Plenty of forage and we appreciate it on every occasion," recounted a satisfied officer in the 86th Illinois. Despite Brevet Major General Davis's official invective against the black refugees, their numbers continued to increase, and several white soldiers found much to admire. "Many of the female slaves who are following the army have marched barefooted through the mud all day carrying their bundles[,] but they did it willingly for 'Liberty,' " said a Minnesota man. The leading division camped tonight some seventeen miles from Milledgeville.

Sherman's headquarters were established on the plantation of a Mr. Vaun,* located some four miles south of the Murder Creek crossing. Unlike most of his peers, Vaun chose to remain with his property, so this night he had General Sherman as his guest. His personal story was a tired variation on one that the General had heard before: Vaun was a Union man at heart who had been swept up in events beyond his con-

---

* A later historian of the region, and even Major Hitchcock in one place, refer to this individual as Mr. Vaughn, while Sherman, in his memoirs, notes him as Mr. Vann.

trol. Sherman pulled no punches in his reply (Hitchcock thought his boss "not heartless, however terribly straightforward"), but he relented enough to proffer some judicious advice. According to Hitchcock, Sherman advised Vaun "to bring all he could, of corn, wheat, etc., into *his house*, for safety from the soldiers; gave him to understand they would take all that lay around loose; gave him sacks to put his wheat in, etc."

Right Wing

Many of the tragic events soon to unfold stemmed from failings on the part of both the Confederate and Union cavalry commanders. Each had been in the saddle and constantly on the move since November 15. Each was tasked with operating on his own hook, almost always in a zone of constant contact with the opposition. Thus far each had handled his assignment with the requisite dash and determination, but this afternoon each would botch critical assignments.

Kilpatrick's main job was to block the road systems coming out of Macon leading to the northeast, where the slow-moving wagons of the Right Wing offered tempting targets. It had been Major General Howard's earnest hope that Kilpatrick would maintain his outposts tight to East Macon, but the cavalry officer opted instead to fall back to the Griswoldville area. There, while some of his men continued the destructive work begun by the 9th Michigan, others struggled to maintain a security perimeter against persistent Confederate probing. At noon Kilpatrick reported repulsing several attacks but promised to hold the line of the railroad. Not long after dispatching this to Howard, he decided to pull back farther east, maintaining his hold on the useless railroad and uncovering Griswoldville, thus allowing Wheeler's men to reoccupy it. The first layer of protection Howard had counted upon to shield his lumbering wagons was not in place anymore.

The ruined village itself was no longer a prize of value, but what was important was the access it provided to the local road network. Once in control of the portal, Confederate Major General Wheeler was well positioned to throw scouts forward to clarify Union dispositions and to concentrate his command to strike a hard blow. He did neither.

Thanks to this failure to undertake a thorough reconnaissance, his superior in Macon had to operate with assumptions and educated guesses, setting the stage for a disastrous clash of arms not twenty-four hours in the future. Rather than making a fist to smite the enemy, Wheeler snapped fingers individually, dissipating his strength into small raiding parties that filled the byways, making life miserable for the Union wagon guards; but at no point did the Rebels do more than menace the Federals.

Isolated in Macon, with his telegraphic connections north and east broken, Lieutenant General William J. Hardee came to several critical conclusions. First, he reckoned that the city was no longer under a direct threat from Sherman's forces. Second, if not Macon, then he reasoned that Augusta must be the true object of the Yankee operation. With each city containing irreplaceable military and manufacturing assets, it was inconceivable that a campaign on the scale that Sherman was waging would not target one or both places. With Macon now off the endangered list, the defensive-oriented Hardee could think only of repositioning his military pieces to protect Augusta.

Third, in the absence of any contrary information from Wheeler, Hardee assumed that the Federal line of march was to the northeast, leaving the Central Railroad clear from Gordon to the coast.* Since time was of the essence, it would be quicker for Macon's now superfluous infantry forces to march the twenty or so miles to Gordon. Once there, Hardee believed they could catch trains to carry them to Augusta.

Orders were issued to the various militia units around the city to pack up in preparation for a move east the next day. One unit of state troops, Brigadier General Reuben W. Carswell's First Brigade of the Georgia Militia, was told to march right away. The citizen-soldiers grumbled as they tramped out of town, but this early departure would save their lives. Hardee then packed his own bags, wanting to return to Savannah as soon as possible, but taking a more prudent course south via rail, then overland by horse to a connecting railroad line that would carry him into the coastal city. Before departing, the

---

* Ironically, even as Hardee was reaching this conclusion, Major General Henry C. Wayne, commanding the patchwork garrison at Gordon, was pulling out the last of his force and heading east to take position behind the Oconee River bridge.

lieutenant general sent off a dispatch to General Beauregard: "Satisfied that there will be no attack upon this place, I leave tonight for Savannah by way of Albany and Thomasville. Main body of the enemy moving on Augusta, the movement in this direction evidently for the purpose of destroying Central Rail Road which has been partially accomplished, stopping for the present all communication with the east."

The mounted raiders dispatched by Wheeler made contact with numerous elements of the Right Wing throughout the afternoon and into the evening. An Indiana soldier in the Third Division, Fifteenth Corps (moving on the direct Gordon road out of Clinton), scribbled in his diary: "Rebs attacked our [ammunition] train & the 48th [Indiana] & 59th [Indiana] had to go back, found Co. K deployed as skirmishers. Rebels left at dark."* Trouble was also brewing for the First Division, en route from Clinton to a bivouac at a crossroads northeast of Griswoldville. "This evening the rebel cavalry made an attack on our train but did not accomplish anything," noted a journal keeper in the 97th Indiana. The Confederate troopers, elaborated a man from the 9th Iowa, "tried to cut off and capture our train but we drove them off without any loss." The Johnnies, bragged an officer in the 25th Iowa, "went off in a bigger hurry than they came."

Following behind the First Division was the Second, which would camp tonight north of Griswoldville, near a small church called Pitts Chapel. These bluecoats encountered some more of Wheeler's men. "The rebels attacked our train while going through town [of Clinton]," wrote one of the 30th Ohio. "We drive them back in less than no time." A few Confederates even struck at the very tail end of the Right Wing, the main wagon train guarded by Corse's Fourth Division. "Met the rebel cavalry," recorded a diarist in the 66th Illinois. "We drove the Johnnie rebs." Howard's orders called for the Second Division to make a demonstration toward Griswoldville on November 22, in the hope of further diverting attention from the wagon trains.

The potential danger posed by these pinpricks was felt as far off as Gordon, where, as a soldier in the 11th Iowa recollected, the men "corralled the wagons four miles in the rear, where the First Division of the

---

* In addition to the primary supply train, which traveled in the rear of the Right Wing, each division maintained its own train, carrying ammunition and other supplies required for immediate needs.

Seventeenth Corps went into bivouac, to safeguard the train, since the rebels' cavalry have appeared both in front and in the rear." However, instead of the recon operations representing a prelude to a more serious attack, the probes were the entire effort.

The head of the Seventeenth Corps column reached Gordon late in the afternoon. The senior Confederate officer at that post, Major General Henry C. Wayne of the Georgia Militia, had been shifting men and supplies east all day, sending everything to the Oconee River bridge, where he planned to make a stand. The last militiamen were clambering onboard the last train when a volunteer aide rode in with word that the enemy was just three miles distant. The scout was a local veteran named Rufus Kelly, disabled by the loss of a leg earlier in the war, though the injury had not quenched in the slightest his resolve to combat the hated Yankees. Having delivered his message, Kelly stared hard at the soldiers climbing onto the train.

"General, what does this mean?" he asked. "Don't we make a stand?"

Wayne tried to explain his plan to defend the Oconee River bridge, but Kelly wasn't hearing a word of it. He launched into a tirade of impressive proportions. "Well, you damned band of tuck-tails, if you have no manhood left in you," he finished, "I will defend the women and children of Gordon."

Kelly wheeled his horse about to ride toward the enemy, most decidedly looking for trouble. Wayne watched him go, waited until everyone had boarded, then signaled the engineer to get moving. As the train pulled away from the platform, Wayne observed a "few scattering shots [from the enemy] . . . dropping harmlessly around it." He and his men would live to fight another day.*

This night Major General Howard sent a positive report to Major General Sherman. He passed along news from his scouts that Milledgeville appeared to be undefended. Howard reported his belief that the Macon garrison numbered between ten and fifteen thousand men;

---

* The unyielding Kelly fought a short engagement with the Yankee advance. He was knocked from his horse, captured, eventually escaped his captivity, and slipped back into Gordon's civilian population. Interviewed thirty years later by one of General Wayne's aides, the doughty Rebel regretted nothing of what he had said that day. Declared Kelly: "I thought so then and I think so yet!"

and that generals Beauregard, Hardee, and Joseph E. Johnston were all present directing the defense.*

Howard's troop movements, along with the estimates of enemy strength circulating around the various Right Wing headquarters, led some officers to credit Sherman with a decision he never made. "General Sherman did not deem it advisable to enter Macon, as it was very heavily garrisoned by Cobb's militia and Hardee's old troops," declared a Fifteenth Corps officer. "It would have cost us many lives to take the city, and of course the wounded would have been left behind. I think it was very wise in General Sherman in avoiding a conflict at that city."

It was Howard's hope that November 22 would see most, if not all, of his vulnerable wagons safely under cover at Gordon. No one was anticipating any significant combat, but the components were in place, and a chain of events already set in motion that would lead directly to a senseless bloody battle.

---

* Even with every available person in place, the Macon garrison likely never exceeded 7,000 men. Of the Rebel leaders cited by Howard, General Beauregard was still in transit, General Hardee on his way out the door, and General Johnston relocated to South Carolina.

CHAPTER 13

"We 'Shot Low and to Kill'"

TUESDAY, NOVEMBER 22, 1864
Milledgeville

——— *Left Wing* ———

The residents of Georgia's capital awoke to the coldest morning in recent memory. The penetrating chill put an edge to the unease everyone felt. Those who had spent the previous days hiding their valuables began to second-guess themselves and wonder if they were so clever after all. Others who had waited to take such drastic steps now feared it was too late. For every voice of calm reason there was another reciting a litany of horrors ascribed to the Yankee horde that was about to descend on the city. It was the anticipation that was hardest.

The nearest to Milledgeville that the Fourteenth Corps would come today was about twelve miles to the northwest, in the area around Cedar Creek. Sherman had decided to let the Twentieth Corps have the honor of "taking" the town, so this day Brevet Major General Jefferson C. Davis's men made abbreviated marches, using the opportunity to tighten their columns, which the lousy weather and bad roads had spread out.

The Union boys greeted a raw day after a bitter night in the open. "Very cold last night," shivered an Ohio soldier, ". . . so cold that sleep

did but little good." The silver lining, as seen by a positive thinker in the 2nd Minnesota, was that "the cold wind last night dried the mud." Nevertheless, recorded another Ohio soldier, the "men really suffered with the cold though we marched rapidly."

The relatively short distances covered by most units, coupled with the general concentration that was taking place and the relative absence of any Rebel cavalry, meant that many wandered from the line of march. "Nearly every man went out foraging and nearly all sorts of delicacies were brought into camp," gloated an Illinoisan. A party from the 75th Indiana "foraged sweet potatoes, sorghum, fodder and salt." A Wisconsin man could not "help feeling pity for these citizens whose every particle of provisions is mercilessly consumed by our troops."

East from the Fourteenth Corps, the Twentieth was tramping on a course set for Milledgeville. Weather conditions were no better for this portion of the Left Wing. "Miserable, cloudy, windy, dreary start of a morning," complained a Garden State quartermaster, "and never I think experienced a colder one at this time of year in N.J." When a New Yorker in the 149th regiment went to sleep last night his "blankets were wet," and when he awoke this morning he "found them froze." The crusty mud road surface proved a mixed blessing, at least according to a Wisconsin soldier. "It told heavily on the shoes and on the half-shod feet; for many of the men had started out poorly shod, or had thrown away their new shoes rather than 'break them in.' " As a result the Federals "hobbled along at a brisk pace."

John Geary's division, which had been on detached service, rejoined the main body near Dennis Station, so the entire Twentieth Corps closed on Milledgeville. The route they followed took them past a tidy plantation owned by a Reverend Jordan. A New Jersey soldier was quite taken with the "extensive gardens . . . well cared for and the house [was] surrounded by some of the most elegant shrubbery and evergreens I ever saw." An Ohioan looked past the elegant facade and did not like what he saw. The Reverend Jordan, he declared, "lives like a *prince* amongst serfs." Added another from Wisconsin, "the good people had left &[,] save in the house which was g[u]arded[,] the boys helped themselves to all they wanted." By the time the trailing division reached Jordan's place, Sherman's men had cleaned "him out of everything available."

The Left Wing pontoniers were on the job at the Little River, near a ruined railroad bridge. The stream here was 250 feet wide, so it took ten pontoons to finish the job. The ground on the bridge's south side was low and swampy, which caused a few problems for the wagons, but nothing as severe as the mud wallow of recent days.

Once the head of the column drew near to Milledgeville, Major General Slocum detailed Colonel William Hawley to forge ahead to secure the town with his regiment (the 3rd Wisconsin) accompanied by the 107th New York. As Hawley later reported, "I immediately proceeded to establish patrols in the streets, and detailed suitable guards for public buildings, including the State House, two arsenals, one depot, one magazine for powder and ammunition, and other buildings containing cotton, salt, and other contraband property."

The occupation plan called for the First and Second divisions to pass through the town, crossing the Oconee River on the wagon bridge (not destroyed) to camp along the river's east bank; while the Third Division would bivouac on the west side near the span. The east side campers settled on Beulah Plantation, owned by a Georgia legislator and lawyer named William McKinley. Major General Slocum set up his headquarters in town at the Milledgeville Hotel. The passage of the troops would extend throughout the afternoon and night and well into the next day, long after Milledgeville's residents went to bed, leading many to date the first day of occupation as November 23.

According to a New Yorker in the first brigade to enter, "we were escorted through the town by the regimental band, which played *Yankee Doodle* for the edification of the remaining inhabitants." An Illinois comrade thought the white residents "a blank-looking set of people, never dreaming that the hated Yankees would ever invade their noble domain." Another Illinoisan, who trudged through a few hours later, recalled white flags everywhere plus an impromptu review by General Slocum, standing on the hotel's steps. The smell of smoke was in the air from the burning State Penitentiary, which had been torched by the inmates left behind who had decided not to volunteer for the Confederate cause.

Then there were the blacks, described by a New Jerseyman as "old negroes and young negroes, males and females, house servants generally, blessing us—cheering us—laughing—crying—praying—dancing and raising a glorious old time generally, even trying to hug the men as they go along." An Indiana officer jotted down some of the different cries of joy he heard: "God bless you! You've come at last. We've been waitin' for you-all more'n four years!" "Lawsee, Massas! I can't larf nuff; I'se so glad to see you!" A few Hoosiers were still chuckling over one of the first sights to greet them, a slave cabin flying a white flag. When one of the soldiers asked a black woman the reason for the signal, she replied: "Why-why, that's to let you'uns know that we'uns have surrendered!"

Not all encounters were so lighthearted. Some African-Americans attempting to connect with Sherman's columns were intercepted by Rebel cavalry, eager to inflict object lessons. One such incident, overstated for effect, is found in the diary of an 8th Texas cavalryman, whose November 22 entry reads: "To-day we followed on [after the Federal columns] and only whipped about 1,000 negroes, who were on their way to the enemy."

For William Tecumseh Sherman the capture of Milledgeville represented the end of the first phase of his grand movement into Georgia. Once he reached the state capital and was debriefed by his principal lieutenants, he would have to make some critical decisions to answer the question: What next? Thus far he had been blessedly detached from day-to-day matters for the most part, free to drift with the great current of events he had set in motion; observing and reacting, but unencumbered by the burdens of command. All that would change when he entered Milledgeville, so uncharacteristically though perhaps understandably, Sherman stole another indolent day. His headquarters moved just a short distance this day, even though, as a bored staff member pointed out, "We had time to get into Milledgeville."

The headquarters party rode slowly, hunched up against the wind's cold bite. "Not so much shooting on the flanks today," noticed Major Hitchcock, "but soldiers all the time out 'foraging' and straggling." As if still trying to convince himself of the rightness of Sherman's philosophy, Hitchcock added: "To a novice there seems much more of this than consistent with good discipline."

Sherman made his lunch stop at the midday headquarters for the Second Division, Fourteenth Corps, where he sat down with the officer in charge, Brigadier General James D. Morgan, and the corps commander, Brevet Major General Jefferson C. Davis. "Sherman was in fine spirits," wrote a divisional officer; "told story of the soldier foraging liberally, and that no one could tell where this army would concentrate."

The General pushed forward after lunch, deciding to call it quits around 4:00 P.M. Instructing his staff to "pick out the place for our camp," he walked over to some slave huts to get out of the cold wind. The blacks told him that there was a nicer overseer's house just down the road, so Sherman set out on foot. Once he arrived at the place, he found that several of his resourceful staff had already scoped it out, settled in, and even had a warm fire going. When they intended to tell their boss was anyone's guess.

Sherman made it his headquarters. Poking around, he turned up a small box with the name "Howell Cobb" written on it. One of the resident slaves was brought forward to tell the General that they were on the plantation named Hurricane, owned by the Confederate leader. As if cued by the revelation, another staff officer, Major George Nichols, produced a recent Macon newspaper containing a Cobb proclamation urging Georgians to assail the Yankee forces "on all sides." That was enough to seal the property's fate. Recollected Sherman, "I sent word back to General Davis to explain whose plantation it was, and instructed him to spare nothing."

Sherman relaxed after supper, while word spread among the plantation slaves that the great officer was in their midst. One black showed up content just to gawk. When he at last walked away, an officer heard him murmuring, "He's got the Linkum head, he's got the Linkum head, he's got the Linkum head." Another slave cautiously approached the gaggle of officers outside the General's room and asked, "Dis Mr. Sharman?" Told that it was indeed him, the man asked for a lit candle. He moved into the room and observed Sherman's face accentuated in light and shadow. According to Sherman, the servant exclaimed: "Dis nigger can't sleep dis night."

After motioning the man to a chair, the General asked why he was so nervous. The black replied that they had been fooled once before by Confederates pretending to be Yankees in order to identify slaves of dubious loyalty, most of whom were subsequently punished. For his answer, Sherman led the slave to the cabin's front porch, where he pointed out a "whole horizon lit up with camp-fires" as proof that the Union army had indeed come. A staff officer present reported that the "General conversed with him for a long time," while Major Hitchcock heard Sherman inform the African-American that "all the darkies" could "help themselves" to the Cobb plantation supplies. When he rose to leave, the slave recognized one of Sherman's escort officers as someone he knew. The two had a warm reunion, and as the black finally departed he was, recalled a staff member, "about the happiest looking individual you ever saw."

It turned out that the escort officer, Lieutenant David R. Snelling, did have a local connection. He was born a few miles away, started the war in the ranks of a Georgia Confederate regiment, and changed sides. Despite this clouded record, Sherman had come to trust his knowledge of the region. Once the slave was gone, Snelling asked Sherman's permission to visit his uncle, who lived about six miles distant near Fortville. Sherman happily granted the request. Before he left, Snelling told Hitchcock that there was little love lost between him and his uncle, who had sternly disapproved of his nephew's lukewarm Southern patriotism.

The young officer rode off with a squad of men, who spared the plantation none of the full Yankee treatment, burning the cotton gin as well as freely appropriating supplies and sundries. The results were reported to Sherman, who wrote that Snelling's "uncle was not cordial, by any means, to find his nephew in the ranks of the host that was desolating the land, and Snelling came back, having exchanged his tired horse for a fresher one out of his uncle's stables, explaining that surely some of the 'bummers'* would have got the horse had he not." To Hitchcock, Snelling confided that his uncle, in a terrible fright, had proclaimed Sherman to be the "greatest general and meanest man in the world."

It was impossible for Sherman to avoid all official business. Once settled in Cobb's plantation, he dictated a message for Major General Howard that summarized the Left Wing's movements, then instructed the Right Wing commander to report in person at Milledgeville on November 23. Howard was to pass a similar request on to Brigadier General Kilpatrick, all in preparation for Sherman's "making further orders."†

Lieutenant General William J. Hardee was not alone in concluding that with Macon now safely behind Sherman's advance, Augusta was the likely target. The telegraph lines between that city and Richmond hummed with urgent traffic. Jefferson Davis sent two messages. One directed that as much valuable machinery as possible be dismantled for relocation to a safer place. The other underscored the Confederate president's determination to cut Sherman off from any sustenance. "All supplies which are likely to fall into the enemy's hands will be destroyed," he commanded.

Still lacking any substantial reinforcements to send to the region, Davis continued his "great men" policy by assigning another notable to the trouble spot. General Braxton Bragg, then overseeing C.S. affairs in North Carolina, received instructions to proceed to Augusta "to direct efforts to . . . employ all available force against the enemy now

---

* This was just the second appearance in Sherman's *Memoirs*, and the first in a conversational context, of the word that would become synonymous with freewheeling foragers.

† Not long after sending this note off, a courier arrived from Kilpatrick with a report on his actions through November 21. The dispatch, which emphasized the positive, brought relief and cheer to Sherman's headquarters.

advancing into Southeastern Georgia." Stopping the enemy effort to capture Augusta was Davis's top priority; as he said, "every other consideration will be regarded as subordinate to that."

A similar sense of urgency now prompted a veteran officer in Augusta to make his own effort to cut through the tangle of semi-autonomous commands scattered before Sherman's columns by placing himself in charge. Ambrose Ransom Wright had been a brigadier in Robert E. Lee's army with service at Antietam, Chancellorsville, and Gettysburg. He was no stranger to controversy, having released a public letter after the latter battle that was harshly critical of several of his peers.

Wright, vindicated at a subsequent court-martial, left the army to win a seat in the Georgia legislature, eventually rising to the position of president of the Senate, making him second in line in order of succession. From where Wright sat, Governor Brown was "disabled" by being cut off in Macon, thus activating a clause in state law empowering him to step in. "I have assumed command of the militia of the State east of the Oconee River, and have ordered all able-bodied men to report to me here," he informed the officer in charge of troops around Savannah.

Wright's move infuriated Governor Brown's partisans, who viewed the action as a blatant attempt to subvert the state's gubernatorial authority. "I need scarcely say that disability is a legal term signifying legal incapacity to do an act—not mere temporary physical hindrance," fumed a lawyer on the scene. The resulting clamor prompted Wright to transmit a request for Brown's approval of his action, something that the governor would not even consider granting. Communication, Brown pointed out, was not disabled, only "lengthened," and therefore did not invoke the "contingency contemplated in the [State] Constitution." Wright's action, while well-meaning, only compounded the confusion.

Confederate response continued to be hampered by the gap at the top. Beauregard, still heading toward Macon, was not in contact with a working telegraph line. Hardee, as one subcommander put it, "was at Macon on Sunday; have not heard from him since." Ripples of panic spread as far as Charleston, where the officer in charge of the post earnestly pleaded with Richmond for reinforcements to meet Sherman's expected assault.

While the top brass dithered, the local press beat the drums of war. In Augusta, the morning newspaper proclaimed that "Georgia's hour of trial has come." Confronted by the Federal depredations, the state's residents faced "the single choice between victory and ruin." Declared the editor of the *Augusta Daily Chronicle & Sentinel:* "There is no alternative left them but to fight."

One area in which Confederate authorities performed with admirable promptitude was the evacuation of Camp Lawton, in business only since early October. Camp authorities had been given permission to ship the prisoners elsewhere on November 19. Camp Lawton's commander reported today that the facility had been completely emptied save for "a few shoemakers and butchers, who will leave in the course of a few hours." The movement of some 10,000 men had been carried out in such a manner that no word of it reached Major General Sherman near Milledgeville, some eighty-five miles to the west. As far as he was concerned, the prison remained a high-priority target and an important objective for the next phase of the operation.

—— *Right Wing* ——

"Cold and snowflakes flying," wrote a diarist with the 11th Iowa as the Seventeenth Corps spilled from its camps into formations taking shape for the march to Gordon. A Wisconsin man in the mass noted that the "ground froze & water ½ an inch thick [with ice]." The units wasted little time sending out foraging parties. A Wisconsin soldier recorded stopping at a large plantation where he had "roasted Chicken Sweet Potatoes Coffee for breakfast." Other observant Federals took notice of a change in the landscape. "We have just left the highlands," said an Illinoisan, "and this is our first introduction to the extensive pineries and swamps that characterize the southern portion of the Empire State of the South." Sherman's men had crossed the fall line; from here on all the rivers led to the Atlantic Ocean.

It was late in the afternoon when the leading elements of the Seventeenth Corps entered Gordon, shooing away a few remaining state militiamen ahead of them. Gordon, also known as Station No. 17 on the Central of Georgia Railroad, was a whistle-stop town—just a couple of buildings out in the middle of nowhere. "The citizens somewhat excited," commented an Ohio diarist with decided understatement. The structures in town linked to the railroad didn't last long, and the track not much longer. "This was a very nice railroad but is fast being destroyed," commented an Iowan.

While they worked, some of the Yankee boys wondered where the army would go next. "If we started south or southwest when leaving Gordon we would go to Mobile [, Alabama,] but if we went east or southeast then we would join our cracker line* at Savanna[h]," mused an Iowa soldier. Others raided the village post office to return with armfuls of recent newspapers. "First, and all-important, was the news that Lincoln had been re-elected to the Presidency," said an Illinois soldier. "[Second:] In order to inflame their passions, the paper contained many . . . scandalous narratives of robbery, rapine and murder [by Sherman's men]. . . . In other columns were found inflammatory appeals from military and civil authorities, calling upon the inhabitants to harass the troops in every conceivable way."

Gordon became a point of concentration for the Right Wing, so before long the surrounding countryside began filling with the impedimenta of war. It was, remembered a Wisconsin officer, "all . . . crowded and in confusion—marching troops, wagons, cannon, ambulances and horsemen being packed together in a mass." Amidst this chaotic scene one image stood out for this officer, the sight of a "little black boy not more than seven or eight years old, running along, dodging this wagon and that horse, and crying, 'I want my mammy! I want my mammy!'" Recalling the event long afterward, the man wondered: "Did he find her that night, or the next morning, or ever? . . . What became of the little fellow? I don't know that, but I've often wondered about it all these years."

Something else claimed attention as sunset approached. Said one of the many who took note of the occurrence in their journals or diaries: "Very heavy cannonading is heard in the direction of Macon."

Some twenty miles to the east, Major General Henry C. Wayne was busy organizing the defense of the Oconee River bridge. Arriving there from Gordon, he found something to cheer him for waiting on the east

---

* Soldier slang for a supply line.

bank was Major Alfred L. Hartridge with a mixed command of cavalry, artillery, and infantry totaling 186 men. Adding the 500 or so
that Wayne had shifted here, he had approximately 700 soldiers to
stop Sherman's march.

It was a daunting prospect. While the river at the bridge crossing
was fringed with broad swampy banks, making it impossible for the
enemy to employ his artillery, there were a number of fording places
both above and below the span. Wayne estimated that he had "twenty
miles at least of line to watch and guard." There was nothing left to do
but try. Wayne afterward reported that his officers and men "cheerfully prepared to do their duty and meet their fate."

As soon as he found a working telegrapher, Wayne began bombard-
ing Savannah with requests for munitions and rations. He also passed
along whatever information came his way, including a late afternoon
flash, "Heavy cannonading now going on in the direction of Macon;
firing rapid."

This day's march spread the four divisions of the Fifteenth Corps
across a broad area. The Third (Brigadier General John E. Smith) literally got off on the wrong foot in its movement toward Gordon. His
men, groused a member of the 93rd Illinois, "marched about a mile
and turned around. . . . Old Gen. Smith got a great many cussings from
the boys for taking us on the wrong road." The relatively unencumbered division overtook the slower-moving tail end of the Seventeenth
Corps, forcing the Fifteenth Corps boys to tramp "through the woods
and plantations, moving abreast with the Seventeenth Corps."

Once the Third Division segued onto the railroad right of way, the
men were set to wrecking it. "The rails are laid on stringers," reported
a soldier in the 10th Iowa. According to an officer overseeing the operation, "the plan adopted was to string out two or three regiments on
one side of the track, and by word of command have every man seize
hold of a cross tie or the stringer, and when all were ready the word
was given . . . and in a few seconds the track rose from its bed; the
stringers were knocked loose from the ties, and the work of piling
the ties across the stringers and building fires was soon accomplished,
the heat expanded the rails while spiked fast."

Coming in behind the Third Division was Corse's Fourth, still shepherding the slothful wagon trains. "We enjoyed a snow storm in Central Georgia this morning," wrote an Ohio soldier in his journal. It was about 9:00 A.M., added an Iowan, when the sky "cleared up & the old Sun came out and with its gentle rays dispelled the blue Noses & white Ears." The slow pace gave lots of time for foraging, so the men did well; a Hoosier recorded finding plenty of pork, while an Illinois boy in the 66th Regiment proclaimed it a "Yankee picnic through Georgia."

What almost all of Corse's troops remembered of this day's march was the Herculean struggle with the wheeled transport. "Roads very bad, trains and artillery mired in mud and men detailed to help extract them," wrote an Iowa man. "As the mules drop down from exhaustion they are rolled out to one side and left more dead than alive," attested a member of the 50th Illinois. The valuable pontoon train was a significant problem. "Every one of the pontoon teams are stuck in the mud," complained an Iowan. An Ohio man recalled it as "hard pulling," while an Illinoisan added, "wagons broke, soldiers laughed, teamsters swore & so it went."

For the Second Division (Brigadier General William B. Hazen), which had spent the night camped north of Griswoldville, today's tramp was east and south toward Irwinton. It was along this route that one of the more clearly documented cases of civil abuse occurred. According to Lieutenant Thomas Taylor of the 47th Ohio, a party of men in Union uniform entered a house "and after robbing the family of every thing to eat, deliberately proceeded to break jars, dishes, [window] sashes, furniture, &c . . . , then robbed the beds of their bedding, wardrobes of their clothing and cut open mattresses. . . . To complete their inhuman and fiendish act [the vandals finished] by driving the lady big with child, her innocent little children and her aged mother from the house." Assigned to return the occupants to their home and to protect them while the division remained nearby, Lieutenant Taylor admitted that the "heart rending grief [they expressed] added to the other touching scenes around filled me too full for utterance."

Griswoldville

It was cold as Lieutenant General Richard Taylor stepped off the Columbus train onto the Macon railroad depot platform early in the

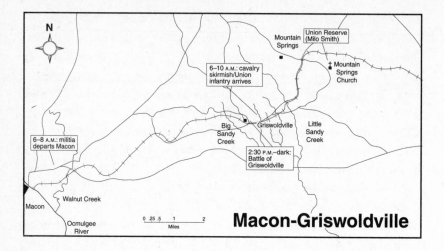

morning. "It was the bitterest weather I remember in this latitude," Taylor later wrote. "The ground was frozen and some snow was falling." Waiting for him was stout Howell Cobb, who commanded the state troops in town and was a political figure of commanding importance. Cobb immediately volunteered that the enemy had been sighted just a dozen miles outside Macon not twelve hours before. He was anxious to take Taylor on an inspection of the defensive fortifications, but the veteran officer stopped the proceedings with a question. "I asked what force he had to defend the place," Taylor said. When Cobb told him how meager it was, Taylor smiled and suggested that everyone—the party at the railroad station and those working on the city's defenses—go inside near a fire. "Macon," Taylor declared, "was the safest place in Georgia."

This did not sit well with the member of Cobb's entourage tasked with directing the construction of the city's defensive works, who immediately challenged the outsider's assessment. "The enemy was but twelve miles from you at noon of yesterday," Taylor explained with great patience. "Had he intended coming to Macon, you would have seen him last evening, before you had time to strengthen works or remove stores." It was as if a great weight had been lifted from Howell Cobb's shoulders. With his own smile he proposed that they repair indoors for some breakfast, a suggestion that Richard Taylor thought was eminently sensible.

Major General Joseph Wheeler, CSA, was mounting the kind of operation he best understood. Yesterday afternoon, after his troopers had pushed the Yankee cavalry out of Griswoldville, the enemy had rolled back a short distance before establishing a picket screen along Little Sandy Creek, east of the ruined industrial center. Wheeler's men had probed this vidette line until 9:00 P.M., providing him with a good idea of its layout. Hardly had dawn come before his cavalrymen swarmed the Federal outposts, scattering the bluecoats caught huddling around small campfires, grabbing horses and prisoners. For a while the sharp tang of gunpowder mingled with the crisp bite of the brisk morning.

It wasn't long after 6:00 A.M. when a column of armed men—perhaps 400 altogether—marched eastward from Macon, the soldiers new to their job and moving quickly to keep warm, even as light snow swirled around them. They constituted a pair of local defense battalions: one recruited from the workmen of the Cook and Brother Armory in Athens, Georgia; the other drawn from the laborers employed at the Augusta, Georgia, powder works. All were under the command of Major Ferdinand W. C. Cook, an Englishman who also managed the Athens arsenal. Cook was operating according to Lieutenant General Hardee's instructions by following the Macon-Gordon road alongside the railroad until he and his men could pick up a train to carry them into Augusta. In their wake, spotted across the city's fairgrounds, the camps for three brigades of Georgia militia were also stirring as these citizen-soldiers prepared to march according to those same orders.

Major General Peter J. Osterhaus and his staff picked their way along the meager Georgia road, the morning ice making passage difficult. Osterhaus was a genuine Prussian officer, having received a military education as a youth in the German state. He emigrated to the United States after picking the wrong side in one of the European revolutions of 1848. Settled comfortably amid the Teutonic community in Saint Louis, Osterhaus went to war as a major in 1861, adding general to that title three years later. He was a serious officer who was enjoying his new command—he was a last-minute replacement to direct the Fifteenth Corps when its regular commander proved unable to return to Atlanta in time for its departure.

Last evening Osterhaus had been instructed by Major General Howard to send his First Division (Brigadier General Charles R. Woods) to block the roads running northeast out of Macon, and, further, to push one of that division's brigades toward Macon to keep the enemy occupied even as the lumbering wagons completed their journey to Gordon. While Woods's First Brigade (Colonel Milo Smith) barricaded itself around Mountain Springs Church,* his Second Brigade (Brigadier General Charles C. Walcutt) was picked to advance. Osterhaus decided to tag along.

Walcutt was not a West Pointer, but as a graduate of the Kentucky Military Institute he knew his job. By the time Osterhaus arrived at Walcutt's headquarters, the brigade's bivouac had nearly completed its transformation from a tent city into a marching column. In short order the brigade—about 1,500 strong—was en route to Griswoldville, perhaps three miles distant.

Cavalry engagements by their nature are mercurial affairs. Formal lines of battle, established defensive strong points—all are of but slight importance in a fast-moving mounted action. An adept attacker can almost always expect a quick success, but the advantage gained is only momentary. An offensive force tends to lose cohesion as it advances, while the defenders are often falling back toward a reserve or even the main body, which has been fully alerted and is expecting trouble.

The Union pickets scrambling rearward before Wheeler's morning attack were from the 9th Pennsylvania Cavalry. When Colonel Oliver L. Baldwin of the nearby 5th Kentucky Cavalry rode over to help, he was assured by the 9th's acting commander, Major Charles A. Appel, that matters were well in hand. Even as Baldwin watched, the Pennsylvanians in reserve mounted a noisy counterattack that drove back the Rebel spearhead.

---

* In the process, the small rural chapel was completely dismantled.

At 8:00 A.M. a heavy column of Georgia militia tramped eastward from Macon, just as Major Cook's two battalions had two hours earlier. This force consisted of three brigades of militiamen, two regiments of the Georgia State Line, and a four-gun battery of the 14th Georgia Light Artillery. Town residents were grateful for the protection these men had provided for the city, but were equally glad to see them go. Facing a cold night and no supplies, the soldiers had helped themselves to whatever was handy. "All the fire we could get was by tearing up stair steps so you can judge what a nice time we had," confessed a militiaman.

Major General Gustavus W. Smith, a Kentuckian who graduated from West Point, was in overall command of these troops, but not with the column. Smith was a nervous man who, earlier in the war, had been physically prostrated by what doctors diagnosed as mental excitement. Ignored for further promotion by Jefferson Davis, he had found a home in Georgia, where a bad mark from the Confederate president was considered by some in authority to be a good thing.

Smith had commanded Georgia's state troops during the Atlanta Campaign, where, if they weren't manning trenches, they were digging them. He was the kind of officer who preferred administration to the rough-and-tumble of field operations. Smith opted to remain behind in Macon to complete his paperwork this day, considering the movement as merely a troop transfer operation. Responsibility for the forces departing the city devolved to the senior militia officer present, Brigadier General Pleasant J. Philips.[*]

A onetime banker and a military veteran courtesy of brief service in Virginia in 1862, Philips owed his seniority to the time spent in the militia. This put him over several other brigadiers in his ranks who had actually seen more combat. Smith's orders to Philips were "to halt before reaching Griswoldville and wait for further orders." There were no cheering crowds or official fanfares to mark the departure of the chilled citizen-soldiers. Philips estimated his marching time to Griswoldville to be about four hours.

---

[*]   Though Philips's name is often spelled with two *l*'s historian William Harris Bragg pointed out to me that this officer's gravestone, many of his signatures, and a special presentation sword all have only one.

The counterattack by the 9th Pennsylvania Cavalry at Griswoldville was short-lived. Hardly had Colonel Baldwin of the supporting 5th Kentucky Cavalry been assured that his help wasn't needed when the officer observed "fugitives . . . dashing down the road and word was brought me that the Ninth [Pennsylvania] was being driven." A Keystone State trooper, who termed this action "severe skirmishing," stated that the "9th lost, in a short time, five killed, twenty-one wounded and forty-two missing." Colonel Baldwin ordered a battalion from his regiment into line across the road "for the double purpose of reassuring the men of the Ninth and of charging the enemy [should he reach that point]."

Richard Taylor enjoyed his breakfast with Howell Cobb, who was a practiced conversationalist with stories reaching back to the administration of James Buchanan, whom he served as secretary of the treasury. As they were eating, an aide brought in the morning intelligence reports, indicating that the Yankee columns were turning to the east, away from Macon. "Cobb was delighted," Taylor recounted. "He pronounced me to be the wisest of generals." Another aide brought less pleasant news: Governor Brown was in town and wanted to meet the pair right away. "Cobb remarked that it was awkward," Taylor recalled, "for Governor Brown was the only man in Georgia to whom he did not speak." Nevertheless, the urgency of the moment overrode personal concerns, so Cobb agreed to see the governor.

The infantry column of Walcutt's brigade, accompanied by Major General Osterhaus, had proceeded about a mile on its diversionary mission when the leading elements reached the 5th Kentucky Cavalry's defensive line, strung across the road. Sizing up the situation, Osterhaus did not hesitate. "General Walcutt was ordered at once to relieve the cavalry, and the advance was sounded," he later reported. Skirmishers hustled forward from the 97th Indiana and 103rd Illinois, backed by the 46th Ohio. Said one of the Hoosiers: "Found Rebel Cav'y at once."

The Macon military elite was now gathered around Richard Taylor. In addition to Howell Cobb and Governor Brown, there were Brigadier General Robert Toombs, advising Brown, and Major General Smith. Taylor knew that Toombs and Smith had seen service with the regular Confederate army. Following the introductions, the group began to review the current situation.

Smith indicated that per Hardee's last instructions before departing for Savannah, the bulk of the militia was heading "east toward Savannah, taking the direct route along the railway." Taylor blanched. Looking at the same data that Hardee had considered, he did not conclude that the enemy had sheared off to the northeast. Taylor saw no reason why Sherman would not keep a sizable portion of his force on the railroad. "I told the Governor that his men would be captured unless they were called back at once," Taylor related.

Brown looked over to Major General Smith, who got the message and hurried from the room.* Able administrator that he was, Smith went to his headquarters to draft the necessary instructions, which he would then send by courier to Brigadier General Philips. As Smith remembered the new orders, Philips "was instructed not to engage the enemy, but, if pressed, to fall back to the fortifications of East Macon." In actuality, his orders were not all that clear-cut.

Faced with the greater numbers and heavier firepower of a full infantry brigade, Major General Wheeler's cavalry gave ground before the advance of Walcutt's men. As one of the Rebel troopers termed the yin-and-yang of this encounter: "We drove back their cavalry but soon the infantry was deployed & advanced against us & we were forced back." "We . . . drove them back through the timber and across an old farm, through another skirt of timber and through the little town of Griswoldville," recollected an Illinoisan on the firing line. Once the village had been cleared, a picket line was established on its western outskirts, allowing the skirmishers to take a breather, while the bulk

---

* "Lieutenant Generals Hardee and Richard Taylor, and other officers of prominence, reached Macon," Smith wrote with some asperity, "but they brought no troops with them."

of Walcutt's command held position to the east just short of the place.

Recognizing that his horsemen had done all that could be done, and that tackling a full Yankee infantry brigade was not a good idea, Major General Wheeler faced a decision. At 8:15 A.M., he sent a message off to Macon, where he believed that Lieutenant General Hardee still commanded: "After finding all the roads leading to Milledgeville occupied by the enemy I wrote you last evening asking if I should move towards Oconee bridge. I have not yet heard from you but have started on my command in that direction and shall move on myself in a very short time. I wait a few minutes to see if any dispatches from you may come."

When none arrived, Wheeler rode off southward, effectively removing his cavalry force from the area. His goal was now to get his brigades around in front of Sherman to help defend Augusta. Wheeler was acting impulsively, but since his troopers weren't tied into any region-wise command structure, he was largely free to operate on his own.

Before they all vacated the area, a few of his troopers encountered Major Cook, leading the two local defense battalions, in time to warm him of the trouble waiting ahead in Griswoldville. Immediately halting his march, Cook put his men into a line of battle. Fortunately, the Yankees weren't showing any aggressive signs. Cook knew that only an hour or two behind him was Brigadier General Philips with a lot more men, so after sending a courier to Macon with a situation report, he settled down to wait.

Major General Osterhaus was a decisive but prudent man. Once he learned that Wheeler's troopers had been brushed away from Griswoldville, he decided that the object of his mission had been accomplished. Furthermore, there was no purpose in keeping Walcutt's men exposed to hit-and-run attacks from the always unpredictable Rebel cavalry. He remembered that earlier they had crossed what he later called "an open prairie," about a mile and a half east of the Griswoldville crossroads. It was a good place to post a brigade—not only did it block the main wagon road and the railroad, it had a slight rise on its eastern side that offered a fine field of fire, with rough or swampy ground off either end to help anchor the flanks. Osterhaus gave orders for Walcutt to pull his brigade back to the timber's edge and dig in. Then, satisfied that all proper arrangements had been made, the division commander rode off to Gordon to report in person to Major General Howard. Behind him, Walcutt's men reversed course, the skirmishers falling back through the town to set up a new screen in the woods on its eastern outskirts.

Riding in advance of his column of militia and state troops, Brigadier General Pleasant J. Philips came up to Major Cook's deployed battalions "at 12 or 1 o'clock within about one mile of Griswolville." Philips learned for the first time that the road forward was not clear, as advertised back in Macon, but blocked by enemy troops. From some of the cavalrymen still hanging around Philips got an estimate of Federal strength at "800 to 1,200 strong."

Not wanting to be caught in marching formation by any sudden attack, the militia brigadier ordered his columns into line of battle. This took the better part of an hour, and when it was completed Philips instructed Lieutenant Colonel Beverly D. Evans, commanding two regiments of the Georgia State Line, to push a skirmish line through Griswoldville. Evans did as ordered, finding, to Philips's great relief, that the Yankees were gone. With no cavalry on hand to advise otherwise, Philips concluded that the route to Gordon was open once more.

The Confederate military force now holding station just west of Griswoldville was a composite division whose constituent parts were emblematic of the different phases of Governor Brown's manipulation of the state's military manpower. Three brigades' worth were Georgia militia, their ranks containing white males between sixteen and sixty years old not in Confederate service.[*] Called to serve a term defined by the current emergency, they could be only appended to regular Confederate forces on a temporary basis. (In this capacity, several units had operated with Hood during the latter phase of Sherman's Atlanta Campaign.) Another segment of the provisional force were two regiments designated as the Georgia State Line. These men were virtual regulars, enlisted for the war's duration. Their allegiance, however, was to the

---

[*] On average. There were younger and older volunteers in the ranks.

state of Georgia. Then there were the two local defense battalions, whose membership came from men exempt from the Confederate draft because of their war industry employment. The cannoneers were the real combat professionals, their four smooth-bore Napoleon cannon having seen active field service in Tennessee and Virginia.

Although Brigadier General Philips had authority over the militia and State Line, the local defense battalions reported to another chain of command, which soon created a problem. Once Griswoldville had been swept clear, Philips was informed by Major Cook that his orders (direct from Lieutenant General Hardee) were to proceed along the tracks to pick up transportation to Augusta, which he intended to do. Lacking any plan of his own, Philips agreed to move everyone through the town. They would march together as far as Griswoldville's east side, where he would halt to seek fresh instructions from Macon.

The slight ridge along which Walcutt's brigade deployed was bisected by a road stretching east to Mountain Springs Church. Walcutt had used the passageway to split his brigade, placing three regiments south of it (left to right: 46th Ohio, 100th Indiana, 40th Illinois) and three on the north side (left to right: 6th Iowa, 103rd Illinois, 97th Indiana).* A two-gun section from the 1st Michigan Light Artillery, Battery B (Captain Albert F. R. Arndt commanding a pair of smooth-bore Napoleons), was posted along the lane, tucked into a hastily constructed lunette. Walcutt established his headquarters in an abandoned farmhouse located just north of the cannon. Although owned by Samuel Griswold, the property was known locally as the Duncan farm after a previous resident.

Some Union skirmishers spooked by Philips's advance scooted out of the far woods to scamper across the broad open field to where Walcutt's brigade was resting. Major General Osterhaus's injunction to erect defensive works had been halfheartedly implemented at best. Word that a sizable body of Rebel infantry was approaching Griswoldville provided much-needed motivation. "We gathered rails, logs and anything we could get for protection," recalled an Iowan. "We were getting dinner, not dreaming of a fight," seconded an Illinoisan.

---

* A seventh regiment, the 26th Illinois, was detached on train guard duty.

The skirmishing gunfire crescendoed in the timber; after a few minutes the field was abruptly dotted with scurrying, hunching figures as the rest of the Federal skirmishers broke cover to skitter toward the Duncan Farm ridge. Now the barricade-building got going in earnest. Said a private in the 103rd Illinois: "We used everything that would check a ball."

The passage of the Georgia state troops through Griswoldville presented the men with disquieting images of the shape of things to come. At its peak of operation, the neat village was something of a showcase for the South's future. Beside the cotton gin manufacturing plant converted to revolver production, the town had boasted brick, soap, and candle factories, a saw- and gristmill, and various shops and quarters for white and black workers. Of the forty-odd structures, now only the two-story wood-frame Griswold mansion and a few other dwellings remained intact. All the others were burned or wrecked to a significant degree. It was a sobering vision of what might happen to Georgians' homes if the Yankee marauders were allowed to operate unchallenged.

There was gunfire near the head of his column, causing Brigadier General Philips to ride forward to meet once more with Major Cook, who informed him that his men had bumped into another line of Yankee skirmishers. These too had been easily driven, chased through the woods across a large fallow field into what looked like a defensive position. The officers and their staffs eased up to the timber's edge, where Cook pointed off to the east. Philips saw, as he later reported, "the enemy posted on the opposite eminence in line of battle behind some temporary intrenchments and fortifications." The militia brigadier decided to bring his command up in battle formation. Counting everyone—militia, State Line, local defense units, and artillery—he had 2,300 to 2,400 men on hand.

Major Cook's battalions of local defense troops, at the head of the column, formed the right flank. In the center Philips put his steadiest infantry, the two Georgia State Line regiments. A pair of militia brigades made up the left flank, with a third held in reserve. The four-gun battery (Captain Ruel W. Anderson in charge of 130 men, with Lieutenant Henry Greaves handling the cannon) was sent to "an eligible

site on the railroad on the north side." Almost immediately after getting into position, the veteran gunners began shelling some Yankee
cannon they could see on the far side of the fallow field, where the road
reentered the woods.

It was at this critical juncture that a staff officer carrying dispatches
from Macon found Brigadier General Philips. The first message, from
Major General Smith's chief of staff, after alerting him that Wheeler's
cavalry had departed the area, instructed Philips to "avoid a fight with
a superior force." A second dispatch, from Smith himself, had been
added after Major Cook's first sighting report had reached Macon. "If
pressed by a superior force, fall back upon this place without bringing
on a serious engagement, if you can do so," Smith advised.

In what remained of Griswoldville, the Macon staff officer composed a situation report for delivery to Major General Smith: "GEN-
ERAL: The whole division, including Cook's battalion, is one mile in
advance of this place on the Central railroad, in line of battle, with the
State Line troops thrown out in front skirmishing with the enemy.
Anderson's battery opened upon them just as I rode up to the line, the
enemy's battery replying. General Philips does not know what their
force is, and, on receiving your instructions, concluded not to advance
farther. On the movements of the enemy depends whether or not he
will fall back to this place or remain where he now is."

Brigadier General Walcutt waved over Captain Albert Arndt, commander of the 1st Michigan Light Artillery, Battery B, whose two-gun
section was assigned to this expedition. Walcutt indicated a party of
enemy soldiers visible at the edge of the woods to the right of a log
house and told the gunner to do something about it. Arndt rode the
short distance back to his guns, where he ordered the section commander, Lieutenant William Ernst, to target the group. Ernst called
out the commands, aimed the two cannon at the distant figures, and
yanked the lanyard. The shells landed close enough to cause the enemy
soldiers to melt back into the woods, so Arndt ordered a ceasefire.

Their appearance provided the officer with a point of reference for
the enemy's possible advance, and he realized that he should shift one
of the guns more to the right to set up a crossfire. Another quick visit
to Brigadier General Walcutt secured the necessary permission, but

even as the captain returned to reposition his artillery, the equation was changing. Four Rebel cannon emerged from the woods, expertly swung into firing positions, then opened on his pair. An Iowa soldier crouching nearby was impressed as the enemy's initial round smashed into one of two caissons carrying munitions, resulting in an explosion that destroyed about half of Arndt's immediate supply.

The first enemy volley also accounted for the Union battery commander. One moment Arndt was assessing the situation, the next he was flat on his back, "lying behind a [tree] stump with one of my men leaning over me unbuttoning my clothes." Stunned by the nearby explosion and believing himself to be fatally wounded, Arndt told the gunner to leave him and help his battery mates. Even as the officer felt himself growing woozy, the air around him was filled with the sharp crack of explosives and the vicious hiss of shrapnel as enemy rounds continued to pummel the Michigan cannon.

Confederate brigadier Pleasant J. Philips now faced one of the most difficult and controversial decisions of his military career. Even as the various regiments and companies making up his composite division moved into places along the tree line, Philips had to decide whether or not to attack. While he had assured Major General Smith's aide that he had no intention of going over to the offensive, Smith's orders had provided the option of doing just that as long as he wasn't being "pressed by a superior force." He wasn't. The Federal infantry blocking his way had made no aggressive moves save for the feeble effort of two Yankee cannon, smothered by the counterbattery blast from Captain Anderson's iron quartet. The open field his men would have to cross was far from flat and level; in fact, two small branches of Big Sandy Creek wriggled north to south, providing sheltered resting places for any advancing line of battle. Its relative openness would also make it easy for the militia units to maneuver, since most had been trained in farm fields such as these.

Philips doubted that the enemy would make a stand here. So far, the U.S. soldiers had demonstrated a marked disinclination to fight, preferring to fall back when pressed, especially as they had done at Griffin and Forsyth. Philips knew from Hardee's assessment that the Federals, no longer targeting Macon, were likely moving toward Milledgeville, so the thin line of enemy infantry across his path was probably a rear guard that would fade away at first push.

Also part of his calculation was the mood of his men. Many had been marching constantly since the campaign opened, abandoning swaths of territory for the enemy to ravage. There were companies in the gray ranks drawn from many nearby areas—Jones, Wilkinson, and Bibb counties, as well as Macon itself—with others from farther away—the towns of Athens and Augusta, as well as Montgomery County, toward Savannah. While not exactly itching for a fight, they were determined to defend their state, tired of those who challenged their courage. According to one Confederate officer, the militiamen dreaded the "jeers and sneers they must encounter . . . more than they do the bullets of the Yankees."

Philips came to the conclusion that the circumstances justified an attack, though he would never share his precise reasoning or proffer any justification for the decision. The plan he settled on was big on simple and direct; his flanks would turn the enemy flanks, while his center would tackle the Federal center. In the only report he would write of this day's actions, his sole comment was that "an advance was ordered."

Recollected an Iowa foot soldier across the way: "The enemy's forces marched out of the timber into the open field with three lines of infantry, either one of which more than covered the brigade front. Their lines were pushed boldly forward, with colors flying and loud cheering by the men, presenting a battle array calculated to appall the stoutest hearts." The martial panoply might have had the desired psychological impact had the opposition been raw troops, but it was a wasted gesture given the nature of these soldiers. "The enemy advanced in three columns," remembered another Iowan, "but the boys who had fought so many battles with Sherman were not frightened at superiority of numbers."

Captain Anderson's Georgia gunners had wreaked havoc on the two Michigan cannon opposing them, clearing the way for the infantry attack. By the time Captain Arndt realized that he wasn't mortally wounded (the fragment that hit him had been deflected by his saber belt plate, leaving him bruised but otherwise okay), his battery had been savaged. His fourteen men paid a terrible price for sticking with

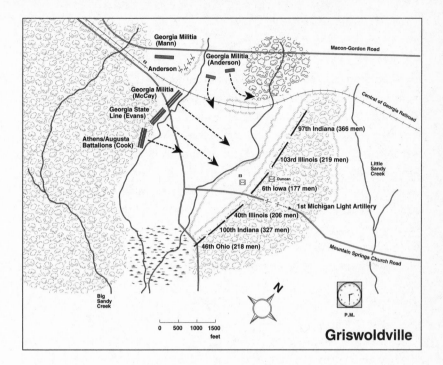

Georgia Militia (Mann)
Macon-Gordon Road
Georgia Militia (Anderson)
Anderson
Georgia Militia (McCay)
Georgia State Line (Evans)
Athens/Augusta Battalions (Cook)
Central of Georgia Railroad
97th Indiana (366 men)
103rd Illinois (219 men)
Little Sandy Creek
6th Iowa (177 men)
Duncan
1st Michigan Light Artillery
40th Illinois (206 men)
100th Indiana (327 men)
46th Ohio (218 men)
Mountain Springs Church Road
Big Sandy Creek
N
P.M.
0 500 1000 1500
feet
Griswoldville

their guns—two lost legs, one an arm, and four more were wounded to various degrees. Even as the still dazed officer watched, one of his gunners, William Plumb, gamely continued to perform his duty even "after the sponge and rammer had been shot to pieces." Although Arndt later reported that he had maintained his position until "the last round of ammunition was fired," evidence suggests that he ordered his tubes out well before the Rebel battle line came within killing range. With six of his horses also down, Arndt's men had to haul the cannon away by means of ropes harnessed to human backs.

Freed of their only real threat, the Rebel cannoneers now ranged freely along the Union line. The Georgia artillerymen, noted an Illinoisan, "made the rails and logs fly pretty lively." "The enemy's well served artillery continued to do serious damage along the entire line of the brigade," seconded a member of the 6th Iowa. "A single shell that struck and exploded in the rail and log barricade at the point where the regimental colors were waving [killed a member of the color guard] ... blowing the top of his head off and saturating the colors with his blood."

As the first, then the second, and finally the third lines of battle emerged from the woods, they were greeted only by the spattering fire from Yankee skirmishers who had holed up in the ruins of some farm buildings located outside the main line of resistance. The militiamen, State Line soldiers, and local defensemen moved steadily, finding comfort in the close presence of neighbors and friends. "The rebel infantry approached . . . at shoulder arms, in good order, as if on parade," recorded one admiring Federal. The Union main line was ominously quiet. "We charged them but were ignorant of their numbers and advantage," declared a member of the Georgia State Line. This state of affairs lasted until the first line was about midway across the field. Then the Yankee position began blinking with gunfire. The time was about 2:30 P.M.

"The music of shot and shell soon began," wrote an Indiana soldier. "As soon as they came in range of our muskets a most terrific fire was poured into their ranks, doing fearful execution," reported the commander of the 103rd Illinois. This first volley, fired at 250 yards, recorded another member of the regiment, "was most terrible; literally mowing down the first line, which halted, wavered, and seemed amazed." Although the majority of Federals were armed with standard single-shot muzzle-loading Springfield rifles, within each Union regiment were special squads of picked men carrying rapid-firing breech-loading rifles. This, allowed an Indiana soldier, "enabled us to keep up a continuous fire." According to a rifleman in the ranks of the 6th Iowa, "we 'shot low and to kill.' "

From his position along the tree line, Brigadier General Philips watched his center units advancing "in fine style under a heavy and galling fire." The two local defense battalions on the right flank, which were slow getting started, lagged behind the State Line troops, who were moving apace with a militia brigade on their left. A shallow gully was encountered where the Confederate line steadied to deliver a volley at the distant foe. Then the advance resumed, the lashing of bullets coming from the enemy position showing no diminution.

After what seemed an eternity, the first line reached a large gully carrying one of the branches* feeding Big Sandy Creek. This deeper trench offered protection from the lead hail spitting in their faces, and for many participants this would be their high-water mark. The advance did force the enemy skirmishers to abandon their forward posts in the farmhouse ruins and scamper into the main position. Within minutes, the second and third lines had pushed into the first, jostling for cover among the gall bushes, scrub pines, and reed cane. Also coming forward was the reserve militia brigade, which was so confused and rattled by the inferno that its first volley was loosed into the backs of some of the Georgia State Line.

A Yankee soldier standing in the ranks of the 103rd Illinois later termed this encounter "quite a hard fight." The enemy infantry, recalled a member of the 97th Indiana, "came at us with force and fury," while a comrade in the nearby 100th Indiana wrote that the Georgians "charged us and fought furiously." "We kept on loading and firing till the smoke got so thick it almost blinded us," added another Hoosier, "and our guns got so hot they burned our hands."

Soon after sliding into the deep gully wriggling roughly parallel to the Federal line (at distances varying from 45 to 100 yards), determined Confederate officers began concentrating on overwhelming the Union right flank. To meet this threat, Brigadier General Walcutt started thinning his left to reinforce his right. He shifted the 46th Ohio from one end of his line to the other, and made two calls on the 100th Indiana—one for three companies to plug the gap created by the withdrawal of Arndt's cannon, and the other to screen the extreme right. Because of these moves, three Hoosier companies had to now cover the frontage previously held by one and two-thirds regiments, but fortunately most Rebel effort seemed directed against Walcutt's right.

Even though Anderson's gunners were operating virtually unopposed,

---

* Afterward given the name Battle Line Creek.

the proximity of the Georgians to the Yankee line forced the artillery-men to choose their targets with care. The abandoned Duncan farm-house was an obvious mark, with the added bonus of its being Brigadier General Walcutt's headquarters. One of Anderson's well-placed rounds exploded near the brigadier, driving a shell shard into the lower part of his right calf, causing a painful and incapacitating wound. The officer was carried off to the field hospital in the rear, near Mountain Springs Church. Command devolved to the senior regimental commander, Colonel Robert F. Catterson of the 97th Indiana.

Making a quick assessment of the situation, Catterson was not happy with what he found. Several units were reporting low stocks of ammunition, and the enemy was continuing to press him hard on the right. "As I had already disposed of every available man in the brigade, and my [thinned] left being so strongly pressed that not a man could be spared from it, I sent to the general commanding the division for two regiments."

Incredibly, the Confederate militia, local defense, and State Line sol-diers maintained their position in the forward gully for nearly two hours. "The firing was incessant," reported the State Line commander. A man in his ranks remembered that "the boys fell one after another." When the man was himself hit, he made himself small behind a tree stump while enemy "bullets . . . cut the ground on either side."

For his part, Brigadier General Philips lost all control of events once contact was made and remained at the tree line. An effort to get Major Cook's local defense battalions to flank the enemy's left "(from some cause of which I am not aware) . . . was never carried out," Philips complained afterward. Also, without any order from him, the militia brigade standing in reserve advanced into the field to join the others in the far gully.

From the few extant reports and accounts of this action, Philips played no role once the engagement was under way. Perhaps over-whelmed by the spectacle of what he had initiated but was unable to manage, the militia officer became a spectator. There would be rumors afterward (but no actual accusation) of alcohol abuse, but this is often a ready excuse to explain errors of judgment. No charges of drunken-

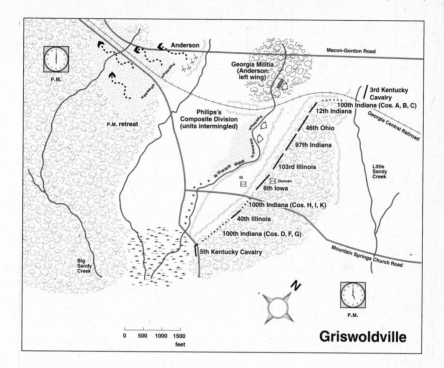

Griswoldville

ness against Brigadier General Pleasant J. Philips are found in any contemporary account from knowledgeable sources.

Of the men filling that broad gully, only bits and pieces of a picture emerge. That there was confusion is attested to by at least one report. Someone must have maintained a firing line near the gully lip to discourage any enemy forays against the position, although Federal sources indicate that their aim was poor, with most shots passing harmlessly overhead. Other officers rallied units together time and again in an effort to drive the invaders away. According to some accounts, at least three and perhaps as many as seven separate assaults lurched out of the gully, only to be beaten down by the torrent of gunfire. The last took place near the end of the engagement, when the left wing of Brigadier General Charles D. Anderson's brigade, which had gotten separated from the other wing, tried to turn the Federal right flank.

By the time of the battle's close, no less than three of the unit commanders—Brigadier General Anderson and colonels James N. Mann and Beverly D. Evans—had been hit. What kept the Georgians trying for so long had little to do with strategy or even tactics. In a telling comment from the battle's aftermath, a mortally wounded militiaman told his captors: "My neighborhood is ruined, these people are all my neighbors."

The Union soldiers were confident but not cocky. "I never saw our boys fight better than they did then," declared a member of the 100th Indiana. "Once when we were so hard pressed that it seemed as though they were going to run over us by sheer force of numbers our boys put on their bayonets resolved to hold their ground at any cost." "At one time it seemed that they would overcome our thin line, as our ammunition [was] nearly exhausted and none was nearer than two miles," reported the commander of the 103rd Illinois, "but fortunately a sufficient amount was procured, and our boys kept up a continual fire."

It was growing dark before the reinforcement Catterson had requested reached the scene of the action. There were three regiments: two cavalry and one infantry. A mounted unit was sent to the left, the others further bolstering the right. Also back was Major General Osterhaus, whose meeting in Gordon with Major General Howard had been interrupted by "a rather severe cannonade in the direction of Griswold[ville]." Osterhaus arrived "soon enough to witness the last efforts and entire rout of the enemy."

There was nothing dramatic about the end of the battle. It was almost as if the men and officers on both sides decided that enough was enough. Some of the militiamen called it quits on their own. Private William Bedford Langford recollected heading across the clearing in the rear toward the woods with a friend. "Just about half way across," he often told his daughters, Yankees began firing at them, about twenty or twenty-five bullets hitting around them, but neither of them was shot. He said neither he nor his companion ran until they reached the woods and then "they surely did run."

Most withdrew under positive commands to do so. One of the Confederate officers in the gully wrote that night came "and, ammunition being well-nigh exhausted, the commands retired in good order." That latter description was repeated in all the Southern after-action reports, suggesting a weary but unpanicked withdrawal, though not without some bitter recrimination from the ranks. A militiaman complained in a letter home of their "leaving some of our killed and wounded on the field exposed to the severities of a very cold night."

Brigadier General Philips claimed his intention was to halt in Griswoldville so he could send out detachments to haul in the wounded, but orders were waiting there for him to return his command to Macon. Thanks to some aggressive track repair, the bone-tired soldiers had to march only two and a half miles from Griswoldville to where trains—and medical assistance—were waiting.

The men began arriving back in Macon at 2:00 A.M., to streets that were as dark and empty as when they had departed. For the citizen-soldiers who had fought with determination but without success, it was a very long and very terrible day.

The volume of fire coming from the Rebel-held gully diminished noticeably after sunset, soon petering out altogether. Federal officers huddled, and at the sound of a bugle, skirmishers from at least four regiments nosed cautiously forward. "The scenes of death, pain, and desolation seen on the field will never be erased from the memory of those who witnessed it," attested an Iowan. "It was a harvest of death," wrote a somber soldier in the 100th Indiana. "We moved a few bodies, and there was a boy with a broken arm and leg—just a boy 14 years old; and beside him, cold in death, lay his Father, two Brothers, and an Uncle." "I was never so affected at the sight of wounded and dead before," added a man in the ranks of the 103rd Illinois. "Old gray haired and weakly looking men and little boys, not over 15 years old, lay dead or writhing in pain."

"I could not help but pity them as they lay on the ground pleading for help but we could not help them as we were scarce of transportation," explained an Indiana soldier to his wife. "The field was almost covered with dead and wounded," contributed a member of the 100th Indiana, "some crying for water, some for an end to their misery." "We took all inside our skirmish line that could bear moving," said an infantryman in the 103rd Illinois, "and covered the rest with the blankets of the dead." Other squads broke up captured arms or brought in uninjured prisoners. "They were badly mixed up in age, ranging all the way from 14 to 65 years," said an Iowan. Among them were several black slave-servants.

Top priority for the Yankees was taking care of their own, as there were both wounded and killed in Union blue. Among the latter was Corporal Aaron Wolford, an older man in the ranks of the 100th Illinois, whom the younger soldiers had fondly called "Uncle." Wolford, who had expressed a premonition of his death the night before, fell early in the combat, shot through the head. His comrades fashioned a rude coffin out of a hollow sycamore log to lay him to rest. Another officer present noted that his men buried their dead, placed the wounded in ambulances, and marched that same night. By midnight only Georgians remained alive on the field east of Griswoldville. One of the last Union soldiers to depart remembered the "mournful sighing of the wind among the pines and the pitiable moans of the wounded and dying."

When the time came to set down the history of this encounter, both sides put their spin on the story, even though most of those who had been through the ordeal fully understood what had happened. Wrote a Confederate participant: "The Militia has been in a very hard fight and got badly whipped." Yet Southern writers, beginning with newspaper reports published within days, stressed that Philips withdrew from the enemy without challenge, that the part-time soldiers had acted with "distinguished gallantry," and that "both sides suffered severely." Northern historians doubled and tripled the size of Philips's force, applying a similar multiplier to his casualties, which, in some estimates, approached 2,000. Federal record keeping was fairly thorough, so Walcutt's losses can be stated with a certain confidence at 13 killed and 86 wounded. Confederate tabulations were much less comprehensive, so here the losses are estimates only: about 50 killed and 500 wounded.

Over the next few weeks, a number of local newspapers dutifully printed letters from some participants containing lists of the injured and dead. The doleful registers filled column after column, often providing the only notification that families or loved ones would receive. In one such column, readers of the *Macon Daily Telegraph and Confederate* learned on November 24 of the battle's impact on the 7th Georgia Militia Regiment, whose commander had been killed. Among the forty-eight individuals listed: T. G. King and J. C. McLeans were dead, William Evans had a slight foot wound, Sergeant D. H. Henly had serious wounds in the thigh and leg, Jack Bussey was hit in the shoulder, William F. Williams in the breast, and M. K. Wilcox was severely wounded "and supposed killed."

Brigadier General Philips remained convinced that had his orders to assail both Union flanks been properly executed, "it would have resulted in dislodging and probably routing the enemy." Although in public Major General Smith praised Brigadier General Philips for his "success in driving before you the enemies of your country," in his official report he complained that the entire fight happened despite his orders "to avoid an engagement at that place and time," and that all things considered, "the troops were very fortunate in being withdrawn without disaster."

For at least one of the participating militiamen, the results of this engagement were clear. "From all the information I can get," he wrote his wife, "the Yanks are making their way to Charleston and Savannah, and I can see no way to keep them from going. My darling Camilla, it is a dark day for the Southern Confederacy."

CHAPTER 14

"The First Act Is Well Played"

WEDNESDAY, NOVEMBER 23, 1864

M ajor General Henry C. Wayne, Georgia's adjutant and inspector general, was not unfamiliar with quixotic endeavors. In 1855, as a United States Army officer, he was put in charge of a program testing whether or not camels could be adapted for military use in the American West. Now, as one of the top officials in the state's chain of command, he had reluctantly drawn a line in the sand at the Oconee River Bridge.

When Wayne first arrived here, after successfully extricating his troops from Gordon, he had every intention of making a stand. However, the large size of the approaching enemy force, coupled with the knowledge that there would be no further help from Savannah, caused him to change his mind. He would have destroyed the bridge and fallen back toward the coast except for the presence of Major Alfred Hartridge, who adamantly refused to even consider taking a backward step with his 186 men. As the major's rank was C.S. Provisional Army reporting directly to Savannah, Wayne (in the state's chain of command) had no direct authority over him. Faced with Hartridge's obstinacy, Wayne reversed himself and prepared to resist the enemy.

Extending work begun by Hartridge, Wayne finished a line of trenches along the river's east bank, covering the bridge. In his communications with Savannah he began referring to the Oconee River Bridge as "the now important point in this neighborhood." He also

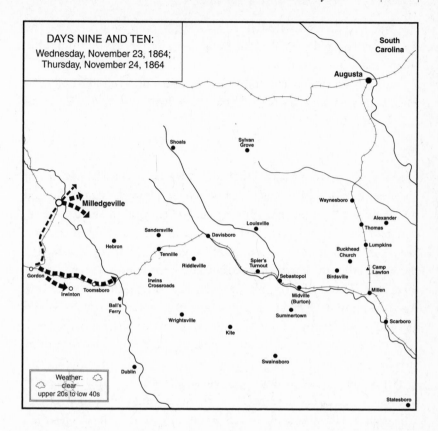

DAYS NINE AND TEN:
Wednesday, November 23, 1864;
Thursday, November 24, 1864

directed the construction of a fortified outpost about two miles west
from the span. This effort, carried out using surplus railroad ties,
resulted in a small but sturdy redoubt. Into this exposed post Wayne
sent a detachment of cadets from the Georgia Military Institute stiffened with eighty Orphan Brigade veterans belonging to the 4th Kentucky Mounted Infantry. "The cadets were, of course, very young,"
recollected acting major John Weller, the senior officer on the scene,
"some of them certainly not over fourteen years of age." Also in the
mix was a group of convict volunteers, still in their prison garb and
"hardened in appearance," according to the Kentuckian.

Wayne had one more trick up his sleeve. The rail line approaching
the bridge on the western side passed along a trestle over a mile of
marshy swamps, making it difficult if not impossible for the enemy to
deploy artillery. Wayne ordered one gun mounted on a platform car to
be pushed forward to support the stockade. He was concentrating
almost all his available strength here, leaving other nearby crossing

places exposed, especially Ball's Ferry, eight miles south. There the state officer posted a small picket detail, with orders to alert him if the enemy made an appearance.

All preparations completed, Wayne's morning situation report to Savannah concluded with the terse assessment: "I am expecting an attack momentarily."

It was 8:00 A.M. by Major Hitchcock's watch when Major General Sherman directed his staff east, toward the Georgia capital. Behind them, plumes of smoke rising in the cold morning air marked the execution of the General's orders that no building on the Cobb plantation (save slave quarters) be saved. Psychologically, Sherman was feeling the great relief of knowing that the initial phase of his grand movement had been concluded pretty much as he had imagined it would be. As he later put it, "The first stage of the journey was . . . complete, and absolutely successful." Physically, he was in minor distress, suffering a flare-up of neuralgia in his right arm and shoulder that made it difficult for him to hold a pen or pencil.

After about ninety minutes in the saddle, the headquarters party passed through an outer ring of the earthworks built to defend Milledgeville. Major Hitchcock dismissed Rebel efforts to defend Georgia's capital with the comment: "not used." Just outside the town boundary, Brigadier General Kilpatrick—never one to miss a chance to make an impression—was waiting with some of his horsemen drawn up along the road. Hitchcock, caught up in the giddy euphoria of the moment, turned to his boss.

"First act of drama well played, General!" he exclaimed.

Answered Sherman: "Yes, sir, the first act is well played."

The 1st Alabama Cavalry (U.S.), riding point for the Seventeenth Corps, came upon the Confederate stockade west of the Oconee River Bridge shortly after 10:30 A.M. Acting major John Weller had pushed out his own skirmish line, which was strong enough to send the Federal riders scattering for cover. When after a few minutes of desultory shooting it became evident that these Rebels weren't taking to their heels, the Yankee cavalry officer called for help.

Many of the Twentieth Corps units camped east of the Oconee River at Milledgeville occupied William McKinley's Beulah Plantation. The house itself, used for headquarters by two division commanders, was protected by a guard of 125 soldiers, but the rest of his holdings were fair game. For young Guy McKinley, there were moments of wonder as he gazed over a large field now filled with the Left Wing's wagon train. To the boy it "looked . . . like a person could have walked all over the field on canvas covered wagon tops without touching the ground, so many of them were there."

Young McKinley witnessed some of the commonplace destruction that occurred. More than a hundred bound and stacked bales of cotton had been plundered for bedding by Union soldiers accustomed to sleeping on the hard ground. An older member of the McKinley clan, a soldier home on sick leave, watched from concealment as the Yankee soldiers carried out well-practiced foraging routines. "Captured wagons, drawn by captured teams, driven by captured teamsters, and laden with captured grain or other stores, rumbled incessantly along toward the camps," he recollected. "Groups of rollicking cavalrymen, nearly hidden beneath great panniers of hay or fodder strapped on before and behind their saddles, passed every moment, singing and laughing as they went. Others with masses of cackling geese or squealing chickens dangling at their saddle-flaps filled up the intervals or accompanied the wagons by way of needless escort."

A heavy infantry skirmish line from the 32nd Ohio, pushing out from Colonel Benjamin F. Potts's brigade of Brigadier General Giles A. Smith's division (Seventeenth Corps), wasted little time chasing the Rebel voltigeurs back into the wooden tie redoubt covering the Oconee River Bridge. The Federals wriggled close enough to bring the position under direct rifle fire, causing some casualties among its garrison.

"The bravery of the school boys was the glory of this fight," reported acting major Weller. "Several of their number were carried off wounded and dying. I can never forget the looks of one little boy as four convicts carried him on a stretcher to the rear. His handsome face, with the flush of fever on it, and the resolute expression of his eyes, indicated that he fully realized the situation."

The appearance of the Union foot soldiers was enough to collapse the screening line of skirmishers, but not enough to force the garrison to abandon the little fort. The Yankee infantry needed more punch, so a request was made for additional firepower.

On the western outskirts of Milledgeville, units drawn from several Twentieth Corps divisions were set to work wrecking the railroad. The men, beginning shortly after midday, had within an amazingly short time "completely destroyed five miles of the road by burning the ties and heating and twisting the rails." "It was really amusing to see 2,000 or 5,000 strong men form in one line on one side of the track," said a New Yorker, "and at the command, see them take hold of the Rails and turn them up, ties and all, as far as you could see, and then pile them up and burn them, forming a continuous line of fire for miles."

Within the town limits bands of soldiers gamboled about, some content to see the sights, others determined to damage, as one New York man put it, "all public buildings considered inimical to the United States." Lieutenant Garrett S. Byrne of the 13th New Jersey was one of the former. "The State House is a rather small building, beautifully located in a square grassy knoll, with its accessory buildings conveniently arrayed around it," he wrote in his best tourist guide manner. "The Executive Mansion is a square brown building with an air of comfort around it. The State Prison is nothing but a long irregular pile of bricks, not even that now for it was burnt down."

Several tourists in blue made note of the state arsenal and magazine (separate buildings) and a few large churches, as well as many well-appointed residences. In some cases the Yankee boys were welcomed as guests in the hope that their presence would deter vandalism. Lieutenant Alfred Trego spent an enjoyable evening in the company of two young women. "All polite and intelligent ladies," he swore afterward, adding that they entertained him with "music on Piano and Guitar."

Mrs. Richard McAllister Orme, of New England stock, answered a knock at the front door of her elegant Doric-columned house to face another Yankee blue blood, Captain Henry Ward Beecher, come to guard the premises. The good captain was given a gracious reception, as were other officers who paid their respects to the daughter of the president of the Phillips Academy in Massachusetts, Beecher's alma mater. Only after they and Sherman's army had departed did Confederate captain James Alexander, Mrs. Orme's son-in-law, emerge from his hiding place, an airless attic cubbyhole.

Other Union soldiers in town had mischief on their agenda. "Stayed in the city all day and lived high," recorded a Connecticut diarist. A comrade in the ranks was fascinated by the "very curious way" in which some of the men sought loot. "Most of the silver and valuables were buried in the gardens and lawns, the earth and grass being very carefully replaced," he explained. "You may see the ingenious Yankee probing the earth about every house with his ramrod. He strikes a hard substance and digs." In this manner, added a member of the 129th Illinois, many "valuable things, dug away in the ground by the owners, were disinterred and taken along or destroyed." Missed in the probing frenzy were two important artifacts of Georgia's government—the state's Great Seal and its legislative records. Both had been hidden by the secretary of state, Nathan C. Barnett; the former under a house, the latter in a pig pen.

It didn't take long for several enterprising Yankees to chance upon large stacks of Georgia state currency—piles of bills printed for use but not yet signed for circulation. That fact made little difference. An amused Ohioan on the scene observed that "many a poor soldier became a millionaire for the time being," while a skeptical New Yorker questioned the wealth, whose "purchasing power . . . is fast departing." Nevertheless, several provost soldiers made the day for a number of unpaid women employees of a town cotton mill when they presented them with wads of bills, making "them happy—for a very short time," commented a Yankee angel.

An experienced foraging officer took as many of the bills as he could carry so he could "pay" for everything his men confiscated. "Settlement was made on the following basis," he bragged afterward; "each meal we had was one hundred dollars, poultry taken $10 each, hams $50 each, grain in the husk one dollar a pound. The ordinary horses & mules 10,000 dollars each." To legitimize all transactions, the officer carefully signed each bill "as Sect'ry of Treasury of the C.S. of America."

Another curious find was a room filled with edged arms—pikes and two-foot-long knives—made for mass distribution when the government ran out of guns. An Ohio soldier was unimpressed, declaring them "miserable weapons," while a Wisconsin man was certain that "if they intended to fight us with those things they must be crazy." It was the estimation of an Illinois veteran that the pikes were "formidable looking weapons, indeed, but of little value when pitted against Spencer rifles." In one regiment the boys hung the long knives at "their sides like officers' swords, but in a few days cast them aside."

Perhaps the most purposeless act of vandalism was that suffered by the state library, located in the capitol building. Lieutenant Byrne of New Jersey reckoned it "a pretty fair sample of libraries generally found at state capitals, but 'tis now in part remembered with things of the past. A great no. of volumes were taken, some for their intrinsic worth and some for their association; some to while away monotony of every day life but [I] should say the most part were taken for mere desecration and despoiling the Confederacy." "Choice literary and scientific works lay piled upon the ground," testified an Illinoisan, "and a crowd of soldiers in selecting from the lot, walked over and trampled upon them, and we observed a horseman ride through the crowd purposely to let his horse trample the books." "Public libraries should be sacredly respected by all belligerents," declared an angry officer on the scene, "and I am sure General Sherman will, someday, regret that he permitted this library to be destroyed and plundered." One soldier thought he recognized General Sherman in the crowd. "He looked pretty rough," the man commented.

At some point in the afternoon, a cadre of officers (many representing the two provost regiments) organized a mock session of the legislature in the actual governmental chamber. "Motions were made, resolutions offered and speeches made, and though the manual was not strictly followed, it was both comical and interesting," wrote a Massachusetts soldier. A Wisconsin officer noted that "Gen. Kilpatrick . . . regaled the convention by an account of his great raid on a [wine] cellar. . . . The committee on Federal relations soon returned with a set of resolutions to the effect that the ordinance of secession was injudicious . . . and void."

The event, thoughtfully organized for all the seeming chaos, made good copy for the reporters on hand, several of whom enthusiastically described it in great detail. The session came to an abrupt halt when the cry went up: "The Yankees are coming." "In a moment all was confusion, and amid shouts, yells and laughter, the multitude rushed for the door," chuckled a Bay State man. In his *Memoirs* Sherman related that he was "not present at these frolics, but heard of them at the time, and enjoyed the joke."

His amusement was not shared by one Milledgeville resident, the sister of Judge Iverson Harris, who managed to make her way into the crowded building to view the proceedings. "How my blood boiled when I entered the State House to see the destruction of property," she exclaimed, "& to see how grandly those wretches sat in state there!"

With the exception of one division still herding the wagons jammed west of Gordon, the Fifteenth Corps spent this day converging on Irwinton. Between the militia forces known to be in Macon, and Wheeler's always pesky cavalry, care was taken at each rest stop to build defensive works. Then, while some of the commands pried up and burned the Central of Georgia Railroad, others ignored the potential danger from roving Rebel bands to go on the prowl. "We got plenty of pork and potatoes," recorded an Iowa soldier.

Brigadier General William B. Hazen, commanding the Fifteenth Corps' Second Division, used the day to issue a flurry of orders meant to address some of the many flaws he had observed in the conduct of the march. Hazen was especially upset at the laxness shown by the divisional supply trains. To cut down on the huge increase in the number of animals being used, he directed that the wagons move more closely with the infantry, which (he hoped) would reduce the herd of pack mules. These surplus animals he instructed be sent to a central divisional corral for distribution where most needed. In addition, Hazen wanted all men not carrying arms to be issued tools and organized into a "brigade pioneer corps" to help with the difficult passage ahead.

The general reserved special scorn for the teamsters who had taken advantage of the situation to lavishly equip themselves with goods and assistants. Singling one out as an example, Hazen asked: "Of what service is this wagon-master, that he should presume to have a wagon [for his own use] and keep two servants and a private horse?" The general also felt compelled to spell out in precise detail the duties expected of the aides-de-camp attached to various headquarters.

Instead of foraging, he wanted them to spend their time closely monitoring and reporting on troop movements as well as carrying out spot inspections to make certain that proper procedures were being followed by all subcommands. Hazen well understood that the coming weeks would be far more difficult and challenging than the recent past. "Too much attention cannot be given to this subject," he announced.

Farther east, the combat was increasing along the approach to the Oconee River railroad bridge. Sweating despite the chill air, gunners from the 1st Minnesota Light Artillery manhandled one of their cannon onto the Central of Georgia railroad track, then began pushing it forward by hand. The Rebel artillery piece mounted on the railroad platform car proved to be ineffective, allowing the Minnesotans to cover about half a mile—within range of the small redoubt barring the way to the Oconee River Bridge. In another few minutes, the Union cannoneers had pumped four shells into the position, causing its occupants to clear out. "We sent a few bullets after them, and considering discretion a cardinal virtue, I withdrew the troops and recrossed the river," declared acting major John Weller, the post's commander, "and this is what we called the battle of Oconee bridge."

A detachment from the 32nd Ohio followed behind the retreating Rebels. "We kept down the railroad till we got about half way to the river and seeing a blockade on the other side with a big gun peeping over, we filed off into the swamp and crept slyly down till we nearly reached the river, laid down, loaded our guns and rested a while," wrote one of the Federals. The Union soldiers set fire to the nearby trestlework, but otherwise remained under cover. As their division commander, Brigadier General Smith, reported, "the enemy could not be dislodged from the opposite side on account of the inaccessibility of the swamp."

Georgia governor Joseph Brown may have at times acted like a man obsessed, but he was no fool. When Major General Sherman entered Milledgeville about 10:00 A.M., he claimed the Executive Mansion for his headquarters, only to discover that the crafty politico had removed most of the "carpets, curtains, and furniture." Determined not to be outmaneuvered by a mere politician, Sherman had his field equipage carted indoors for his short sojourn in the capital city.

The General did a little sightseeing and a lot of decision making. One of these decisions proved how flexible he could be when applying his rules of war to cotton, which was burned indiscriminately during the march. In Milledgeville, however, Sherman spared much of what was there, allowing himself to be swayed by the most transparent stratagems. Major Hitchcock was instructed to draw up orders of protection, even though the General knew full well that the promises he received in return not to use the cotton to aid the Confederacy were worthless. He also decreed that the Georgia State House was not a legitimate object for destruction, much to Major Hitchcock's relief. "It would have been wrong and a blunder," he declared.

There were weightier matters demanding Sherman's attention. He had heard from Major General Howard, who had opted not to report in person, but instead sent a brief narrative of the Right Wing's progress through November 23. The news was basically good, as was that from Major General Slocum of the Left Wing. Nothing in the Confederate response so far required any modification in Sherman's original arrangements—he was still free to chart a course with no reference to outside influences.

The biggest question facing him was whether or not to mount a serious effort against Augusta. That the Confederates would actively defend the city he had no doubt. That he had sufficient military muscle to take it by storm he also had no doubt. What he didn't have was time. He would be landlocked before Augusta, and once he was held in a static siege, his logistical problems would rapidly intensify. So far his men had moved across a fertile and generally well drained region, plentifully supplied with farms and plantations. That would change once they entered the coastal lowlands, where swamps predominated and the number of well-stocked farmsteads diminished in dramatic fashion.

"Augusta [was not] of sufficient value to delay the great object an hour," Sherman later explained, "indeed, remaining in the hands of the enemy, it compelled him to guard it." He still intended to convince the Rebel authorities that he had serious designs in that direction, obliging them to scatter their strength to defend not only it, "but Millen, Savannah and Charleston." Characteristically, once he decided, Sherman quickly issued his Special Field Orders No. 127, specifying the routes to be followed in the next phase of the operation. As he later summarized them: "These were, substantially, for the right wing to follow the Savannah Railroad, by roads on its south; [and,] the left wing was to move to Sandersville, by Davisboro' and Louisville."

This directive also addressed some of the shortcomings Sherman had observed during the operation's initial phase. Too much of the railroad destruction had been haphazard. "Great attention," he declared, had to be given to thoroughly wrecking these lines, for "it is of vital importance to our cause." Not caring if he repeated himself, Sherman spelled out what needed to be done to accomplish this, and to allow more time for the soldiers to properly do the job, he reduced the daily marching distances from fifteen miles to ten.

His orders highlighted the increased danger to the supply trains in the days ahead by urging that any Confederate action against the wagons be met with prompt, harsh retaliation, declaring that "we should . . . punish him severely for the first attempt, as it will deter him from repeating it." Sherman additionally turned his critical gaze on the need to better control the foraging process ("more attention must be paid to this subject"), control excess wagons and unnecessary animals ("All . . . should now be destroyed"), and improve security for engineer and pioneer details whose road repairs would become increasingly important as the columns encountered the coastal swamps, and he took off the gloves for officers responding to any effort—military or civilian—to delay the march. His men were authorized to "deal harshly" with such individuals "to show them that it is to their interest not to impede our movements."

Sherman spent time with Brigadier General Kilpatrick, who was not the bearer of good news. Kilpatrick claimed that several of his men had been murdered by the Confederates after they had surrendered, so the hot-tempered officer sought permission to respond in kind. Sherman wasn't ready to go that far. He would monitor the situation, he said, and if circumstances warranted, retaliation would be sanctioned.

Sherman next gave Kilpatrick his instructions: "I want you to move right on, straight for Augusta. Strike the railroad at Waynesboro, between Millen and Augusta. Move well in toward the city, and at the same time send a force and, if possible, rescue our prisoners at Millen, but don't risk your command; don't give or receive battle unless under the most favorable circumstances. The Fourteenth Corps will follow in your track, while Howard will destroy the railroad from the Oconee [River] south to Millen. There is another railroad still further south; I wish we could reach that, and then all communication with Richmond and the west would be forever severed."

Kilpatrick left to bring his troopers through the Georgia capital and off on their new mission. Sherman's marching orders for the infantry made it clear that he had no intention of lingering long in Milledgeville—just about everyone would begin moving tomorrow, November 24.

Confederate major general Henry C. Wayne was gratified by the stubborn defense his mixed force of cadets, veterans, and convicts were mounting at the Oconee River Bridge, but his troubles were far from over. Even as the enemy was making a first move against the west-bank stockade, word arrived that another party of Federals had successfully forced a crossing to the south at Ball's Ferry. Wayne immediately organized a reaction force of cavalry, artillery, and infantry under the command of Major Alfred Hartridge, which he dispatched to the trouble spot.

It wasn't until well after dark that Wayne learned how well Hartridge had done. Reaching the threatened point at about 3:00 P.M., the major took up a defensive position blocking the only road out of Ball's Ferry, then set about gathering intelligence. When more than an hour passed without any aggressive movement by the enemy,* Hartridge decided to attack. "I advanced on the ferry," he later related, "and, after a fight of about one hour and a half, I forced the enemy to recross the river." One of Wayne's staff officers, who debriefed participants, wrote that the Yankees "became panic stricken and left the opposite side in a hurry, and our men crossed and picked up twenty-three cavalry guns, several overcoats and a number of knapsacks and other rigging and captured one man."

Wayne's losses thus far had been seven wounded and three killed at the railroad bridge, with another two dead and seven wounded at

---

* The size of this force was estimated by Wayne at two hundred, by Hartridge at four to five hundred, and reported to be at battalion strength by Major General Frank Blair, commanding the Seventeenth Corps.

Ball's Ferry.* Round one had gone to the Confederates, but Wayne knew there would be a round two. Now that the enemy leaders realized he was holding the line of the Oconee, they would come at him with everything they had. His situation report sent off to Savannah at 9:00 P.M. noted that even though the Yankees had been repulsed at Ball's Ferry, they retained possession of the flatboats used to cross there. He concluded his brief update: "Send me 5,000 [caliber] .54 cartridges."

This day ended with a bang for both the Right and Left wings. On the right, foragers prowling through Toomsboro "found about a half bushel of powder hid away, which the boys put a fuse to & fired it making the whole town shake," reported a bemused artilleryman. In Milledgeville, the government's evacuation had ignored the munitions stored in the state's arsenal and its magazine—both brick buildings located near the capital. The magazine was emptied of its contents, which were then unceremoniously dumped into the Oconee River, while the arsenal was set ablaze. "I heard a loud explosion," said a Wisconsin soldier, "and on going to the window, I saw the arsenal on fire, and soon it was wrapped in flames." Several churches, located around the same square as the arsenal, were damaged by the explosion.

THURSDAY, NOVEMBER 24, 1864

In Richmond, Virginia, news that Sherman had captured Milledgeville was changing from unsubstantiated rumor to likely probability. It was considered highly credible intelligence in the War Department, while a well-placed editorialist deemed it a "correct" opinion "in well-informed circles." Nobody, publicly at least, thought it amounted to much. "Milledgeville is a very small town of about twenty-five hundred inhabitants," announced the *Richmond Sentinel*. "Its only consequence is derived from its being the seat of Government." The *Richmond Examiner* was certain that the Yankee excesses were merely driving lukewarm Southerners back into the Confederate fold. "General Sher-

---

* There is no report of any Federal casualties for the day's engagement at the bridge, while there is an estimate of "10 or 12 killed and wounded" at the ferry crossing.

man is not conquering Georgia back into the Union," it proclaimed; "but many hitherto unbelieving Georgians by him [are] getting themselves baptized into the true Confederate faith."

Taking in the big picture, the writers for the *Richmond Whig*, noting that Macon had been bypassed and that Hood's army was left unchallenged to operate in the Union rear, decided "that SHERMAN'S march looks more like a retreat than an advance; more like a defensive than an aggressive movement." President Jefferson Davis wasn't quite as complacent. In a telegraph sent to Savannah he insisted that "every effort must be made to obstruct the route on which [Sherman] . . . is moving, and all other available means must be employed to delay his march, as well as to enable our forces to concentrate as to reduce him to want of the necessary supplies."

Delay was very much on the mind of Major General Oliver O. Howard, commanding the Right Wing, in receipt of Sherman's orders to get marching along the railroad toward Sandersville. It was becoming increasingly evident that the route following the railway was effectively barricaded at the Oconee River Bridge. Howard decided to flank the roadblock on both sides, sending Osterhaus (Fifteenth Corps) on a southern swing via Ball's Ferry, while Blair (Seventeenth Corps) would jog north to a crossing place shown on the Federal maps as Jackson's Ferry.

Meantime pressure would be maintained on the bridge itself, lest the enemy get wise to the other actions. Just to hedge his bets, the Right Wing commander sent his brother and aide, Lieutenant Colonel Charles H. Howard, to Sherman with the warning that he "might have to ask him to threaten the enemy from the north," if it proved impossible to get over the Oconee. By the end of the day Major General Howard had his aides packing up the headquarters preparatory to moving closer to the river.

On the Confederate side of the Oconee River Bridge, relations between Major General Wayne (Georgia state troops) and Major Hartridge (C.S. Provisional Army) continued to deteriorate. The tone had been set on November 23, when Hartridge had hectored Wayne into remaining here. Today, each kept the telegraph operator busy with messages to Savannah.

Wayne began by reporting his belief that he was facing Kilpatrick's cavalry division of "3,000 men," then wondered if he and his men would ever "get out of this pickle." When daylight arrived, the enemy began shelling his bridge defenses. Wayne reported the attack and requested 1,000 reinforcements. By day's end, the militia officer believed he now had "more than Kilpatrick's division in front of me," and he passed along disturbing intelligence suggesting that the enemy was in his rear.

Hartridge ridiculed Wayne's strength estimates, guessing that they were confronted by no "more than 800 men." "My men are in good spirits," he later asserted, "but I cannot depend much on the militia." The Confederate Army major's tone throughout was truculent, Wayne's more resigned. Then, at about 8:15 P.M., the enemy across the Oconee suddenly lashed at them with "heavy volleys of small arms." It wasn't an assault, however, but covering fire for a bold party that set fire "to the far end of the trestle on this side." After that things became ominously quiet.

Thus far in the campaign, Sherman's columns had been able to navigate the central Georgia road system with a good measure of success. Large-scale maps, prepared and distributed by Captain Poe at the beginning of the operation, provided a general orientation and direction. These charts were supplemented almost daily by scouting reports and tracings of regional guides taken from Georgia county courthouses and other governmental offices. This process had served the Union officers well, but the accuracy of the county maps was a function of local government, and sometimes they were out of date. Usually it was only a minor inconvenience, the matter of a few extra miles to be marched by a column. Today, however, Major General Howard found his entire operational plan thrown into disarray because of incorrect map information.

Howard had decided to bypass the Oconee River Bridge on either side, with the Seventeenth Corps swinging north to use a crossing identified as Jackson's Ferry. The problem, as he learned this day, was that Jackson's Ferry had not operated in a long time, and the road to it was in terrible shape. Men might make it, but not men with wagons.

The Fourth Division commander, Brigadier General Giles A. Smith, the first to recognize this setback, voiced his suspicions late on the afternoon of November 23. His immediate superior, Major General Frank Blair, refused to accept this negative assessment, citing "positive information from citizens" as his source. It took additional probes of the area before Blair finally agreed with Smith's reiterated declaration, sent at midday, that "there is no Jackson's Ferry, nor any practical crossing for ten or fifteen miles above" the Oconee River Bridge. The bad news took several more hours to work its way up the chain of command.

The vacuum at the top of the Confederate leadership ended on November 24. In Savannah, Lieutenant General William J. Hardee stepped off the train arriving from the south to once more take personal charge of affairs along the coast. As soon as he learned that President Davis was sending another brass heavyweight, General Braxton Bragg, to Augusta, Hardee opted to remain in Savannah to concentrate on its defense. Told of the fighting taking place at the Oconee River Bridge and Ball's Ferry, he determined to visit there at once.

Back to the west, the city of Macon was further heartened this morning by the arrival of General P. G. T. Beauregard. After descending from the train, he went into what he later termed "a long and important conference with Generals [Howell] Cobb and [Richard] Taylor." Based on the information in hand, Beauregard reasoned that Sherman was probably following "the most direct route to Port Royal[, South Carolina]." Like all his colleagues, Beauregard saw little profit in harrying the rear of Sherman's columns and so concentrated on putting all his available force in front. He approved Hardee's plan to transfer the Georgia militia then in Macon to the Atlantic coast, although this time they would move south and east, alternately marching and riding. Beauregard, also deciding that Lieutenant General Taylor could be more helpful to Hardee in Savannah, ordered him there.

Finally, the overall commander once more nudged the distant General Hood to do something: "Sherman's movement is progressing rapidly toward [the] Atlantic coast, doubtless to re-enforce Grant. It is essential you should take [the] offensive and crush the enemy's force in Middle Tennessee soon as practicable."

Another opportunity to seriously upset Sherman's timetable was playing out not forty miles to the east, at the Oconee River, but there is no evidence that anyone in authority recognized it as such. The influx of "pinch-hitting" generals necessitated by Beauregard's absence meant that there was no continuity of command, a problem exacerbated by first Hardee's and then Richard Taylor's self-limiting definition of their responsibilities. With each concentrating on Macon's defensive zone, neither felt compelled to act in the wider arena.

Hardee's abrupt departure created a void that put Wheeler on his own hook. The cavalry officer acted according to character by marching toward the guns; in this case, moving to place his force in front of Sherman's columns. This led his command off on a march twenty miles south of the Oconee River Bridge to a ford near Dublin. What might have been accomplished by assailing the rear of the Right Wing while its front was pressed against the river was not even a theoretical possibility, since the critical tool for such a plan—Wheeler's cavalry— was no longer on the scene.

This lack of focus on the part of the Confederate commanders in central Georgia was a boon to Sherman's operation; a factor he never considered in his planning, but which in many ways was key to his continuing success.

It was late afternoon before Major General Oliver O. Howard learned that there was no fordable crossing at Jackson's Ferry, or at any other spot within two days' march north of the Oconee River Bridge. That left Ball's Ferry to the south as the Right Wing's only option; it was to Howard's credit that he acted swiftly to reroute Blair's Seventeenth Corps there to join Osterhaus and the Fifteenth Corps. As Howard reported to Sherman, "I will be obliged to cross everything in the vicinity of Ball's Ferry." One problem though—the enemy held the east bank, and had been improving his defenses for twenty-four hours. The fate of the Right Wing of Sherman's grand movement now depended on finding a way across the Oconee River.

Tracking Sherman's movements was a constant challenge for Confederate authorities, but there were two organizations outside the military that were equipped and motivated to monitor the enemy's progress—the Georgia Railroad (running between Atlanta and Augusta) and the Central of Georgia Railroad (connecting Macon with Savannah). It was in their interests to know where the enemy was and his likely course, in order to assess damage and protect rolling stock by getting it out of harm's way. With an audacity that would be unthinkable in a later age, trains were kept running, as much to move passengers and cargo as to pinpoint the changing boundaries of the enemy's penetration. Information gleaned by the railroad agents and from passengers formed much of the intelligence that crackled along the telegraph network to distant centers like Richmond.

The November 24 issue of the *Augusta Daily Chronicle & Sentinel* carried a wealth of information from both railroads. According to "an intelligent gentleman who arrived last night by the passenger train up the Georgia [Rail]road," the paper's editors learned that the Federal Left Wing had turned south off the rail line at the Oconee River, that rumors of many Union troops in Greensboro were wildly exaggerated, and that the track remained open to Greensboro and Athens. "A gentleman who arrived last night from Savannah" supplied details from the Central of Georgia. He not only reported the fight at the Oconee River Bridge but confirmed the capture of Milledgeville.

The two Georgia railroads continued to observe and report on Sherman's progress, even as those actions were inexorably grinding up the tracks and infrastructure that represented the very lifeblood of those companies.

In his later years, Major General Oliver O. Howard would shake his head at the emerging story of Sherman's campaign as one unbroken lark. The Left Wing, under Slocum, he explained, "had enjoyed a fine march, having had but little resistance. The stories of the mock Legislature at the State capital, of the luxurious supplies enjoyed all along, and of the constant fun and pranks of 'Sherman's bummers,' rather belonged to that route than ours." Howard's case had merit this day as the Left Wing crossed the Oconee at Milledgeville to begin marching south and east, with only some bad stretches of road and poor traffic control to delay the movement.

The Yankee boys of the Twentieth Corps awoke to a "dense, penetrating fog" that was slow to burn off. "The roads are frozen and the air frosty," complained a New York soldier. The Third Division, which had been camped along the Oconee River's west bank, had to use a covered bridge, which provided much amusement. One soldier said that "a continuous medley of cheers and yells broke from the troops as they traversed the long passage while brigade followed brigade debouching from the exit and making away into the woods."

At this point in the operation the supply gathering system was operating with few hitches. "Each regiment had its detail for foraging, duly authorized and supplied with passes, two or three from each company, which would start off on roads to right and left of the road on which the reserve of the regiment and the teams were to move," explained a Connecticut soldier. "The boys would separate in parties of four or five upon each road, and visiting farm-houses would thoroughly ransack the place and get not only all the rations and forage which were needed but teams, horses, and mules to draw them to the road on which the main line of march was made, and there transferred to the regimental wagons and issued by proper authorities. . . . Besides the authorized foraging for general supplies, there was a great deal of individual foraging done." Recorded a Wisconsin diarist of this day's pickings: "We had pancakes and honey, potatoes and pork for supper."

By the time the tail end of the Third Division moved out, the narrow roads had been thoroughly churned by the two divisions moving ahead of it. This slowed the wagon train to a crawl, forcing the soldiers to keep pushing them along until well into the night to cover the assigned distance. This resulted in one of the more striking scenes of the march, as a long stretch of road was illuminated after sunset by parallel pyres of pine fence rails running along the shoulders of the lane. It was, recorded a Massachusetts soldier, "a grand scene; . . . two walls of fire . . . extending as far as the eye could reach, with here and there burning cotton gins and out buildings, and the heavens above, and all before, around and behind them, light as day with the flames of the burning pitch."

Behind the Twentieth came the Fourteenth Corps, two divisions moving on a parallel route several miles to the left, a third holding station in Milledgeville. Orders for the First and Second divisions to march came as an unpleasant surprise for some soldiers. When the members of the 17th New York "saw no signs of moving we commenced cooking Thanksgiving dinner," recollected one of them. "Just as we had it nearly started orders came to move, and as we could not carry a half-cooked dinner we had to throw it away."

Images of women ran like a red thread through the skein of today's events, from the mysterious, to rebellious, to forlorn. According to Brigadier General William P. Carlin, just as his division was marching over the Oconee River "a woman on horseback crossed at the same time with a pass from General Sherman, from which circumstances it was understood that she was a spy for him." For some of the units marching behind Carlin's division the women they encountered were subtly and unsubtly defiant. The ladies watching the Fourteenth Corps pass through Milledgeville "were quite numerous but they were very rebellious," reminisced an Ohio boy. "One of them covered her face as the stars and stripes were carry by." "In passing through Milledgeville a woman threw a large stone from a two story window at Pvt. John Cooper, Co. I, barely missing him," reported a member of the 104th Illinois, who was silent on the fate of the rock chucker. Another female gave vent to the tremendous strain of the past days. East of the capital, as a column including the 113th Ohio was passing a residence, "a soldier asked a woman if supper was ready," said a Buckeye. "She burst into tears and replied that she had not a morsel of food in the house."

The lucky members of the Third Division got to spend the day in Milledgeville. Even though all the Twentieth Corps and most of the Fourteenth had already left, these Yankees had no compunctions about taking anything they deemed "duly confiscated or contraband. As a result the city was pretty well ransacked and things torn up generally." Still, necessary military routine was not ignored, at least by an officer in the 2nd Minnesota who found himself drilling new recruits who, having joined the regiment at Atlanta, had been marching ever since. "The morning was quite frosty and handling the polished steel of our gun barrels with bare hands was cold business," he recollected. "Some of the men were gray men. One never had drilled before and some of them had only been on drill a few times."

A number of small foraging parties that ventured away from the town found the countryside spotted with roving bands of Confederates. One that tangled with about thirty Rebels had to call for help. "Two of our boys were wounded," noted an officer. "Their wounds will probably prove fatal. One half of the rebel squad were dressed in our overcoats." Other gunfire, this in town, denoted a tragic incident, recorded in the annals of the 75th Indiana: "A very unfortunate affair occurred here in the shooting of two negresses (half white) by a member of one of the Regiments of our Brigade, while standing upon the balcony of a house viewing our troops marching through the streets." The unfortunate individual who fired the shot was held at brigade headquarters until the incident was investigated. "Subsequently it was proven that the shooting was purely accidental, and the man was released."

Major General William Tecumseh Sherman led his headquarters out of Milledgeville at 10:00 A.M. Noting that it was Thanksgiving, Major Hitchcock offered a silent prayer: "God hasten the day when we shall all unite, North and South, East and West, in heartfelt thanksgiving for Peace and Victory over these accursed rebel leaders!" In one last piece of necessary business, Sherman called in Dr. R. J. Massey, who ran the city's biggest hospital, to inform him that he was now responsible for twenty-eight Union soldiers deemed too sick to travel. When Massey asked what Sherman wanted done with them, the General answered: "If they die, give them a decent burial; if they live, send them to Andersonville, of course." Catching the doctor's surprised look, Sherman added: "They are prisoners of war, what else can you do? If I had your men I would send them to prison."

After traveling from Atlanta to Milledgeville in the company of the Fourteenth Corps, Sherman now shifted over to the route of the Twentieth. Before long the command party began overtaking the tramping files. "General Sherman passed our column at 12 M., and was cheered heartily by all the troops," wrote a Pennsylvanian in the Second Division. A Wisconsin man from the First Division paid more attention to the moment. He wrote: "General Sherman rode along through the division, wearing his slouched, black hat, black cloak with high collar nearly hiding his face, looking neither to the right or left, buried in deep thought, unheeding the remarks of the men, who queried loud enough for him to hear, whether 'Uncle Billy knows where he is going?' "

"We are now in the regular pine region," Major Hitchcock observed, "dense growth of pines on all sides, save where cleared." The volunteer aide, who was taking part in his first military operation, got a bit of a fright when the staff suddenly came upon the spectacle of a division deploying across a field. "What, they are coming into line!" Sherman exclaimed. A closer examination showed that it was only a midday rest stop. "But for five minutes H.H. expected a fight 'then and there,' " Hitchcock commented, enjoying the joke on himself. "Knows now how the *expectation* feels."

Since they had outdistanced the headquarters baggage train, Sherman's aides found him a house for the night near the west bank of Gumm Creek.[*] The occupants, a woman of sixty-five and her unmarried daughter of thirty-five, were initially frightened, but Sherman calmed them. The older woman's story had a sad ring to it—husband dead, no boys in the war, the women opposed to it all. Even as they conversed inside with Sherman, practiced foragers swept the outside area clean. "Rascals *borrowed* all her pots and kettles, even tea-kettle," exclaimed Major Hitchcock. He got a chuckle when the older woman, learning that Sherman's surgeon was a bachelor, began to advertise her daughter's good points.

"If one stopped to think over all the losses or estimated all the real anxiety and suffering caused by the *simple march* of an army like this, it would be sad enough," Hitchcock reflected afterward. "But it's no use." He found himself recalling something Sherman had told him only the other day. Said Sherman: "Pierce the *shell* of the C.S.A. and it's all hollow inside."

---

[*]   Most contemporary accounts spell it "Gum."

PART THREE

Milledgeville to Millen

NOVEMBER 25–DECEMBER 4

CHAPTER 15

"We Went for Them on the Run"

FRIDAY, NOVEMBER 25, 1864

Four days earlier, while piecing together his defense of the Oconee River Bridge, Confederate major Alfred L. Hartridge realized that his right flank was vulnerable to an enemy force moving toward Sandersville from Milledgeville. To impede such a move, he sent his cavalry (the Ashley Dragoons) to wreck the bridges over Buffalo Creek, a natural choke point. Hartridge's men returned after carrying out their mission, leaving behind several outposts to watch and report. The importance of this slight action would exceed anything the major might have imagined.

Left Wing

Major General Henry W. Slocum's Left Wing continued its drive toward Sandersville—the Twentieth Corps now on the inside track, the Fourteenth running outside. Operating on a roughly parallel course well off the left flank of the Fourteenth was Kilpatrick's cavalry, on a mission without reference to the infantry routes. These troopers were up early, one of them long remembering how the bugles this day "rang out beautifully, clear as bells, first from Division head-quarters, quickly repeated at Brigade head-quarters, and quickly again at the head-quarters of the regiments, and still again at the headquarters of the

Milledgeville to Millen

DAY ELEVEN:
Friday, November 25, 1864

UNDER THE GUN
[LW] Hebron
[RW] Toomsboro

Weather: clear
mid-30s to mid-40s

companies, . . . and then the fires began to gleam everywhere, like the
gas-lights of a great city. . . . It was a beautiful day, and, with no enemy
in front or rear, the command marched rapidly."

The infantrymen were also stirring. "Morning cold but not so bad as
the last four nights," groused a member of the 102nd Illinois. As the
two long columns began twisting their way eastward, the tail end of
the Fourteenth Corps pulled out of Milledgeville to follow its compatriots. Bands were playing despite the early hour, leading one Ohio boy
to reflect that its citizens "doubtless breathe a sigh of relief as they witness our departure." There was some unfinished business as the state
magazine, emptied of its contents, was dynamited. Another Ohio soldier, in the process of crossing the Oconee, recalled hearing "two
explosions." "Blew up the powder house and burned the bridge across
the Oconee," added a Minnesota soldier, whose memoir highlighted a
final act that many in the capital would later find the most reprehen-
sible of Sherman's brief stopover.

Among those watching the Yankees leave was Anna Maria Green, whose father was superintendent of the Georgia Lunatic Asylum. Hardly had the last Federal soldier disappeared into the woods across the river when the cry went up, "Our cavalry is coming." A few mounted men brandishing pistols entered the town, announcing themselves as part of Wheeler's cavalry. Miss Green was one of those whose anger at enduring the enemy occupation was transformed into a fierce Confederate patriotism. "How can they hope to subjugate the South!" she exclaimed to her diary. "The people are firmer than ever before." Green also recorded the name of the only victim of rape mentioned by name in the annals of Sherman's march—a certain "Mrs. N." "Poor woman," commented Green. "I fear she has been driven crazy."*

The Confederate troopers belonged to Brigadier General Samuel W. Ferguson's brigade of Iverson's division in Wheeler's command. They didn't cut an especially martial figure. One Milledgeville resident described them as "mere boys," while another thought they were "very ragged and for the most part . . . bare footed." Still, they were Confederates after all and welcomed as such. Brigadier General Ferguson was pleasantly surprised to witness how the "women ran out [of their houses] and knelt on the side walks, with hands joined in prayer, and tears streaming down their cheeks, and . . . these were tears of joy." The troopers quickly checked the town, then congregated at the river's edge to stare at the wrecked bridge. Ferguson needed to know where the Yankees had gone, so at his orders, a party of scouts swam their horses across the rain-swollen Oconee to chase after them.

Next the Rebel troopers got down to the business of supplying their needs. A local boy named Willie, mounted on a mule left behind by the Federals atop a nice McClellan saddle he had been given, was asked by a trooper to dismount so he could better admire the boy's fine animal. Hardly had Willie slid off his mule before the trooper climbed on and, according to a witness, "told him he had [just] swapped mounts." A property owner just outside the town would later complain to Governor Brown about the "plundering band of horse stealing

---

* Other sources identify the victim as Mrs. Kate Nichols, said to have been raped by two Federal soldiers. One or two other such accusations are so vague as to be unverifiable.

ruffians" who had cleaned him out. Given the choice of occupation forces, the citizen would much "prefer to trust to the generosity and justice of the Yankees."

General Sherman and his staff were in the saddle early. Per his orders, their unwilling host was rewarded with $50 in Confederate notes, to which one officer added $5 in U.S. bills. Major Hitchcock got in the last word during a parting exchange with the young lady of the house, who reproached him for waging war on hapless women. When the good major got her to admit that she would have shamed any man who didn't enlist in the Confederate cause, he had her. "Then you have done all you could to help the war," he announced as he departed, "and have not done what you could to prevent it."

The command party had ridden perhaps ninety minutes when a rider came from ahead, seeking Captain Poe. There was a problem at Buffalo Creek, where the chief engineer's skills were sorely needed. From the outrider Major Hitchcock learned that the bridge or bridges over the creek had been burned. Already the leading elements were grinding to a halt, while behind them, the other segments of the Twentieth Corps were slowing to a crawl.

The road that the corps was following led through the village of Hebron. An Illinois soldier mentioned that it consisted of "a few houses on each side [of the road] numbering altogether about six is all that can be seen of a town and all there ever was." To this a New Jersey quartermaster contributed that Hebron had "the usual amount of negro huts and corn cribs." He also remarked on the number of "very well made cotton gins and presses blazing away, to the right and left of us."

About three miles east of Hebron, Captain Poe reined his horse in before Buffalo Creek to assess the problem. "This Creek of itself is not to exceed thirty feet wide but the crossing is at a point where it overflows a space of 60 or 70 acres making it necessary for a bridge nearly a quarter of a mile in length," wrote a later-arriving telegrapher. Actually, the puzzle confronting Poe was more complicated than building a single bridge. "The stream or swamp is here divided into eight channels, which are spanned by as many bridges, varying in length from 30 to 100 feet each," wrote another officer. "Between these earthen causeways are thrown up."

Poe's assessment told the tale. The eighty-foot main bridge, which spanned the central creek channel, was burned beyond repair. The damage to much of the approach bridging was less severe; in most cases, while the planking was gone, the supporting trestles were only partially damaged. The corduroy ramps leading over the fringing swamps had been thoroughly trashed, but were also the easiest to repair. Fortunately, Poe had with him Lieutenant Colonel Joseph Moore plus his section of the 58th Indiana pontoon train, as well as all the willing hands he could muster from nearby regiments.

Security was not a concern thanks to the prompt action of the first unit on the scene. Lieutenant Colonel John B. Le Sage of the 101st Illinois had pushed a detachment to the creek's east bank, where they chased away a few Rebel videttes. More trouble occurred around noon when several Southern mounted bands threatened the lodgment, but Le Sage's reinforced perimeter held firm. There just weren't enough Confederates in the area to cause a serious problem.

Captain Poe kept his unskilled workers busy stabilizing the approach ramps. "The first thing to do was to get logs and rails to throw onto that mud to make it possible for the engineers to get their [pontoon] boats and other material to the river bank," recollected one of those conscripted foot soldiers. The pontoniers started repairing the secondary trestle bridges "using timber procured from the woods" and laying down planking using balk and chess from their pontoon kits. Once a clear pathway to the central channel was established, three pontoon boats were deployed to stretch the eighty-foot gap. Then the process was repeated on the opposite side.

The men worked in a well-organized fashion; nevertheless, there was a delay of four and a half hours that stacked troops up all the way back to Gumm Creek. "People are silly in destroying those bridges for we generally tear down the nearest house to build them again, and the longer we carry on our march the more time we have to prey on the miscreants," declared a New Jersey officer. They made the most of the delay in the 29th Ohio. "While waiting here the boys amused themselves in various ways," wrote a regimental diarist, "some by playing cards, others by betting largely at the 'chuck luck' board, while others would get several 'Darkies' of both sexes to 'patting' and dancing, we have enough of them in our Regiment to get up quite a 'Cotillion.' "

Major General Sherman passed the time waiting with his staff in a deserted house west of the creek, listening to two of his officers—Major Hitchcock and Colonel Charles Ewing—debate whether or not they should torch the structure when they depart. The pair were unaware that their boss was listening until he broke into their conversation.

"In war everything is right which prevents anything," Sherman announced. "If bridges are burned I have a right to burn all houses near it."

Hitchcock, feeling argumentative, countered that there had to be a link between the home owner and the bridge burners to justify such a course, but Sherman was having none of it. "Well, let him look to his own people," he shrugged, "if they find that their burning bridges only destroys their own citizens' houses they'll stop it."

Ten miles north from where Sherman's officers were debating the finer points of military ethics, Kilpatrick's mounted column was also approaching Buffalo Creek, albeit the stream's more shallow upper reaches. "Long Bridge, over Buffalo Creek," according to a reporter traveling with the cavalry officer, "was found destroyed, but by cutting down the bank we crossed by fording." Kilpatrick's men would be delayed hardly at all.

In between the cavalry and the Twentieth Corps marched the Fourteenth. Just about the time— 2:00 P.M.—that Captain Poe declared the Buffalo Creek bridges open for Twentieth Corps business, the engineers with the Fourteenth Corps were coming to terms with their crossing challenge. Here the main channel had been spanned by a fifty-foot bridge (burned) approached via trestles (wrecked) running over a stretch of swamp. The 1st Michigan Engineers and Mechanics got the job of fixing the trestles and corduroying the banks, while the second section of the 58th Indiana tackled the bridge itself. Here the work would last nearly seven hours.[*]

Considering the complexity of the task completed under Captain Poe's direction, the four-and-a-half-hour delay for the Twentieth Corps ranked as a solid engineering achievement, causing but a minor inconvenience for the infantry column. It did save Sandersville from being occupied for another twelve hours since it allowed time for scouting

---

[*] Brevet Major General Davis had a bad habit of staging his pontoon trains well back in his columns. While this enabled his forward elements to make good time, it also took longer to bring the pontoons forward when needed.

detachments from Major General Wheeler's command to establish a loose screen three and a half miles west of the town.

Wheeler had pushed hard toward Augusta after crossing the Oconee near Dublin. He paused with most of his riders at Tennille, where he conferred with Lieutenant General Hardee, but not before sending scouts ahead to Sandersville. This force pounced on groups of mounted outriders, who proved to be foragers eager to be the first into the town. Wheeler's men promptly attacked, driving the Federals back to their infantry columns, then about three or four miles east of Buffalo Creek.

The infantry was alert for trouble, with skirmishers well forward, and even as their fire brought Wheeler's troopers to a halt, heavier lines of battle scissored out, perpendicular to either side of the road. Once these had been aligned and steadied, a stronger line of skirmishers pushed ahead. Among them was John Smethurst of the 31st Wisconsin.

"We went double quick through the bush and briers, over fences with our knapsacks on," he recollected. "It was a good deal like work. We found the Rebels about a mile from the Brigade in line in a strip of woods. We had to advance on them over a large open field. They kept up a steady fire on us but did very poor shooting for not a man of us was hurt. Although the balls came rather close we did not get orders to fire until we were within two hundred yards of them. We could see them plain standing by their horses firing at us. At last the order came to fire. We gave them two or three volleys and then went for them on the run yelling like fury. They could not stay with us any longer so they mounted and left."

Sherman wished the Twentieth Corps to reach Sandersville this day, but the delays at the burned bridges, compounded by the late-afternoon scrap, meant that for the first time his schedule had been upset by enemy action rather than natural obstacles. Major Hitchcock recognized that something had changed in the overall military equation. "From this on we shall be impeded and harassed and have skirmishing every day," he silently prophesied.

While the foragers up front had gotten their noses bloodied, those operating to the sides and rear of the Twentieth Corps did quite well. "Forage plenty and men and animals faring sumptuously," crowed an Indiana soldier. "We are now in 'Peanut land' and we not only had them by the peck but by the bushels." "Among the variety of plunder which the boys have found at the farm houses in this vicinity were gamecocks, which have been brought into camp and distributed in great abundance," contributed a Connecticut man, "and there is a cock fight at the cook's fire in almost every company this evening."

Now that the Fourteenth Corps held the extreme left flank of Sherman's movement, its foragers were more exposed to armed bands operating just a short distance from the main road. "The rebel bush-whackers shot several foragers to-day," noted a record keeper in the 34th Illinois. "The foragers from the Brigade were attacked by about 100 rebel cavalry and driven back," observed a member of the 104th Illinois, "leaving 8 or 10 men wounded or missing." Yet, somehow, the determined Yankees managed to cope. "We get meat fresh and salt, Sorghum, Honey, Sweet Potatoes, and meal," proclaimed a Michigan man. "The camp is full of provisions." When a picket for the 86th Illinois was taken to task for killing a hog while on duty, he contested the charge. "The d——d old rebel wouldn't give the countersign," he protested to his captain. "So we . . . brought him down."

Incidents with children dominated this day's record of soldier-civilian encounters, some of them heart-wrenching. One Michigan forager encountered a "little girl [who] said she wanted a postage stamp to send her co[u]sin a letter. He was a prisoner." Two black children were brought to a brigade headquarters, as their mother "had left them and gone," no one knew where. An Illinois soldier visited a nearby house, where he found a woman with several youngsters, one of whom "kept up a continual crying for something to eat." The Yankee did what he could, even though he "had but one hard cracker to give them."

Sherman and his staff had their own close encounter with the locals. After crossing Buffalo Creek and waiting for the skirmish to end, they stopped at a house whose matron whined so much that Sherman chose to tent in the field this night. Not long after the camp had been set up, the General enjoyed a serenade from a regimental band. The only intrusion of work occurred when the aide sent by Major General Howard, his brother Charles, appeared to update Sherman on the Right Wing's progress.

Well to the north and east of this tranquil scene, Kilpatrick's column reached the Ogeechee River at a point known as the Ogeechee Shoals. Scouts from the 2nd Kentucky Cavalry surprised a Rebel picket posted at the crossing, capturing most of them, including a dozen horses, which were welcome as many of Kilpatrick's were jaded and sore. It had been an uncharacteristically quiet day for the troopers, who, encountering few of the enemy, had enjoyed good foraging. However, once at the shoals there was work to be done. "Here we destroyed a large cotton factory, mill and other buildings," wrote a member of the 9th Pennsylvania Cavalry. In the house being used as operational headquarters, Kilpatrick allowed a member of his staff to scrawl a sentiment on the wall. The graffiti read: "May all the names engraved here / in the golden book appear." Kilpatrick signed it, as did members of his staff.

As the Left Wing infantry settled in for the night, full security was implemented. "The 1st and 3rd Divisions camp in line of battle semi-circle," wrote a gunner in the Twentieth Corps. Officers were admonished "to have your picketing most thoroughly and carefully performed—pickets thrown well out." One of those pickets was an Ohio private named John W. Houtz, who did his duty while he kept his diary up-to-date. "I got on a post by a swamp and a cold chilly place it is these frosty evenings," he scribbled, adding that he "heard cannonading on our right [which] appears to be on the railroad."

This morning saw two of Jefferson Davis's key generals positioned on the front line against Sherman. In Augusta, General Braxton Bragg took charge of the city's defenses. Bragg was damaged goods. Once the great hope for Confederate aspirations in Kentucky and Tennessee, he delivered a major victory at Chickamauga, only to lose all the laurels and his command two months later when he was routed outside Chattanooga. His abrasive character created more fissures than bonds among western theater commanders, and only the president's reluctance to retire West Point professionals kept Bragg on the active list. For a while the general served as the president's military adviser, but when trouble loomed on the North Carolina coast in October 1864, Davis sent Bragg there. Now the president wanted his experience in Augusta.

The threat posed by Sherman's army loomed large enough in Davis's calculations that he broke his own rule by allowing Bragg to bring with him some regular Confederate States units assigned to defend the

North Carolina coast near Cape Fear. He also suspended a law restricting the use of militia reserves to their own states, so that there would be nothing to hinder South Carolina units from coming into Georgia or vice versa. Bragg himself had recently pointed out to South Carolina's governor that the two states were joined at the hip. "If Georgia is saved South Carolina cannot be lost," he informed the politician. "If Georgia be lost South Carolina cannot be saved."

Protective earthwork construction was accelerated, using a labor force made up of impressed slaves and Union prisoners who had volunteered to receive better treatment. At least one resident was less than thrilled with the galvanized Confederates, whom he described as "a great nuisance in this neighborhood. They steal, visit negro quarters and tamper with slaves, & in one instance committed robbery." The city's largest circulation newspaper did its part to boost morale with an editorial exhorting all citizens, "Now is the time, if ever, to defend their homes, their families and their all against future invasions and devastation."

Another town paper reported that the all-important Confederate Powder Works had been dismantled and relocated out of danger. Incredibly, especially for anyone who chanced by the massive twenty-six-building complex stretching for two miles along the Augusta Canal, the story was true. With Sherman's threat looming, the man responsible for operating the complex—Colonel George Washington Rains—had ordered the facility's critical machinery, supplies, and inventory packed onto trains for shipment to a safer location. Even with the Confederacy's transportation resources stretched to the limit, the importance of the powder works was such that its relocation was given the highest priority.

Bragg at once set to work examining scouting reports and poring over maps. His initial assessment was that while one enemy wing was being blocked by Wayne at the Oconee, the other had crossed the river at Milledgeville and "seems to be tending south." Later in the day, when news of Sherman's crossing at Buffalo Creek was confirmed and he learned of the clash outside Sandersville, Bragg recognized that Federal movements on November 26 "will determine whether he designs attacking here or on Savannah."

Savannah's chief defender, Lieutenant General William J. Hardee, arrived at Tennille Station on the Central of Georgia Railroad around

1:00 A.M. Here, also known as Station No. 13, the general was little more than three miles south of Sandersville and a dozen from the Oconee River Bridge. Morning reports suggested that Confederate forces were holding their own; enemy columns were still being blocked by Major General Wayne before and below the railroad bridge, while the destruction of the Buffalo Creek crossings promised to delay if not halt enemy movements in that quarter. Hardee ordered up munitions and rations from Savannah, though he prudently had them cached at Davisboro (thirteen miles east) and Millen (even farther toward the coast). Although this is not explicit in the official records, Hardee seems to have convinced Major General Wayne to pay more attention to the fighting at Ball's Ferry, since, at 11:00 A.M., the increasingly stressed militia officer dispatched reinforcements there.

Having made his moves, Hardee now waited to see what the enemy would do next.

Right Wing

Throughout the day the Fifteenth and Seventeenth corps concentrated at Ball's Ferry. The Federals were learning that the profusion of pine forests throughout the region represented a very mixed blessing. In a long entry for this day's events, a garrulous Illinois soldier wrote that a "thick haze of black pine smoke" settled like a fog over the morning encampments, producing a "somber film that envelops the skin," so darkening everyone's complexions that "you could scarcely distinguish them from the dusky African." Soap now headed the want lists as a "very necessary article of forage."

"Countermarched at 4 A.M.," scrawled a weary Seventeenth Corps soldier. "Long and tedious march." Per Major General Howard's orders, Major General Blair's men were disengaging from the railroad bridge and looping around toward Ball's Ferry. This brought them onto the routes already being used by the Fifteenth Corps, which had gotten there first. As a consequence, recorded a brigadier under Blair, his men "had to cut two roads [through the woods], one for wheels, one for men, much of the way had to be corduroyed in swamp." The snaky route followed by the Seventeenth Corps brought it alongside a stretch of Central of Georgia Railroad tracks which hadn't yet been touched.

That wouldn't do, so, reported one infantryman, they "had to tare up Rail road in the evening." About four miles of track were wrecked in this manner.

Getting his troops across the Oconee at Ball's Ferry looked impossible to Major General Peter J. Osterhaus. The terrain was so unforgiving that he could only squeeze forward two regiments—the 57th Ohio and 116th Illinois—and those in a widely dispersed skirmishing formation. They at once engaged the enemy forces dug in on the opposite bank, who replied with an impressive volume of musket and cannon fire. It would cost a lot of lives, and even then Osterhaus wasn't certain he could force his way across in the face of such determined opposition.

The worried officer made his way back toward Major General Howard's headquarters to deliver the bad news. Spotting the Right Wing commander dismounted by the side of the road, writing dispatches, Osterhaus rode over. Without getting off his horse, he blurted out: "General Howard, how can we get any further?" Snapping back that this "was no way to talk," Howard motioned him down. Listening to his subordinate's assessment, the Right Wing commander realized that Osterhaus had a case of tunnel vision. Everything was focused on crossing at Ball's Ferry, forgetting that there were other uses for all the men lined up behind those skirmishing along the river. The trick was to utilize that strength to locate the enemy's weak points, not to try to bull through a strong point.

Howard explained that he wanted Osterhaus to use his numerical superiority to "extend his skirmish line north and south, pressing them in, till they could get sight of the other bank or clearing beyond the river." It was really very simple. "Deploy your skirmishers more and more till there is no reply," said Howard, certain that somewhere they would run out of Confederates. The Prussian officer hurried off to carry out the task. Howard would later state, without equivocation, that the "Oconee crossing was the most difficult that we had to encounter."*

A few miles west of Howard's headquarters, the villagers of Irwinton were finding out what it meant to be in the path of Sherman's

---

* Howard did make one defensive move in response to unconfirmed reports of Rebel cavalry south of him. He had a detachment sent off to burn a key bridge over Big Sandy Creek to forestall any surprises from that direction.

storm. A member of the 81st Ohio recalled their "burning the Court House and other public buildings, and also a lot of cotton." A soldier in the 12th Illinois described the town as "mostly burned," while one in the 50th Illinois proclaimed it "now in ruins." However, what the Federals could take they could also give back. Early in the evening a shanty fire spread to an adjoining two-story residence, prompting nearby Union soldiers to save it. "We . . . carried out the goods and then knocked the siding off the porch and got the fire out," recorded an Illinoisan. "We then carried back the goods. There was an old man and young lady and child living in the house."

It was late in the afternoon when Osterhaus reported to Howard that his constantly extending skirmish line had finally outstretched the Confederate defensive zone at a point two miles north of the ferry. Said Howard: "I then instructed him to send in a brigade with the canvas [pontoon] boats, already put together, and push over the men rapidly into the clearings beyond, then come down the river and take the enemy in the flank." It turned out that the critical site was closer to the camps of the just arriving Seventeenth Corps, so Major General Blair's men got the assignment.

Pontoniers from the 1st Missouri Engineers with about thirty infantrymen led by Lieutenant Colonel Kirby of Blair's staff made their way to the river's edge, where they learned why the Rebels had not bothered to post a guard. The Oconee narrowed noticeably here into a stretch of rapid-flowing white water, making a pontoon bridge difficult, if not impossible. Finally, one of the Missouri engineers plunged into the swift rapids with a rope tied to his waist. He managed to secure his end to a stout tree on the other bank.

Using this as a guideline, a "flying ferry" was set up to hand-haul across an officer with thirty men. They established a security perimeter that provided cover while the engineers transported an additional 170 soldiers. This armed party then began picking its way through the swamp in the gathering darkness toward the Ball's Ferry road, hoping to trap the stubborn Confederates against the river.

Although unopposed, the Federal crossing of the Oconee was not unnoticed. Even as he was considering a request from the officer commanding at Ball's Ferry for ammunition and reinforcements, Major General Henry C. Wayne learned that the enemy had secured a lodgment on the east bank. He reported this to Lieutenant General Hardee at Tennille, who was also mulling over reports from Wheeler's scouts that placed an enemy column near Sandersville. It was clear that the defensive scheme holding the Federals back along the Oconee had been compromised, leaving nothing to do but preserve the fighting forces. Hardee allowed Major General Wayne to withdraw the Ball's Ferry defenders while instructing Major General Wheeler to reinforce his advance party at Sandersville to buy time for Wayne's men to clear the area. He then ordered his headquarters relocated eastward to Millen. "I think," Hardee concluded by late afternoon, "that the enemy is moving on Savannah."

Before nightfall the scouts Brigadier General Ferguson had sent off from Milledgeville returned with information about the Yankee movements as well as a straggler they had captured. The officer was unimpressed with the specimen of Yankeehood, who had been caught with "a ladies handsome opera cloak, opera glass and other plunder in his possession." The cavalry officer made his disgust known and turned the prisoner over to a trooper, who promised to take care of the matter. Ferguson had rafts to build, and paid no attention when he heard a shot not long after dismissing the guard and his prisoner. The next morning, seeing a crowd standing at the riverside, he asked the reason and was told they were staring at a dead enemy soldier. With a sudden chill, Ferguson knew whose body it was.

CHAPTER 16

"Poor Foolish Simpletons"

SATURDAY, NOVEMBER 26, 1864

A bout an hour after midnight, the Confederates holding the line at Ball's Ferry and the Oconee River Bridge began pulling back toward Station No. 13 (Tennille) on the Central of Georgia Railroad. When the first elements arrived there at 5:30 A.M., they received new orders to continue westward as far as Station No. 10 (Sebastopol). It would take several more hours for all the troops that had been holding the Oconee River line to complete their withdrawal through Tennille, which was itself under threat from a Yankee force descending on it from the north.

Before departing for Millen, Lieutenant General William J. Hardee, now fully in his Savannah-defense mode, sent Wheeler's cavalry to delay the enemy outside Sandersville. Once again, in the absence of any comprehensive strategic plan, senior Confederate officers were acting to protect their own areas of specific responsibilities. Hardee's overriding concern at this moment was to preserve military assets to augment Savannah's pitifully small garrison, then estimated at "less than 1,000 men of all arms." He was virtually certain that Sherman was going to bypass Augusta in favor of Savannah, but he still released Wheeler's mobile force to assist in defending the northeastern city and arsenal, based on a strategic analysis several days old. General Beauregard, whose job it was to choreograph the military pieces to maximize their impact, was isolated in Macon and unfamiliar with affairs west of

Milledgeville to Millen

DAY TWELVE:
Saturday, November 26, 1864

UNDER THE GUN
[LW] Sandersville/Tennille
[RW] Irwins Crossroads

South
Carolina

Augusta

Shoals

Sylvan
Grove

Hayes

Milledgeville

Waynesboro

Alexander
Thomas

Louisville

Sandersville   Davisboro

Hebron

Tennille
Riddleville

Spier's
Turnout

Lumpkins

Buckhead
Church

Camp
Lawton

Gordon

Irwins
Crossroads

Sebastopol

Birdsville

Irwinton   Toomsboro

Ball's
Ferry

Wrightsville

Kite

Midville
(Burton)

Summertown

Millen

Scarboro

Weather:
cloudy
mid-30s to upper 40s.

Dublin

Swainsboro

Statesboro

the Oconee River. His principal activity this day was to harangue General Hood (via telegraph) to help him identify someone to better manage Wheeler's cavalry.

The cavalry leader, who warned Sandersville's residents on November 25 "to send off all movable property of value," now reached the threatened place. A little girl who saw him remembered the officer as "a very small, very erect man, dressed in grey, wearing a crimson sash and a large black plumed hat." "There was not an adult male citizen to be seen," recorded a trooper in the general's escort, "but the terror-stricken women swarmed in the street around Wheeler, crying and begging him to leave the town and not bring on a fight there. One woman swung to his horse's neck, begging him not to fight." Orders to buy time overrode any humanitarian concerns, so Wheeler ignored the protestations and prepared to resist the enemy's advance.

Left Wing

Afterward, when the fighting was over, a Yankee wit cracked that *Sander*sville "was well named, for it was the only place thus far that gave indications of having any 'grit.' " The jaws of the Left Wing closed on the Georgia town with conviction. From the west the Twentieth Corps pressed in, while the Fourteenth closed from the north. Both were expecting trouble. Mounted Infantry of the 9th Illinois screened the Twentieth Corps, making first contact with Wheeler's troopers. The Rebels, who had blocked the road with felled trees, were fighting dismounted from behind cover along a creek bed. At least one Illinoisan was killed in this initial encounter. Hustling up behind the mounted infantry was the 13th New Jersey, leading the way for Colonel Ezra A. Carmen's brigade. Three companies fanned out in skirmishing formation, "and with shouts and yells," swarmed forward. "Presently, the pop-pop-pop of carbines was heard," reported an anxious soldier in the column. "Then a volley of musketry told that the cavalry were not doing all the shooting." Men weren't the only creatures keyed up by the action; as the New Jerseymen pressed back the dismounted Confederates, "the sound of horses neighing was perfectly audible." An impromptu Yankee squadron formed of "all the mounted officers of the corps" swooped in to assist the foot soldiers.

To the north, Colonel Robert F. Smith, commanding the First Brigade, Second Division, Fourteenth Corps, had the good sense to lead the way with foraging parties drawn from two regiments—the 16th Illinois and 17th New York—closely succored by their reserves. Once these detachments tripped the enemy's outpost line, they fell back a short distance to their supports before the combined force then surged ahead. More men were fed into the advance from the 113th Ohio; it was, according to a Buckeye, "warm work."

Major General Sherman kept position just behind the Twentieth Corps skirmishers. "I myself saw the rebel cavalry apply fire to stacks of fodder standing in the fields at Sandersville," he later attested. Major Hitchcock, riding at Sherman's side, termed this morning's affair "not a battle,—only skirmish firing, but that pretty rapid and constant for twenty or thirty minutes." Pure serendipity coordinated the converging attacks of the two Left Wing corps, forcefully shoving the thin Rebel line back on its heels.

The crescendo of firing brought some Sandersville residents to windows or onto porches in curiosity and consternation. Two white women and several female slaves huddled in a town building. One of the whites, who for a long time was known only as "L.F.J.," was spotted at her window by a passing Confederate cavalryman who rushed into the house. "For God's sake, ladies, go into your cellar!" he cried. "Don't you know those bullets will kill you?" The curious young lady, a recent war widow and mother, suddenly realized her danger. "We have no cellar," she told the trooper.

"Then take that poor baby, and put him on a pillow in some of the back room chimneys, and you ladies stay there," he responded. "We are fighting Sherman's whole army, and we've got to run, and that fast. We thought we were fighting a skirmishing party, but its the whole army."

As he turned to go, the young widow begged him to stay with them. "I would gladly do so if I could help you, but I'd only be captured," he answered. "Lock your doors; stay in the house; if the soldiers try to come in speak politely to them, and ask for a guard. I don't think the Yankees will harm you. Good-bye." He paused at the door. "God bless you ladies!" he called out. "To run is the hardest thing I ever did."

Run he did, as files of Northern infantry entered Sandersville. "There was a wild chase through the town, our skirmishers broke down the fences & rushed through the back yards & streets in line of battle," wrote a New Jersey soldier. "The Reb. Cavalry galloped ahead for dear life. Of course the women & children were frightened entirely out of their wits & increased the confusion by their screams." According to a Massachusetts soldier the "women were in great trepidation, wringing their hands saying, 'The Yanks are coming, the Yanks are coming.'" Giving way to temptation, "L.F.J." peeked through a window. "Looking out, I screamed in terror," she related. "It seemed as if the whole world was coming down upon us."[*]

Elements of the Twentieth and Fourteenth corps passed the town limits at about the same time, with a slight edge to Brigadier General

---

[*]   Casualties for this action were not comprehensively reported. Federal losses can be pegged at two killed and a half dozen wounded, while Wheeler's Confederates suffered at least three dead and an unknown number injured.

Alpheus S. Williams's troops. Hardly had the last shot died out before Sherman, followed by his staff, entered Sandersville. "Saw the 20th [Corps] coming in on a road to our right," recollected an Ohio soldier in the Fourteenth Corps, "and pretty soon Old Billy Sherman came riding down the street with a whole cigar stuck in his mouth, supposed to be the same one he took Atlanta with, as he never lights one." The General's party rode through the town square "and went to [a] large brick house set back in [a] yard, with [a] large garden in front and on both sides," reported Major Hitchcock.

The aide received an instant lesson in Yankee resourcefulness as he helplessly rattled the locked front door, only to have it opened a moment later from the inside by a Union soldier who had broken in through the rear. The owner, a Southern matron, appeared in the hall demanding that Sherman protect the house because he was a Catholic like her.* "Madam, it's a pity the Catholics in the South have not acted so as to protect themselves," Major Hitchcock huffed. Sherman's orders directed the Twentieth Corps to pass around Sandersville toward Tennille, while the Fourteenth was to camp in the town itself.

Some of those taking the bypass marched as far as the Central of Georgia Railroad tracks, which only a short time earlier had carried Confederate fighters west to safety. "We immediately commenced repairing the RR," commented a Wisconsin soldier with what now passed for standard humor. This stretch of the line also employed the cheaper strap iron with the metal pads spiked to long pine stringers. The tracks were pried, piled, burned, and bent, "and that in very quick time too," the soldier reported, "for it didn't take quite as long for an army to spoil a road as it does to build one." Even this noncombat activity was not without risks. A soldier in the 31st Wisconsin was reported fatally injured when a pile of railroad ties fell on him, breaking his back.

Other Federals who missed their chance to pick through Sandersville did quite well in its environs. "This evening we got chickens, pork, yams & molasses," recorded a satisfied Minnesotan in the ranks. While a few groups of foragers did scrap with bands of Confederate cavalry roving the periphery of the Federal occupation, others had social rather than military quandaries. A New York soldier, who had just decapi-

---

* Actually, it was Sherman's wife, Ellen, who was a Catholic. The General himself, raised an Episcopalian, lived by a personal code that was secular and deist.

tated a chicken with his hatchet, knocked on the back door of the farmhouse in search of some water to wash his hands without thinking about the implications of his act.

When the door was opened, he found himself facing a group of women "transfixed with terror at the sight of my blood-smeared face and hatchet." Remembering his upbringing, the Federal politely asked for a basin of water, which was brought out to him by one of the younger women in the group. Now suffering from acute embarrassment for intruding into their lives, the Yankee boy mumbled thanks, and as he hurriedly cleaned up he lamely explained that the lack of army rations forced the soldiers to live off the land. That broke the ice somewhat, so for the next few minutes the Northern boy and the Southern girl engaged in empty small talk, as if they were chatting at a garden party. Then the soldier, finishing his ablutions, turned to go. He briefly considered leaving the bird for the women to eat but then thought "it would probably be my last opportunity for the day to get food, and—hunger got the upper hand of sentiment, and the fowl went with me."

Wheeler's holding action outside Sandersville, which successfully helped facilitate the escape of Confederate forces to the south, was misread by Sherman as being without purpose. This offense was compounded when the fast-moving combat spilled into the town itself, where several civilian buildings were used for cover by the withdrawing Confederates. Also annoying to him was the destruction of useful supplies by the retreating Rebel cavalry. Several of Sherman's rules of war had been broken, a fact that made the General, in Major Hitchcock's words, "very angry."

It was fortunate that his staff set up headquarters in an occupied house, since its female owner put a human face on the town's civilian population, taking them off the retributive table as far as Sherman was concerned. Anything else even remotely "official," however, was fair game. "The co[u]rt house & jail is on fire," scribbled an Ohio diarist. "Bands are playing[.] The church bell's tolling."

A stone monument in the town to native son and former state governor Jared Irwin was not touched, save some chipping it suffered from random shots fired during the engagement. Not so lucky were businesses located near the government center, and all cotton stocks. One Federal "went into a large drug store after the boys had cleaned it out and I never saw such a mixture of medicines and glassware. I would hate to take some prescriptions which were compounded." The only resident who benefited from the Yankee occupation was a prisoner released from the jail before it was torched. "He was a happy man I assure you when we let him loose," declared a Union soldier.

Contrary to popular notions, Sandersville's Masonic lodge enjoyed no special protections. The building had been entered and ransacked by the time a couple of Union officers who were Masons learned of it. They managed to salvage a number of ceremonial artifacts, which they left in care of Mrs. "L.F.J.," whose father had been a member of the order. The biggest beneficiary of this plunder was probably the supply train managed by a New Jersey lieutenant named Garrett S. Byrne. Hardly had the officer learned of the incident when he returned to his train to discover that some prankster "had made odd fellows or masons of all my mules by pulling the aprons around their heads, adorning one of my wagons with a huge representation of a skeleton and . . . for a few days there was nothing used around the train for towels but aprons and scarves, and the mules looked like so many marshals in a 4th of July celebration."

Perhaps the most viewed corpse of the entire campaign was encountered in Sandersville. Major Hitchcock observed the body lying in front of a church, as did a half dozen other diarists and journal keepers. "Should judge the poor fellow was about 40, powerfully built man, in a dark colored homespun uniform and a ball had gone though his heart," recorded an officer. "We laid him out on the church steps near where he fell, [and] placed a bible on his bosom." Soon afterward, when the 2nd Massachusetts passed the dead man, "one of Co. C went & pulled off his shoes." Later still, when a Wisconsin soldier was wandering through the town, he reached the church just as a few Federals were "putting him into a rough coffin, and his grave was being dug near the church."

"So sudden an advent of so many 'Yankees' seems rather to astonish the natives both black & white," observed an Ohio man, "the latter looking on sullenly at a distance while the former rush out upon the sidewalks with expressions of great satisfaction." A New Yorker deemed the white citizens to be "strong secesh," while a Michigan surgeon fell in with "an intelligent half blood who testified that slaves here were bred same as stock. . . . A crime to be able to read. Such we find slavery in central Georgia."

Major General Sherman spent this night in Sandersville. He patiently

endured a rambling discourse from a local preacher intent on interced-
ing for the town's helpless females and youngsters. Sherman finally
waved him away with a terse statement: "I don't war on women and
children." Remembering the sight of Wheeler's troopers burning fodder
outside the town, he told other residents "that, if the enemy attempted
to carry out their threat to burn their food, corn, and fodder, in our
route, I would most undoubtedly execute to the letter the general orders
of devastation made at the outset of the campaign." Sherman was certain that those listening to him "would be sure to spread the report."

It was here that the General learned of Howard's long delay at the
Oconee River, causing him to halt the Left Wing until he "heard that
the right wing was abreast of us on the railroad." Ahead of his columns
was the line of the Ogeechee River, a natural obstacle more formidable
in places than the Oconee. At least one staff officer in the Fourteenth
Corps worried that if the Rebel defense of that river was as stubborn
as that they had just encountered, "it may give the whole army considerable trouble to get across."

Left Wing (Cavalry)

Twenty miles or so north of Sandersville, Brigadier General Kilpatrick's men continued their mission. Riding with them were several
reporters; the one writing for the *Philadelphia Inquirer* had been traveling with the infantry but managed to wrangle a spot on this expedition in search of some adventure. This day provided plenty: "We
marched at 7 A.M., crossed the Ogeechee, and passed through Gibson,
a small place, where the militia of that county had been ordered to
assemble that day. We captured there a Colonel, Major, Captain, Lieutenant, and some privates. We crossed Rocky Comfort Creek; deep,
but not wide, and camped on Big Creek. In the morning, about two
hundred men were sent as an advance to cut the railroad between
Augusta and Savannah, at a place called Wainsboro.* The county was
very thickly timbered with pine, but the roads good."

There's an air of mystery surrounding this special operation mentioned by the correspondent. Ostensibly, and as reported by Brigadier

---

*   Misspelling of Waynesboro in original.

General Kilpatrick, it was aimed solely at the railroad bridge over Brier Creek, just north of Waynesboro, linking that place and points south with Augusta. However, a postwar account by one of the cavalrymen who took part strongly suggests that there were really two schemes in motion at the same time.

The first strike group, the "official" one, was the railroad-wrecking sweep to Brier Creek Bridge. The second, the "unofficial" one, was described by that trooper—Julius B. Kilbourne—as a "forced march to rescue the Union soldiers then prisoners at Millen." Kilpatrick assigned two members of his staff to lead these strikes; his assistant adjutant-general captain Llewellyn G. Estes, and one of his aides-de-camp, Captain Edward M. Hayes. The soldiers taking part were drawn from several regiments, principally on the basis of their good health and having horses in sturdy condition. Extrapolating from the fragmentary evidence in hand, it would seem that Captain Hayes led the bridge-burning party, while Captain (later Major) Estes headed south for Camp Lawton. Both groups departed camp well before sunrise.

"The roads were dry, and it was a bright moonlight night," recollected Kilbourne. "We silently moved on during the long night through forest and towns, with nothing to break the silence save the tread of the horses or clatter of our sabers and sound of the bugle to dismount and lead our horses on coming to a stream, and then to close up and move on." The small column continued pressing southward in the daylight. "About the many plantations which we passed we saw no one but now and then some old gray-headed man walking about the house, looking at us as we passed."

It was about 4:00 P.M. when they first glimpsed the Camp Lawton stockade. Reflecting on the suffering captives, Kilbourne related: "How our hearts leaped with joy at the sight and at the thought that we should be able to effect their release!" Captain Estes eased forward with a few men. After a short scout he returned with the disappointing news that the camp was empty of living Union prisoners; the officers had been transferred to Columbia, South Carolina, the enlisted men (those not exchanged) moved into Florida. It was a bitter pill for everyone. After wrecking a few camp buildings, the special operation group turned back to link up with the main body.

Somewhat after Estes and his men made their discovery, Captain Hayes with his command reached the Brier Creek Bridge. Here they "destroyed a portion of the track and partly burned the railroad bridge," as well as pulling down the telegraph wires before reversing course.*

The bulk of Kilpatrick's command camped this night about Sylvan Grove, covering the road to Waynesboro. Unknown to the Union general, Confederate major general Wheeler, having disengaged from the fighting around Sandersville after leaving one brigade behind to shadow and harass the Union infantry, had marched north with all the troopers he could muster. His scouts had told him of Kilpatrick's incursion, and this time Wheeler was determined to hit his impudent opponent hard.

───── *Right Wing* ─────

It wasn't long after dawn when a few frantically signaling figures on the west bank of the Oconee River indicated that the way across at Ball's Ferry was clear of Confederates. The flanking force sent to trap them had found the defenses empty, the enemy gone in the early morning hours. The Rebs, scribbled a gleeful Ohio diarist, "had lit out." At 7:15 A.M. the officers with the pontoon sections of the 1st Missouri Engineers were ordered to set down both bridges at the ferry site. It took a while to recall the equipment that had been used overnight to get the flanking party across the river, so it wasn't until after 9:00 A.M. that the bridge builders plus equipment were on the scene. The swift-running Oconee River here was nearly 250 feet wide and 10 feet deep. The plan was for one bridge to be used by the Fifteenth Corps, with the other reserved for the Seventeenth. With Major General Osterhaus nettling everyone with his fretting the engineers went to work.

This meant that most of the troops on the east bank were in a holding pattern. In the 55th Illinois the boys took the opportunity presented by the idle time and nearby river "to wash their clothing, for which there was certainly great need." The impulse was less sanitary in the 30th Ohio, whose members were "busy chucklucking." The soldiers of the Second Brigade, First Division, Fifteenth Corps were read a letter from Major General Howard to Major General Osterhaus con-

---

* Cavalrymen were notoriously poor railroad wreckers. The telegraphic communication between Waynesboro and Augusta was restored in less than twenty-four hours, and a traveler passing between the two towns on November 29 reported the railroad operational.

gratulating them for the Griswoldville victory. "Officers from other commands who were looking on say that there never was a better brigade of soldiers," Howard's note enthused. One Illinois soldier in the Seventeenth Corps spent time gazing at a solitary civilian, whose plight added a poignant incident to his daily diary entry: "Old man to right of road—arms folded, looking over his silent home and desolate fields!"

By 11:00 A.M. the double pontoon was finished, with the first troops crossing before noon. The passage itself was not without some anxiety. An Iowa man tramping across never forgot how the weight of the column "would settle the frail [pontoon] boats low in the water, but the pontoons proved to be reliable." For a second occasion in this operation, Right Wing officers took advantage of the bottleneck "to take in all horses where they had no proper papers for them," related a foot soldier. This time, however, many of the Yankee boys were wise to the move. "We . . . went to the river & tried to swim our horses across, as it was the order to corral all extra horses," recorded an Illinoisan, who added, "I lost mine."*

*   *   *

According to Major General Howard's chief of staff, an old word was given a new meaning this day. It was the recollection of Lieutenant Colonel William E. Strong, assistant inspector-general for the Right Wing, that it happened as the command party was waiting impatiently to cross the Oconee at the pontoon bridge. Holding up the group for the better part of an hour was an "immense cavalcade of mounted foragers" clogging the limited crossings with their plunder. It was all too much for a surgeon in the group, Dr. Edward A. Duncan, who exclaimed: "Damn the bummers they are always bumming around when they are not wanted." Strong declared that the word "seemed so appropriate that it was accepted from that moment and within two days was in every body's mouth."

Strong's reminiscence is likely too pat, but it does pin down a time and a place to introduce the word that would become inextricably bound into the fabric of the March to the Sea. Indeed, those participants who penned postwar memoirs avoided mentioning it at their

---

* Also, animals deemed too broken down to continue were killed. One soldier estimated that 400 were destroyed at this place.

own peril. Yet there was no general agreement on what the word actually meant. For some it referred to low-ranking headquarters personnel who used the relative freedom of their positions to scrounge around. Others were equally certain that it was best applied to the regular details specified in Sherman's orders on foraging. Still more lined up askew, agreeing that the bummers were foragers, but not part of any official detachments.

It was not a freshly minted word, but one that was repurposed. Sherman believed it came out of New York City, where (he said) it referred to loungers who sold their votes on election day. In a letter he wrote in 1883, the General related that the vote sellers sat around firehouses on their "bums" waiting for the highest bidder. A more modern writer traces it back to a German word (*bummler*) referring to tramps. Where all the postwar users of the word agree is applying it to the task of foraging.

The word *bummer* is virtually absent from contemporary diaries and letters written by campaign participants. It does appear in the text of a field order issued on December 1 by the Third Division of the Seventeenth Corps. Referring to officially designated foragers, the orders read: " 'Bummers' are entitled to a position in the ranks, and must be provided with it." Any other reference in orders to the men detailed to gather supplies for the columns terms them *foragers*.

The word caught on because it fit so well. "He was a logical product of this campaign," wrote a Michigan veteran. "The Georgia forager, a unique character such as the world has never seen before, coined for himself the name of Sherman's Bummer," contributed a Hoosier officer. "To provision his army on the way Sherman made use of a new organization, which may fairly be said to have been his invention; though I have never heard that he claimed a patent on it," cracked a New Yorker. Underlying the lightheartedness attached to the word was a grim reality as expressed by a soldier in the Fourteenth Corps: "The typical military bummer was a character full of good humor and the milk of human kindness, but with a soul sternly set upon the duty of despoiling the country."

*   *   *

Once past the river, the Seventeenth Corps angled northward to intersect the Central of Georgia Railroad at Station No. 14, also called

Oconee. The Fifteenth Corps turned more to the northeast to reach a map reference called Irwins Crossroads. It was slow going for both corps; just getting all the men, wagons, and animals (including cattle herd) over the river would take all night. "It was an almost bottomless swamp and there were no fields in sight so that rails to corduroy were not to be had," complained an Iowa infantryman. "Many of the worse places were corduroyed with small trees but it consumed a great deal of time to thus fix the roads." Even on the eastern side there were marshy areas to navigate. This led a member of the 47th Ohio to conclude that "Georgia now seems to be all swamps." A comrade in those Buckeye ranks let propriety slip when he wrote in his diary that the men were "obliged to wade in the mud and water up to our a—es."

While a few of the horticulturally inclined marveled at their first encounters with palm leaves and Spanish moss, others scattered about in search of food. "Here we had plenty of forage, molasses and sweet potatoes," wrote a soldier in the 50th Illinois. As they were looking for potable water near their night camp, a party of the 66th Indiana came upon a cache of stashed furniture: "a lot of chairs, a nice side table for a parlor, some meal, 3 saddles & some other things." The Yankees hauled the goods back to camp to enjoy their dinner in fine style. "Poor foolish simpletons," remarked one of the Hoosiers, "if they had left them in their house they would have been guarded by our provost guard, but when they hid such things out in the wood we appropriated things as we actually used for our own especial benefit."

The stubborn defense of the Oconee River proved something of a wake-up call for most of the soldiers, who up to this point in the grand movement had seen little evidence of a Southern will to fight. From this day forward an infantryman in the 50th Illinois fully expected to "have a skirmish nearly every day . . . as the Johnnies are getting quite thick in front." "It is reported that the rebels are concentrating some fifty miles ahead of us and are strongly fortifying themselves on the Ogeechee river," added a soldier in the 11th Iowa. A comrade in the 81st Ohio got hold of a local newspaper proclaiming that Sherman was desperately seeking an " 'out let,' and if 10,000 resolute Georgians will only come to the rescue, Sherman's whole army can be captured."

This soldier's editorial riposte: "Let'em come!"

CHAPTER 17

"I Never Was So Frightened in All My Life"

SUNDAY, NOVEMBER 27, 1864

In Richmond, President Jefferson Davis made an effort to sort out the tangle of overlapping and interlocking jurisdictions that were undermining any effective response to Sherman's march. With General Beauregard west of the Oconee giving every indication of remaining there for the present, even as Sherman's forces maneuvered east of the river, Davis wanted some centralized decision-making out in front of the Yankee horde. Military protocol dictated that the job go to the senior officer on the scene, so General Braxton Bragg in Augusta was informed today that he had been given full authority over "all combinations [aligned] against the present movements of the enemy."

Accepting the assignment with great reluctance, Bragg in his blunt assessment made it clear that his heart wasn't in the effort. "In assuming it I must candidly express my belief that no practicable combinations of my available men can avert disaster," he prophesied. Monitoring these changes in Virginia, an experienced War Department clerk and observer of political infighting anticipated a scrap when Beauregard returned east to pick up the reins. "Here, then, will be war between the two B.'s—Bragg and Beauregard," he snorted; "and the President will be as busy as a bee. Meantime, Sherman may possess the land at pleasure."

In Washington, planners were sifting through the conflicting Confederate press reports, trying to predict where along the Atlantic coast

Milledgeville to Millen

DAY THIRTEEN:
Sunday, November 27, 1864

UNDER THE GUN
[LW] Davisboro
[RW] Riddleville
[Cavalry] Waynesboro

Weather: clear
upper 30s to low 50s

Sherman would appear. It was anticipated that the Union force would be short of munitions and supplies, so the objective was to stage everything in depots located close to where Sherman was expected to show himself. This day, President Lincoln's military adviser, Major General Henry W. Halleck, directed the Commissary and Ordnance departments to begin stockpiling goods at Hilton Head, South Carolina. In a related move, the officer responsible for getting the mail delivered to Sherman's men felt that he no longer had to maintain the pretense that the general was going into Tennessee. All deliveries intended for Sherman's force had been forwarded to Nashville, but now that it was patently obvious that the Federals were not headed in that direction, the postal authorities were authorized to reroute everything to Baltimore, Maryland. From there it could quickly be put onto ships for transport to any port on the Atlantic coast.

Combined Left/Right Wings

For the first time in the current campaign, the two halves of Sherman's grand army were operating in close concert. Although still functioning as independent wings, their movements were those of a single entity headed in one direction. Today each wing assigned a division to wreck the railroad; each sent a division to guard its wagon train (both moving along the main road through Davisboro), and each sent divisions off on parallel routes—the Left Wing swinging around toward Louisville by way of Fenn's Bridge, the Right Wing using plantation roads to reach Riddleville, some six miles southwest of Davisboro.

Brigadier General John W. Geary's division (Twentieth Corps) had the railroad duties for the Left Wing, tasked with demolishing the stretch between Tennille and Davisboro. "Here tearing the track, burning ties, twisting iron, &c.," wrote one of Geary's Ohio soldiers. It was Brigadier General John M. Corse's men (Fifteenth Corps) who were handed the same job, but from the Oconee River to Tennille. There was something about this work that prompted three different members of the 50th Illinois to consider it worth mentioning. Frederick Sherwood, a musician in the ranks, thought it "Good work for a Sunday's job." Charles F. Hubert, who later wrote a history of the regiment, remembered that the men carried out their task to a rhythmic chant: the line, "Soldier, will you work?" answered by, "No, I'll sell my shirt first." All this labor gave Lewis F. Roe cause for ironic reflection. "This is the Sabbath, a day set apart for the worship of God & probably my folks have been to Church to-day, while I have been engaged in a far different occupation, that of tearing & burning the Macon Railroad."

Other soldiers were set to work on the South's reigning cash crop, fondly known as King Cotton. A Massachusetts soldier noted that "a great deal of cotton was destroyed," while a Minnesota boy marching with a different column recalled passing two "large buildings stored full of bales of cotton [which] were burning." This may well have been the Hodgson plantation, where a meticulous staff officer counted 580 bales incinerated. "As the dense columns of smoke roll up toward the sky," related an Illinois soldier, "we mentally exclaim 'Cotton is *not* King'!"

The columns moving slowly, Sherman's hungry men scattered across the countryside. "Country very level, fertile & well cultivated," recorded an Ohio soldier. "Great abundance of forage, provisions, mules, horses &c. captured to day." By now the ever pragmatic infantrymen had adapted to the official and unofficial ways of carrying out the "forage liberally" directive. "There is strict orders for soldiers in the ranks to do no private foraging," declared an Iowa man, "but there is scarcely a private that does not forage from noon till night if he can get a chance." "Country good, abounds in sweet potatoes, yams, molasses, fresh pork," added an Illinoisan. "Desolation we leave behind in their stead." The tendency toward casual excess was beginning to bother some of the Yankee farmers. "I think we destroy as much or more than we eat," worried an Ohio soldier. The image was even starker for an Iowan in the Seventeenth Corps, who wrote this day: "I think a katydid, following our rear, would starve."

It was another deadly day for the unfit horses and mules rounded up after the river crossing. "These animals were in daily use," explained a Fifteenth Corps brigadier, "but every regiment had an excess of pack animals beyond the allowance in orders, and while forage was now easily obtainable for all of them, it would only be a few days when the whole army would be on short rations for both men and animals. . . . I was informed the orders were that these [extra or unserviceable] animals were to be killed by the rear guard after the balance of the troops had passed. This was not a pleasant duty, but the order was imperative, and was obeyed to the letter."*

One small item on Sherman's personal agenda was a ride into Tennille to investigate a cryptic remark made the previous evening by a local black man. Recounting what he had seen of the various waves of destruction visited upon the railroad station, the slave concluded by exclaiming that not only did the Yankee soldiers burn the depot and wreck the tracks, but they "sot fire to the well!" Checking it out this morning, Sherman found the well was more a pit lined by wooden scaffolding with steps leading down to a "fine copper pump." Thorough Federals had filled the pit with flammable material and, as the black had accurately described, "sot fire to the well!"

---

* This officer estimated the number of animals put down at 200–300, though some sources suggest a total as high as 500.

Sherman's anecdote in his *Memoirs* masked a grim awareness throughout the ranks that the black refugee problem was not going away. A "great crowd of miserable squalid negroes, women and children, are following us," wrote a Wisconsin diarist. "I do pity these poor helpless creatures. . . . I hope they may gain what they so ardently desire—their freedom—but I fear they will in the thousands of cases, find their freedom in death." "Women came with large bundles on their heads, children also carried quite large packages on their heads, and some of the larger ones carried the little ones," contributed another Wisconsin man. "They would not leave us if told to do so," added a third Midwesterner. "Where they lived from I don't know, but they managed to live somehow." Their eagerness to help was exploited by soldiers who took them along as personal servants. "It makes but little difference to the private what wages he's agreed to pay," commented one observer; "he won't do it."

Sherman's overall scheme moved the combined wings in as tight a formation as possible. That meant taking advantage of every available parallel route, far more than were shown on any of the maps in use. The result was that both halves experienced some serious cases of faulty navigation. In the Fifteenth Corps, Brigadier General John E. Smith's division was a good two miles along the wrong road before anyone noticed. "If ever Old Smith got a cursing he got it today," growled a limping Illinois soldier.

Making matters worse for the officers leading the Twentieth Corps was the fact that the person who discovered that an entire brigade had gone astray was their Left Wing commander, Major General Henry W. Slocum. "About noon Slocum came along at full speed and halted our Reg[imen]t and kept on calling for the Brig[ade] to halt until he reached the head of the Brig[ade]," recorded a member of the 102nd Illinois. "Had quite an exhibition of General Slocum's temper," added a soldier from the 105th Illinois. Lieutenant Alfred Trego was close at hand when Slocum encountered the errant guide. "Gen. Slocum came up and gave one of his aid[e]s a terrible cussing for leading the column on the wrong road. He was very angry—told him he was unfit to be an aide and sent him to headquarters under arrest."

The Right Wing finally completed crossing the Oconee River this day; the Seventeenth Corps was done early, the bigger Fifteenth Corps took until noon. When they had finished, the Missouri engineers pulled up the bridges, packed their gear, and readied themselves to do it all over again at the Ogeechee. As the last Fourteenth Corps units pulled out of Sandersville, they burned several government warehouses that had been used overnight by Federal soldiers for shelter. Most of the town's citizens were glad to be rid of the men, but Mrs. "L.F.J." was actually sorry to see them go. The youth assigned to guard her house had shown sympathy toward the young woman and her child, making sure they obtained a generous helping of rations, including flour and real coffee. Special permission was granted allowing the sentry to join "L.F.J." and her mother for a home-cooked meal. She never forgot how, "asking God's blessing upon our food, he ate his supper."*

William Tecumseh Sherman was among those departing Sandersville, traveling only as far as Tennille, where he set up his headquarters. While short in distance, the journey was greater in symbolism, since he was also shifting his flag from the Left Wing to the Right. For the moment the General and his staff would accompany Blair's Seventeenth Corps.

It was a pensive day for Sherman, who was anxiously reviewing his troop dispositions in light of the enemy's recent combativeness. One of the Confederacy's more skilled officers, Lieutenant General William J. Hardee, had been as close as Tennille on November 26. Residents living near the station claimed to have heard Hardee vow to hold the line of the Ogeechee River at Louisville, a possibility that had to be treated with sober consideration. Sherman rode so lost in thought that, as Major Hitchcock watched with openmouthed astonishment, he ignored a woman standing at her front gate frantically trying to get his attention. "If she spoke, it was not audible," remembered Hitchcock, "and he rode along looking straight forward *and did not see her.*"

Among Sherman's other frustrations this day was the sketchy nature of the maps he had to use. Another was making certain that his generals were literally burning their bridges behind them to bolster the

---

* Fifty-five years after the war, Mrs. "L.F.J." used the columns of the *National Tribune* (a newspaper for veterans) to locate her benefactor. She had by then remarried and was living in nearby Madison as Mrs. L. F. Harris. Her appeal resulted in what the paper's editors termed "many letters from different men . . . and every day or so more . . . are coming in." Based on details known only to the participants, Mrs. Harris identified her compassionate sentry, but the newspaper account garbled the name as M. C. Canney. Given the facts as known, Private Michael Carney of the 61st Ohio seems the likely angel.

security of the trailing wagon trains. When a casual conversation with one division commander suggested that the Oconee River and Buffalo Creek crossings hadn't been destroyed, Sherman fired off a petulant dispatch to the wing commander to make certain that they had. His mood wasn't helped by some of the information contained in recent Rebel newspapers confiscated in Sandersville. Several reprinted accounts taken from Northern dailies accurately gauged the size of his force, how it was organized, and his likely objectives. Speaking with Major Hitchcock, Sherman had complained, "It's impossible to carry on war with a free press."

He was presently moving his forces in three columns, the middle and right ones supporting each other as they tramped to take up a line between Davisboro on the left and Riddleville on the right.* The third, a pair of divisions from the Fourteenth Corps, followed a slightly diverging route north of the others. This column's aim was to get across the Ogeechee River at a place called Fenn's Bridge. If Hardee was making a stand at Louisville, they would turn his flank; if Wheeler came pounding down from Augusta hoping to pounce on the wagons, they would block the thrust, so much depended on how well the column carried out its mission, and how lucky it was.

Major James A. Connolly, a Third Division staff officer riding at the head of that column, was hoping for a little excitement. The morning's march had been without incident, the men even joking about eating too many of the persimmons that littered the roadsides. Matters became decidedly more serious as they drew near to the Ogeechee River, where scouts pointed out to Connolly how the Rebel cavalry tracks they had been following (easily visible in the sandy road) suddenly split left and right, suggesting an ambush ahead. The column halted while a skirmisher screen nosed forward with Connolly following. "Being as full of curiosity as a woman, and being anxious to get the first sight of the rebels, I rode along with the skirmish line, watching every tree and stump, listening very intently, and moving as quietly as a cat in the sandy road, expecting every moment to hear the crack of a rifle from some concealed rebel."

All was quiet. The voltigeurs reached the river, where the major beheld an astonishing sight—Fenn's Bridge was intact, "not a plank

---

* The rearmost units would not arrive until nearly midnight.

disturbed, and not a rebel in sight." With Connolly was Colonel George P. Este, commanding the division's Third Brigade. The pair grinned at each other before putting spurs to their horses' flanks to see who could race across first. In his account, Connolly diplomatically implies the result was a tie. The infantry humped after the officers to spread out along the east side, protecting the precious gift.

Connolly afterward encountered a local woman who identified herself as the toll collector. She told him that there had been Confederate cavalry here this very morning, but they had headed west to burn a span toward Sandersville, saying they would return later to wreck Fenn's Bridge. The swift advance by the Fourteenth Corps' men cut off the Rebels, allowing the Federals to gain control. "The Lord was 'on our side' this time, surely," sighed a relieved Connolly. "For if that rebel brigade had burned the bridge this morning when they were here, we would have been compelled to build one before we could cross, and we could not have built one at all if there had been a regiment of rebels on the east bank to oppose us."

Both flanking divisions utilized Fenn's Bridge. An Indiana soldier remembered it as "an old wooden bridge none to[o] sound but all crossed safely." Once over, the pair angled south toward Louisville on parallel roads, camping for the night in a defensive posture. There were smiles at Sherman's headquarters when news of the successful crossing was confirmed. With the Ogeechee line now breached, all planning aimed toward the next potential trouble spot: Millen. As Major Hitchcock settled down at the end of a long day, his only thought was that "tomorrow the second Act of the Drama will be fully under way."

Cavalry

For all his acumen as an operational planner and strategic visionary, Sherman had a blind spot when it came to handling cavalry. His entire army career never intersected with that branch of arms; consequently it was a weapon he did not know how to employ wisely. He failed to understand the combat strengths and limitations of cavalrymen, never grasped what they did effectively or what they did poorly, and had no practical appreciation of their special problems.

There was no integration of his cavalry division with his infantry corps. Scouting duties for the foot soldiers were handled, for the most part, by mounted infantry, engineers, detached cavalry companies, or staff officers; flank protection came from the swarms of foragers who effectively cocooned the line of march; while picketing duties were given to foot soldiers or mounted infantry. The jobs Sherman tended to give his troopers were railroad wrecking (which they did poorly), infrastructure demolition (also difficult without adequate tools), and attracting the attention of the enemy's cavalry (which they did exceedingly well). Kilpatrick's current mission parameters contained all three, though the one Sherman most emphasized was number four—freeing the prisoners at Camp Lawton.

After breaking contact with the Yankee infantry around Sandersville on November 26, Confederate Major General Wheeler pushed his riders north and west, toward Ogeechee Shoals. Shortly after midnight his men began scrapping with the two regiments Kilpatrick had posted to watch the back door.

Trooper Leroy S. Fallis in the 8th Indiana Cavalry (one of the two rearguard regiments; the 2nd Kentucky Cavalry was the other) recalled the Rebel strikes as "unexpected, and in the darkness things became somewhat mixed." Hoping to realize maximum effect under the cover of night, the few Confederates involved made a substantial ruckus. Confusion reigned on both sides; at one point a section of the 8th Indiana Cavalry bluffed its way out of a tight spot by pretending to be a Rebel detachment; at another, a different Hoosier section was flanked out of its barricaded position and, in the words of a trooper, "fell back in some confusion." Disruption rather than attack was the objective; once the Federals stabilized a situation, Wheeler's men sought another weak point, allowing the Yanks to proclaim a successful defense while the Rebs enjoyed a successful harassment. According to Private Fallis, "we could hear the old rebel yell as they attempted some new move which was invariably met and repulsed."

At dawn Brigadier General Kilpatrick continued his assigned mission toward Waynesboro and Millen. However, the information Wheeler had gathered convinced him that Kilpatrick's real objective was to raid Augusta. "Being mindful of the great damage that could be done," the Confederate general adopted a strategy of "pressing him hard [so that] he might be turned from his purpose." Here again the absence of any overall coordination squandered a valuable military asset. Wheeler made his own decision to concentrate on defending what was probably the best-prepared potential target along Sherman's track—this at a time when more and more Confederate leaders on the scene recognized that Savannah was the most likely object of the enemy's attentions.

Even more ironic was the fact that the enemy Wheeler was protecting Augusta against was clearly thinking of defensive, not offensive, measures, as his march arrangements made evident. Before breaking camp, Kilpatrick's Second Brigade formed behind a barricade across the road, and at the word of command, the hard-pressed First passed through the Second. While the First took over the advance, the Second staved off Rebel dashes at the column's rear. A member of the 92nd Illinois Mounted Infantry described the process:

> *A company of fifty men would form at some point in the thick brush, with open fields in rear; in the road a squad of six or eight mounted men would halt, fire at the enemy at long range, then turn and retreat on the column; and on would come their confident pursuers at a gallop. When close up, the fifty concealed horsemen, cool and quiet from much similar practice, would volley them with their repeating rifles. Then the enemy would . . . deploy his skirmishers, and carefully feel his way . . . while the fifty mounted men were leisurely closing up on the column.*

"Marched thirty miles and built 9 or ten barricades," recorded an exhausted Ohio trooper. At one creek the Federals were able to destroy a bridge before the pursuing Confederates could reach it, forcing them to find an upstream ford, thus buying perhaps an hour of peace until the familiar sounds returned. "The rebels followed close . . . hooping and yelling terribly," recollected an Illinois man. "It was evident that the Johnnies in our rear were becoming desperate and wrathy in the highest degree," agreed a Pennsylvanian.

It wasn't just the Rebels who were testy. Even before reaching Waynesboro, Kilpatrick's men passed the Whitehead plantation, where the Yankee troopers helped themselves with the extreme discourtesy of soldiers pressed for time. When they departed, Catherine White-

head declared them "certainly the vilest wretches that ever lived
& must be overtaken in their wickedness, but if they are not punished in this world, God will certainly punish them in the world to
come."

For reasons unexplained, Wheeler today limited himself to a stern
chase, allowing the head of Kilpatrick's column to enter Waynesboro
in the early afternoon, where some railroad equipment and associated
buildings were set ablaze. It was about this time that the Federal general heard from Captain Estes that there were no Union prisoners to
be liberated from Camp Lawton. In later reporting this revelation to
Sherman, Kilpatrick tried to allay his chief's anticipated disappointment. "It is needless to say that had this not been the case I should have
rescued them," he said; "the Confederate Government could not have
prevented me."

With his prisoner-liberation mission scratched, Kilpatrick led his
men south from Waynesboro following the railroad. Roughly three
miles outside the town he found a good location for a defensive camp;
there he established a barricaded line with one flank anchored on the
railroad and the other resting on a pond. Rather than allowing his
weary troopers time off their feet, Kilpatrick kept every available man
busy tearing up the tracks, so that he could claim some accomplishment of his assignment. It was not a decision welcomed by the officers,
whose men were "sadly in need of rest and sleep." They would not get
much of either.

Behind Kilpatrick's column, Major General Joseph Wheeler entered
Waynesboro just after sunset. "The town was in flames," he recounted,
"but with the assistance of my staff and escort we succeeded in staying
the flames and in extinguishing the fire in all but one dwelling, which
was so far burned that it was impossible to save it." Wheeler planned
some nasty surprises for the Federals in the morning; meantime, he
would continue to badger the rear guard, "to keep them in line of
battle all night."

While Wheeler continued to act as if the enemy were itching to
turn toward Augusta, Kilpatrick's intentions were in a different direction. With U.S prisoners gone from Camp Lawton, there was no longer
any compelling reason to keep his command exposed to Wheeler's
assaults. Accordingly, as the Federal reported, "I deemed it prudent to
retire to our infantry." He intended his next day's march to close on

Louisville, where he expected to reach the protective umbrella of Sherman's main columns. That was, if Joe Wheeler would let him go.

MONDAY, NOVEMBER 28, 1864

The three cities directly under Sherman's shadow reacted to the threat in different ways. The mood in Augusta was positively bullish. "The enemy's position is becoming developed at last," announced the *Augusta Register.* "Whatever may be his opinion of our strength, we are conscious that our force is not only able to protect stated points, but will be able to meet him in open combat, and make him rue the day he toyed with the iron spirit of the Southern people." The paper's editors also heaped praise on Lieutenant General William J. Hardee. " 'Old Reliable' is too well informed of SHERMAN'S tactics to be outwitted by him," they boasted. "He is one of the most vigilant and energetic officers in the service, and knows how and when to operate."

In contrast to Hardee's studied equanimity, Major General Samuel Jones, the officer commanding in Charleston, was in a near panic. Once more today he fired off a telegram to Richmond reiterating his imperative want of reinforcements. "I cannot too strongly urge my need of them," he pleaded. This prompted a stern and immediate rebuke from the Confederate secretary of war. "It is impossible to afford re-enforcement," James Seddon answered in no uncertain terms. "You must rely on your own resources."

Self-reliance marked the tone of a proclamation issued under this date by the mayor of Savannah, Richard D. Arnold. "The time has come when every male who can shoulder a musket can make himself useful in defending our hearths and homes," it read. "Our city is well fortified, and the old can fight in the trenches as well as the young, and a determined and brave force can, behind intrenchments, successfully repel the assaults of treble their number."

——— *Combined Left/Right Wings* ———

Sherman's headquarters moved fifteen miles today, departing Tennille on a rambling course that jogged southeast for two or three miles, then picked up the old Savannah Road heading northeast, before turning southeast again to camp in the field roughly three miles outside Davisboro, not far from New Hope Church. The General was still gingerly coming upon the Ogeechee River with the Fourteenth and Twentieth Corps closing on Louisville, even as the Fifteenth and Seventeenth Corps marched in parallel a few miles to the south. "Thus we approached [the] Ogeechee [River] at two points," wrote Major Hitchcock, now a more confident strategist, "one column at Louisville, which is ten to twelve miles above [the] railroad Bridge,—and [the] other . . . coming towards [the] railroad Bridge across the Ogeechee which is at Station 10."*

The command party traveled "on sandy roads, and through woods chiefly pine, though as yet we still see oaks and other trees," continued Hitchcock in his travelogue mode. "Good farms along the traveled roads, and crops have all been good." They crossed paths with Major

---

*   Sebastopol.

General Frank Blair, commanding the Seventeenth Corps, who showed them some captured correspondence from soldiers in Hood's army representing a low state of morale and generally poor conditions. If Sherman gave any thought to what was happening to George Thomas in Tennessee, he gave no indication.

The officers lunched at a farm owned and occupied by one J. C. Moye, who received a guard detail to protect his residence; everything else on the place that could feed man or beast was appropriated. This night Sherman enjoyed a conversation with General Blair and two of his principal subordinates. An ever more admiring Hitchcock found the General to be "one of the most entertaining men I ever heard talk—varied, quick, original, shrewd, full of anecdote, experience and general information."

Just about all the railroad wrecking this day fell to the Twentieth Corps, which tackled the line beginning west of Davisboro, continuing east to Spier's Turnout.[*] Much of the right-of-way, recorded a Connecticut soldier, "runs through a dismal swamp on a bed of transported sand." "We tried various modes of destruction," contributed a Massachusetts man; "tipping the whole track over, passing the men down from left to right & keeping it going like a row of bricks & then piling up the ties & lifting the whole length of stringer & rail on top to burn the whole; lighting a continuous fire of pitch rails along both sides of the stringer & rail to burn & warp them. This was very effectual as the rails, being laid very closely together, sprang up from the stringer, drawing out the spikes, & bent & twisted themselves very considerably. Some of the reg[imen]ts, who had axes, cut the stringer where the joint of the rails came & laid the lengths on fires. This is, on the whole, the best way."

"The troops moved in haste save at the creek crossings where army wagons and teams, horsemen and infantry were blended in a confused jam from which a constant stream emerging closed hurriedly with the fast receding column," contributed a Wisconsin soldier in the Twentieth Corps. The toughest marching was turned in this day by the Fifteenth Corps, which, constituting the extreme right flank of the army, picked its way along roads that were only visible on maps. "I think the Div[ision] has been lost nearly all day," groused an Illinoisan. "We have

---

[*] Modern Bartow.

followed old Indian trails ⅘ of the time." To another midwesterner, this was a "wilderness. It is all large pine timber and no underbrush, only along the ravines. The land is very sandy . . . and thickly covered with a kind of grass resembling long thin wire. It is 10 to 30 inches high and very hard to walk through—slippery and tough."

"In making the order of march for the day the map of Georgia was consulted and the right[most] division was directed to move to 'Johnson's,' " explained an officer. "General Howard and staff moved with this division. We soon found the column was moving more south than appeared proper, and no man we could find, white or black, had ever heard of Johnson's. We were in Johnson county and assuming the county seat was intended, we found that was Wrightsville and moved the column there." The result of this confusion was that one brigade (the Second, Colonel Robert N. Adams's) spent the night at Wrightsville, while the rest of Corse's division bivouacked along the Little Ohoopee River, seven miles northeast. (What caused the whole foul-up was, according to an Ohio soldier: "Colonel Adams followed General Corse, who was following General Howard.")

Once the Right Wing commander managed to sort things out, the wayward brigade was directed east to rendezvous with the rest of its division near Swainsboro on November 29.* "These roads are generally mere trails and in many cases they are barely, if at all, distinguishable by a person unaccustomed to the country in riding on them," acknowledged the weary but wiser staff officer.

The units operating along and north of the railroad reported a number of brief sharp encounters with Rebel cavalry, perhaps from the same force that should have burned Fenn's Bridge. When a squad of mounted Confederates made a dash at the 137th New York, the "men immediately fell in, and taking arms, were ordered to load, the first time since leaving Atlanta," reported the regiment's commander. Another such strike caught Private William James Lockhart of the 22nd Wisconsin and his buddy Jotham Scudder lugging that night's intended supper, a large Muscovy duck. Lockhart was veteran enough to keep his priorities straight. When his buddy asked what they should do with the weighty bird, Lockhart replied, "Hang onto it until the ball actually opens for us, then if it comes to that we can drop it after

---

* The junction took place near modern Kite.

we are marched close to the front." His experience served him well, for his regiment was never called into action, leaving the men to enjoy a fine duck dinner.

Six miles east of Davisboro, elements of the Twentieth Corps swept across the Herschel V. Johnson plantation.* The owner, a past Georgia governor (active Confederate senator and no friend of the current Executive Mansion occupant), was not at home when the Yankees called. "Large quantities of stores were found buried on it & much plunder was carried off by the stragglers ahead of our column," recorded a New Jerseyman. That was only part of the story. According to a Wisconsin soldier, the "foragers got lots of stuff to eat here but not finding the usual amount of finery in the house the[y] suspected that it was hid some where. The officer in charge of the party persuaded an aged darkie by threatening to hang him up (rather persuasive argument) to tell him where the stuff was. The Ex-Gov[ernor] had worked it pretty sharp. He took up a bed of cabbage in his garden, there dug holes and deposited his goods in boxes and barrels in said holes, and then set the cabbages out nicely again. But it wouldn't work." A New Jersey officer mused that Johnson "must have lived like an old Baron on the grand old feudal lines and having almost all of the privileges of those saucy old fellows."

Louisville, Georgia's state capital immediately prior to Milledgeville, was the point of concentration for the two Fourteenth Corps divisions, pressing in from the north, with a Twentieth Corps division following the wagon road from Sandersville. Both found their routes blocked. The problem confronting the Twentieth Corps was a replay of Buffalo Creek; the river bridge gone along with another seven smaller ones carrying ramps over tributaries and marshes. "Here we had to lay our pontoons for a bridge, the rebels having burned the bridge & blew up the embankment through the swamp over which the road lay," recorded a Twentieth Corps Connecticut diarist.

A section of the 58th Indiana under Lieutenant Colonel Joseph Moore reached the site at about 1:00 P.M. The engineer estimated that between the river pontoon of 100 feet and approaches, he had to repair about three-quarters of a mile of roadway. The officer commanding the division reported the "pontoniers and pioneers at work all afternoon." In some cases the secondary bridges were entirely bypassed via

---

* This was likely the "Johnson's" sought in vain by the Fifteenth Corps.

corduroy lanes pushed through an adjacent swamp. Watching the workers overcome the obstructions, an Indiana volunteer was suitably impressed. "The facility in crossing this country of many rivers and insufficient roads was one of the hardest blows inflicted on the Confederates," he proclaimed.

Just to the north of Louisville, the adventurous Major James A. Connolly was once more seeking action. He had attached himself to a small scouting party that was operating about an hour ahead of the Third Division, Fourteenth Corps. Connolly and his crew had hoped to secure the Rocky Comfort Creek bridge into Louisville, but this time their luck ran out. When he arrived at the span right after daylight, Connolly found it ablaze. "I . . . was probably 20 minutes too late and couldn't save it," he reflected. "I could have reached it in time, but as we found the road barricaded about every mile by fences built across it, we had to approach very cautiously for fear of an ambuscade; and in this way we lost time."

With only five others with him, Connolly had no intention of trying to secure the opposite bank; so while one of them carried word back to the main column, the rest hunkered down to observe. When the leading infantry reached Connolly a little after 8:00 A.M., two regiments (23rd Missouri and 89th Ohio), in the words of one soldier, "crossed the river on timbers of the bridge, still standing although burning." According to an Ohioan in the 105th Regiment, the creek was "a deep stream, full of snags, with swampy banks, making very bad passing." A section of the 58th Indiana under Major William A. Downey arrived to construct the crossing. "It was a very long bridge (50 yards) spanning a swamp & river," recalled an Illinois soldier. Passage over the creek would not be ready until nearly 4:00 P.M.

This did not bode well for Louisville. The burned span was but a minor impediment for foot soldiers, so even as pontoniers and pioneers set to work, squads of men roamed the town with time on their hands. The result was a rough handling. "The boys made quite a raze," summed up a Missouri man. "Books, clothing, cutlery, medicine, etc., etc., were brought into camp in profusion," testified a Minnesotan. "It mattered not that the articles taken were of no use to anyone, they will take them anyway." "One fellow played on the piano while his comrades danced a jig on the top of the instrument and then he drove an axe through it," reported an Ohio infantryman.

Several sources recount that a female resident had spat on one of the first Yankees to enter Louisville. No one who set down the incident actually witnessed it, making it most likely a bogus justification for the destructive excesses of the Union soldiers. One Indiana soldier may well have put his finger on the more probable motive when he confided to his diary: "We burnt some of the town[,] just a little to keep our hand in you know." "I never can sanction such proceedings," wrote a conscious-stricken Illinoisan in his journal, "believing that no man who ever was a gentleman could enter a private house & disgrace our uniform and the service as many of our men did today." "I [am] getting ashamed to see such outrages committed," declared one thoroughly riled staff officer, "and made up my mind to sho[o]t the first scoundrel whom I may catch."

According to Brevet Major General Jefferson C. Davis's official report, it was just "before night the troops and trains were passing both streams into their camps around Louisville. The road, running as it does here through an immense cypress swamp, required considerable labor to put and keep it in condition for the passage of trains, and it was not until noon the next day that the entire column succeeded in getting into its camps." Not in his report was a fortunately nonlethal case of friendly fire occurring when Fourteenth and Twentieth Corps patrols, prowling their respective sides of the river, opened fire on each other. A bemused Indiana engineer recorded that "old general [James D.] Morgan run in and put a stop to the firing though they were so far apart that they did not hurt any one."

Also not reported was another incident just after dark, when the town jail, located near Davis's headquarters and supposedly guarded by the 34th Illinois, burst into flames. A staff officer he sent to investigate had words with the 34th's commander. "General Davis then summoned the combatants and delivered them a lecture the purport of which we did not learn," recorded an Illinoisan. "Neither did we discover who fired the jail."

Cavalry

Confederate Major General Joseph Wheeler was in his element. Behind him were civilian centers to be protected; in front was the enemy to be vanquished. Well before morning he had portions of his command in motion seeking to encircle and envelop the Yankee position, while he waited for first light to press the foe's rear guard. Marring this other-wise perfect picture was a heavy fog; "so much so," reported a *New York Herald* man with the Union expedition, "that we could not see fifty yards in advance." Wheeler's opposite number, Brigadier General H. Judson Kilpatrick, had no intention of waiting around for the Rebels to come charging. With his main mission of rescuing Federal POWs scrubbed, and his men having ripped up enough railroad track to record it as mission accomplished, it was time to find sanctuary.

Kilpatrick had his men marching well before dawn, still heading south from Waynesboro along the railroad. It would be another leap-frog operation, with one brigade holding a barricaded line until the other passed through it to establish a new position a few miles farther along, then falling back itself to repeat the process. Just to be certain that the enemy was actually in his rear, Kilpatrick pushed out two reconnaissance battalions. As soon as they encountered Wheeler's force, the battalions promptly fell back through the rear guard, closely pressed by the Rebels. Kilpatrick himself held station with the shield-ing units—elements of the 8th Indiana Cavalry and 9th Michigan Cavalry.

His prompt departure this morning effectively negated Wheeler's effort to encompass his command. The Rebel general sent two units to get in front of the Yankees. Hung up by the darkness, unfamiliar with the roads, and plain exhausted, the pair were unable to close the circle. They almost netted a big prize, however, as the equally weary Federals mishandled the tricky leapfrog maneuver. The officer holding one bar-ricade, losing count of the units passing through, prematurely with-drew, leaving Kilpatrick's group isolated from the rest. Then some of Wheeler's troopers galloped in from a side road, blocking the route Kilpatrick had to use.

The cavalry general, according to one of his troopers, "seeing that he was cut off, led his men on at once in a charge with the saber and cut his way through." A newsman on the scene for the *Philadelphia Inquirer* recorded that at one point the enemy riders were "not twenty-five yards from us firing their pistols as they came." The *New York Herald* correspondent added that "only hard fighting and swift paces saved him; as it was he lost his hat, which the rebels use as a foundation for loud brags in [the] Augusta papers." Kilpatrick's abrupt charge carried along only the riders closest to him. A section of the 8th Indiana Cavalry was left behind in the rush, forcing these men to fight their own way out.

Even as this formation of Yankee cavalrymen pounded down the narrow lane in their flight, squads of Confederates swarmed to the roadsides, some even forming along a bordering fence. Leroy S. Fallis was one of those who ran the gauntlet. Writing in 1903, the Hoosier said, "I have to this day a vivid remembrance of on this run looking into the muzzle of a revolver in the hand of a reb but a few feet away, and hearing the undesirable summons 'Halt, you Yankee,' but I did not halt until I had passed through the danger point. How rapidly thoughts passed through my brain on that occasion, and how quickly my thoughts were put into action. Believing my time had come, I sat almost straight in the saddle, again sending my spurs into my horse's flanks to hasten his speed, if possible, so that when shot he might carry me out to the boys before I fell. The revolver clicked, but no discharge, and I was safe."

Caught in the ebb and flow of these cavalry actions was Bellevue plantation, home of Judge John Wright Carswell and his wife, Sarah Ann. A brief skirmish around the house between Yankee and Rebel troopers shattered some windows and left a bullet crease in the hand-carved mantel in the parlor. The Confederates were driven off, giving the Federals a brief window of opportunity to forage the farmstead. Several tied their animals to Sarah Ann's beloved rosebush, which stretched along the side of the main house. While the raucous Union men carried out their searches, the horses, growing restless, increasingly pulled at the bush. Knowing that he could not stop the depredations, the judge determined to do something to protect what his wife held dear. He went outside, quietly untied the reins, and held the horses in place until the invaders finally took their leave. From that time on, the living token that he preserved for his wife became known as Sherman's rosebush.

Once the head of Kilpatrick's column reached a crossroads about thirteen miles south of Waynesboro,* it turned west toward Buckhead Church, near where a bridge carried traffic across Buckhead Creek.

---

*   In the area of modern Perkins.

Here the 5th Ohio Cavalry and 10th Wisconsin Battery were detailed to provide security until the entire column had cleared the choke point. Trooper Jacob A. Gilberg of Company D was among those assigned to hold it. Recollecting events afterward, he wrote that the bridge planks were wet and would not burn, so the cavalrymen loosened the flooring but left everything in place until the last minute. "As company after company passed over the bridge we could see evidences of the struggle in which they had been engaged," Gilberg wrote. "A Colonel came riding by, and in a loud voice exclaimed: 'Any one who says the First Brigade is demoralized is a ——— liar!' "

The firecracker sounds of the stern chase drew closer and closer. (In one of those free-for-all melees, Wheeler's chief of staff, Brigadier General Felix H. Robertson, was shot in the arm but still managed to kill his assailant with a sword blow to the head.)* Finally, a weary squad clattered over the bridge. "Is this the rear guard?" they were asked. Said one of them: "Yes, we are the last, and the Johnnies will be on you in a moment." The Ohio boys scrambled onto the span to begin flipping the loosened floorboards into the water, until only the stringers remained. "Company D, fall back!" barked an officer, while the Wisconsin gunners pumped some shells into the fringing woods on the other bank to cover them.

Kilpatrick decided to make a stand about three miles west of Buckhead Church, on the grounds of a plantation owned by a family named Reynolds. To a squad of 8th Indiana cavalrymen he said, "Boys, make you some coffee, we are not going away from here until after supper." As the general later reported, "I . . . took up a strong position and constructed a long line of barricades, with my flanks thrown well to the rear." Not mentioned was that Kilpatrick, according to Indiana trooper Fallis, "put about 100 negroes to work" building it.

More information was provided by a member of the 92nd Illinois Mounted Infantry, who wrote: "By the side of the road stood a large house, and around the house, in circular shape, were constructed rail barricades, [Colonel Eli H.] Murray's [First] brigade on the left, and [Colonel Smith D.] Atkins's [Second] Brigade on the right of the road, dismounted. In front, on the right of the road, was an open field, and

---

* It was a war-ending wound for the sturdy officer, who died on April 20, 1928, making him the last surviving general officer of the Confederacy.

the ground was, for twenty steps, rising, so that the Yankee barricades could not be seen any distance off. The barricade . . . furnished an excellent protection against musketry, and a complete barrier to a cavalry charge, as no horse could leap it, or throw it down by impact from the outside."

Kilpatrick's men had time to build the defensive work, since the dismantling of the Buckhead Creek bridge forced Wheeler to locate a ford for his men, a process that chewed up the better part of an hour. Ironically, even as his horsemen began wading through the stream, others had managed to repair the bridge using pews taken from Buckhead Church. A few bold Confederates scouted the enemy position, one of whom was seen well off to the right by the commander of the 92nd Illinois Mounted Infantry. He borrowed trooper William Black's carbine to pot away at the distant observer, who showed no signs of being under fire. The enlisted man finally snatched back his weapon, exclaiming, "Colonel, you are disgracing my gun; give it to me." The regimental history continues: "Will took his gun—one quick glance along the barrel from his dark eye, and the rifle cracked; the Rebel fell, and away went the horse, riderless."

In his after-action report, Major General Wheeler noted that "night was fast approaching" before he launched his attack against Kilpatrick's fortified position. His plan was to turn the enemy's right flank while pressing ahead with the bulk of his force, which he estimated at 1,200 riders, though a later (friendly) writer set the figure at 1,900.*

Once again, the turning effort failed to achieve its objective, leaving those attacking head-on to bear the brunt of the Yankee firepower. "Reaching the open," recalled a Tennessee cavalryman, "our bugler . . . sounded the charge, and at our foe we went like an avalanche, but our entire line was driven back in defeat. Retiring and re-forming, a second assault was made with the same result, we both times sustaining fearful loss in men and horses in a hand-to-hand encounter across the breastworks." One of the Yankee boys on the receiving end recorded that the Confederates had attacked "with great fierceness and boldness,"

---

* Many Federals believed they were being attacked by three or four times that number.

Milledgeville to Millen

DAY FIFTEEN:
Tuesday, November 29, 1864

UNDER THE GUN
[LW] Spier's Turnout/Sebastopol
[RW] Summertown

South
Carolina

Augusta

Shoals

Sylvan
Grove

Milledgeville

Waynesboro

Louisville

Alexander
Thomas

Sandersville

Davisboro

Lumpkins

Hebron

Buckhead
Church

Tennille

Spier's
Turnout

Riddleville

Sebastopol

Birdsville

Camp
Lawton

Gordon

Irwins
Crossroads

Millen

Irwinton

Toomsboro

Midville
(Burton)

Ball's
Ferry

Wrightsville

Summertown

Scarboro

Kite

Swainsboro

Weather:
clear
mid-40s to low 60s

Dublin

Statesboro

while another stated that "they made charge after charge." During a
short lull in the action, the Federals found a dead Rebel officer "shot in
seven different places."

Dusk was obscuring everyone's vision as Wheeler regrouped for
another lunge at the Union line, while Kilpatrick, satisfied that he had
sufficiently punished his opponent, continued his trek toward Louisville. When it was finally launched, a third Confederate attack overwhelmed the barely manned barricades, leaving Wheeler in control of
Reynolds's plantation. "The rebels seemed somewhat discouraged,"
observed trooper Fallis. "Although they followed us they kept at a
respectful distance, while the 8th Ind. Cav., bringing up the rear, would
blaze away when the rebels came within range of their Spencers."

Wheeler himself stopped for the night at 9:00 P.M. to send a situation report to his superiors: "We fought General Kilpatrick all night
and all day, charging him at every opportunity. Enemy fought stub-

bornly, and a considerable number of them killed. We stampeded and came near capturing Kilpatrick twice, but having a fleet horse he escaped bare headed, leaving his hat in our hands. Our own loss about 70, including the gallant General Robertson, severely wounded. Our troops all acted handsomely."

Kilpatrick continued another six miles before camping for the night. Louisville, and the protection of the main column, was about ten miles distant. In the words of one Ohio trooper, "It was a night of anxiety."

The extremely fluid nature of this day's engagements allowed each side to claim the advantage, with each reporting having inflicted casualties on the other that, if true, would have crippled them. Since neither was put out of action, the figures reported as suffered by each will have to do: 70 for the Confederates and losses of "over 100" for the Federals. The fact was that few on either side were much interested in counting bodies once the firing died down this night. Speaking for himself, but reflecting every man, a trooper in the 8th Indiana Cavalry closed his diary entry for November 28: "We are very tired to-night."

TUESDAY, NOVEMBER 29, 1864

Cavalry

The thrill-seeking staff officer Major James A. Connolly was getting some much-needed sleep in his tent outside Louisville when he was abruptly awakened by a voice calling his name. As Connolly later related, "It proved to be one of Kilpatrick's staff officers, and he was very much excited. He told me in broken sentences that they had been fighting day and night for the past three days; that Wheeler's cavalry was all around them with a vastly superior force; that they were out of ammunition, and men and horses were utterly worn out; that Kilpatrick didn't know where our infantry was but had started him off at midnight last night to try and make his way to some infantry column and beg for support or they would all be lost."

Like most infantrymen, Connolly did not hold the mounted arm in especial esteem ("their stories of hard fighting are cut after Baron Munchausen's style"); however, knowing that the Federal cavalry was out on a raid, he surmised that the relatively light opposition his men had faced thus far lent some plausibility to the supposition that the enemy's main force was targeting Kilpatrick. The major took the messenger over to the tent of Brigadier General Absalom Baird, who commanded the division. After hearing him out, Baird agreed that this could be a serious matter.

Even as one aide raced off to the headquarters of Colonel Morton C. Hunter with orders to have his brigade ready to march at a moment's notice, another escorted the cavalry officer over to the camp of the Fourteenth Corps commander, Brevet Major General Jefferson C. Davis. After listening to a third telling of the tale, Davis approved the rescue mission for Hunter's brigade.

Not surprisingly, Major Connolly attached himself to the enterprise, which got under way just before sunrise. According to Kilpatrick's officer, the cavalrymen were holed up some ten miles distant. The infantry column had trouped for about two hours when the pop-pop-pop of carbines ahead signaled danger. Hunter deployed his leading regiments, whose battle-wise veterans promptly built some light breastworks, threw forward skirmishers, and then waited for whatever would come next. It was Kilpatrick's column.

The cavalry officer passed over the rescue operation without comment in his report. Connelly's recollection of the moment was more vivid. The instant that the troopers "saw the line of blue coated infantry drawn up in a line across the road, and extending off into the woods on either side, they knew that they were saved, and sent up such shouts as never before were heard in these 'Piney Woods' which our infantry responded to with right good will." "This is one of the times when our cavalry was happy to see the infantry come to their relief," bragged an Ohio soldier, an expression with which trooper Leroy S. Fallis had no argument. When they first sighted the grinning infantrymen, "I can assure you we were not sorry." The small force that Wheeler had detailed to harry the Union cavalry reversed course at the sight of the barricaded infantry.

Combined Left/Right Wings

A cautious calculation marked Sherman's troop moves this day. Enemy leaders knew with certainty that he had no designs on Macon, and they were growing more certain that Augusta would also be bypassed. The wide dispersion of Confederate forces that Sherman had used to his advantage during the first phase of his grand movement was no longer something he could factor into his schemes. A much more plausible assumption would be that his opponents were actively concentrating all their available military assets in front of him. The delay he had suffered at Ball's Ferry underscored the danger that a determined force in the right position posed to his hitherto steady progress.

There was also the disquieting reality that Sherman had no clear picture of the enemy's deployments. Wheeler and his cavalry were out there along with an unknown number of Georgia militia, and, if various Southern newspaper reports were to be believed, veteran troops who were brought in from the Atlantic coast as well as other parts of the Confederacy. Unconfirmed intelligence gathered by Major General Howard put an experienced corps from Virginia under Confederate lieutenant general Jubal Early standing fast at Millen.

Sherman decided to hold back one of his corps from crossing over the Ogeechee in order to give him a mobile force capable of flanking any enemy effort to make a stand along the river's east side. Orders sent to General Howard directed him to gather the Fifteenth Corps "about one day's march ahead, ready to turn against the flank of any enemy who should oppose our progress." As Sherman told Major Hitchcock, this was all he would do until he could "learn definitely the state of affairs north and east of the Ogeechee."

The General was likely mulling over such matters when he was spotted by passing soldiers from the Seventeenth Corps, one of whom never forgot the sight of Sherman "pacing to and fro in front of a large house with a cigar in his mouth." Not long afterward, headquarters was packed and moving east toward Station No. 9½ (also called Burton)* on the Central of Georgia line.

The group quickly passed along the artillery guns and wagons attached to Major General Blair's corps. It was characteristic of Sherman that he was able to disconnect and relax once he had sifted through the variables to make his decisions. Catching sight of one of the battery officers, he rode over to the man to inquire how the foraging was going. They shared a laugh as his roving eye took in the pile of corn fodder

---

*   Modern Midville.

stashed on one of the cannon caissons. After complimenting the officer on the excellent condition of the unit's horses, Sherman continued
down the marching column. He came upon a pair of gunners (one on
horseback, the other on foot) who were talking about nothing in particular. Spotting the General, the mounted enlisted man pulled his
own animal to a stop, just as his companion commented, "This is
pretty good land here." Not missing a beat, Sherman segued into the
chatter. "Yes," he answered, "it is very good land, only a little too
sandy." The marching gunner turned on the interloper, to find himself
face to face with the general commanding, "looking as smiling as you
please." When telling this story later, the gunner confessed "that about
that time he felt like getting into a very deep hole."

A ride of a few hours brought Sherman and his staff to the crossroads home of a Judge Tarver, where they decided to stop for lunch.
The good magistrate had absented himself, but several women and
children held the post. Sherman took a look at the fearful gaze of one
of the older girls, counseled her to haul as many provisions into the
house as she could manage, then assigned a guard to watch over the
building. Major Hitchcock chatted briefly with the teenager, who con-
tradicted her mother's testimony by confirming that there had been
some Rebels here just the other day. Hitchcock judged that if this girl
had "been brought up in [a] city [she] would be very lady-like and
refined looking."

He was snapped out of his reverie by a female slave who implored
him: "Please, Sir, soldiers robbing me of all I got, clothes and everything." The major followed the woman to her cabin where he found
"four or five soldiers turning things over." He ordered them out; "all
obeyed at once," one even volunteering that he had been against the
scavenging raid and had tried to prevent his associates from entering
the cabin. Hitchcock watched them depart without further comment.
Perhaps drawn by his action, another slave, an older man, recounted
that a number of Wheeler's cavalrymen had passed through here just
two days earlier, but not before confiscating all the mules and horses
they could lay hands on.

Hitchcock was still shaking his head as the group mounted to continue forward, eventually stopping for the night by Rocky Creek. The
intelligence arriving was positive but still incomplete. There was no
word about Kilpatrick, though from a black man Hitchcock learned

that the Federal riders had fought with Wheeler's cavalry about thirty miles outside Augusta. Major General Slocum had pushed a brigade south from Louisville toward Station No. 9½, where he expected to take control of the bridge from the north side. A late-arriving courier brought an update from Howard, necessitating Hitchcock wake Sherman, who dictated a response. The major had just finished writing the orders when he espied his boss taking a night constitutional and joined him.

The General was anything but martial in appearance—"bare feet in slippers, and red flannel drawers . . . , woolen shirt, over which [he put] his old dressing gown, and blue cloth (½ cloak) cape." As long as Hitchcock had known Sherman, he had never seen him sleep through an entire night. Other members of the staff guessed it was his neuralgia acting up, but Sherman just accepted it as the way of things. Chatting with Hitchcock, he said that he had come to appreciate the stillness at 3:00 or 4:00 A.M. It was, he claimed, the "best time to hear any movement at a distance." As the two talked about nothing special, all around them the campfires of the great army flickered and dimmed.

Even as Sherman's headquarters moved from west to east, the forces around him continued the choreography begun on November 28. Immediately south of the rail line the Seventeenth Corps closed on Station No. 9½. The men generally made good time until they got close to the river, where they encountered its bordering swamps, which caused delays while the pioneers laid down corduroy paths. An Iowa man with an eye for topography observed that the landscape had definitely changed. "The country from Atlanta to the Oconee [River] is high land with considerable range of hills, principally rocky, the streams clear," he noted. "From the Oconee river the country becomes low, mostly sandy, the streams yellowish and turbid, the bottoms and banks of streams generally muddy, swampy and in some places nearly impassable."

Farther south marched the Fifteenth Corps, a portion of which unintentionally intersected with the Seventeenth, forcing it to chop a bypass through the pine thickets. This day's marching was generally easy on the legs, but tougher on the soul. "All day in an awful pine forest, hardly broken by fence or clearing," grumbled an Illinoisan. "I never saw such a lonesome place." "Trees tall and stately, with no underbrush," added another Midwesterner. "One can see the troops and trains moving along, beneath them like a huge reptile." "Only saw three houses to-day and they were nothing but dilapidated log cabins inhabited by tall sallow complected Georgia damsels," said an Ohio boy.

What there was to consume was absorbed by the columns as they plodded eastward. "Poor people live here and are losing all their provisions," commiserated a Missouri officer. One surprise came when they reached the swampy belt fringing the Ogeechee. There the persistent foragers "found the refugees' camps who were trying to hide from the Yankee invaders, but we hunted them out most effectively." According to an Iowan, the prowling Yankees "got 60 horses & 40 negroes [and] got lots of cattle."

While these animals were being driven back to the main column, one of the horned cows decided to charge a file of marching infantry. A farm boy from the 50th Illinois got in front of the onrushing beast, planted himself with bayonet fixed, and prepared to meet the foe. "It was more of a shock than he had bargained for but he stood it manfully," reported a comrade, "amid the cheers of the spectators."

The major exception to the generally unencumbered Fifteenth Corps' passage was that undertaken by the wayward brigade at Wrightsville, which had a lot of ground to cover to close the gap with its parent command. "Had to make right angle to the left in order to join the rest of the Div[ision]," related an Illinois soldier. "Every mile or oftener was a slough that delayed & vexed all. Took a north & north east course around & among swamps for ten miles. . . . A very pleasant day—got with the rest of the Div[ision] this evening. But little encouragement to know that we took the wrong road yesterday & required all of today's work to get us right again."

Two divisions of the Twentieth Corps continued to grind up the Central of Georgia Railroad track. "Our course is marked by a line of fire," wrote a New York officer. This proved to be a problem, as noted by a Massachusetts officer in his journal. "The marching by the side of the burning track was perfectly infernal, & the word may be taken in a very literal sense," he scribbled. "There was a swamp on each side in many places so that we could not get away from it." The swath of destruction stretched as far east as Station No. 10½, also known as Bethany.* One major find was a yard full of cut timber, stored in readiness to repair the line once the army had passed. An officer on the scene estimated the cache at three million board feet. "Burned it," reported a New Yorker. "It made a splendid fire."

The Third Division of the corps, babysitting the wagons and cattle, reached Louisville on November 19. The evidence of stubborn but futile resistance, and the feeling that Louisville's citizens had asked to be taught a lesson, loosened the already slack restraints on the men's behavior. "Hung an old man to try to make him tell where he hid his money," related an officer. "Many are becoming highwaymen by their mode of life." "It is really heart-rending to enter some of these houses and see how like demons our soldiers have behaved," said a Wisconsin officer. "On the other hand, we find many noble incidents, where privates, as well as officers, generously alleviate the suffering of the inhabitants."

All of the Fourteenth Corps was now settled around Louisville. Save for the one brigade shunted off to succor Kilpatrick's cavalry, most of the other men not on duty spent the day foraging. A number scrapped with bands of Rebel cavalry roving around the outside of the picket perimeter. One Ohio officer was in charge of fifty men tasked with clearing out an unoccupied plantation a few miles beyond the security zone. "But as we were filling a cart large enough to haul one half of the Southern Confederacy," he recollected, "a squad of Johnnies appeared and commenced firing on us. We soon were in condition to return the compliment. We were annoyed but a short time when they withdrew. We were not long in finishing our business at that point I assure you, but we got all we could haul away."

Louisville was the first Southern town that the Fourteenth Corps had been able to pause in during the current campaign, so a sense of unwinding spread all along the chain of command. "Col. [James W.] Langley . . . Brigade Commander, and his whole staff, were on a big drunk tonight," complained an Illinois soldier. "They have been out to a wine distillery and had imbibed to beastly intoxication, and are play-

---

* Modern Wadley.

ing the fool on a large scale. If they were reported to their superiors they would be unstrapped* and sent home in disgrace." Perhaps it was a coincidence, but back in the peaceful camp of the 52nd Ohio, a relaxed soldier was writing in his diary that the regimental band "is just now playing their evening tune and the lively notes of 'Coming through the rye' float gently on the breezeless air."

WEDNESDAY, NOVEMBER 30, 1864

———— *Interlude in Violence* ————

In one of those awful coincidences of war, a pair of bloody battles were fought this day—November 30—on opposite ends of Sherman's march. Each was a product of the General's decision to undertake the grand movement, though neither would have any immediate impact on his operations. One dwarfed the other in terms of numbers engaged or losses sustained, but in each scenes of carnage were terrible and commonplace.

The "lesser" of the two had its origins in Sherman's ability to see several moves ahead on the chessboard of war. Writing on November 11 to the army's chief of staff, Major General Henry W. Halleck, Sherman anticipated that as he approached the Atlantic coast, Southern leaders might try to concentrate a force in his front using the railroad running between Savannah and Charleston. To prevent that from happening, the General wanted a Union column from the Department of the South to raid inland in order to cut the route "about December 1." Prodded by this request, a divisional-strength expedition was organized by cobbling together units borrowed from Charleston to Florida. The plan was to penetrate the coastline using the Broad River near Hilton Head, South Carolina, land at a peninsula-like bulge called Boyd's Neck, and from there march west just seven miles to strike the railroad near Grahamville, South Carolina.

Simple enough in concept, the operation proved a disaster in execution. Staffed at the top with second- and third-rate commanders prone

---

* I.e., stripped of their rank.

to timidity, consisting of units that had never functioned together before in a large-scale expedition, and requiring effective coordination between the army and navy, the scheme was further crippled by dollops of bad luck. Delayed in landing thanks to a thick fog, then sent out initially on the wrong road, the weary invasion force—which should have reached the railroad on day one—flopped into camp a few miles short of the goal on the night of November 29. These proved to be critically important miles and hours for the Confederacy.

Between the Federal troops and the vital railroad route was a low ridge that provided a natural bastion, which eager hands had improved. Named Honey Hill, it was manned by a mix of South Carolina and Georgia troops, the latter just rushed there—including some Peach State units that had been mauled at Griswoldville. How these determined Georgians reached Honey Hill was a story in itself. Even as Sherman's forces had pushed through Milledgeville, then on to Louisville, these units had marched south, then east, from Macon, eventually reaching a rail line to board cars that carried them into Savannah. Once there some courageous decision-makers realized that the threat to communication with Charleston overrode issues of parochial sovereignty, so they routed them into South Carolina just in time to meet the Federal advance on November 30.

The payback was all the sweeter when it became known that the Yankee force included black units. While Sherman himself was willing to defy his commanders in chief (Grant and Lincoln) by refusing to take any African-American units with him on the march, the broad strategic implications of his campaign thrust a number of them into harm's way, including perhaps the most famous of all—the 54th Massachusetts (Colored). Of the eleven infantry regiments engaged on the Union side at Honey Hill, six were African-American.

The Confederates had a naturally strong position, were well dug in, and were highly motivated. Thanks to poor leadership, the bewildered Federal infantrymen were committed to the fight in a piecemeal fashion, with no overall plan. The engagement, begun at midday, ended at dusk when the bloodied, battered Federals withdrew. The Rebels defending the railroad (who never numbered more than 1,500) counted some 200 casualties, including 8 killed. The Union expedition (which totaled more than 5,000 men) lost 750, nearly 90 of these fatalities.

The critical rail line between Charleston and Savannah remained in operation. The next day, the victorious Georgia militiamen returned to Savannah, where they were added to the city's garrison.

While it was more directly related to Sherman's operation, the battle of Honey Hill paled in comparison with the grand-scale combat that also occurred this day in south-central Tennessee at Franklin. The quixotic General John B. Hood, ignoring Beauregard's entreaties and adhering to a schedule of his own making, launched his much-anticipated invasion of the Volunteer State on November 21—the day before Sherman entered Georgia's capital. Hood's first goal was Nashville, after which anything seemed possible—at least to John B. Hood.

The same storm systems that brought discomfort to Sherman's men in central Georgia struck Hood's legions with even more misery. Snow, ice, and punishing cold pummeled the Rebel warriors. For the first ten days of this operation, Hood's men shadowboxed with a small Federal army under Major General John M. Schofield that Major General George Thomas had positioned near the southern border to monitor enemy movements.

Hood, proving more determined and resourceful than Schofield, actually managed to get between the Union force and Nashville at a place called Spring Hill on November 29. The poor condition of Hood's army, the matter of his personal exhaustion and professional shortcomings in command of so many troops, and a panic-inspired animation on Schofield's part resulted in the Federals eluding the trap to take up a defensive position nearby at Franklin, with the Harpath River to their rear.

Furious at his missed chance at Spring Hill to deal the U.S. cause in Tennessee a serious blow, Hood ignored legitimate concerns and alternate strategies offered by his subordinates to hurl his army directly at the enemy's defensive works at Franklin in a series of sledgehammer assaults that buckled and bent but did not break them. Of the approximately 22,000 Federals engaged, roughly 10 percent were killed, wounded, or missing/captured. In contrast, Hood's army, numbering here some 23,000, suffered losses that exceeded one-third of its strength, including six irreplaceable generals.

Incredibly, Franklin was not the end of Hood's campaign, merely an appalling midpoint. On December 1, Schofield would continue his withdrawal into the defenses of Nashville, where George Thomas

Milledgeville to Millen

DAY SIXTEEN:
Wednesday, November 30, 1864

UNDER THE GUN
[LW] Waynesboro
[RW] Midville

Weather: clear
mid-40s to upper 60s

waited, still unsatisfied with the hand Sherman had dealt him and not
at all confident he could stop Hood. For his part, Hood trailed after
Schofield. Despite the awful damage done to his army at Franklin,
given the stakes that were on the table and the absence of any alternatives, he really had no choice. Very soon now, Sherman's cavalier allocation of troops to hold the line in middle Tennessee would be put to
the ultimate test.

*   *   *

At this juncture, Sherman worried most that the enemy was going to
mount a significant defense along the line of the Ogeechee River. He
need not have concerned himself. Almost as if it had been designed
this way, the zones where Sherman was expecting trouble fell outside
those where Confederate leaders were focusing their attention. General Beauregard, in overall command, had departed Macon for Mobile,
Alabama, where he believed his presence was urgently required. His

sole contribution to affairs near the coast was to advise Lieutenant General Hardee not to expect any more help in Savannah than he had already received.

Hardee's attention was fully occupied by reports of an enemy raid against his rail connection to Charleston,* and the pressing need to build up his landside defenses. General Braxton Bragg in Augusta, temporarily tasked with directing operations against Sherman in Beauregard's absence, limited his strategic initiatives this day to ordering repairs to the Georgia Railroad and urging Wheeler to keep hitting the enemy's cavalry.

Whatever potential there was in a stout defense of the Ogeechee River line would be unrealized and unimagined by the men who, in Jefferson Davis's way of thinking, should have been combining resources and coordinating efforts to stop Sherman. Instead, each had created a self-imposed arena of responsibility, beyond which no thought was given. It was as if none of the officers desired to impinge in the slightest on the prerogatives of the others. While courteous in the extreme, it was also not a very effective way of putting obstacles in Sherman's path. As a member of the General's staff observed about this time: "Every place we come to we fear that the rebels are fortifying such and such points always about two days march from us but we still continue our journey over a country having a greater natural capacity for protection than any I have yet seen."

Combined Left/Right Wings

Two divisions of the Fourteenth Corps remained encamped around Louisville along with Kilpatrick's bone-tired cavalrymen. The remaining infantry division followed its leading brigade southward toward the station on the Central of Georgia line known as No. 10, or Sebastopol. The security perimeter ringing Louisville was tested throughout the day by small bands of mounted men engaged in hit-and-run attacks. "There are not many rebels around us but they are slowly collecting in the hope of impeding our progress," observed a Minnesota man.

Soldier Levi Ross was part of the 86th Illinois roused from its camp

---

* This was the operation that resulted in the Battle of Honey Hill.

reveries by a sudden uptick of firing on the picket line. The men were hustled into formation, then hurried toward the sound of the guns. "As we filed up the road we saw the enemy in line of battle and mounted for a charge," remembered Ross. "Soon we reached the picket line, and deployed for the reception of the charge. Our entire regiment had come out and likewise deployed at short intervals on either side. The sight of reinforcements deterred the enemy from his intended charge yet he remained in line exposed to our fire. Occasionally he would dash down toward us, then suddenly wheel about and get out of range."

This "game," continuing throughout the day, was repeated at various points along the security boundary. Infantryman Ross had two close calls and a chilling reminder that the enemy was playing for keeps. He viewed four bodies of Union foragers, "all shot through the head and powder burnt. I saw them with my own eyes and therefore it needs no confirmation." All this hostile activity grated on the nerves of the officer commanding the corps, Brevet Major General Jefferson C. Davis, who complained to his boss that his "foragers are circumscribed to the limits of the picket-lines; so the general commanding will see the necessity of our getting out of this soon."

The division sent to Sebastopol managed to avoid all these problems as the enemy's focus remained on Louisville. "Any quantity of forage on the road, in the way of potatoes, meat, sorghum, honey, &c.," wrote a member of the 104th Illinois. Another in that regiment never forgot the celebration that greeted them when they reached the railroad station area. "The negroes had a grand jubilee after dark; the boys built a platform, provided a fiddle, and the darkies more than hoed it down, one old fellow dancing on his head, and keeping time to the music."

Also congregating at Louisville was the Twentieth Corps. One division had already arrived; the other two finished wrecking the railroad as far as the Ogeechee River, where they destroyed the railroad bridge. The men then marched north to cross to the Louisville side below the city, using Cowart's Bridge. To the west of the town engineers took up the pontoon bridge that had carried the wagons of the Left Wing across the Ogeechee.

Sherman made the decision to pause the Left Wing at Louisville entirely on military grounds. Yet it had an unintentioned humanitarian impact, as slaves from the whole region began congregating there. "Thousands of colored people joined the columns every day," recorded a New Yorker, "many of the women carrying children in their arms, while older boys and girls plodded by their side." "Supposed to be 2,000 along with Army," added an Illinois comrade. "Coming in very fast."

For the Fifteenth Corps, this day's marching kept the men entirely on the south side of the Ogeechee River, as Sherman intended. This was his ace in the hole should the enemy make a stand at Millen behind the natural obstacles created by the merging there of Buckhead Creek and the Ogeechee. If the Confederates did stand fast, the Fifteenth would be in position to cross the river below to flank them. For the men of the corps, that meant spreading across trails in Jefferson, Johnson, and Emanuel counties, pushing through a region of pine forests that gave way to swamps.

The "roads a complete wilderness," complained a Missouri soldier, "only pine trees[,] the most stupid place God created." According to an Ohio comrade, "during that whole distance [marched this day] only one log hut greeted our vision and that was inhabited by a 'love lorn widder' with six tow headed children." A member of the 103rd Illinois encountered a German-American who professed complete loyalty to the Union. The sound of a passing band brought tears to his eyes and anger to his tone. "This is the first music I have heard in four years; it makes me think of home," he blubbered. "D——n this Georgia pine woods."

There were delays as numerous patches of swamp ground necessitated either a detour or corduroy path. "Have to make our roads," groused a soldier in the 48th Indiana. "The sloughs are called creeks but they spread out like swamps," complained an Ohio officer. "I do not think an army could move with any rapidity through this country during the wet season." It all lent an air of exasperation to some of the men. "The roads are desperate," scrawled one, "our supplies are becoming shorter and shorter, darkness seems to be falling on our path."

Darkness fell across the path of the Sample plantation, seven miles below Summertown, where South Carolinian Sue Sample was visiting her sister-in-law. For days the ladies had been emotionally whipsawed by conflicting rumors—first that the Yankees could be expected any day, then the reassurances that they were passing at least sixty miles away. The pair had just returned from visiting a neighbor when one of the plantation slaves cocked his ear and said, "Listen Miss Sue, what dat?" It was the sound of military drums beating, more like six miles than sixty distant. Sample went into the house to lie down, for she had hardly slept the previous night from anxieties. Hardly had she closed her eyes before she was shaken awake with someone saying, "Get up, the Yanks are in the yard."

Sue Sample hurried downstairs to the sitting room. The sun had set, it was dark, but she could clearly make out that "a Yank was at each window with a cocked pistol in their hand, swearing all the time." Large sweaty men pushed their way into the house, helping themselves to loose items and having a dinner prepared for them under protest. Recalled Sample: "I never was so frightened in all my life."

The Fifteenth Corps finally settled in for the night around Summerville. Just to the north, the Seventeenth Corps was crossing the Ogeechee River at Station No. 9½, Burton. "The railroad bridge at this point had been burned but was easily repaired and quickly covered in a sufficiently safe and substantial manner to admit of the cavalry and infantry crossing, while a pontoon bridge was laid a few rods above over which the artillery and trains were expeditiously moved," reported a staff officer.

Among those crossing with the Seventeenth Corps was Sherman and his headquarters. By the time the command group had reached the bridge, its approaches were a confused tangle of "wagons, footmen and horsemen," which forced the party to pick its way "through slowly in single file, often having to stop," recorded Major Hitchcock. Once settled on the other side, Sherman encountered one of the memorable characters of the campaign. Major Hitchcock identified him as "old Johnny Wells," the former stationmaster here. Another staffer, Major George Nichols, thought him a "shrewd old fellow, with a comical build, he was evidently born to be fat and funny—as he was."

Even though his story was a well-worn one—a quiet Union man opposed to the war—his winning ways had even Sherman enjoying his company. "Never met a man more quick, in his way, in shrewd and odd 'points' and laughable sayings," noted Hitchcock. "There's John Franklin went through here the other day, running from your army," Wells declared. "I could have played dominoes on his coattails." Accepting the pilfering and destruction that was going on even as they conversed, Wells said, "It'll take the help of Divine Providence, a heap of rain, and a deal of elbow-grease to fix things up again." According to Sherman's military telegrapher, Wells "came into camp soon after tea and chatted with the General and staff until Eleven O'clock."

Somehow Sherman did find time to attend to military matters. As late as 3:00 P.M. he was still fretting over a possible enemy effort at Millen. When he provided movement directions to Left Wing commander Major General Henry W. Slocum, Sherman also advised him to keep an ear cocked toward Millen "in case you hear the sound of battle." Some time later, a courier arrived from Major General Howard with the best possible news. One of Howard's most trustworthy scouts, Captain William Duncan, had just reported in from a recon to the east. Duncan with his men had penetrated to "within three miles of Millen, on this side [south] of the river, and found no enemy." Along the way, the Yankees fell in with a Rebel lieutenant whom they took prisoner. "Not much information could be got from him," Howard related. Still, if Duncan's report held up and the enemy wasn't making a stand at Millen, then another important hurdle would have been cleared.

Not far from where Sherman's campfires flickered, the passage of the Seventeenth Corps continued well into the morning hours. Major Hitchcock went to the river's edge to watch the soldiers "crossing by light of fires on either side, striking scene, and sounds too." With him was fellow staffer George Nichols, a sometime correspondent for the *New York Post*, who (writing anonymously) would produce a lengthy account of the campaign that was reprinted many times:[*] "A novel and vivid sight was it to see the first of pitch pine flaring up into the mist and darkness, the figures of man and horse looming out of the dense shadows in gigantic proportions. Torchlights are blinking and flashing away off in the forests, while the still air echoed and re-echoed with the cries of teamsters and the wild shouts of the soldiers. A long line of the troops marched across the foot bridge, each soldier bearing a torch; their light reflected in quivering lines in the swift running stream."

---

[*]   These accounts became the basis for a successful memoir of Sherman's March, published in 1865.

CHAPTER 18

"Give Those Fellows a Start"

THURSDAY, DECEMBER 1, 1864

Every element in Sherman's operation was in motion. The most provocative was a double-barreled column pushing out from Louisville that started at 12:15 P.M., following the most direct road to Waynesboro. The leading portion consisted of Brigadier General Kilpatrick's cavalry division. Marching in their dust along the same route was Brigadier General Absalom Baird's Third Division of the Fourteenth Corps. Exactly what the movement portended depended on who was asked.

It was Sherman's intention to keep Wheeler's cavalrymen so occupied that they wouldn't harass him as he pivoted on Millen to turn southeast toward Savannah—essentially exposing the logistical tail of his operation to enemy units operating out of Augusta. Griswoldville had shown him that the Rebels weren't averse to sallying forth from a stronghold to strike at his rear.* So his directive to Kilpatrick was to move "in the direction of Augusta, [and] if Wheeler gave him the opportunity, to indulge him with all the fighting he wanted."

Kilpatrick's sense of the mission was more circumscribed. According to his official report, its object was "to cover the movements of our troops, marching in several columns on Millen." Brigadier General

---

* At least, that is how Sherman read the incident. The fact that it was an accidental collision between his rear guard and Georgia militiamen trying to get around him was not known until much later.

Milledgeville to Millen

DAY SEVENTEEN:
Thursday, December 1, 1864

UNDER THE GUN
[LW] Waynesboro/Millen

South
Carolina

Augusta

Shoals

Sylvan
Grove

Milledgeville

Waynesboro

Alexander
Thomas

Sandersville

Louisville

Lumpkins

Hebron

Davisboro

Buckhead
Church

Tennille

Camp
Lawton

Riddleville

Spier's
Turnout

Gordon

Irwins
Crossroads

Sebastopol

Birdsville

Millen

Toomsboro

Irwinton

Midville
(Burton)

Ball's
Ferry

Summertown

Scarboro

Wrightsville

Kite

Weather:
clear
mid-40s to upper 60s

Dublin

Swainsboro

Statesboro

Baird had his own opinion, which he shared with his staff officer, Major James A. Connolly. Said the aide: "The General pointed out to me on the map, this morning, our line of march for the next few days, and I find that our Division, together with Kilpatrick's cavalry is to form a flying column,* to be detached from the main army, and strike ahead boldly toward Augusta, fighting Wheeler, and everything else that comes in our way, stubbornly, driving them before us, and demonstrating in such a way as to confirm the impression that the army is advancing on Augusta."

The determined Confederate campaign of misinformation regarding Augusta's defenses resulted in no one on the Union side really knowing what to expect. Enthusiastic newspaper accounts of troops

---

* A military column without supply wagons or other impedimenta to allow for the maximum possible speed.

arriving there from distant points were not taken at face value, nor were they dismissed out of hand. Connolly realized that "Sherman didn't know what is at Augusta, or between here and there; neither do we know. A rebel army of 50,000 men may be on us before daylight tomorrow morning, for all we know, but I suppose that is just the reason Sherman has sent us off this way, and it will probably all turn out right."

What was actually standing in the way of the combined cavalry/infantry column were observation detachments sent out by Wheeler, who was holding his main body along Rocky Creek, perhaps twenty miles east from Louisville and five west from Waynesboro. The units assigned to shadow the flying column contested the advance using all their skills and advantages of ground. The Johnny Rebs, admitted an Indiana trooper, "fought us real stubbornly." In one of the day's first encounters, which took place some four miles out, the 5th Kentucky Cavalry came upon a roadblock situated so as to make a saber charge impossible and where, reported the Union commander, "nothing save bulldog fighting could do me any good."

It soon became apparent that the infantry was better suited to this kind of combat, so Kilpatrick asked Baird to take over the point. The column was rearranged—infantry in the center, cavalry on the flanks—and the march resumed. "We then moved rapidly," Baird reported. It was getting dark by the time they reached Buckhead Creek—twelve miles west of Louisville and thirteen from Waynesboro—where they coiled up for the night in a defensive alignment. As fighting went, the day had been more noise than anything else, but everyone suspected that it would get worse.

The rest of the infantry on the north side of the Ogeechee River—Sherman's entire force save one corps—tramped eastward in three columns. The Seventeenth Corps was closest to the river, following the Central of Georgia Railroad. Moving in tandem north of it on the road from Louisville to Millen via Birdsville was the Twentieth Corps. Utilizing the next road system farther north were the two remaining divisions of the Fourteenth Corps, which were also shepherding most of the Left Wing's wagons as well as those for the cavalry. Off to their left were Baird and Kilpatrick.

These movements brought blessed relief to the Louisville area residents. The past days had been an endless roulette of incursions into homes accompanied by the firing of unoccupied structures that often threatened adjacent houses. It took courage, determination, wit, and luck for people to hold on to as much of their property as they could without inciting further violence from marauding Yankees. When one woman rushed into her burning house to rescue belongings, she met a Federal soldier on his way out, clutching some of her best gingham cloth. To her great surprise, he thrust it at her as they passed, saying: "Here, I'll give this to you." "Thank you," she answered, "it is mine anyhow."

On the outskirts of the town the Holt family had suffered a great deal. Convinced that Judge Holt, the clan patriarch, had hidden valuables, some foragers strung up and dangled him until he nearly passed out, all to force him to reveal the hiding place. Only the presence of a fellow Mason among the pillagers saved the roof over the family's heads. Nora Holt, the plantation matron, learned that even their faithful servants had not been spared. One of the black women she owned came to her in tears, saying that the recent grave of her deceased child had been dug up in the search for plunder, the tiny coffined body left discarded next to the pit. "What kind of folks dese here Yankees?" she asked Mrs. Holt. "Dey won't even let de dead rest in de grave."

Since the Seventeenth Corps was following the railroad right-of-way, it got the job of wrecking the line. "Broke camp at 7," scrawled a diarist, "moved to railroad station and filed down track—troops tearing it up—reach our point—tear up, burn and twist—hard work—hot sun—hot fires!" "The rail was of the light pattern, such as is generally used now for horse-car tracks," observed an Illinois man. This more malleable material made possible one of the enduring symbols of Sherman's March. An Iowa soldier related that after the rails had been "heated in the middle for about 10 or 12 feet of their length they would fasten a piece of telegraph wire on either end and 6 or 8 of them would get hold of each end and take it to a tree or telegraph pole and going around in opposite directions would wind the rail around the tree. The boys called them neck ties."

While some soldiers "repaired" the railroad, others foraged. Gunpowder, however, was a critical item that could not be replenished through seizures. Orders issued today by the Seventeenth Corps commander addressed that issue. "The practice of indiscriminate firing must be stopped," it proclaimed. Officers, who were strictly enjoined to monitor cartridge usage, were authorized to impose a penalty on those who acted irresponsibly. "The cartridge-boxes of forage parties will be inspected on their return from duty each day," the directive continued, "and the men will be charged 50 cents for each cartridge missing that cannot be satisfactorily accounted for." The orders proved to be another layer of paper control, difficult to enforce, and ignored by officers who did not regard the measures as serious enough to warrant attention.

The Twentieth Corps and the two divisions of the Fourteenth not supporting Kilpatrick conducted their marches in the standard pattern—organized parties of foragers spread far and wide, with the main column taking care of cotton to be burned or structures to be demolished. Private Rumor walked in the ranks, this day with tales of Hood's fate in Tennessee, possible destinations for the campaign, and the story of a wealthy widow willing to put up $40,000 for the return of her husband's body from the battleground at Gettysburg.

Despite Wheeler's focus on protecting Waynesboro by stopping Kilpatrick, there were still enough mounted Rebel bands infiltrating the line of march to make it a gamble for a small foraging party and a scrap for a larger one. "On the 1st of December, three men, belonging to the regiment, were murdered," reported a member of the 21st Ohio. Adding to the litany was a diary entry by a soldier in the 79th Pennsylvania who recorded that the "Rebels . . . captured our Brig[ade] Q[uarter] M[aster] & 3 men, shooting them all, some of them with their throats cut from ear to ear." The officer commanding the 88th Indiana reported that his foraging party "numbering thirty-two men and one officer, were attacked some five miles out by a squad of rebel cavalry, but succeeded in getting off with a goodly supply of forage and no loss."

The Seventeenth Corps would bivouac for this night near the Burke County line on the grounds of the Joseph B. Jones plantation, "said to be one of the finest in the state." The two Fourteenth Corps divisions reached Reynolds's plantation, scene of Kilpatrick's fierce holding action. The Twentieth Corps paused in Burke County, about two-thirds of the way from Louisville to Birdsville. As the soldiers settled down for the evening, a member of the 129th Illinois was treated to an impromptu vocal concert by some of the Rebel prisoners he was guarding, with lyrics tailored to the occasion:

Come, Come, Come, Rain, Come
Come 'till you flow o're our boots
Come and we'll thank 'ye to keep back Yankee
Until our ranks are filled up with recruits.

South of the river the Fifteenth Corps matched general course and speed with the rest of the army, managing to avoid much of the forager problems happening north of them, but passing over a landscape clearly not intended for military traffic. "This was a busy day for the Pioneer Corps," related an Illinois soldier. "Many bad sloughs were bridged or corduroyed with rails and poles, to make them passable for the artillery and trains." "We . . . have to wade the swamps every two or three hundred yards," seconded a weary Buckeye. For the next few days this corps would operate in two columns moving on a pair of roads that, according to Major General Osterhaus's map, ran "substantially parallel to and south of the Ogeechee River and the Savannah railroad." If true, this route would carry the men almost to the very outskirts of Savannah itself.

The major encounters on this leg of Sherman's March were between man and creatures. An Ohio soldier reported finding "American scorpions" in the camp, while a Minnesotan recorded the death of a twelve-foot pine snake. Food gathering went well, a member of the 66th Illinois recalling the sight of "the foragers coming in loaded down with bee-hives on their shoulders, the open end of the hive to the rear, and bees flying back to their master's plantation; some of the boys have young porkers on their horses." This night the corps' encampments were roughly in line with Millen, on course toward Statesboro.

The passage east of the Fifteenth Corps meant that peace finally returned to the Sample plantation and its neighbors, though a high price had been paid. When the morning passed without incident, Sue Sample with her sister-in-law Rachel went calling on Rachel's aunt, who lived next door. The Yankees here had been especially destructive. "The beds were torn open, feathers all out," Sample recollected. "The bedsteads were chopped to pieces, books stolen, and not a thing left worth sleeping on." It was all too much for Rachel, who "fell across the bed and wept."

There was worse to come. Another wave of foragers (these on foot) passed through the area to take care of everything that the mounted men couldn't carry. "They shot all the hogs in the pen," remembered Sample. "We could hear nothing but guns all day and the squeals of hogs." She at last encountered an officer whom she identified as being Brigadier General John E. Smith. "Our Men are carrying on a great destruction," he remarked. Observing soldiers loading wagons with precious stocks of corn, Sample begged them to leave something for the women and children to eat. When the foragers finally departed, they left enough corn on hand to guarantee that the family would not starve, though many of her neighbors told Sample that they had been cleaned out. Sue Sample always wondered: "Was it my entreaties that saved it?"

The closest anyone in Rebel authority came to Sherman's advance today was Station No. 7 on the Central of Georgia Railroad, also called Scarboro. Major General Henry C. Wayne of the Oconee Bridge action arrived on a special train from Savannah. All he could gather before reversing down the line were unconfirmed bits of news; that the enemy was already in Millen, and that Sherman had split his army in order to advance along both sides of the Ogeechee. His arrival and departure were observed by Union scouts sent out by Major General Howard, who was then just across the river. The scouts noted that Wayne's train was operating "with great caution."

North of Wayne, at his camp along Rocky Creek, Major General Wheeler mulled over a dispatch from General Bragg's adjutant that seemed to put the entire responsibility for stopping Sherman on his small command. Not only was the cavalry general expected to "cover the enemy's front," but he was also supposed to "retard his movements much, whatever may be his line of march." In addition, Wheeler was tasked with spreading the word that "we are very largely re-enforced here [at Augusta] and at Savannah, and are preparing for any movement on us."

This day had an emotional start for Sherman, who began it by biding farewell to "old Johnny Wells." The General, recollected a staff member present, "took the trouble to go round by his house[,] shake hands & say good bye. The scene was quite affecting. The tears trickled down [Wells's] . . . face and all he could say was God bless you and make you successful."

Sherman accompanied the Seventeenth Corps, and likely stopped from time to time to proffer unsolicited advice on the proper way to destroy a railroad. Camp for this night was at the Jones plantation, where Major Hitchcock had nothing but scorn for the master, a fire-breathing Rebel legislator who took himself off to safety in Savannah, while leaving his property in the care of his wife, "sick in bed; infant *four days old*, eight other children [present] . . . oldest only *ten or eleven* years old." Sherman spoke to the invalid mistress to set her mind at ease, then arranged for supplies to be stocked in the house. He took no action to halt the foraging that was otherwise stripping the Jones holdings.

A Georgia citizen named Mallory visited with the General this evening. He did not impress Hitchcock, who thought him "rather hang-dog and cowed looking." Mallory's presence prompted another of Hitchcock's moral self-examinations as he charted how far his feelings had changed in the course of the past weeks. "Evidently it is a material element in this campaign to produce among the *people of Georgia* a thorough conviction of the personal misery which attends war, and of the utter helplessness and inability of their 'rulers,' State or Confederate, to protect them. And I am bound to say that I believe more and more that only by this means the war can be ended,—and that *by this means it can*."

Doing what was necessary to finish things was much on Sherman's mind as he dictated a message this evening intended for Brigadier General Kilpatrick. Perhaps sensing in the cavalryman's report a plaintive tone seeking approval, Sherman took care to assure him that his operations to date "have been entirely satisfactory to the general-in-chief." He repeated his desire that Kilpatrick not hold back from giving the "enemy all he wants when he offers you battle." Finally, Sherman felt compelled to address a subject raised by Kilpatrick: acts of terror against his troopers.

The cavalry officer recounted more instances of the murder and mutilation of his men after they had been taken prisoner. Sherman was not yet convinced by the anecdotal evidence he had been given, yet he could not ignore the increasing number of incidents. He wanted to be sure that Kilpatrick put Wheeler on personal notice that the atrocities had to stop. Once Kilpatrick had alerted Wheeler, should he obtain substantial proof that Rebel soldiers were committing the excesses, the cavalry general would receive official approval to retaliate. In such a circumstance, said Sherman: "You may hang and muti-

late man for man without regard to rank." The edge of a terrible abyss had been reached, and Sherman was fully prepared to cross it if the situation—according to *his* rules of war—justified such a course of action.

FRIDAY, DECEMBER 2, 1864

By the day's order of march, Major General Joseph A. Mower's First Division (Seventeenth Corps) had the lead following the railroad along the Ogeechee River. His division would be the first to reach Millen, which still wasn't good enough for Captain Oscar L. Jackson, commanding a company in one of Mower's regiments, the 63rd Ohio. Jackson, who also happened to be in charge of the regiment's foragers, was determined to get into Millen before anyone else in order to secure the best supplies for his men. His brigade commander gave him the okay to proceed, cautioning the captain to keep his group "well together and be cautious as . . . the enemy had been there a few hours previous and it was not yet known that they were gone."

Jackson's party arrived at the railroad bridge across Buckhead Creek several hours ahead of the main column. The floor planking had been thrown off and a feeble attempt made to torch the span, but, stepping gingerly, Jackson was able to get his "men across the creek in single file on the standing timbers." To his great relief, there were no Rebel soldiers in the town. Posting a detail to watch the roads, the officer sent the remainder of his small command off to forage.

Besides the usual goodies, they found a lot of honey bee hives. "We would set a hive off the stand and split it open and brush the bees away and fill the heavy comb into vessels," Jackson recollected. "It was warm and the bees [were] able to fly but seemed too much frightened to sting." The Ohio boys had the town to themselves for only a short while before a patrol from the 1st Alabama Cavalry, on detached service with the infantry, ambled in to join the fun.

Jackson was comparing notes with the cavalry leader when one of his men came running over to report that a train that had come up the line from the south was stopped just outside the town. It must have been a scouting mission since its conductor was walking ahead to gauge the lay of the land. He paid for his boldness when he ran into Jackson's picket line and was taken prisoner. Several of the cavalrymen galloped out to try to capture the train, but the alert engineer reversed gears in time to back out of danger.

When the head of the heavy column arrived at the creek by mid-afternoon, it was halted while engineers from the 1st Michigan repaired the bridge to handle bulk traffic. "Some of the boys had to get down and 'coon it over,' " remarked a soldier in the 32nd Ohio. "One fellow fell off into the creek and came near losing his life." Once the bridge had been restored, and the columns were passing through the town, serious attention was given to the legitimate targets of war. "The railroad and all government property destroyed," commented an infantryman in the 43rd Ohio. The three divisions of the Seventeenth Corps camped this night in the Millen area.

South of the Ogeechee, the Fifteenth Corps marched in two columns operating roughly parallel to the river. Although the course of one was along what was grandly styled the Old Savannah Road, passage was anything but routine. "We had to wade a great many swamps," recorded an Ohio diarist. "The roads very bad and we was obliged to make corduroy [roads] across the swamps," added a journal keeper in the 47th Ohio. The point where the road crossed Scull's Creek posed a significant challenge, requiring the construction of a log bridge for the wagons and ammunition. A mile or so beyond the creek, the leading brigade reached Clifton Ferry on the Ogeechee, diagonally across from Scarboro. The 1st Missouri Engineers were on hand, and in a remarkably short time a pontoon bridge had been laid over the Ogeechee, allowing a large mounted party to go across, reach the Central of Georgia track, then scout southeast as far as Scarboro.

The Federals galloped into the small station town to learn that the last train to Savannah had departed not two hours earlier. The local post office yielded a fine selection of recent Savannah newspapers, which were forwarded to Major General Howard. A civilian telegraph operator named Jonathan Lonergan was riding with this group. Lonergan found that his enemy counterpart had thought to take his instrument with him, but when he hooked his own device to the wires, the circuit south was still functioning.

For the next fifteen minutes the Yankee listened as Confederate operators down the line exchanged chatter without any helpful context. Now and again Lonergan heard an interrogatory for operator "9," and it finally dawned on him that it referred to the Scarboro station. Tapping an acknowledgment, he was rewarded with the query: "What is the news? What is going on?" Lonergan promptly replied: "The Yankees have not yet crossed the river, and all is quiet." Hoping to glean some fresh intelligence, he continued: "What is the news from the East? How are things looking in Savannah?"

The distant operator, growing suddenly suspicious, demanded to know the identity of his correspondent. Fortunately, an officer with the scouting party had learned the Scarboro telegrapher's name. Lonergan promptly identified himself as the man, but any hopes he had of reaping a harvest of information were dashed when the man himself broke into the circuit from the next station to the south and exposed his deception. With the ruse exposed, Lonergan exchanged ironic pleasantries with the distant operator, spiced with barbed comments and patently false information. "Darkness approaching and camp being some distance off, the conversation ended," reported Lonergan.

Across the Ogeechee from where he was sitting, the Fifteenth Corps settled into camp, the northern wing near Scull's Creek, the two divisions to the south in Bulloch County. An Illinois veteran resting near the Right Wing headquarters scribbled in his diary: "While soul stirring music is being dispensed by Gen. Howard's band—A warm day & pleasant evening,—Have heard the news from a Rebel paper today—They pretend to think that Sherman's army is surrounded & about to be captured."

North of the Seventeenth Corps' line of march, the columns constituting all of the Twentieth Corps and two-thirds of the Fourteenth merged at a crossroads about two miles northeast of Birdsville, with the former having the right-of-way. The roads posed no exceptional problems, so the foragers were especially active. One incident this day offered a case study in how soldiers drawn from different regiments could work together for their own defense and self-interest.

It began with a decision by Sergeant Lyman Widney to undertake an unofficial foraging expedition with his messmate. The two set off at sunrise, hoping to prove the childhood adage that the early bird gets the worm. They encountered their first house after a tramp of several miles, only to find that it had just been visited by a five-man foraging party, so the pair trudged on. As they approached a small woods, they heard several shots. Soon two Federal soldiers came running toward them, exclaiming that their group of five had been ambushed by Rebel cavalry.

"We now considered ourselves in a predicament," related Widney, "five miles ahead of our army and almost face to face with the enemy." Looking over their shoulders, they saw not a relief column, but scattered clumps of men—other foraging parties like themselves. A bit of frantic signaling brought many to them on the run; before very long there were fifty or more soldiers on hand from perhaps a half-dozen regiments. A skirmish line was organized, and the group, representing several units and without any officers present, moved aggressively into the woods. The extended skirmish line pushed through the little forest, locating the bodies of the ambushed foragers as well as the remains of the Rebel cavalry's night camp. Popping out of the belt of trees, the Yankees found themselves on the edge of a clearing, with mounted Rebels formed along the opposite side.

Neither group seemed anxious to press the issue, which worked to the advantage of the Federals, for more and more foragers joined them until the size of the battle line was imposing enough to scare away the enemy riders. With the danger removed, the impromptu formation dissolved as the soldiers picked up where they had left off. When Sergeant Widney and his messmate rejoined their regiment that night with their spoils, they were welcomed as lost souls, since their comrades "had heard just enough of our encounter to believe that the worms had caught the early birds."

After dispersing a few Rebel pickets near Buckhead Church, the combined Twentieth/Fourteenth Corps column settled in for the night, a short march from the rail line connecting Millen with Augusta through Waynesboro. Just to their north was the flying column of infantry and cavalry, which had itself had a very busy day.

The formation—aligned like yesterday, infantry in the middle, cavalry watching the flanks—set off shortly after sunrise. "Commenced skirmishing with the enemy before we had gone a mile," noted the enterprising staff officer, Major James Connolly. Brigadier General Baird, in overall charge of the expedition, wasn't one to take chances. Connolly noted that "our movement was slow and extremely cautious, the ground ahead being well reconnoitered by our advance parties and skirmishers." The enemy made every effort to justify Baird's caution. "We have had sharp skirmishing with the rebels all day," recorded an Indiana trooper. "They would take advantage of every creek, swamp, or any place they could retard our march."

Brigadier General Baird, a Pennsylvanian, was something of an abolitionist. He made it a point to personally question as many slaves as possible, even allowing one named Jerry to tag along as a guide. Major Connolly thought him "a lively, rollicking, fun loving fellow, with a good deal of shrewdness." Jerry and Baird had been riding together chatting amicably for the entire morning when the black man suddenly erupted in a loud laugh. "Golly," he said in response to Baird's questioning look, "I wish old massa could see me now, ridin' wid de Ginrals."

Eight miles on the flying column approached Rocky Creek, behind which Confederate General Wheeler was waiting with some of his men. The fight for the crossing unfolded in two short phases. In the first, Kilpatrick's cavalry cleared the Rebel outposts away from the creek's south side. These advance posts existed solely to sound the warning, so the Southern riders wasted little time getting across when challenged. "We made them fly," boasted a Pennsylvania trooper.

Phase two was a little trickier, since General Baird was careful with his men's lives. After probing the length of Wheeler's line and locating an undefended stretch, Blair sent one regiment across Rocky Creek. Once over, the unit—the 74th Indiana—immediately made its presence known to Wheeler, who, finding his line breached, pulled back toward Waynesboro. In Major Connolly's words, the Rebs "lit out."

Several of Kilpatrick's regiments charged across the creek to hurry the Rebels along. They brought back with them a wounded Texan who under interrogation admitted that everyone was expecting an attack on Augusta. "He also told us that there was no rebel infantry outside of Augusta, and that Wheeler's cavalry was scattered all over the country," reported Connolly.

The combined column pressed forward a mile to a crossroads where generals Baird and Kilpatrick argued about the next move—Kilpatrick wanting to follow the most direct route to Waynesboro, Baird preferring to swing below it in order to establish contact with the middle columns coming toward them from Birdsville. Since Baird was senior, his opinion prevailed, so everyone jogged a short distance south before setting up for the night. "If we get any communication from the rest of our Corps tomorrow we *may* turn toward Augusta again," observed Major Connolly.*

Sherman's headquarters tent for this night was located on the west bank of Buckhead Creek, just outside Millen. After tending to his duties, Major Hitchcock came upon the General engaged in a lively conversation ("wish I could note it," said the aide) with five or six black men, who let one of their number do most of the talking. They had reasoned through the question of whether or not to accompany the Union army and had concluded it would be better for them to stay put. Sherman endorsed their decision, and was clearly impressed by the insight shown by the group's spokesman.

The elder slave displayed his knowledge of African-American history by citing the military service performed by blacks for General Andrew Jackson at New Orleans in the War of 1812. Sherman men-

---

* Baird's decision to close with his support allowed General Wheeler's advocates to proclaim that his defense of the Rocky Creek line compelled the Yankees "to turn their course" away from Waynesboro.

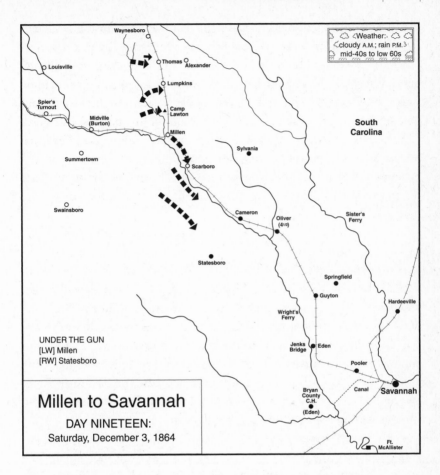

Waynesboro

Weather: cloudy A.M.; rain P.M. mid-40s to low 60s

Louisville

Thomas Alexander

Lumpkins

Spier's Turnout

Midville (Burton)

Camp Lawton

Millen

South Carolina

Summertown

Sylvania

Scarboro

Swainsboro

Cameron

Oliver (4½)

Sister's Ferry

Statesboro

Springfield

Guyton

Hardeeville

Wright's Ferry

UNDER THE GUN
[LW] Millen
[RW] Statesboro

Jenks Bridge

Eden

Pooler

Bryan County C.H. (Eden)

Canal

Savannah

Millen to Savannah

DAY NINETEEN:
Saturday, December 3, 1864

Ft. McAllister

tioned that the Rebel president had announced his intention to arm the slaves to help the Confederacy. If Jefferson Davis went ahead with his plan, Sherman wondered aloud, would blacks fight against the Union? "No, Sir," said the spokesman with emphasis, "de day dey gives us arms, *dat day de war ends!*"

When he wasn't chatting with his black visitors, Sherman was making some key decisions regarding the campaign's ultimate objective. To Major General Henry W. Slocum of the Left Wing, Sherman designated a pair of roads to be used by the Fourteenth and Twentieth corps in order to "continue to march toward Savannah." General Kilpatrick, he told Slocum, "will be instructed to confer with you and cover your rear."

Major General Oliver O. Howard also learned for certain that the "next movement will be on Savannah." He was to keep the Fifteenth Corps marching along the west side of the Ogeechee River, as the Seventeenth was to continue to chew up the railroad along the opposite bank. Sherman, believing that the Confederate leadership remained uncertain whether he intended to strike for Macon, Augusta, or Savannah, authorized Howard, if feasible, to send raiding parties well south of Savannah to disrupt the rail links with lower Georgia and Florida. Speed was now becoming a watchword. Sherman remarked on the Savannah garrison: "The fewer the men and the sooner the party starts the better."

SATURDAY, DECEMBER 3, 1864

An American eagle of a military bent, loitering high over the confluence of the Ogeechee River and Buckhead Creek, would have observed a decided, even decisive, change in the direction of Storm Sherman. Fully three-quarters of his force was either now committed or in the process of being committed to roads that led unerringly to the south and east—toward Savannah. The course so clearly delineated ran along a peninsula-like corridor, bounded to the east by the Savannah River and to the west by the Ogeechee. Into this region Sherman now steered three infantry corps and his cavalry division.

Both flanks were protected by difficult-to-cross water systems, which provided the principal tactical advantage of this movement. The main disadvantage was that Sherman was clearly showing his hand, so his enemy, who had been stumbling and struggling to pin down his front, would soon know precisely where to find it. The closer to Savannah Sherman's columns marched, the more the land became favorable to the defense. The number of swamps and swampy streams increased to the point where moving the wagons was limited to narrow strips of built-up roadways, making a situation ideal for delaying actions.

It was partially to offset this defensive advantage that Sherman kept one corps moving along the southwest bank of the Ogeechee, ready to turn any line of resistance the Confederates might try to establish. An almost textbook example of this plan working was provided this day by Confederate Major General Henry C. Wayne, who was nervously monitoring the Federal movements in person. On December 2 Wayne retreated from Station No. 7, Scarboro, to No. 4½, in the area of modern Oliver. There, at the junction of the Ogeechee River and Ogeechee Creek, Wayne was joined by several militia units under Colonel Robert Toombs,[*] forwarded from Savannah. About 10:30 A.M., after receiving a briefing about the advances of the Union Fifteenth Corps along the Ogeechee's opposite bank, Wayne recognized that this column "would cut my rear," so he conferred with Colonel Toombs. They agreed on a strategic withdrawal of approximately twenty-seven miles, to Station No. 2, Eden.

Sitting in Savannah with his maps spread before him, Lieutenant General Hardee realized at once that Wayne's precipitate maneuver ceded a strong defensive position behind Ogeechee Creek, so when the militiaman arrived at Eden, he was met by one of the general's staff officers "with instructions to return to No. 4½, and that further re-enforcements would be sent to me. Obeyed the instructions, though in opposition to my own judgment and that of my officers, and re-occupied No. 4½ about 7 P.M.," Wayne reported. Sherman could read maps as well as Hardee. Even though he had no knowledge of Wayne's back-and-forth actions, he saw the same potential at Station No. 4½ as did his opposite number. He pointed it out today to Major Hitchcock, commenting: "There we must cross a creek and there they have the shortest line to hold from river to river." Added the aide: "Perhaps we shall fight them then—*perhaps not.*"

Overall, the General was well satisfied, with one or two caveats. As he later related, "the whole army was in good position and in good condition. We had largely subsisted on the country; our wagons were full of forage and provisions; but, as we approached the sea-coast, the country became more sandy and barren, and food became more scarce; still, with little or no loss, we had traveled two-thirds of our distance, and I concluded to push on for Savannah."

The marches made by the Fifteenth Corps, south of the Ogeechee, had positioned its columns roughly opposite Millen and Scarboro, points only just reached today by units on the north side, so for many of Major General Osterhaus's men this was a day of rest. Clothes washing figured in several diary agendas, as did bathing in the river and some of its tributaries. "There was a forage party sent out, they brought

---

[*] Toombs had been a brigadier general while in Confederate service, but upon his return to Georgia had entered the state military as a colonel.

in pork, potatoes, & corn and fodder," recorded a journal keeper in the 63rd Illinois. The history of the 53rd Ohio noted the discovery of a citizen who secreted himself underground with his goods. "He was buried with his valuables," recounts the history, "but the sharp nose of the Union boys discovered the 'stiff' and brought it to the surface, together with the valuables. It was amusing to see the foragers going around prodding the ground with their ramrods or bayonets, seeking for soft spots, and when such were struck, they soon found a shovel to see what was buried beneath."

The exceptions to this pattern were two brigades—one each from the First and Fourth divisions—sent across the Ogeechee on the pontoon bridge to wreck the railroad between Millen and Scarboro. Viewing the railway route outlined by pyres of burning ties, an Illinois man reflected, "How terrible the sweep of an unchecked army!" The Fifteenth Corps brigades joined with others from the Seventeenth on the same mission. "At Millen there was a junction, one branch to Augusta, the other to Savannah," reported a Wisconsin soldier. "We tore up the junction, burned the depot and five large buildings that were used for prisoners." "Broke camp at daylight," contributed a comrade in the 10th Illinois, "moved down railroad three miles and tear up, burn and twist—twenty eight rails first . . . , forty rails second time."

North of Millen, the roads followed by the Twentieth Corps took its columns to an intersection with the branch rail line between Millen and Augusta, just outside the former, where the men did what by now came naturally. "Having stacked arms and posted pickets, some distance from the [rail]road, we went to work; half of the regiment remaining at our arms, while the other half was at the work of destruction. As soon as a few rods of the road had been destroyed, the party at work was relieved by the party guarding the arms. Fence rails were set afire and the iron rails laid across, whereby the latter soon became bent and unserviceable. The road had been repaired by the rebels but a few days before, as we saw from the newly made ditches on both sides of the track, not supposing that we would be there so soon."

The course followed by the Twentieth Corps brought many of its units near enough to Camp Lawton that curious soldiers flocked to the place like tourists to a popular attraction, though the images they recorded were anything but pleasant ones.

Samuel Storrow, 2nd Massachusetts

Visited the Stockades where the Rebels confined our prisoners. The one we saw was 450 or 500 yards square on a gentle slope with a brook at the bottom. On the hill opposite was a fort which commanded the whole of the interior of the Stockade, within easy grape range.* The stockade was of pine logs a foot thick & 20 feet high, with sentry boxes perched on top & outside. . . . A slight railing ran all the way around about 25 feet from the stockade; this was the "dead line;" any man crossing or leaning on this was liable to be shot without any warning.

John Potter, 101st Illinois

The prisoners were compelled to erect houses or sheds for their own shelter. The material was soon all worked up and the later arrivals could not do any better than to scoop holes in the sand, and many of them died and were left, as it were, actually in graves of their own digging.

George S. Bradley, 22nd Wisconsin

The huts were built in all manner of shapes. Some had walls of logs, with a covering of timber, and over these a good layer of sand. Some had walls of turf, again others were cut into the ground perhaps two feet and then covered, sometimes with pine slabs, sometimes with sand, and some were simply thatched with pine boughs, while others were bare sheds. It made my heart ache to look upon such miserable hovels, hardly fit for our swine to live in, and here our brave soldiers had to stay.

Rice C. Bull, 123rd New York

There was not a soul around the place when we arrived and the only things left were a few dirty, filthy-looking rags. Not a long distance from the prison I was amazed to see the largest spring I ever saw; from it gushed a stream that would be called a small river in the North . . . , the stream from the spring ran near the stockade and I think furnished water for the prison; if so, they had at least good water.

---

* The reference is to grape shot, an antipersonnel cannon munition containing golf-ball-size lead balls that spread out on discharge like a shotgun blast.

Peter K. Arnold, 28th Pennsylvania
We saw one of the stockades where they had kept our prisoners. Many
was the curse that was recorded against the Rebels by our troops on
that day.

David Anderson, 19th Michigan
We found the bodies of several of our men lying unburied in this loath-
some den; consigning them to the parent earth, our bugles sounded, and
falling in line, solemnly and sadly we moved away.

Once reports were confirmed that Camp Lawton no longer held any Union prisoners, Sherman's interest in the place waned. Even though he and his staff spent several hours in Millen proper, he did not bother to make the short ride north to view the abandoned compound. All of which is not to say he had banished it from his reckoning. Individuals who had visited the place passed along their impressions, which was sufficient for Sherman to assign culpability to the rail junction that switched so many onto tracks carrying them to the prison. According to an officer in the 63rd Ohio, Sherman's verbal instruction to Major General Frank Blair, commanding the Seventeenth Corps, "was to make the destruction [of Millen] 'tenfold more devilish' than he had ever dreamed of, as this is one of the places they have been starving our prisoners."

The punishment meted out by Sherman nearly had fatal consequences for Major Hitchcock, who was present in the town when the hotel (not normally a legitimate target) was set ablaze. He was watching it burn with some fellow staffers when word spread that a crazy old woman who lived in the town was still inside. Hitchcock raced into the burning building with two others, where they saw a few hardy foragers taking care of business before the flames consumed everything, but no victim was found. They finally located her outside the burning hotel, holding a goose on a makeshift leash and talking to herself. Before he departed, the conscious-stricken major left some U.S. money with a black woman, who promised to take care of her.

The slow passage of the Twentieth Corps past Camp Lawton backed traffic using the roadway running past Buckhead Church, forcing the two trailing divisions of the Fourteenth Corps to seek an alternative route. This led Brevet Major General Jefferson C. Davis's men to improvise a course north and then east, a path that took them into a region of swamps, dim roads, and two significant stream crossings.

"Got lost, turned back, and cut across fields & woods, struck several woods, left them, kept cutting across," scribbled a weary Illinois boy. Added a Wisconsin comrade: "Moved at 6 A.M. again over roads leading in almost every direction, sometimes almost in a circle apparently." The tramp became even more of an ordeal for several Yankees who decided to emulate the blacks they saw chewing on sugar cane. "In a raw state the juice acts as a physic and the men were ignorant of the fact," chuckled another Wisconsin soldier, "and besides not being used to it became the more readily its victim. After a few hours it was amusing to observe how anxiously the men would dodge aside in the woods or swamps which was the cause of much joking and merriment."

It required a small pontoon bridge to carry the two divisions across Buckhead Creek, after which there was another bridge needing repair to allow the columns to pass over Rosemary Creek. Both were provided by the pontoniers of the 58th Indiana. "While crossing the pontoon at Buckhead, a mule loaded with sweet potatoes, lost his equilibrium and fell into the stream," reported a member of the 113th Ohio. "He was fished out by the boys, more on account of the load he carried than for their love of the animal."

The bottleneck passing over Buckhead Creek provided General Davis with the opportunity to cut down on the size of the black host following his column. Davis, a Kentuckian, was not counted among the more racially enlightened members of the officer corps. Like many of his white peers, he had greeted President Lincoln's Emancipation Proclamation with profound skepticism, worrying that it "can do nothing but mischief." His views on the matter of the proper status for the newly liberated African-Americans did not differ much from those of his immediate superior, Major General Sherman.

Obeying verbal orders from higher up the chain of command, provosts kept blacks off the pontoon bridge while the soldiers and their wagons were using it. Then, after the military procession had completed passage, the pontoons were quickly pulled over to the far side of the stream, leaving the refugee column with no easy means of getting over. However, as an Illinoisan noted, "Nothing could induce them to turn back." Buckhead Creek was simply too insubstantial a barrier to a determined people. By some accounts, about 500 "were left on the wrong side of the river sure enough, but when we broke camp next morning they were there again all the same." There is some secondhand testimony that a few blacks drowned attempting to cross, and doubtless several turned back, but most persisted. Unfortunately for the refugees, the message understood by the officers who had ordered the action was to wait for a bigger stream before trying it again.

Major General Sherman was seen in Millen by an Ohio officer who recollected him as a "very plain, unassuming man and [who] today is in undress uniform but has that big shirt collar on as usual." Trying to read something in his expression, another Buckeye concluded that the General was the "most incomprehensible man I ever met with." Yet beneath that implacable exterior, he was coolly calculating his enemy's strength. "At Millen I learned that General Bragg was in Augusta," Sherman stated, "and that General Wade Hampton had been ordered there from Richmond, to organize a large cavalry force with which to resist our progress. General Hardee was ahead, between us and Savannah, with [Major General Lafayette] McLaws's division, and other irregular troops." That accounting left out what was probably the greatest immediate threat to Sherman's movements—Wheeler's cavalry.

Twice now Sherman had sent Kilpatrick's men forward with orders to seek out and engage Wheeler's troopers. The first time the Federal riders had been deflected in their course by Wheeler's attacks, which forced them to seek refuge under the guns of the infantry. The second effort, this time backed by an infantry division, had not fared much better. After shoving Wheeler away from his defenses along Rocky Creek, the infantry/cavalry column had swung to the south of Waynesboro to camp around Thomas Station on the Millen-Augusta railroad.

Although there is no evidence that Sherman met this day with either Kilpatrick or Baird, his intentions were made clear. As recollected by Baird's staff officer, Major James Connolly, the infantrymen and cavalrymen "are to move up the R.R. tomorrow and drive Wheeler across Briar Creek, 5 miles north of Waynesboro." Kilpatrick also got the message, instructing his two brigade commanders "to send surplus animals and all non-combatants to the wagon train; that in the morn-

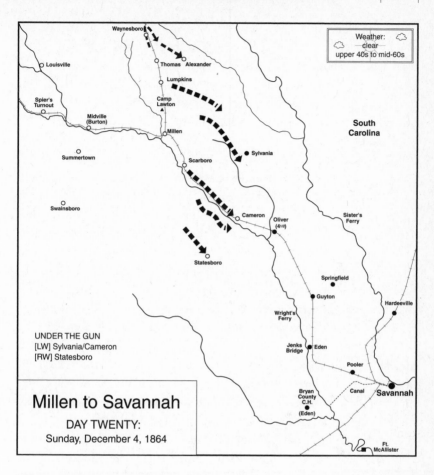

Weather:
clear
upper 40s to mid-60s

South
Carolina

UNDER THE GUN
[LW] Sylvania/Cameron
[RW] Statesboro

Millen to Savannah

DAY TWENTY:
Sunday, December 4, 1864

ing the command would move to engage, defeat, and rout the rebel cavalry" then defending Waynesboro.

SUNDAY, DECEMBER 4, 1864

At about noon, Sherman indulged himself by doing something he did often during the grand movement into Georgia—he took a nap. There were things to worry about, but as matters stood this December day, his attention to them was not urgently required. It was a time to drift with the random flux of events and not second-guess decisions already made. Writing in his journal, Major Hitchcock caught the gist of the moment: "Roads good generally except some heavy sand, and now and then wet swampy spots, but nothing bad. Trains move very well, animals all in good and most in splendid condition. Abundance of forage—chiefly fodder." Sherman's eyes may have been closed, but many of his men were convinced that his mind was never still. A diarist in the Seventeenth Corps scribbled today that he "passed 'Uncle Billy' sitting in porch of farm-house with his heels over the railing and his big head uncovered; thought he was asleep, but am not so sure about that."

Even as Sherman was resting, events were unfolding some twenty miles away that would cause him to wake up and counter an enemy action. A scouting party from the Seventeenth Corps, operating about a half day's march ahead of the main column, approached Ogeechee Creek near Station No. 4½, where Sherman had anticipated trouble. Trouble there was, in the person of the reluctant warrior Major General Henry C. Wayne accompanied by perhaps 4,000 Georgia militia backed by three cannon. All were snugly dug in behind fresh earthworks running along the eastern side of the creek. Although the railroad bridge had been burned, Wayne fretted over his right flank, which he thought could be turned, as the stream "was fordable above us."

At 1:35 P.M. by his watch, the crackle of musketry announced the arrival of Federal troops along the creek's opposite bank. As Wayne later reported, "Skirmishing began on our left and in front of the bridge on the railroad." The Yankee scouts took stock of the situation, estimated Wayne's strength at between 2,000 and 5,000 men, then sent a rider with the information back to Major General Frank P. Blair.

It was early evening before Blair's summary reached Sherman, who had been mentally preparing for just such a situation. Couriers departed his headquarters bearing fresh instructions for both wing commanders. Major General Slocum, with the Twentieth Corps approaching Sylvania, was alerted to be ready to switch over to a road that would carry him along the east side of Ogeechee Creek, leading into the enemy's rear area. At the same time Major General Howard was instructed to have the Fifteenth Corps prepped to cross the Ogeechee River below the Rebel strong point.

Sherman would not have the satisfaction of seeing how well his contingency plans performed. Back at Station No. 4½, Major General Wayne was relieved of command at 4:00 P.M. by Major General Lafayette McLaws, who had been sent up the line from Savannah by Lieutenant General Hardee.

McLaws had served well under General Robert E. Lee at Gettysburg, but, following that battle, arguments with a superior during a campaign at Knoxville, Tennessee, cost him further service with Lee. Despite winning his case in a court of inquiry, McLaws was bundled off to his home state of Georgia to help as best he could. The experienced officer saw at once how exposed Wayne's command was at Station No. 4½.

Sherman's turn toward Savannah had altered the entire paradigm of the campaign. Before his pivot at Millen, when a multitude of destinations seemed possible, Confederate strategy was to harass and delay. Even though President Jefferson Davis still believed that to be the operating principle, a subtle variation had been added. No longer was it considered acceptable to expose a command in a delaying operation. Maintaining an armed force in the field was assuming paramount importance, even to the extent of sacrificing cities.

McLaws knew that Sherman's threat against Station No. 4½ was merely potential on the evening of December 4, but the 4,000 men with Wayne were too important to risk losing. A fast-moving raiding force thrusting from above or below could cut the Savannah road, isolating Wayne's men, leaving them with no place to go. That was unacceptable. Just ninety minutes after taking command, McLaws ordered everyone to fall back to Station No. 1½, near Pooler. In his *Memoirs*, Sherman commented that the veteran McLaws "must have seen that both his flanks were being turned, and prudently retreated to Savannah without a fight."

Even as the wheels of strategy whirred throughout the day, the main business of the march continued unabated. After destroying the Central of Georgia depot and associated buildings in Scarboro (Station No. 7), the Seventeenth Corps proceeded slowly along the railroad right-of-way, with one brigade from each division detached to break it up. Brigadier General Manning F. Force, in charge of one of those brigades, observed that the day's labor left his men "exhausted but lively as ever." Yankee ingenuity was on display as an Illinois regiment put a gristmill into operation to process the kernel corn that was being gathered. General Force's observation was borne out by the 68th Ohio, which settled in for the night "on a large plantation, where, finding molasses in untold measure, and kettles in abundance, we invited ourselves to an old-fashioned taffy-pulling party."

Marching in parallel across the Ogeechee River, the left two divisions of the Fifteenth Corps had no problem keeping apace. "We could see the smoke of the burning railroad all day on the other side of the river," wrote a member of the 50th Illinois. There were few encounters with civilians to record, for, as a member of the 103rd Illinois noted, "Almost all of the people from this section have sloped." Still, security remained high on routine agendas. "Went into camp," wrote an Iowan, "built some light works this evening."

The need for continued vigilance was made apparent this afternoon as the two divisions constituting the right column of the Fifteenth Corps approached the small village of Statesboro. Those at the head of the column were greeted with the sight of a party of mounted Union foragers coming helter-skelter toward them, closely pursued by a larger detachment of Rebel horsemen. A volley from the 70th Ohio scattered the enemy, followed by a charge from the 55th Illinois that shooed them through Statesboro. The Illinois soldiers liberated one of their own, grabbed while foraging. Convinced his abductors intended to murder him, the Yankee, according to the regiment's history, "kept wrathfully blackguarding his captors." The instant he was set free, the former victim "picked up his gun again and gave the fleeing rebels a parting shot."

The opposition failed to dampen forager ardor. "They loaded their wagons with anything they could find to eat for man or beast," remembered a resident. "Corn and cured hams and bacon were their choice. They shot all the chickens and killed all the fat hogs and steers they could find, often cutting off the hams and leaving the rest for the buzzards to eat." Prior to the arrival of the blue horde, area farmers had secreted their best animals and most critical supplies in the Mill Creek swamp, known as Old Bay. According to one local, for all their activity the Yankees never bothered to search through the thick swamp. One Bulloch County matron even boldly walked into the Federal camp, where she "bought used coffee grounds from them so as to have some real coffee again."

Statesboro marked the end point for this day's march by the two right divisions, while the left pair settled along the river across from Cameron, itself the night camp for the leading elements of the Seventeenth Corps. Some sixteen miles north and slightly west of Cameron, the forward units from the Twentieth Corps would call it a day after one of those grueling tramps, the kind that wouldn't figure into the pleasant memoirs that emerged decades later. The columns were passing through a region that was aptly described by an Ohio soldier as "swamp, swampy, swampier." A new twist to the problems facing the wagon masters and their escorts was recognized by a New Jersey officer who "found roads or ground good for traveling except in some places where a wagon and mules would gradually sink down one or 2 feet with perfect ease and without any previous warning, breaking through the crust and necessitating some hard work and a little swearing to extricate the same."

An infantryman with the train guard witnessed "teams at bad holes doubled up and pioneers to facilitate progress built bridges of pine corduroy." Held to their task by the physical labor necessary to keep the wagons moving, one of the regiments guarding trains, missing out on all the goods being collected, had to content itself with a raid on the army's hardtack reserve. "The crackers were being carried for us and were needed then, full as much as on any subsequent time and why should we go hungry in the presence of plenty?" a soldier rationalized. "At any rate we took the crackers."

A major delay in the December 4 schedule occurred at a point where the road being used by the Twentieth Corps passed over a mill dam holding back Horse Creek. The earthen barrier had not been constructed with heavy military convoys in mind, so hardly had the first division completed its passage when the stressed dam gave way. According to a Wisconsin diarist, the breach "overflowed the road—so that we lost several teams." An Illinois soldier on the scene soon observed that the watercourse was "swelling at so rapid a rate that it was impossible to cross on pontoons, and [we] had to remain there for about three hours." "Every one wet and mad and disgusted with the general run of things," griped a New Jerseyman.

The delays did allow time for some detachments to carry out the sad necessity of burying soldiers who had died during the march. Chaplain Lyman Ames was among those who took care of the sick and injured for the Second Division of the Twentieth Corps. Since leaving Atlanta, he had presided over the interment of nine Union soldiers, most for illness or accidentally inflicted wounds. In Sherman's calculations, those unable to make the march because of sickness or injury were supposed to have been culled out before the movement began, but in reality, not everyone who was unwell chose to be separated from

his comrades. With treatment facilities barebones, the constant movement over dirt roads put added strain on those being conveyed in
unsprung wagons.

It was a cruel dilemma. "We have not the transportation to spare to
carry wounded men, and to leave them in the hands of the rebels would
be worse than death itself," explained a Wisconsin soldier. Before setting out this morning, Chaplain Ames gave final rites to a boy from the
29th Ohio who died of fever. During the long break waiting for the
dam flood to subside, a second Ohio soldier passed away. "A large
number present at the burial," Ames noted. "Addressed them briefly."

The two divisions of the Fourteenth Corps moving in sync with the
Twentieth left Lumpkin's Station this morning, but not before "burning the ties and bending the iron." "No forage of any account," grumbled an Ohioan. An Indiana officer termed it "a very poor country,
sandy and marshy." The fact that Union forces only controlled areas
actually occupied was demonstrated this day when the Union column's
rear guard was challenged by a detachment of mounted Rebels as
it began moving out. "Rebs make their appearance ½ mile from
us," wrote an Ohio diarist. "Some little firing between them and
stragglers. . . . Lieut. Hubley left his sword, belt & pistol in field where
we lay. Rebs were so close he could not get it."

Waynesboro

One part of the "game" that Confederate Major General Joseph
Wheeler deftly handled was psychological warfare. He understood
that the enemy was anxiously aware of being deep in Rebel territory
and very much on their own. Anything he could do to increase their
discomfort level might lower their combat efficiency, thus improving
his odds in battle. He had put theory into practice during Kilpatrick's
first Waynesboro raid by maintaining harassment of the Yankee column
both day and night. In Wheeler's reckoning, these efforts had paid
dividends, leaving the enemy "too much demoralized to again meet
our cavalry" without close support. With the Federals once more
knocking on Waynesboro's front door, the Confederate general was
still trying to keep them off balance.

The Federal infantry was camped near Thomas Station, with Kilpatrick's men posted a mile farther north. About midnight, Wheeler's men manhandled one, maybe two, artillery pieces as close to the Union picket line as they dared and opened fire on the cavalry bivouacs, clearly delineated by their campfires. This provoked a rapid response from the pickets, causing the cannon to withdraw, but the damage had been done. Two members of the 92nd Illinois Mounted Infantry were dead, and a lot of officers went without much sleep this night.

Heading that list was Brigadier General Absalom Baird, commanding the Fourteenth Corps division supporting Kilpatrick. Roused from his slumber by the shelling, Baird and his staff rode out to the infantry picket lines to investigate, guided by the stalwart Major James A. Connolly. Baird was nervous. After they had ridden in silence for a while, he became convinced that they had actually passed through their outpost ring and were in imminent danger of being captured. Connolly, who had personally placed the pickets, knew better. "After some parleying I convinced him I was right and we went ahead to our pickets. But as this fuss was all over, and we could see nothing, we returned, getting to bed again, in bad humor, about 2 this morning," he said.

An Indiana soldier reported that "General Kilpatrick was at General* Hunter's headquarters during the time of the bombardment and said he would give them something to do in the morning." True to his word, just a couple of hours after Baird and his officers tossed about in a restless sleep, the bugle notes of "Officer's Call" sounded throughout the cavalry camp. While the company commanders gathered, the enlisted men brewed their coffee and managed breakfast. Then the meeting broke up as the officers scattered back to their units. The troopers in Company L of the 9th Michigan Cavalry listened as Captain David P. Ingraham explained that Kilpatrick had warned them "to prepare for a fight; that he was going out to whip Wheeler." Not long afterward the bugles were at it again. This time they were announcing "Boots and Saddles."

The infantry became bemused spectators when Kilpatrick insisted on having his entire division assemble in formation, filling the open fields near the railroad station. While it may have boosted the morale of his riders, the watching foot soldiers were less impressed. "So many cavalry in line in an open plain make a beautiful sight," Major James

---

*   Actually, *Colonel* Morton C. Hunter.

Connolly admitted. "But it's all show; there's not much fight in them." His opinion reflected that of his boss, Brigadier General Baird, who had advised the Fourteenth Corps commander that the cavalry would only act if the infantry was nearby "in order to accomplish what is necessary to be done." The troopers began moving off toward Waynesboro a little before 8:00 A.M.

The 10th Ohio Cavalry had the advance. Hardly had its leading section passed through the Federal picket line before it struck a slight barricade manned by a regiment of dismounted Confederate cavalry. After a blast of gunfire sent the Ohioans packing, the rest of the regiment deployed, losing time in the process. A second advance found the barricade hastily abandoned, allowing the column to continue northward. About a mile farther the Federals encountered Wheeler's main line of resistance, which a reporter present described as "a splendid defensive position with heavy rail barricade, with a swamp on one flank and the railway embankment on the other." Wheeler afterward insisted that it was a single regiment holding the position, though another Southern source puts several regiments from Brigadier General William Wirt Allen's division there. The enemy soldiers were ready and waiting, so there was no chance of overwhelming them by a quick rush. Kilpatrick ordered his Second Brigade (Colonel Smith D. Atkins commanding) to take the barricade.

Atkins's plan was conventional but effective: pin down the enemy front with heavy fire while mounted columns turned the flanks. In this case the 92nd Illinois Mounted Infantry (backed by the 10th Wisconsin Battery) was given the task of hammering the center, while the 9th Ohio Cavalry was to sweep around the enemy's right, with the 9th Michigan Cavalry and the 10th Ohio Cavalry tackling the Rebel left. Even as his units were deploying, Kilpatrick rode out to his vidette perimeter to taunt Wheeler, a fellow West Pointer. A writer for the *New York Herald*, who doubtless polished the language for publication, recorded the tirade as: "Come on now, you cowardly scoundrel! Your [news] organs claim you have thrashed Kilpatrick every time. Here's Kil himself. Come out, and I'll not leave enough of you to thrash a corporal's guard!"

The fight began in the center as the dismounted battle line of the 92nd Illinois Mounted Infantry made contact. "We moved up through a slough and were well covered until we got within 200 yds of the

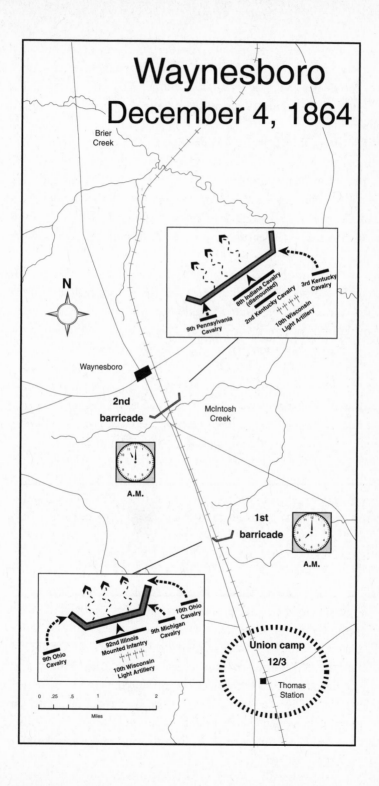

Waynesboro
December 4, 1864

Brier
Creek

N

8th Indiana Cavalry
(dismounted)

3rd Kentucky
Cavalry

9th Pennsylvania
Cavalry

2nd Kentucky Cavalry

10th Wisconsin
Light Artillery

Waynesboro

2nd
barricade

McIntosh
Creek

A.M.

1st
barricade

A.M.

10th Ohio
Cavalry

9th Michigan
Cavalry

92nd Illinois
Mounted Infantry

9th Ohio
Cavalry

10th Wisconsin
Light Artillery

Union camp

12/3

Thomas
Station

0   .25   .5   1   2

Miles

works when they opened with Artillery and musketry but shot too high," reported an Illinoisan. The Yankee troopers levered their Spencers frantically to lay down a heavy suppressing fire, a process that an officer later described as "grinding out the shot from your coffee-mill guns."

The 9th Ohio Cavalry swept around the enemy's right flank. "I ordered my bugler to sound the charge," recollected Colonel William D. Hamilton. "The companies began to move in an awkward irregular line, looking back for me. . . . Waving my hat, I called 'come on, boys.' A shout went up all along the line, and the glitter of their sabers following the fire of the carbines showed the mettle of the men, when the charge was on." "Away we went on the gallop," added another Ohio officer, "carbines firing, sabers flashing." Trooper F. J. Wentz in Company H became an unwilling spectator when his horse, attempting to jump a small ravine, "landed lengthwise in the bottom of this excavation." Wentz could only observe as his regiment "swept on close up to the edge of the swamp, driving everything before it."

The attack of the 10th Ohio Cavalry came against the Rebel left. "At the word of command 200 bright blades leaped from their scabbards, and with a yell away we flew . . . like the sweeping cyclone, until the intervening space had been passed," declared a trooper. "Moments seemed hours. . . . Suddenly a sheet of flame shot out from the . . . barricade . . . , and as suddenly horses and riders were in the last agonies of death, blocking the way." "We could see an officer dashing down the [enemy's] line with his saber raised and hear his voice, calling on his 'brave men' to 'stand and fight the invaders,' " recorded a Buckeye. "This officer, we afterwards learned from the prisoners, was General Wheeler." It was here that one of Kilpatrick's favorites, Captain Samuel E. Norton, was seriously wounded. Just prior to the charge he had proclaimed: "Now for a name for our regiment."

Wheeler riposted with his reserve regiments to stiffen the flanks. In response, the 9th Michigan Cavalry added its weight to the combat on the Union right. The Michigan men, said a report, "had to form while on the run from column of fours to that of battalions." This was accomplished despite the fact that the "fog and smoke was now so dense as to almost totally obscure the enemy's position." Attempting to capture an enemy battle flag, the regiment's adjutant, William C. Cook, "was knocked from his horse, and had his horse shot," before being taken prisoner. The Rebel color bearer had tried to spear the impetuous Yankee with his flagstaff, but it bent double instead. "I was glad I did not kill him for he was a handsome fellow," remarked the Confederate.

While this was unfolding, the men of the 92nd Illinois Mounted Infantry rushed the barricade. The dismounted regiment overran it "and pumped their Spencers at the backs of the retreating Rebel soldiers." In a brief melee along the barrier, the Illinois color bearer was killed, the flag he was carrying seized by an enemy officer. According to one account the dying color bearer shouted: "I'm shot. For God's sake save the flag!" Before the Rebel could claim his trophy, one end of the flagstaff was grabbed by a Yankee trooper and the two engaged in a deadly tug-of-war, each masking the fire of comrades behind them. The impasse was only broken when the Illinois soldier fumbled out his revolver, compelling the Confederate (armed just with a sword) to surrender. Also killed in this action was George "Wait" Downs of Company I. "He never spoke after he was struck," wrote a friend. "It will be sad news for his folks, but you know in battle, there is no distinction."

Said Kilpatrick, Wheeler "made several counter-charges to save his dismounted men and check our rapid advance." The Union general committed his ready reserve, the 5th Ohio Cavalry, yelling to its commander: "Col. Heath, take your regiment; charge by column of fours down that road and give those fellows a start." The chronicle by the *New York Herald* reporter recounts that Kilpatrick went in with them. "They rode over the rebel barricade, hewed men down and used their pistols in a close engagement."

It was during this part of the action that the leading files of Baird's infantry reached the scene in time to be interested spectators. "The charge by our cavalry across the open field was a most sublimely grand, never-to-be-forgotten scene," recorded an Ohio foot soldier; "no words of the writer can describe or paint the picture." An Indiana infantryman present noted that some of the Rebels "had to retreat across a large swamp about a mile and the road was graded high and about wide enough for three or four men to ride abreast. They was in such a hurry they crowded each other off."

Kilpatrick's men now controlled the roadblock, but Wheeler wasn't finished. A second, even stronger barricade had been erected just outside Waynesboro, along McIntosh Creek. Into this position the Confederate cavalry leader funneled his men (most from Brigadier General

William Y. C. Humes's division), where they waited for round two. It wasn't long in coming. Kilpatrick moved his First Brigade (Colonel Eli H. Murray commanding) into the fore, and it was these men who first espied the enemy's position. "Between us and Waynesboro was a valley, through which ran a small creek," remembered an Indiana trooper. "On the north or opposite side of this creek the rebels had taken their stand, having their artillery well posted."

To his credit, Kilpatrick realized that he could not repeat the tactics that had served him so well at the first barricade. This time, Wheeler's "flanks [were] so far extended that it was useless to attempt to turn them. I therefore determined to break his center." Colonel Murray deployed his brigade, sending the 3rd Kentucky Cavalry against the Confederate left, the 9th Pennsylvania Cavalry around to the other flank, and the 8th Indiana Cavalry (fighting dismounted) straight up the middle. Once more the 10th Wisconsin Battery was on hand for fire support, with the 2nd and 5th Kentucky Cavalry in reserve.

It took time to get all the units into position. Murray erred in setting up the 3rd Kentucky Cavalry first, halting it in full view of the enemy, where it became the object of their full attention. "No body of men ever stood fire any more resolutely; not a man faltered," reported the regiment's commander. "At length, the enemy's fire becoming fierce and many of their comrades falling around them, they disregarded the restraints of discipline and rushed, with wild shouts, upon the enemy in their front."

A dismounted Indiana trooper recalled that the 3rd Kentucky cavalrymen "moved rapidly upon the works of the enemy, without firing, and received such a shower of lead that they were thrown into confusion and hurled back upon the 8th Ind. Cav. which stood firm, and letting the Kentucky boys through, closed up their ranks and moved upon the works of the enemy, under heavy fire, which was returned from their Spencers. . . . At this time the 10th Wis. Battery was run into position and opened a fire of canister upon the enemy."

Some of the resistance to this effort was directed toward the 9th Pennsylvania Cavalry, which now struck the Rebel right. Just as in the case of the 3rd Kentucky Cavalry, the Pennsylvanians were goaded into action after being forced to wait under a galling fire. Suddenly, said one of the troopers, "our whole line commenced to move forward without orders, at a slow walk of our horses at first, but faster and faster until we were charging at full speed." The regiment's commander, Colonel Thomas J. Jordan, was very much in his element. He found validation in the sound and fury of battle, writing afterward that during this engagements he "enjoyed the sweetest draught of pleasure that can enter a soldier's heart." In an open letter to the folks at home, a Lancaster County boy bragged that they "whipped" the Rebels "handsomely at Waynesboro."

With both flanks engaged, the middle of Wheeler's line became the dramatic focus. Under the cover of unrelenting volleys from the 8th Indiana Cavalry and artillery rounds sent over by the 10th Wisconsin Battery, the 2nd Kentucky rode forward, ripped passages through the barrier, and penetrated the enemy's center. Wheeler's second position collapsed as the various units disengaged to make their way through Waynesboro toward safety behind Brier Creek.

"Through the streets of Waynesboro we rushed," crowed an Indiana rider, "through the streets of Waynesboro they retreated." Wheeler himself admitted that his men "were so warmly pressed that it was with difficulty we succeeded in withdrawing." Even as the 2nd Kentucky Cavalry pushed through the town, Colonel Murray abruptly detached half the regiment for a mission to the right, a fact the unit's commander did not realize until he cleared the streets and drew his men into a line, only then realizing that he had just fifty or sixty troopers to take on all of Wheeler's command. Fortunately, the Confederates were more intent on getting behind Brier Creek than beating up on a lone Union regiment, plus help was on hand in the form of Baird's infantry. "Kilpatrick stopped; we marched thru his lines, formed in line, and went about a mile," recollected a Missouri soldier. "We found neither works nor rebs and fell back and got dinner."

In the town, Brigadier General Kilpatrick was relishing the moment. An Indiana man recalled him "rushing around like a child with a new toy, saying: 'I knew I could lick Wheeler! I can do it again!'" "I seen one old Reb laying along the road (quite an old man) that had been [struck by] a saber stroke across his back and [he] was not dead yet but mortally wounded and under other circumstances his grey hairs would have appealed to my heart for sympathy," said one of Baird's infantrymen, "but we are not here to sympathize with men who brought it on themselves." Another foot soldier saw a "woman [who] was kneeling over the dead body of a Confederate cavalryman; perhaps it was her husband."

North of Waynesboro, Wheeler's men retreated across Brier Creek, closely shadowed by Kilpatrick's two reserve regiments, the 5th Ohio Cavalry and the 5th Kentucky Cavalry. While the Kentuckians covered them, the Buckeyes destroyed the wagon and railroad bridges. Back in the town, some of the Pennsylvania troopers "amused themselves by examining the contents of the fine houses in town and making several bon fires of buildings, &c." A seventeen-year-old female resident was drafted to entertain on her family's piano, relocated into the street. "They made me play.a long time," she recalled, "but I never played anything but Southern airs. I must say I was not afraid of them, and I told them so, but they laughed it off." Neither Baird nor Kilpatrick had any intention of sticking around very long, so by 3:00 P.M. the Federals were hustling away to the southeast, toward a small place on the map named Alexander.

As the foot soldiers departed Waynesboro, an Indiana man marveled that the streets, empty right after the fight, were "alive with women and children who had on their Sunday clothes and it reminded me of home. They had hid in cellars while the fight was going on and come out to see us." The next day a small group of these civilians would gather to bury a Georgia officer killed in the fighting. A young girl present remembered that "as there was no minister in the town, Judge Lawson read the funeral service and the ladies sang some hymns."

Kilpatrick's troopers formed the column's rear guard. On top of today's combat decisions, the cavalry commander faced a difficult personal matter. The promising officer Captain Samuel Norton, who was too badly wounded to be moved, would have to be left behind. A 10th Ohio cavalryman volunteered to remain with him. Kilpatrick's contribution was a note to be given to Joseph Wheeler. "For the memory of old association," Kilpatrick asked that Wheeler see that Norton received care and that the trooper be allowed to care for the officer he termed "very brave and a true gentleman." In return for Wheeler's courtesies, Kilpatrick promised "the thanks of your old friend."

In their after-action reports, both Wheeler and Kilpatrick claimed to have been fighting against a numerically superior enemy, and each was certain that they had inflicted grievous casualties on the other. Wheeler never bothered with a head count, but a cavalry veteran and later historian of his campaigns pegged his strength at about 2,000. Kilpatrick had left Atlanta on November 15 with some 5,000 riders; attrition and detachments had likely lowered the number engaged at Waynesboro to perhaps 3,700. So the advantage in numbers was with Kilpatrick, though the force multiplier enjoyed by defenders was in Wheeler's favor.

The reckonings of the Confederate losses made by Union participants ranged from less than 100 to more than 500. A fair estimate of the killed, wounded, or captured would be around 250. Wheeler claimed inflicting 197 casualties on the Federals. A tally of the losses recorded in the various regimental accounts totals 79, suggesting that the Rebel fire, while enthusiastic, was not especially well aimed. Various regimental histories and contemporary newspaper accounts peg the total Union loss in this day's action at between 125 and 190.

One target that Wheeler's men did hit sported four legs. Saber charges against log barricades may have looked impressive from a distance, but close up they were hell on the horses. Kilpatrick reported "upwards of 200 in killed and wounded." In a note to Major General Sherman, the cavalryman complained that his continuing duties as rear guard allowed the infantry to scour the country of livestock, leaving nothing for his troopers. "I . . . respectfully urge that a few hundred horses be turned over to me from one or more of the army corps marching on roads parallel or near to my line of march," Kilpatrick requested.

Other than thinning the Yankee horse herd, what was accomplished? Some of Wheeler's adherents stake the saving of Augusta on the outcome of the action, but it was never in either Baird's or Kilpatrick's brief to push beyond Brier Creek. Even had Wheeler offered no opposition, the destruction of the Brier Creek bridges would have completed the mission and turned the Union column to the south. Inflicting damage on the Yankee cavalry, while perhaps quenching a warrior's thirst, left the core of Sherman's striking force untouched; besides, with Baird's infantry on hand Wheeler had no chance of delivering a telling blow.

One of the Federal infantrymen on the scene was certain that on this memorable day "the rebel cavalry have learned a lesson they will not soon forget." However, the only changes that would come to Wheeler's operation had everything to do with topography and nothing to do with any learned lessons. Kilpatrick, anxious to feather his cap, could crow about thrashing his opposite number, though the close presence of strong infantry supports dims any luster of that accomplishment. A stretch of a branch railroad had been wrecked (mostly by the infantry), some bridges destroyed, and a few buildings trashed in Waynesboro. Not a victory of any substance, though both Bragg (in Augusta) and Sherman viewed it as necessary to shield their more important assets from enemy interference.

Perhaps most critical for Sherman's grand movement, the tricky pivot toward Savannah was accomplished without any significant challenge to the lengthy tail that was his true weak point. A few mounted bands made some uncoordinated rushes at wagons that were easily repulsed by the train guards; at no point were the supply vehicles imperiled by anything other than the broken dams, sucking mud, or lousy trails.

None of which diminishes the fortitude and courage shown by the fighting men on both sides. Compared with infantry combat, cavalry actions were fast moving, briefly violent, and given to abrupt reverses of fortune. A momentary repulse or a charge generally meant little in the overall ebb and flow of the action, though it did spice up an official report. Still, at the point of sharpest contact the combat was as fierce as any of the more celebrated mounted engagements of the war. Yet in many ways the infantry officer Major James Connolly was not far off the mark when he observed: "A cavalry fight is just about as much fun as a fox hunt; but, of course, in the midst of the fun somebody is getting hurt all the time."

PART FOUR

Millen to Savannah

DECEMBER 5–10

CHAPTER 19

"Splendid Sight to See Cotton Gins Burn"

MONDAY, DECEMBER 5, 1864

Left Wing

The immediate result of the combat at Waynesboro was a separation by both sides: Wheeler to regroup and resupply, Kilpatrick to screen the rear of Baird's column marching through Alexander to Jacksonboro. "No trouble from the Rebels so far," a relieved Ohio trooper commented about midday. His summary would hold true through nightfall. A Pennsylvanian observed that they were "entering the swampy country lying between the Savannah and Ogeechee rivers," while an Illinois trooper saw the change in more immediate terms with the comment, "Good water . . . begins to be a scarce article as we find swamps instead of streams."

An answer to Kilpatrick's departing request on behalf of Captain Norton was making its way forward. Wheeler assured Kilpatrick that the suffering officer would "receive every attention which can be bestowed upon a wounded soldier." A Waynesboro physician who had taken Norton into his house, Dr. Edmund Byrne, passed back to Wheeler that the Yankee "was doing well and [was] out of pain at last accounts." Sadly, this brief rally preceded a dramatic decline, and before this day was out the valiant officer would be dead.

Coordinating Baird's marching infantry column with Kilpatrick's

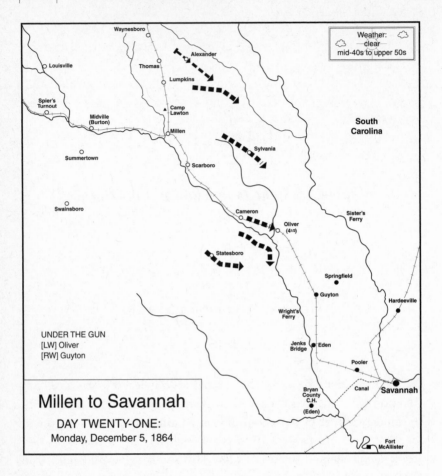

UNDER THE GUN
[LW] Oliver
[RW] Guyton

Millen to Savannah

DAY TWENTY-ONE:
Monday, December 5, 1864

Weather: clear
mid-40s to upper 50s

screen kept Major James A. Connolly in regular contact with the cavalry officer. If anything, the infantryman's low opinion of the mounted
units in general and their leader in particular took on an even sharper
edge. "Kilpatrick is the most vain, conceited, egotistical little popinjay
I ever saw," Connolly declared. "He has one redeeming quality—he
rarely drinks spirituous liquors, and *never* to excess. He is a very
ungraceful rider, looking more like a monkey than a man on horseback."

Baird's men were slowly closing the gap with the rest of the Fourteenth Corps, strung out along the main road between Waynesboro
and Savannah. "Two or three plantations were all we passed, and they
very poor ones," wrote an Illinois diarist. "The whole surface of the
earth is sand and the roads are almost ankle deep and marching diffi-

cult." "All our bed clothes and our dishes are full of sand," complained a Minnesota soldier. Still, the column made steady progress until it reached the crossing of Beaverdam Creek, where the enemy had burned the wagon bridge and clogged the creek with brush. While pioneers cleared the obstructions, a detail from the 58th Indiana set to work rebuilding the bridge. The job wasn't completed until nearly 10:00 P.M., so the Fourteenth Corps settled down for the night around Jacksonboro, a small village that once had been the Screven County seat.

Black refugees continued to flock to the corps. "The number of negroes with us is perfectly astonishing and all have tales of the most barbarous cruelty at the hands of their master," commented an Illinoisan. "They were a motley crowd, with clothes dirty and patched with many colors," added an Indiana trooper, who continued, "Some of the women had young babies with them, and they were a nuisance in the army; but we could not drive them back, as they were seeking their freedom, and so they trudged on after us and we divided our rations with them." "However they do not evoke my sympathy," contributed an infantryman, echoing the sentiment of those commanding the corps. "I think them far better off with their masters than dragging along with the army."

Matching general course and speed just a few miles to the south was the Twentieth Corps, which today passed through Sylvania, though it was a tough slog for many. "Streams or water swamps are so numerous that we can not learn their names any more," grumbled an Illinois foot soldier. A Pennsylvania comrade recorded that "much of the road [was] being corduroyed through the interminable swamps." "The wagons often get stuck in the mud, causing long and tedious marches . . . to come up with the advance," contributed a New Yorker. "Some of the boys occupy their time during these waits playing chuckluck, draw and whiskey poker."

Foragers reported mixed results; one termed the pickings "scarce," while another inventoried a bounty that included "sweet potatoes, five pigs, hens, honey, bacon, etc., etc." "Stop at house," scrawled a diarist in the 129th Illinois. "Everything moveable taken, the women crying. Tell them they should have immigrated from this country before the war. They say that the women had nothing to do with the trouble. We can't see it. Consider them our worst enemies." Standing orders for rearguard units were to destroy all bridges once the column had passed. For one Pennsylvania regiment, this meant burning a short span and breaching a mill dam to flood the roadway. Hardly had these soldiers begun their task when "three foraging teams came in sight on the other side of the road. The men were ordered to cross the burning bridge, which they did, and succeeded in backing the flames and brought their teams and horses across in safety," reported the officer in charge.

A new problem arose that was identified by a surgeon in the 19th Michigan, who wrote: "Uncultivated land is covered with a sort of vine grass about a foot high & so plenty that the fire readily burns the country over giving us a fine smoke to march in." Fresh orders directed officers to halt all unauthorized arsons, nothing that "such fires occasion great delay, especially to the ammunition train." There were other related issues as well, though less readily apparent. "Seen far in advance at night, these fires often lead the weary soldiers to believe that they are approaching camp, and they press on with renewed vigor, only to be deceived, and to discover other fires still farther ahead," said an Illinois man. "The dead pine trees often catch fire, and the creeping, writhing flames ascend from their base to the topmost branches. They may be seen miles away. These scenes are indelibly impressed upon the mind." Reflecting on the daytime wagon jams and evening conflagrations, a New Jersey quartermaster quipped that his options were reduced to either being "Trampled by day . . . [or] liable to be burnt up at night."

Right Wing

The biggest question hanging over the Seventeenth Corps this day was: How much of a fight was awaiting them at Ogeechee Creek? The answer, to everyone's great relief, was not much of one at all. "After considerable maneuvering of troops and some skirmishing by the 35th New Jersey, the enemy retired and we crossed the creek and went into camp," recorded an Ohio officer. According to a signal officer present, word of the enemy's departure was brought by foragers who had filtered across the creek even as units were deploying to storm the position. This intelligence, he noted, "of course was pleasant to all but those preparing for the attack." The Rebels, chortled an Iowan, "concluded that they had better mover on, or they would get hurt, and the infantry left without firing a gun." The railroad bridge had been burned, but the wagon crossing only de-planked, requiring a little labor by pioneer detachments before it was again carrying traffic.

Once over the creek, Seventeenth Corps soldiers not assigned to railroad wrecking went into bivouac to call it a day. Gunners from the 1st Minnesota Light Artillery enjoyed some poetic justice. "We got a number of the wooden spades they had used [to build their sand works] & burned them to cook our sweet potatoes by." A member of the 10th Illinois recorded that four members of one company, who exceeded orders, were "tied by thumbs in front of [the] color-line for pillaging." Others, under orders, took care of the railroad buildings as well as additional authorized targets. A Wisconsin man thought it a "splendid sight to see cotton gins burn."

Sherman spent much of the morning on the porch of a two-story wood-frame house gazing over a well-tended garden while hoping for positive tidings from Ogeechee Creek. "Sat waiting for what might turn up," noted Major Hitchcock. "General and staff on piazza talking,—General sometimes looking at map, and awaiting news from Blair." The all-clear was sounded at 10:30 A.M., allowing Sherman to proceed with his entourage. They reached Ogeechee Creek about a half hour later to find, as Major Hitchcock put it, "the birds had flown." "This is better than having to fight those fellows in these bushes, ain't it?" Sherman joked as they made their way across the rebuilt wagon bridge. Once on the other side, Hitchcock marveled at the now empty earthworks, which had been professionally sited to oppose any effort to ford the creek. A direct attack against a determined foe here would have been a slaughter. "Now you understand what a *flank movement* means," a smiling Sherman told his aide.

As soon as his headquarters were established in the home of Mr. Matthew Lufburrow, Sherman drafted messages for major generals Howard and Slocum, canceling prior instructions to envelop the enemy position at Station No. 4½. He also wanted to tighten up the overall deployments. Now that they were approaching Savannah, whose garrison held the greatest number of enemy soldiers he had yet faced, Sherman was determined to keep his columns well in hand. The last thing he wanted was for any component to become so isolated from the rest that a Rebel force, striking out from Savannah, might engage the Union soldiers with a force approaching numerical parity. If that meant halting one or two corps to allow the others to catch up, then so be it. In the note to Major General Howard explaining his thinking, Sherman emphasized that "we must move in concert, or else [all] will get lost." Overall, however, the General was well satisfied with how affairs were progressing. Everything, he later wrote, "seemed to favor us. Never do I recall a more agreeable sensation than the sight of our camps by night, lit up by the fires of fragrant pine-knots."

The one corps separated from Sherman by the Ogeechee River marched south and east in two columns of its own. While the Fourth Division of the Fifteenth Corps led the left half (nearest to the river) this day, its partner—the First Division—used as many "catch roads" as it could to keep abreast. By now experienced officers knew that railings needed to corduroy the lanes were hard to find in swampy areas, so when a fence was encountered, the soldiers were instructed to each shoulder a board, lugging it until needed. Foraging on this side of the river was generally good, with sweet potatoes and beef in ample supply.

"Negroes swarmed to us to-day," declared an Illinois officer. "I saw one squad of 30 or 40 turned back." Passing by a farm said to date to the Revolutionary War, another Illinois boy took notice of "a negro on the place who was over a hundred years old." Other African-Americans were later remembered for their tragic experiences. This night an injured female slave reached the camp of the 103rd Illinois. She had helped other Union soldiers find the livestock hidden by her mistress, one Milly Drake. After the Yankees had departed, a member of the regiment reported that "gentle Milly took half a rail and like to wore the wench out. Broke her arm and bruised her shamefully. That was all the reason the girl had for running away."

In one of the more remarkable personal journeys of the campaign, the officer on whom President Jefferson Davis pinned his greatest hopes of stopping the Yankee juggernaut was crossing Sherman's wake to reach the front. General P. G. T. Beauregard had been in Montgomery, Alabama, on December 1, traveling toward Mobile, when he was handed a dispatch from Richmond placing him in direct command of all coastal forces opposing Sherman's march. Beauregard, acknowledging the new instructions on December 2, then plotted a bold course to reach the crucial area. A train carried him from Montgomery to Macon on December 3. From there the trail was by horse, departing Macon for Milledgeville, thence to Sparta and Mayfield, the latter about a day's ride from Augusta. In his last message to Savannah before breaking contact, Beauregard had offered Lieutenant General Hardee advice on improving the city's defenses besides urging him to use every effort to obstruct the roads. Further instructions would have to wait until he reached Augusta on December 6.

One of the irregular military assets available to Beauregard was touted today in a letter written in Louisville for publication in the *Augusta Daily Chronicle & Sentinel.* The unit, not part of any formal order of battle, was called Hazzard's Scouts. These soldiers, proclaimed the missive's author, "have kept the enemy terribly annoyed on his rear and flank—dashing into them at unexpected places and capturing prisoners. The Hazzard Scouts are notorious for their gentlemanly deportment. They are never found away from their posts of duty or danger. Capt. Hazzard having been long engaged as a scout, seems to understand all the tricks of a Yankee and how to take advantage of them. He is certainly a terror to Yankees, knowing as he does how to handle his gallant scouts. There are few, if any, who surpass him as a commander of scouts. He is a gentleman and a soldier."

In Richmond, the December 5 issue of one of the city's dailies, the *Sentinel,* offered an upbeat analysis of events in Georgia. "Sherman's campaign, which was daringly conceived, has been timidly prosecuted," it announced. The writers pointed to the slow pace plus numerous delays that had marked the operation thus far. "It has given us time to concentrate our means of resistance and to obstruct his path with daily increasing obstacles. SHERMAN seems to have realized his peril, and to be concerned now only to make his escape. The hero has turned fugitive." While the government may not have embraced every conclusion reached by the newspaper's editors, there was a guarded optimism coursing through the War Department. "We are . . . hopeful of the defeat of Sherman—a little delay on his part will render it pretty certain," wrote a clerk in a position to hear all that his bosses were

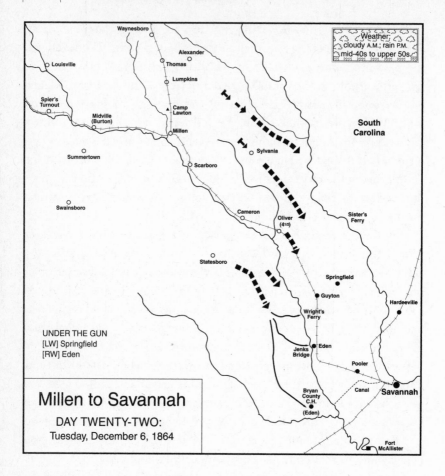

Weather:
cloudy A.M.; rain P.M.
mid-40s to upper 50s

South
Carolina

UNDER THE GUN
[LW] Springfield
[RW] Eden

Millen to Savannah

DAY TWENTY-TWO:
Tuesday, December 6, 1864

hearing. However, unlike those running things, the clerk was left with a nagging question: "If it should occur, will it give us peace?" he wondered.

TUESDAY, DECEMBER 6, 1864

Left Wing

The bulk of Sherman's forces continued to press along the peninsula formed by the Savannah and Ogeechee rivers leading to Savannah. The Twentieth Corps, operating in the center, reached a spot about twelve miles northwest of Springfield, while the Fourteenth Corps, running about a day behind on the outside flank, followed the Augusta Road, which wriggled along the Savannah River. The tails of both columns were now being screened by Kilpatrick's cavalry, with his First Brigade tasked with watching over Brigadier General Williams's men, while the Second Brigade held its place behind Brevet Major General Davis's columns.

Everyone was reporting an increasing number of obstructed roadways. There was little rhyme or reason in these efforts to stymie the Federal movements. In some stretches the Rebel activity was a momentary nuisance. "Before going into camp [we] ran into a place where the enemy had felled about 2 acres of timber to prevent our progress," recorded a New Jersey officer, "and it was just so much time thrown away for our pioneer corps removes it about as rapidly as they can walk." In other places, the Confederate blockages were more significant. "Were delayed much during the day by obstructions placed in the roads by the enemy," complained a New York officer. In no case, however, did the delays result in any column not reaching its assigned objective. A major factor in this achievement was the absence of any opposition to the unarmed pioneer squads sent to clear the routes. "There is nothing new in the military line," declared the New Jersey officer, "we don't meet any rebels behind every fence and bush dying on behalf of their altars and homes."

Which is not to say that there weren't any encounters with the locals. "Stopped at the home of a woman whose son is in our Army & her husband a Confed[erate] Soldier," wrote a Michigan diarist. In another incident, an Illinois soldier arrived on the scene after a property owner had fled after firing on a forager, then abandoning his house with four women inside. The deed had been done, the residence was forfeit—no pleading could overturn that judgment—but several sympathetic soldiers managed to delay the arson long enough for the women to resettle themselves nearby. One of those men who spoke with the ladies reflected that a "woman under such a trying ordeal [does her] talking with a pathos that is truly eloquent."

Food gathering went well, though the variety left something to be desired. "Yam, yam, yam," grumbled an Illinois boy. "Confound the yams." An Illinois officer declared that "the worst of swamp water [was] enough to kill the devil himself was he compelled to drink it, but by boiling it making coffee strong the wigglers and other vermin were destroyed." More critical to this day's progress were the swamps, increasing both in number and size. When the officer commanding the Second Division, Twentieth Corps, bumped into the wagons belonging to the Third Division, he found the procession stopped "waiting for a long swamp to be corduroyed." No one else seemed interested in clearing the way, so the officer assigned "a portion of my command at working, giving my personal superintendence until it was finished at dark."

By now the men moving with this wing were becoming increasingly certain of their objective. "We are on what is known as the middle road to Savannah," recorded a New Yorker, "which city, the rank and file have concluded, is our destination." "I got a rebel paper . . . ," recorded a journal keeper in the 75th Indiana, "it . . . says Sherman is trying to get to Savannah and I am thankful for the information as I did not know before where we were going." Nevertheless, Major General Sherman was still determined to keep the enemy guessing. His instructions today to Brigadier General Kilpatrick included orders for him to send detachments to several Savannah River fords, where they were to "make a good deal of smoke and fuss . . . as though threatening to cross into South Carolina."

The cavalry commander, still waiting on word from Sherman concerning his request for more horses, took matters into his own hands by allowing parties of dismounted troopers to cross the Savannah River in small boats to search for them. Yet, even as these efforts were under way, another squad of troopers was handed the onerous job of dispatching animals no longer able to keep up. It was especially hard on one Ohio cavalryman, whose horse had been a faithful companion since leaving Atlanta. Now it was clubbed down with thirteen other unfortunate beasts. The column moved on and had covered several miles when, to the trooper's amazement, the ever faithful steed, his head "covered with blood, and the brains . . . oozing out from his broken skull," rejoined the procession. No one could bring himself to shoot the creature, who gamely hobbled along until the bivouac was reached, where he finally expired. "He belongs to the long roll of forgotten heroes," eulogized the cavalryman.

Kilpatrick's headquarters this night were at the home of a Captain Brown, where, it was said, George Washington had slept. An officer with the Fourteenth Corps' rear guard listened with bemusement as the cavalry officer informed the mistress of the house "that her children could say in after years that Kilpatrick had stayed there." Not to be outdone, the woman retorted that "Washington was father to his country while [Kilpatrick] . . . was a desolator."

—— *Right Wing* ——

Major General Oliver O. Howard's command continued its bifurcated mission. One corps, the Seventeenth, remained yoked to the Twentieth and the Fourteenth by marching down the right side of the Savannah corridor, following the Central of Georgia Railroad. The command made only short marches this day, with Sherman's headquarters near Station No. 4½ not moving at all. "There is a considerable washing and cleaning up being done," recorded an Iowa diarist, "and considerable gambling too."

It was an enduring part of army life that even on rest periods, someone would get the short end of the stick. It fell to a couple of brigades to spend today railroad wrecking, an assignment putting several units on a reverse course. "As we are performing our retrograde movement, we are accosted with numerous interrogatories as to our destination and the object to be achieved, which elicited numerous witty replies," contributed a wordy Illinois soldier.

Foragers could no longer count on having a successful expedition. Some efforts met with no problems, procuring "plenty of sweet potatoes and fresh pork," while others returned empty-handed, leading a few to worry for the first time about the "danger of having to go hungry." Yet again, efforts by civilians to conceal their valuables were undone by what one soldier called "the inevitable Yankee."

Throughout this entire operation, Sherman had shown a marked disinclination to stray from the line of march. This day was no exception, with the General content to spend it at his headquarters issuing orders or reading reports. He continued to bring the pieces of his expedition closer together. "I have been dividing my army so long as I knew there could be no serious opposition to either column," he explained to Major Hitchcock, "now that they must make whatever opposition they can, I concentrate; tomorrow all my columns will be within sound of cannon and in supporting distance."

Kilpatrick's Waynesboro report reached Sherman while he was

here, along with his request for more horses. Sherman promptly shot off a circular to his corps commanders instructing each to gather "100 horses, the best adapted to cavalry uses, together with a sufficient number of mounted negroes to lead them . . . for delivery to the cavalry command of General Kilpatrick." In a follow-up message to his mounted chief, Sherman vowed that "in order to keep you well mounted" he was fully prepared to "dismount every person connected with the infantry not necessary for its efficient service, and take team horses, even if the wagons and contents have to be burned."

Among today's visitors to Sherman's headquarters was George N. Barnard, a civilian photographer attached to the operation to document it in pictures. While he had a lot of images to show of captured Atlanta, Barnard had yet to take any of the March to the Sea. He had nearly recorded some scenes of the prison pen at Camp Lawton, but there hadn't been sufficient time for him to set up the equipment or prepare the chemicals necessary for the job. Nonetheless, the sight of the graves and living pits used by some of the POWs left a powerful impression on the experienced war photographer. Barnard shared his thoughts on Camp Lawton with Major Hitchcock: "I used to be very much troubled about the burning of houses, etc., but after what I have seen I shall not be much troubled about it."

Across the Ogeechee River from Sherman's headquarters, offensive operations were under way, carried out by the Fifteenth Corps. In a series of actions that would foreshadow a future generation's amphibious end runs, Major General Howard pushed forward a pair of fast-moving columns toward crossing points on the Ogeechee River, while a third was sent well south to undertake a similar mission at the Canoochee River.

One advance party, closely supported by a full brigade, headed for Wright's Bridge, just below Guyton. "When we got there we found the bridge on fire and the rebels gone," reported an Iowa soldier. "We built works on the bank of the river and went to repairing the bridge so we could cross. We sent six men across in a canoe. They got a shot at the rebs on the other side. As soon as we could cross on the bridge, Captain McSweeny took three companies and went out to the railroad, which was about four miles from the river, on a reconnaissance." Continued a comrade: "While they were out the rebs came from [station] two and a half and attacked us at the bridge cutting off the three companies that were out." However, the enemy promptly fell back, allow-ing the detached party to return later without incident.

The second fast-moving party targeted another Ogeechee crossing, this one at Jenks' Bridge, near Eden. "Upon arriving at the river found the bridge destroyed," reported the expedition's commander, who made no crossing attempt. His men entrenched in an all-around defense, ready to take on any attacker from any direction. The smallest force, sent farthest south to the Canoochee River, determined that this crossing was destroyed and the opposite bank strongly held. The group retired "without doing the work." Still, the Confederates in Savannah were on notice that Sherman's army was drawing near.

Two of the Confederacy's top military leaders were in Augusta this day. General Braxton Bragg spent his final hours in overall charge of stopping Sherman by coordinating several defensive moves along the vital Savannah-Charleston corridor, then under pressure from another Federal raiding force operating from the coast. At the same time he advised Joseph Wheeler to "press well on the enemy's left flank, so that if he crosses [the] Savannah River you will know it immediately, and advise me."

Bragg's reluctant tenure came to an end this evening when General Beauregard rode into town to assume overall command. Now in touch with a working telegraphic connection to Richmond, Beauregard loaded it with a lengthy report, most of which justified his decision to allow John B. Hood to invade Tennessee instead of trying to engage Sherman. A small portion of the note addressed the growing crisis in eastern Georgia. Here Beauregard declared that "all that could be [done] has been done . . . to oppose the advance of Sherman's forces toward the Atlantic coast. That we have not thus far been more suc-cessful none can regret more than myself, but he will doubtless be prevented from capturing Augusta, Charleston, and Savannah, and he may yet be made to experience serious loss before reaching the coast."

In Washington today the protocols of a democracy were satisfied as the Congress informed the Executive Branch that a quorum was present, allowing it to receive communications. President Abraham Lincoln promptly dispatched his annual State of the Union message. The lengthy document covered the course of foreign and domestic affairs, reviewed national finances, commented on agricultural conditions, and even welcomed Nevada as the nation's newest state. Progress of the war was not ignored. "Since the last annual message all the important lines and positions then occupied by our forces have been maintained," Lincoln announced, "and our arms have steadily advanced."

Continued the president: "The most remarkable feature in the military operations of the year is General Sherman's attempted march of three hundred miles directly through the insurgent region. It tends to show a great increase in our relative strength that our General-in-Chief [Lieutenant General Ulysses S. Grant] should feel able to confront and hold in check every active force of the enemy, and yet to detach a well-appointed large army to move on such an expedition. The result not yet being known, conjecture in regard to it is not here indulged."

As he often did, Lincoln masked his anxieties with humor. It was in this period, when he had a meeting with the Pennsylvania politician and publisher A. K. McClure, that Lincoln asked if the newsman would like to know Sherman's whereabouts. When McClure eagerly said that he would very much want to know, Lincoln replied: "Well I'll be hanged if I wouldn't myself."

Lincoln followed his State of the Union message with a short speech this evening from the White House in response to a band concert given in his honor. "I have no good news to tell you, and yet I have no bad news to tell," Lincoln said. "The most interesting news we now have is from Sherman. We all know where he went in at, but I can't tell where he will come out of." Drafted but cut from his annual message was an attempt to lower expectations about the operation and its leader: "We must conclude that he feels our cause could, if need be, survive the loss of the whole detached force; while, by the risk, he takes a chance for the great advantages which would follow success." For the crowd gathered at the White House, Lincoln chose to end his remarks by calling for three cheers for "Gen. Sherman and the army."

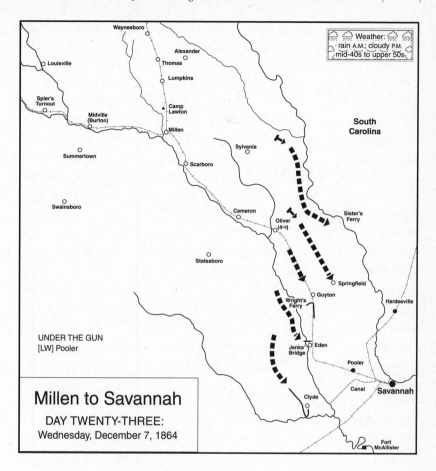

Waynesboro

Alexander
Louisville Thomas
Lumpkins

Spier's
Turnout
Midville
(Burton)
Millen

South
Carolina

Sylvania
Summertown Scarboro

Swainsboro Cameron Sister's
Ferry
Oliver
(4½)

Statesboro

Springfield
Wright's Guyton
Ferry Hardeeville

UNDER THE GUN
[LW] Pooler

Jenks' Eden
Bridge
Pooler

Millen to Savannah

DAY TWENTY-THREE:
Wednesday, December 7, 1864

Clyde Canal Savannah

Fort
McAllister

Weather:
rain A.M.; cloudy P.M.
mid-40s to upper 50s

WEDNESDAY, DECEMBER 7, 1864

Left Wing

Heeding General Bragg's admonition to press the enemy's forces nearest the Savannah River and South Carolina, Major General Wheeler
renewed his campaign of harassment aimed at the Federal Fourteenth
Corps. His troopers ran up against Kilpatrick's Second Brigade, which
absorbed much of their attention during the day. There was a short but
sharp skirmish first thing in the morning, followed by a larger-scale
scrap late in the afternoon. In the latter, the Union riders were struck
as they were feeling their way across a stream and threading gingerly
through a swamp.

The afternoon fight began when Wheeler and his escort ventured too near the Federal rear guard—the 9th Michigan Cavalry—which reacted by charging the enemy party. Wheeler's group retreated to the Rebel main body, which returned the compliment by driving the Michigan men back to their fully alerted reserve, the 9th Ohio Cavalry. For the next few minutes charge was met by countercharge as small groups of riders engaged in briefly violent combat to the accompaniment of shouts, screams, and the crack of pistols firing. One officer in the 9th Ohio Cavalry recalled the events in broken fragments—a lazy column of march suddenly transformed by shouted orders to form a line of battle, followed by the breathless command: "Draw saber, forward charge!" A Tennessean with Wheeler long remembered the civilian they had along as a local guide, an embittered old man whose property had been wrecked by marauding Yankees. Caught in the whirl of the fight, the noncombatant used both barrels of his shotgun to bring down two of the enemy, one of them a young officer. "He is very proud of his feat," wrote the Tennessee trooper, "and feels that he had taken partial satisfaction for the burning of his house and turning his family out of shelter."

During the engagement Wheeler's men put enough pressure on the Union troopers that they called for infantry help. The added heft proved more than enough to squelch the fighting. Wheeler's losses were eleven killed, wounded, or missing, while the two Federal cavalry regiments suffered thirteen casualties. The Union officer felled in this affair was the "gallant" Captain Frederick S. Ladd. For all the sound and fury, the effect on today's movements by the Fourteenth Corps was negligible.

Far more bothersome for the foot soldiers were the swamps and occasional stretches choked by chopped timber. A Wisconsin soldier recalled how he and his comrades, after one swampy section, were "bespattered with mud from heels to crown." The officer commanding the leading Fourteenth Corps division reported that the roadway was "badly obstructed by fallen trees, but by heavy details removed them, causing but little delay."

A few of those marching in Baird's division, still traveling last in line, worried about rumors that Braxton Bragg, with 10,000 soldiers from the Augusta garrison, was driving hard on their heels. It probably wasn't a coincidence that when the division bivouacked for the night, extra details were assigned to erect defensive barricades. The head of the Fourteenth Corps column settled in about two miles shy of Ebenezer Creek, where, scouts reported, the bridge had been destroyed. Poor staff work had allowed the pontoniers of the 58th Indiana to make their camp before it was realized that their talents would be needed. "We were aroused at 11:30 [P.M.] and ordered to 'fall in,' " groused one engineer. "Four Companies were sent to Ebenezer Creek to make a bridge."

There was emotion in the ranks of the 87th Indiana this night regarding the noncombat death of a popular soldier, Sergeant Kline Wilson. A friend who sat with him just before he died asked if he had any special message for his parents. "He said he was too weak to talk but to say to his father that he died in a good cause." In a letter to the sergeant's hometown newspaper, the friend wrote that "Sergt. Wilson was a brave, good soldier and his loss is deeply regretted by the officers and soldiers of his regiment, and especially of his own company."

Marching parallel to the south of the Fourteenth Corps, the three divisions of the Twentieth encountered some especially bad sections of ground. A Michigan foot soldier complained that "in places [the swamp] was almost impassible." In the Second Division, one brigade commander had to assign every man to be "distributed along the [wagon] train," where they "rendered material assistance in pushing them along." An Ohio infantryman, who termed the swampy surface "quicksand," noted that "many teams [were] getting [stuck] fast." It had rained off and on throughout the morning and as a result, attested a Wisconsin man, "we had to pry and pull whip & shout, to extricate the wagons . . . sunk to the axles in the soft quicksand." Along one mucky patch, a New Jersey officer was struck by the sight of forty or fifty wagons "looking like so many stranded ships, stuck to their beds in the mud, with their mules resting quietly."

For the Twentieth Corps soldiers this day's big distraction came when they passed through the small town of Springfield, which one Illinois soldier described as "a poor looking distracted, woe begone place." An officer in a companion regiment recollected "white flags flying at all inhabited houses." Once they entered the town, a few of the boys discovered the pleasant charms of its female residents. A soldier in the 102nd Illinois had to laugh at the citizens who remained safe and unmolested in their houses, while having to helplessly watch as the inquisitive Yankees found all their outdoor hiding places. "An almost endless variety of articles have been exhumed," chuckled the infantryman. "Some are bringing any clothing, others blankets, others fine dishes, silver spoons, etc. One man has just passed us dressed as a lady, only his toilet was rather rudely made."

For one little girl in the path of Sherman's men, the impressions of this day stayed with her. The enemy's approach triggered a variety of responses from her neighbors; some tried to hide their valuables, while others seemed resigned to whatever would happen. "All were in a wild state of expectancy, moving hither and thither, knowing not what was best to do," she recalled years later. The Yankees at last arrived with the suddenness of a thunderstorm. "In a few minutes the broad grounds were literally alive with soldiers—rushing in all directions like wild Comanche Indians," she remembered. "Parties searching through the house from garret to cellar, in every niche and corner, through drawers, closets, trunks, wardrobes, and even under beds, taking everything of any value. Outside the house, the burning of fencing and outbuildings, and the firing of guns and pistols, slaying of cows, calves, hogs, pigs, chickens, and turkeys, while others were robbing the smokehouse, dairy, syrup house and store room."

Right Wing

Assigned to follow the Central of Georgia Railroad tracks and river road along the Ogeechee River's east bank, the Seventeenth Corps encountered both swamps and roadblocks. A member of the 11th Illinois remembered it as "a very wet swampy country," while another in the regiment wrote that they "had to build four or five small bridges, and also had to do some corduroy work." "Stopped often and long while the roads are cleared of trees etc felled by the rebels," added a man in the 20th Illinois.

The tougher traveling and diminishing prospects of locating adequate forage for the animals led to another culling of the herds. A diarist in the 12th Wisconsin noted the shooting of 100 horses and mules this day; another in the 16th Wisconsin added 200 to the sum, while a third, in the 64th Illinois, estimated the entire number of unfit animals dispatched at "about 2,000."

The leading elements of the Seventeenth Corps camped around Station No. 3, Guyton, near where Sherman set his headquarters for the night. During the ride from Station No. 4½, Oliver, Major Hitchcock had been both sobered and amused. One of the first sights to meet his gaze this morning was a roadside burial detail setting to rest "some poor fellow's remains. . . . Perhaps by some once happy fireside his place is now empty forever, and loving eyes will look vainly for his return." The diversion was provided at midday, when the General took lunch at the Elkins residence. The matron of the house, "a regular Georgia woman," admitted to Hitchcock that she took snuff and let her children eat clay.

Mrs. Elkins hoped that Sherman would find Savannah undefended, but he thought otherwise. "McLaws' division was falling back before us," he reflected, "and we occasionally picked up a few of his men as prisoners, who insisted that we would meet with strong opposition at Savannah." When he sent Major General Slocum his movement objectives for the next few days, Sherman added the thought: "We hear that the enemy is fortifying in a semi-circle around and about four miles from Savannah." Some of the General's concerns percolated to his staff, so that his principal telegrapher observed today that "indications now point to a fearful & determined battle to make that harbor a base."

It speaks to the flexibility of Sherman's troop arrangements that while fully three-fourths of his force did little this day but march and change camps, the remainder executed several offensive missions. Yesterday the Fifteenth Corps had secured one Ogeechee River crossing at Wright's Bridge and positioned itself near another (Jenks' Bridge). Today the Fifteenth Corps exploited the first and forced the second.

At Wright's Bridge, below Guyton, Colonel James A. Williamson took his all-Iowa brigade over the rebuilt span, crossed to the river's east bank, advanced to the railroad, and turned south. The Union officer was taking no chances. "All the way down the Ogeechee we kept out flankers and skirmishers in front," recollected a member of the 4th Regiment. This action got under way about midday. Farther south, midwesterners from Brigadier General Elliott W. Rice's brigade (Brigadier General John M. Corse's division) mounted a successful crossing at Jenks' Bridge.

It was no casual operation. A slight enemy force held the opposite bank, and the old bridge was unusable, necessitating a pontoon. The call went back to Wright's Bridge for the 1st Missouri Engineers to come forward. The pontoniers arrived at 10:30 A.M., and their presence triggered the action's first phase. Under a covering fire of musketry and artillery, the engineers pushed their pontoon boats into the river to ferry several companies of the 2nd Iowa to the east bank, where they engaged the Rebels, then established a security perimeter.

Now the engineers were able to use their canvas boats for the purpose they had been designed; by 1:00 P.M. the military bridge was carrying traffic. The rest of Rice's brigade trouped over, with the 2nd Iowa covering the front. One of those soldiers in the advance recalled marching "about ½ mile over 5 or 6 [foot] bridges which the planks had been taken off so that we had to cross on the timbers and then deployed and advanced through the swamp knee deep in water for about 1½ miles when we came onto dry land." Here the Rebels had concentrated to impede the advance, positioning themselves behind a rail barricade.

The 7th Iowa supported the 2nd, which attacked in open skirmishing order. A soldier in the regiment recollected having to "charge over an open field of several rods in extent. We did not wait for a second volley, but got to the barricade before they could reload and 19 prisoners were taken, and the company hurried after the rest of them." According to this soldier, both generals Howard and Corse were on hand, the latter applauding them and exclaiming: "Brave boys, brave boys; never saw such brave boys."

The retreating Confederates had a last trick up their sleeves. A train was waiting for them on the Central of Georgia tracks. Much to the wonderment of the pursuing Federals, the Rebels clambered aboard and clattered off. "They took the cars for Savannah," marveled an Iowa soldier. Once Rice's men reached the railroad, they made contact with scouts from Williamson's brigade marching down from Wright's Bridge. The combined force took possession of a railroad station known as Eden. Experienced soldiers who did the math reckoned they were now within a day's march of Savannah.

The First, Third, and Fourth divisions encamped this night near Jenks' Bridge. The Second had turned south to follow roads taking it to the Canoochee River crossing probed on December 6. Leading the way for the Second Division was Colonel John M. Oliver's brigade, whose route led across Black Creek, where another enemy party was waiting, the bridge ablaze with the streambed tangled with tree pieces and brush. Hardly had the enemy skirmishers been driven off when a cloud of pioneers attacked the blockage with a vengeance. "At Black Creek," reported the colonel, "the obstructions in the ford were removed, so that our ambulances and ammunition wagons crossed the ford before the troops could get across on the stringers of the still burning bridge."

Savvy field officers, knowing there was a second bridge just ahead at Mill Creek, rushed the pace so that the leading Yankees and retreating Confederates reached it at the same time. The Federals took the crossing intact, allowing them to continue as far as Bryan County Court House, also known as Eden.[*] Here most of the division would spend the night with pickets forward about two miles to the Canoochee River. While the unsupported thrust had no greater objective than securing the river crossing, it did cause the enemy to spread his defending forces southward to cover that approach to Savannah, thus reducing the concentration in the northwest quadrant, where Sherman had massed most of his men.

It fell to the 83rd Illinois to picket the river this night, always a dangerous operation in the close presence of the enemy. Already this evening there had been a firing incident when a party of Rebel scouts attempted to slip past the cordon. Joseph Grecian of Company A had just reached his post at one of the posts involved when he observed five riders heading toward him. "There they come, boys!" he shouted and pulled the trigger, only to hear the percussion cap snap without igniting the gunpowder. Quickly recapping the piece, the soldier tried again with the same result; however, a comrade next to him successfully fired his rifle. A verbal exchange with the intruders established they were Yankee scouts who were allowed to come in. The officer commanding them said that one sentry's bullet had hissed close to his head, yet when his men had tried to shoot back, their guns too had only popped their percussion caps. "It seems providential, indeed, that so many pieces were snapped, but only one shot was fired and all our lives were saved," noted Grecian.

---

[*]   Not to be confused with the railroad station town of the same name. When enough Georgians became confused, the name of this Eden was changed to Clyde.

Across southeastern Georgia, life went on in the wake of Sherman's passage. It was business as usual in Augusta, as a member of Wheeler's staff discovered when he cooled his heels for twelve hours in the offices of the government powder works before he could satisfy the rules of the bureaucracy in order to secure a requisition of ammunition for the troopers at the front. "An apparently small trifle sometimes wields the destiny of nations," he fumed.

In Milledgeville, Governor Joseph Brown, back in his office, took the offensive against local citizens who had helped themselves to State House and Executive Mansion property during the Yankee occupation. Unless everything was returned right away, Brown vowed to search any household suspected of colluding and punishing those responsible.

In Savannah, the time had come for Lieutenant General William J. Hardee to man the city's battlements. Into the field works guarding the northwest approaches Hardee sent the Georgia militia, now commanded by Major General Gustavus W. Smith. One of the approximately 2,500 civilian-soldiers so assigned took the opportunity to dash off a letter to his wife. Wrote Felix W. Prior:

> We are camped here, where we have some fortifications, awaiting Sherman's advance on this city. It is feared he may succeed in cutting the roads and deprive us of communication from without. . . . Savannah is now rather a dull place, every thing remarkably dear in the way of provisions. It requires a good deal of money to get but very little even of something to eat. The militia have seen a rough time indeed since they have been out this last time and the prospect ahead is not flattering though if the enemy would pass over into South Carolina the Ga. Militia might stand a chance of going home. . . . I don't think I shall enjoy life much while this great war lasts, but I desire to live through it, especially on account of my wife & children. I have seen men killed on the battle field who had heavy responsibilities at home, clever, good men who had dear and near wives & children at home. I hope God in his goodness will spare me.

Major General William Tecumseh Sherman *(above)*. He was forty-six years old at the time of the Savannah Campaign and about to undertake an operation that he described as "smashing things to the sea." Before setting out, Sherman reviewed his cavalry arm *(below)*, commanded by Brigadier General H. Judson Kilpatrick. The General considered Kilpatrick a "hell of a damned fool."

Working from orders by Captain Orlando Poe, Union soldiers destroyed Atlanta's manufacturing and transportation systems *(top)*. On November 15, the Twentieth Corps (one-half of the Left Wing) left Atlanta, heading due east *(above)*. Many facets of this operation are depicted in the composite sketch of the march *(below)*.

GENERAL SHERMAN'S GRAND MARCH THROUGH CENTRAL GEORGIA.—[SEE PAGE 780.]

Peaceful Georgia villages such as Madison *(left)* played unwilling host to the Yankee invaders. "Colored people are pleased to see the Yanks," wrote an Ohio soldier. "Whites look sour & sad."

"Cotton stored near the railroad station [in Madison] was fired, and the jail near the public square gave up its whips and paddles to increase the big bonfire in the public square," noted an Ohioan *(right)*. On November 22, Sherman's Left Wing entered Milledgeville, where the Stars and Stripes were raised over the capitol building *(below)*.

Union soldiers held a mock session of the legislature in the capitol building *(left)* and repealed Georgia's act of secession. Sherman spent the night of November 23 in the Governor's Mansion *(below)*, where he had to use his field equipment, since Joseph Brown had hidden the furniture.

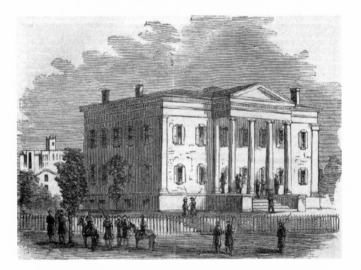

After resting just a day in Milledgeville, Sherman had his Left Wing marching on November 24. The crossing of the Little River *(right)* was accomplished by means of a pontoon bridge.

The first real opposition to the Left Wing came at Sandersville *(top)*, where Wheeler's cavalry skirmished with Federal infantry. At Tarver's Mill *(middle)* Major Hitchcock watched *Harper's* artist T. R. Davis sketch the scene, sitting under the branches of a fine live oak. The Seventeenth Corps crossed the Ogeechee River *(bottom)* utilizing both a trestle *(left)* and pontoon *(right)* bridge.

Major General Oliver Otis Howard *(left)* commanded Sherman's Right Wing during the Savannah Campaign. Even without a right arm (lost in battle in 1862), Howard projected an image of professional competence not always borne out by his combat performance. Nevertheless, Sherman designated him his second-in-command over Henry Slocum, who ranked Howard.

Major General Henry W. Slocum *(right)* was described by one Sherman aide as "brave, cool, experienced." Sherman's Left Wing commander was competent but prickly, so much so that his career went on hold when he refused to serve under an officer he personally despised. Slocum's command included the largest contingent of eastern soldiers to participate in the March to the Sea.

Camp Lawton *(top)* was supposed to replace Andersonville, but the approach of Sherman's columns forced its evacuation. What the Federal soldiers saw inside the compound *(above)* stirred widespread anger, some of which vented itself on the nearby town of Millen *(below)*. Sherman told his Seventeenth Corps commander to make Millen's destruction "'tenfold more devilish' than he had ever dreamed of."

Flamboyant and controversial, Brigadier General H. Judson Kilpatrick *(right)* led Sherman's cavalry in the Savannah Campaign. Quick to anger and a fighter, Kilpatrick was also, in the words of one Federal officer, "the most vain, conceited, egotistical little popinjay I ever saw." Kilpatrick's men were in almost constant skirmishes with Rebel cavalry under Major General Joseph Wheeler. The largest-scale encounter between the two came at Waynesboro on December 4 *(below)*, when Kilpatrick personally led one of the attacks against Wheeler's barricaded position.

GENERAL SHERMAN'S ARMY DESTROYING THE MACON RAILROAD BETWEEN ROUGH AND READY AND JONESBOROUGH, GEORGIA.—[SEE NEXT PAGE.]

A miscellany of scenes common during Sherman's March: destroying railroad tracks *(top)*, foragers heading out and returning to camp in the evening *(middle pair)*, an infantry column crossing a river via a pontoon bridge *(bottom)*.

Brigadier General William B. Hazen *(left)* commanded the force assigned to capture Rebel Fort McAllister. The *Harper's* image of the assault *(below)* was based on a sketch by its artist, T. R. Davis. Seen in the depiction is the outer ring of abatis (piled treetops) and the inner palisade of sharpened wooden stakes. Near the abatis, the smoke blooms mark explosions of deadly land mines then known as torpedoes. Watching across the flat marshes from several miles distant, Sherman was moved by what he saw. "There they go grandly," he said with pride, "not a waver."

One striking incident of the Savannah siege occurred when a Federal battery dueled with C.S. gunboats on the Savannah River *(below, top)*, resulting in the capture of the tender *Resolute*. Fort McAllister's capture opened a river supply route and also resulted in a sizable haul of munitions *(below, middle)*. Finally, on December 21, Sherman's army entered Savannah *(below, bottom)*.

The final defense of the besieged city came from the Rebel ironclad *Savannah*, which blew itself up *(above)* late on December 21. "It lit the heavens for miles," said one of its sailors. Among the variety of Savannah scenes depicted *(below)* is the image in the center showing the Green Mansion, Sherman's headquarters during his occupation, and the one below it depicting the Rebel evacuation.

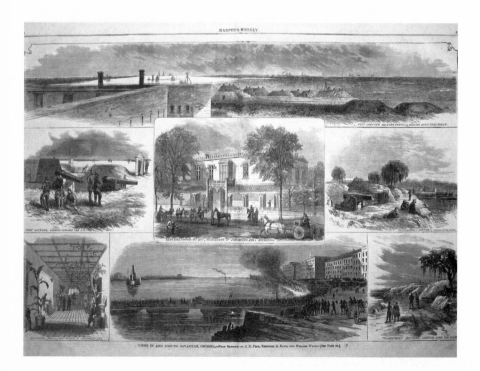

GENERAL SHERMAN REVIEWING HIS ARMY AT SAVANNAH.—SKETCHED BY WILLIAM WAUD—[SEE PAGE 83.]

To officially close his Savannah Campaign, Sherman reviewed each of his four corps, one of which is shown marching past him *(above)*. On Christmas Day, Sherman entertained his officers at the Green Mansion *(below)*.

The darkly impressionistic sketch *(above)* depicts Brigadier General Kilpatrick's headquarters near Savannah. Immediately prior to setting up shop here, Kilpatrick and his men liberally foraged through Liberty County to the south of the city. New Year's Day in Savannah called for an official reception by Sherman, held in the spacious Green Mansion *(below)*.

Chosen to oversee Confederate operations aimed at stopping Sherman, General Pierre Gustave Toutant Beauregard *(left)* had to manage a principal subordinate determined to pursue his own strategy, a collection of Confederate brass spread across southeastern Georgia with differing agendas, and a well-equipped, able, and active enemy. Facing critical actions occurring at either end of Sherman's March, Beauregard struggled against a decrepit transportation system and unpredictable communications to fashion a coordinated response to the Yankee invasion.

Confederate cavalry under the command of Major General Joseph Wheeler *(right)* represented the principal force opposed to Sherman's March. A fierce competitor (he was wounded three times, lost sixteen horses in combat, and had thirty-six staff officers wounded by his side), the youthful Wheeler had to live down a popular sobriquet as the "War Child." He answered to a number of officers and officials during Sherman's March, and the poor discipline of his men led to their being dubbed "Wheeler's robbers."

It fell to Confederate president Jefferson Davis *(below, left)* with his vice president, Georgia's Alexander Stephens, to rally dispirited Georgians and put together a winning team to defeat Sherman's forces.

Among those Davis called upon was William J. Hardee *(above, left)*, a past commandant of cadets at West Point who was known as "Old Reliable." Another ordered into the breech by Davis was General Braxton Bragg *(above, right)*, whose military strictness, personal insensitivity, and notable battlefield failures cast him as one of the most detested of Confederate generals.

Davis put much of his hope for turning things around with General John B. Hood *(below, right)*, who gave up making defensive moves against Sherman and went on a high-risk offensive into Tennessee.

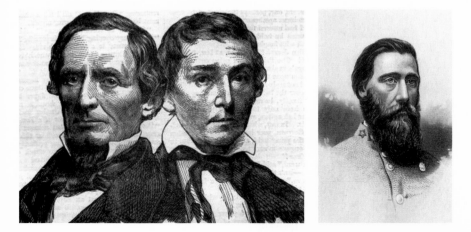

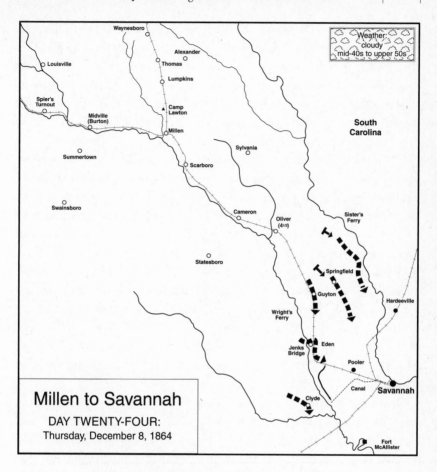

Millen to Savannah
DAY TWENTY-FOUR:
Thursday, December 8, 1864

THURSDAY, DECEMBER 8, 1864

—— *Left Wing* ——

Advancing along the center of the Savannah peninsula, the Twentieth Corps met little opposition from enemy fighters, but a great deal from the land itself. In an effort to keep things moving, the Second Division—the first in line—was shunted onto a "small road branching off to the right, with a view of finding some middle road." The route, more a question mark on the map, did not exist; at least, no one was able to locate it. As a consequence, the division plowed ahead, carving its own byway out of the forests and swamps in the general direction of Savannah.

That left the only known thoroughfare clear for the First Division, followed by the Third, which was also dragging along the wagons. The former had a rather uneventful tramp; forage was good, and the sections of blocked passageway were swiftly cleared by what a Wisconsin soldier called "the lusty black pioneers." The First Division's passage served mainly to churn up the already fragile road bed, making matters exponentially worse when the Third finally came along.

A musician marching with the Third's First Brigade pronounced them "the worst roads I ever saw." Matters were so bad that the division commander, Brigadier General William T. Ward, was described by one staffer as "cussing mad." If an officer with the 85th Indiana is to be believed, the frustrated Ward turned to drinking. The soldier and his company were busy corduroying a swampy swath of road when the general rode up to supervise. "Captain," he slurred, "corduroy it good, its shaky down here. Corduroy it good, its shaky. The first wagon will go down, down, and the next wagon will go clear to the hub, and the next wagon will go down to H——l. I tell you Captain, its shaky." With that Ward rode off, now possessing a nickname. From here on the men of the 85th Indiana referred to their commander as "Old Shaky."

Running behind time with the Twentieth Corps was the Fourteenth, which held the extreme left flank of Sherman's movement. A combination of treacherous ground and Rebel opposition (including a surprise appearance by the Confederate Navy) guaranteed that Brevet Major General Jefferson C. Davis's men would not close the gap this day.

The path followed by the Fourteenth Corps snaked alongside the Savannah River, where it slithered through a latticework of creeks and accompanying swamps. It was especially bad near Ebenezer Church, where Ebenezer Creek emptied into the Savannah, but not before splitting into several miry branches. The lone bridge here was approached by a corduroy causeway with occasional culverts and drains. The Confederates, reported a Wisconsin man, "had raised 'Hail Columbia' here in general. The corduroy was torn up the whole length; the bridge burned and not satisfied with that they had slashed the cypresses from both sides across the road and making a complete tangle of it."

Somehow, four companies from the 58th Indiana had reached the bridge (a trestle affair) and were busily fixing it up, even as pioneer details replanked the corduroy sections. Among the first units to arrive when the crossing was declared open at noon was a pontoon detail from the 58th. There was another wrecked crossing a few miles farther on at Lockner Creek requiring their skills. Hardly had the initial regiments begun tramping over the Ebenezer Creek trestle when the Confederates surprised everyone. "Like a flash of lightning out of a clear sky, a loud explosion was heard a short distance down the stream, and a sixty-four pound shell came whizzing over our heads," recorded an engineer on the spot.

It was the Confederate gunboat *Macon*, operating on orders from Lieutenant General Hardee to do what it could to interdict the progress of the Federal columns along the Savannah River. "Our Brigade just got over when a rebel gun-boat opened on the bridge and stopped operations for a while," said an Ohio soldier. The enemy craft fired perhaps a half dozen times, more for show than effect. Its distant gunners could only aim in a general direction, without any sightings for corrections to improve accuracy. The warship became more of a novelty than a threat. "The curiosity of all to see a live Rebel Gunboat in operation overcame whatever alarm might have been felt and there was a rush to the river bank in such numbers that the boat was frightened away and soon disappeared up the river," chuckled an Illinois soldier.

More serious was an accompanying crescendo of carbine and rifle fire to the north as several groups of mounted Rebels attacked the rear guards, both cavalry and infantry. A number of Yankee pickets were gathering pine knots for lunchtime fires when the enemy appeared, among them a captain in the 101st Indiana who promptly dropped his load to scramble for safety with his men. "I dare say the captain was scared but he done some pretty fast running to get away," commented an amused observer. "We had our dinner ready but not eaten when the reb cavalry made a charge on us," growled a Minnesotan. "Most of the coffee was spilled in the hurry to get into line."

The Confederates had driven in Kilpatrick's cavalry screen as far as Baird's infantry rear guard. Once it became plain that the foot soldiers were holding their line, the mounted Rebels eased up, allowing the Federals time to sort out a defensive alignment with the cavalry on the right and the infantry to the left. Each side glared at the other for the rest of the day. Words replaced bullets after sunset, as opposing pickets exchanged banter. "The Rebels said they would drown the whole pack of Sherman's thieves in the swamps about Savannah, and our men replied that Savannah would be in our possession within three days," said an Illinois trooper.

"The negroes come into our lines by hundreds," continued that cavalryman, "but we cannot do anything for them. They are of all sizes, all ages, all sexes, and all colors, from the whitest white to coal black; women of all ages, and little children, all barefooted, and with scarcely clothing enough to cover them." "Up to this time the Darkies have been following the army from sections through which we passed and have accumulated thousands of all sizes and sex," added an Indiana infantryman guarding the Ebenezer Creek bridge, "and our orders is not [to] let them cross the river." Another Hoosier, this one an officer in a different Indiana regiment, marched past the growing refugee crowd near the checkpoint. "The groups gathered around the bridge presented a picture of misery seldom equaled," he attested.

The officers who had tried and failed to stem the unwanted procession at Buckhead Creek on December 3 now looked to the crossings at Ebenezer Creek and Lockner Creek as presenting them with another, even better opportunity.

Right Wing

Major General Sherman moved his headquarters with the sweep of the Seventeenth Corps along the Central of Georgia Railroad, today's objective being Station No. 2, Eden. It was steady but slow progress. "Trees had been felled in the road, and our march otherwise obstructed," related an Ohio soldier. "A good deal of corduroy built," commented a brigade commander in the Third Division. "Houses of two men burnt, neighbors informed on them as the men who had obstructed the roads." The torching of one of the two residences was noted with approval by Major Hitchcock.

After the General's staff broke camp at 7:00 A.M., they soon observed firsthand the challenges presented by the sandy crusted roads crossing the lengthening patches of swamps. The relatively placid pace did not bother Sherman, as he was more concerned about keeping his army concentrated. With the Fourteenth Corps lagging behind, it would not do for the other columns east of the Ogeechee River to travel too fast. "The army has been advancing slowly and surely," observed a member of Sherman's staff, "but as cautiously as if a strong army were in our front."

For lunch break Sherman's party stopped at the home of a Reverend Heidt, who proved to be one of those duplicitous civilians that Major Hitchcock had come to loathe. When Union infantry foraging his property came to the General with handfuls of rifle cartridges found hidden in his hen coop, the good cleric loudly proclaimed them planted by the Yankee soldiers. Sherman's aide-de-camp, Major Lewis F. Dayton, examined the evidence with a grim smile. "We don't draw ours from the Macon Arsenal," he said, displaying the manufacturing stamp on the cartridges. Heidt stammered a new excuse, but Sherman was utterly uninterested in dispensing any justice this day. The good reverend's house would be spared, much to Major Hitchcock's amazement.

Headquarters night camp was along the wagon road near Station No. 2, where Sherman received a verbal report from his Left Wing commander, Major General Slocum, who promised to tighten up his deployments. From Major General Howard came copies of recent Savannah dailies with news reprinted from New York sources about the fight at Franklin, Tennessee. The Southern sheets also contained full copies of Sherman's Special Field Orders No. 120, issued at the start of the campaign. "General very much provoked, and quite bitter on newspapermen everywhere," observed Major Hitchcock. "I don't wonder."

Once more it was the Fifteenth Corps that most aggressively carried the fight to the enemy. It was now operating in four separate detachments. For the Third Division, herding the lumbering wagons, today would be spent in camp near Jenks' Bridge. An officer and diarist in the 59th Indiana wrote that his men "had washing done and a general cleaning up." "We sent our forage detail & wagon out this morning," recorded an Illinois captain. "We got plenty of corn, sweet potatoes, beef, & sheep."

The Second Division, supported by the First, continued to drive south toward the Canoochee River. Since the Confederates still seemed determined to contest the stream crossing, Brigadier General William

B. Hazen, commanding the Second Division, decided to consolidate a short distance away at Bryan County Court House. "Our camp was in a pine woods, where we put up breastworks of logs," reported an Ohio soldier. The supporting division swung east to the Ogeechee River to bivouac near a historic fortification site known as Fort Argyle, where the Yankee boys made some nineteenth-century improvements. The Federals, wrote a member of the 9th Iowa, "built works [and] sent out a foraging party that had a fight but nothing serious."

It fell to the Fourth Division to knock on Savannah's front door. Setting out from its encampment on the west bank of the Ogeechee, the division crossed at Jenks' Bridge to take up a rapid march following the River Road. The men, recorded one of them, "moved without supply trains, but with two days' rations in their haversacks." Opposition was light, "not sufficiently serious . . . to occasion much detention," said the expedition's commander, Brigadier General John M. Corse. He continued that the "first line of [enemy] works . . . we found evacuated." The lack of any resistance allowed some of the soldiers to slip into their best tourist mode. "Around us are magnificent live oaks, beautifully hung with festoons of Spanish moss," marveled an Illinois diarist.

Corse's column made it as far as Dillon's Bridge, near where the Savannah-Ogeechee Canal met the Savannah River. The crossing here was still in flames, but it was routine by now for pioneers and engineers to extinguish the fire in order to quickly get it back into operation. A small force was established on the city side of the canal, with scouts reporting a manned Rebel barricade farther down the road. Corse, deciding he was far enough out on a limb, ordered his division to entrench along the canal's country side. Things were so quiet that a few of the boys took it easy. "Went in swimming to-day," reported an Illinois soldier. "The water was quite warm."

A rider raced back with a report for Major General Howard, who promptly passed the news to Sherman. "This is an important point gained," declared Major Hitchcock. The General was already looking ahead to making contact with the Union fleet off Savannah. In a note to General Howard, Sherman authorized risking a scouting party to navigate the Ogeechee River to its mouth in order to "inform the naval commander that we have arrived in fine condition and are moving directly against Savannah." Major Hitchcock believed that it would only be a matter of "two days [before] we shall know whether Savannah will stand a siege."

The effort Wheeler was making to keep up the pressure on Sherman's Left Wing stretched Confederate logistics well past their breaking points. Keeping his troopers in constant contact with the slowly moving Federal columns was all that mattered; consequently, Wheeler never questioned how his men kept themselves supplied. After this campaign had ended, one exasperated citizen wrote the C.S. secretary of war to protest "against the destructive lawlessness of members of General Wheeler's command." He continued: "Beeves have been shot down in the fields, one quarter taken off, and the balance left for buzzards. Horses are stolen out of wagons on the road, and by wholesale out of stables at night. . . . It is no unusual sight to see these men ride late into camp with all sorts of plunder."

Still, it was results that mattered, and this day Wheeler delivered something. A Union rider bearing a communication from Major General Slocum to Brevet Major General Davis ran afoul of one of Wheeler's detachments, which sent the captured missive all the way up the chain of command to Lieutenant General Hardee in Savannah. The note sketched the proposed alignment of Federal forces once contact had been made with Savannah's principal defensive ring. The dispatch contained accurate intelligence, but it presented only a slight advantage to Hardee, who now had a better idea where to best concentrate his scant resources. All his efforts were aimed at buying time—time for somebody somewhere else to do something that might upset Sherman's schemes. That someone else was General Beauregard, who attempted a strategy conference in Charleston that Hardee declined to attend, pleading "injury to the service" if he left his post. Beauregard realized that he would have to travel to the threatened city.

One key question was answered this day: Savannah would not be held to the last ditch. General Beauregard made that clear in a message he sent Hardee from Charleston: "Having no army of relief to look to, and your forces being essential to the defense of Georgia and South Carolina, whenever you shall have to select between their safety and that of Savannah, sacrifice the latter."

Hardee had allowed one exception to Beauregard's directive.

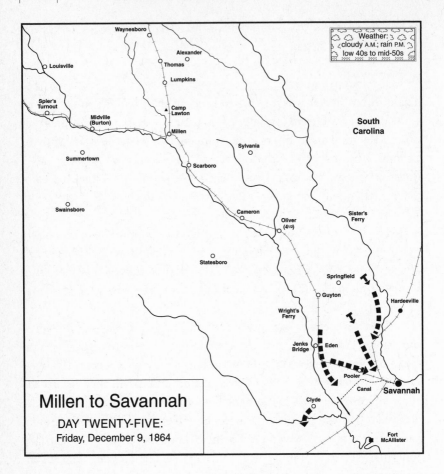

Millen to Savannah

DAY TWENTY-FIVE:
Friday, December 9, 1864

Located on Genesis Point near the mouth of the Ogeechee River, Fort McAllister had successfully blunted seven different Union naval efforts in 1862 and 1863 to penetrate the river system it protected. The earthen fort lay some four miles outside Savannah's intermediate defensive ring and could expect no help if attacked on its land side. Abandoning the position would open the Ogeechee River for Federal craft, which could easily range inland as far as King's Bridge, where it would be possible to establish a depot for Sherman's army. Once Sherman tapped into a source of fresh supplies and—even more important—large-caliber siege guns, Savannah was doomed.

Hardee never explicitly ordered the Fort McAllister commandant (Major George W. Anderson) to hold until the last, but his actions left no other interpretation. This day Hardee dispatched to the fort rations of bacon, bread, whiskey, molasses, salt, and sundries amounting to what one Southern officer calculated was "thirty-two days' rations for two hundred men." The implication was clear: Fort McAllister was to be held to the bitter end.

FRIDAY, DECEMBER 9, 1864

Savannah's defensive scheme was laid out in four zones. Outermost was a fringe region where the primary components were passive: roadway obstructions and bridge demolitions. Closer to the city came a more active exterior "outpost" line about twelve miles out from Savannah's western boundary. "Detached field works had been hastily prepared at important points, and some light artillery and infantry put in position," recorded an officer with Hardee's garrison. No one expected this exterior line to stop the Federals, only delay or deflect them. Arcing about five miles west from town (and up to twice that to the south) was the intermediate or "overflow" line. The latter name acknowledged that large sections of it had been rendered impassable by the simple expedient of flooding heavily irrigated rice fields or cutting dikes to inundate low-lying areas. According to the garrison officer, the defenses here "consisted of detached works, located at prominent points, commanding the established avenues of approach to the city, crowning causeways and private crossings over these lowlands and offering resistance wherever the swamps were practicable." The final line, tight to the city itself, was best considered a rallying point in case of a breakthrough or a rearguard position covering an evacuation into South Carolina.

Left Wing
Monteith Swamp

Brigadier General Nathaniel J. Jackson's First Division had the lead today in the general movement of the Twentieth Corps from around Springfield toward Monteith Station on the Savannah and Charleston Railroad. No one needed a compass to recognize that their general course was changing from south to east. Taking the point for Jackson's command was the 123rd New York, a veteran unit nearly five hundred strong. "The boys were marching along, joking, laughing and singing as usual, when all at once a shell exploded directly over their heads," related a member of the unit. "If ever soldiers were surprised it was the boys of the 123d Regiment, about noon on the 9th of December, 1864."

Ahead of them the thoroughfare was pinched on its left by a wide swamp and on its right by a mixture of swamps, woods, and rice fields, a region known locally as Turkey Roost Swamp. The passage directly ahead was clogged with heavy slashings—chopped trees and brush promiscuously piled together. Behind this was a piece of high ground on which the Confederates had constructed two redoubts, with one field piece manned by veteran North Carolina artillerists, part of the reinforcements that General Braxton Bragg had brought with him from the Wilmington area.

The cannon fire brought Brigadier General Jackson to the front to assess the situation. The Rebel position was well sited; its gun commanded the road, while the heavy slashings discouraged any effort to tackle the position straightway. Tactical doctrine called for getting the enemy's attention head-on, then working another force around the side to take it from the flank. Jackson saw no reason not to go by the book. His leading unit—the First Brigade under Colonel James L. Selfridge—was told to "occupy the attention of the enemy in front," while the next in order—Colonel Ezra A. Carmen's Second Brigade—was sent into the swampy mess on the right side of the road "with instructions to advance well around the enemy's left flank and endeavor to get in his rear."

Both assignments were easier said than done. A member of one of Selfridge's regiments recollected the men wading through the "swamp just at the left of the road, [and] jumping from bog to bog, sometimes miring in the black, inky mud and water to their waists." Officers with the flanking brigade had troubles of their own. "After plunging around a while on horse back, we concluded to dismount & send our horses to the rear," wrote one of them. A short New Yorker found the swamp deep enough that he was "obliged at one time to swim or sink."

Growing impatient at the slow pace of Colonel Carmen's maneuver, Brigadier General Jackson decided to hedge his bet. Three regiments from Colonel James S. Robinson's Third Brigade (two advancing, one in support) were peeled off the column to be sent into the mire on the enemy's right. "We waded through a swamp," related a soldier in the 31st Wisconsin, who also noted that he and his comrades "had quite a lively time of it."

The Confederates blocking the roadway were getting jumpy. Their instructions were "not . . . to fight the enemy, but merely to hold them in check for a few hours." How long this meant was a function of their commander's nerves. It was apparent that the Yankees were flanking them; however, the trick was to hold until the artillerymen could get in their last lick in time to withdraw their piece before it became impossible to do so.

Along the road, Colonel Selfridge's men were doing their best to keep the enemy's focus on them. "Advanced as skirmishers, crawling on our hands & knees through brush & water, through the swamp," recalled one. On the right, Colonel Carmen reached the enemy's rear, where he spent some time aligning his five regiments for the charge. On the left, the two regiments—61st Ohio and 31st Wisconsin—had wormed their way through the morass to confront a stretch of open ground leading to the Rebel right flank.

Luck played its part in this little action. The time it took Colonel Carmen to move his brigade across the swamp, then line it up to attack, allowed the later-starting pair from Colonel Robinson's brigade to wriggle close enough to the enemy redoubt to open fire. A few minutes of taking hits from the front and right was enough for the Tarheels in the forward redoubt. A soldier in the 31st Wisconsin long remembered the "most magnificent view of their coat tails standing out at right angles to a pair of legs that were doing their best to take their owner to a place of safety."

Even as the two regiments raced forward to claim the forward redoubt, Colonel Carmen's battle line closed on the second. Had the first still been manned with Confederates, his job would have been more bloody; but with no force firing into their flank, Carmen's men surged ahead. "The enemy kept blazing away with his gun from the fort, as valorous in his effort as he was poor in his shooting," scoffed a soldier in the 3rd Wisconsin. By now some details from the First Brigade had scrambled into the emptied first redoubt to open fire on the other position. They only managed to hit Captain Wilson S. Buck of the 3rd Wisconsin. Enough was enough. A soldier in the 2nd Massachusetts remembered seeing "the Johnnies break over the parapet & make for the rear."

Hoping to slow the pace of the Yankee advance, a thin line of Tarheels from the 10th North Carolina Battalion briefly barred the way. Playing it by the book, Captain C. M. T. McCauley took station eighty paces to the rear of his skirmishers, directing things from behind a large tree stump. Once the Federals got into range, the captain's position was fully exposed. A bullet chipped the bark on one side of the stump, then the other. McCauley carefully peered over the top when, as he recollected, there came "three or four baskets full of bullets all around and over him." He also noticed that his men were expeditiously retrograding, "and not desiring to go contrary to the tactics, maintained his distance pretty well."

Racing ahead of Colonel Carmen's brigade were skirmishers from the 3rd Wisconsin led by Sergeant Wilbur F. Haughawut. "As I came splashing out of the water under [a] full head of steam," he recollected, "I beheld several heads exposed above the works, and though they were prepared to riddle me with bullets, my comrades' cheers so elated me that I slackened not till I had cleared the 15-foot ditch filled with water to protect the fort. I scaled the ditch and works and secured the three prisoners with my empty musket." This trio, plus one more, would prove the only prisoners taken, for, as the sergeant's regimental commander reported, "the swamp was so deep, and the enemy had a good road at his command, it was impossible for us to overtake him."

At a cost of one man killed and seven wounded, the Twentieth Corps had cracked through its sector of the outpost line. Ahead of them lay the intermediate line, a much tougher proposition.

Ebenezer/Lockner Creeks

Brevet Major General Jefferson C. Davis was feeling the pressure. The Kentucky-born commander of the Fourteenth Corps had problems galore this December day. His columns were still struggling to bull through the melange of limited roadways, pervasive swamps, and tricky stream crossings in the area where the Augusta Road crossed the Ebenezer and Lockner creeks. As a direct consequence, his corps—

and his corps alone—was running behind Sherman's schedule, a failing that Davis felt personally.

He was an officer who needed friends with friends in Washington, where the decision rested whether or not to confirm him in the rank of major general or leave him in an "acting" or brevet capacity. While Davis's combat record was solid, his career would forever bear the mark of his actions on September 29, 1862, when he shot his former commander dead after a quarrel. His connections were strong enough to sweep the matter under the rug; Davis was not punished, but it was a blemish that would always be there. Having Sherman in his corner was important, but he wasn't scoring any points as long as his corps was slowing up the entire enterprise.

It didn't help that Wheeler's cavalry appeared to have singled out his command for special attention. His rear guard had been skirmishing constantly over the past few days, further slowing down the pace of his progress. Then there were the slave refugees, more and more of them every day, increasingly retarding the movements of his men and wagons. While in Eatonton, on November 20, Davis had issued a special order on the subject that read in part: "Useless negroes are being accumulated to an extent which would be suicide to a column which must be constantly stripped for battle and prepared for the utmost celerity of movement. . . . Our wagons are too much overladen to allow of their being filled with negro women and children or their baggage, and every additional mouth consumes food, which it requires risk to obtain. No negroes, therefore, or their baggage, will be allowed in wagons and none but the servants of mounted officers on horses or mules."

His directive had been but indifferently enforced, and now Davis found his column handicapped by a crowd of fugitives numbering in the hundreds, if not a thousand or more. Like his commander as well as many of his soldiers, Davis believed that the blacks would be better off returning to their home plantations. There would be time once the war was over for the government to sort out what would happen to this abruptly freed race, but the middle of an active military campaign was not it.

Six days earlier, at Buckhead Creek, his officers had tried to halt the trailing refugees by preventing them from using the military bridge before it was dismantled. Buckhead Creek had not been enough of a barrier to discourage many, and since then the problem, as Davis saw it, had only worsened. Any sympathetic consideration of their plight was lost on a man imbued with an urgent sense of military necessity and raised in a society that dehumanized its African-American members.

The bridging of the Ebenezer and Lockner creeks offered Davis a better opportunity than had Buckhead Creek to free his infantry columns from the freed slaves' clinging embrace. Even as the trestle bridge over Ebenezer Creek was being finished on December 8, Davis positioned provost units at the entryway with orders to turn back any unauthorized blacks. When Brigadier General Absalom Baird's aide, Major James Connolly, learned of this he was livid. "I . . . knew [this] must result in all these negroes being recaptured or perhaps brutally shot down by the rebel cavalry to-morrow morning," he fumed. "The idea of five or six hundred black women, children and old men being thus returned to slavery by such an infernal copperhead as Jeff. C. Davis was entirely too much for my Democracy; . . . and I told his staff officers what I thought of such an inhuman, barbarous proceeding in language which may possibly result in a reprimand from his serene Highness, . . . but I don't care a fig." Connolly stormed off, his conscience assuaged, but Davis's orders remained unchanged.

Human nature being what it is, orders to prevent the blacks crossing at Ebenezer Creek were not entirely effective. "Some hid in the wagons and passed by the officers," noted an Indiana teamster, but a majority were halted. "As soon as the army was across, the planks were taken up," reported a member of the 2nd Minnesota. To keep anyone from clambering over the bridge skeleton, what was left was burned. "It was really pitiful to see them and they are afraid of the Rebels and begged hard to get over," related a Hoosier. "Some of them swam the river but the women and children could not get over."

Just as at Buckhead Creek, resourceful individuals began to organize their own crossing. "The Negro men constructed a raft by tying ropes to each end, [and] would pull it back & forth loaded with families of negro women & children," scrawled a Minnesota diarist. "They would 'bress the lord' as soon as they was over." "The raft would carry only half a dozen and sunk a foot under water then," added another Minnesotan. "One young fellow slightly deformed crossing with his wife, she stumbled and fell off the raft going to her neck in the water, her husband caught her and dragged her on board again. . . . They came on shore, she dripping and smiling, and he remarking that he would rather lose his own life than that sweet darling should be drowned." Tragically, if those who did get over Ebenezer Creek thought that the worst was behind them, they hadn't reckoned with the cold determination of Davis's officers.

A short way down the Augusta Road was Lockner Creek, where Federal engineers had laid a pontoon bridge. Here mounted infantry from the 16th Illinois constituted the rear guard, under the command of Captain Charles D. Kerr. "As soon as we were over the creek, orders were given to the engineers to take up the pontoons, and not let a negro across," he admitted afterward. "The order was obeyed to the letter." Weary blacks who had made it from Ebenezer watched in horror as a second crossing was denied them. "Rushing to the water's brink, they raised their hands and implored from the corps commander the protection they had been promised," said Kerr. Once the pontoons had been secured, the rear guard moved off, the men closing their ears to the plaintive wails that gradually faded out behind them.

Later, when this day's events became widely known and infamous, more lurid details would be added to the story, none of which came from eyewitnesses. Sadly, what had happened was bad enough. Given the determination they had already demonstrated, it is beyond doubt that some number of the blacks did make it across both creeks to remain with the column. It is also tragically probable that a number drowned in the attempt, while others either slipped away or allowed themselves to be rounded up by Wheeler's troopers. In his official report, the Confederate cavalryman noted only that "a great many negroes were left in our hands, whom we sent back to their owners." That some were shot or physically abused by their captors is not out of the question; it is even more likely that most of those so corralled were returned to face whatever retribution their owners thought to inflict.

There was never any argument that Brevet Major General Davis was exceeding Sherman's guidelines, as there is no evidence that the General ever voiced any disapproval of his subordinate's action. Davis was not ever compelled to account for what he did that December day. Whether or not this action was a factor, Congress eventually declined to confirm Davis's promotion, so he ended the war holding just a "temporary" rank of major general.

Even as this humanitarian tragedy was playing out at the tail end of the Fourteenth Corps column, its leading elements were making contact with another piece of Savannah's outpost line. It happened near or on the plantation of a Dr. Cuyler, at a natural choke point where the wagon road meandered between two swamps. Here the Confederates had built a small earthwork manned with artillerists. The Rebels, reported an Ohio soldier, "opened upon us in a lively manner, and for a time we were at a standstill."

While regiments branched away from the column to splash into the swamp to engage the enemy skirmishers, Battery I of the 2nd Illinois Light Artillery came forward to challenge the enemy tubes. Its young commander, Lieutenant Albert L. Coe, acting with what one soldier called "his usual rashness," galloped ahead of his men. "Sitting there on his horse, fearless of danger, looking for a good position for the battery," related an onlooker, "a solid shot came whirling along and tore his right shoulder off." "He was literally torn to pieces," related a gunner, "and had only time to say, 'My God, boys, I am killed.'" Once it became clear that the Confederates weren't going to obligingly clear out, the decision was made to hold station until morning.

Right Wing

The soldiers in Brigadier General William B. Hazen's division, Fifteenth Corps, awoke this morning to find that the Confederates defending the Canoochee River crossing had departed during the night. After sending a brigade to secure the stream's opposite bank, Hazen ordered up his pontoniers, who had a bridge ready for traffic by late morning. Even as his main body deployed on the other side, Hazen set his leading brigade, Colonel John M. Oliver's, marching hard for King's Bridge, an important crossing point of the Ogeechee River.

Oliver's force was organized for speed, so the men passed over the Savannah and Gulf Railroad tracks without stopping. Not so the brigade coming behind them, which, after reaching the right-of-way at 3:00 P.M., immediately stopped to wreck it. The "order was for every man to take hold of a railroad tie;" recollected an Ohioan, "then at the command we turned the railroad upside down. . . . We threw rails of pine in the track then set the whole mass on fire." An incident here reminded the soldiers that injury could happen at any time and in any fashion. "While this was being done, one man in Company E[, 47th Ohio,] was struck in the bowels by a tie, some of the spikes coming out." The brigade racing to King's Bridge arrived there to find that much of the sizable structure was ablaze. After dropping off a regiment to guard what remained, the rest of the brigade marched east to take out its frustrations by destroying the "magnificent . . . railroad bridge across the Ogeechee . . . 500 yards long." North of this activity, the troops of Brigadier General John M. Corse's division began to exploit their lodgment across the Savannah-Ogeechee Canal. Two brigades probed forward, hoping to gain control of a strategic intersection with the Darien Road, possession of which would speed up communication with Hazen's men away toward King's Bridge. The only problem was that the Confederates had anticipated this move, with another of their detached works barring the route.

According to one of Corse's regimental commanders, the leading Union elements "soon encountered the enemy's pickets and a brisk skirmish ensued." The Rebel voltigeurs were steadily pressed back into the defensive work, which one Federal officer described as "breastworks hastily constructed of logs and rails, though in some places dirt had been thrown up." "The rebels open fire from a mask[ed] battery," wrote an Illinoisan. "Battery H, 1st Missouri [Light Artillery] replies with vigor and dismounts a rebel cannon." It was a remarkable display of shooting, considering that the Yankee artillerymen had to set up in a dense woods and had "to fire altogether by the sound of [the enemy] . . . guns." Companies from the 81st Ohio and 66th Illinois, in widely spaced skirmishing order, darted ahead to overrun the position, whose defenders had lost heart once their cannon had been knocked out. Pursuit lasted until the Federals reached a wrecked bridge over a branch of the Little Ogeechee River, where they halted to wait for orders.

While the troops were resting here, they heard the whistle of a railroad train. Some of the soldiers caught sight of an engine pulling cars moving slowly southward on the Savannah and Gulf tracks, not more than a mile distant. The Missouri gunners hastily set up for a shot, but by the time they fired, the train was at extreme range, so no hits were registered.

The train conductor may have thought he had left his troubles behind him, but his luck was definitely spent. A short while earlier, after the barricade had been overrun, Brigadier General Hazen released his mobile unit, the 7th Illinois Mounted Infantry, for a dash to the south and east. This put the troopers ahead of the train, so when they heard it coming, a few quick-thinking members of the regiment managed to pry up one rail. This was enough to alert the railroad engineer to his danger; he stopped and reversed, hoping to back into Savannah. "The Brigade was too far away to prevent him by its [gun]fire," said a soldier in the 81st Ohio, "and he would have succeeded, but for the thoughtfulness of a soldier who happened to find a citizen's mule team near a road crossing. He drove the wagon on the track and shot the mules, forcing a complete blockade. By the time the train reached this, re-enforcements came up and the train was a prize. Colonel [Robert N.] Adams made prisoners of the male passengers, gallantly released the ladies unconditionally, and burned the cars." Among the haul of male citizens was Richard R. Cuyler, president of the Central of Georgia Railroad.

For days the Seventeenth Corps had been marching without serious incident along the Central of Georgia, wreaking havoc on President Cuyler's charge. Resistance was token for the most part, but today the iron rails unerringly led Major General Frank Blair's men into Savannah's outpost line for a fight and a deadly discovery.

This on a day that began on a positive note. "Strong sea breeze in our faces," wrote an optimistic Illinois diarist. At first, the Rebel videttes manning small barricades were content to fire a shot or two before scampering rearward. That all changed after about five miles, when the Federals encountered another of those Confederate outpost forts. "We found the enemy in position behind an earth-work at the end of a causeway leading through a swamp, the swamp extending around on both their flanks," reported Major General Joseph A. Mower, commanding the First Division. Mower followed the standard playbook, ordering one brigade "to engage the enemy in front," while two more waded into the swamp to flank the enemy's right.

The result was no different from any of the other outpost line encounters this day. Once the flanking force made its presence known,

the Rebels pulled back. The soggy Yankees closed on the road behind
the barricade, re-formed their lines, then continued the advance toward
Savannah. Behind them, however, a defensive weapon was making its
murderous debut in this campaign.

From the very first days after Sherman commenced his grand movement into Georgia, Confederate president Jefferson Davis had
reminded his subordinates that their arsenal included what he termed
"subterra shells," also known as torpedoes (in modern times called land
mines). Several munitions officers familiar with the workings of these
devices were assigned to Savannah to oversee the weapon's deployment. It was on the causeway fronting the Rebel earthwork that Sherman's soldiers blundered into one of several minefields that had been
seeded at selected points along the city's outpost perimeter.

Sherman, closely monitoring the movement of the Seventeenth
Corps, arrived on the scene not long after the barricade had been captured. His habit of yielding right-of-way to combat units on the march
paid an unexpected dividend as he and his headquarters party
approached the position via an adjacent clearing rather than using the
roadway. "Rode into the field," noted Major Hitchcock, "when we saw
by a group of men in the road on our right that something was the
matter." Sherman spurred forward to find himself joining "a group of
men standing around a handsome young officer whose foot had been
blown to pieces by a torpedo planted in the road."

The weapon came in a number of shapes and sizes. A passing artilleryman described one kind: "These torpedoes were 8 inches in diameter and had three wire prongs which stuck up above the surface of
the earth just enough so that the pressure of a man's foot was sufficient
to explode the torpedo." Similar versions were observed by Major
Hitchcock, who found them "13 in. long x 7 in. diameter, and at one
end were fitted on two brass nuts on which were screwed some sort of
friction tube . . . [with] a sort of nipple projecting from the fuse-
hole. . . . They would hold four or five lbs. powder and explode with
terrible effect."

The victim in this case was a member of the 1st Alabama Cavalry,
which provided a forward screen for much of the Seventeenth Corps.
"He was waiting for a surgeon to amputate his leg," continued Sherman, "and told me that he was riding along with the rest of his brigade-

staff of the Seventeenth Corps when a torpedo trodden on by his horse had exploded, killing the horse and literally blowing off all the flesh from one of his legs." "Poor fellow lay on the ground, covered all but his face with a blanket, only pale, but without a groan or complaint," added Hitchcock. Even as they were contemplating the fallen officer, a squad of Confederate prisoners with armed escort reached them.

Sherman now applied *his* rules of war to the situation. Under certain conditions he accepted his enemy's use of land mines, but this was not one of them. The finer points of his reasoning were later articulated by two of his staff officers, majors George W. Nichols and Henry Hitchcock:

Nichols

In the entrance to forts, or in a breach made in line of works, such implements may be used to repel the assault, but the laws of war do not justify an attempt of the kind which has been so disastrous to-day.

Hitchcock

Torpedoes at the entrance to a fort are perhaps justifiable, for the fort itself is a warning. But here they run away, refuse to defend the road, but leave hidden in an open public road, without warning or chance of defense, these murderous instruments of assassination—contrary to every rule of civilized warfare.

Sherman

This was not war, but murder, and it made me very angry.

The General turned to the prisoners, ordered them issued picks and shovels, then put them to work digging up the remaining torpedoes. "One of the Rebels asked where the General was and wished to see him," wrote an Ohio soldier on the scene. "The guards informed him that it was General Sherman who set him at digging up torpedos. The Rebel looked rather astonished." According to a gunner in the 1st Minnesota Light Artillery: "A Rebel major, who was in the squad, complained bitterly at this treatment, saying that he was not responsible for what the Savannah Confederates had done. 'Go on with your digging,' said Gen'l Sherman, 'you had no business to be caught in

such company.' " Major Hitchcock counted seven torpedos successfully excavated by the Rebel prisoners, who accomplished their task
without any injury. "This is a new mode of killing Yanks that us western fellows ain't used to," sighed an artilleryman. "We have to step
light now."

Even as this tableau was playing to its curtain, the head of Major
General Blair's column was running into more of the Confederates'
improvised arsenal. As the Federals neared Station No. 1, Pooler, the
Rebels shelled them using a field piece mounted on a railroad car. The
unexpected barrage panicked a company of short-timers—men due to
be soon mustered out of service—who promptly "disappeared like a
covey of partridges in the thick underbrush." The situation was far
more serious for a quartermaster officer, Lieutenant W. F. Hamrick,
who came forward from his position of safety to observe the action.
The soldier "was on his horse when a 12-pounder shot passed through
his chest," reported an Ohio soldier. "The event distributed a painful
shock throughout the whole division," said an officer.

As soon as Blair's men spread out in battle formation, the railroad
car and its cannon scuttled toward Savannah. The Yankee boys now
took possession of Pooler, which Major Hitchcock observed was "simply
a small neat station house or shed, say fifteen or twenty feet square, by
side of track." What most impressed the staff officer was the way the
soldiers automatically prepared their position for defense. The men,
said Hitchcock, "went to work and built [a] barricade all along their
line, made of three rows of logs one above another, about four feet high
in all, and in front were placed on end, sloping forward from top log,
sticks of cord wood of which they found [a] large pile ready cut and
corded for R.R. use at the Station."

Now that Savannah's outpost line had been overcome at each point
of contact, Sherman prepared to maneuver his columns for his operation's next phase. The time had come to begin to link together the
various strands of his army in order to tighten his grip on Savannah's
principal defensive ring, its intermediate line. Toward that end, pontoniers marching with the Seventeenth Corps threw a floating span
across the Ogeechee at the site of the wrecked Dillon's Bridge, linking
Blair's men with the Fifteenth Corps. "To-morrow we may expect to
concentrate our army so as to form a continuous line about the city of
Savannah," Major Nichols declared.

There was one more incident to play out before fading sunlight closed this day's operations before Savannah. A small group of men gathered behind the newly established Union front at the place where the Savannah-Ogeechee Canal intersected the Ogeechee River. Three men stood apart from the others: Captain William Duncan and Sergeant Myron J. Amick, 10th Illinois Cavalry, and Private George W. Quimby, 32nd Wisconsin. A correspondent who saw them later reported that they were "dressed in what may be considered the habits of Confederate citizens, not omitting in their make-ups a moderate allowance of rents and tatters, to give their garb an air of plausibility."

The plan was simple enough. Using a small dugout, Duncan and his companions were to descend the Ogeechee River to its mouth, where they expected to contact the Union fleet, hungry for word of Sherman's arrival. The officer carried with him a short message from Major General Howard as well as instructions for the fleet signal officers regarding the codes to use for communicating with the land forces.

The three squeezed into the small craft; one in the stern to steer, one in the middle to paddle, and one up front to provide relief for the other two. It wasn't the most stable of vessels, so the men worried as much about capsizing as they did being captured. Everyone on shore crossed their fingers as the trio pushed off just before sunset. All three were landlubbers born and bred. "I don't think the two men had any more experience on the water than I had," admitted Duncan, "and I did not have any."

After an hour or so of paddling and drifting on the inky black river, the scouts passed under King's Bridge, still smoldering from the Rebel torching earlier in the day. Fortunately for them, their passage went unnoticed by the Federal infantry overwatching the place, though the picket fires on the shore gave the reluctant sailors some tense moments. By midnight, the tide having turned against them, they realized they were making very little headway. Any hope they had this night of slipping past dangerous Fort McAllister was extinguished by the surging current.

The men steered for the right bank, grounded on the shore, then went searching for assistance. They found some slave cabins and, counting on the help they had received so willingly from other blacks during the march, boldly entered one of the huts. "We were not disappointed in finding the occupants friendly and as we required information, we told them who we were," related Sergeant Amrick. The slaves described the river's course downstream, then, when the trio proved unable to locate their dugout (which had drifted a bit), the knowledgeable blacks fetched it for them. A glance at the still incoming tide convinced the scouts to hold up until the next evening. The obliging slaves helped them secrete their craft before leading them to a piece of dense timber where they would be safe for the day. "We were very tired and wrapped ourselves in our ponchos and went to sleep," said the sergeant.

General P. G. T. Beauregard spent this day in Savannah receiving all the bad news. The briefing he heard from Lieutenant General Hardee contained nothing that could be construed as positive. The enemy, whose strength Hardee had seriously underestimated at 35,000 to 40,000, was clamping down on the city's "overflow" line. To oppose them he had maybe 10,000 soldiers of all types, from veterans to armed civilians. He reckoned he had supplies sufficient to feed his force for about thirty days. In order to garrison his intermediate line at even minimum levels, Hardee was shortchanging positions north of the town shielding the all-important connection with Charleston. Finally, Wheeler's cavalry was off on its own, operating somewhere behind Sherman's force.

Beauregard, who already regarded Savannah as lost, chided Hardee for not having made adequate preparations to evacuate his garrison into South Carolina. Apparently, it had been Hardee's intention to rely on river craft to ferry his soldiers with their accoutrements across the Savannah River, while Beauregard much preferred a floating bridge. At his insistence, Colonel John G. Clarke of his engineering staff was put in charge of the project. Beauregard yet again reminded his subordinate that his orders were "to defend the city so long as consistent with the safety of his command." He pledged to have the Charleston commander, Major General Samuel Jones, extend his forces closer to Savannah to better protect the all-important corridor north.

There was an unintended indignity when the time came for Beauregard to depart Savannah that evening. He had entered town on a Charleston train, but the latest reports indicated that during the day the enemy had cut that rail line near the South Carolina border. Used by now to having his travel plans complicated by Sherman's designs, Beauregard commandeered a launch to carry him up the Savannah River as far as the railroad bridge, where he changed over to a train to carry him to Charleston. As one of his aides later summed up the situation: "The outlook for the immediate future of the Confederacy had become very alarming."

SATURDAY, DECEMBER 10, 1864

Left Wing

The Rebel roadblock that had cost the impetuous Lieutenant Coe his life and held up the Fourteenth Corps was very silent this morning as Federal skirmishers brought it under fire, then edged closer. "The battery that annoyed our march last night fell back during the night toward Savannah," noted a relieved Illinois soldier. "They had earthworks thrown up across the road and embrasures for four guns." The idling columns began shuffling southward, following the Augusta Road, toward a link-up with the Twentieth Corps near Monteith.

The Yankees were now passing through a rice-producing region where the residences were few and far between. Supply parties prowling close to the Savannah River found one, described by an Ohioan as "a splendid plantation well stocked with forage." Continued an Illinois comrade, "The proprietor had fled to an island in the river, which is a part of his plantation, taking with him most of his effects, but the boys succeeded in capturing a large flatboat loaded with rice, meat, &c, which was duly appropriated without a trial by jury." All the men knew their business, for, as the Ohio man explained, "if we did not clean it out on short notice it was our own fault."

For one successful forager, today was a lesson learned about the prerogatives of command. William Bircher's division had stopped near a stretch of the Charleston and Savannah Railroad, where some detachments got busy prying up the rails, while the others were warned to remain close because of reports of Rebel cavalry in the neighborhood. Bircher, in the 2nd Minnesota, cheerfully ignoring the restrictions, wandered about a mile and a half before he came upon an abandoned farmstead not yet visited by other Federals. A few helpful blacks loaded the boy with potatoes and eggs, and as he departed, he gazed longingly at a pair of plump cows destined for some regiment's commissary.

Returning to where his comrades were working the road, Bircher tried to sneak in with his stash, but instead ran right into his colonel, who was sitting on a pile of track ties, supervising the line's destruction. The officer eyed the youngster lugging a rubber poncho filled with something.

"What have you got in your blanket?" he asked evenly.

"Potatoes," answered Bircher, knowing that it would do him no good to lie about something that could be easily checked.

"What have you got in your handkerchief?" continued the colonel.

"Eggs." They had arrived at the moment of truth. If Bircher was to keep his plunder, he had to convince the colonel that no rules had been broken. He was mentally ready when the officer popped the next question.

"Where did you get them?"

"Oh," said Bircher in his most casual tone, "about two hundred yards from here."

The colonel smiled. "Is that so?" he said.

"That's so."

"About two hundred yards from here?"

"Yes, sir."

Hoping to close the sale, Bircher began to describe the stout bovines he'd seen, but the colonel cut him off, saying that they'd talk about cows later. For the moment he instructed the young man to place his goods on the ground, then join the regiment tearing up the tracks. "I never got humpbacked from the amount of work I did," Bircher recollected in later years. "I principally kept one eye on the colonel and the other on the potatoes and eggs." The colonel's cook made an appearance, gathered in his takings, then headed toward camp. Bircher intercepted the man, but his protestations of ownership carried no weight with him. "Well," reflected the young soldier, now imbued with a veteran's philosophical skepticism, "that was the last I saw of the eggs and yams."

Some of the units assigned to the railroad job were told to follow the line to the river in order to destroy the bridge. "We tore up the track to the bridge and a detail was sent to fire it and the bridge but the Rebs had a Gun Boat laying in the river and they shelled us so we abandoned it," reported an Indiana soldier. Actually, corrected an Ohio comrade, it was so dark when the arsonists reached the span that no one was "certain what was firing on them." It could have been a gunboat; equally, it could have been a battery on the South Carolina side. Whichever it was, the Hoosier avowed that the Rebels "made it 'red hot' for us."

Having cleared the Rebel outpost blocking the way at Monteith Swamp, the Twentieth Corps bypassed the station to press toward Savannah's principal line of defense. The trick now was to recognize the difference between the lightly held outer works and the firmly held main position, then knowing when to stop. A soldier in the 129th Illinois who was part of this process recollected slogging "through thick underbrush and thorns in the pines, without a single shot being fired at us by rebel infantry. We could not explain this any other way than that the enemy's intention was to get us within easy range, and then pepper away at us to kill as many as possible. . . . We advanced until a swamp prevented all further progress, from the other side of which the enemy stationed there now opened on us. The enemy, being secure behind the swamps, answered three or four times to our shots, but all balls went overhead." The officer commanding a Connecticut regiment in the same predicament sent for something to eat once the line had stopped advancing, "for he 'knows it will be a week before we will get out of this d——d swamp.' "

The encounter of the day was turned in by a detail from the 150th New York, which was ordered toward the Savannah River by its brigade commander, who was hoping for a good haul to replenish depleted supplies. What happened instead was a land-river action, whose only eyewitness account was the brief unpublished report filed by the officer in charge, Captain Henry A. Gildersleeve:

Camp 150th NYV
Dec 11th 1864

Colonel

I have the honor to report that while foraging yesterday with my company, which numbers forty-two muskets, we discovered a steamboat, making her way up the Savannah river, and captured her with her officers and crew, eleven in number. Col. Clinch (said to be a bearer of dispatches to General Beauregard) and orderly were also taken from the vessel.

She proved to be the Rebel dispatch boat "Ida"—a sidewheel steamer about one hundred and twenty feet in length.

As soon as the "Ida" came in sight we opened fire on her with our muskets and were assisted some by a detachment of the 9th Ills. Cavalry. The bullets were so effective they caused her to turn around and endeavor to make her way back. In this attempt she struck ground and being still in range, considered her case hopeless, and pulled up the white flag.

Colonel Clinch then came ashore in a small boat and surrendered himself and the vessel.

As soon as the tide came up she was brought along side the wharf. By a very careful search nothing of any value was found on board but a small amount of rations for the crew.

Considering it unsafe to hold my company there until support could be obtained I fired the boat and returned to my regiment.

The prisoners were all turned over to the Provost Marshal of the Corps and I hold his receipt for the same.

I remain Very Respectfully,
Your Obd't Serv't
H.A. Gildersleeve
Capt. 150th NYV
Comd'g Co. C

Afterward, one of the captured Southern officers passed through the camp of the 86th Illinois, where he struck up a conversation with a Yankee after learning they both had connections to the town of Buffalo, New York. The Rebel had little good to say about C.S. currency (terming it "Confederate trash"), and confessed that he was "d——d glad to be captured," because he "was tired fighting for a country that was already gone to h——l."

——— *Right Wing* ———

The four constituent parts of the Fifteenth Corps, which had been operating on independent tracks for the past few days, began to merge across the face of Savannah's southwestern defensive sector. The men of Major General Peter J. Osterhaus's corps would occupy the extreme right flank of the investment Sherman planned for Savannah.

Those of the command operating this morning along the Canoochee River awoke to a heavy fog. "The weather is cold and a chilly mist is above and around us," recorded a Minnesota man, "which, rising from the flow water of the swamp and canal, gives a spectral appearance to the long lines of blue-coats." At numerous points the probing screen ahead of the main columns encountered the city's hard defensive shell. In a pattern repeated all up and down the line, Rebel cannon let loose at the first sight of the Federal voltigeurs. "We then commenced firing and skirmishing with the enemy," related a member of the 63rd Illinois. "The balls flew pretty thick but none of our boys were hurt." One slight exception was a private clipped by a tree branch severed by a cannonball, though the man "was not hurt bad, merely scared."

This was the sloppy phase of the process of grappling the enemy's main line of resistance. Units advanced by rough maps and compasses, with scant knowledge of what lay ahead. The men of the 100th Indiana found themselves having to entrench in the middle of a rice field. "Every thing is a black muck," griped a Hoosier. "We had just got settled when the Captain of a couple of guns which were in the embrasures close at our right told us to lay low. He was going to wake up the Johnnys. He fired both of his guns at a Battery perhaps half a mile away. He woke them up all right. They replied, knocked the muzzle off the gun next to us, the wheel of the other, blew up the caisson standing in the rear of the guns, and threw one shell into the muck in front of us which exploded and covered us with about 20 tons of black mud."

Even though the main part of the Fifteenth Corps was concentrating in an area bounded on its right by the Little Ogeechee River, several detached units extended Union control as far south as the ruined remains of King's Bridge. Already Sherman was looking at his maps and realizing that the Ogeechee River represented his best chance for establishing an accessible supply link with the Federal fleet at the stream's mouth. All that stood in the way was Fort McAllister. The first step toward eliminating that strong point was to restore King's Bridge to allow troops to cross. So an advance party from Major General Howard's headquarters, headed by his chief of engineers, Captain Chauncey B. Reese, now stared thoughtfully at the wrecked crossing.

It was a daunting prospect. The stringers and supporting timber were gone; all that remained were the log pilings, stretching like parallel dotted lines to the opposite shore. The distance to be bridged was about 700 feet; with approaches, nearly 1,000. The river here was really an estuary of the Atlantic, with a daily tidal rise of six to eight feet. At low tide the water was fourteen feet deep. While the tools needed were part of the kits carried by the engineers, all the timber would have to be manufactured on site. The final product had to be sturdy enough to carry a full division plus wagons and artillery.

The group with Captain Reese broke up, each member hurrying off to begin the process of measuring, surveying, mapping, and planning. When the bridge was first constructed the schedule had been measured in weeks. Now it would be counted in hours and days.

For their part, each of the three divisions in the Seventeenth Corps pressed hard today against Savannah's defenses. Likely the first in contact was the Fourth Division, which learned firsthand that many of the city's seaward-facing heavy-caliber guns had been shifted over to the land side. "The rebels shelled us quite lively, their large 32 and 64 lb shells tearing through the tops of the tall pine trees hurling branches and splinters in all directions," attested an Iowa soldier. "It was demoralizing but the damage was slight." Next into the line of fire was the Third Division, one of whose soldiers had a less than fond memory of plowing "pell mell through a big swamp up to my crotch in water." The typical situation facing the men was described by a Third Division soldier when he wrote: "In our front was a large ricefield partly covered with water, on the opposite side of which was a slight elevation, on which the enemy were entrenched." Substitute "swamp" for "ricefield," and the model fits nearly all.

Major General Sherman was still tagging along with the Seventeenth Corps; now that they were encountering the enemy's main line of resistance, his curiosity drew him into the combat zone. "He had dismounted," recalled an Illinois soldier, "and was walking nervously up and down the side of the road, his head bent over on his breast, his hands crossed behind him. He seemed intent upon his own thoughts, and oblivious to the volleys of shell and shot which tore down the road." "The boys thought that he was exposing himself unnecessarily and wished for the sake of all concerned that 'the Old Man' would look a leedle out and seek a safer place," seconded an Iowan.

All of which would have found no argument with Major Hitchcock, shadowing his restless boss this eventful day. Things had started out without any problems. Headquarters was on the move with Major General Blair's corps at 8:00 A.M., but once it became clear that the head of the column was fighting and not marching, Sherman brought everyone to a halt at a frame farmhouse. The women inside appeared more curious than anxious about what was happening around them, even when a field aide station began treating wounded men in their front yard. Hitchcock was taking in the scene, which he would later record in his journal, when he suddenly noticed that the General had gone off on foot to where there was shooting.

The frantic aide ran forward, searched for a while, then retraced his steps to discover that Sherman had returned ahead of him. However, it wasn't more than thirty minutes before he was again on the move, again heading toward the front. This time, Hitchcock walked alongside. They had covered maybe one hundred yards when there was the *boom-thud* of a cannon firing nearby. Sherman stopped, looked toward the source of the sound, and quickly stepped to one side. Hitchcock, hearing a "loud *rush* and whizzing in air over and in front of us," hit the deck. The solid shot struck elsewhere before bounding toward the rear. Hitchcock rose, dusted himself off, and joined his boss. "This place is not safe," Sherman said, "they are firing down the road—we had better go back."

The pair returned to the frame house, which abutted the Central of Georgia Railroad in its backyard. There they found the rest of Sherman's staff, spooked by the same skipping iron ball, clustered nervously behind the psychological cover represented by the flimsy structure. Just as a column of soldiers began cutting diagonally across the tracks, Sherman sighted down the right-of-way toward Savannah. The road ran straight and true, making it a perfect targeting guide for any alert Rebel gunner.

"I could see the cannoneers preparing to fire, and cautioned the officers near me to scatter, as we would likely attract a shot," remembered Sherman. "Very soon I saw the white puff of smoke, and, watching close, caught sight of the ball as it rose in its flight, and, finding it coming pretty straight, I stepped a short distance to one side, but noticed a negro very near me in the act of crossing the track at right angles." Major Hitchcock watched, frozen in horrific anticipation, as the cannon round hit the ground some distance off, but continued ricocheting along the right-of-way. A bounce carried it past the huddled staff and their boss; it hissed close to the infantry file, and with what seemed an eerily precise aim, struck the black man in the head, killing him instantly. Remarked Sherman: "A soldier close by spread an overcoat over the body, and we all concluded to get out of that railroad cut."

The incident of the near misses was not the only noteworthy moment for Major Hitchcock this day. Ever conscious of his self-appointed role as chronicler/historian of the enterprise, he realized that December 10 marked a milestone. Now that Sherman's forces were coming into contact with Savannah's fixed line of defenses, this day "may be considered as ending our *march* on this campaign." As reports came in through the evening citing the strong resistance being met by all corps, Hitchcock also wondered: "How long will it take us to get over the *last* five of our '300 mile march'?"

There were those in the Savannah garrison who were content to carry out their job assignment without much reference to what was happening around them. Edwin Ledyard was one. He worked in the Savannah Arsenal, where his duties included delivering ordnance to the main line of defense. "I was driving out . . . in a light wagon belonging to the arsenal and was near our intrenchments when a cannon [shell] suddenly exploded some distance in front," he recollected.

"What is that?" Ledyard asked a passing soldier.

"That's Sherman," was the answer.

The stranger suggested that he drive his wagon elsewhere. "I took his advice," said a suddenly frightened Ledyard.

Now that Sherman was closely investing Savannah, Lieutenant General William J. Hardee's options had much simplified. There were only five narrow corridors along which to approach western Savannah—the two railways, as well as the Augusta, the Louisville, and the Ogeechee roads—so Hardee blocked them all. Taking full advantage of the low-lying land and irrigated rice fields in between those access points, his engineers had flooded the intervening ground, making it hugely difficult, if not impossible, to penetrate the defensive perimeter through those regions. In addition, recognizing that there was little chance that Federal naval elements would attack the city, the Confederate commander had reoriented a great deal of his most powerful ordnance to point inland.

Hardee divided his intermediate line of trenches and strong points into three sectors. On the right, to garrison two and a half miles of front from the Savannah River to the Central of Georgia railway, he put 2,000 militia and twenty cannon under Major General Gustavus W. Smith. On the far left, covering a seven-mile stretch anchored on the Little Ogeechee River, were 4,000 men (and thirty-two guns) commanded by Brigadier General Hugh W. Mercer, who was superseded today by Major General Ambrose R. Wright, presumably recovered from his earlier power tussle with Governor Brown. The units under Wright were a mix of veterans, militia, and local defense outfits. Holding down the four critical miles in the center were 4,000 mostly veteran soldiers under Major General Lafayette McLaws. Backing him up were twenty-nine cannon of various calibers. A land approach from the south was deemed impossible because of the extensive swamps; vessels attempting to penetrate the lower barrier through its various streams or small rivers would encounter powerful detached batteries at critical choke points.

In situation reports dispatched today to General Beauregard, Hardee said that the "enemy is in heavy force all along my front." He noted that there was skirmish and "artillery firing throughout the day," and feared that he might, at any moment, "expect a determined attack." Hardee also informed Beauregard that every soldier in the city's garrison was at his post on the front. Said the lieutenant general: "I have not a reserve."

Captain Duncan, Sergeant Amick, and Private Quimby—the scouts sent by Major General Howard to contact the Union fleet—spent most of this day hidden in the woods not far from Fort McAllister. They were concealed near a road in military use; not long after dawn they watched a couple of mounted enemy soldiers on their way to relieve a picket post farther to the west. No one with the party had thought to bring anything to eat, so by midafternoon stomachs were growling. Sergeant Amick went to see if he could get some vittles from the slaves living nearby. When more than an hour had passed without his return, Duncan and Quimby went looking for him. They found the noncom crouched under one of the stilted, whitewashed slave cabins. They also spotted a Confederate patrol approaching the shack, so they hurriedly joined their comrade.

Amick passed around the food parcel he had with him as they waited for the Rebels to finish inspecting the cabin. The blacks had provided "some roast pig and rice bread. We never before tasted a morsel that seemed so delicious," declared the sergeant. Overhead the enemy troopers had paused while one of their number had his revolver repaired by a slave blacksmith. As the man worked, a soldier in the group causually asked him if he had seen any Yankees hereabouts. The hidden Federals gagged as the slave answered: "Yes, Massa, I see'd some." Hands reached for revolvers, but relaxed as he went on to explain that the bluecoats in question were all "Ober de ribber."

By the time the patrol finally moved along, the sun had set, but there was enough twilight that the three scouts decided to wait a while longer before continuing their journey down the Ogeechee River. When it was dark enough, another young slave led the Union soldiers back to their dugout. Duncan tried to talk him into joining them as a guide, but when he refused Quimby pulled out his gun to force the boy into the craft, only to realize that it was too small to hold four, so they turned him loose.

The Yankees pushed into the Ogeechee River, where they nearly bumped into a steam tug anchored mid-channel. Duncan recalled that they "lay down flat in the bottom of the dugout and let it drift by." The next obstacle was Fort McAllister, whose shoreline was illuminated by several fires lit to facilitate continuing efforts to strengthen the land-side defenses. "The tide was rapid and strong from the obstructions as it swirled through," related Amick. After successfully eluding a sentry boat, the three slipped past any watchful eyes on shore and eased through over a line of nautical torpedoes set for the pressure of much bigger game.

More hours passed, the men alternately rowing and drifting. They were also becoming increasingly thirsty, as no one had bothered to bring along anything to drink, forgetting that at McAllister the river water became salty from the ocean. Navigating toward the cry of nearby roosters crowing, the three grounded their craft on what turned out to be a marshy island. Then, exhausted by their labors and facing a rising sun, they pulled their boat under cover and, crammed together, all fell asleep.

PART FIVE

Savannah

DECEMBER 11–JANUARY 21

CHAPTER 20

————

"I Was Soon Covered with Blood from Head to Foot"

SUNDAY, DECEMBER 11, 1864

The malevolent rumble of artillery firing woke Savannah's citizens early this morning. "It was supposed in the city that a heavy engagement was going on," reported a resident, "but it proved to be only a general shelling from the heavy guns on our lines." All along Savannah's defensive perimeter, the Yankee boys were becoming acclimated to their new condition. Among those learning lessons were some soldiers from the Fourteenth Corps, positioned where the Central of Georgia tracks ran straight into the city. "We found by trial that every time a man set foot on that road, a ball or shell came whizzing down it," observed an Illinois man. Farther south along the Fourteenth Corps line the Confederates had mounted a massive seacoast howitzer whose shell, recalled a Georgian, made "noise enough to wake the dead." A Rebel soldier was posted close enough to the Yankee pickets to hear them warn newcomers: "Better keep quiet or the Rebs will turn that wash tub loose on you again."

Daily rhythms began to adjust to the new reality and the unpredictability of a situation where boring routine could be suddenly interrupted by tragedy. "One man had his forearm knocked off by the butt of a musket, which was stuck in the ground by the bayonet and struck by a piece of shell which cut the butt off the musket, throwing it against the man," recorded an officer in the 63rd Ohio. Among the prides of the 4th Minnesota were its fighting cocks, the fiercest of which was tended by an officer's black servant named "Little Abe." The rooster greeted this new day by crowing "lustily," drawing an enemy shell "which exploded in front of Capt. D. L. Wellman of Company I and a piece of it cut off the front of his hat, skinned his nose and hit him on the shoulder, cutting a hole in the cape of his overcoat. The captain picked up the piece of shell. . . . Turning to Abe, he told him to 'Choke that rooster and stop its crowing.' "

Elsewhere along the still-forming Union siege lines men were thinking of their stomachs. "Rations are very scarce," wrote an anxious diarist in the 123rd New York. "The forage in the country is the only grub we eat, and that is getting rather scarce." "All that was issued to the men today was a little rice and a little poor beef that was picked up on the march," added another journal keeper in the regiment. "An old rice mill up the river is run night and day, hulling rice for the army. It will give but a small quantity to each man. When there is any for sale brought into Camp it brings a dollar a pound quick." It was a double nuisance for some of the artillerymen of the Seventeenth Corps. "Our infantry came round tonight begging for ears of corn we had to feed the horses," wrote one, "while we were but little better off." Declared a Fourteenth Corps soldier: "Foraging is played out."

Still, there was a war on, so military operations continued apace. Several units were ordered to block access to the rear areas of the Federal deployment by cutting down trees and wrecking bridges. Others were part of a beefed-up security force now watching over the supply wagons. It was not an idle concern. According to one of Wheeler's troopers, today his squad "found the enemy ten miles from Savannah; captured two wagons and three prisoners."

There were numerous reconnaissance efforts undertaken as officers worked to fix the exact locations of enemy strong points. A two-regiment probe headed out from the Twentieth Corps lines. "As we filed into the pike a round shot from a battery up the road struck just in front of the reg't & ricocheted over us hurting no one," wrote a relieved member of the 2nd Massachusetts. The Federals "found the rebels in a line of works on the other side of a flooded rice-swamp, and then returned."

A more ambitious assignment was handed to Colonel William Hawley, commanding the 3rd Wisconsin. He was to take his regiment across the Savannah River onto Argyle Island, a large rice plantation formed by a split in the river channel. Once there he was to secure as much of the rice as possible, then check out the enemy's strength on the South Carolina side. The officer was ready for the task, his men were prepared, but the facilities came up short. The "crossing was slow," related a Wisconsin man, "as only two small skiffs could be found." About ten men per boat per trip was the limit, so by the time nightfall put an end to river operations, just two companies had been ferried over. The rest would have to cross in the morning.

It was also a busy day for Sherman, who spent much of it conferring with his Left Wing commander, Major General Slocum, at the latter's headquarters. While there he had a conversation with a recently captured Confederate officer, Colonel Duncan L. Clinch, who, having known Sherman before the war, was mistakenly hoping for better treatment. The "General . . . gave him the sharpest talk I have heard lately," observed Major Hitchcock, "not personal abuse, but very bitter denunciations of the rebel leaders, and a scathing rebuke to the 'Southern gentlemen' who had allowed themselves to be dragged by such men into rebellion. . . . General told him [that] . . . having voluntarily entered rebel service and being a prisoner of war he must take the lot of a prisoner,—that he could do nothing for him more than for any other, but he would be treated kindly, etc."

More guests, the Cuyler brothers, were waiting when Sherman returned to his own headquarters later in the day. The elder, a doctor whose unoccupied property along the Savannah River had been cleaned out by one Yankee column, was, according to Hitchcock, "very quiet, and almost sullen." The younger Cuyler was Richard R., the recently captured president of the Central of Georgia Railroad. In what must have been a streak of masochism in the man, he asked Sherman "what portions of the railroad we had destroyed." Cuyler listened without emotion as the General went into exquisite detail "step by step how much had been burned, how thoroughly the rails had been torn up, bent and twisted, etc., etc.," noted Hitchcock. The aide was surprised to see the railway official take the news "very philosophically." (He even deciphered the railway distance markers, explaining to Sherman that they were calculated using Savannah's courthouse as the starting point.) At the end of their chat, the General provided each with a pass to allow them to exit through the rear of his lines.

Sherman still found time to monitor progress toward eliminating

Fort McAllister. Ever since reaching Savannah's defenses, he had been obsessing about the post, making, said Hitchcock, "every inquiry about this fort, its exact location, strength, etc." In a remarkable stroke of luck, scouts operating on December 10 procured what Sherman's chief engineer termed "a plan of Fort McAllister."* Now having a good idea of the layout of the place, Sherman fretted over the best way to approach it. Poring over his maps instead of sleeping, he realized he couldn't find King's Bridge, so at 2:00 A.M. he had an aide chase after Major General Howard for the information. At the crossing itself serious construction was underway with four companies present from the 1st Missouri Engineers.† While two of them prepared the timber, the other pair set to work on the bridge itself. From here on the job would proceed around the clock.

In a closely related event, a signal corps detachment serving with Major General Howard's headquarters, following up on a December 10 scouting report, marched out to the plantation of Dr. Langdon Cheves, where the men established an observation post in a rice mill located on the Ogeechee River's northern bank. From here the communications party could see across the flat salt marshes well down toward the river's mouth and had a direct view (some two and a half miles below on the opposite bank) of Fort McAllister. As they established the station, the officer in charge realized that they were in something of a no-man's-land between the Federals and Confederates. When he reported this to Major General Howard, a battery and some infantry were hustled down to enhance security.

The Rebel bastion was also the object today of a stealthy visit by scouts attached to Brigadier General Kilpatrick's command, which had begun moving south once the Left Wing infantry it had been screening assumed static positions. In an untimed December 11 report to Sherman, Kilpatrick estimated a garrison of "about 200 men and

---

*   A postwar account credits a sketch map contained in a letter from a member of the fort's garrison, which was confiscated while the Federals were near Macon. The account does not cite its source for the story.

†   In recollecting his visit some two months later for his official report, Sherman made a mental slip that has been perpetuated in several histories of the campaign. Perhaps because of his extended association with the unit during the period of the march he spent with the Left Wing, the General identified the engineer regiment working on the bridge as the "Fifty-eighth Indiana." The Hoosiers were, in fact, resting in camp with the Left Wing at the time. The bridge builders, correctly noted by Captain Poe in his report, were from the 1st Missouri Engineers.

thirteen guns mounted." He opined that with a force of infantry added to his cavalry, and the element of surprise, he could take the fort. All he needed was Sherman's approval.

In the fort, commandant Major George W. Anderson kept abreast of increasingly ominous tidings. He had only just learned that the Confederate forces blocking nearby crossings of the Canoochee River had been withdrawn to the city, leaving that route of approach to McAllister wide open. Also, until recently Anderson had been able to call on the scouting services of several small cavalry units stationed close at hand, but they too had been reassigned, forcing the Confederate officer to improvise. He organized his own detachment out of some of the mounted men under his direct command (most drawn from the artillery batteries, since they had the horses). Said Anderson: "I was thus thrown upon my own resources for all the information relative to the strength and designs of the enemy."

In Savannah itself, accurate information on the enemy's strength and designs was as much the product of wishful surmise as hard evidence. "I have been obliged to extend my line," Lieutenant General Hardee warned his superior. "It is impossible to hold it without immediate reinforcement." Even as he griped, Hardee was manufacturing some of the help he needed by dismounting one of Wheeler's cavalry brigades to use as infantry. "It was a bitter pill to my men to be separated from their horses and they marched into Savannah in no good humor," recollected the cavalry commander, Brigadier General Samuel W. Ferguson. To ease the tension, Ferguson waited until his footsore troopers had tramped into their new camp, then in a loud voice commanded: "Rear rank open order. Prepare to dismount. DISMOUNT." "When they broke ranks they gave a cheer," Ferguson remembered, "showing that they appreciated the joke."

Many civilians believed that Sherman's army had arrived at the city's gates in an exhausted and hungry condition. Each day that the siege was prolonged, went their argument, the weaker the Federals became. "Sherman was in no condition to attack our works," declared a civilian. "He was scarce of ammunition and had no heavy guns as well as other difficulties in the way of his giving battle." This thread of thinking wound its way as far as Richmond, where a War Department clerk, thinking also of the militia forces he imagined were gathering behind Sherman, prophesied that a "battle must certainly occur near

Savannah, Ga. Sherman *must* assail our lines, or perish between two fires."

Captain Duncan, Sergeant Amick, and Private Quimby awoke at dawn, cold and wet—very wet. It had rained some, and the dugout they were using leaked a lot. To compound matters, Quimby fell overboard as they bailed out the craft, though the water was shallow enough that he could stand up. What they could see, or could not see, was disheartening. No sign of the Union navy; instead, an expanse of water roiling with the wind and current. "Our situation at this time did not look very encouraging," said Duncan; "we had too much water and not enough boat."

Once more the sound of roosters crowing gave them a direction to pursue. This time it appeared to emanate from the opposite shore. Somehow the sodden trio paddled the sievelike dugout across the undulating expanse and landed. They found themselves on the grounds of a deserted plantation; no people and, as they shortly discovered, no water either. "We were quite despondent by this time," Duncan admitted, "and would have been glad to be captured by anyone." Their efforts had consumed much of the daylight, but with no other choice other than to continue the mission, the three drained the dugout and set off. Now the current was carrying them away from land.

"We are entering the ocean," Duncan stated. "That cannot be," Amick reported, "as I can see trees in front." There was a moment of confusion before they all realized that the trees were ship masts. What was even better was that one of the vessels had spotted them. It lowered a small launch that began working toward the three waterlogged landlubbers. "When I told the men this," Duncan recollected, "Amick gave a start that nearly upset our dugout." The craft approaching flew the Stars and Stripes. "Never had the national colors looked so beautiful to us," declared Amick.

No sooner had the ship's launch pulled alongside than the three scrambled aboard. Amick was all for sinking the dugout, but the amused sailors towed it back with them to their armed steamer, the USS *Flag*. Hardly had the trio reached the *Flag*'s deck when the steam tug *Dandelion* arrived, plucked them off, and immediately set course for Union fleet headquarters at Port Royal, South Carolina. Duncan,

Amick, and Quimby were given fresh clothes, "abundantly supplied with food and drink," then allowed to catch up on some much-needed sleep.

MONDAY, DECEMBER 12, 1864

From: Flag-Steamer Philadelphia
Port Royal Harbor, S.C., December 12, 1864

To: Hon. Gideon Welles,
Secretary of the Navy
Sir: It is my happiness to apprise the Department that General Sherman, with his army, is near Savannah, and I am in communication with him.

In view of his probable arrival I had stationed several steamers at different points, and had come down from the Tulifinny [River] yesterday in order to be at hand. I had not to wait many hours.

This morning about 8 o'clock the Dandelion arrived with Captain Duncan and two scouts, Sergeant Myron J. Emmick and George W. Quinby, bearing the following lines from General Howard:

To: Commander of U.S. Navy Forces,
Vicinity of Savannah, Ga.

HEADQUARTERS DEPARTMENT OF ARMY OF TENNESSEE,
Near Savannah Canal, Georgia.

Sir: We have met with perfect success thus far. Troops in fine spirits and near by.
Respectfully,

O. O. Howard
Major-General, Commanding

Captain Duncan states that our forces were in contact with the rebels a few miles outside of Savannah. He says they are not in want of anything.

Perhaps no event could give greater satisfaction to the country than that which I announce, and I beg leave to congratulate the United States Government on its occurrence.

It may, perhaps, be exceeding my province, but I can not refrain from expressing the hope that the Department will commend Captain Duncan and his companions to the honorable Secretary of War for some mark of approbation for the success in establishing communications between General Sherman and the fleet.

It was an enterprise that required both skill and courage.

I have the honor to be, very respectfully, your obedient servant,

J.A. Dahlgren,
Rear-Admiral, Comdg, South Atlantic Blockading Squadron

Declared a member of the admiral's staff: "The excitement, the exhilaration, ay the rapture, created by this arrival, will never be forgotten by the officers and crews of the Federal vessels who saw the beginning of the end of the war." Dahlgren's covering note, along with Howard's brief communication, was immediately put aboard a fast ship headed north. An officer on board later told a reporter that the entire fleet was firing a salute as they departed, "and the vessels were decorated with flags."

Along the U.S. lines outside Savannah, "the Corps and Division Commanders are getting their troops gradually in front of the rebel lines as far as yet known," recorded Major Hitchcock at Sherman's headquarters. Most were cautious probes, but one division commander, Brigadier General John W. Geary in the Twentieth Corps, planned a two-brigade assault on a Confederate fortification in his front. The selected troops were roused at 2:30 A.M., then moved into a swamp bordering the objective preparatory to the charge. Apprehensions went up several notches when word spread that the water in the front was nearly neck deep. Finally, at 4:30 A.M., the attack orders were canceled. Sputtered one well-soaked Ohioan: "Ambitious Geary baffled again!!!"

For many of those not engaged in siege activities, the name of today's game was "Find the food." It wasn't that the army was out of supplies, it was just that what was on hand was not appealing to men accustomed to the rich variety enjoyed during the march. For instance, there remained a sizable beef herd, but the quartermasters always killed the

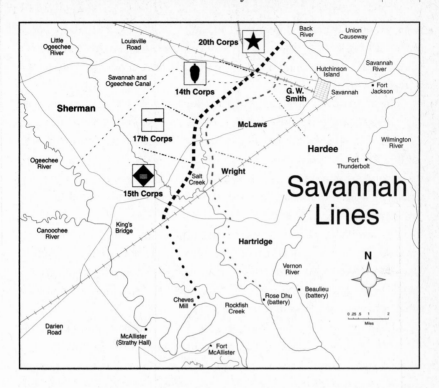

most scrawny beasts first, leading one soldier to complain that they were getting "*dried beef on foot.*"

Some Wisconsin boys got an unexpected education in differing cultures when they visited a community of slaves recently arrived from Africa, where they were given rice cooked with a tangy meat. The soldiers' pleasure was ruined when they learned that the distinct flavor came from chicken entrails—often the only portion of the bird allowed the blacks by their owners. Along the section of the line held by the 39th Ohio, the Buckeyes were taunted by Confederate pickets, who boasted that there was plenty of bacon in their camps. A Federal present recalled that "one of our boys replied if you have so much bacon why in hell dont you grease your britches and slide back into the union?"

Since the various corps had approached the main line of resistance in something of a pell-mell fashion as their differing routes of march converged, some readjustment of positions was necessary to tidy up the deployments. The late-arriving Fourteenth Corps today occupied a section previously held by the Seventeenth, which slid to the right.

One group of Major General Blair's infantry and artillery had to choose either a long roundabout march out of range of the enemy's guns, or a shorter path across their sights. The officers opted to wait for nightfall to risk the direct passage.

Those involved described the experience as either running the "blockade" or the "gauntlet." "As soon as it was nearly dark we moved out," recollected an Ohio infantryman, "making as little noise as possible and just before merging into the open plain we were ordered to carry our arms muzzle downwards so they could not be seen and not to speak above a whisper lest the Rebel battery should open up." The infantry went first, followed by the artillery. "You may judge of our feelings as we he[a]rd time and again of the strength of the [rebel] fort and that it was near to our rout[e]," said a member of the 1st Minnesota Light Artillery. "We pass at a quick walk and they only fired 5 times at us and did not hurt one of us. But you ought to see the heads bow, when we saw the flash of the guns."

On the far left of the Union siege lines, the tedious process of getting the 3rd Wisconsin transferred onto Argyle Island was further slowed by dramatic events. A short distance above where the dogged Midwesterners were about to resume crossing twenty at a time, a Federal battery had taken a position on the river bluff, supported by the 22nd Wisconsin. It was still before dawn when infantry lieutenant W. H. Morse made his way about a mile north of the camp to check on an outpost. Once there he "spied a light some distance up the river which appeared and disappeared several times. I waited and watched and soon I saw smoke, and, daylight approaching, I saw the vessels."

The boats in question, part of Savannah's ad hoc naval squadron, consisted of the gunboats *Sampson* and *Macon*, accompanied by the tender *Resolute*. They had initially been ordered up the river from the city to protect the Charleston and Savannah rail bridge, but once it became evident that Sherman's men were astride the line, new orders came to destroy the span. With that mission completed, Lieutenant General Hardee had recalled the craft to Savannah in order to add their firepower to the city's defenses.

Sampson was leading the column, followed by the *Resolute* and the *Macon*. It had proven to be a sobering journey for the Confederate sailors. "As we went along we saw at the different places smoking ruins," reported the squadron's commander. Intelligence gathered from civilians met on the way suggested that the Yankees had yet to establish any artillery positions along the riverbank.

In fact, the four rifled Parrott cannon guarded by the 22nd Wisconsin had been rolled into position on the Colerain plantation just the previous afternoon. The tubes represented Battery I of the 1st New York Light Artillery, Captain Charles E. Winegar commanding. On paper the Confederate squadron's heavier-caliber guns seriously outmatched what the Federals had, but Winegar had picked a good spot for his cannoneers. They were positioned on a bluff in a bend of the river where the channel narrowed, forcing the enemy craft to approach head-on, significantly limiting how many of their weapons could bear on the target. Still, the Confederates knew their business. As the three vessels drew within range, the *Macon* swung out somewhat to starboard to unmask its forward piece. Captain Winegar, a Gettysburg veteran, opened fire at 2,700 yards, while the gunboats remained menacingly silent until within 800 yards.

Winegar's opening shot was somewhat anticlimactic, bursting in the air well short of the targets. This brought some unsolicited advice from the Wisconsin colonel to the New York captain that he was cutting his fuses too short. Winegar retorted that he was using percussion shells, which exploded on impact, and guessed that a defective firing pin caused the premature detonation. The rest of the colonel's boys were well under cover and enjoying the fireworks display. A member of the regiment recollected most of the enemy's return fire "falling short, but some struck in the bank just under the battery, and some went high above us. . . . None of us were hurt in the least, for when we saw the white smoke from their guns, we either jumped down behind our breastworks or got behind the big trees near the shore."

No one counted how many times the *Sampson* and *Macon* fired, but Captain Winegar logged 138 rounds from his guns. The fact that the Confederate craft, approaching head-on, were essentially stationary targets, simplified the firing solution for the Yankee cannoneers, who scored with 5 percent of their shells. The Rebels scored no hits, even though a midshipman aboard the *Sampson* recollected a "terrific fire" from both sides. As later reported by the Southern squadron commander, *Sampson* "was struck three times—on her hurricane deck, near machinery and steam drum, and once in her rudder. . . . C.S.S. *Macon* was struck twice, once under her bow and one shot passing through [her] smokestack. C.S.S. *Resolute* [was] struck twice, one shot injuring her wheel so as to disable her." Hoping to push through to Savannah before the Federals closed the river, the Confederates had instead run into a hornets' nest. It was evident to the squadron commander that "we could not pass the batteries."

Orders were given for the three ships to reverse course. Struggling to maneuver in the narrow channel while still under fire, *Sampson* collided with *Resolute*, "damaging both vessels." Adding insult to injury, the *Macon* also sideswiped the tender making its U-turn. "The C.S.S. *Resolute* being unmanageable, drifted ashore [on Argyle Island]," continued the squadron commander's report. "It being impossible to render her any assistance without endangering the safety of the other vessels from the fire of the enemy . . . , we were compelled to leave her, with orders for the crew to escape in their boats if it was impossible to get her off."

The frantic efforts by the crew of the *Resolute* to lighten the craft by throwing every loose object overboard was observed with very great interest by some recently arrived spectators on the shore—Company F of the 3rd Wisconsin, which had hurried up Argyle Island from where the rest of the regiment was crossing from the Georgia side. The Wisconsin boys were enjoying the spectacle when the Rebel sailors signaled their intention to abandon ship by piling into two lifeboats. At this several riflemen waded into the shallows, parted the reeds, and called out: "Turn back, Cap, turn back." When the captain of the *Resolute* ordered his men to continue rowing, he was shot in the shoulder for his trouble, which was enough to convince his men to surrender. A couple of overeager infantrymen waded into the neck-deep water to take possession. The Wisconsin colonel in charge later tallied five naval officers and nineteen sailors taken prisoner.

The *Macon* and *Sampson* successfully steamed the 200 miles to Augusta, though they were reduced to burning bacon in their boiler furnaces to finish the home stretch. The *Resolute* itself was repaired by its captors, and despite stories that it was burned shortly thereafter, actually remained in U.S. service throughout the siege, providing useful services transferring troops and supplies. Chatting afterward with Major Hitchcock, Captain Winegar bragged that this was "the first *naval* engagement he ever took part in, and that he wants more of the same sort."

Just about all that Sherman could think about now was Fort McAllister; so, after seeing the Cuyler brothers on their way, he rode to Major General Howard's headquarters to be closer to the action. Work on King's Bridge was continuing, with Captain Reese expecting to be finished early on December 13. Security on the opposite bank was now courtesy of Brigadier General Kilpatrick's First Brigade, which had crossed the Ogeechee higher upriver, followed by a crossing of the Canoochee on a hastily re-erected pontoon bridge to get there. His advance detachment had surprised Fort McAllister's commander, Major Anderson, who was undertaking a scout of his own. "We were hotly pursued by their cavalry," Anderson later reported; nevertheless, the detail accompanying him had time enough to burn two barns full of rice and a steam tug anchored three miles above the fort.

The Yankee troopers stopped for the night on the plantation owned by Captain Joseph L. McAllister of the Confederate army, which one Pennsylvanian declared "a beautiful place," though this did not prevent it being ransacked by other less appreciative cavalrymen. Some members of the 8th Indiana drew coffee water out of the Ogeechee but then had to spit it out since it was "too salty to drink." In the near distance they could hear the irregular but constant boom of cannon fire as the Union tubes positioned at Cheves' Rice Mill* opened a harassing bombardment on the fort. (The Yankee cannoneers also hoped that the sound of their guns firing might serve to signal the navy downriver of their presence.) At this extreme range there was little chance of doing any significant damage, but a couple of Federal shells came close enough to one of the powder magazines that Major Anderson ordered a protective traverse wall thrown up. Return fire from the fort was equally wild, managing only to scatter a pile of sweet potatoes collected by the Union gunners for their dinner.

The fort commander was at his moment of truth. There was no doubt that the enemy's sights were set on McAllister, but with fewer

---

* A two-gun section from Battery H, 1st Illinois Light Artillery, Captain Francis DeGress commanding, operated throughout the day, joined for a period by a section from Battery H, 1st Missouri Light Artillery, Lieutenant John F. Brunner in charge.

than 200 defenders* the result was a foregone conclusion. There was still time to spike the guns, then evacuate the soldiers, but Anderson rejected that option. "I determined under the circumstances, and notwithstanding the great disparity of numbers between the garrison and the attacking force," he vowed, "to defend the fort to the last extremity."

Whether Anderson abandoned or fought mattered little to Sherman, who was set on taking the place. "We wanted the [commissary] vessels and their contents," Sherman declared, "and the Ogeechee River, a navigable stream, close to the rear of our camps, was the proper avenue of supply." After a quick consultation with Major General Howard, he decided to pass on Brigadier General Kilpatrick's offer to assault the fort and rely instead on the Second Division of the Fifteenth Corps—Brigadier General William B. Hazen's—to do the job. Howard had been holding it off the front line in reserve, and besides, Sherman, who had once commanded the division, thought very highly of it.

Hazen, a thirty-seven-year-old West Point graduate, was summoned from his headquarters a couple of miles away. When he arrived, Howard and Sherman explained the role his division was to play in the next day's work and, as Hazen remembered, they "gave me a little map of the country about the mouth of the Ogeechee River." Then, recounted Sherman: "I gave General Hazen, in person, his orders to march rapidly down the right bank of the Ogeechee, and without hesitation to assault and carry Fort McAllister by storm. I knew it to be strong in heavy artillery, as against an approach from the sea, but believed it open and weak to the rear. I explained to General Hazen, fully, that on his action depended the safety of the whole army, and the success of the campaign."

Before Hazen could depart to begin organizing matters at his headquarters, Sherman proffered one last piece of advice. He indicated on the map how the ground on the southern edge of Genesis Point was veined with small streams and creeks. Pushing a force of any size through that region would be fraught with difficulties. Sherman was determined that not one piece of the plan go awry, so repeated his

---

* In addition to the 150 men who were assigned to the garrison, Anderson likely had some extra hands on board from some of the local militia units.

injunction, as Hazen phrased it, "not to find myself behind any creek, so that we could not get forward."

TUESDAY, DECEMBER 13, 1864

Throughout southeastern Georgia, good news was where one could find it. It was reported in today's *Augusta Daily Chronicle & Sentinel* that solid progress was being made on reestablishing telegraphic communication with Macon. More than sixty-five miles of chopped poles and smashed insulators had already been repaired by the Southern Telegraph Company. However, even the upbeat newspaper writers had to admit that "some time must elapse" before the task was finished.

In Savannah, there was increasing concern in high military places regarding Union efforts to cut the narrow communication corridor with Charleston. The Yankees had been island-hopping in the Savannah River like so many fleas; even though their few forays to the South Carolina shore were small-scale, limited in scope, and easily batted away, they portended much worse to come. Such was General Beauregard's concern that he diverted the last reinforcements he had been able to scrape together (450 men, more or less) to bolster its defense. Echoing Beauregard's concern, Lieutenant General Hardee informed Major General Wheeler in no uncertain terms that the proper place for his cavalry was on the South Carolina side of the Savannah River, not pecking at Sherman's rear guard. Wheeler at once began the laborious process of ferrying his mounted units across the stream to consolidate them at Hardeeville. All would transfer over save for Iverson's division, which would continue to harass the Union rear areas. The net result was that the best military asset capable of inflicting real damage on Sherman's logistical apparatus was off the chessboard.

One of those irritants that so bothered Beauregard and Hardee was the 3rd Wisconsin, now entirely installed on Argyle Island. Most of the men were set to work getting the island's three rice mills into operation. This was accomplished in short order and soon, bragged a soldier, they were running the "rice-mills to their full capacity, thrashing out rice for our hungry comrades." One squad had already returned from an unopposed December 12 landing in South Carolina at a place called

Izard's Plantation. Today there was fighting near Izard's landing dock as the Argyle Island Yankees tangled in a cross-river exchange with a Rebel reaction force. "We drove them off without much trouble," snorted a Wisconsin officer.

Closer to the city, Hutchinson Island was also the scene of some limited combat. Rebel snipers had established themselves in several buildings, and one had killed a popular officer in the 134th New York. That was enough for Brigadier General John W. Geary, commanding this sector, who sent sixty men onto the upper island to clean out the murderous nests. When this force proved too small to do the job, Geary promptly reinforced it. The pop-popping of men engaged in a deadly game of hide-and-seek would continue throughout the day.

In a myriad of ways, efforts were made all along the siege line to strengthen positions or improve the flow of supplies. Technicians from the 1st Michigan Mechanics and Engineers labored to close the locks that Confederates had busted open to flood the fields now occupied by Sherman's men. Other units spread along the wrecked railroad right-of-way, transforming the useless track bed into a valuable wagon road. Abandoned rice mills were put into operation to process the stacks of the confiscated raw product into something edible. All across the rear zones of Sherman's lines, wagon corrals, cattle herds, and supply caches were secured with earthworks or fortified posts. In a hundred different ways, his men were signaling that they had come to stay.

There were mini-actions all along the main siege lines, few large enough to warrant mention in official reports unless men died. The soldiers in the 63rd Illinois would puzzle for a while about the mission they executed this afternoon. The regiment was called into line not long after 1:00 P.M., then marched toward Savannah following the railroad tracks. The column halted short of the enemy's position, where it deployed to the left of the road bed in an open skirmishing order. One more advance was undertaken, bringing the men within extreme rifle range of the Rebels. The order to halt was followed by one to commence firing toward the city. Forty rounds apiece were loosed off before the shooting was halted, the men re-formed in column along the railway line, and then returned to camp "covered with mud up to our forks," said one. The soldiers guessed they had carried out a diver-

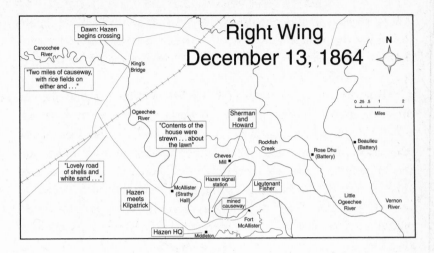

sion for an operation somewhere else. Not until the next morning would they understand the reason for their curious action.

Fort McAllister

William Tecumseh Sherman stood silent and unseen in the obscuring morning shadows, watching Hazen's division pass on its way to Fort McAllister. There were other pressing matters awaiting the General's attention this day, but he would entertain none of them. Opening communication with the fleet was the only item on his personal agenda, and Fort McAllister was all that stood in the way. Sherman's earlier confidence had waned somewhat. He now acknowledged that McAllister "will be found [to be] a strong work," so he cut orders for Brigadier General Kilpatrick to try to establish contact with the fleet at the next inlet to the south.

The divisional pioneers and Missouri engineers, who had labored hard through the night to complete the crossing in time, were almost through. The span lacked guardrails, but no one in charge was willing to hold things up the extra couple of hours it would have taken to install them, so the soldiers crossed with no handholds. The finishing work, now undertaken in the breaks and pauses of the movement, would have the protections in place by December 14. No one seems to have been hurt or any material lost in the crossing.

Brigadier General Hazen made the passage at about 5:00 A.M. There is nothing to indicate that he met with either Sherman or Howard this morning, but given the very high level of expectation on the part of the two leaders, some kind of leavetaking would not have been out of the question. Most of the foot soldiers marched in ignorance of their objective; only Hazen and his key officers knew what lay ahead. "There was a general notion [among the ranks] that we were going to assail and capture some obstacle separating the army from its food and raiment," recollected the brigadier. There were seventeen regiments marching this morning; for eight there would be little to note in journals and diaries save for another stretch of Georgia countryside visited. For the other nine, however, this day would produce the mix of anxiety, determination, fear, adrenaline, and relief that embodied combat.

Once across King's Bridge, the infantrymen tramped along what Hazen described as "about two miles of causeway with rice fields on either hand." "While we were going along the causeway," he continued in a later memoir, "the column was beset by a great crowd of rice plantation people, a simple race, small, ignorant, of all shades of color and speaking a peculiar patois. They were entirely unique and distinct from any other people, and their chatter was . . . almost unintelligible."

The officer in command at Fort McAllister, Major George W. Anderson, greeted the new day with foreboding. A sudden increase in Union cavalry patrols to the west had effectively shut down his own scouting efforts, so the major had no idea what was going on beyond his picket outpost about a mile distant. The two enemy cannon at Cheves' Rice Mill continued to annoy the garrison with an occasional shell. The Federal navy had not made an appearance below the fort, but Anderson wouldn't put it past them to be cooking up some combined operation. His one grim satisfaction was knowing that the ordnance experts from Charleston had arranged for a deadly surprise along the causeway leading directly to the fort. That, plus the defenses his men had worked so hard to erect, added to the difficulty the enemy would have getting through the swampy areas surrounding the place, gave him some hope that Sherman would find Fort McAllister too costly to capture.

Not long after the tail of Hazen's column—including six cannon in one and a half batteries—crossed King's Bridge, Major General Sherman and his staff headed off along the plantation roads, paved with crushed oyster shells, to Cheves' Rice Mill, from where the General intended to observe operations. Missing from the entourage was Major Hitchcock, who, to his everlasting regret, chose to remain at the main headquarters closer to Savannah. Also with the party were Major General Howard and his staff. Once there, they would be joined throughout the day by a gaggle of officers and aides from the other Fifteenth Corps divisions and the Seventeenth Corps. A crowd of braid and glitter was about to descend on Cheves' Rice Mill.

With no immediate decisions requiring his attention, Brigadier General Hazen took in the sights as his column trudged south from King's Bridge. "The day was bright," he wrote later; "and the march, after leaving the rice-farms, was along a lovely road of shells and white sand, under magnolias and wide-branching live oaks draped in long hanging moss." Probably around 6:15 A.M. the Yankee boys passed near Strathy Hall, the formidable residence of Joseph L. McAllister, a portion of whose property had been donated to the Southern cause for the eponymous fort. Kilpatrick's cavalrymen had already paid the mansion a visit, Hazen observed, "and the contents of the house were strewn upon the floors or scattered about the lawn." Even though the horse was already out of this barn, Hazen (who had enjoyed a slight prewar acquaintance with the McAllisters) posted some guards anyway, perhaps thinking he might need the structure for a headquarters later on and did not want anyone burning it.

There was corresponding activity among the handful of Union vessels watching over Ossabaw Sound, where no less than three rivers—the Vernon, Little Ogeechee, and Ogeechee—terminated. Steam was up and the crew ready on the tug *Dandelion*, which had just been turned over to Lieutenant George A. Fisher of the army signal corps for his mission to establish contact with Sherman's forces. Fisher logged the time at 8:00 A.M. when he came aboard. Following a discussion with the boat's skipper, the party departed the anchorage. Their likely course followed first the Vernon River then the Little Ogeechee River before ducking into a narrow passageway called Harvey's Creek. It wasn't long before the eager signal officer was "looking closely in every direction with my glass for some signal or sign of General Sherman's army."

Not far south from Strathy Hall was the turnoff for Genesis Point and Fort McAllister, four and a half miles distant. It was near here that Hazen met up with Brigadier General Kilpatrick, whose men had carried out a crucial and largely unheralded assignment by keeping prying enemy eyes away from the approaching infantry column. The cavalrymen, Hazen noted, "had reconnoitered the fort and confirmed what General Howard was able to tell me about the situation."

If Kilpatrick was unhappy at Sherman's decision to deny him a role in the upcoming assault, he did not show it. Perhaps he shared his thoughts with Hazen about how the job should be done—use sharpshooters with fast-firing breech-loaders to suppress the enemy cannon, then rush the place. If he did pass anything along, Hazen never saw fit to acknowledge the fact, and Kilpatrick never tried to claim any credit. The best news was that the route was clear to within about a mile of the fort.

Hazen's column made the turn toward Genesis Point. About a dozen mounted men—signal corps officers, some orderlies, and aides—galloped forward to scout the way.

For the moment, the tug *Dandelion* had gone as far as its captain was prepared to go. Across the marsh to the north and east, at long cannon range along the Little Ogeechee River, was the enemy's Rose Dhu Island battery, making further movement foolhardy. Lieutenant Fisher, who could see nothing of Sherman's army, realized that he needed to get closer to Fort McAllister. The *Dandelion*'s skipper agreed to loan him a lifeboat with four sailors to row. Accompanied by two other signal corps men, Fisher pushed off about 10:00 A.M.

After passing along the plantation road through the marshland, Sherman, Howard, plus their staffs reached Cheves' Rice Mill around 10:30 A.M. The General's first thought was of the Union navy just a few miles away. "Have you seen anything of the fleet?" he queried the post's senior officer, Captain James M. McClintock, of Major General Howard's signal detachment. "Nothing definite, General," the captain replied; "but, at times have thought I could dimly discern the tops of masts far out upon the sound." This was not the news Sherman wanted to hear. "I don't believe they are looking for us," he complained aloud. Sherman, McClintock observed, "was quite restless and seemingly impatient."

There was a small shed attached to the rice mill that had a flat roof; without being directed there Sherman and some of those with him clambered onto it to better observe Fort McAllister. Their efforts were punctuated by DeGress's gunners, who continued with their own program by occasionally blasting a round toward the enemy redoubt. From his perch atop the shed, Sherman noted that McAllister could be "plainly seen over the salt-marsh, about three miles distant." A soldier with the group attested that with "the use of the glass I could see the fort[,] rebel flag & even the men very distinctly." Added an officer with Major General Howard's staff, the "timber in rear of the fort had been cleared off so, not only the fort, but the movements of the troops in rear of it, could be seen from the mill."

For the moment, however, there was very little to see. Sherman, anxious for some sign that Hazen was on the case, could only mutter that "the place looked as peaceable and quiet as on the Sabbath."

Perhaps three miles southeast of where Major General Sherman was glaring at Fort McAllister, Lieutenant Fisher's party was picking its way through the marsh, struggling against the sharp-edged grass and the falling tide. There was nothing recognizable to navigate by at water level, so the boat stopped from time to time to allow the officer or one of his men to stand on some passably firm ground to fix their position. When the time came to write his report of this adventure, Fisher described this process as taking "a careful and close reconnaissance of the forts and the surrounding country."

It was a testament to the effectiveness of Kilpatrick's cavalry that the dozen advance riders from Hazen's column came within a mile or so of Fort McAllister before they encountered any of the enemy—a small mounted picket guarding the entrance to a narrow causeway running parallel to the river bank. Using the cover provided by the trees lining the road, the Federals, led by Lieutenant William H. Sherfy, overran the post before those manning it could react. When the captured Rebels showed a marked disinclination to walk on the causeway itself, the Union officers began to suspect the presence of torpedoes.

One of the captured Confederates, Thomas J. Mills, now confirmed the presence of the deadly devices. They had been laid here to draw first blood when the Union soldiers took to the causeway, as they had to do to reach Fort McAllister. When Brigadier General Hazen was notified of this, he halted the column to consult the helpful POW. Mills not only showed where the torpedoes had been placed, he also assisted in digging them up. "This humane and proper act gained for him, as it deserved, the kind consideration of all," remarked Hazen.

While a detail gingerly excavated the deadly packages, Hazen directed his column into open fields near a house belonging to the Middleton family. It was apparent that he had more troops in hand than there was room for in the constricted area of dry ground across the causeway, so eight regiments took station at the Middletons', which became Hazen's headquarters. Thanks to the helpful Mills, Hazen had also gleaned several helpful details about McAllister's armament and defensive scheme that would guide him in shaping his mission plan.

The time was approaching 2:00 P.M. when the causeway was declared safe for passage. Hazen ordered forward the nine regiments he had selected to attack the fort, led by three from Colonel Wells S. Jones's Second Brigade: 47th Ohio, 54th Ohio, and 111th Illinois. There was a slight rubbernecking delay as the men passed by the excavated mines, "and large, black, ugly-looking things they were," wrote a gunner who saw them later in the day. Immediately upon debouching from the narrow causeway, Jones's column fanned out to advance as skirmishers, quickly bringing Fort McAllister under direct rifle fire.

Hazen had decided against sending out a flag of truce with a surrender demand, "believing that it would merely advertise our intentions, and be met with a boastful refusal."

As soon as Hazen's men opened a scattering fire,[*] Major George W. Anderson understood that it was the beginning of the great trial for his little command. Considering, as he later reported, "the feebleness of the garrison of the fort, . . . it was evident, cut off from all support, and with no possible hope of reinforcements from any quarter, that holding the fort was simply a question of time." Anderson reckoned his grim options as "death or captivity."

Major General Sherman reckoned it as roughly 2:00 P.M. when he "observed signs of commotion in the fort, and noticed one or two guns fired inland, and some musket-skirmishing in the woods close by." A staff officer under Howard with an eye for the poetic took note of how the skirmish line was marked "by the little round puffs of blue smoke that roll out from the cover of the wood full rifle range away from the Rebel Fort, and which float lazily up towards the tree tops."

The crescendo of musketry about Fort McAllister, punctuated by the boom of its landside cannon firing, caught Lieutenant Fisher's full attention. Once he determined that the enemy wasn't firing at him, he began to swing his binoculars over a wider area. "I . . . saw, about three miles northwest of where I was lying in the marsh, a flag upon the top of an old rice mill, but there being no air stirring I was unable to make out of what nature it was," he reported. "I could then indistinctly see persons through a broken part of the roof, one of whom, taking hold of the end of the flag, drew its folds out so I could see our own glorious Stars and Stripes." Taking a deep breath, the young officer told the sailors to row back to the *Dandelion*. He had found Sherman's army!

---

[*]   Major Anderson reported that his men were suffering from rifle fire as early at 8:00 A.M. If the time is correct, it is improbable that the shooters were Hazen's men; more likely, they belonged to Kilpatrick.

Two mistakes had been made in designing Fort McAllister's rear defenses and in preparing the ground adjacent to the earthwork that made matters even worse for the garrison. The landside guns, like most of those along the river and seawalls, were positioned behind an unnotched fort wall; in military terms, they were en barbette. While this allowed the individual cannon to traverse to a greater degree than those constrained by a narrow opening, or embrasure, it was hell on the men who operated the weapons. They were fully exposed while handling the reloads, which might not have been so fatal a miscalculation were it not for the other decision that had been made.

A fort ultimately depends upon the strength of its walls, the effectiveness of its firepower, and the courage of its garrison to survive. Adding to that defensive scheme were the obstructions placed outside the fort, designed to slow up any attackers, increasing the attrition as they came closer. Fort McAllister was not without these layers of defense.

There was a ditch running close to the walls, where the land was firm enough to support it; a dozen feet deep, nine feet wide at bottom, and twice that at top. Studded in a ragged row along the ditch floor were sharpened wooden stakes, four feet long, embedded perhaps two to three inches apart. Out from the ditch (ten yards at some points, up to twenty-five at others) was a ring of abatis—chopped trees left with upper branches intact, laid in parallel with the tops interlaced and pointing toward the enemy. Two more such rows were planned but not even begun by December 13. Just outside this barrier was a narrow field of sub-terra shells—torpedoes—diabolically sited where advancing troops would slow down and congregate to pick their way through the maze.

In the process of preparing the abatis, the fort's garrison and slave laborers cleared a further field of fire by chopping down trees for several hundred yards more, as well as razing some wooden outbuildings. A detached mortar battery located off the fort's southeast corner was to be dismantled to prevent its use by the enemy. Major Anderson's men had not gotten around to removing the stumps, dismantling the mortar battery, or finishing the building demolition, an oversight that provided Federal sharpshooters with ample places of cover to shoot at the exposed artillerymen. In some cases, the riflemen were able to set up within 200 yards of the fort. A veteran marksman in the 47th Ohio sized up the situation at once as his company scuttled ahead to bring McAllister under fire. Nestled safely behind one of the tree stumps, he brought his rifle to his shoulder with the comment, "watch me make the Johnnies get off the works."

In his after-action report Major Anderson cited the worst case of one of his batteries along the landside wall where "out of a detachment of eight men three were killed and three more wounded. The Federal skirmish line was very heavy, and the fire so close and rapid that it was at times impossible to work our guns."

It was Brigadier General Hazen's intention to encircle the landside of Fort McAllister using nine regiments; three from each of his three brigades. The first across the causeway, Colonel Wells S. Jones's Second Brigade, were assigned "position on the left of the road, the left resting on the river." The next to arrive were the three from Colonel Theodore Jones's First Brigade—30th Ohio, 6th Missouri, and 116th Illinois. In many ways theirs was the toughest task, for they had to pick their way through the swampy mire south and east of the fort in order to take their place on the extreme right. Last over the causeway were the 70th Ohio, 48th Illinois, and 90th Illinois from Colonel John M. Oliver's Third Brigade, which were to link the two flanks.

(In addition, eight regiments were designated as reserves, shown on contemporary maps as positioned behind the first wave. However, given the constricted and congested staging area, and referencing regimental accounts, it seems that perhaps only three actually lined up to backstop the attack. Based on admittedly sketchy accounts, it appears that each battle line was directly supported by one regiment.)

Prior to leaving the Middleton house area, each colonel was briefed by Hazen on the deployment he intended to employ in the assault. "To make the chance of hits by the enemy as small as possible, the formation was in single rank, resembling a close line of skirmishers," he later explained. Hazen had a special reminder for Colonel Theodore Jones, echoing Sherman's admonition not to march his men "behind any creek, so that [they] . . . could not get forward."

Hardly had the engagement begun when Hazen's chain of command was struck a blow. Colonel Wells S. Jones and his acting assistant adjutant general, Captain John H. Groce, were advancing the skirmish line when one "magic bullet" from a Rebel sharpshooter took both of them out. Groce was killed, Jones badly wounded with a ball lodged in his right lung. Command devolved to the next senior colonel, James S. Martin of the 111th Illinois, who took charge of the three regiments.

Matters were progressing, but slowly. Hazen, already stressed, now had Sherman breathing down his neck. About the time the working parties were clearing the torpedoes off the causeway, Hazen's signal corps detachment established a station along the Ogeechee where they very quickly made contact with their opposite numbers at Cheves' Rice Mill. Hazen's first message was an inquiry whether or not Sherman was present. "On being assured of the fact," the General continued, "and that I expected the fort to be carried before night, I received by signal the assurance of General Hazen that he was making his preparations, and would soon attempt the assault." Hazen urged his subordinates to complete their deployments, fully aware that high-powered eyes were upon him.

Lieutenant Fisher reached the *Dandelion* with his exciting news. It was enough to convince the tugboat's captain to risk taking his craft closer to Fort McAllister. Orders were given to stoke up a full head of steam and raise the anchor. The *Dandelion* descended the Little Ogeechee and Vernon rivers, passed through Hell Gate, and cautiously ascended the Ogeechee River.

According to a soldier with Colonel Theodore Jones's three regiments, they moved "south and east, then north through the cane that grew very thick around there." Once his column disappeared into the marsh, Jones's men became lost from Hazen's control, as more than one courier sent to chart their progress failed to locate them. (A portion of the 116th Illinois, assigned to screening duties, appears to have taken a more direct route. "I and others of the 116th Ill. were on the skirmish line for what seemed to me to be a long time before the signal to charge was given," recollected one of them.)

By 4:00 P.M. the two other elements were in their positions at the edge of the woods bordering the cleared zone and ready to go. Ironically, by hacking down the trees within accurate range of their guns, the Confederates had unintentionally designated a safe area for the attackers in the still-standing woods.

Sniping between the Yankee voltigeurs and enemy sharpshooters in the fort was constant, with only occasional accents provided by the beleaguered cannon. Toward 4:00 P.M. the call "cartridges" was repeated along the 47th Ohio's front. Private Louis Shuttinger from Company A volunteered to get more. He dodged back to the main line, loaded his blouse with fresh ammo, and worked his way forward, following the riverbank, until he reached the skirmish line's left flank. Calling out, "Keep them down, boys, here I come," Shuttinger stood up to begin walking methodically along the irregular row of crouching men, dropping a handful of cartridges to each as he passed. He completed the mission, reached the right flank, and dropped to the ground, unhurt. "Shuttinger was our smallest man," declared a comrade, "but he had the heart of a lion."

Others along Hazen's perimeter prepared for the ordeal to come. Moving among the recruits who joined the 47th Ohio after Atlanta had fallen, Captain J. H. Brown "cautioned his men to keep close to the Veterans." Stepping out from the files of the 70th Ohio, Colonel Henry L. Philips said: "My comrades, knowing that you have been prompt in the discharge of every duty, I deem it a waste of words to urge upon you the importance of continuing to do so." Pointing out toward Fort McAllister, he continued: "You see what is before you, and you know your duty."

As Philips stepped back into the crowd, he was intercepted by Private John Compton. Although designated early on as a regimental color bearer, the boy, having spent most of his service as a teamster, had yet to see any combat. "Colonel," he said, "you know I am not used to this kind of work; please excuse me." "John," answered Philips, shaking his head, "were it in my power God knows I would gladly excuse every man in this regiment."

Hazen's anxiety to get things started almost matched Sherman's. The sun was dipping toward the horizon, daylight was running out—and still no word from the right that Colonel Jones's regiments were coming into line. (As Hazen later learned, Jones's command "found itself behind a long stream, or sluice, and was a long time getting across it and into position.") Deciding to stick with the plan for as long as possible, Hazen held off giving the go-ahead to attack.

One of the signal officers at Cheves' Rice Mill, spotting a wispy column of smoke marking the tug *Dandelion*, quickly spread the word. Sherman, aiming his glasses in that direction, soon made it out, giving the lowly tug an instant upgrade by exclaiming, "Look! Howard, there is the gunboat!" At the other end of the link, Lieutenant Fisher signaled a desire to communicate that was acknowledged by the distant post. He was in touch with Sherman's army! His first message was not the stuff of legend.

WHO ARE YOU?

MCCLINTOCK, GENERAL HOWARD'S SIGNAL OFFICER, was the reply.

HOW CAN I GET TO YOU? WHAT TROOPS ARE AT FORT MCALLISTER?

WE ARE NOW INVESTING FORT MCALLISTER WITH HAZEN'S DIVISION.

Speaking now with the authority of Major General Foster and Rear Admiral Dahlgren, Fisher asked how he could help.

CAN YOU ASSIST US WITH YOUR HEAVY GUNS? This time the name tagged to the message was "Sherman."

Fisher considered his answer and was unable to resist a small joke.

BEING ONLY A TUG-BOAT, NO HEAVY GUNS ABOARD.

The silence that followed at the other end made Fisher wonder if he had misjudged his man. The flags at the post began waggling again, but this message was not directed toward him. Aimed at the opposite shore, it was addressed to Brigadier General Hazen:

> It is absolutely necessary that the fort be taken immediately. The Stars and Stripes must wave over the battery at sundown.
>
> Sherman,
> General

Hazen had run out of time. First Brigade or not, he was ordering the attack. Telling his signal officer to transmit that he was assaulting at once, Hazen hurried to his command post for the action, which one soldier described as "a big [tree] stump." His bugler, J. A. Vaughan of the 55th Illinois, looked at him expectantly. With a nod from Hazen, Vaughan sounded the call "Attention." All along the two-thirds-complete ring, the men chosen for the attack moved to the edge of the tree line that had hid them from most of the enemy's attention. In response, the decimated Confederate cannon crews did their best to step up the rate of fire.

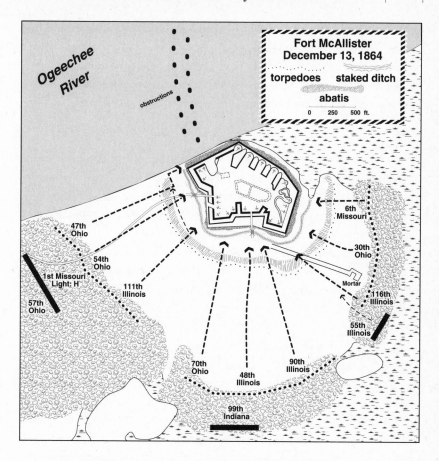

Fisher to Sherman: IS FORT MCALLISTER TAKEN?

Sherman to Fisher: NOT YET, BUT IT WILL BE IN A MINUTE.

After another nod from Hazen, bugler Vaughan sounded "Forward." "To my great surprise and joy the right brigade, under Colonel Theodore Jones, moved out accurately at the same moment," sighed a vastly relieved brigadier. "It had crossed the stream and formed in line just in time to receive the order." Hazen's 3,000 men now faced an advance of six or seven hundred yards. "The forward movement began promptly at the sound of the bugle," recorded an Ohioan in the center, "with varying speed from a brisk walk to double-quick and from that to a run." The Buckeye officer on the left who was worried how well his recent recruits would behave noted with pride that "they all started off in fine style something like old soldiers."

There were some uninvited but welcome guests, as a portion of one reserve regiment—the 55th Illinois—impulsively tagged along. "There was no firing," Hazen added, "and the line was well up to the fort before its defenders were ready to resist, so well had the sharpshooters, who now advanced with the main line, done their work."

To Sherman's anxious eyes, Hazen's men came "out of the dark fringe of woods that encompassed the fort, the lines dressed as on parade, with colors flying, and moving forward with a quick, steady pace." An aide with the General remembered "a long line of blue coats and bright bayonets, and the dear old flag was there, waving proudly in the breeze." A cannoneer standing in the jump-off area recollected seeing "a single line of men advancing, gun in the right hand, in a stooping posture, at a fast walk, toward the fort, but they did not go far in this way before they straightened up and broke into a fast run."

Some 150 yards out from their objective, the various Union regiments began firing, which triggered a response from Fort McAllister. "The musketry from the assaulting force and the musketry and artillery from the fort showed [that the fight] . . . was being made in earnest," declared a staff officer with Howard. "Our troops fired but one volley, the enemy fired continually." To a soldier charging in the center, McAllister "seemed alive with flame; quick jets of fire shooting out from all its sides, while the white smoke first covered the place and then rolled away from the glacis."

Added another soldier present: "This was the moment the General looked for."

At different points along the converging assault lines Hazen's men entered the narrow torpedo zone.

L. C. Huffine, 30th Ohio
When we got up close to the fort, we saw the wires above ground, and the boys sang out, "Watch out!"

T. N. Stanley, 48th Illinois
One of my company was torn to pieces by a torpedo and I was almost covered with dirt.

Lyman Hardman, 30th Ohio

I had arrived near the edge of a small ditch around a mortar bed, when I exploded a torpedo that had been placed in the ground by stepping on it. On recovering from the effects of the shock I found that the shoe of my left foot [was] blown off and the foot very badly burned. My face and one ear [were] considerably cut and burned.

Y. R. Davies, 70th Ohio

Some 50 yards out from the fort we crossed a line of torpedoes buried in the sand, and [the reluctant color bearer] John Compton . . . stepping on one of them, was instantly killed. His body was mangled almost beyond recognition.

John Booth, 116th Illinois

I was knocked down by one of the torpedos, and a piece of the limb that was attached to the torpedo struck in the corner of my left eye, which when I pulled it out caused the blood to flow. I was soon covered with blood from head to foot.

J. H. Horner, 30th Ohio

I remember very distinctly of jumping over a pile of fresh earth while on the charge. The man just behind me jumped over it all right, but the man behind him struck the cap of the torpedo as he ran and it exploded and blew off his foot above the ankle joint, leaving the bone bare of flesh for two or three inches above the joint.

Then the thin, long lines pressed into the snarled strip of slashed trees. The soldiers struggled to get through what one of them called "the netted abatis work," while another recollected "crawling under and over the trees that were felled with their tops pointing out from the fort." The Yankees emerged from the scratching tangles to sprint the ten to twenty-five yards to the next obstacle, the spiked ditch girding McAllister's land sides. Hazen had anticipated this moment, instructing his officers that once they had broken through the abatis they were "to charge with a rush, every man for himself."

To one gasping Yankee the row of sharpened stakes resembled "a tangle of buckhorns shining in the sun." He continued: "There was no passing this barrier until a few brave men bending over their guns crawled under and through, lifting and pushing the logs apart and leaving gaps through which the regiment[s] speedily rushed." Another soldier struggling at the obstacle wrote "that it would take four or five men to break one of them of[f] So that we could get through." "Some got through the small openings," added an Ohioan in the 70th, "some were held up by comrades, and fell over, others were helped over by those on the other side."

Not everyone was struggling to get out of the ditch. Alert members of the leftmost regiment, the 47th Ohio, noticed that the staked strip ended at the riverbank, and with the tide out there was an unobstructed beach fronting the fort, wide enough for a charging column. Without hesitating, Colonel Augustus C. Parry bawled out orders that halted the forward rush, then reoriented it into a compact column that the officer with his second in command led onto the beach toward McAllister. Scrambling in with them were some soldiers from the 111th Illinois, equally glad to have found a way forward that saved them "from the bullets and [we] gained the fort from the river side, where there was not a man to keep us out," declared one of them.

At Cheves' Rice Mill, Sherman was reacting to the sights like an avid sports fan: "There they go grandly; not a waver." "See that flag in the advance, Howard; how steadily it moves; not a man falters." "There they go still; see the roll of musketry. Grand. Grand."

Then it was up the wall and onto the parapet. A member of the 116th Illinois recalled this as "the most difficult part of the work—to climb up the side of the fort, which was loose earth." Frantic defenders tried to fire over the parapet edge or hurled objects on the yelling, scrambling mass of blue men swarming the fort's outer walls. Along the river side's northwest face, where no one was expecting trouble, a ragged cheer and shouts announced the arrival of the 47th Ohio and portions of the 111th Illinois.

From his perch at Cheves' Rice Mill, Major General Howard found the sight of the fighting both appalling and irresistible. "They crossed the ditch, then over the parapet," he said. "The wind lifted the smoke," added a Sherman aide. "Crowds of men were visible on the parapet, fiercely fighting—but our flag was planted there."

Soon afterward, claims would be made by the 47th Ohio, 70th Ohio, 90th Illinois, and 111th Illinois on the honor of having placed the first flag on the Confederate works. None would be able to definitively prove their contention. More to the point, flags on the parapet did not signal an end to the fighting. Groups of the McAllister garrison fought around their cannon, while others fell back to the interior to fort up in bombproofs and magazines.

For a short time, recalled a member of the 47th Ohio, the attackers "were all engaged in [a] fierce hand-to-hand encounter, fighting with the bayonet and the butt of muskets." Seconded another soldier in the melee, "we had to bayonet them before they would stop fighting." Several gun commanders who refused to abandon their tubes were engulfed by the blue flood. One who died under the onslaught was Lieutenant Richard C. Hazzard of Clinch's Light Artillery. His commander was also felled at the very end of the fighting, but not before a combat notable enough to merit mention in Major Anderson's final report:

> I would . . . most respectfully call the attention of the general commanding to the gallant conduct of Captain [Nicholas B.] Clinch, who, when summoned to surrender by a Federal captain, responded by dealing him a severe blow on the head with his saber. (Captain Clinch had previously received two gun shot wounds in the arm). Immediately a hand to hand fight ensued. Federal privates came to the assistance of their officer, but the fearless Clinch continued the unequal contest until he fell bleeding from eleven wounds (three saber wounds, six bayonet wounds, and two gun shot wounds), from which, after severe and protracted suffing, he has barely recovered.

Major Anderson almost added his own name to the list of killed. Cornered on the parapet, he threw down his sword but then was jabbed at by a bayonet-wielding Yankee. When Anderson protested, the soldier reversed his gun and clubbed the fort commander in the head before moving on. Fortunately, the next Federal on the scene was Brigadier General Hazen himself, who knew Anderson before the war. "Get to the rear, George," Hazen told the groggy Confederate, "and report to me later." Hazen also encountered another acquaintance wearing the other uniform, the human pincushion Captain Clinch. Somehow the Rebel officer "recognized and spoke to me," recorded an astonished Hazen. "He was lying on his back, shot through the arm, with a bayonet wound in the chest, and contused by the butt of a gun."

Sherman recalled that "the parapets were blue with our men, who fired their muskets in the air, and shouted so that we actually heard them, or felt that we did." "Then all of us who had witnessed the strife and exalted in the triumph, grasped each the other's hand, embraced, and were glad, and some of us found the water in our eyes," said Major Nichols of Sherman's staff. Howard's communications chief, Captain McClintock, was tempted to tell everyone to pipe down, for "so wild and boisterous were their demonstrations that the old building was so shaken that it was next to impossible to hold a glass with sufficient steadiness upon a flag at that distance to distinctly read it." McClintock complained to his boss, Major General Howard, who found a way to settle things down. Howard then dictated a message for Lieutenant Fisher on the *Dandelion:*

> *FORT MCALLISTER IS OURS. LOOK FOR A BOAT. GENERAL SHERMAN WILL*
> *COME DOWN TO-NIGHT.*

The twilight had deepened to the point that Lieutenant Fisher could barely read the flag waggles, and he realized that he had neglected to pack any torches for night signaling. The officer decided that the tug should retire to the river's mouth, where he could deliver his news before returning to pick up Sherman.

The fighting inside Fort McAllister sputtered fitfully for a few minutes as the last defenders were prised out of their hiding places. On his way to the Union rear, POW Major Anderson encountered Colonel James S. Martin, one of the three brigade commanders. Martin afterward claimed to have accepted Anderson's surrender of the post. Before leaving the fort area, the Confederate commander observed a company of Union soldiers marching out of McAllister on a course that would take them right into the torpedo belt. Anderson, recalled the young lieutenant in charge of the detail, "held out your hand and told me not to go out that way and you told me the way to go out and I found out afterwards that if I had . . . went out the way I first started I would have been blown up with torpedoes."

Instead of destroying their flags, the garrison had tried to hide them, not a smart thing to do when confronted by some of Sherman's most experienced scroungers. Captain George E. Castle of the 111th Illinois found one stuffed in the fireplace of a bombproof, while Captain J. H. Brown of the 47th Ohio located another tucked away with stored gunpowder, and yet a third was taken by Captain George Nelson, a Third Brigade staff officer.

In the final accounting, Hazen put his losses at 24 killed (most by the torpedoes) and 110 wounded. The fatalities were especially heavy among the color bearers, who, because their duty put them in the van of the advance, were among the first to reach the torpedoes. Three of them—two in the 48th Illinois and one in the 70th Ohio—died. Major Anderson counted sixteen of the fort's defenders killed, and twenty-eight wounded. The rest, including himself, were prisoners. Taken also were twenty-four cannon, one mortar, sixty tons of ammunition, some fine Havana cigars, and thirty days of food supplies, including a small but select wine cellar.

When he had calmed down somewhat, Sherman waved over his aide-de-camp, Major Lewis Dayton, to sketch a note for Major General Slocum, holding down the left flank. "Take a good big drink, a long breath, and then yell like the devil," read the message. "The fort was carried at 4:30 P.M., the assault lasting but fifteen minutes." Dayton went on to say that contact had finally been made with the Federal fleet.

Sherman now committed an act of utter folly. So anxious was he to be in touch with the outside world that he commandeered one of the small boats used by the signal corps men at the rice mill with the intention of reaching Fort McAllister via the Ogeechee River. No one present seems to have calculated the potential risk for a small party in a rowboat on an unfamiliar river in the dark traveling to the site of a fierce battle not thirty minutes ended. Compounding the imprudence, Major General Howard insisted on going along. There was a streak of vanity in the man who, writing long after the war, would take great pains to claim much of the credit for the successful attack. The prospect of Sherman's going alone to the site of one of his (Howard's) triumphs was just unthinkable.

So the pair—representing two-thirds of the top leadership of the forces that had marched from Atlanta to the gates of Savannah—piled into the small skiff that the signal men provided. Somebody had to row, so Major Nichols and Captain Nehemiah Merritt of Sherman's staff volunteered for the duty, claiming, according to Sherman, that "they were good oarsmen." Somehow room was also found for Howard's chief of staff, Lieutenant Colonel William E. Strong, and another Sherman aide, Captain Joseph C. Audenried.

The group set off on a voyage of what Sherman estimated to be six nautical miles, rowing against a flood tide. Strong, Merritt, Nichols, and Audenried constituted the galley, while Sherman—no surprise here—sat in the stern and steered. It was a tough pull against the river current, so to help them ignore their exertions, the rowers sang songs. Strong's recollection was that "even Generals Sherman and Howard entered into the spirit of it and joined in the chorus of many an old and familiar air." It was not long after 9:00 P.M. when they somehow found their way to a landing point about a mile and a half above the captured fort.

Sherman's luck was still running strong, for the sentry they encountered on the shore was not trigger-happy, and the party was soon brought to Brigadier General Hazen's Middleton house headquarters. They found the brigadier preparing to eat dinner with his staff; "he invited us to join them," wrote Sherman, "which we accepted promptly, for we were really very hungry." Hazen asked permission to allow the fort's captured commandant, Major Anderson, to join them. Since it was Hazen's party after all, Sherman offered no objection. The only awkward moment came when Anderson, noticing that among those serving the table was one of his house slaves, asked him what he was doing. "I'se workin' for Mr. Hazen now," was the answer that spoke volumes about changing fortunes.

A group of couriers and aides, riding north from Cheves' Rice Mill, spread the word of the Union victory. While most would find out next morning, many heard about it this night. "When the news was received we raised such a loud and long cheer that we made the whole country resound," declared a Seventeenth Corps man. Someone had to come out of the picket line of the 64th Illinois to explain why everyone in camp was celebrating. "I would the world could have heard the whole joyful yells pass around the lines which encircle Savannah," proclaimed a happy member of the 39th Ohio.

Word spread through the Left Wing, anchored on the Savannah River. "I hear the troops cheering and the bands playing Yankee Doodle," noted a diarist in the 38th Ohio. Few were thinking of this in any strategic sense; for most it meant that supplies would soon begin to flow. Near the 74th Ohio the cry was: "Fort McAllister is taken and the cracker line is open!" A Pennsylvanian in the 147th regiment "felt that "a great load was lifted from our shoulders, and the rejoicing in our ranks was very great." In the 21st Michigan, the pickets shouted "Hardtack!" at the doubtless perplexed Confederates opposite them, but the Michigan boys knew full well what it meant. " 'Hardtack' was really a jubilant cry of real meaning, a just cause of exultation as it foreshadowed the full fruits of victory," predicted one soldier.

Sherman was determined to obtain "some news of what was going on in the outer world." Having already survived one foolhardy adventure this night, he saw no reason why he shouldn't undertake another. Hazen, remembering that the spoils of war included a yawl in good condition tied up on the far side of the fort, led his guests toward it. As they crossed along the causeway, a guard warned them to watch out for torpedoes. It was Sherman's recollection that a soldier seeking a wounded pal had actually been killed while he was there, though Howard remembered it as being "an ambulance with mules hauling it" that triggered the explosion. Either way, Sherman promptly authorized Hazen to use some of the captured garrison to clear the minefield in the morning.

This infuriated Major Anderson, who branded it "an unwarrantable and improper treatment of prisoners of war." Perhaps as a sop to the offended commander, or maybe as a little psychological warfare, Brigadier General Hazen allowed McAllister's Confederate signal officer to send news of the surrender to his counterpart at the Rose Dhu Island battery. The unsigned message quickly worked its way up the Confederate chain of command, "reporting the loss of the work and representing the officers unhurt [save one]."

Sherman and Howard clambered aboard the yawl, which was crewed by fresh arms provided by Hazen, leaving the former rowers— Strong, Nichols, Audenried, and Merritt—on shore. Once again the brain trust of a major military operation was committing risky business, but Sherman was adamant. Luckily for all involved, Lieutenant Fisher was a responsible and proactive officer. After delivering word of the army's arrival to the other vessels in Ossabaw Sound, he returned with the *Dandelion* to a point just below the captured fort. They had not been on station very long when the splash of oars heralded a small craft heading toward them.

"What boat is that?"

"Sherman."

The yawl scraped alongside, allowing the generals to climb onto the deck. The two, noted Fisher, "were welcomed with twice three cheers by those on board." Fisher launched into a short briefing of current events, indicated that Major General Foster was eager to get in touch, and that he had sent back word of Sherman's arrival. The generals also learned that the intrepid Captain Duncan, Sergeant Amick, and Private Quimby had, recalled Howard, "succeeded in avoiding all dangers and hindrances and had reached the fleet the morning of the 12th." Asking for paper and a place to write, Sherman sat down to personally compose dispatches to the secretary of war and the army's chief of staff. Lieutenant Fisher also remembered notes for Major General Foster and Rear Admiral Dahlgren.

Sherman's dispatches opened with news of McAllister's capture, then summarized his forces' position outside Savannah. He declared that his "army is in splendid order, and equal to anything." He went on in more detail in the note intended for Major General Halleck (knowing it would be shared with Lincoln and Grant), adding that the newspaper "editors in Georgia profess to be indignant at the horrible barbarities of Sherman's army, but I know the people don't want our visit repeated." Typical of Sherman's rapid-fire mind, suggestions were advanced for the next phase—either a course reversal to Montgomery, Alabama, to draw Hood down from Tennessee; or a march into the Carolinas to force General Robert E. Lee to abandon the fortifications protecting Richmond and Petersburg.

Before that, however, Sherman wanted to finish with Savannah. "I will try and see Admiral Dahlgren and General Foster before demanding the surrender of Savannah, which I do not propose to make till my batteries are able to open," he said. Sherman closed each missive with the confident assertion: "I regard Savannah as already gained."

Leaving the dispatches for delivery with Lieutenant Fisher, Sherman and Howard returned to their yawl to be rowed back to Fort McAllister. Once ashore, they were guided again to the Middleton house, where, said Brigadier General Hazen, they "shared my blankets, spread upon the floor."

It had been a very long day.

An anticlimactic footnote to this tumultuous day was provided by Brigadier General Kilpatrick, who, following his brief conference with Brigadier General Hazen, took his troopers south to the mouth of the Medway River in St. Catherines Sound. There, at Kilkenny Bluff, he spotted some Federal warships on patrol. According to a soldier with the party, "Signals, shots and fires failed to attract any response from them. A six-oared boat was soon found, and when the tide set out [Captain Lewellyn G.] . . . Estes, with seven volunteers (six at the oars and one at the helm) started for the ship. They beat a cavalry march for speed, too. In about an hour we received signals that they were there and in communication with Uncle Sam's jolly sailors."

Estes carried a copy of Howard's dispatch already delivered by Captain Duncan. In a message to Sherman time-dated 1:30 P.M., Kilpatrick made a case for setting up the army's supply base in the St. Catherines area, a suggestion that became moot once Fort McAllister fell. Howard's note was forwarded to Major General Foster by the USS *Fernandina*, while the unidentified contact vessel remained in touch with the shore. Even though nothing would come of this exchange, it did demonstrate that Sherman had more options than connecting with the fleet via Ossabaw Sound.

The happy cavalrymen at Kilkenny Bluff entertained some of the boat's crew the next day. "The officers and sailors wanted to ride our horses, and we thoroughly enjoyed seeing them do so," said a Michigan trooper. "When they left us many of them were sore and lame from the tumbles they had received while riding."

WEDNESDAY, DECEMBER 14, 1864

Major General Sherman had been sleeping one, maybe two hours when he became aware that there was someone in the room asking for him. Sherman called the stranger over and rubbed the exhaustion from his face while the messenger explained that a staff officer from Major General Foster was waiting with a boat at Fort McAllister. Foster wished very much to see him, but he was incapacitated by an old war wound, so could not come ashore. Could Sherman come to him? "I was extremely weary from the incessant labor of the day and night before," recalled Sherman, "but got up, and again walked down the sandy road to McAllister, where I found a boat awaiting us."

The man who greeted him aboard the revenue cutter *Nemaha* had a very mixed war record. He was the kind of officer who stood out while acting as a subordinate, but when promoted to top command fell prey to excessive cautions and concerns. "He may have been a lion in his day," observed a soldier who had served under him, "but his day is past." Thus far Major General John G. Foster had fumbled his two military missions connected with Sherman's March. The expeditionary force he had dispatched under Brigadier General John P. Hatch to cut the Charleston-Savannah railroad at Grahamville had been repulsed at Honey Hill. A follow-up effort (also led by Hatch) against the railway farther north had been stopped short of the goal, though within extreme cannon range, allowing Foster to claim that his guns now "commanded" the passage. Foster's hope was that Sherman would be too preoccupied with resupplying his army, capturing Savannah, and moving to the next phase of his campaign to take him to task for his failures.

An officer with Foster's staff recalled Sherman as "the most American looking man I ever saw, tall and lank, not very erect, with hair like a thatch, which he rubs up with his hands, a rusty beard trimmed close, a wrinkled face, sharp, prominent red nose, small, bright eyes, coarse red hands, black felt hat slouched over the eyes . . . , brown field officer's coat with high collar and no shoulder-straps, muddy trousers and one spur."

By Sherman's account the meeting was amicable. Foster, after providing the most up-to-date intelligence he had regarding Savannah's defenses, indicated that troops under his command were "strongly intrenched, near Broad River, within cannon-range of the railroad." The officer hastened to assure Sherman that the warehouses at Port Royal contained "ample supplies . . . awaiting your orders." For his part, Sherman told Foster about the capture of Fort McAllister, indicated his army's positions, and was, according to Foster, "perfectly sure of capturing Savannah." Sherman's shopping list included bread, sugar, coffee, and heavy-caliber siege guns. Foster added that twenty tons of mail were at Port Royal awaiting delivery to his men.

From the moment he arrived before Savannah, until just a few hours prior to meeting with Foster, Sherman had been obsessed with taking Fort McAllister. With that accomplished, he immediately segued to a new all-consuming focus: capturing Savannah. The rough plan he shared with Foster would have the bulk of Sherman's force blocking all western approaches to the city, while one division would be detached to cut off Hardee's escape route north to Charleston. The staff officer present recollected the strategizing in more colorful terms. Sherman, he wrote the same day of the meeting, "says the city is his sure game and stretches out his arm and claws his bony fingers in the air to illustrate how he had his grip on it."

Sherman's problem now was logistical. Capturing Fort McAllister was a step—albeit an important one—toward setting up the supply pipeline. The Ogeechee River still needed to be swept clear of torpedoes, and obstructions had to be removed, plus a flotilla of shallow-draft craft was necessary to carry the goods as far as King's Bridge, where Sherman expected to establish his distribution hub. Getting the navy's help was, as Sherman put it, "indispensable." He agreed to journey with Foster into Ossabaw Sound in the hope of meeting the commander of the blockading squadron, Rear Admiral John A. Dahlgren.

The fifty-five-year-old naval officer was on station outside Savannah, supervising the placement of buoys to guide an attack in which he was planning to use his ironclads. At 8:00 A.M., after being informed that communications had been opened with Sherman, he made the decision to steam down to Ossabaw Sound in his flagship, the USS *Harvest Moon*. Not long after reaching the sound, he spotted Major General Foster's steamer and learned that Sherman was aboard. "Anchored immediately," Dahlgren wrote in his diary, "and in a few minutes the steamer came alongside, and I jumped aboard, walked into the cabin, and met General Sherman." The rear admiral, quite Sherman's equal when it came to self-confidence and vanity, added: "He had left his army to see me."

"I was not personally acquainted with him at the time," reflected Sherman, "but he was so extremely kind and courteous that I was at once attracted to him." Dahlgren had come to his sea command through his brilliance at a Washington desk job as director of naval ordnance development and manufacture, a position that placed him in regular contact with President Lincoln, who took a personal interest in furthering his career. His appointment to take command of the South Atlantic Squadron had been over the objections of the secretary of the navy, backed by many serving admirals who felt that Dahlgren had not earned his spurs. Like his predecessor, Dahlgren had been unable to conquer Charleston from the sea, so it is not improbable that he saw a partnership with Sherman to capture Savannah as beneficial to his record of achievement.

According to Sherman, "There was nothing in his power, he said, which he would not do to assist us, to make our campaign absolutely successful." The rear admiral could not have been more cordial, even when Sherman touched a traditional rivalry by commenting that his "division had just walked into McAllister . . . , but that no ships could have taken it, so powerfully was it fortified toward the water."

Dahlgren ordered a list complied of shallow-draft vessels capable of reaching King's Bridge, then offered to personally oversee the clearing of the waterway. He and Sherman discussed the possibility of a joint action against some of the Rebel river redoubts, with Dahlgren promising to undertake preliminary surveys of the enemy's defenses. The rear admiral happily agreed to transport Sherman to Fort McAllister, freeing Major General Foster to return to Port Royal to begin opening the floodgates of supplies, ordnance, and mail.

Sherman spent the night aboard the *Harvest Moon*, where he was joined in the evening by his dedicated aide and faithful chronicler, Major Henry Hitchcock, who had found his way from headquarters to Cheves' Rice Mill to Fort McAllister to the flagship. It took but a short time for Hitchcock to conclude "that navy officers are luxurious rascals compared to us dwellers in tents."

It was during these visits with Foster and Dahlgren that Sherman was handed a note from Lieutenant General Ulysses S. Grant, addressed from near Petersburg, Virginia, on December 3. The message had been written before any word had been received regarding the fate of Sherman or his forces. "Not liking to rejoice before the victory is assured I abstain from congratulating you and those under your command until the bottom has been struck," said Grant. There followed a short summary of events in Virginia and elsewhere, along with a troubling assessment of Thomas's lackluster performance in Tennessee. The man appointed by Sherman to hold the line against Hood had forted up in Nashville after ceding much of the territory to the south without a fight. "Part of the falling back was undoubtedly necessary," Grant grumbled, "and all of it may have been; it did not look so, however, to me." Of Sherman's yet-to-be-revealed accomplishments, Grant expressed a sentiment sure to please its recipient: "I have never had a fear of the result."

With the dawn word of McAllister's fall spread afresh along the Union siege lines outside Savannah. "News came about 10 o'clock of the capture of Fort McAllister," recorded a Michigan diarist. "Sherman had been on board the fleet. . . . Our communication is opened with the north again. We gave 3 hearty cheers." Major James A. Connolly noted in his journal that the soldiers in Brigadier General Absalom Baird's division (Fourteenth Corps) "have been cheering and yelling like Indians all day. Everybody feeling jolly—bands playing, batteries all firing, flags all flying, and everybody voting everybody else in this army a hero." "Now we are knocking at the gates of Savannah," crowed an Iowa boy. "We are going in before long too, for we have the means and Sherman will not be long in putting the same into requisition."

At the captured fort, a detail of prisoners headed by McAllister's engineering chief were clearing the minefield. "They would make a mark around the torpedo with their fingers, then dig it out," related one of the Yankee guards, "and when they were on the ground they looked like camp kettles." When General Beauregard later learned of this incident, he applied to Brigadier General John H. Winder, commissary general of prisons, for a like number of Federals "to be employed in retaliation." According to Beauregard, "Gen. Winder answered, that under his instructions from the Confederate War Department he could not comply; also, that in his belief, prisoners could not rightfully be so employed."

Before McAllister was taken, the men may have grumbled about their condition, but it was always with a sense of resigned acceptance. Now that the door to the army warehouses was open, resignation was replaced with impatience. "We will soon have rations again," proclaimed a New Yorker, "and what we wish for fully is letters from home." The capture of McAllister, added a hopeful member of the 105th Ohio, "must soon end our season of scarcity of rations which now reigns to such an extent as to make anything welcome that is possibly eatable." "Our food line should now be open again," contributed a Wisconsin comrade. "We now have too little to live on. . . . We have only a small amount of rice and an ounce of meat per day."

Still, not everyone was thinking about mail or their stomachs. An Ohio soldier found time today to enjoy his surroundings. "Almost every tree is draped with Spanish Moss," he wrote in his journal. "It is long & sways to & fro in the breeze. Live oaks look green & splendid." A few members of the 22nd Wisconsin were celebrating their good fortune this day: "We captured a yawl boat—it had in it 5 chickens, one gobbler and one good blanket." Another captured boat was the object of a turf war between the infantry and engineers. Acting on orders from Major General Slocum, Colonel George P. Buell with a detail from the 58th Indiana Pontoniers came aboard the captured tender *Resolute*, intending to tow it to the mainland to repair the engines. Buell's deputy was met at the gangplank by Colonel William

Hawley, who claimed possession for the 3rd Wisconsin. After a bit of verbal tussle, Slocum's orders trumped Hawley's claim, so the captured craft was hauled to the mainland.

Brigadier General Kilpatrick's headquarters this day were located in historic Midway Church, Liberty County, some fifteen miles southwest of Fort McAllister. He and his riders had arrived here yesterday, having had no problem dispersing the two Confederate militia units assigned to the region, the 29th Battalion Georgia Cavalry (Lieutenant Colonel Arthur Hood commanding), and members of the Remount Detachment of the Liberty Independent Troop. Muttered one frustrated Rebel: "If Hood's Battalion ever fired a shot at a Yankee in Liberty County, I have never been able to find out where it was."

One bold detachment from the 9th Pennsylvania Cavalry raced nearly thirty miles along the Savannah and Gulf Railroad with orders to destroy the bridge at the Altamaha River. However, this time the militia had managed to concentrate on the opposite bank in sufficient strength, so the 120 or so Union troopers had to content themselves with wrecking the approaches on their side.

Kilpatrick's men found themselves in something of a forager's paradise. Their commander looked across Liberty County and saw many wealthy plantations. The area had been relatively untouched by the war, and even more important, it was far enough distant from Savannah that no Union infantry units had ranged this far, so the troopers had it all to themselves. Add to the mix the absence of Wheeler's cavalry and the impotency of the local militia, and the result proved to be a catastrophe for Liberty County's property owners.

One of the more affluent of them was Mrs. Mary Jones Jones,* recent widow of the influential cleric and planter the Reverend Dr. Charles Colcock Jones. (Dr. Jones made the conversion of slaves to Christianity his life's work. Through his efforts there was some improvement in their living conditions, even as he taught his converts a Christian obedience to their owners.) The holdings he had passed to his wife consisted of three plantations plus associated slaves: Arcadia in northwestern Liberty County, Montevideo near Riceboro, and May-

---

* Mary Jones had married her cousin, hence the "Jones Jones."

bank, closer to the coast. Mrs. Jones, a fervent secessionist like her husband, had managed the estates since his passing in March 1863. The abrupt Yankee invasion forced some hard choices. The family decided to remain at Montevideo, which lay along the most likely route for any invader, but to store their goods at the more remote Arcadia. Maybank, presumably, would be left in God's hands.

Mrs. Jones had spent the previous day in remote Arcadia, preparing for the goods and valuables she intended to place there. She set off for Montevideo at sunset in a carriage driven by her house slave, Jack. They were about seven miles north of Riceboro when an armed Union officer gestured them to a halt. After enduring a hasty inspection, Mrs. Jones, despite her imperious ways, was advised by the Federal of a roadblock ahead manned by less understanding Yankees. Thus forewarned, she had Jack take her on a roundabout path that led them to a Confederate picket post. Her hopes that a Southern gentleman would see to her needs proved wishful thinking once the officer made clear that he had his orders, which did not include providing her with an armed escort.

The black servant of a family friend offered to help; with him operating as a scout, Mrs. Jones and Jack were able to get to about four miles west of Riceboro, where they encountered another C.S. picket who said that the town bridge was down. A nearby couple who knew the family urged her to stay with them for the night, but Mrs. Jones was determined to reach Montevideo. She was ready to continue on foot when the picket learned that the bridge had been sufficiently repaired to handle her carriage. The town itself was occupied by Union troopers, necessitating another detour, but by 9:00 P.M. she had reached her daughter, son-in-law, and grandchildren at the Jones family homestead.

Her travails were far from over. The wagons carrying the goods intended for Arcadia had found the route closed by enemy checkpoints, so the family members now hustled to secrete what they could on the Montevideo grounds. Other neighbors passed through with ominous tidings of where the Yankees were operating. Then her son-in-law, the Reverend Robert Quarterman Mallard, insisted on leaving to join his militia unit. Left alone, the women prepared to greet the next day with what Mrs. Jones's daughter later wrote of as a "fearful anxiety." It was not a misplaced concern.

Ahead of Liberty County would be six weeks of almost constant exposure to Yankee raiding parties and foraging expeditions. The ordeal, the most extensive suffered by any region during Sherman's march, was just getting started.

Once the fall of Fort McAllister had been confirmed, Lieutenant General Hardee feared it presaged an all-out assault. Work on the now-critical floating bridge was not progressing as rapidly as everyone hoped it would; only the first leg (from the city to Hutchinson's Island) was completed. Worried that he was almost out of time, Hardee ordered a temporary wharf built on the north side of the island to allow him to evacuate troops by boat if need be. (When the dawn of December 15 revealed that the Federals were not mounting a major operation, Hardee canceled the wharf to continue building the bridge.)

A turf war now erupted over management of the bridge project. Lieutenant Colonel B. W. Frobel, a Confederate States Army engineer on detached service with the Georgia state forces, caught the ear of the militia commander, Major General Gustavus G. W. Smith, to convince him that he could do a better job than Beauregard's man, Colonel Clarke. Smith pressed Hardee, who passed the buck by foisting Frobel on Clarke. Neither had anything good to say about the other, and not until Clarke concocted some make-work to keep Frobel out of his hair was the chief engineer able to devote his full attention to finishing the job.

THURSDAY, DECEMBER 15, 1864

Now that the emotional high of Fort McAllister was behind them, Union soldiers returned to the often tiresome and sometimes deadly business of the siege. "No change from yesterday," noted a diarist in the 129th Illinois. "Occasional shots from Rebel gun. They do no harm. One man wounded on skirmish line." "The frogs are peeping at night, the mosquitoes kiss us on our cheeks and leave a smart which is quite uncomfortable at times," added a Massachusetts comrade. "The birds are leaping from tree to tree and warble forth their sweetest notes of praise." "This morning I go and see the tide come in," wrote an Illinois boy.

Along some sections of the opposing lines the philosophy was live and let live. "We were stationed on the east side of the swamp & Ogeechee canal," wrote an Ohioan with the Fourteenth Corps. "Lieutenant Heath of Co. A made an agreement with the Rebel picket in our front that either party should give the other warning before firing." Not so at other points. According to a member of the 68th Ohio (Seventeenth Corps), "a heavy detail from our regiment was assisting to build a line of heavy earthworks, when the saucy enemy threw a number of shells among the working party; but the boys hugged the ground and escaped injury." On a portion of the Fifteenth Corps line, the heavier-caliber Rebel cannon had their way with a section from the 12th Battery, Wisconsin Light Artillery which "lost three men today all of them being badly wounded."

Behind the front lines, the men grumbled about the food and indulged in the general gripe of being located in the midst of a swamp. "Rations getting scarce," complained a Hoosier. "Living on rice and short on 'hard tack,' groused an Ohio man. "We are now living on plain rice, without salt," contributed a Minnesotan. "We first chopped a trough-like hole in a log, then laid the heads of the rice-sheaves in it, and with a club threshed the grains out; then we rubbed the kernels between our hands to clear it of hulls; after which we used our lungs for a fanning mill, placing the rice, hulls, sand, and all, in a tin plate and blowing until we had it free from hulls; but the sand still remained, and, like the rice, sunk to the bottom and could not be cleaned out; so we had to cook the rice with the sand in it."

Many of the Yankees manning the Fourteenth Corps lines were wondering today what to make of some unusual prisoners taken early in the morning. "The story they tell is this," related a soldier in the 79th Pennsylvania. "Some six hundred Federal prisoners, confined in the 'Bull Pens' at Charleston, took the oath of allegiance to the confederacy, and were formed into a battalion. . . . For a long time they were not allowed arms. On Tuesday last [December 13], however, 250 were taken from the battalion on trial, and ordered to hold the fort in front of our lines. On Wednesday evening [December 14] while the officers were asleep, a guard was placed over them, one of the guns was spiked and filled with mud, and off they started in squads for our lines." "There is much diversity of opinion as to what should be the judgment in their cases," continued a Wisconsin soldier in the 21st regiment.

"They have undoubtedly done wrong in their enlisting but they claim they have never been disloyal at heart to the U.S. and I believe in this they are honest."

When evening settled in along the lines, a number of Union patrols edged ahead to fix the locations of suspected enemy strong points. One such was drawn largely from the 104th Illinois. "The boys waded in [the swamp] for a considerable distance," recalled a member of the expedition. "In places the water was deep, reaching to the armpits of some. The route taken was found to be impracticable, and the enemy becoming alarmed and opening fire, the command was ordered back to camp, where it arrived wet, cold and disgusted with Georgia swamps."

Closer to the Savannah River, Colonel Ezra Carmen was making his way to the headquarters tent of the Twentieth Corps commander, Brigadier General Alpheus S. Williams, his head fairly buzzing with glittering prospects. Carmen led the brigade that now had a two-regiment foothold on Argyle Island, thanks to the transfer of the 2nd Massachusetts to join the 3rd Wisconsin. Carmen saw Argyle Island as the perfect launching point to break the enemy's communication link with Charleston in order to trap the Savannah garrison inside its battlements. He found Brigadier General Williams with Major General Henry Slocum, the Left Wing chief. Both listened eagerly to Carmen talk as he pointed to a rough map he had drawn showing the city, the river, and the thin line representing the planked Union Causeway—Savannah's only connection to the outside world.

There were, Carmen explained, "boats enough in the river to cross a brigade every hour." Despite the firefights ignited each time a Federal touched the South Carolina shore, Carmen had been assured by Colonel William Hawley (commanding the 3rd Wisconsin) that the Union Causeway "could be reached by a brigade." Even as Carmen was explaining this, a courier arrived with a message from Hawley confirming everything that had been said. Carmen's enthusiasm was becoming infectious; even cautious Henry Slocum saw the possibilities clear enough. "Damn it!" he exclaimed at last. "Let us take this plank road and shut these fellows in." Before departing for his headquarters, he alerted Carmen to have the rest of his brigade ready to move on a moment's notice.

Back at his camp, Slocum sent a situation report to Sherman, at

9:00 P.M. Summarizing the current situation plus his plans for Carmen's brigade, the Left Wing commander strongly recommended moving at least a division, and possibly an entire corps, across the Savannah River via Argyle Island into South Carolina. Such an action, he emphasized, would enable the Twentieth Corps to "seal up that side of the city and be in a position to shell every portion of it." For one of the few times in his professional military career, Slocum was raring to go. He was anxious to know what Sherman thought of the enterprise.

Today's *Augusta Daily Chronicle & Sentinel* printed an assessment from Savannah that was both sobering and encouraging. The account, after listing a number of the wounded recently admitted to the principal military hospital (seventeen altogether), reported the death of one of the principals in the Griswoldville fight, Major Ferdinand W. C. Cook, who had directed the Athens Local Defense Battalion. Savannah's citizens were cautioned against hoarding food, and those with a surplus were asked to share with those in need.

Still, there was nothing in the present circumstances that gave Savannah's authorities any cause for alarm. Said the writer: "The citizens of Savannah have only to discharge their duty, and act in concert with the brave and gallant veterans in defending our homes and firesides from the pollution of a hostile foe, the enemy will be driven back in dismay and confusion, and our city rendered secure from future trouble."

This cheery outlook was not shared by General P. G. T. Beauregard in Charleston, who put Richmond on the spot today by officially requesting validation for his plan to preserve Lieutenant General Hardee's forces, even if it meant abandoning Savannah. "I desire being informed if these instructions are approved by the War Department, and are applicable to Charleston as well as Savannah," Beauregard wired President Davis's military adviser. Working off the same page, Hardee chimed in a separate message, warning that unless his communication and supply line to Charleston could be held open, "I shall be compelled to evacuate Savannah."

In another note sent this day to Major General Samuel Jones, the man principally responsible for keeping the corridor open, Hardee confessed, "I feel uneasy about my communications." Now that matters were moving inexorably toward an evacuation, Hardee wanted to be sure that there were no misunderstandings, so he asked Beauregard to "come here and give me the benefit of your advice."

Amid the day's bustle, one of the chief actors in the drama quietly slipped off the stage. General Braxton Bragg, rushed over from the North Carolina coast by Jefferson Davis to guide efforts from Augusta, packed his bags to depart from Charleston, where he had conferred with Beauregard. With no real authority for him to wield, Bragg was feeling very much like a fifth wheel. Declaring that his "services [were] not being longer needed in this department," he transferred himself back to North Carolina. Watching him go, a clerk in the Richmond War Department mused that Bragg's principal contribution had been to play "the part of chronicler of the sad events from Augusta."

As promised, the USS *Harvest Moon* steamed up the Ogeechee River from Ossabaw Sound, carrying Major General Sherman and Rear Admiral Dahlgren. Breakfast was served and consumed by the time the boat hove to near the captured redoubt. Dahlgren now played the part of tourist, with Sherman his guide. The naval officer thought McAllister "a truly formidable work; so crammed with bombproofs and traverses as to look as if the spaces were carved out of solid earth, a very strong and complete work." Also taking the tour was Major Hitchcock, who spent a while gazing at the spiky ditch alongside the steep fort wall and thinking about that awful climb to the parapet. "How on earth they ever did what they did is wonderful," he proclaimed. The biggest surprise for Dahlgren was the sight of the surrendered Rebel garrison, "still there cooking, etc., as if nothing had happened."

Sherman's break from the war ended as the group piled aboard the admiral's barge to be rowed up to Cheves' Rice Mill, where horses and more staff were waiting. Here the two leaders parted; Sherman continued on to Major General Howard's headquarters, while Dahlgren returned to Fort McAllister. When the rear admiral reached it, he noticed approvingly that the *Dandelion* was already "very busy pulling up the piles driven across the river by the rebels [to obstruct the channel] . . . and the most labored device of torpedoes I have yet seen, stout piles being secured slanting down river, with an iron shell on the head. Much ingenuity exercised."

Sherman reached Howard "about noon, and immediately sent orders to my own headquarters, on the Louisville road, to have them brought over to the plank-road, as a place more central and convenient; gave written notice to Generals Slocum and Howard of all the steps taken, and ordered them to get ready to receive the siege-guns, to put them in position to bombard Savannah, and to prepare for the general assault." The effort of getting his hands back on the reins of authority, controlling operations against Savannah, kept Sherman occupied well into the evening.

There was some time for a little healthy unwinding. Major Hitch-cock was part of a "group of twenty-five or thirty officers around the campfire, . . . chatting, telling stories, singing songs—and there was some excellent singing to a guitar, —and having a good time generally, which nobody enjoyed more than the General, though he took chiefly a listening part, with intervals of the most entertaining reminiscences of former campaigns, etc. Besides this, the Headquarters band . . . gave us some very pretty music."

Probably between 10:00 and 10:30 P.M. Sherman received Major General Slocum's request to push a division (backed by the rest of the corps) into South Carolina using their foothold on Argyle Island. At roughly 11:00 P.M. Sherman finished dictating his response to Major Hitchcock. "For the present do not send more than one brigade," he told Slocum. There were a number of variables involved in the proposed strike that Sherman needed to consider. Even as Major Hitch-cock began composing the note for delivery, Sherman fell fast asleep. But not for long.

Colonel Maxwell Van Zandt Woodhull, an aide on Major General Howard's staff, was sitting by a campfire burning between the tents of his boss and Sherman. It being a pleasant evening, the colonel was "thinking of various things, and of nothing in particular, but not sleepy enough to seek my cot." Two riders materialized out of the darkness, drawing up at the fire, where one of the pair dismounted. Woodhull saw that the stranger was a lieutenant colonel.

"I am Colonel Babcock, of General Grant's staff, and I have just arrived with dispatches for General Sherman," he announced. "Is the General here?"

Woodhull indicated Sherman's tent. "Please inform him of my arrival," the newcomer said, with an air suggesting he expected to be obeyed. There was no one from Sherman's staff on hand, so Howard's man knocked on the tent pole, lifted the closed flap, and went in. Sherman, coming awake quickly, listened to Woodhull's explanation for the interruption as he slipped on his coat. "Get me a light," the General said. "Show Babcock in."

As Grant's aide entered Sherman's tent, Woodhull sat back down in front of his fire "with something fresh to think of." Inside, Babcock produced a page of foolscap and handed it over. It was a note from Grant dated December 6. Up to this instant the General had been the lord and master of his fate, but Grant's dispatch was an abrupt reminder to Sherman that even he answered to a higher authority. Sherman scanned the letter.

It was the worst possible news. Looking at the total military picture, Grant had concluded that "the most important operation toward closing out the rebellion will be to close out [General Robert E.] Lee and his army." Toward that end, Grant wanted Sherman and his best troops to join him, in Virginia, right away. "Unless you see objections to this plan, which I cannot see, use every vessel going to you for purposes of transportation."

"The contents [of this letter] . . . gave me great uneasiness, for I had set my heart on the capture of Savannah, which I believed to be practicable, and to be near," related Sherman; "for me to embark for Virginia by sea was so complete a change from what I had supposed would be the course of events that I was very much concerned." Asking Babcock for a moment, Sherman stepped outside, where he again came under the scrutiny of Colonel Woodhull.

"He now stood before me without a hat, with his military coat buttoned loosely across his breast, in gray drawers and gray stockings without his boots," recalled the aide. "He was utterly unconscious of physical comfort or discomfort, lost completely in the great thoughts which filled his mind. . . .

"He stood in the warm ashes, at times unconsciously brushing the ashes over one foot with the other, and he drew as close to the campfire as his subconsciousness deemed to be prudent, but with the exception of this automatic and purely physical impulse he was lost to every surrounding."

At last Sherman turned and reentered his tent. A short while later the word was passed for Major Hitchcock to join them. There was much to do.

CHAPTER 21

"*I Beg to Present You as a Christmas Gift the City of Savannah*"

FRIDAY, DECEMBER 16, 1864

William Tecumseh Sherman spent much of the morning crafting his response to Grant's December 6 message. Just as before, when he obtained permission for the march through Georgia, he did not directly debate his superior's proposition; rather, he provided him with information that he hoped would lead him to Sherman's preferred option, even as he took only small steps toward actually carrying out Grant's directive. When he had written in haste from the *Dandelion*, Sherman was intent on capturing Savannah. Now that he better understood Grant's priorities, Sherman began his note with the assurance that he had "initiated measures looking principally to coming to you with 50,000 or 60,000 infantry, and, incidentally, to take Savannah, if time will allow."

Sherman made sure that Grant understood what a magnificent military force he had: "four corps, full of experience and full of ardor, . . . equal to 60,000 fighting men." He mentioned how well his men had supplied themselves on the riches of Georgia's bounty—most of which he'd have to leave behind, along with Kilpatrick's cavalry. Sherman guessed that if he undertook a northward march "to Columbia, S.C., thence to Raleigh, and thence to report to you," it would require six weeks. Putting these same legions on transports would take about four—assuming enough ships could be found. In his *Memoirs*, Sherman estimated he needed a "little less than a hundred steamers and sailing-vessels," representing a very significant drain on such resources at the same time Grant was mounting a combined army-navy assault on North Carolina's Fort Fisher, which guarded Wilmington, the Confederacy's last still functioning seaport.

Grant's request meant that Sherman would have to abandon any serious effort to cut Savannah off from South Carolina because of the risk it represented of his becoming entangled in an operation that he couldn't easily shut down once it began. He did mention in his response Major General Slocum's proposal to put a corps north of the city, "but, in view of the change of plans made necessary by your order of the 6th, I will maintain things in statu[s] quo till I have got all my transportation to the rear and out of the way, and until I have sea transportation for the troops you require." However, just to be sure that there was no question where he stood, Sherman closed the lengthy note with the comment: "I feel a personal dislike to turning northward."

In his summary, Sherman continued to play loose with the facts—glossing over the condition of his army and highlighting the imminent collapse of the Savannah garrison. Grant's parting shot at George Thomas in Nashville mandated a response. Here Sherman was less than supportive of his senior subordinate, professing to being "somewhat astonished at the attitude of things in Tennessee." Thomas was "full of confidence" when he left him with more than enough force to stop Hood. "I know full well that General Thomas is slow in mind and in action, but he is judicious and brave, and the troops feel great confidence in him," Sherman declared, in something less than a ringing endorsement of the officer he had hand-picked to hold that state for the Union.

This time Grant did not need Sherman's memoranda to sway him. He had already had second thoughts about his call for his friend to join him. "I had no idea originally of having Sherman march from Savannah to Richmond, or even to North Carolina," Grant later admitted. "The season was bad, the roads impassable for anything except such an army as he had, and I should not have thought of ordering such a move." Still, for the moment Grant put his order on hold. He informed Major General Henry W. Halleck in Washington, who in turn told Sherman that for the present he was to "retain your entire force [in Georgia] . . .

and . . . operate from such base as you may establish on the coast." Almost as an afterthought, Halleck closed his dispatch with late-breaking news: "It is reported that Thomas defeated Hood yesterday near Nashville, but we have no particulars nor official reports, tele-graphic communication being interrupted by a heavy storm."

*　　*　　*

The battle referred to by Halleck actually took place over two days—December 15 and 16—across the open fields and hills just south of Nashville. Following the bloody fight at Franklin, General John B. Hood had stubbornly stuck to his plan by trailing after the retreating Union force until he stopped just short of Nashville on December 1, where he ran out of ideas. Major General George Thomas had used the time allotted him to ring the city with a belt of defensive works that would have given pause to a fresh, well-equipped enemy. Hood's was neither. More to the point, many of the troops that Sherman had long ago credited in the plus column had finally arrived. Despite his disadvantageous position, Hood, in a decision that remains controversial and perplexing to this day, spread his 21,000 infantry across the high ground in sight of Nashville's defenses, boldly confronting Thomas's 50,000.

The period from December 1 to 14 was marked with useless side actions initiated by Hood, much suffering on the part of his men, and an increasingly acerbic barrage of messages from Washington to Thomas, urging him to attack. Hardly had Hood's foot soldiers settled into place before he sent off his 6,000 cavalry under Major General Nathan B. Forrest to chew up some strategically unimportant railroad blockhouses as well as keeping an eye on 8,000 Yankees occupying Murfreesboro. Thomas, taking great care to properly position his forces, still hoping to get sufficient horses for his mostly dismounted cavalry, and trying to gauge the fickle weather for a viable operational window, had his deliberate progress interpreted as fatal indecision by a nervous War Department and U. S. Grant.

On December 6, Grant ordered: "Attack Hood at once and await no longer the remount of your cavalry." Thomas dutifully set December 10 as the date to commence operations, only to see his force pummeled on December 9 by a sleet and ice storm that made all movement treach-erous. Fuming at his fair-weather central command near Petersburg,

Virginia, Grant vented his impatience by lining up a replacement for Thomas in the person of Major General John A. Logan, who should have been marching with Sherman, but who had been caught away on leave when the army decamped from Atlanta. Logan was dispatched to Nashville with orders to relieve Thomas if no offensive was under way by the time he arrived.

After he had departed, Grant, who shared Sherman's lower opinion of political generals (of which Logan was one), decided that he had better go in person. He left Petersburg on December 14, reaching Washington that evening. There he found that telegraphic communication with Thomas was cut owing to the terrible weather. There was nothing to do but wait until the situation was clarified. The message that finally came through on December 15, followed by others the next day, carried news of victory—a great and complete success.

Thomas attacked Hood on December 15, feinting against his enemy's right, which enabled him to fall like an avalanche on his left. Badly outnumbered, debilitated by lack of supplies, and stung by the same weather that had slowed Thomas, Hood's men savagely resisted. By day's end, however, the Confederate army had not only been shoved off its line but pressed back two miles into a second, more compact defensive position. Thomas repeated the offensive program on December 16, this time crushing Hood's left flank. At the end of the day, the Army of Tennessee wasn't in retreat, it was in flight. In the words of one Indiana soldier: "They all scampered."

Hood's initial report to Richmond regarding the debacle was an exercise in denial. Yes, his army had retreated from Nashville, but its casualties had been very small, and he was moving to a new defensive position. Had Hood bothered to ask the common soldiers in his ranks, he would have learned that his once-proud legions were now, according to one of them, "the worst broke down set I ever saw." The only saving grace for the Rebel army was the less than vigorous pursuit by Thomas. Bedeviled by bad weather, snarled logistics, and quibbling commanders, Thomas's men did little more than herd the remnants of Hood's force southward. Only Major General Forrest seemed to know what to do and how to get it done. Several times his men successfully executed delaying actions that further slowed the triumphant pursuers.

The campaign ended on December 28, when Hood withdrew into

Alabama, allowing Thomas to halt his exhausted command at the Tennessee River. At the cost of 6,000 killed, wounded, or missing, George H. Thomas had whittled down Hood's army from the 21,000 soldiers fighting to hold outside Nashville to less than 15,000 dispirited men who crossed the Tennessee River, heading south.

Thomas had done what Sherman had asked of him; indeed, what Sherman had needed done if his own campaign was to be crowned with success. In the years following the war, while Sherman would readily acknowledge the importance of the Nashville victory, there was always a qualification in his praise. Thomas, said the General in his *Memoirs*, "was slow, deliberate and almost passive in the face of exasperating danger, but true as steel when the worst came."

* * *

Sherman's operational orders for December 16 included the return of an old theme—railroad wrecking. Captain Poe was told to finish the remaining track-twisting in the immediate Savannah vicinity. For the men of Poe's primary unit, the 1st Michigan Engineers, the new orders merely extended what they had been doing since December 11. This day proved a little more exciting. "Our company tore down a bridge," scribbled one Michigan technician. "The Rebs fired upon us, and we returned the fire." Major General Howard was instructed to select two Right Wing divisions to knock out the Savannah and Gulf Railroad as far south as the Altamaha River. Howard picked Hazen's division from the Fifteenth Corps, plus Major General Joseph A. Mower's from the Seventeenth, for the task. Since the latter had drawn the stretch nearest the Altamaha River, those soldiers set off today.

There was major construction to match the destruction. By Special Orders No. 308, Lieutenant Colonel Andrew Hickenlooper, inspector general for the Seventeenth Corps, was "hereby placed in charge of the building of the wharf at King's Bridge." Hickenlooper found himself commanding what he later tallied as "a total force of about 600 skilled mechanics, 150 experienced axemen, 300 detailed men, six wagons, two saw mills, and a fleet of boats of various sizes." Within three days, his laborers completed what he proudly described as "fine a dock and wharf as was ever constructed for the accommodation of the commerce of any city."

On the siege lines the business of war continued with few interrup-

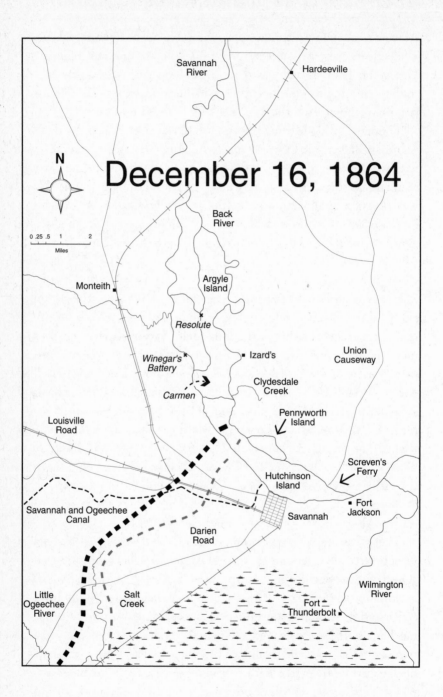

December 16, 1864

Savannah
River

Hardeeville

Back
River

Argyle
Island

Resolute

Monteith

Izard's

Union
Causeway

*Winegar's
Battery*

Clydesdale
Creek

Carmen

Pennyworth
Island

Louisville
Road

Hutchinson
Island

Screven's
Ferry

Savannah and Ogeechee
Canal

Savannah

Fort
Jackson

Darien
Road

Little
Ogeechee
River

Salt
Creek

Fort
Thunderbolt

Wilmington
River

tions. "Johnnies have thrown a few shells most too close to be really safe," wrote an Ohioan in his journal. "Sharpshooting rather sharp today." Farther along the line a Michigan soldier noted that the Rebels "make us lay uncomfortably low some times & between shot, shell, grape & canister & sharp shooters we have all we want to do to avoid them."

While most of the diary keepers recorded only routine matters this day, at least one stared death in the face. Captain William E. Fisher received orders this evening to take his command (Company D, 17th New York) to occupy some breastworks situated within point-blank range of a large Rebel fort. "Now thinks I," wrote Fisher, "the man who ordered me there must be a D——d fool, but go I must." To make matters worse, the only approach was along a narrow road with swamps on either side. Fisher cautioned his men "to keep closed up and march without noise." A providential cloud blocked the moon, so the detail made it undetected to the breastworks, which proved to be "nothing but a hole with a bank about three feet through to cover my company from the shots of a 64-pounder," said Fisher. His men dubbed the place "Fort Useless," and the young officer was certain that when they were discovered at daylight, the Rebel cannon would blast his little company out of existence. Nature now intervened by providing a thick blanket of fog to accompany the recall orders, which reached the officer in the early morning. Sighed Fisher when they had all safely returned to their camp, "We were very lucky."

Finding the next meal was still very much on everyone's mind. "Rations are getting shorter every day," worried a New Yorker. "The men are anxious to take the city as they know they will have plenty of rations when they get there." Some officers decided not to wait until the cracker line was operating, so a number of foraging parties were dispatched this day. It was a brigade-sized force that left the Fourteenth Corps' rear area, crossed the Ogeechee River at King's Bridge, then set course for Hinesville. For others the effort and results were on a smaller scale. "I manage to get potatoes enough for supper, by digging about an hour in an old potato patch," said one Illinois soldier.

A number of fortunate units would remember December 16 for reasons having nothing to do with food. "Received a large mail from our Northern friends," exclaimed an Illinois diarist. "What a scene our camp presents as the boys are scattered here and there, perusing the letters just received from loved ones a thousand miles or more away, and talking over with each other the news from home; some, it is true, mingled with sadness, as they learn for the first time of the death of some near or dear friend, or other misfortune . . . , but, with very few exceptions, all seem happy, and we all utter the silent prayer, deep down in our heart, 'God bless our dear ones at home.' "

"This last trip through Rebeldom had made letters a priceless boon," contributed a Wisconsin man, who also engaged in the complementary pleasure of responding. "I never knew what luxury there was in writing, until I was debarred the privilege," he said. The postmaster for the First Division, Fourteenth Corps, reported that the "three hundred dollars' worth of stamps which I obtained for the Division was only a fraction of what were wanted for the first mail out from Savannah and I was kept busy franking letters that there were no stamps for." Homesickness washed across the letter-reading camps, a feeling accentuated that evening when a Rebel band on the other side played "Home, Sweet Home." Confessed one Yankee after that performance: "Some of us felt blue."

Included among this day's letter writers was William Tecumseh Sherman, who wrote to his wife, Ellen. Sherman's pride in his own accomplishments and that of his men was evident as he described the cheers the sailors gave him ("the highest honor at sea"), the trust his men placed in him ("The soldiers think I know everything and that they can do anything"), and his strong feelings for them ("I never saw a more confident army"). It was clear to the General what his army had accomplished in the March to the Sea and why: "We have destroyed nearly 200 miles of Railroad and are not yet done. . . . We lived Sumptuously, turkeys, chickens and sweet potatoes all the way, but the poor women & children will starve. All I could tell them was, if Jeff Davis expects to found an empire on the ruins of the South, he ought to afford to feed the People."

Sherman also shared insights with his wife regarding his next military moves. "I have some heavy guns coming from Port Royal, and as soon as they come I shall demand the surrender of Savannah, but will not assault, as a few days will starve out its Garrison about 15,000, and its People [about] 25,000," he told her. In closing, he revealed an impish side not often seen by his men or staff: "Await events and Trust to Fortune. I'll turn up when & where you least expect me."

Sherman didn't mention the visit he'd had with his postmaster, Colonel A. H. Markland. "I've brought you a message from the President," Markland said at their meeting. "He asked me to take you by the hand wherever I met you and say 'God bless you and the army.' He has been praying for you." Sherman thought a moment. "I thank the President," he said at last. "Say my army is all right."

In a subsequent reference to Lincoln's gesture, Sherman added that he felt "thankful for his high favor. If I disappoint him in the future, it shall not be from want of zeal or love to the cause."

Argyle Island was the hot spot along the opposing lines. Taking full advantage of the limited sanction Sherman granted him, Major General Slocum upped the Union presence there from two regiments to a full brigade. By now Colonel Carmen and his staff had a system of transferring men across from the Georgia mainland down to a fine art, so little time was lost in transporting them. Once they were landed, the newcomers were treated to a somewhat unsettling sight for soldiers used to seeking cover. "A rice field as far as the eye could reach," was a New York soldier's assessment, "level as a plain." A diarist in a companion Empire State regiment added that the troops crossed the broad rice fields in single-file formation.

Once they reached the small building complex where the rice was being processed, the Yankee boys encountered the local slaves, who were getting a crash course in capitalism. At first, commented a Federal, "any quantity of rice was to be had, and at almost any price, as the negroes did not know a ten-cent stamp from a five-dollar bill." Before long, however, the slaves "knew enough to say 'one dollah' whenever they were asked the price of rice." Hardly had the brigade assembled near the mills when the Rebels across the river opened an artillery battery from the opposite shore; meanwhile, a gunboat downriver joined in the chorus, catching Colonel Carmen's men in a vicious crossfire.

A Massachusetts soldier termed the enemy's barrage "annoying, stopping the rice-mill, and forcing the troops to lie all day behind a dike." "They made excellent practice & set one of the storehouses on fire, burning it to the ground," confirmed a comrade in the Bay State regiment. "Even while lying near that old mill under the splinters flying thick in every direction," chimed in a New Jersey officer, "[I] had to laugh at a negro, dropping in, get under a big load of bed clothes as a shell whistled occasionally by me."

Colonel Carmen decided to do something about his predicament by detailing some riflemen from the 3rd Wisconsin to harass the land-based gunners. "I was sent with my Company to get as close as possible to them on our side of the river, and either silence them or drive them off," reported Captain Julian Hinkley. "I got up within about a hundred and fifty yards of them and opened fire. They immediately turned their guns on us, and for a few minutes gave it to us hot." Hinkley's firing line was along the riverbank, with the men standing in the cold water. One of the shooters later avowed that the "lads of the company made it interesting for the rebels, in spite of chattering teeth." By the time a relief party from the 2nd Massachusetts replaced the Wisconsin riflemen, the enemy battery had departed for more peaceful climes. "We blazed away, but were replied to only by musketry," said a Bay Stater. "I think we hit some of them as we could hear them holler several times just as we fired."

The exchange of gunfire eventually sputtered into a sullen silence. For what it was worth, Carmen's brigade was now in undisputed possession of Argyle Island, though most of the soldiers who had made it so could not imagine why anyone cared. Observed one New Jersey officer: "Gen. Sherman does not seem in any hurry to take the city."

One officer who was in a hurry to get into Savannah was General Beauregard, who left Charleston at 8:00 A.M. bound for the city. He tarried a bit at the headquarters of Major General Samuel Jones, whose troops were holding the roadway open between those two points. When Beauregard got near Pocotaligo, he detrained for a transfer to wagons in order to sidle past the section of track threatened by the Yankee batteries. The long-distance enemy fire had yet to damage the line, but Beauregard did not want to risk a lucky hit that could close the passageway. Once beyond the danger zone, Beauregard's staff piled onto another train that carried them near to the now destroyed Savannah River Bridge, where they took to the roads.

When Beauregard reached the city at 11:00 P.M., he could not help but notice that the pontoon bridge he had told Hardee to build was, in the estimation of one of his aides, "only about one-third constructed." The problem was a lack of boats. Hardee's engineers had decided that the flat barges used to transport rice or cotton would serve the purpose, so the search was on to find enough of them. When one of Hardee's subordinates protested that assigning troops to gather in the craft would disrupt plans he had to strike the enemy occupying Argyle Island, the general answered that the "attack is of no importance when compared with that of getting the flats into the river and down to Savannah."

The clock was ticking. There were ominous signs that Savannah's once firm resolve was beginning to soften. Anticipating the orders to evacuate, some overeager officers ordered warehouses stocked with army provisions opened, "and all persons were told to help themselves." A soldier on the scene thought it a "very questionable mode of defending a city, but a good example to be followed in good time and in good order by any who prefer to give or sell provisions to Confederate soldiers and their families rather than to hoard them up for raiders and Yankee invaders and plunderers." Even more chilling, there were additional desertions from the battalion of enemy POWs—twenty-seven of them in one instance. Two of the unfortunates, captured before reaching the Union lines, were subjected to interrogation, where they revealed a plot that threatened to compromise Savannah's defenses.

SATURDAY, DECEMBER 17, 1864

The officer commanding the leading division in the Gulf and Savannah Railroad wrecking expedition was less than pleased with his assignment. "My time [for this operation] was limited to five days," complained Major General Joseph A. Mower. "This limitation of time would make it necessary for me to march twenty miles per day, and give me one day in which to destroy twenty miles of railroad." Still, orders were orders. "Broke camp at daylight," recorded an Illinois soldier, "heavy fog—country flat—bog—trees dripping with dew—small bridge broke through—halt." The forced pace took its toll. "Saw Men sun struck," scrawled an Illinois diarist. Mower's command camped for the night around Midway Church, where the foraging began to resemble former times during the March to the Sea. "We got some sweet potatoes and negro peas so we had a good supper," commented a Hoosier in the 25th regiment.

Those soldiers in Brigadier General William B. Hazen's Fifteenth Corps division, part of the same mission, were no more pleased with their assignment than was Mower. "Leaving camp before the steamers with commissary supplies had arrived at King's Bridge, the regiment could draw no government rations and the country afforded very little besides rice," growled an infantryman in the 55th Illinois. "The very fatiguing labor of tearing up the track, added to the insufficiency of food, proved severe upon the men." An officer in the nearby 47th Ohio reported that one "man in Company B gave out on this march and died tonight."

Moving in parallel with these two divisions was a brigade of soldiers from the Fourteenth Corps whose sights were set solely on foraging. These columns moved through "a low level[,] wet & mostly timbered country" that so disoriented the men that several were certain that "we are in the state of Florida." For most it was a hungry tramp until late in the day, when they struck bonanza. "I shot a hog as the Regiment camped and skinned out a ham and Lieut. Starbuck had some yams and we got a square meal and we done it Justice," sighed a contented member of the 75th Indiana. "I thought I was hollow to my toes." A comrade in the 105th Ohio agreed that "there was plenty & such a time as we had eating. It's wonderful how often & how much a half-starved man can eat in a given time."

Back along the siege lines more and more regiments bid welcome to their mail carriers. "Card-playing stopped," noted an Indiana man in the 22nd regiment, "and all read the news from home." In the 85th Illinois "the hearts of the men were made glad" by the mail, while a soldier in the 147th Pennsylvania would affirm "how glad we were to hear from our loved ones again." "The 29th presents the appearance of a vast reading room today," marveled an Ohioan, "as our mail has once more arrived and it is greedily devoured after some five weeks being passed without hearing from the 'outer world.'" One reader-respondent was rather rudely reminded that there was a war going on. "Rebels shell while I was writing and [hit] the limbs of a tree right over me so I change position," recorded a nonchalant correspondent in the 16th Wisconsin.

Almost all the Confederate defensive effort this day was limited to artillery. "We lie in a swampy piece of woods within good musket [range] (though for the heavy timber out of sight) of the Rebel works," wrote an Ohio soldier. "By way of amusement they shell the heavy timber we are in and [today] . . . they fired half a dozen times into our camp with grape-shot. Nobody was hurt. These shells splinter the trees nastily." "Our pickets are so close that they call to each other," added a New Yorker, "and when they send a shell the rebels will say 'How do you like that, Yanks?' and the first thing you know, over goes a shower of bullets from our boys."

On Argyle Island, Colonel Ezra Carmen began the day with orders to land a hundred-man recon force on the South Carolina shore. To his immense frustration, the tide was ebbing, dropping the river level too low for the heavy barges he intended to use; since there simply weren't enough shallow-draft craft to be found, the operation had to be scrubbed. Today's main accomplishment was to keep the rice mills operating despite harassing fire from a Rebel horse battery that once more appeared across the way. "One of ours answered," noted a Massachusetts soldier, "& soon shut them up."

In sharp contrast to taking Fort McAllister, Major General Sherman initially approached the capture of Savannah in a very methodical and thorough manner. With a supply line now open, he was already receiving the heavy-caliber siege cannon he needed to pound the city into submission. The bulky, unwieldy tubes took time to wrestle along the marshy roads into firing positions, which also had to be prepared. Still, Sherman saw no reason why he shouldn't go on the record with an official call to Lieutenant General Hardee to capitulate in order to save Savannah's citizens from harm. Accordingly, as Sherman recollected, "I rode from my headquarters . . . over to General Slocum's headquarters, . . . and thence dispatched (by flag of truce) into Savannah, by the hands of Colonel [Charles] Ewing, inspector-general, a demand for the surrender of the place."

HEADQUARTERS MILITARY DIVISION OF THE MISSISSIPPI
In the field, near Savannah, Ga., December 17, 1864.
General WILLIAM J. HARDEE,
Commanding Confederate Forces in Savannah:

GENERAL: You have doubtless observed from your station at Rosedew that sea-going vessels now come through Ossabaw Sound and up

Ogeechee to the rear of my army, giving me abundant supplies of all kinds, and more especially heavy ordnance necessary to the reduction of Savannah. I have already received guns that can cast heavy and destructive shot as far as the heart of your city; also, I have for some days held and controlled every avenue by which the people and garrison of Savannah can be supplied; and I am therefore justified in demanding the surrender of the city of Savannah and its dependent forts, and shall await a reasonable time your answer before opening with heavy ordnance. Should you entertain the proposition I am prepared to grant liberal terms to the inhabitants and garrison; but should I be forced to resort to assault, and the slower and surer process of starvation, I shall then feel justified in resorting to the harshest measures, and shall make little effort to restrain my army—burning to avenge a great national wrong they attach to Savannah and other large cities which have been so prominent in dragging our country into civil war. I inclose you a copy of General Hood's demand for the surrender of the town of Resaca, to be used by you for what it is worth.

I have the honor to be, your obedient servant,

W. T. SHERMAN,
Major-General.

[Inclosure]

HEADQUARTERS ARMY OF TENNESSEE
In the Field, October 12, 1864.
TO THE OFFICER COMMANDING U.S. FORCES AT
RESACA, GA.:

SIR: I demand the immediate and unconditional surrender of the post and garrison under your command, and should this be acceded to, all white officers and soldiers will be paroled in a few days. If the place is carried by assault no prisoners will be taken.

Most respectfully, your obedient servant,

J. B. Hood,
General.

After dispatching the message, Sherman was talking with Slocum when an aide appeared with a matter for the Left Wing commander's attention. Receiving a nod in response, the staff officer waved over Colonel Ezra Carmen, who had arrived from Argyle Island to better understand how his little effort fit into the larger picture. Not one to be intimidated by high rankers, Carmen stood before the two senior commanders to explain how feasible it would be to push two brigades onto the South Carolina shore to cut the Union Causeway. When Sherman mentioned the danger from Rebel gunboats, Carmen expressed confidence in the field artillery's ability to drive them off. Sherman lapsed into a moody silence, and Carmen shut his mouth. "My rank did not permit me to press the matter," he later wrote, "though I thought a great opportunity was being lost."

William J. Hardee had his hands full this day suppressing a mutiny in the battalion of troops recruited from disaffected Union prisoners of war. The two would-be deserters captured yesterday revealed an imminent plot among the men to immobilize their officers, spike their cannon, then surrender en masse to the Federals. Wasting no time, Hardee struck fast and hard. According to an officer in the city's garrison, the battalion camp "was suddenly surrounded by detachments from the 55th Georgia, and by Jackson's Augusta battalion, and two field-guns loaded with canister were brought to bear on them. The men were deprived of their arms, and the ringleaders, five in number . . . were seized. These, and the two privates apprehended the previous night in the act of deserting to the enemy, were tried by a drum-head court martial, on their own confessions convicted of mutiny and intended desertion to the enemy, sentenced and executed." The impressed battalion was then "marched under guard to Savannah where it was closely watched during the rest of the siege."

When he wasn't handling this matter, Hardee was planning the military evacuation with Beauregard. Both officers were operating with consciences cleared by official sanction from Richmond. Beauregard had received the confirmation he sought for his decision to abandon Savannah after making "the fullest possible defense consistent with the safety of the garrison." Hardee was the recipient of a personal note from President Jefferson Davis, assuring him that the cupboard had been scoured for possible reinforcements but that the shelves were bare. Davis cautioned Hardee to "make the dispositions needful for the preservation of your army."

The arrival of Sherman's surrender demand forced them to set aside their work, and "after full consultation," a response was crafted. Though dated December 17, it would not pass through the lines until the next day. One of Beauregard's aides thought that Hardee's riposte was "clear, firm, to the point. It was written with moderation and dignity, and in that respect was in contrast with the communication of the Federal commander."

HDQRS. DEPT. OF S. CAROLINA, GEORGIA, AND FLORIDA,
Savannah, Ga., December 17, 1864.

Maj. Gen. W. T. SHERMAN,
Commanding Federal Forces, near Savannah, Ga.:

GENERAL: I have to acknowledge receipt of a communication from you of this date, in which you demand "the surrender of Savannah and its dependent forts," on the ground that you have "received guns that can cast heavy and destructive shot into the heart of the city," and for the further reason that you "have for some days held and controlled every avenue by which the people and garrison can be supplied." You add that should you be "forced to resort to assault, or to the slower and surer process of starvation, you will then feel justified in resorting to the harshest measures, and will make little effort to restrain your army," &c. The position of your forces, a half a mile beyond the outer line for the land defenses of Savannah, is, at the nearest point, at least four miles from the heart of the city. That and the interior line are both intact. Your statement that you "have for some days held and controlled every avenue by which the people and garrison can be supplied" is incorrect. I am in free and constant communication with my department. Your demand for the surrender of Savannah and its dependent forts is refused. With respect to the threats conveyed in the closing paragraphs of your letter, of what may be expected in case your demand is not complied with, I have to say that I have hitherto conducted the military operations intrusted to my direction in strict accordance with the rules of civilized warfare, and I should deeply regret the adoption of any course by you that may force me to deviate from them in the future.

I have the honor to be, very respectfully, your obedient servant,

W. J. HARDEE,
Lieutenant-General

A Union staff officer familiar with the exchange of messages afterward noted that "both [Sherman and Hardee were] 'only talking,' and both knew it."

SUNDAY, DECEMBER 18, 1864

Messages between Grant and Sherman crossed each other in transit today; Grant's gracefully conceding to Sherman, Sherman's still tactfully pressing his argument. Now that it was official that Sherman's force had safely reached the coast, Grant was able to formally praise his subordinate "on the successful termination of your most brilliant campaign." Then, after grumbling again about how hard it had been for him to get George Thomas moving, Grant did allow that he "has done magnificently [at Nashville], however, since he started." This victory, coupled with some minor successes elsewhere, caused Grant to reconsider, and then cancel, his earlier orders for Sherman to join him in Virginia. Once more he was ready to defer to the older man's judgment. "I want to get your views about what ought to be done and what can be done," he wrote. Grant closed his note: "I subscribe myself, more than ever, if possible, your friend."

Sherman's missive, composed before Grant's arrived, opened with a summary of recent events. The General felt the need to rebut several points made by Hardee in his rejection of Sherman's demand. Then he went on to make sure Grant understood that the obstacles standing in the way of his transferring his army to Virginia—dense fogs, mud banks in the Ogeechee River, only six feet of low-tide water at the loading wharf—would inevitably result in "more delay than you anticipate."

Regarding the capture of Savannah, Sherman's thinking had jumped from slow but sure, to faster even if more costly. "I still hope that events will give me time to take Savannah," said Sherman, "even if I have to assault with some loss." In his *Memoirs*, Sherman said that from the moment he received Hardee's "letter declining to surrender" he had decided that "nothing remained but to assault." Orders were issued this day to his wing commanders "to make the necessary preparations at once for assaulting the place." Sherman's planning at this stage had little finesse. "I . . . resolved to make the attempt to break his line of defense at several places," he said, "trusting that some one would succeed."

For all his tough talk, Sherman was loath to spend lives on taking Savannah if there was a less costly way of winning the prize. "Of course I must fight when the time comes," he admitted to his daughter Minnie before the start of the Georgia campaign, "but wherever a result can be accomplished without Battle I prefer it." The best way to achieve that result was to pinch off Hardee's connection to Charleston, and the force best placed to do that was Foster's. Sherman said to Foster: "It is all important that the railroad and telegraph wire should be broken between the Savannah River and Charleston." Sherman was hoping for a "bold rush," but he was realist enough to realize he was pushing a weak reed. If a bold rush wasn't possible, Sherman was content to let Foster's men "whale away with their 30-pounder Parrotts and break the road with cannon balls," something they hadn't been able to accomplish in several days of trying.

The longer Sherman mulled it over, the greater seemed the risks in allowing Major General Slocum to pursue the same objective by sliding the Twentieth Corps across the Savannah River via Argyle Island, or even Hutchinson Island just below it. In making this argument to himself, the General reasoned that "the enemy held the river opposite the city with iron-clad gunboats, and could destroy any pontoons laid down by us between Hutchinson's Island and the South Carolina shore, which would isolate any force sent over from that flank." Haunted by a notorious defeat in the first year of the war when a Federal force was pinned against the Potomac River and almost annihilated, Sherman vowed not "to make a mistake like 'Ball's Bluff' at that period of the war."

Had he not been so determined to push the Foster option, a thoughtful review of his initial objections to Slocum's suggestion would have revealed greater possibilities than he imagined. The Confederate Savannah River Squadron had but one fully operational ironclad in its arsenal, which could only reach Argyle Island with its guns from extreme range at high tide. The next largest gunboat (wooden) was in a similar fix. Slocum's men had already demonstrated with the capture of the *Resolute* that a well-sited land battery could successfully engage timbered gunboats. Also, Colonel Carmen's men had become very adept at moving troops by barge, a process that could be easily halted and concealed when an enemy smokestack was sighted. There were risks in such an operation. Where Sherman misjudged was in assessing them. Ultimately, his decision to push Foster to do more would take extra time—something, as it turned out, he did not have.

On the southern front, the first elements of Hazen's division (Fifteenth Corps) "commenced taring up the [rail]rode and twisting the irons," according to an Indiana soldier. The brigade he was in, added an Ohio comrade, "went to work at once tearing, burning the railroad, twisting the iron rails, and destroying the telegraph wires and poles." Farther south along the right-of-way, Mower's division of the Seventeenth Corps was yet tramping to reach its assigned work zone. Still, the soldiers managed to find time to forage liberally on the countryside. Several regiments visited Walthourville, which one Yankee described as "a small aristocratic village, situated in a pine grove—pretty churches—residences vacated." "There we got some corn meal and killed hogs," added a Hoosier, "as they were the first chance we had to kill hogs since we had been in the [county], . . . we lived sumptuously that night and grew fat."

Operating in the same neighborhood was a brigade from Baird's Fourteenth Corps division, whose sole concern was getting grub. The men located all they needed near Hinesville, where one of them remembered that they "found plenty of sweet potatoes, rice & corn with which we loaded up our teams." One detachment swung around toward Riceboro, passing Midway Church, which provided an Indiana boy a cause to meditate upon the people who built and used it. In the end, he was "glad after all to know that the citizens once knew one who was able to help in time of trouble."

More than one of Baird's soldiers took stock of the large number of alligators lurking in the swampy areas. This night a 75th Indiana enlisted man decided to play a joke on his recently acquired black servant, who was terrified of the creatures. Sending him into the swamp to fetch wood, the soldier trailed along out of sight, waiting until they had gone deep enough into the morass before making a convincing splashing sound in the water. The servant immediately dropped his load of kindling to race back to camp, where he babbled a vivid tale of his encounter with the terrible monster. The laughing soldier tried to explain it was all a joke, but the frightened black refused to reenter the swamp. The prankster now had to fetch his own firewood, leaving him to wonder "whether the joke is on him or me."

Immediately west of Savannah, the throaty grumble of artillery provided a steady backdrop to the day as the city's defenders reacted quickly to provocative acts or just followed a prearranged program of harassing fire. The members of one Wisconsin regiment found themselves camped with Yankee guns behind them and Rebel cannon in front. The enemy's "bombs, shells, and balls . . . would go over our heads," said one in the unit. "Our batteries would reply by also shooting over our heads, so we were between two fires. But we were safer than if we had been on the firing line. Sometimes a ball would come low and break off a limb of a tree, but we could dodge the limbs."

The engineers of the 58th Indiana labored throughout this day building fascines—stout bundles of rice straw fifteen inches in diameter, seven and a half feet long, stiffened with a pole through the center core, all held together by Confederate telegraph wire. Soldiers advancing to the attack would each tote a bundle for deposit into ditches or quicksand marshes as instant corduroy. The officer in charge, Colonel George P. Buell, set up something of an assembly line in the camp. The various fascine components were stacked in construction order so that the men could walk from one workstation to the next, building their bundle as they progressed. The task continued well after sunset, as the engineers turned out 700 of them. "It looks very romantic this evening to see the men making fascines by candle light," observed a member of the regiment.

Sometimes directives to *prepare* for an assault were corrupted in transmission into orders to *launch* an assault. One such instance this day was recollected by a soldier in the 147th Pennsylvania: "Our Division was drawn up in line of battle and arrangements were made to carry the enemy's works in our front by a night attack. The night was cold, dark and dreary, and as we were not allowed to build fires to keep warm, for fear of arousing the suspicions of the enemy, and as may readily be conceived, we suffered considerably. At about 12 o'clock midnight the order was countermanded and the men were allowed to break ranks and retire for the night well pleased with the turn affairs had taken."

There was more action on Argyle Island as Confederates on the South Carolina side of the river made it clear that they didn't appreciate the Yankee squatters. During the night Colonel Carmen had hauled Captain Charles E. Winegar's Battery I, 1st New York Light Artillery, from the Georgia mainland to reposition it on the island. The gunners whose enthusiastic barrage had disabled the *Resolute* were equal to the task of suppressing the Rebel horse artillery that had been harassing the work details.

Even as the two sides were exchanging their mini-broadsides, Brigadier General Alpheus S. Williams, commanding the Twentieth Corps, met with Carmen and, as the colonel recollected, "informed me that Sherman had heard from Grant; that all was uncertainty at headquarters, and that for the present I make no effort to cross, and meanwhile to examine further up the island for an additional crossing, as he thought more men would be sent over." Later, about 9:00 P.M., Carmen received fresh orders. He was authorized to cross just two regiments to the South Carolina shore at dawn to establish a beachhead. The brigade commander was cautioned not to advance farther into the country than was consistent with establishing a prudent defensive line.

The aggressive officer, knowing that employing just two regiments would be enough merely to stir up a hornet's nest of trouble, strongly suspected he would have to commit his entire brigade before the little foray was over. He had already sought a blank check to reinforce any party he put over, and while he had not received specific approval, neither had he been told that he couldn't do so. Even before the operation began, Carmen had decided that unless otherwise directed, he would assume he had the necessary authority to reinforce the two regiments. Major General Sherman may have hesitated to directly challenge Rebel forces north of Savannah, but Colonel Carmen was proceeding with no such qualms. What it would do to Sherman's developing plans remained to be seen.

In Savannah, the Confederate high command was focused on getting out of town. "Active, urgent preparations for the evacuation were instantly begun," said a Beauregard aide. "It was now but a question of a few days." For once, Beauregard's anger had gotten some results. Work on the all-important pontoon bridge between Savannah and the South Carolina shore was being "prosecuted with . . . vigor," said his aide-de-camp. As part of the planning, Beauregard today completed a memo indicating where the various parts of Savannah's garrison were to report once they had left the city. Also given their life-or-death instructions were the ships of the Savannah River Squadron. The shallow-draft wooden gunboats were to try to break out upriver to Augusta; the deeper-drawing ironclad *Savannah* was to seek the open sea; and the nearly immobile ironclad *Georgia* was to be scuttled. A number of warships still under construction were to be burned to prevent their capture.

Even though he already knew the answer, General Beauregard addressed an appeal to Richmond for more troops, suggesting they be detached from General Robert E. Lee's army for service with him. Specifically requested were the divisions of major generals Robert F. Hoke and Bushrod R. Johnson, both of which contained a large proportion of Georgia, North Carolina, and South Carolina regiments. Beauregard's request was forwarded to Lee, who promptly threw the matter back into the lap of Jefferson Davis with the ultimatum: "If Hoke and Johnson are sent south it will necessitate the abandonment of Richmond with the present opposing force." There the matter ended.

Amazingly, only a few leaks about the ongoing planning reached the rank and file. A Confederate marine posted near the Little Ogeechee River wrote after the fact: "Of our weakness I was fully sensible and was convinced all along that should Sherman with his disciplined and hardened troops storm us, he could carry our works, yet the idea of evacuation had not entered my head, for we had been told that Genl. Hardee had decided to hold the City [at] all hazards. So when I was informed privately by a friend . . . [on December 18], even [before] some of our higher officers dreamed of it, that the place was to be abandoned, I could not realize it." A military telegrapher working in the city, in a letter written this day, acknowledged that Savannah's only hope was a miracle. "Our works are very strong," wrote Thomas Carolin Clay, "but pray we may look to the Almighty & not trust to our weak arms of flesh."

MONDAY, DECEMBER 19, 1864

Sherman's growing impatience to take Savannah, his nagging frustration over Foster's inability to close the back door, and the inevitable delays in communicating with the North now led the General to a fateful decision. As he had yet to receive Grant's December 18 note, he was still operating under the assumption that he would be personally taking the bulk of his army to Virginia. Sherman very much wanted Savannah in his pocket before then; believing that the only way he could motivate Foster was to confront him, the General decided to visit the timorous subordinate at his Hilton Head Island headquarters.

Before departing, Sherman dictated identical messages to major generals Howard and Slocum, advising them of his absence and instructing them "to push the preparations for attacking Savannah with all possible speed, but to await orders for the attack." Not specifically addressed was his earlier approval to Slocum's request to push a brigade across Argyle Island into South Carolina, "seemingly threatening in flank the movement of troops attempting to escape from Savannah." Either it slipped Sherman's mind or else he did not consider such an action sufficiently provocative to trigger a Savannah evacuation; otherwise he would have either called it off or refrained from visiting Foster until the enemy's reaction was known.

Sherman reached King's Bridge with his party at midday, just in time to prevent a major disruption to the all-important supply system. It required approximately 1,600 men to handle the security as well as manage the unloading and transfer of goods from boats to wagons sent by the various commands. Since December 16 these duties had been performed by Colonel Benjamin F. Potts's brigade (Seventeenth Corps), but when Sherman arrived at King's Bridge he was told by the acting provost marshal that Major General Blair had recalled Potts's troops, sending only two regiments (600 men) to replace them. Sherman was very annoyed. After ordering the two regiments back whence they came, he told Potts not to go anywhere. He fired off notes to Howard and Slocum, apprising them of the problem and directing them to detail one regiment (approximately 350 men) with 50 black pioneers from each corps to handle the workload at King's Bridge. Only when this body of men was fully assembled could Potts be released.

(Sherman's actions and orders ignited a tempest in a teapot, as it took time for the instructions to make their way through the wing commanders to their subordinate corps commanders. Before matters were straightened out, Major General Blair had ordered Colonel Potts arrested for failing to obey orders to join him, and the commissary of subsistence had figuratively crossed swords with Blair by refusing to release Potts's men from their duties.)

Sherman boarded an army tug at King's Bridge, then headed down the Ogeechee. He was anxious to contact Rear Admiral Dahlgren, who was scouting the Vernon River, planning the joint operation against its defensive batteries that he had discussed with Sherman during their meeting. When Sherman's tug finally located the *Harvest Moon* toward evening, the General came aboard. Dahlgren now learned that the combined army-navy push (Howard was to supply some troops) was canceled (a "great disappointment" to the rear admiral); but more importantly, he was informed of Grant's intention to transfer most of Sherman's army to Virginia. Dahlgren agreed to transport Sherman to Hilton Head for his personal meeting with Foster, a journey that the rear admiral estimated would take until dawn.

The destruction of the Savannah and Gulf Railroad remained on the daily agenda. "Still taring up the rode," scribbled a diarist in the 83rd Indiana, while others in the division set down their tools and "loaded the [wagon] train with corn & potatoes." Southward, Mower's division of the Seventeenth Corps finally arrived at its designated zone. "Moved out on the rail road and tore up track all day," recorded a member of the 64th Illinois. Liberty County's ordeal continued, as the soldier added: "Got lots of flour and meal." The Fourteenth Corps brigade that had been scouring the county as well made the turn for home today, "our teams all loaded," according to a Minnesota man. Their only complaint was that they had to "drink the water along the side of the road, which is nearly black as tar."

Now that supply vessels were arriving at King's Bridge, someone had the idea to fill them with contrabands for the return trip to Hilton Head, where Northern abolitionists had set up a model African-American community. For several days the blacks had been shunted into staging camps near King's Bridge. A soldier assigned to watch over one encampment never forgot how the escaped slaves "would sing hymns, pray and preach and hold out till nearly midnight, unless we ordered them to stop." Others enjoyed "plantation dances and frolics." The white soldiers found their "amusements . . . quite interesting."

The Fourteenth Corps staff officer, Major John A. Connolly (still drafting a note for newspaper publication regarding the incident he'd heard about Ebenezer Creek), watched with interest as the first contingent of blacks slated for transport were marched down to the departure wharf. "It was a strange spectacle to see those negroes of all ages, sizes, and both sexes, with their bundles on their heads and in their hands trudging along, they knew not whither, but willing to blindly follow the direction given to them by our officers." Once the procession reached King's Bridge, other Federal officers went among them, observed an Ohio guard, "and the men and boys, able bodied, are taken out to work for the government."

Up and down the siege lines preparations went ahead for the upcoming Savannah assault. In the Second Division, Twentieth Corps, there was a staff conference today "with view to the adoption of a plan for storming the enemy's works." Orders were issued to other commands to "make thorough reconnaissances of the grounds in their front; [and to] examine the approaches of the enemy's works which give the greatest promise of successful assault." In one such expedition, a detachment from the 7th Iowa used a small boat to ease up to the Rebel lines along Salt Creek. They found that "the opposite shore was low and marshy in many places, waist deep in mud," ruling out this avenue of approach. In returning to their supports, the reconnaissance party was spotted by Rebel artillerymen who "threw their shells among us, pretty lively for a while, but without doing us any injury," wrote a relieved Iowan.

Along with all this focused activity, typical siege operations continued as if nothing else were happening. An Iowa soldier noted that there was "some heavy cannonading and brisk skirmishing all along the lines." "We lay within 100 yds of their forts under constant fire and they don't hurt anybody," boasted a Michigan man this day, "only chop off trees with their shots. Our pursuits go on the same as if no enemy within 50 miles except when shells come down too close, everybody is out of sight into their holes like so many gophers."

Fate yet played an unpredictable hand. In the sector held by the First Brigade, Third Division, Seventeenth Corps, Major John M. Price of the 12th Wisconsin had just been promoted from captain, relieving him of all duties on the picket line. Nevertheless, he insisted on one final tour of duty, partly in order to examine an area being considered for a possible attack. According to Brigadier General Manning F. Force, who looked into the matter, Price, returning from his scout, approached a two-man picket post "upon one of the thread-like narrow dikes, [when] they took him for a rebel and challenged. He answered 'a friend' and kept advancing taking them for our men. As he came near they said something which he did not hear. He then observed one going around as if to get behind him, supposed he had come upon rebels, turned to run off and was shot." Price died the next day. "He was a fine officer in both appearance and soldierly qualities," mourned a comrade, "and was much beloved by all the men of the regiment."

The stakes were being dramatically raised this day on Argyle Island. At dawn and pursuant to orders, Colonel Ezra Carmen landed the 3rd Wisconsin followed by the 2nd Massachusetts onto the South Carolina shore at Izard's Plantation, near where a Rebel horse battery had been driven off by Captain Winegar on December 18. Incredibly, the Confederates had not picketed the place, so the Wisconsin boys splashed ashore "without opposition," as one of them stated. Behind them the 2nd Massachusetts piled onto the riverbank, also without trouble. "If they had had their guns where they were yesterday they could have knocked Hail Columbia out of us," observed a Bay State officer.

Skirmishers took up the advance, followed by the rest of the two regiments. "The rebs made but little opposition," said a Wisconsin officer. Colonel Carmen was about to stick his neck way out. Soon after the two regiments cleared the landing area, he signaled for the 13th New Jersey to come across as well, an action that he fully realized "exceeded . . . [my] instructions." The New Jersey soldiers began changing banks at 7:00 A.M. "It was known that the only avenue of escape left to Hardee, was across the river in our front," said one, "and it was intended, if possible, to cut them off." Confederate reaction may have been slow to develop, but develop it did. Beginning around 11:00 A.M., "the contest became severe and stubborn," reported Carmen, as his men began meeting more and more of Major General Wheeler's troopers supported by local militia. Nevertheless, by noon Carmen had advanced his line nearly two miles inland.

This despite a difficult terrain. "We came right across rice fields all cut up with ditches from 1 to 10 ft. wide," related a Massachusetts soldier, "which we had to get over as best we could; part of the way was through rice as high as our heads & all wet with dew." By 1:00 P.M. Carmen's progress was halted by an increasing enemy force backed with artillery. Seeing his bluff called and his bet raised, Carmen upped the ante. Orders went to Argyle Island for the rest of the brigade—the 107th and 150th New York regiments—to join their compatriots. As fast as the 107th landed, Carmen parceled it out; four companies to assist the 2nd Massachusetts, two to aid the 3rd Wisconsin, and five to extend the line. The men, said a member of the 107th, "had some severe work skirmishing."

By 4:00 P.M. Colonel Carmen had pushed his command to its limits. His four regiments (the 150th New York stood in reserve) held a "line nearly two and a half miles long, front and flanks well covered, and securely resisting Wheeler's persistent attempts to dislodge it." The officer dispatched a situation report to his division commander, admitting what he had done and requesting entrenching tools. With an entire brigade now fully committed to an enterprise authorized only for two regiments, Carmen's superior had little choice but to back him up by sending the tools along. Night found the colonel's men well posted, but isolated on the South Carolina shore. There was plenty of activity in the darkness as two cannon were hauled across the river to be positioned before more combat the next day. "I had not reached the [Union] causeway," Carmen later wrote, "but had given the enemy a good scare."

His evacuation plan finished and nearly ready for implementation, General Beauregard departed Savannah this morning for Charleston. The all-important floating bridge was almost completed. The first and longest leg (about 1,000 feet) began at the bottom of West Broad Street to connect with Hutchinson Island. On Hutchinson, a newly raised causeway snaked across the island to a second section of bridge carrying traffic to Pennyworth Island. A short causeway plugged into the third bridge between Pennyworth and the South Carolina shore. From there yet another temporary roadway linked up with the planked road known as Union Causeway—the Savannah garrison's only escape route.

The engineering detail under Captain Robert M. Stiles was still hustling to finish the last bridge section when Beauregard left. Lieutenant General Hardee accompanied his superior as far as the head of the elevated passageway, where they encountered Major General

Wheeler, with a report on his battle at Izard's—Colonel Carmen's fili-
bustering affair—now several hours old. Beauregard's sole focus was
successfully abandoning Savannah. "Gentlemen," he said, indicating
the smoke and musketry sounds coming from the river, "this is not a
demonstration; it is a real attack on our communications. You must get
out of Savannah as soon as possible."

The floating bridge upon which so much depended was not exactly
built to standard specs. Normal construction would have deployed
relatively small pontoon boats oriented perpendicular to the roadway,
but here the seventy-five- to eighty-foot-long barges (all that was available) were lined up end-to-end, moored in place with railroad car
wheels as anchors. Existing city wharves and associated buildings were
stripped for planking to be laid as flooring, which was then covered
with rice straw to muffle the sounds of wheels, feet, and hooves on
wood. There was a near tragedy when a number of the precious flats
intended for the crossing were destroyed by some of Wheeler's over-
zealous cavalrymen, who believed they were keeping them out of the
enemy's hands. The time it took to locate replacements, coupled with
unexpectedly heavy morning fogs along the river, further slowed completion of the bridge sections.

Hardee desperately wanted to evacuate this very night, but Captain
Stiles still wasn't finished at sundown. The experienced lieutenant
general, who had a good idea how long it would take for the entire
10,000-man garrison to make it over to the South Carolina shore, did
not want there to be anyone caught in the city at daylight. When the
engineers couldn't promise having the bridging task accomplished
until after 8:00 P.M., Hardee reluctantly rescheduled the military
movement to sunset December 20. That is, unless the enemy had
something to say about it.

TUESDAY, DECEMBER 20, 1864
Midnight–Sunset

The *Harvest Moon*, carrying Major General Sherman, arrived at Port
Royal about 8:00 A.M. A reporter present noted that there was "a general rush . . . to the dock to get a sight of the illustrious visitor. . . . The
General was looking peculiarly well, and seems fresh for another
march more extensive than the one he had just finished." Following a

breakfast at Foster's headquarters, and a "casual inspection of the Post," the two officers retired for a serious discussion.

Exactly what transpired between them is not recorded. Sherman in his *Memoirs* wrote that he "represented the matter to General Foster," who "promptly agreed to give his personal attention to it." Major Hitchcock was a tad more specific, noting that Sherman agreed to provide Foster with extra men to cut "off the only remaining avenue open from Savannah—the 'Union Causeway,' an old plank road running N.E. from the city to Hardeeville." These and other discussions kept Sherman occupied throughout the day.

Savannah's evacuation began at daylight. A Georgian serving with the provost guard remembered observing the long "lines of army wagons" that trundled onto the floating bridge "to seek the safety of the river on Carolina soil. Here and there could be seen a carriage whose owner had been fortunate to secure a passport." According to a South Carolinian who escaped: "Very few of the citizens [of Savannah] left the city. . . . All was uncertainty and doubt. Hope was mingled with fear, and it was difficult for any one to decide which preponderated in his own mind. . . . There was a pretty general hope that the city would be spared, but no one could give any substantial reason for this hope, having no certain grounds upon which to base it, and ignorant of the real condition kept them from arriving at a different conclusion and preparing for the worst."

Munitions were being shipped across with a haste that resulted in several boxes breaking open to spill their contents on the dock. When Lieutenant General Hardee observed this, he "became quite incensed, thinking the guns had been insecurely packed or piled up loose on the wagons," said an ordnance official. This individual realized the end was near when he received orders several days earlier to issue rattail files to the army. To anyone experienced with weapons, this could only mean "the spiking of artillery."*

---

* Muzzle-loading cannon ignited gunpowder through a small touch hole drilled into the barrel. Driving a pointed "spike" into the vent jammed it, or sometimes widened it, rendering the weapon useless.

Included in the evacuation scheme was all the light, easily portable artillery. Excluded were the much harder to move large-caliber guns, whose crews operated today free of previous restrictions on ammunition expenditure. "Our batteries were awake early this morning, even before I got up," wrote a member of the 50th Illinois. "Our skirmishers kept up their part of the tune." Another diarist, in the 9th Iowa, recorded that the opposing batteries "have kept up a regular war all day." "On account of getting so many shells into our camp they thought best to build breastworks in front . . . although we lay back in reserve in the woods," commented a soldier in the 29th Ohio. "Heavy cannonading all around the lines," added yet another soldier, this one in the 93rd Illinois, "so much it makes me nervous so that I can hardly write."

Cornelius R. Hanleiter, serving a battery along Savannah's southern river defenses, received orders at noon to destroy all government property that could not be quickly moved, then to prepare the light artillery for rapid movement. "This intimation of the intention of the Confederate authorities to evacuate Savannah, though suspected for a day or two, was anything but pleasant," he remembered. The orders caught the battery without sufficient horses to transport everything, so Hanleiter had the unenviable task of deciding what would be left behind. One easy decision was to ship provisions and bedding kept at the post to the part of town where many of the batterymen lived with their families. The officer consoled himself that at least the women and children would enjoy some comfort after the gunners were obliged to abandon them "to the tender mercies of the invaders."

It proved a nerve-racking day for Colonel Ezra Carmen, whose brigade was fighting hard to maintain its toehold on the South Carolina shore opposite Argyle Island. The Rebels in front were in greater strength and acting more aggressively than at any time since the Yankees had come ashore. Adding to his problems, a Rebel gunboat reached extreme range at high tide to begin pumping its monster shells into Carmen's cramped perimeter. The enemy gunners, noted the officer, "opened on our positions, and in fact on any object they could see, firing in nearly every direction of the compass." Only the falling tide forced the enemy ironclad to pull out of range.

What had begun as a grand adventure was being turned into a grim holding action. An increasingly frantic Carmen fired off three or four dispatches to his division commander requesting reinforcements, "yet I have not even an answer," he lamented in the afternoon. The once bold officer was now thinking the unthinkable. "If my command is sacrificed it will be because I have been left in an exposed position unsupported," he said.

At the same time, reports were reaching Carmen suggesting that something was stirring in Savannah. According to an officer from the 3rd Wisconsin, "From one portion of our line wagon trains can be seen leaving the City." Eager to view it for himself, Carmen climbed into the loft of a barn on his line. Scanning toward the Union Causeway he "could see wagons, family carriages, men and women on foot, singly and in groups, moving north along the road."

There were signs throughout Savannah that all was not well. A "crowd of women" gathered around the city's main arsenal, "supplied with pails and buckets," in response to a rumor that the building "contained provisions." Until the officials in charge managed to convince the women otherwise, it looked as if they intended "carrying it by storm," said an arsenal employee. No formal announcement had been made, yet the indications were plain enough. The daughters of one artillery commander helped their father distribute hoarded stores of clothes and blankets to his men. Late this morning the ladies called on acquaintances with the signal corps, only to find the men "busy burning dispatches."

The concern on everyone's mind was given voice by one of the provost guards, who said, "Sherman had burned Atlanta and had driven the helpless women and children into exile. What he would do to Savannah was a question often asked, but no one could answer."

A trickle of Confederate deserters made their way today through the no-man's-land to the Federal lines. "Sick of war and the rebel cause," recorded one Federal interrogator. "There has been a rumor to-day that they are evacuating the city, but the report is not credited," added a Wisconsin soldier. "It is stated by a deserter that the inhabitants are very anxious that the city should be surrendered, probably fearing that if they hold on, it will share the fate of Atlanta." Likely from such sources, Brigadier General John W. Geary was able to ascertain "that the enemy had completed a pontoon bridge from Savannah across to the South Carolina shore." The brigadier promptly "notified the general commanding corps of the discovery."

It was approaching 5:00 P.M. before Major General Sherman finished his business on Hilton Head Island, then reboarded Rear Admiral Dahlgren's flagship for the return run to Savannah. Atmospheric conditions outside had taken a turn for the worse, with a stiff wind blowing up from the southeast. In consequence, the General's party, recorded Major Hitchcock, "lost considerable time both in starting and on the way by very rough weather."

Sunset–Midnight

According to the master evacuation plan, as soon as darkness fell, all "light batteries will . . . be withdrawn by hand from their positions in line with as little noise as possible, and will be sent over the pontoon bridge to Hardeeville."

Also after sunset, Savannah's Board of Aldermen met with Mayor Richard D. Arnold in the City Exchange on Bay Street, where they received official notification that the army was decamping. With the news came the sobering realization that responsibility for the city's safety was passing from military hands into theirs. Somebody at Hardee's headquarters had copied them on Sherman's surrender demand, so the elected officials were only too aware of his threat to bombard Savannah, then turn his soldiers loose on the population. They quickly resolved to send a small delegation headed by the mayor to enter the Union lines at daybreak to surrender the city.

Up and down the Union siege lines, the coming of darkness left individual soldiers alone with thoughts of their own mortality. "It is feared that General Sherman contemplates an assault on these works of the enemy soon," reflected an Ohioan. "That means death to many of us, and we dread to hear of it." For many units, the only offensive plan was a straight-ahead advance through waist-deep waters under full obser-vation of the enemy. "I feel a cold shiver yet when I think of that order for the assault before daylight," recalled a Wisconsin man.

On the Seventeenth Corps front someone had the bright idea to have the men try out small ladders to help them cross the ditches and fortifi-cation walls. Watching the soldiers awkwardly rehearse with the clumsy objects, a Wisconsin officer realized with a start that the higher-ups were serious. "When we came to think how the Confederates could sweep the surface of the water with their cannon . . . , and that those who were, perhaps, only slightly wounded, must surely drown in their helplessness, the prospect of such a charge was not at all pleasing to us," he said. "I could not go to sleep again for a long time after that."

Per the Hardee-Beauregard evacuation plan, between 8:00 P.M. and 10:00 P.M. the troops manning the various river forts were to spike their guns, dump munitions in the water (no fires or explosions to alert the enemy), and march into South Carolina, using either the floating bridge or boat transport. Additionally, the 4,000 soldiers under Major General Ambrose Wright, holding the southernmost seven miles of the intermediate line, were to withdraw, pass through the town, and cross the river using the pontoon bridge. The last to leave would spike all cannon being abandoned, while the skirmish line screening the operation would remain in place until at least 10:30 P.M.

"I have no words to picture the gloomy bitterness that filled my breast on that dreary march through water, mud and darkness," related one of Wright's men. About the only ones glad to go were Brigadier General Samuel W. Ferguson's dismounted cavalry, who knew that once across the Savannah River, they would be reunited with their horses.

Before the city council's emergency session adjourned, those pres-ent (some prominent citizens had been invited to join the elected ones) heard from Captain Josiah Tattnall, commanding the Savannah River Squadron. Voices rose in protest when he mentioned a plan to burn several vessels still under construction in the shipyards, as it was pointed out that there was a great danger that flames would spread to nearby residences. Tattnall allowed that if the aldermen could round up fifty workmen, he would be able to sufficiently damage the ships to avoid having to set them ablaze. But it was too late for such deals. Even as the aldermen were departing from the City Exchange, a fire was seen in the distance where the shipyards were located, set by retreating troops under orders to leave nothing of military value behind. Three officials from the affected districts raced off to organize bucket brigades.

Elsewhere in Savannah the hundred-man provost detail was finding itself seriously overmatched by the mobs of mostly white looters. The unit had been divided into smaller squads that patrolled the downtown district. They would key in on the sounds of entryways being smashed open. "Men, women and children would force open a door but like hungry dogs after a bone, each for himself, indifferent to the property or rights of others, they would grab, smash, pull, tear, anything & everything, shoes, meat, clothes, soap, hats, whatever came to hand," said one of those tasked with maintaining order.

Many of the Rebel artillerists chose to dispose of their excess munitions by discharging it at the enemy. "The shelling to-night from the river battery and from their works in our front is unusually severe," recorded a New Yorker in the Twentieth Corps, "the flying pieces striking our tents and barking the trees." An Ohio comrade never forgot how the Rebels "opened their batteries full blast upon us," while a Pennsylvanian termed it "a severe artillery fire," and commented that "the shot and shell flew in and around us in liberal profusion."

Lieutenant General Hardee departed from Savannah with most of his staff on the steamer *Swan* not long after 9:00 P.M. One aide remained behind with a small detail charged with the responsibility of seeing that the escape route was held open long enough for the skirmish lines to pass through the city. An officer with the garrison took note of one unfortunate reality: "By reason of the lack of transportation many of the Confederate sick and wounded were left in hospital when Savannah was evacuated."

At 10:00 P.M. it was the turn of Major General Lafayette McLaws's 4,000 men, holding the critical center of the intermediate line, to commence their evacuation. Here too the cannon were to be spiked (at 11:00 P.M.), while the skirmish line held its place until half past midnight. "Our camp fires were left burning and our entire army . . . marched into Savannah," wrote a Georgia soldier. "I will never forget the event."

It fell to W. H. Mendel, a young man in the ranks of the 1st Georgia Reserves, to warn the ambulatory wounded in the hospitals along the retreat route. "Since my father was very ill and not expected to live, after performing my duty, I went to see him and to bid the family good bye," he recollected.

When the hour arrived for Baker's North Carolina Brigade to withdraw, the headquarters band got in its last licks by launching into a spirited rendition of "Dixie." In response, nearby Yankee pickets groaned, then shouted: "Played out! Played out!" One Tarheel long remembered the silent tramp along the road to the city "lined by the great live oak trees, with their long festoons of waving moss and vines which swing backward and forward, in the pale moonlight, and seemed to be ghosts of our departed hopes."

Not far offshore, those strong winds were piling up the waves, making it a slow and uncomfortable journey for the USS *Harvest Moon*, transporting Major General Sherman's party. The General's host, Rear Admiral Dahlgren, knew from experience that they would not reach the Savannah area until daylight. Sherman was unfazed. With his orders to Howard and Slocum not to initiate any offensive activity while the heavy siege guns were being installed, he wasn't expecting any dramatic changes in the situation there for at least the next twenty-four hours.

Major General Gustavus W. Smith was designated to extricate his 2,500 men from their positions northeast of the city starting at 11:00 P.M.

Guns being left behind were to be spiked by midnight, and the skir-mish line was to maintain the covering screen until 1:00 A.M. "I can't describe my feelings when we had to leave," wrote a Georgian, "desper-ate to think after 4 years of service that I have to leave my native state to the mercy of a ruthless enemy."

Neatly calculated schedules had a way of unraveling when faced with reality, and this night was no exception. Even with an hour or more head start, the troops coming up from Major General Wright's sector took a while to reach Savannah, so there was a tendency for the various streams of men to converge in town at about the same time. "The scene of our army crossing the Savannah river at midnight, with the aid of bonfires to prevent the horses and men from marching into the river and off the dikes into the water surrounding them, presented a panorama that I will always remember," wrote a Georgian. Said another: "As we passed through the city guns were firing in every direction, doors were being knocked down, women and children were screaming, and the devil to pay generally."

An artilleryman thought the "night was exceedingly dark, and everything seemed to move without system or direction. In the city, as we passed through, men were discharging their fire-arms and making the night hideous with their oaths and blasphemies; horsemen gal-loped about apparently without object and women . . . going hither and thither. On the roadside and alongside of the pontoons, all night long, men and horses were strewn in confusion—some struggling in the mud and water, others worn down with fatigue, and perhaps sick at heart and in body, resting or asleep."

WEDNESDAY, DECEMBER 21, 1864

More and more it was becoming apparent to the Union soldiers man-ning the siege lines that something out of the ordinary was happening in Savannah. An Illinois diarist in the Fifteenth Corps spotted a large fire burning there, while Brigadier General Geary of the Twentieth Corps could hear sounds that he intepreted as the movement of troops and wagons across a pontoon bridge. Inside the tight beachhead his men were holding on the South Carolina shore, Colonel Carmen could hear "the curses and yells and tramping of men . . . indicating plainly that the city was being evacuated."

Now the Confederate skirmish lines began to evaporate as the various commands slipped away into Savannah. When one Georgia officer made the rounds to pull in his posts, he found that all his men except one had already fled "to parts unknown." That one, an "old tried and true soldier," had grimly held his position even as those around him bugged out. Another officer nervously stared at his watch and worried that he was waiting too long. "I don't know what in the hell to do!" he muttered to one of his men. That soldier's advice was brief and to the point: "Obey orders."

Whether from exhaustion or the presence of so many armed men in the streets, the number of incidents in Savannah diminished notice-ably after midnight, until some of the retreating Rebels thought they were passing through a ghost town. A Confederate States marine put the time at near 1:00 A.M. when he and his comrades "fell into the long line of silent men who were pouring in a continuous stream over a pontoon bridge which had been erected between the city and the Car-olina shore." An artilleryman jostling nearby recalled that the "con-stant tread of the troops and the rumbling of the artillery as they poured over those long floating bridges was a sad sound, and by the glare of the huge fires at the east of the bridge it seemed like an immense funeral procession stealing out of the city in the dead of night."

Beginning a little after 2:00 A.M., curious Federal pickets began real-izing that the Rebel lines had become very, very quiet. On the far right, Private V. Thornton Ware of the 6th Iowa was remembered as the first to poke his nose into the empty enemy trenches to bring back word that the way was clear. Another comrade in those ranks cast his vote for Private Robert Barr, whose less than lofty intentions in scout-ing forward were "after getting something to eat and foraging a little."

Holding the Union left astride the most direct route into Savannah was Brigadier General John W. Geary's division (Twentieth Corps). This night's picket detail fell to the 102nd New York, several of whom took notice when no one from the other side "answered their calls." Colonel Henry A. Barnum, commanding the Third Brigade, autho-rized Lieutenant Colonel Harvey S. Chatfield to send out a ten-man patrol to confirm whether or not the Rebels had gone. Sergeant Alexander Hunt was one of those who "crawled up to their works about 3 A.M., [and] found them deserted." Chatfield informed Barnum, who passed word along to Geary, who immediately put together a flying column to push "forward rapidly in the direction of Savannah, hoping to overtake and capture a part of the enemy's forces."

Even as the last pockets of Confederate infantry were retreating through the city, the plucky Savannah River Squadron was dying. One of the first to go was the ironclad CSS *Georgia*, a formidable behemoth whose engines could not adequately power the ship, condemning it to spend much of its service as a adjunct floating battery to Fort Jackson. Its crew now helped nature take its course by opening valves to allow the vessel to disappear into the river muck.

More spectacular was the end of the wooden gunboat *Isondiga*, which had grounded above the bridge while providing protection for the crossing. Set afire by its crew, the *Isondiga* exploded before dawn. Still afloat as the sun rose were the steamer *Firefly* and the ironclad CSS *Savannah*. The latter had tried to break out to sea and failed because a path could not be cleared in time through the minefield designed to protect it. Now the warship lurked in position along the South Carolina shore.

Striding at the head of Brigadier General Geary's flying column was the 102nd New York, with Sergeant Hunt near the front. "Soon we met two men coming toward us in a buggy, one carrying a white flag, which he waved excitedly," remembered the noncom. "We sent them to the rear under guard and hurried on. It was still dark. A few shots were fired at us from the brush, but we did not stop."

The party consisted of two of the aldermen, who, having gotten separated from the mayor, ran first into the Yankees. Their meeting with General Geary was something of a nonevent, since they lacked the authority to deliver the city into his hands. Another carriage was intercepted, this one bearing Mayor Arnold. Said Geary: "Just outside of the city limits, near the junction of the Louisville and Augusta

roads, I met the mayor of Savannah and a delegation from the board
of aldermen bearing a flag of truce. From them I received, in the name
of my commanding general, the surrender of the city. This was at
4:30 A.M."

Mayor Arnold handed over an official note addressed to Major General Sherman:

> SIR: *The city of Savannah was last night evacuated by the Confederate
> military and is now entirely defenseless. As chief magistrate of the city
> I respectfully request your protection of the lives and private property of
> the citizens and of our women and children.*
>
> *Trusting that this appeal to your generosity and humanity may
> favorably influence your action, I have the honor to be, your obedient
> servant,*
>
> R. D. ARNOLD
> *Mayor of Savannah*

An unknown officer belonging to Major General Gustavus W.
Smith's command was the last to transit the floating bridge. Behind
him was an empty passageway, rocking slowly in the river current.
Rockets were fired, signaling the last of the river battery crews to spike
their guns and take to their boats. Then the bridge itself was broken
up, its anchor cables cut, and the sections allowed to scatter with the
river current. Some sections sank, others caught fire, still others drifted
aimlessly.

In the town, the small provost guard detail clustered nervously near
its transportation, the steamer *Swan*. Someone had remembered at the
last minute that there was a detachment still guarding the old Confederate Powder Magazine, but even as a courier was making ready to
recall the unit, spotters in the City Exchange steeple yelled that they
could see the first Yankee skirmishers entering the town. It was too
late to recall the unfortunate party, whose members would become
prisoners of war.

The provost men piled into the *Swan*. There was a melancholy leave
taking between one officer and his black servant, who promised to
look after the white man's family until he could return. When the
little steamer at last pushed away from the city wharf, it seemed to one

soldier as if they were departing a world of flame. There were small fires at various places along the shore, as well as several large ones. Pieces of the bridge were drifting past; "some were still linked together and were burning fiercely. Others were floating down the river like huge torches." The soldiers found their eyes watery and "weary with looking at the flames, which the river, like a huge mirror, reflected from beneath. The men were subdued in spirit, quiet in voice and sad at heart."

"We rushed to the pontoon bridge just in time to see our end swinging off in the river," recollected Sergeant Hunt of the 102nd New York. "Then with my little command still intact I ran to the foot of East Bay street, to a large mill filled with flour and meal, which was being stolen, left a guard there and hurried back to the Custom[s] House just in time to assist Gen. Geary in raising 'Old Glory.' "

Close at hand was the 137th New York. "We entered the city just at break of day," wrote Charles Engle of the regiment. "We found the streets filled with men women children and negroes. All seamed pleasd to see us." After dispatching detachments to various trouble spots, Brigadier General Geary assembled as much of Barnum's brigade as remained at City Hall, where, reported one officer, "he took formal possession of the city, complimenting our brave brigade and its courteous and thorough commander in a fine speech, and soon after Col. H. A. Barnum addressed the brigade in a neat and appropriate speech." It was a colorful affair, for waving over the heads of those assembled, their folds flapping in the strong southwest breeze, was "every flag of the brigade," recalled another New Yorker.

Rear Admiral Dahlgren returned from a conversation with the bridge crew of the *Harvest Moon* to let Major General Sherman know that the weather was such that the pilot did not feel confident trying to cross the sandbar into Ossabaw Sound. It would be much safer, he argued, to turn into the coast sooner at Tybee Roads, there to follow an inland passage taking them south. Dahlgren had concurred, so that was the decision. It would be a less dangerous journey, but also a slower one. Sherman expressed no anxiety.

Behind Barnum's brigade came the rest of Brigadier General Geary's division. "We passed through the city amid the shouts and cheers of the colored people and not a few of the white citizens of both sexes, welcomed us by waving white handkerchiefs and many seemed much pleased to see the old Stars and Stripes again," commented an Ohio man in the First Brigade. The Federal arrival was announced in dramatic fashion in the Elizabeth Basinger household, when her black maid burst into the room. "Oh, Miss! Oh, Miss Lizzie!" she said, her words in a tumble, "de Yankees is come, dey is as tick as bees, dey is so many on horses and de horse's tails is stannin out right straight, you just come look out de winder."

Watching from the window of her father's home off Lafayette Square was twenty-four-year-old Fanny Cohen, who chose this day to begin keeping a journal. The one flag-raising by the Yankee troops that she observed left her underwhelmed. In her opinion, the response of the Federals to their banner was "three very orderly and unimpulsive cheers."

Among those who fled Savannah with Hardee's garrison were the editors of the town's two newspapers: the *Savannah Republican,* and the *Savannah Morning News.* The *Republican's* editor had the foresight to anticipate the circumstances, so the December 21 sheet contained his bittersweet editorial, which read in part: "By the fortunes of war we pass today under the authority of the Federal military forces. The evacuation of Savannah by the Confederate army, which took place last night, left the gates to the city open. . . . It behooves all to keep within their homes until Gen. Sherman shall have organized a provost system and such police as will insure safety in persons as well as property."

A ten-man squad from the 29th Ohio made its way out along the river to the eastern edge of the city, where they took possession of Fort Jackson, still smoking from fires set by the departing Rebel garrison. The Ohio boys, said one, raised "the old flag on that fort once more." Behind them several hundred more Federals were coming to complete the job.

Peering across to the South Carolina shore, the soldiers could observe the hulking menace of the CSS *Savannah*. Once the ironclad's captain observed the U.S. flag flying, he ordered several rounds fired. Ironically, this was the only time in the entire war that Fort Jackson came under direct attack.

The Rebel warship was observed from downtown Savannah by Major J. A. Reynolds, chief of the Twentieth Corps artillery, who wasn't averse to picking a fight with the iron-sided vessel. Reynolds ordered forward Captain Thomas S. Sloan's Battery E, Pennsylvania Light Artillery, which, he reported, "took position on the lower end of Bay street and opened fire on her." When the *Savannah* tried to return the favor, its gunners found they couldn't sufficiently elevate their cannon to reach the nuisance. Major Reynolds was certain that Sloan's battery scored some hits, though the *Savannah*'s commander did not report any.

As word of Savannah's evacuation raced along the Union lines, soldiers from the other three corps found excuses to come into town. A Wisconsin man in the Seventeenth Corps admitted that he and his comrades "tried to behave ourselves, but the poultry, flour, molasses &c that lay in our way caused us to take considerable. . . . A woman, laughingly pointing to our plunder, exclaimed 'You have more to eat than we.' "

Iowans from the Fifteenth Corps passed through one of the sections yet to be visited by provost guards. An infantryman noted that "the white women and negroes and our soldiers seemed intent on cleaning the stores of everything but the officers are doing their best to stop it." Pennsylvania troops of the Fourteenth Corps found a more secure area of town. "The people of Savannah seemed to be satisfied with this change of military rulers," said Captain William S. McCaskey. "They seem to like 'the Yankees' reasonably well; fed most of our boys during our short visit; giving them their dinners with a cheering welcome. They are not so blind as not to know the advantages to be gained under the shadow of the old flag."

For hour after hour, the *Harvest Moon* picked its way along the scramble of creeks, small rivers, and twisting streams through swamps that were collectively termed "the inland passage." It didn't seem that things could get any worse, but they did late in the afternoon when, as Rear Admiral Dahlgren noted, "the channel was so narrow and winding that the *Harvest Moon* stuck fast." They were in Romney Marsh, maybe four miles from Ossabaw Sound and the Ogeechee River. This close to the end of his journey, Sherman at last expressed his impatience, so the decision was made to use the admiral's barge to continue the trip.

In the decade or so before the war began, John W. Geary amassed a strong résumé in civil administration, serving as San Francisco's first mayor and later as governor of the Kansas Territory. It wasn't random chance that placed his division with the most direct access to the city. No sooner had Geary reported his presence in Savannah than Major General Slocum put him in charge of maintaining order. "My eventful career is still upon its everlasting whirl," Geary bragged to his wife in a letter in which he referred to himself as "*Commandante* of the City."

Orders issued today began the process of governance. Savannah was divided into five subdistricts, with units assigned to each. Patrols were established to "protect all peaceable persons and public and private property, quell all disturbances, arresting all disorderly persons and turning them over to the . . . provost guard. . . . Every officer of the command is enjoined to put forth the most strenuous efforts to establish and maintain perfect order and subordination."

This wasn't always achieved. A squad of Indiana infantry came upon civilians scrapping among themselves over loot from a sacked warehouse. "I saw some fights between the women, and the air became sulphurous from the curses," said an amused Hoosier. "Our soldiers stood in groups taking in the scene. When a fight occurred among the Amazons, they would cheer and encourage the weaker ones, and despite the roughness of the scene would get some enjoyment out of it."

It was growing dark before Rear Admiral Dahlgren's barge, whose soggy passengers included Major General Sherman, nosed out of Romney Marsh into Ossabaw Sound. Not long afterward a steamer was sighted, signaled, then drew alongside. It was the army tug *Red Legs*, whose crew bubbled with the amazing news that Savannah had been evacuated by the Confederates and was now occupied by Federal troops. A message they were carrying from Sherman's aide Dayton confirmed matters.

HEADQUARTERS MILITARY DIVISION OF THE MISSISSIPPI

In the Field, December 21, 1864—9 a.m.

DEAR GENERAL: I have sent you two dispatches via Fort McAllister in hopes of reaching you. General Slocum reports enemy gone from his front and he had got eight guns—this report at 4 a.m. He is also gone from this front and General Howard reports [his division commander] Leggett near the city, and no enemy. General Woods also got six guns. General Slocum is moving and General Howard the same and I have no doubt both are in Savannah now. I will ride with General Howard, at his request, and leave our camp until the matter is more definite and you make orders.

I am, general, &c.,
L. M. DAYTON
Aide-de-Camp

There was no more time to be lost. Transferring to the *Red Legs*, Sherman ordered it to take him to Cheves' Rice Mill.

This was another stressful day for Colonel Carmen, with his men holding on to their small patch of South Carolina real estate. Early this morning he observed a detail from the 58th Indiana setting up a pontoon bridge linking his beachhead to Argyle Island. Instead of reinforcements, Carmen received orders to pull his brigade back to the Georgia mainland. The withdrawal was fraught with difficulties. The wind was high and the tides treacherous, slowing everything to a crawl. Then, rather than standing back to watch them go, the Rebels who had kept Carmen's little foray pinned in place began pressing his lines. "A great danger soon threatened us," declared a New Yorker, "for we were only a mile from the *pike* upon which the whole Rebel army were marching out." For a time matters appeared so grim that the Union officer was mentally prepared to count his casualties in the hundreds, but after sunset the enemy's efforts ceased. It was nearing midnight when, as Carmen recollected, "the last man crossed safely to Argyle Island and my campaign in [the] So[uth] Car[olina] Rice Swamps ended."

Time had run out for the CSS *Savannah*. Unable to sortie because no one could clear a path through "friendly" minefields, the warship had been granted a short reprieve from destruction on the night of December 20 solely to prevent the Federals from quickly repairing the floating bridge. As long as a Rebel force held Screven's Ferry at the head of the Union Causeway, the ironclad's crew had an escape route. Not long after sunset, the *Savannah*'s captain was told that the soldiers guarding Screven's would be withdrawn at 8:00 P.M. Thirty minutes before that time, the captain followed his crew in a boat carrying them to shore. Then the Screven's Ferry wharf was fired, taking with it the little steamer *Firefly*, which was lashed alongside. Behind them, in the bowels of the warship, sparks sputtered as a slow fuse burned toward carefully stacked charges. At 11:30 P.M. flame and gunpowder met. "It lit the heavens for miles," said one refugee sailor. "We could see to pick up a pin where we were and the noise was awful." A Union soldier across the river thought "it made a fearful and tremendous explosion."

THURSDAY, DECEMBER 22, 1864

Major General Sherman's headquarters party reached Fort McAllister before midnight, but had to stew until the ebb tide had sufficiently diminished to allow the tug *Red Legs* to continue to Cheves' Rice Mill. Someone had the presence of mind to use the signal tower near the fort to inform the mill station that Sherman was on his way, so horses were waiting when the General landed at 2:30 A.M. A slow ride in the dark brought everyone to headquarters, where breakfast was served while tents were struck and baggage packed. Finally, at 7:00 A.M., Major General Sherman mounted to lead the way into Savannah.

While significant steps had been taken to preserve order in the city there was still room for improvement. An Illinois soldier taking a stroll this morning observed others getting into "grocery cellars where there was molasses, lard &c and the poor whites and Negroes were helping themselves as well, grabbing and dipping in pails, getting the molasses and lard over each other. It was grand fun. In one place . . . they got it on the floor almost ankle deep." "The boys got plenty of tobacco," added an Illinoisan. "The citizens went for plunder as hard if not worse than the soldiers." "The rebels left everything in the stores," exclaimed an officer, "and, of course, the boys rigged themselves out."

In other instances there was a more formal interaction between North and South. "Took dinner with a secesh family," scribbled a New York diarist. "Had a good dinner and a warm argument." A Connecticut man found other civilians not interested in arguing, merely proclaiming that they were "heartily sick of the war." When Frances Thomas Howard answered a knock on the door of her family's home, she found a Yankee officer on her steps preparing to requisition the place for Colonel Barnum's headquarters.

"There are eight children here, all under five years of age," protested Mrs. Howard's companion. "I don't think you would find a stay in this house very pleasant."

The staff officer threw up his hands. "Good God!" he exclaimed. "Eight under five! I'll go *anywhere* else!"

The women directed him to a vacant house across the street. As he departed, they smiled at their little joke. Yes, there were eight little children in the house—four white and four black.

Sherman reached Savannah at 9:00 A.M., according to Major Hitchcock's watch. Entering from the south, the General's party turned onto tree-lined Bull Street, which they followed to the river. At Bay Street they went inside the U.S. Customs House, whose roof offered a panoramic view of the captured city. "The navy-yard, and the wreck of the iron-clad ram *Savannah* were still smouldering, but all else looked quiet enough," observed Sherman.

The General had served in the area as a young army officer, so he knew the best places to stay. The party rode directly to the Pulaski House, where Sherman was soon holding court in the same building that Confederate president Jefferson Davis once occupied. Hitchcock quickly lost count of the number of people who craved an audience with their conqueror. There was a brother of Lieutenant General Hardee, the town's mayor, and other citizens of importance. Most intriguing was Mr. Charles Green, a banker and British citizen who offered his spacious, well-furnished house for Sherman's headquarters. (Green later stated that he made the offer to spare a Georgia citizen indignity, though the Pulaski House manager seemed willing enough to provide the General with space. Less charitable wags viewed Green's gesture as an effort to win a favorable opinion regarding his seized cotton holdings.) At first Sherman was reluctant to accept the proposal, but he was easily persuaded. The Green mansion—richly appointed with expensive furniture, pricey art, and exotic plants—would serve as the General's command post throughout his stay in Savannah.

It wasn't long before Savannah's white residents began to experience changes in the order of their society. Mrs. Caro Lamar had always been suspicious of William, one of her house servants. This day, she wrote, "as I feared and expected, William proved to be a traitor." Mrs. Lamar's husband had been engaged in the risky but lucrative business of bringing commodities through the blockade; as one of the perks of the work, he had amassed a sizable store of liquors and wines. Barely four hours after William vanished, the first Yankees appeared at her door, polite but insistent, and they knew where to look. This party was followed by another, and before sunset much of the Lamars' liquid capital (along with a quantity of food) was confiscated. This night, Mrs. Lamar "felt so awfully weak, and peculiarly that I dreaded sickness and evil consequences." She would survive.

"You can form no conception of the utter demoralization of the servants," declared another Savannah resident, Mrs. G. W. Anderson. "Many families are left without a single one, & in every household several have taken leaves. . . . All the petted servants of all the Owens have left for 'freedom.' . . . All the country negroes are crowding into the city, & must plunder for a living. With such a population we have much to dread if left without proper police regulations."

Viewed through the other side of the lens, sentiments were quite different. "When the morning light of the 22d of December, 1864, broke in upon us, the streets of our city were thronged in every part with the victorious army of liberty;" declared a black Baptist preacher, "every tramp, look, command, and military movement told us they had come for our deliverance, and were able to secure it to us, and the cry went around the city from house to house among our race of people, 'Glory be to God, we are free!' "

Squads of Yankee troops continued to secure the Savannah area, occupying defensive works and locking down caches of munitions. A detail from the 58th Indiana Pontoniers was handed the task of repairing Hardee's floating bridge linking Savannah to Hutchinson Island. Most of the sections had survived, though some had been lost, while others were drifting loose. Much of it now lay snagged against the cityside bank, held there by the current. The existing segments were reattached, and long ropes were strung preparatory to swinging it back into place. One of the engineers noted approvingly that it had been constructed with docks on either end, "so the rising and falling of the tide does not lengthen or shorten the bridge."

"The amount of property left behind is enormous," crowed a Connecticut soldier, "especially cotton[,] also RR machinery[,] cars[,] engines &c[;] so fast they left all & fled[,] even the guns in the forts were so poorly spiked out boys pulled them out with their fingers." A correspondent on the scene reported that the "depots of the Savannah and Gulf Railroad, and of the Georgia Central Railroad were captured, with all their furniture etc. intact. Thirteen locomotives, in good order, and one hundred and ninety-three cars of various description were taken." A final accounting would add 167 artillery pieces captured and 38,500 cotton bales to the tally. The latter would prove an embarrassment to Lieutenant General Hardee, who was taken to task for allowing so much to fall into enemy hands. Hardee argued, none too convincingly, that most of it was in small batches, privately held, so to have torched it would have destroyed many residences.

Miss Frances Thomas Howard stared out her window at a ragged line of Confederate prisoners being held under guard opposite her house. "They looked tired and hungry, and we determined to feed them," she said. Food was gathered, but how to carry it past the Yankee guards without having it hijacked? Approaches to several senior officers were rebuffed, until she at last decided to target the man commanding the guard detail. To his pleased amazement, Miss Howard and two of her female companions invited him to dinner, where they made him comfortable.

"Do you know why we invited you to dine?" asked one of her friends.

"Because you like us, I suppose," answered the officer.

"No, indeed!" explained the Southern lady. "We hate you as all good Confederates should!"

"Then what made you ask me to dinner?"

The ladies sprang their velvet trap. "Because you are the captain of the guard, and now that we've fed you, our enemy, you cannot refuse to let us feed our friends, the Confederate prisoners."

The officer reluctantly agreed, and issued the necessary orders. "Our poor fellows were nearly starved, but waited patiently and quietly to be helped," said Miss Howard. "Hungry as they were, there was no snatching or pawing, although they saw that the supply of food we had brought was not half enough."

When numbers of Sherman's soldiers took stock today of what they had achieved, all felt good about it. "General Sherman, the bravest and best military man in the United States, has again won a victory which the nation ought to be proud of," puffed an officer. An Illinois soldier writing today to his wife said: "I . . . feel as if it were an honor to belong to Sherman's Army." Not far away an artilleryman was penning thoughts to his spouse: "Savannah has fallen! . . . Thus one more Rebel stronghold has succumbed to the Union army, and we are nearing the termination of this rebellion."

Besides the scores of civilians seeking assurances, or officers requesting orders, Sherman was also visited this day by a determined agent for the United States Treasury, one A. G. Brown. On behalf of his department, Agent Brown staked a claim for all captured Confederate property, especially cotton. Sherman agreed only insofar as his quartermaster and commissary officers had first pick; then the Treasury could have whatever was left. Having few cards in his hand to play, Agent Brown agreed.

Before departing, Brown mentioned that he was about to catch a fast steamer for Fortress Monroe, an army post on the Virginia peninsula in telegraphic communication with Washington. Knowing of President Lincoln's fondness for the whimsical gesture, Brown suggested that Sherman might consider a Christmas offering for the chief executive. That being all the hint Sherman needed, he immediately wrote out a message:

SAVANNAH, GEORGIA, December 22, 1864

To His Excellency President Lincoln, Washington, D.C.:
I beg to present you as a Christmas gift the city of Savannah, with one hundred and fifty heavy guns and plenty of ammunition, also about twenty-five thousand bales of cotton.

W. T. SHERMAN, Major-General

CHAPTER 22

"But What Next?"

DECEMBER 23, 1864–JANUARY 21, 1865

At the time Sherman's forces arrived, Savannah's population was 20,000-plus—the plus representing an unknown number of refugees, said by some to number in the thousands. The Yankees promptly set up shop, the officers finding space in vacant houses or rooms in occupied ones, the enlisted men building shantytowns in available open spaces. Nearby outbuildings and various loose construction goods soon found their way into the designs, which were as diverse as the soldiers themselves. "All hands are working like bees this morning getting material to build houses and clearing the camp ground," said a Wisconsin soldier. "Nails had been collected from houses or taken out of the stores, and nothing prevented us from having more commodious quarters than the pup tents," added an Illinoisan. "The lovely square in front of our house soon became a village with [the] streets its parade ground," grumbled one resident. Other parts of the town were less orderly. "All of our Squares [are] built up with wooden houses so that I scarcely recognized the streets," complained another citizen.

The military administration headed by Brigadier General Geary took care of security issues, while Mayor Arnold's people maintained city services, including the water and gas supply. Commandante Geary kept a measured distance from his civilian charges, looking down on them as a "spectacle of humbled aristocracy." Still, he ruled with an even hand, prompting Mayor Arnold to term him "noble Geary." For his public face, Geary professed to be "activated by no motives but which were in every respect compatible with those of a soldier, dictated by the true principals of charity and humanity." The bottom line was performance, and here Geary's details delivered. "In fact, 24 hours after its occupation it was as orderly as any New England city," boasted an Illinois soldier.

Savannahians divided between those resigned to the way things turned out and those who mingled defiance with a grudging compliance. The female species of the latter could usually be identified by their mourning dress or walking route. "On the street, at church, or in the drawing-room nearly every lady you meet is dressed in black," observed one newspaperman. For these women a simple promenade around the block could mean a complicated zigzag course, for according to one of them, high on the list of "things that seemed hard for us to bear was the suspending of [U.S.] flags across the streets so as to compel us to walk beneath." Still, the generally soft hand of Union occupation presented many diehards with a quandary. "They are all astonished at the generosity of General Sherman's orders," chuckled a New Yorker, "and some seem indignant that he was not a barbarian, that they might vent their pent up spleen on him."

The leading voice for reconciliation in the town came from its mayor, Richard D. Arnold, whose pragmatic philosophy was: "Where resistance is hopeless it is criminal to make it." He was a leading speaker at an assembly of citizens that met in late December to set the agenda for the coming months. Resolutions were passed that acknowledged the Union victory, heaped praise on Brigadier General Geary for his "uniform kindness," and urged Governor Brown to call a special constitutional convention to reconsider secession. All those who signed the resolutions vowed to lay "aside all differences" and bury "bygones in the grave of the past" in order to "once more . . . bring back the prosperity and commerce we once enjoyed."

(Lest Mayor Arnold come across as a rubber stamp for Federal rule, he bristled when asked to help turn out crowds to cheer Union soldiers marching in review, knowing full well that many still had family or friends fighting for the other side. "Do you think I would order them out to see your soldiers parade?" he exclaimed. "Sir, I'll be damned if I do!")

The conciliatory declarations from captured Savannah did not sit well with others throughout the Confederacy who were still resisting. "Oh it is a crying shame, such poltroonery!" exclaimed one Southern matron upon reading the declarations. In distant Richmond there was anger aplenty—aimed at the surviving Southern newspapers that were permitted to reprint the material. "The proceedings will be used as a 'form,' probably, by other cities—thanks to the press!" griped an official. The editors of the *Augusta Daily Constitutionalist* chose to ignore how close they had come to sharing Savannah's fate when they thundered: "If there is one sink lower than any other in the abyss of degradation the people of Savannah have reached it."

The biggest problem facing city leaders was maintaining the food supply. At first, Sherman wasn't interested. "No provision has been made for the families in Savannah, and many of them will suffer from want," he declared on Christmas Eve, "and I will not undertake to feed them." Cooler heads prevailed, and within two days Sherman had struck a deal with Mayor Arnold, granting the civilian leader access to all captured rice among the Confederate army stores. An arrangement was worked out, allowing Savannah's leaders to sell the rice in New York with the proceeds applied toward food purchases.

The man entrusted to carry out this mission was Julian Allen, a northern social activist and entrepreneur who used his commission to solicit a broader collection of aid for a starving Savannah. Allen's call to action snagged heartstrings in New York, Boston, and Philadelphia, so that by mid-January ships were docking in Savannah filled with donated foodstuffs. While some Savannahians were embarrassed at becoming national objects of charity, most welcomed the helping hand.

These civilian events were background noise to the Union occupation. There was much work to be done, including sanitation, infrastructure repairs, and clearing the river channels. Men badly wounded in the course of the march or otherwise incapacitated were put onto hospital boats for transport north. When it became evident that the army would be moving on, Captain Orlando Poe was set to work designing a ring of fortifications running close to the city making it possible to hold the place with a division-sized garrison. Taking advantage of the existing Confederate inner line, Poe incorporated much of it into his scheme.

Some soldiers were employed putting these defenses into shape, but most found themselves with time on their hands. Many became tourists. "The city is beautifully laid out, with broad streets densely shaded, interspersed with numerous parks, squares and monuments," proclaimed a member of the 50th Illinois. "Many of the parks were lined with beautiful trees," added an Ohio comrade, "while others contained large marble shafts, erected to the memory of noted men of American history." "Every alternate square is a public square fenced, with entrance gates at each of the four corners," contributed another Buckeye, "with walks leading from each gate to the center where benches and seats were provided for the use of the public."

A Fifteenth Corps soldier was drawn to the Catholic cemetery, "a place of somber beauty long to be remembered," while a Twentieth Corps comrade was much taken with Jasper Springs, a historic site marked by a "wonderful spring . . . noted for its beautiful crystal water."

Mentioned by almost every soldier-tourist was the impressive monument honoring the Revolutionary War hero Casimir Pulaski, killed in a failed assault on the then British bastion in 1779. Located in Monterey Square, it reached toward heaven with a thirty-foot white Carrara marble shaft crowned by a statue of Lady Liberty, set atop a twenty-foot-square limestone base. Numerous carvings adorned the shaft and foundation stones, freighted with symbolic meanings that struck a sympathetic chord with one Indiana visitor. "The guns, the shot, and the spears are emblematic of war—the profession of the gallant dead," he wrote. "The wreath represents the reward of those who perish in the cause of liberty. The flame and the color of the [green-painted iron] fence call to our minds the immortality of the deeds of those who give their lives that men may be free." Another Hoosier visitor could not resist the ironic observation that the residents who built and maintained this temple to American liberty "have been exposing their lives for American slavery."

Beyond the cultural stops, there were lighter forms of entertainment for the soldiers. The camp of the 66th Ohio was located next to "one of the theaters of the City, which was occupied every night by either an amateur variety troupe or by some leading band of the army giving a concert," said one. "One thing I must mention and that is the most beautiful levee all along the river front proper," observed a Wisconsin soldier. "I have seen many thousands sit there on the morning after pay day gambling with all kinds of games." "Oh the wickedness that is practiced in the army," proclaimed an Illinoisan. "We have [a prayer] meeting at times while others are right under our notice gambling and swearing all around us." South of the town a racetrack opened for business. "Thousands of soldiers every day witnessed these races until some fist-fights occurred," reported a Hoosier, "when they were discontinued by order of the commanding general."

A local seafood soon became an exotic staple of many a Federal dinner. "Our squad was well provided for . . . ," wrote a Minnesota diarist, "went out foraging and found some oysters." "There is a hundred and twenty men detailed out of the Brigade to go to Thunder Bay to rake Oysters for us," added a Wisconsin man in the Twentieth Corps. "Listen to the *menu* from my diary of Sunday, January 1, 1865, and pity the poor soldier," kidded an Illinois officer. "Dinner for headquarters' mess. Oyster soup, oysters on the half shell, roast goose, fried oysters, roasted oysters, rice, raisins, and coffee, with condensed milk, of course. A little top-heavy as to oysters, but we don't complain."

More than one Yankee boy had eyes for Savannah's opposite sex. "There was quite a lot of citizens out," wrote an Illinois diarist on Christmas Day, "[including] some very good looking young ladies." A member of Sherman's staff retained fond memories of the "delightful entente cordiale between the officers and ladies," while a line officer deemed Savannah's women "the tastiest Secesh I have ever seen." "Each little knot of soldiers made acquaintance with fair ones," recorded another officer, "glad to entertain and be entertained with cards, dance, and song." Sometimes the entertainment went further. "There is the most hoars here that I saw in my life both black and white," exclaimed an amazed Federal. "I thought that Washington had enough but this beats that."

One spontaneous amusement took place on a rainy December 28; in fact, a Pennsylvania soldier went so far as to proclaim it "the best joke of the season." This day, recorded a Federal officer, "a rebel blockade runner came into port, not having heard that the city had changed hands, with a cargo of tea, coffee, sugar and bacon." Continued an Illinois man: "They did not find out that things had changed until they saw at Fort Jackson (several miles below the river,) the stars and stripes flying from every prominent house and steeple; but it was too late then to return." "She was a long, low, three masted schooner, painted a dull grey color, her long, slender masts and otherwise trim appearance, indicated speed," reported an observer from the 50th Illinois. "Cannon upon her deck gave her a warlike appearance, and as she passed up the river in custody of Uncle Sam's navy, reminded us of a culprit arrested for some crime."

The timing of Sherman's march put 60,000 Yankee boys in the Savannah area at holiday time. "While I am writing this Christmas eve, guns are firing all around and the boys are having a fine time of it," scribbled a Minnesota correspondent. Signal corps men added to the merriment by shooting off some of their rockets. Things got so raucous in one Fourteenth Corps division that neighboring units belonging to the Seventeenth Corps, thinking an attack was under way, scrambled into a line of battle, which they maintained most of the night. "Quite a joke on Granny Blair," snorted an Illinois soldier.

In the 26th Wisconsin's camp, the men on Christmas Eve "cleaned our quarters. Each person planted a Christmas tree in front of his tent." Attending Episcopal services, an Indiana volunteer eyed the collection plate as it was passed. "I saw one hundred dollar Confederate bills spread out on the basket; that kind of money was cheap; but I saw many [U.S.] greenbacks in that basket." Another soldier present at services where civilian and military intermingled in the pews thought aloud: "It did not seem as though we were enemies." Pennsylvanians in the 147th regiment attended a Catholic church where they "witnessed the imposing ceremony of celebrating 'High Mass', after which we partook of a royal dinner, especially prepared for the occasion."

Not every holiday repast was so fine. Christmas supper for the 63rd Illinois consisted of "rice boiled in water, baked beef, coffee and hard tack." For some of the soldier boys the thought of loved ones at home was hard to bear; one Iowan pronounced this day the "most awful lonesome for Christmas," and an Indiana man proclaimed it "rather a dull Christmas—not like our Northern merry makings."

It was Sherman's wish that the campaign be consummated with a grand march past him by each corps in turn. The ceremonies began on Christmas Eve with the Fifteenth Corps. "Had a Review today," noted an Iowa diarist. "Sherman looked pleased." "The arms glistened in the sunshine," contributed a Minnesotan, "banners gaily fluttered in the breeze." Three days later it was the turn of the Fourteenth Corps.

"The troops made a good appearance," bragged an Ohio participant. "Uncle Billy's dolled up like a duke," exclaimed a Michigan boy. Another Buckeye reported that the General "is a keen looking man of about forty five with short sandy beard and red face—though not caused by whiskey." The next day the Seventeenth Corps assembled for the occasion. "The Generals looked well and I think the men did too," said an Iowan, "considering the campaign that they have just ended by taking this city."

The infantry proceedings ended on December 30, when the Twentieth Corps stepped off. " 'Uncle Billy' is the pet of this command," proclaimed a New Englander. "Gen. Sherman was very much pleased. Each Brigade Band of course wheeled out in front of the General and played till the brigade had passed," wrote a proud New Jersey officer. "One regimental column after another passed all as one man, in perfect time with the soul stirring music. As each tattered flag is dipped on passing Sherman, the drums beat the roll 'to the colors' & the General raises his hat." According to another soldier present, "Gen'l Sherman himself, who was often rather careless in dress upon the march, was resplendent in full dress, and presented a commanding and inspiring presence as he returned the salutes and cheers of his admiring columns."

With many of its units drawn from the more protocol-conscious eastern states, the Twentieth Corps prided itself on its appearance. "They call us the 'paper collar and white glove fellows' and of course said we would beat them in show," boasted the corps commander, Brigadier General Alpheus S. Williams. "And we did! . . . My corps . . . was the last reviewed and all the world and his family came to see it. . . . Hundreds of officers have told me it was the finest and most splendid review they ever saw. Gen. Sherman confesses it was the best of all. . . . I was quite a lion! Think of it—a lion!—a lion!"

Bad weather forced the cavalry review to be postponed until January 12, when the skies finally cleared. "We went to the sity and was reviewed by Genl. Shirman," recorded a Pennsylvania trooper. A New York infantryman thought the riders "did very well," while an Illinois foot soldier was more enthusiastic. It was, he declared, "a splendid sight. . . . It took them about an hour and a half to pass." The infantryman was awed by the sight of the horsemen "all in uniform decorated with burnished weapons. . . . Oh, it was a grand scene!"

Savannah's garrison trudged into South Carolina about forty-five miles, until the line of the Salkehatchie and Combahee rivers was reached. The movement was an ordeal for everyone. "Such a march as it was, through rain and mud," grumbled a Georgia soldier. "Expressed my feelings in no complimentary terms. I certainly felt like cursing somebody and did not care who." Following Beauregard's plan, a new line of defenses was built behind the two rivers.

Many of the Georgia troops who had served in Savannah's trenches were sent off to Augusta, while South Carolina militia units tramped along to Charleston. Those that were left, which included Wheeler's cavalry, took defensive positions while everybody waited for Sherman's next move. When confirmation of these events reached Richmond, a government official, thinking too about verified news of Hood's Nashville defeat, remarked that together they made "up a tale of disaster which has filled the land with gloom."

For Sherman the Savannah sojourn was a time to savor his accomplishments, revel in the majesty of a conqueror, and plot his next move. The newspapers for which he had little use during the campaign now sang his praises to a grateful nation.

Chicago Tribune, *December 26, 1864*
Well and nobly done, gallant Sherman.

Boston Post, *December 27, 1864*
It is an important event, crowning a successful march; and the more welcome it is a bloodless victory. It fills up the measure of the fame of the gallant Sherman, his corps of noble officers and . . . [his] invincible [army] . . . ; and undoubtedly it is the herald of other and of still more important successes.

Quincy Daily Whig & Republican, *December 27, 1864*
The news of another magnificent victory will thrill through the nation, awakening again the echoes of enthusiastic applause from every hill-top and every valley. Sherman, at the head of his heroic legions, has

marched into the city, with scarce a breathing spell after his great
march.

Philadelphia Inquirer, *December 26, 1864*
Sherman has triumphed again, and this time with no loss to himself. . . .
This is a great and glorious achievement for Sherman and his heroic
army. No such campaigning has been undertaken during the war as
that through which Sherman has led his army, and no campaign has
had a more successful termination. *

The spouses and relatives of many of the officers who had recently
fought him now presented themselves seeking favors. This greatly
amused Sherman, especially in light of some of the proclamations
signed by these officers branding his soldiers as vandals. "Therefore it
struck me as strange that Generals [William J.] Hardee and [Gustavus
W.] Smith should commit their families to our custody, and even
bespeak our personal care and attention," he chuckled. Sherman did
what he could, though in no case did he intervene when the issue
involved seized property. He did inquire about some of the people he
knew when he was posted here as a young army officer, "but when I
ask for old & familiar names, it marks the Sad havoc of war," he told his
wife.

The long campaign through Georgia had not dulled Sherman's
sharp distinctions of right and wrong. Efforts by British citizens resident in Savannah to protect their cotton holdings especially riled him.
"I treat an English subject with [no] more favor than one of our own
deluded citizens," he informed Washington authorities, "and that for
my part I was unwilling to fight for cotton for the benefit of English-
men openly engaged in smuggling arms and instruments of war to kill
us." Speaking to a Savannah gathering that included several British
subjects, Sherman avowed that there "was not a man in his army who
would not eagerly join in invading England and punishing her for her
insidious conduct." "I would not be surprised if I would involve our
government with England," he informed his wife. Still, he had no

---

* It was Sherman's way not to drink too deeply of these popular accolades. "A single
mistake or accident, my pile, though well founded, would tumble," he wrote to his
wife.

inhibitions about staying in Charles Green's mansion, which, he told Ellen, was "elegant & splendidly furnished with pictures & Statuary."

Sherman's isolation from the outside world was shattered on December 30 when he opened correspondence from his wife's family and his brother, John, informing him that the ailing son he had never seen— Charles Celestine Sherman—had died on December 4. In writing to his wife, Sherman noted that Charles had "gone to join Willy, for he was but a mere ideal, whereas Willy was incorporated with us, and seemed to be designed to perpetuate our memories. . . . I should like to have seen the baby of which all spoke so well, but I seemed doomed to pass my life away so that even my children will be strangers."

While Sherman was coping with this personal tragedy, a political storm was swirling about his attitude concerning African-American integration into U.S. society. At first it seemed that he could keep the matter at arm's length. "It would amuse you to See the negroes, they flock to me old & young they pray & shout," he told his wife on Christmas Day, "and mix up my name with that of Moses & Simon, and other scriptural ones as well as Abram Linkum the Great Messiah of 'Dis Jubilee.' " Major Hitchcock noted, "Frequently they come in a dozen or twenty at a time, to his room up-stairs [in the Green mansion] where he usually sits. He has always had them shown in at once, stopping a dispatch or letter or a conversation to greet them in his off-hand— though not undignified way—'Well, boys, —come to see Mr. Sherman, have you? Well, I'm Mr. Sherman—glad to see you'—and shaking hands with them all in a manner highly disgusting, I dare say, to a 'refined Southern gentleman.' "

The same mails that brought Sherman word of his dead son also conveyed warnings from supporters in Washington that his often professed opinions against blacks were not winning him friends. Major General Henry W. Halleck, the army's chief of staff, reported that Radical Republicans were publicly stating that Sherman had "manifested an almost *criminal* dislike to the negro, and that you are not willing to carry out the wishes of the government in regard to him, but repulse him with contempt!" A political friend allied with the Radicals piled on as well. "You are understood," he said, "to be opposed to their employment as soldiers and to regard them as a sort of pariahs, almost without rights."

Replying to the politician, Sherman noted that on "approaching

Savannah I had at least 20,000 negroes, clogging my roads, and eating up our subsistence. . . . The same number of white refugees would have been a military weakness. Now you Know that military success is what the nation wants, and it is risked by the crowds of helpless negroes that flock after our armies. My negro constituents of Georgia would resent the idea of my being inimical to them, they regard me as a second Moses or Aaron. . . . Of course I have nothing to do with the Status of the Negro after [the] war. That [is] for the law making power, but if my opinion were consulted I would Say that the negro should be a free race, but not put on an equality with the whites." Sherman was less circumspect when answering Halleck, a fellow professional and member of the white military brotherhood. "But the nigger?" he asked. "Why, in God's name, can't sensible men let him alone?"

If Sherman had hoped to get going with the next phase of his grand scheme before any more of this controversy got in the way, he was to be sorely disappointed. On January 11, 1865, the day's ship landings included a revenue cutter from Washington bearing the secretary of war, Edwin M. Stanton. In addition to clarifying official policies regarding confiscated material (cotton, especially), Stanton wanted a face-to-face with Sherman about race relations. During that January 12 sit-down, Stanton listened intently as the General talked about blacks by relating "many interesting incidents [during the march], illustrating their simple character and faith in our arms and progress." When the secretary brought up Brevet Major General Davis, Sherman quickly assured him that his subordinate "was an excellent soldier, and I did not believe he had any hostility to the negro."

Stanton produced newspaper clippings critical of Davis's actions at the Ebenezer and Lockner creeks. "I had heard such a rumor," Sherman responded, and immediately sent for his Fourteenth Corps commander. The story Davis related to Stanton, strongly seconded by Sherman, said more about their biases than it illuminated the truth of what had happened. Davis explained that "old and young" blacks were indeed following his column "in droves." The route assigned his corps took the men along the swampy Savannah River Road, necessitating constant use of the pontoon trains. In order to keep on the schedule expected of him, the temporary bridging had to be pulled up the instant the last soldier passed over, then rapidly pushed forward to the next crossing so as not to delay the march. That was why the bridges had to be disassembled so quickly on the day in question. Davis allowed that some blacks were stranded on the far bank, but only because they were "asleep" when it was dismantled; further, that it was only "mere supposition" that any were drowned or picked up by Wheeler's cavalry. What had happened to him, Davis said, could have happened to any of the senior officers in a similar situation, even to Major General Howard, who was one of the "most humane commanders who filled the army." In Sherman's recollection, Stanton ended the conversation by professing that the unfortunate affair had been explained "to his entire satisfaction."

That wasn't the end of it, however. Stanton insisted on meeting some black leaders, so Sherman arranged a gathering that very night, mostly attended by Methodist and Baptist preachers. With the General looking on, the group of twenty responded to a series of questions posed by Stanton regarding their understanding of the Emancipation Proclamation, their views on black military service, and their aspirations for the future. Then, to Sherman's surprise and quiet fury, he was asked to leave the room. Once he had gone, Stanton asked those assembled for their opinion of the General. Perhaps not surprisingly, given their natural wariness of white men and recognizing that Sherman was not going away, the selected black leaders, after pronouncing the General "a friend and gentleman," assured Stanton that they "could not be in better hands."

Sherman never forgave Stanton for putting him on trial before a black jury. Just because he had conducted his recent campaign on purely military principles, untainted by political considerations, by refusing to burden his army with "hundreds or thousands of poor negroes, I was construed by others as hostile to the black race."* Still, in a very public gesture, Sherman stood in the reviewing stand for a parade mounted by the city's all-black fire companies. A reporter on hand recorded: "As they marched one or two of the most musical darkies sang various songs, of a didactic character, narrating the brave deeds of the companies in conflagrations of the past days, and the companies took up the chorus and filled the streets with their loud refrain."

---

* Writing afterward to his wife about these incidents, the General made it clear that any self-examination was not on his agenda. Said Sherman: "I am right and won't change."

Also, as a sop to the war secretary (and to keep refugee blacks from following his army) Sherman signed his name to Special Field Orders No. 15, which established a framework for black refugee families to settle on abandoned plantations located on the South Carolina and Georgia coast, as well as along Florida's St. Johns River.

Sherman later claimed that he viewed this policy as providing only "temporary provisions for the freedmen and their families during the rest of the war," a distinction that, tragically, was withheld from most participants. Their efforts at a new life would come to an abrupt halt within a year when directives from the Andrew Johnson administration returned much of the land to its former (white) owners.

In the face of these vicissitudes, Sherman could still find solace in the warm support of President Abraham Lincoln as expressed in his reply to the General's "Christmas gift" of "the city of Savannah":

EXECUTIVE MANSION,
Washington, December 26, 1864.

MY DEAR GENERAL SHERMAN: Many, many thanks for your Christmas gift, the capture of Savannah. When you were about leaving Atlanta for the Atlantic coast, I was anxious, if not fearful; but feeling that you were the better judge, and remembering that "nothing risked, nothing gained," I did not interfere. Now, the undertaking being a success, the honor is all yours; for I believe none of us went further than to acquiesce. And taking the work of General Thomas into the count, as it should be taken, it is indeed a great success. Not only does it afford the obvious and immediate military advantages, but, in showing to the world that your army could be divided, putting the stronger part to an important new service, and yet leaving enough to vanquish the old opposing force of the whole—Hood's army—it brings those who sat in darkness to see a great light. But what next? I suppose it will be safer if I leave General Grant and yourself to decide. Please make my grateful acknowledgments to your whole army, officers and men.

Yours, very truly,
A. LINCOLN

PART SIX

Finale

CHAPTER 23

"The Blow Was Struck at the Right Moment and in the Right Direction"

On January 21, 1865, William Tecumseh Sherman boarded the army steamer *W. W. Coit*, which carried him to Beaufort, South Carolina, where he would begin what he later called "the active campaign from Savannah northward." Some hundred or so miles inland from where he came ashore, a Union prisoner of war in a stockade outside Columbia put pen to paper to praise the man he much admired and, by so doing, helped transform the March to the Sea from another military campaign to an American epic.

Samuel H. M. Byers was soldiering with the 5th Iowa when he was captured in fighting near Chattanooga in 1863. By his own account, he subsequently made several escape attempts, "only to be retaken" each time. Perhaps as a way of combating the psychological debilitation of confinement, Byers became obsessed with Sherman's successes, as he gleaned them from camp rumors and occasionally smuggled newspapers. He had actually viewed Sherman just before his capture, and never forgot the General's apparent fearlessness. Once it became known that Sherman's Savannah campaign had accomplished its objective, Byers funneled his emotions into a five-stanza lyric poem with chorus that took considerable liberty with the facts, but which was unabashed in its adoration of this great American hero. The verse-poem concluded:

Oh, proud was our army that morning,
That stood where the pine darkly towers,
When Sherman said, "Boys, you are weary,
But today fair Savannah is ours!"
Then we sang a song of our chieftain
That echoes o'er river and lea,
And the stars of our banner shone brighter
When Sherman camped down by the sea!

A fellow POW set the verse to music to produce a song that the other prisoners enjoyed singing to mock their guards. According to Byers, the piece "soon reached the soldiers in the North, and before I knew it, it was being sung everywhere." He would successfully escape captivity, and when Union forces reached Columbia, he actually met his hero, who added him to the headquarters staff. Sherman, who far preferred myth-making to objective reporting, informed Byers: "You hit it splendidly."

The Union men who marched with Sherman to the sea expressed equal fervor when it came to evaluating what they had together accomplished. "The importance of the march through Georgia has never been overestimated," wrote H. Judson Kilpatrick in 1876. "The very moment that Sherman reached the sea, demonstrating the fact that a well-organized army, ably led, could raid the South at pleasure; there was not a man in all the land but knew the war was virtually over, and the rebellion ended." Much closer to the actual events, a triumphant Illinois soldier, writing from the streets of Savannah, had no hesitation in stating that the campaign "will go down in history, and be told over and over again as one of the greatest achievements on record." Another Illinoisan was equally unequivocal that the "march has been the greatest blow to the Confederacy that has yet been struck."

Few of the Yankee boys shed a tear over what they had done to the central and eastern portions of the state. "This part of Georgia never realized what war was until we came through on this expedition," said a Minnesota man. "It is terrible to think of," professed a Connecticut officer, "but only as an act of retributive justice to these people here." "As you are aware," a Wisconsin boy told his parents, "we have . . . made a big hole in the Confederacy. Will not the North rejoice when it realizes the effects of this great movement? . . . [N]o more [a] terrible blow has been dealt the South than that has just been given it in Ga."

Recent memories of heavily laden foraging parties or the sights of pillaged homesteads were amplified in the imagination until many Federal participants became utterly convinced they had scoured Governor Brown's state to the bedrock. "Georgia [is] in a helpless condition, not to recover from the terrible shock of war till reconstructed," said a Wisconsin soldier, while a staff officer reflected that it "looks hard to see a large, prosperous, fruitful country thus laid in utter ruins, but it is the only way to conquer rebellion." "On our march to the coast we have ploughed through [the] garden and granary of the Confederacy, laying waste the country and cutting things up root and branch," reported a Pennsylvania officer to the folks back home. "We have effectively severed their railroad lines of communication; we have swept off thousands of their slaves; and not to put too fine a point upon it, Sherman's scythe has cut a clean swath just fifty miles in width." "On the entire route, the destruction was more devilish than you can imagine," a Seventeenth Corps staff officer assured his family. "The Union army was a besom of destruction, sweeping across the country, leaving in its wake devastated farms and the smoke of burning buildings," said another soldier.

The ever-present Major Hitchcock penned his assessment of the campaign before Savannah was captured. Overall, he decided that Sherman's columns had been "most fortunate in weather. . . . The health of the whole army . . . has been unusually good, —and mortality very small. . . . We have escaped more than was thought possible the obstacles which might have been interposed. . . . The great object of the march, —the destruction of R.R. on the vital chain of rebel communication from E. to W.—has been more than accomplished, and it is shown that a large army can march with impunity through the heart of the richest rebel state. . . . Our supplies are yet hardly drawn on at all, our . . . men are in the finest spirits, ready for anything 'Uncle Billy' orders. . . . I do not forget, and God knows I am sorry for the people of the regions we have traversed [but this] . . . Union and its Government must be sustained at any and every cost. . . . To do this implies . . . war now so terrible and successful that none can dream of rebellion hereafter."

Sherman's final report on the Savannah Campaign was measured in its praise for his officers and men. Generals Howard and Slocum were described as "gentlemen of singular capacity and intelligence, thorough soldiers and patriots, working day and night . . . for their country and their men." Those leading Sherman's divisions and brigades received his "personal and official thanks," while the rank and file were lauded for carrying out their duties (be it combat, road fixing, foraging, or track wrecking) "with alacrity and a degree of cheerfulness unsurpassed." Sherman singled out Brigadier General Kilpatrick in both his final report and in a personal message sent on December 29.

In the latter, the General said: "I beg to assure you that the operations of the cavalry have been skillful and eminently successful. . . . [At] Thomas' Station, Waynesboro', and Brier Creek, you whipped a superior cavalry force, and took from Wheeler all chance of boasting over you. But the fact that to you, in a great measure, we owe the march of four strong infantry columns, with heavy trains and wagons, over three hundred miles through an enemy's country, without the loss of a single wagon, and without the annoyance of cavalry dashes on our flanks, is honor enough for any cavalry commander."

The first reactions to the campaign from the other side were often a mixture of concern and disbelief. Many a distant Georgian's letters home during this period echoed the sentiments of one coming from Petersburg in early December: "I am nervous and exceedingly anxious to hear from you." Some who wrote wondered why the state had apparently lain supine before the Yankee advance. "The people of Georgia should all unite and repel Sherman and destroy him at every post, destroy and carry off provisions and forage from his front," wrote a bellicose member of the 3rd Georgia fighting under General Robert E. Lee. Another in the regiment was more acidic. "Even Georgian soldiers in Virginia don't understand why Sherman marched through the State without resistance," he wrote on Christmas Day. "Was it a lack of patriotism in the people that they did not fly to arms to stop the invader?" "I feel very little inclined to call myself a Georgian any more," ruminated one more, "and if it were not that you all live in Macon I should disown the state *in toto* and transfer my allegiance."

When Governor Joseph Brown stood before the reconvened Georgia legislature in early 1865, he was compelled to officially rebut imprecations against his state's will to resist "because her people did not drive back and destroy the army of the enemy." The fault, Brown insisted, lay with the central government in Richmond, which held back fifty regiments of Georgia veteran soldiers in Virginia when they were urgently needed to defend their homes. Brown's prideful bitterness found an echo in a young Georgia militiaman on picket duty after Savannah's fall when he was confronted by a South Carolina squad who asked "what in the hell we meant by letting Sherman march through Georgia. I told them; allright, You will have a chance of it in a few days, for he is sure coming, and you will not be able to stop him either."

Only later would people become aware of the extent of destruction along portions of the march route. Where it was bad, it was often really bad. "All around the grove were carcasses of cows, sheep and hogs, some with only the hind quarters gone, and the rest left to spoil," remembered a resident living near Louisville. A neighbor suffered much the same, recollecting that the hogs were "killed, mules taken, corn taken to feed the horses, anything, everything to eat." Even the preponderance of homes that survived the passing storm were nonetheless badly treated. "Where there were no houses burned, they destroyed all the fencing and palings, so that when they left, the houses stood out in the bare yards and fields," reminisced a Bulloch County civilian. "Many of us are utterly ruined," contributed a Clinton homeowner. "What the people in this country are to do God only knows for starvation is certainly staring them in the face," wrote a woman near Sandersville. A neighbor added that it "was now winter, too late for crops; what were we to do?"

Once the shock had passed, however, a determination to survive emerged. Hardly had the last Yankee soldier disappeared down the road than most Georgians caught in their path began picking up the pieces. One resolute household existed on scraps scavenged from abandoned Union camps until "kind relatives in another part of Georgia, who had not been robbed, came to the relief." For those who lived off the land, the prospect of a sudden catastrophe was never far from their thoughts, so recovering from Storm Sherman was no different. "Now I reckon you want to know what the Yankees did for us," scribbled a McDonough mother to her daughter. "Well, bad enough but no worse than I expected. . . . You must not be uneasy. We will live but not so Plentiful as we used to." "There was a great crop raised in 1864," a

Bulloch County farmer reminded his readers in 1914. "It was one of the most fruitful years in my memory . . . and even the Yankee army could not eat it up and carry it off in two days."

Sherman always believed that his march helped break Georgian support for the Confederate cause. State governor Brown might well have agreed, at least based on some of the petitions he received. One submitted in mid-January, from Wilcox County in the south-central portion of the state, declared that the "time has come when our authorities should go boldly to work to negotiate a peace before we are entirely ruined." The great losses suffered outside the state by Georgians under arms lent an urgency to this appeal, which demanded that talks begin "before the whole white male population is butchered." Other citizens were equally determined to keep resisting. "I hope that S.C. will accomplish what Ga. should have done, capture Sherman and his vile pack," wrote a Rockbridge resident in February 1865.

Just about everyone wanted the outsiders to go away. A Georgia soldier's wife, living just outside the zone of Sherman's destruction, reported a rumor making the rounds in mid-January that France and England were ready to guarantee Confederate independence if a policy of gradual emancipation was adopted. "I would rather do that than continue fighting or go back to Lincoln," she declared. A northern man visiting conquered, conciliatory Savannah in late January 1865 observed that the "real Union sentiment in this city, I fear, is small. The people look upon the Confederate cause as lost, and therefore come forward and take the oath of allegiance to the United States; but they still retain their Southern sympathies and have no love for the Union."

Sherman's March dramatically fractured the social fabric by shattering the binds of custom and coercion that held together white and black Georgia. The placid exterior of antebellum southern life masked a balance of terror coursing underneath—terror felt by blacks who were arbitrarily subject to cruel punishments unto death for any sign of resistance; terror felt by whites who viewed themselves as living atop a dormant but active volcano. Three years of war had already slackened the bonds by siphoning away many white males (the chief enforcers); the passage of Sherman's columns severed most (but not all) of the remaining ones.

"We fear the negroes now more than anything else," declared a

Sandersville resident in late November 1864. Yet amazingly, in the often complicated chronicle that was Sherman's March, minor incidents of black-on-white retribution were rare, major ones virtually nonexistent. "When Sherman's army marched through the South, did we take advantage of this (as we might) to commit acts of lawlessness and violence?" asked a black Augusta newspaperman right after the war. "No, never!"

Blacks who voted with their feet met a reception from Sherman's men that ranged from a bemused paternalism to outright racism. "They thronged the line of march wide-eyed and wondering," wrote a Pennsylvania soldier. "It was very amusing to see the darkies in the city [of Savannah] and villages," wing commander Henry W. Slocum told a New York friend. "They came out in groups and welcomed us with delight, they danced and howled, laughed, cried and prayed all at the same time."

While some Yankees looked at the refugees with sympathetic eyes, many more were captives of the racial stereotypes of their age. Brigadier General William P. Carlin, commanding a division under Brevet Major General Jefferson C. Davis, thought of them as "useless creatures . . . encumbering the trains and devouring the subsistence along the line of march so much needed for the soldiers." A soldier marching under Carlin described the escaped slaves as the most "unadulterated miserable wretches as I ever saw." "The soldiers had no little fun at the expense of black people on that march," said a Fifteenth Corps staff officer. A benign incident was recorded by a member of the 100th Indiana who watched as a uniformed orderly stopped before a throng of blacks waiting at a crossroads to tell them that General Sherman was coming, wearing a fancy uniform and riding a mule-drawn carriage. "The poor Darkies took it all in," chuckled the soldier, "and when . . . one of our bummers came along dressed in a captured uniform that no doubt had been some cherished family keepsake . . . they marched along by the side of the road singing their songs till some one told them the truth."

The presence of a compliant and eager-to-please black population was a boon for Sherman's March. "We find the colored population our friends at all times," said an Ohioan. "When, as often happened during the march, information was given by the slaves, it could always be relied upon," recollected an Illinois comrade. A Connecticut officer in charge of one foraging party recorded how his command relied on black guides to avoid Rebel cavalry patrols. They enjoyed a peaceful bivouac after cleaning out two plantations. Only in the morning did the local blacks reveal to the officer "that a large Rebel force had passed on a cross-road, less than a mile from me, during the night. These negroes had, on their own hook, gone out beyond my pickets and stood watch for our additional safety."

Back with the main column, blacks made themselves useful in a variety of ways. "Two Sergeants in Co. C picked up a colored man at Madison, who wished to cast his lot with Sherman's army," recorded a member of the 123rd New York. "The very next day he 'confiscated' a good horse, and the Sergeants transferred their heavy knapsacks, tents and blankets, pots, kettles, frying pan, coffee pot, etc. to the back of the horse. At night Jack, the name of the colored man, came in with plenty of sweet potatoes, fresh pork, etc., and fodder for his 'mool' as he called him. . . . He said he was going to get a cook next day, and sure enough, next night he brought in two colored girls, one of them a house servant, who was quite aristocratic, the other a field hand. . . . Those two Sergeants had an easy time of it all the way to Savannah."

When Sherman's forces closed on the coastal citadel to plunge into its spongy barrier of swamps and flooded rice fields, the brawn of male blacks became a major asset. "New negro pioneer squads have been temporarily organized & [a] Serg[eant] is detailed from the regiment to take charge of them," reported a man in the 105th Ohio. An artilleryman with the Seventeenth Corps took note of the "Pioneer Corps now numbering some 600 negroes picked up on the march." This labor force enabled the Yankees to push through the zone of Confederate road obstructions with relative ease. "Rebels have blockaded roads along the swamps," recorded a Minnesota soldier, "but they are soon cleared away by our negro pioneers, who carry axes & spades." "The roads were nothing but quagmires," added a Fifteenth Corps infantryman. "We had 400 negroes, who constructed of pine logs and poles a double corduroy [road] from our front to the rear."

The one laboring job that blacks were not allowed to perform was railroad wrecking. Sherman made this task one of the highest, if not the highest, of priorities for his troops. Whenever it was possible, the march route followed a railroad right-of-way so that units—from single regiments to whole divisions—could be assigned to wrecking duties. "I attached much importance to this destruction of the railroad," Sherman said, "gave it my own personal attention, and made reiterated orders to others on the subject."

Major General Henry W. Slocum, commanding the Left Wing, reported that his men had destroyed 119 miles of rail, principally following the Georgia Railroad from outside Atlanta to where the line crossed the Oconee River, east of Madison. An additional six miles' worth came out of the Eatonton branch of the Central of Georgia around Milledgeville. The infantry of the Right Wing, under Major General Oliver O. Howard, claimed 191 miles destroyed. Their path of destruction followed the Central of Georgia, starting east of Macon, continuing to the crossing of the Little Ogeechee, forty-six miles west of Savannah. Twenty-four miles were ripped out of the Augusta and Savannah line, with more than forty pried from the Savannah and Gulf Railroad beds.

The traditional story of Sherman's March reckons each of these stretches wrecked with exquisite care. Indeed, when Sherman personally supervised, or the work was carried out by the 1st Michigan Engineers, destruction was total. However, when the job was left to the infantry without Sherman's presence, the results varied—from a thorough ripping of beds, burning of ties, and twisting of rails to a far more cursory vandalism, which often consisted only of flipping the track over and setting the sleepers on fire.

This helps explain why, on January 3, 1865, Confederate engineer chief Major General J. F. Gilmer was able to report that "cars now run from Macon to Milledgeville." By the end of the month, a determined traveler could complete a rail journey from Rutledge to Augusta. While it is true that whole sections between Gordon and Savannah would have to be abandoned, it was only because the Federal garrison in the latter place constituted a threat to working parties. This is not to say that the railroad wrecking was superficial. It wasn't; but it was several degrees less than the absolute destruction usually portrayed. Much the same could be said for the Confederate telegraph system, dismantled along with the railroads. By dint of hard work, the Southern Telegraph Company had service restored between Richmond and Mobile on January 1.

The notion that Sherman's March to the Sea was the first to display characteristics of widespread destruction is a persistent generalization grafted onto the saga soon after its completion, projected to an even greater degree in the century following the Civil War. Sherman's inclusion of civilian and commercial property on his list of legitimate military targets led some historians to proclaim that his campaign was one of "total war." This is to misread Sherman's intentions and to misunderstand the results of what happened.

"Total war" implies a military operation meant to obliterate civilian infrastructure preparatory to imposing a new order on that society. Sherman had no such desires. His more limited goal was to make any continuance of rebellion so unpalatable to southern civilians that they would view a return to the Union as the lesser of two evils. The overwhelming force he applied made it clear to all that the so-called Confederacy lacked the wherewithal to guarantee personal security. Sherman's decision to add civilian property to the mix stemmed from his belief in collective responsibility and his determination to punish the Southern leaders who should have been looking out for the welfare of their people by finding an accommodation with him.

Ironically, from Sherman's standard of values the March to the Sea was a failure. It was his hope to end the Civil War in such a way that the country would be able to turn back the clock to the idealized society that had (in his opinion) existed prior to the outbreak of the conflict. Political and social changes that he neither understood nor could control doomed that aspiration.

Sherman's metaphor that war was like a fight between two adolescents that ended when one was fairly beaten and agreed to henceforth play by the other's rules proved not to apply. Beaten Southerners may have rejoined the Union, but they had not renounced the essentials of the social system that had bound their society in 1860. New ways would be found to restore the old balance of white authority and black subservience, through manipulation of law and other forms of physical coercion that would restore the old order for nearly a century.

Sherman's way of war, however nontraditional in its means, was essentially conservative in its ultimate objectives. It is perhaps the supreme irony that the General departed Atlanta utterly convinced that his way would set things right again, when in fact he helped usher in changes whose implications must have appalled him.

*   *   *

In 1875, when it was far too late to do anything about it, Sherman tried to discourage the public's continuing fascination with the March to the Sea. "I only regarded the march from Atlanta to Savannah as a 'shift of base,' as the transfer of a strong army, which had no opponent, and had finished its then work, from the interior to a point on the sea-coast, from which it could achieve other important results. I considered this march as a means to an end, and not as an essential act of war." Nobody paid much attention to his declaration because everybody knew better. The March to the Sea, at least in the popular imagination, was seen as a defining moment in American history. Its significance was promoted by Northerners and Southerners, though for decidedly different reasons.

Those in the North were in the process of enshrining an enduring image of the common men who preserved the Union. From the halls of Congress (where veteran pensions were a hot topic) to the mainstream press (who found that printing soldier recollections often boosted circulation), the picture of "Billy Yank" was taking shape. One problem was that most such chronicles often ended in an untidy and bloody battle. The March to the Sea offered size and scope without the gore— at least, without much. As one veteran officer (though not a march participant) wrote in an article aimed at "Young Folks," "The romantic character of the march is unsurpassed. That an army should disappear from sight for a month, marching unharmed through hostile regions, its whereabouts unknown to its friends, and emerge at last as if out of a wilderness, with undiminished numbers and increased renown, is a circumstance that equals in interest any in history; and so long as America's boys and girls read the account of the nation's achievements, they will find no chapter more fascinating than that which tells of Sherman's March to the Sea."

Many of the common soldiers who afterward recounted their experiences in this campaign both shaped and were shaped by its popular conception. "We had a gay trip through the State of Ga.," wrote an Ohio boy to his "Coz" Sallie in December 1864. "Plenty of fat hogs, sweet taters, molasses, pea nuts, scared niggers and other eatables too numerous to mention on the whole route." Twenty-four years later, a best-selling soldier memoir (*Hardtack and Coffee*, by John D. Billings) would remark that "this traveling picnic of the Western armies was unique." Also enshrined was the image of the bummer as a carefree warrior, ingenious in his means of acquisition, dogged in his determination to fight when challenged.

Usually forgotten in the retellings were the days of miserable weather that accompanied travel along rudimentary roads, the ever-present fear of murderous irregulars lurking just outside the picket lines, the back-breaking toil of shoving loaded wagons by hand through clay gumbo, the almost constant crack of muskets as enemy cavalry pressed the column's rear, the miles of corduroy lanes, and the briefly violent roadblock actions. While contemporary accounts make it clear that no one was untainted by the foraging operations (if a soldier didn't personally appropriate the food, he ate it without compunction when it was brought into camp), the passage of time led participants to assuage any lingering guilt by writing about such incidents in broad strokes or illustrating them by means of a humorous anecdote.

In sharp contrast, the other side's story of the march emphasized and amplified every encounter to an outrage. A sympathetic historian, writing in the 1950s, commented that a "bitter feeling toward the North, a belief that Yankees were barbarians, an utter detestation of Sherman, lived long in the minds of Southerners." An 1875 Augusta newspaper review of Sherman's *Memoirs* concluded that the General's reputation would be forever sullied "by acts of cruelty and brutality which would have disgraced the chieftain of a tribe of Indians or the leader of a band of brigands." When, in 1911, the U.S. Post Office issued a stamp bearing Sherman's image, outrage throughout the South was palpable. "If W. T. Sherman's face must be held up to view, send it to those who love his character and celebrate his victory in song, but not to those whose homes he robbed, whose daughters he insulted, whose sons he murdered, and whose cities and homes he burned," thundered one editorial.

Perhaps *the* lightning rod for rage at Sherman's Savannah Campaign was the song "Marching through Georgia," written in early 1865 by a Chicago-based composer named Henry Clay Work. Although he was a successful creator of melodic material for the commercial marketplace, Work was no hack. He was a meticulous, painstaking tunesmith, whose war songs were often animated by a humanitarian abolitionism. Unlike many peers who milked black stereotypes for all their minstrel-show guffaws, Work strove for more humane characterizations. Those strains of high craftsmanship coupled with an underdog sympathy came together in "Marching through Georgia." To an original and compelling melody, the composer set his own verse, which in a remarkably short span managed to touch many of the campaign's high points. He referenced the slaves who abandoned their owners ("How the darkies shouted when they heard the joyful sound!"), the foraging ("How the turkeys gobbled which our commissary found!/ How the sweet potatos even started from the ground"), and the hapless opposition ("Treason fled before us, for resistance was in vain").

In the North, much to Sherman's displeasure, the song became a hit, as well as an obligatory accompaniment to his public appearances. "I wish I had a dollar for every time I have had to listen to that blasted tune," he was heard to mutter on one such occasion. Its reception farther south was quite different. A human face was put on the issue in 1902 when Miss Laura Talbot Galt, a thirteen-year-old student in the Louisville, Kentucky, school system, refused to sing the song in class. She even put her hands over her ears while her classmates performed the piece. "I did that because I would not listen to a song that declares such a tyrant and coward as Sherman and his disgraceful and horrible march through Georgia . . . to be glorious," she declared in an open letter to the press. Fifteen years later, a Macon assembly representing "Children of the Confederacy" passed a resolution protesting "against the use of the so-called 'hate song,' *Marching through Georgia*, and [we] urge its suppression and elimination in all schools and on all public occasions."

Time has neutralized much of the acid in these sentiments, but the phrase *Sherman's March* has morphed into a comfortable metaphor for a scorched-earth policy, and its architect has become an accepted synonym for a pariah. A series of damaging Georgia floods in the twentieth century were said to represent "probably its worst devastation since Sherman's Civil War march to the sea," and an Atlanta sportswriter, speaking of a disgraced Braves ballplayer, called him "the most disliked person hereabouts since William Tecumseh Sherman." A T-shirt sold during the 1996 Summer Olympic games in Atlanta sported a fiery image of the General with the legend: "Atlanta's Original Torch Bearer."

It seems that Sherman's "shift of base" will forever be best remembered for everything that it wasn't.

*   *   *

Sherman's March to the Sea was a highly organized, carefully planned operation that also allowed ample room for improvisation. The columns departing Atlanta on November 15–16 were not traveling lean and mean. Packed into more than 2,500 wagons were a twenty-day supply of bread; forty days of sugar, coffee, and salt; and three days' worth of animal feed. Moving with the lengthy wagon trains were 5,000 cattle, representing a forty-day beef supply. Writing to his surrogate father from Savannah, Sherman rejected the notion that he had been "rash in cutting loose from a base and relying on the country for forage and provisions. I had wagons enough loaded with essentials, and beef cattle enough to feed on for more than a month, and had the census statistics showing the produce of every county through which I desired to pass. No military expedition was ever based on sounder or surer data."

Solving the problems in getting so many heavy, awkward vehicles over the watercourses large and small, along dirt tracks that were roads in name only, or through the sucking swamps outside Savannah represented a logistical achievement of unparalleled accomplishment. Sherman's "secret weapon" (secret only from most of the popular postwar accounts) were the two pontoon detachments and the pioneer units, the latter of which began the march mostly white and ended up largely black in composition. Without the skillful hard work of the army's bridge makers and road fixers, the march would have become a dispiriting slog through Georgia. The fact that Sherman could plan a route across fifteen significant creeks, streams, or rivers, requiring bridging at an average 230 feet per crossing (many more smaller water crossings were built), along with nearly 100 miles of corduroy paths, most of which was accomplished without serious delay to the columns, speaks to the effectiveness of this arm of the General's operation. Not surprisingly, Sherman's chief engineer, Captain Orlando Poe, was afterward jumped two ranks to colonel for his work.

Foraging was a double-edged sword during the March to the Sea. On the one hand, Sherman's supply situation required it. On the other, if it was allowed to take place without controls, the army's combat effectiveness would be seriously degraded. By making use of his personal currency with his officers and men, aided by a few strongly worded orders on the subject, Sherman was able to keep something of a lid on the activity. He accepted the inevitability of some excesses, while he also distanced himself from any direct responsibility, which allowed him to focus on operational matters as his columns passed from the well-drained red clay region above the fall line into the sandy bogs and swamps of the coastal lowlands.

In his official report of this campaign, Sherman put the damage done to the Georgian infrastructure at $100 million. It was a number without context, meant more to suggest the grand scale of his wrecking rather than a sober assessment of its costs to the Confederacy. The property consumed by Sherman's men was, for the most part, the result of a focused targeting. Food-refining or product-manufacturing buildings were high-priority objects, as well as just about any structure that could be associated with the railroads. Also topping the hit lists were government assets at all levels—town, county, state, and national. Almost everything else that suffered—in the built-up areas, at least—was what a later generation of military planners would term collateral damage. Houses unfortunate enough to be located adjacent to priority targets were often caught up in the flames and the general disinclination of Union officers to expend any effort to protect them. Exceptions, where dwellings safely distanced from the approved targets were torched, had a lot to do with circumstances or plain bad luck. The unexpectedly sharp Rebel rearguard action at Sandersville exposed much of the town to Yankee wrath, while blocked roads that held a Federal column in place for a while in Louisville also spelled trouble when bored soldiers turned to mob vandalism. When the columns kept moving and priority targets were sufficiently isolated, collateral damage was minimal.

Not accounted for in any of the quantitative measurements was the psychological impact of what was, to all intents and purposes, a home invasion on a grand scale. One Illinois soldier never forgot how the white property owners viewed the looting of their holdings "with grim despair depicted on their countenances." "We were the first live Yankees many of them had ever seen," recorded Henry Slocum, "and our long columns filling through their quiet country towns inspired almost as much curiosity as terror." "Some few look and act scornful and indignant to think that the Yankees should have dared to tread the sacred soil of Georgia," added a Seventeenth Corps soldier, "others terrified and frightened stand mute as Egyptian mummies and stare . . . with disheveled faces upon the passing and conquering army."

Devastation of crops and animal stock was significant, but not on the scale of a great plague. For all the acumen they showed at winkling out hidden goods, Sherman's foragers missed much. That some families suffered serious losses cannot be denied, but neither can the fact that most found ways to make it through the winter of 1864–1865, with no cases of starvation reported. Many a little boy or girl who viewed the outrages with wide-eyed horror lived to write about those experiences when they were old and gray. The Civil War devastated much of the South, and, sad to say, there were other regions which could match wrecked economies with the 60-by-300-mile swath marked out by Sherman's columns. War, it must be said, is an equal-opportunity destroyer; a Pennsylvania farmer visited by Confederates on their way to Gettysburg would have much in common with a Georgia farmer caught in the path of the March to the Sea.

*   *   *

Confederate resistance to Sherman's campaign was fatally hampered at the very outset thanks to the defensive scheme imposed by Jefferson Davis. By parceling out authority among several regional commanders who enjoyed supreme oversight within their domains, while allowing his designated overall chief (Beauregard) to self-limit his authority, Davis virtually guaranteed that what scarce assets were available to oppose Sherman's March would be used in the most inefficient manner. The question must be asked: Could Confederate forces have inflicted such damage on Sherman's force that he would have contemplated turning back? The answer is a firm no. Sherman's troops were simply too good and too experienced, their commander too fixed in his purpose. There is no questioning the fortitude and determination of the Georgia militiamen who attacked a numerically inferior Federal force at Griswoldville; still, the outcome was a terrible defeat.

Yet Confederates could have inflicted some serious damage on Sherman's operation. Wheeler was the key. If his mounted units (arguably the best fighters available on the Rebel side) could have been concentrated against the Federal logistical tail (the pontoon train especially), there is little doubt that the Union columns would have been considerably impeded. This might have resulted in Sherman reaching Savannah in a much less vigorous condition than he did, which would have forced him to take much more time to subdue the coastal fortress. All of which might well have pushed his departure from Savannah into the Carolinas into March, if not April. What the Confederacy might have done with such a delay is another question altogether.

Such speculation is ultimately moot, because Wheeler was juggled from regional commander to regional commander, who required him to spread his units thin to carry out what they designated as his primary mission—intelligence gathering. The times he met Kilpatrick with anything approaching parity, there was a sharp combat. Given the volatile nature of cavalry engagements, the side that retained the battlefield at the end of the fight (a traditional measure of victory) meant very little. In virtually every mounted engagement of any consequence in this campaign, each side would legitimately claim its mission objectives had been achieved. When a unit making a retrograde movement is attacked, success for both sides is assured, since each completes its assignment. Given the practical impossibility of assessing losses absorbed and inflicted in such a continuous campaign, each cavalry commander let his imagination fill in the blank spaces, resulting in claimed totals that would have wiped out both sides. The fact that save for operational wear and tear, the opposing horsemen were ready to renew the combat right after Savannah says all that needs to be said about the casualty exchange.

Even as the mounted forces picked up where they had left off after Savannah to continue the action in the Carolinas, Georgia's Governor Brown was fuming over reports of excesses committed by Wheeler's men while in his state. Given his naturally litigious personality, Brown launched an investigation, documented his case, then filed a lengthy brief with General Beauregard, who promptly forwarded the matter along to Major General Wheeler. Wheeler counterattacked by submitting affidavits from his subcommanders blaming other parties (including Georgia militiamen, roving bandit gangs, and even a special unit of Wheeler impostors organized by Sherman to spread discontent) that completely exonerated his command from any misbehavior. By the time this all came to a head, it was April 1865, so there was no prospect that the competing claims would ever be impartially examined.

In a note included in the case file he had amassed, Governor Brown allowed himself the observation: "I cannot withhold the expression of my surprise, that General Wheeler should pronounce all the important charges of horse stealing, breaking open houses and stealing property of citizens, which are made against his command, to be basely false."

*   *   *

Adding up the numbers for the March to the Sea is more an exercise in conjecture than it is a computation of data. For all his careful details of damage inflicted and generous estimates of the destruction done, Sherman was remarkably lax when it came to counting the cost to his army. What tables and tabulations are to be found in the *Official Records* are all partials, and there is no consistent time frame applied to what reports are given. Missing entirely are any overall summaries for the entire Right Wing.

A 1908 calculation by a Union veteran named Frederick H. Dyer, who was obsessed with what today we would call "number crunching," provides a useful starting point. Dyer figured that the Savannah Campaign (November 15 to December 10) cost Sherman 136 killed, 673 wounded, and 280 missing, for a total of 1,089. Additionally, Dyer tacked on another 200 losses in combined killed and wounded for the siege itself. Dyer seems not to have accounted for death from disease and accidents; fortunately, here we have a report from the Right Wing's medical director (there is no corresponding report for the Left Wing) that records 32 soldiers dying from disease and adds that 29 of those initially tagged as wounded succumbed to their injuries. Making appropriate allowances for the Left Wing, the best estimate becomes approximately 240 killed, 650 wounded, and 280 missing, totaling 1,170.

Such a patchwork of incomplete hard data and extrapolations applies also to the extant Confederate information. A Southern version of Dyer by the name of Edwin L. Drake ran some Confederate numbers in 1878. Working only with general tabulations (killed/ wounded/missing), he put Wheeler's campaign losses at 596. Turning to the mix of infantry forces opposing the march, Drake estimated losses during the Savannah siege of 800. To these lists of losses we can add Griswoldville's 550, Fort McAllister's 200, and another 100 for various skirmishes, to reach an estimated total of 2,300. It's a useful number to keep in mind when hearing Federal assessments term the Confederate efforts as "feeble."

How much Georgia vengeance was visited upon Union foragers is difficult to assess with any precision. Most Union accounts of men murdered while gathering supplies are secondhand; reliable primary testimony is rare. That some Yankee boys were killed while in the act of foraging is undoubtedly true. One modern historian puts the body count at 64 found in such a condition as to suggest execution. However, most of the significant incidents reported by Southern civilians or cavalrymen seem to exist more to counter deprecations against Georgia manhood than to accurately relay facts.

One account relates how some property owners banded together to jump the foragers at their night camp. "They would kill whole small parties of foragers and bury them in the woods," he declared, conveniently explaining why no bodies had been found. There is another recollection of the slaughter of a number of captured foragers in the town of Sandersville just before the Union occupation—an incident unreported by the Federal soldiers who flooded the area afterward, assiduously probing into every pile of freshly turned earth seeking buried treasures.

Georgians needed to believe that they had resisted the invaders to some degree; Union officers allowed the rumors of such killings to circulate in the hope it would discourage unofficial foraging. Thus it was in the interests of both sides to leave unchallenged the various claims of wandering soldiers waylaid and murdered. Assuming the number of Union soldiers missing to all be captured or killed foragers, and eliminating reasonable combat losses from the mortality total with the residue due to foraging, it can be estimated that on average, 14 soldiers were either killed or captured foraging each day between November 15 and December 10. Using a formula applied in the Fourteenth Corps of 1 man in 20 being assigned to these duties on a daily basis, roughly 3,000 infantrymen were actively foraging on any given day. (Given the number of "unofficial" foragers, the actual number could easily be double that.) Nonetheless, using the conservative number, the chance of a forager running into serious trouble was about one-half of one percent.

*   *   *

Sherman's successful completion of the march further strengthened his great friendship with Ulysses S. Grant. Grant had expended much political capital with President Lincoln in helping to convince the chief executive to approve the operation at a time when some of the lieutenant general's senior staff opposed it. Even though the public record made clear that it initially took Grant a while to become comfortable with the March to the Sea concept, after the war he would loyally insist that he had been "in favor of Sherman's plan from the time it was first submitted to me."

Sherman actually passed two tests in Grant's way of measuring things. The first was his demonstration of professional competence in managing the campaign. The second was the public manner in which he resisted the kinds of boosters who would have had him competing with his friend's accomplishments. When Sherman's senator-brother John reported some talk about promoting him to the same rank as Grant, the General would hear none of it. "I will accept no commission that would tend to create a rivalry with Grant," he declared. "I want him to hold what he has earned and got. I have all the rank I want." "How few there are who when rising to popular favor as he now is would stop to say a word in defense of the only one between himself and the highest in command," Grant confided to his wife at this time. "I am glad to say that I appreciated Sherman from the first feeling him to be what he has proven to the world he is."

While honest in his respect and affection for what he called "the singular friendship of General Grant," Sherman also noted that the lieutenant general was "almost childlike in his love for me."

*   *   *

Sherman's generalship for the first portion of the march (Atlanta to Milledgeville) showed him at his thoughtful, self-confident best. Both wings moved under instructions drafted beforehand, with neither encountering anything to cause them to alter the program. Kilpatrick's mounted command operated with the Right Wing, where it provided invaluable service when Howard's columns passed closest to Macon. Wheeler's failure to interdict the Federal procession to any serious degree owed as much to the dispersion of his forces (thanks to conflicting priorities imposed on him by the Confederate leadership) as it did to the effectiveness of Kilpatrick's screen. Had the Rebel leaders clustered in Macon used their combined militia-infantry and cavalry with a coherent and targeted plan, Sherman's dispositions might have proven inadequate to shrug off the blows, but as events played out, the disorganized enemy was never able to do anything more than annoy isolated Federal units.

Once at Milledgeville, Sherman rapidly assessed the condition of his forces as well as the Confederate response, then made adjustments. He clearly expected much more trouble coming out of Augusta than he had registered from Macon. (From contemporary communications, the intensity of the fighting at Griswoldville was very much underreported at the time.) Sherman's willingness to switch Kilpatrick's command from the Right Wing to the Left shows the flexibility the General applied to his thinking. While he afterward downplayed any danger from Confederate troops gathered in Augusta, his decision to closely support Kilpatrick's forays with infantry suggests that he viewed the threat seriously.

The cavalry commander's inflated claims of success at Waynesboro were accepted without question by army headquarters, and based on that assessment of damage, Sherman left his vulnerable logistical tail open to attack by spreading Kilpatrick's men thin across the entire rear of the Left Wing. Once again, what might have proven to be a fruitful opening for enemy thrusts coming out of Augusta became no more than a mild bother as Braxton Bragg steadfastly refused to release any infantry from the earthworks protecting his temporary charge. Bragg's tunnel vision was compounded by Hardee's decision (firmly seconded by Beauregard) to transfer most cavalry operations to South Carolina, leaving just a few mounted units to harry the Federal logistical tail. It was another opportunity squandered.

(Ironically, Sherman scored a significant success against a target not even on his hit list. On November 21, workers began dismantling the irreplaceable machinery at the Confederate Powder Works in Augusta for transportation out of danger. For the next month no gunpowder was produced there. Everything was returned in early December so that the mill complex was back in business by the end of the year. Still, for thirty critical days, the South's largest gunpowder maker was virtually shuttered. Production in November 1864 topped 101,000 pounds; that for December was little more than 13,600 pounds.)

Sherman's equanimity was showing cracks by the time he confronted Savannah's formidable defenses. Fort McAllister was assaulted without any thought given to less costly alternatives. Luck was again riding with Sherman as the Rebel defenses proved more theoretical than actual. Smart, potentially murderous preparations had been made, but here Union courage and determination overwhelmed any positional advantages enjoyed by the Rebels.

The completely unexpected news that Grant wanted him to break off operations short of finishing the job further upset Sherman's equilibrium. His thinking on the capture of Savannah veered all across the spectrum. At first he was prepared to tighten his grip in order to starve the garrison into submission. Then, when Grant's bombshell message was received, he considered a quick assault heedless of the casualties. Sherman finally settled on a third option—a direct assault combined with a strong move against Hardee's sole link with Charleston, before the Confederate officer saved him the trouble.

Throughout the march, Sherman demonstrated the ethical inconsistency of a person whose strong general principles had to personally confront individuals affected by those policies. His sparing of cotton holdings in Milledgeville, and the varying degree of sympathy he showed to families he encountered along the way, speak to a moral drift that doesn't match the traditional image of stone-faced devastator. Except on those cases where his acutely personal standard of right and wrong was violated, Sherman never sanctioned destruction outside the limits he had established. Yet he had accepted from the outset that damage would occur that he could not control. Much to the discomfort of those near him who expected a rigid consistency, Sherman embraced the seeming contradictions, assuaging his conscience by blaming southerners for their complicity and deeming himself powerless in the random destructiveness of the storm he had unleashed.

Most of these rough spots were progressively forgotten by Sherman as he later wrote and talked about the March to the Sea. As well written as they are, his *Memoirs* grant him a degree of insight and calm reasoning that is not always borne out by more contemporary correspondence and actions. Sherman eventually distilled his recollections into a summary overview that trimmed off the dross, leaving only hard certainties. His thoughts were clearly expressed in a speech he gave at a reunion of the Army of the Tennessee (Howard's wing) that took place in Des Moines, Iowa, on September 30, 1875. On that occasion he delivered what in many ways were his valedictory thoughts on the campaign that would forever define him and set his place in history.

The "March to the Sea," as it is called, is a kind of an epoch in the history of the country, and occupies a prominent place in our memories. But this march began early. When you moved from Vicksburg to [Fort] Donelson, in a very early period of the war, you were moving to the sea. . . . And so the grand march went on till we found ourselves in Atlanta, in possession of a town. Now, up to that time it had been the policy of all to sow peace and prosperity wherever our armies trod. Indeed, we were playing into the hands of our enemies. We made up the roads after us. . . . We had tried kindness, but it seemed to be entirely lost. The stern rule of war must be applied to those who deserved the switch, and we did it. We had gone on stage line, on wagon line, and on railroad. We had hundreds of miles of roads to defend, consuming and absorbing our own strength, and it became necessary to stop that right there. . . . It must have entered into the minds of many that this was the time when something could be done. I therefore say that I determined to send back enough of that army which was then at my command to enable Gen. Thomas to defeat Hood and let Tennessee live, while the rest of us should go on to crush in that body of our enemies which was there before us between the two great conquering armies of the Union. . . . Now, gentlemen, that March to the Sea, so beautiful and poetical, was an example for armies. We went to the sea with some opposition, it is true, but well provided for, suffering but little; but in so doing we transgressed the rules of war that armies should not be more than 100 miles from their head-quarters. . . . But we had a journey of 300 miles to take, and we determined to make it and to subsist on our friends and enemies while making it. Now, so far as this is concerned, it is a subject rather of mirth than of serious moment. Georgia was at that time regarded, not only here but all over the world, as the arch stone of the South. That once destroyed, and the Southern Confederacy dwindled down to the little space between the Savannah River and

Richmond. The consequences of this march were felt all over the country. All acknowledged that when Savannah should be taken the road to Richmond was clear, and that the war was at an end. And I appeal to those who remained at home if they did not feel that victory was near— if their hearts did not throb more warmly, and if their whole nature was not stirred to its very depths when they heard that the Army had reached Savannah? It was felt that the solution of this great problem of our civil war was assured, and that the people of the United States could not only vindicate their laws but could punish the traitors. The thoughts arising here overflow—spread like the waves of the sea, circling wider and wider till they inclose the whole field of our toils. Certain it is that this march was great in its conception and in its execution grand—that the blow was struck at the right moment and in the right direction.

UNION FORCES ROSTER

MILITARY DIVISION OF THE MISSISSIPPI

Maj. Gen. William T. Sherman, commanding

ARMY HEADQUARTERS

Lieut. Col. Charles Ewing, inspector general
Capt. Lewis M. Dayton, adjutant general
Capt. Orlando M. Poe, chief of engineers
Capt. Thomas G. Baylor, chief ordnance officer
Brevet Brig. Gen. Langdon C. Easton, chief quartermaster
Col. Amos Beckwith, chief commissary
Dr. John Moore, chief medical director
Maj. J. C. McCoy, aide-de-camp
Maj. Henry Hitchcock, aide-de-camp
Capt. Joseph C. Audenried, aide-de-camp
Capt. George W. Nichols, aide

ARMY OF THE TENNESSEE (RIGHT WING)

Maj. Gen. Oliver O. Howard

PONTONIERS

1st Missouri Engineers
Lieut. Col. William Tweeddale

FIFTEENTH ARMY CORPS [15,894]

Maj. Gen. Peter J. Osterhaus

FIRST DIVISION

Brig. Gen. Charles R. Woods

FIRST BRIGADE

Col. Milo Smith

12th Indiana
Maj. Elbert D. Baldwin

26th Iowa
Maj. John Lubbers
27th Missouri
Col. Thomas Curly
29th Missouri
Lieut. Col. Joseph S. Gage

31st/32nd Missouri Battalion
    Maj. Abraham J. Seay
76th Ohio
    Col. William B. Woods

SECOND BRIGADE

Brig. Gen. Charles C. Walcutt (w)
Col. James S. Martin

26th Illinois
    Capt. George H. Reed
40th Illinois
    Lieut. Col. Hiram W. Hall
103rd Illinois
    Maj. Asias Willson
97th Indiana
    Col. Robert F. Catterson
    Capt. George Elliott

100th Indiana
    Maj. Ruel M. Johnson
6th Iowa
    Maj. William H. Clune
46th Ohio
    Lieut. Col. Isaac N. Alexander

THIRD BRIGADE

Col. James A. Williamson

4th Iowa
    Lieut. Col. Samuel D. Nichols
9th Iowa
    Capt. Paul McSweeney
25th Iowa
    Col. George A. Stone
30th Iowa
    Lieut. Col. Aurelius Roberts
31st Iowa
    Lieut. Col. Jeremiah W. Jenkins

SECOND DIVISION

Brig. Gen. William B. Hazen

FIRST BRIGADE

Col. Theodore Jones

55th Illinois
    Capt. Charles A. Andress
116th Illinois
    Lieut. Col. John E. Maddux
127th Illinois
    Capt. Charles Schryver
6th Missouri
    Lieut. Col. Delos van Deusen
8th Missouri
    Capt. John W. White
30th Ohio
    Capt. Emory W. Muenscher
57th Ohio
    Maj. John McClure

SECOND BRIGADE

Col. Wells S. Jones (w)
Col. James S. Martin

111th Illinois
    Col. James S. Martin
    Maj. William M. Mabry
83rd Indiana
    Lieut. Col. George H. Scott
37th Ohio
    Lieut. Col. Louis von Blessingh
47th Ohio
    Col. Augustus C. Parry
53rd Ohio
    Capt. David H. Lasley
54th Ohio
    Lieut. Col. Israel T. Moore

THIRD BRIGADE

Col. John M. Oliver

48th Illinois
    Maj. Edward Adams
90th Illinois
    Lieut. Col. Owen Stuart
99th Indiana
    Lieut. Col. John M. Berkey

15th Michigan
Lieut. Col. Frederick S. Hutchinson

70th Ohio
Lieut. Col. Henry L. Philips

THIRD DIVISION

Brig. Gen. John E. Smith

FIRST BRIGADE

Col. Joseph B. McCown

63rd Illinois
Lieut. Col. James Isaminger
93rd Illinois
Lieut. Col. Nicholas C. Buswell
48th Indiana
Lieut. Col. Edward J. Wood
59th Indiana
Lieut. Col. Jefferson K. Scott
4th Minnesota
Col. John E. Tourtellotte

SECOND BRIGADE

Bvt. Brig. Gen. Green. B. Raum

56th Illinois
Capt. James P. Files
10th Iowa
Lieut. Col. Paris P. Henderson
10th/26th Missouri
Col. Benjamin D. Dean
80th Ohio
Lieut. Col. Pren Metham

FOURTH DIVISION

Brig. Gen. John M. Corse

FIRST BRIGADE

Brig. Gen. Elliott W. Rice

52nd Illinois
Maj. Wesley Boyd
Lieut. Col. Jerome D. Davis
66th Indiana
Lieut. Col. Roger Martin
2nd Iowa
Lieut. Col. Noel B. Howard
7th Iowa
Lieut. Col. James C. Parrott

SECOND BRIGADE

Col. Robert N. Adams

12th Illinois
Lieut. Col. Henry van Sellar
66th Illinois
Lieut. Col. Andrew K. Campbell
81st Ohio
Maj. William C. Henry

THIRD BRIGADE

Lieut. Col. Frederick J. Hurlbut

7th Illinois
Lieut. Col. Hector Perrin
50th Illinois
Capt. Henry Horn
57th Illinois
Capt. Frederick A. Battey
39th Iowa
Maj. Joseph M. Griffiths

ARTILLERY BRIGADE

Maj. Charles J. Stolbrand

1st Illinois Light Artillery: Battery H
Capt. Francis De Gress
1st Michigan Light Artillery: Battery B
Capt. Albert F. R. Arndt (w)
1st Missouri Light Artillery: Battery H
Lieut. John F. Brunner
Wisconsin Light Artillery: 12th Battery
Capt. William Zickerick

SEVENTEENTH ARMY CORPS [11,732]

Maj. Gen. Frank P. Blair Jr.

FIRST DIVISION

Maj. Gen. Joseph A. Mower

FIRST BRIGADE

Brig. Gen. John W. Fuller

64th Illinois
  Capt. Joseph S. Reynolds
18th Missouri
  Lieut. Col. Charles S. Sheldon
27th Ohio
  Capt. James Morgan
39th Ohio
  Capt. Daniel Weber

SECOND BRIGADE

Brig. Gen. John W. Sprague

35th New Jersey
  Col. John J. Cladek

43rd Ohio
  Col. Wager Swayne
63rd Ohio
  Maj. John W. Fouts
25th Wisconsin
  Lieut. Col. Jeremiah M. Rusk

THIRD BRIGADE

Col. John Tillson

10th Illinois
  Lieut. Col. McLain F. Wood
25th Indiana
  Maj. James S. Wright
32nd Wisconsin
  Col. Charles H. De Groat

THIRD DIVISION

Brig. Gen. Mortimer D. Leggett

FIRST BRIGADE

Brig. Gen. Manning F. Force

30th Illinois
  Lieut. Col. William C. Rhoads
31st Illinois
  Lieut. Col. Robert N. Pearson
45th Illinois
  Maj. John O. Duer
12th Wisconsin
  Lieut. Col. James K. Proudfit
16th Wisconsin
  Maj. William F. Dawes

SECOND BRIGADE

Col. Robert K. Scott

20th Ohio
  Capt. Lyman N. Ayres
68th Ohio
  Lieut. Col. George E. Welles
78th Ohio
  Col. Greenberry F. Wiles
17th Wisconsin
  Maj. Patrick H. McCauley

FOURTH DIVISION

Brig. Gen. Giles A. Smith

FIRST BRIGADE

Col. Benjamin F. Potts

14th/15th Illinois Battalion
  Lieut. Alonzo J. Gillespie
41st Illinois Battalion
  Maj. Robert H. McFadden
53rd Illinois
  Col. John W. McClanahan
23rd Indiana
  Lieut. Col. George S. Babbitt
53rd Indiana
  Capt. Henry Duncan
32nd Ohio
  Lieut. Col. Jefferson J. Hibbets

THIRD BRIGADE

Brig. Gen. William W. Belknap

32nd Illinois
  Maj. Henry Davidson

11th Iowa
  Capt. Benjamin Beach
13th Iowa
  Capt. Justin C. Kennedy
15th Iowa
  Maj. George Pomutz
16th Iowa
  Capt. Crandall W. Williams

ARTILLERY BRIGADE

Maj. Allen C. Waterhouse

1st Michigan Light Artillery: Battery C
  Lieut. Henry Shier
Minnesota Light Artillery: 1st Battery
  Lieut. Henry Hurter
Ohio Light Artillery: 15th Battery
  Lieut. George R. Caspar

ARMY OF GEORGIA (LEFT WING)

Maj. Gen. Henry W. Slocum

PONTONIERS

58th Indiana
Col. George P. Buell

FOURTEENTH ARMY CORPS [13,962]

Bvt. Maj. Gen. Jefferson C. Davis

FIRST DIVISION

Brig. Gen. William P. Carlin

FIRST BRIGADE

Col. Harrison C. Hobart

104th Illinois
  Lieut. Col. Douglas Hapeman

42nd Indiana
  Capt. Gideon R. Kellams
88th Indiana
  Lieut. Col. Cyrus E. Briant
33rd Ohio
  Capt. Joseph Hinson

94th Ohio
  Lieut. Col. Rue P. Hutchins
21st Wisconsin
  Lieut. Col. Michael H. Fitch

SECOND BRIGADE

Lieut. Col. Joseph H. Brigham

13th Michigan
  Lieut. Col. Theodoric R. Palmer
21st Michigan
  Maj. Benton D. Fox
69th Ohio
  Capt. Lewis E. Hicks

THIRD BRIGADE

Col. Henry A. Hambright
Lieut. Col. David Miles

38th Indiana
  Capt. James H. Low
21st Ohio
  Lieut. Col. Arnold McMahan
74th Ohio
  Maj. Joseph Fisher
  Maj. Robert P. Findley
79th Pennsylvania
  Lieut. Col. David Miles
  Maj. Michael H. Locher

SECOND DIVISION

Brig. Gen. James D. Morgan

FIRST BRIGADE

Col. Robert F. Smith

16th Illinois
  Lieut. Col. James B. Cahill
60th Illinois
  Col. William B. Anderson
14th Michigan
  Maj. Thomas C. Fitzgibbon
17th New York
  Lieut. Col. Joel O. Martin

SECOND BRIGADE

Lieut. Col. John S. Pearce

34th Illinois
  Capt. Peter Ege
78th Illinois
  Lieut. Col. Maris R. Vernon
98th Ohio
  Capt. James R. McLaughlin

108th Ohio
  Maj. Frederick Beck
113th Ohio
  Capt. Toland Jones
121st Ohio
  Maj. Aaron B. Robinson

THIRD BRIGADE

Lieut. Col. James W. Langley

85th Illinois
  Maj. Robert G. Rider
86th Illinois
  Lieut. Col. Allen L. Fahnestock
110th Illinois
  Lieut. Col. E. Hibbard Topping
125th Illinois
  Capt. George W. Cook
22nd Indiana
  Capt. William H. Snodgrass
52nd Ohio
  Lieut. Col. Charles W. Claney

THIRD DIVISION

Brig. Gen. Absalom Baird

FIRST BRIGADE

Col. Morton C. Hunter

82nd Indiana
  Lieut. Col. John M. Matheny
23rd Missouri
  Lieut. Col. Quin Morton
17th Ohio
  Lieut. Col. Benjamin H. Showers
31st Ohio
  Capt. Michael Stone
89th Ohio
  Lieut. Col. William H. Glenn
92nd Ohio
  Col. Benjamin D. Fearing

SECOND BRIGADE

Col. Newell Gleason

75th Indiana
  Maj. Cyrus J. McCole
87th Indiana
  Lieut. Col. Edwin P. Hammond
101st Indiana
  Lieut. Col. Thomas Doan
2nd Minnesota
  Lieut. Col. Judson W. Bishop

105th Ohio
  Lieut. Col. George T. Perkins

THIRD BRIGADE

Col. George P. Este

74th Indiana
  Lieut. Col. Thomas Morgan
18th Kentucky
  Lieut. Col. Hubbard K. Milward
14th Ohio
  Lieut. Col. Albert Moore
38th Ohio
  Capt. Charles M. Gilbert

ARTILLERY BRIGADE

Maj. Charles Houghtaling

1st Illinois Light Artillery: Battery C
  Lieut. Joseph R. Channel
2nd Illinois Light Artillery: Battery I
  Lieut. Alonzo W. Coe
Indiana Light Artillery: 19th Battery
  Capt. William P. Stackhouse
Wisconsin Light Artillery: 5th Battery
  Lieut. Joseph McKnight

TWENTIETH ARMY CORPS [13,741]

Brig. Gen. Alpheus S. Williams

FIRST DIVISION

Brig. Gen. Nathaniel J. Jackson

FIRST BRIGADE

Col. James L. Selfridge

5th Connecticut
  Lieut. Col. Henry W. Daboll
123rd New York
  Lieut. Col. James C. Rogers
141st New York
  Capt. William Merrell

46th Pennsylvania
  Maj. Patrick Griffith

SECOND BRIGADE

Col. Ezra A. Carmen

2nd Massachusetts [316/136]
  Col. William Cogswell

13th New Jersey
   Maj. Frederick H. Harris
107th New York
   Capt. Charles J. Fox
   Lieut. Col. Allen N. Sill
150th New York
   Maj. Alfred B. Smith
   Col. John H. Ketcham
3rd Wisconsin
   Col. William Hawley

THIRD BRIGADE

Col. James S. Robinson

82nd Illinois
   Maj. Ferdinand H. Rolshausen

101st Illinois
   Lieut. Col. John B. Le Sage
143rd New York
   Lieut. Col. Hezekiah Watkins
61st Ohio
   Capt. John Garrett
82nd Ohio
   Lieut. Col. David Thomson
31st Wisconsin
   Col. Francis H. West

SECOND DIVISION

Brig. Gen. John W. Geary

FIRST BRIGADE

Col. Ario Pardee Jr.

5th Ohio
   Lieut. Col. Robert Kirkup
29th Ohio
   Maj. Myron T. Wright (w)
   Capt. Jonas Schoonover
66th Ohio
      Lieut. Col. Eugene Powell
28th Pennsylvania
   Col. John H. Flynn
147th Pennsylvania
   Lieut. Col. John Craig

SECOND BRIGADE

Col. Patrick H. Jones

33rd New Jersey
   Col. George W. Mindil
119th New York
   Col. John T. Lockman
134th New York
   Lieut. Col. Allan H. Jackson

154th New York
   Maj. Lewis D. Warner
73rd Pennsylvania
   Maj. Charles C. Cresson
109th Pennsylvania
   Capt. Walter G. Dunn

THIRD BRIGADE

Col. Henry A. Barnum

60th New York
   Maj. Thomas Elliott
102nd New York
   Lieut. Col. Harvey S. Chatfield
137th New York
   Lieut. Col. Koert S. Van Voorhis
149th New York
   Maj. Nicholas Grumbach
29th Pennsylvania
   Lieut. Col. Samuel M. Zulich
111th Pennsylvania
   Lieut. Col. Thomas L. Walker

THIRD DIVISION

Brig. Gen. William T. Ward

FIRST BRIGADE

Col. Franklin C. Smith

102nd Illinois
  Maj. Hiland H. Clay
105th Illinois
  Maj. Henry D. Brown
129th Illinois
  Col. Henry Case
70th Indiana
  Lieut. Col. Samuel Merrill
79th Ohio
  Lieut. Col. Azariah W. Doan

SECOND BRIGADE

Col. Daniel Dustin

33rd Indiana
  Lieut. Col. James E. Burton
85th Indiana
  Lieut. Col. Alexander B. Crane
19th Michigan
  Lieut. Col. John J. Baker
22nd Wisconsin
  Lieut. Col. Edward Bloodgood

THIRD BRIGADE

Col. Samuel Ross

20th Connecticut
  Lieut. Col. Philo B. Buckingham
33rd Massachusetts
  Lieut. Col. Elisha Doane
136th New York
  Lieut. Col. Lester B. Faulkner
55th Ohio
  Lieut. Col. Edwin H. Powers
73rd Ohio
  Lieut. Col. Samuel H. Hurst
26th Wisconsin
  Lieut. Col. Frederick C. Winkler

ARTILLERY BRIGADE

Maj. John A. Reynolds

1st New York Light Artillery: Battery I
  Capt. Charles E. Winegar
1st New York Light Artillery: Battery M
  Lieut. Edward P. Newkirk
1st Ohio Light Artillery: Battery C
  Capt. Marco B. Gary
  Lieut. Jerome B. Stephens
Pennsylvania Light Artillery: Battery E
  Capt. Thomas S. Sloan

CAVALRY DIVISION [5,063]

Brig. Gen. H. Judson Kilpatrick

FIRST BRIGADE

Col. Eli H. Murray

8th Indiana Cavalry
  Lieut. Col. Fielder A. Jones
2nd Kentucky Cavalry
  Capt. Joseph T. Forman
  Capt. Robert M. Gilmore
3rd Kentucky Cavalry
  Lieut. Col. Robert H. King

5th Kentucky Cavalry
  Col. Oliver L. Baldwin
9th Pennsylvania Cavalry
  Col. Thomas J. Jordan

SECOND BRIGADE

Col. Smith D. Atkins

92nd Illinois Mounted Infantry
  Lieut. Col. Matthew van Buskirk

3rd Indiana Cavalry
  Capt. Charles U. Patton
9th Michigan Cavalry
  Col. George S. Acker
5th Ohio Cavalry
  Col. Thomas T. Heath
9th Ohio Cavalry
  Col. William D. Hamilton
10th Ohio Cavalry
  Lieut. Col. Thomas W. Sanderson
McLaughlin's (Ohio) Squadron
  Capt. John Dalzell

UNATTACHED

1st Alabama Cavalry
  Col. George E. Spencer
9th Illinois Mounted Infantry
  Lieut. Col. Samuel T. Hughes

ARTILLERY

10th Wisconsin Battery
  Capt. Yates V. Beebe

CONFEDERATE FORCES ROSTER

[G=*Griswoldville*, H=*Honey Hill*, O=*Oconee River Bridge*, S=*Savannah Defenses*]

DEPARTMENT OF SOUTH CAROLINA, GEORGIA AND FLORIDA

Lieut. Gen. William J. Hardee

Hartridge's (Independent) Command
Maj. Alfred L. Hartridge [O/S]

Ashley (South Carolina) Dragoons
Captain George C. Heyward

27th Georgia Battalion [detail]

Maxwell's Light Artillery Battery
Lieut. Joseph A. Huger [section]

FORT MCALLISTER

Maj. George W. Anderson

Emmett Rifles
Capt. George A. Nicoll

Clinch's Light Artillery Battery
Captain Nicholas B. Clinch (w)

1st Georgia Reserve Regiment:
    Company D
Capt. George N. Hendry

1st Georgia Reserve Regiment:
Company E
Capt. Angus Morrison (w)

GEORGIA STATE TROOPS

FIRST DIVISION GEORGIA MILITIA

Maj. Gen. Gustavus W. Smith

UNATTACHED

Factory and Penitentiary Guards [O]
Williams's (Militia) Company of
    Infantry
Talbot's (Militia) Company of Cavalry

FIRST BRIGADE GEORGIA MILITIA [H/S]

Brig. Gen. Reuben W. Carswell

1st Georgia Militia Regiment
    Col. Edward H. Pottle
2nd Georgia Militia Regiment
    Col. James Stapleton
3rd Georgia Militia Regiment
    Col. Q. M. Hill

SECOND BRIGADE GEORGIA
MILITIA [G/S]

Brig. Gen. Pleasant J. Philips
Lieut. Col. Dexter B. Thompson

4th Georgia Militia Regiment
  Col. James M. Mann
5th Georgia Militia Regiment
  Col. S. S. Stafford
6th Georgia Militia Regiment
  Col. J. W. Burney

THIRD BRIGADE GEORGIA
MILITIA [S]

Brig. Gen. Charles D. Anderson

7th Georgia Militia Regiment
  Col. Abner Redding
8th Georgia Militia Regiment
  Col. William B. Scott
9th Georgia Militia Regiment
  Col. J. M. Hill

FOURTH BRIGADE GEORGIA
MILITIA [G/S]

Brig. Gen. Henry K. McCay

10th Georgia Militia Regiment
  Col. C. M. Davis

11th Georgia Militia Regiment
  Col. William T. Toole
12th Georgia Militia Regiment
  Col. Richard Sims

GEORGIA STATE LINE BRIGADE
[G/H/S]

Lieut. Col. Beverly D. Evans (w)
Lieut. Col. James Wilson

GEORGIA MILITARY
INSTITUTE, CORPS OF
CADETS [O/S]

Maj. Francis W. Capers

ARTILLERY

14th Georgia Light Artillery [G/S]
  Capt. Reul W. Anderson
Pruden's Battery [O/S]
  Capt. William H. Pruden
Pulaski Artillery [S]
  Lieut. R. H. Brown [section]
Hamilton's Battery [S]

MCLAWS'S DIVISION

Maj. Gen. Lafayette McLaws

BAKER'S NORTH CAROLINA
BRIGADE [S]

Brig. Gen. Lawrence S. Baker

10th North Carolina Battalion
  Maj. Willon L. Young
36th North Carolina
  Maj. James M. Stevenson
40th North Carolina
  Maj. William A. Holland
50th North Carolina
  Lieut. J. C. Ellington
77th North Carolina
  Col. Washington Hardy

LEWIS'S KENTUCKY MOUNTED
INFANTRY ("ORPHAN"
BRIGADE) [S]

Brig. Gen. Joseph H. Lewis
2nd Kentucky Mounted Infantry
4th Kentucky Mounted Infantry
9th Kentucky Mounted Infantry
Worthen's North Carolina Battalion
3rd Battalion Georgia Reserves
1st Regiment Georgia Reserves

ARTILLERY

Capt. J. A. Maxwell

Daniell's Light Artillery Battery [S]
  Capt. Charles Daniell

Abell's Light Artillery Battery [S]
  Capt. Henry F. Abell
Barnwell's Battery [section] [S]
German Artillery Battery [S]
  Capt. F. W. Wagner [section]

WRIGHT'S DIVISION

Maj. Gen. Ambrose R. Wright

MERCER'S BRIGADE

Brig. Gen. Hugh W. Mercer

Athens Local Defense Battalion
  [G/H/S]
  Maj. Ferdinand W. C. Cook (k)
Augusta Local Defense Battalion
  [G/H/S]
  Maj. George T. Jackson
Nisbet's Local Defense Regiment [S]
Brook's Foreign Battalion (paroled
  Union prisoners) [S]

JACKSON'S BRIGADE

Brig. Gen. John K. Jackson

Columbus Local Defense Units [S]
  Colonel Leon von Zinken

Dismounted Cavalry Brigade [S]
  Brig. Gen. Samuel W. Ferguson
  (also see Wheeler's Cavalry)

ARTILLERY

Capt. John W. Brooks

Guerard's Light Artillery Battery [S]
  Capt. John M. Guerard
Maxwell's Battery [section] [S]
Barnwell's Battery [section] [S]
Terrell Light Artillery Battery [S]
  Capt. John W. Brooks
Hanleiter's Light Artillery Battery [S]
  Capt. Cornelius R. Hanleiter

CAVALRY CORPS

Maj. Gen. Joseph Wheeler

ALLEN'S DIVISION

Brig. Gen. William Wirt Allen

CREWS'S GEORGIA BRIGADE

Col. Charles C. Crews

1st Georgia Cavalry
  Col. Samuel Davitte
2nd Georgia Cavalry
  Col. George C. Looney
3rd Georgia Cavalry
  Col. Robert Thompson

4th Georgia Cavalry
  Col. Isaac Avery
6th Georgia Cavalry
  Col. John R. Hart

HAGAN'S ALABAMA BRIGADE

Col. James Hagan

1st Alabama Cavalry
  Lieut. Col. David T. Blakey

3rd Alabama Cavalry
  Col. Josiah Robins
4th Alabama Cavalry
  Col. Alfred A. Russell
7th Alabama Cavalry
  Capt. George Mason

19th Alabama Cavalry
  Capt. Warren S. Reese
51st Alabama Cavalry
  Col. M. L. Kilpatrick

HUMES'S DIVISION

Brig. Gen. William Y. C. Humes

HARRISON'S BRIGADE

Brig. Gen. Thomas H. Harrison

3rd Arkansas Cavalry
  Col. Anson W. Hobson
4th Tennessee Cavalry
  Lieut. Col. Paul F. Anderson
8th Texas Cavalry
  Lieut. Col. Gustave Cook
11th Texas Cavalry
  Col. George R. Reeves

ASHBY'S BRIGADE

Col. Henry M. Ashby

1st Tennessee Cavalry
  Col. James T. Wheeler
2nd Tennessee Cavalry
  Capt. William M. Smith
5th Tennessee Cavalry
  Col. George W. McKenzie
9th Tennessee Cavalry
  Capt. W. L. Bromley

IVERSON'S DIVISION

Brig. Gen. Alfred H. Iverson

FERGUSON'S BRIGADE

Brig. Gen. Samuel W. Ferguson [S]

2nd Alabama Cavalry
  Lieut. Col. John N. Carpenter
56th Alabama Cavalry
  Col. William Boyles
9th Mississippi Cavalry
  Col. Horace H. Miller
11th Mississippi Cavalry
  Col. Robert O. Perrin
12th Mississippi Battalion
  Col. William M. Inge

LEWIS'S KENTUCKY MOUNTED INFANTRY ("ORPHAN" BRIGADE) [O/S]

Brig. Gen. Joseph H. Lewis

2nd Kentucky Mounted Infantry
4th Kentucky Mounted Infantry

9th Kentucky Mounted Infantry
Worthen's North Carolina Battalion
3rd Battalion Georgia Reserves
1st Regiment Georgia Reserves

ANDERSON'S CONFEDERATE BRIGADE

Brig. Gen. Robert H. Anderson

3rd Confederate Cavalry
  Lieut. Col. John McCaskill
8th Confederate Cavalry
  Lieut. Col. John S. Prather
10th Confederate Cavalry
  Capt. W. J. Vason
12th Confederate Cavalry
  Lieut. Col. Marcellus Pointer
5th Georgia Cavalry
  Col. Edward Bird

DIBRELL'S TENNESSEE BRIGADE

Brig. Gen. George G. Dibrell

4th Tennessee Cavalry
  Col. William S. McLemore
8th Tennessee Cavalry
  Lieut. Col. Paul F. Anderson
9th Tennessee Cavalry
  Capt. James M. Reynolds
10th Tennessee Cavalry
  Maj. John Minor

11th Tennessee Cavalry
  Col. Daniel W. Holman

YOUNG'S BRIGADE

Brig. Gen. Pierce M. B. Young

10th Georgia Cavalry
20th Georgia Battalion
Cobb's Legion Cavalry Battalion
Phillip's Legion Cavalry Battalion

Chapter Notes

Note: Complete information for material cited in the chapter notes can be found in the bibliography. All references to Series I of *The War of the Rebellion: A Compilation of the Official Records of the Union and Confederate Armies* are here designated OR, followed by the volume and number of the series. Similarly, all references to *Official Records of the Union and Confederate Navies* are abbreviated ORN, and to the *Supplement to the Official Records of the Union and Confederate Armies*, ORS. Other frequently used source abbreviations appearing herein are as follows: AAS (American Antiquarian Society), AHC (Atlanta History Center), ALL (Abraham Lincoln Presidential Library), BHS (Bureau County Historical Society), CHI (Chicago Historical Society), CHS (Chemung County Historical Society), CIN (Cincinnati Historical Society), CSL (Connecticut State Library), DU (Duke University), EU (Emory University), GHS (Georgia Historical Society), GSA (Georgia State Archives), HFL (Henry Ford Library), HL (Huntington Library), IHS (Indiana Historical Society), ISL (Indiana State Library), IU, (Indiana University), KNP (Kennesaw Mountain National Park), KNX (Knox College), LHS (Lancaster County Historical Society), LOC (Library of Congress), LSU (Louisiana State University), MAS (Massachusetts Historical Society), MCA (Fort McAllister Historic Park), MHI (United States Military History Institute), MHS (Minnesota Historical Society), NA (National Archives), NJH (New Jersey Historical Society), NYH (New-York Historical Society), NYL (New York State Library), OHS (Ohio Historical Society), PAH (Pennsylvania Historical Society), RU (Rutgers University), SHC (Southern Historical Collection), SHI (State Historical Society of Iowa), TSL (Tennessee State Library), UDC (Georgia Division, United Daughters of the Confederacy: Confederate Reminiscences and Letters, 1861–1865), UGA (University of Georgia, Athens), UMB (Bentley Historical Library, University of Michigan), UIA (University of Iowa), UMC (William L. Clements Library, University of Michigan), UWA (University of Washington), WHS (Wisconsin Historical Society), and WRS (Western Reserve Historical Society).

CHAPTER 1. A GATHERING OF EAGLES

3   "view to judging": Davis, *Rise & Fall*, 2:478.
4   "sovereignty of the State": Quoted in Parks, *Joseph E. Brown*, 219.
4   "a traitor": Quoted in ibid., 281.

4   "prolonged applause": Rowland, *Jefferson Davis*, 341.
4   "poor man": Cooper, *Jefferson Davis*, 526.
4   "Our cause": Macon speech in Rowland, *Jefferson Davis*, 341–44.
5   "the [sad] face": Williams, *Diary from Dixie*, 297.
6   "to all human calculations": Quoted in McMurry, *John Bell Hood*, 152.
7   "not unreasonable hope": Rowland, *Jefferson Davis*, 378–79.
7   "rode forth": Hood, *Advance and Retreat*, 253.
8   "I now ask": Quoted in Hughes, *General William J. Hardee*, 245, 248.
8   "The time for action": Rowland, *Jefferson Davis*, 345–47.
9   "I . . . warned him": Taylor / Davis meeting described in Taylor, *Destruction and Reconstruction*, 242–44.
9   "I can say,"/ "best which can be": Quoted in Hughes, *General William J. Hardee*, 248, 250.
10   "There are those": Quoted in Boritt, *Jefferson Davis's Generals*, 53.
11   "perfectly feasible": Roman, *Military Operations*, 2:278.
11   "he would be": Roman, *Military Operations*, 2:279.
11   "the hero": Augusta speech in Rowland, *Jefferson Davis*, 358–61.
12   "man . . . who looks": Williams, *Diary from Dixie*, 438.
12   "great struggle": Columbia speech in Rowland, *Jefferson Davis*, 351–55.
13   "spoke very candidly": Williams, *Diary from Dixie*, 440.
13   "If every man fit": Rowland, *Jefferson Davis*, 351.
13   "There are no vital": Richmond speech in Richardson, *Messages and Papers*, 1:271.

CHAPTER 2. CAPTIVE AUDIENCES

14   "Our town": Jones, *When Sherman Came*, 5.
15   "I can see nothing": Lunt, *Woman's Wartime Journal*, 3–14.
15   "The winter": Jones, *When Sherman Came*, 15.
16   "whether the State of Georgia": Quoted in Iobst, *Civil War Macon*, 330.
16   "It was very astounding": Felton, *Country Life in Georgia*, 89–90.
17   "We know what terrible": Jones, *When Sherman Came*, 20.
17   "But the misfortunes": Brown speech quoted in Parks, *Joseph E. Brown*, 307.
17   "six different wards": *Sunny South*, 11/30/1901.
18   "a sock a day": Quoted in Walters, *Oconee River*, 284–86.
19   "much more pleasant": Barber, *Army Memoirs*, 177.
19   "Disease and starvation": Quoted in Bailey, *War and Ruin*, 44.
19   "Let us not judge": Davidson, *Fourteen Months*, 334.
19   "a merry hearted girl": UDC, 3:73.
19   "tranquil old city": Quoted in Lawrence, *A Present for Mr. Lincoln*, 4.
20   "altogether the most": Ibid., 165.
21   "His only answer": Quoted in Stampp, *The Peculiar Institution*, 91.
21   "I know that": Quoted in Federal Writers' Project, *Georgia Narratives*, 192.
21   "shot, burned and drowned": Howe, *Marching with Sherman*, 64.
21   "Massa hates": Nichols, *Great March*, 59.
21   "The whites who were left": Harris, *On the Plantation*, 49.

22 "I got way up": Quoted in Federal Writers' Project, *Georgia Narratives*, 168–69, 235–36.

CHAPTER 3. THE STORMBRINGER

23 "You must continue": Sherman on Willy quoted in Fellman, *Citizen Sherman*, 199–201.
24 "forced into prominence": Ibid., 117.
24 "I am full of passion": *Weekly Missouri Democrat*, 7/10/1866.
24 "I would feel rejoiced": Quoted in Fellman, *Citizen Sherman*, 68.
24 "I look on myself": Quoted in Hart, *Sherman: Soldier, Realist, American*, 49.
25 "You are rushing into war": Quoted in Davis, *Sherman's March*, 15.
25 "wore very common": McConnell, *John D. Martin's Journal*, 25.
25 "With his large frame": Temple, *Campaigning with Grant*, 290.
26 "He is a very nervous man": Bohrnstedt, *Soldiering with Sherman*, 142.
26 "He twice rose": Temple, *Campaigning with Grant*, 290.
26 "I'm too red-haired": Quoted in Davis, *Sherman's March*, 5.
26 "To the casual observer": Howe, *Marching with Sherman*, 421–422.
26 "Sherman was the professional": Boyd, *Life of General . . . Sherman*, 9.
26 "Without being aware of it": Quoted in Kennett, *Sherman*, 240.
26 "Gen. Sherman": Elliott, Diary and Letters, MHI.
26 "Every man": Cutter, Letters, MHS.
27 "we felt as though": Gross, Journal and Letters, MHI.
27 "The true way": Quoted in Lewis, *Sherman*, 434.
27 "War is the conflict": Sherman, "Grand Strategy of the War," 582.
27 "See the books": Quoted in Hart, *Sherman*, 309.
27 "No goths"/"too much looseness": Quoted in Grimsley, *Hard Hand of War*, 63, 100.
27 "My idea of God": Quoted in Brinsfield, "Military Ethics," 46.
28 [The] northern people": Ibid., 43.
28 "prospered beyond precedence"/"We veterans believe": Sherman, "Grand Strategy of the War," 583, 582.
28 "On earth": Quoted in Bower, "Theology of the Battlefield," 1015.
28 "Satan and the rebellious saints": Quoted in Marszalek, *Sherman*, 251.
    "army commanders": Sherman, *Memoirs*, 2:175.
29 "Even yet"/"If the United States": Quoted in Force, *General Sherman*, 252.
29 "endowed with intellect": Quoted in Fellman, *Citizen Sherman*, 147.
29 "We must *Kill*": Quoted in Hirshson, *White Tecumseh*, 240.
29 "The law is": Quoted in Brinsfield, "Military Ethics," 45.
29 "war is on our part": Howe, *Marching with Sherman*, 74.
30 "this fair land": Quoted in Marszalek, *Sherman*, 296.
30 "mobs, vigilance Committees": Simpson and Berlin, *Sherman's Civil War*, 755.
30 "is intensifying the greatest fault": Quoted in Merrill, *William Tecumseh Sherman*, 260.
30 "free press": Sherman, "Grand Strategy of the War," 592.
30 "I say with the press": Quoted in Spore, "Sherman and the Press," 2:31–35.
30 "As the press": Ibid., 3:30.
31 "I would prefer": Quoted in Fellman, *Citizen Sherman*, 156.

31 "I have had the question": Quoted in Merrill, *William Tecumseh Sherman*, 253.
31 "I care not": Simpson and Berlin, *Sherman's Civil War*, 688.
31 "which party can whip": Quoted in Bower, "Theology of the Battlefield," 1024.
31 "when peace does come": Sherman, *Memoirs*, 2:127.
31 "My children": Quoted in Fellman, *Citizen Sherman*, 199.
31 "I do think": Simpson and Berlin, *Sherman's Civil War*, 791.
31 "If I have attained": Howe, *Home Letters*, 327.
31 "People write to me": Quoted in Merrill, *William Tecumseh Sherman*, 268.
32 "You might as well appeal": Sherman, *Memoirs*, 2:126.
32 "We have accepted the issue": OR 39/2:248.
32 "Talk it over": Simpson and Berlin, *Sherman's Civil War*, 688.
32 "To make war": Quoted in Bower, "Theology of the Battlefield," 1024.

CHAPTER 4. THE PLAN

33 "most spicy": *New York Herald*, 5/13/1875.
33 " 'cutting their way' ": Quoted in Boynton, *Sherman's Historical Raid*, 160.
34 "I have no doubt": *New York Times*, 10/22/1883.
34 "knock Jos. Johnston": Sherman, *Memoirs*, 2:27.
34 "Atlanta is ours"/"The political skies": Quoted in Castel, *Decision in the West*, 534, 543.
34 "Now that we": Quoted in Boynton, *Sherman's Historical Raid*, 143.
35 "not designed"/"studious and ingenious cruelty": Quoted in Marszalek, *Sherman*, 285.
35 "it is kindness": Sherman, *Memoirs*, 2:120.
36 "this act of Sherman's": Quoted in Bailey, *War and Ruin*, 26, 44.
37 "If once in our possession"/"Either horn": OR 39/2:412.
37 "spare the state": Sherman, *Memoirs*, 2:137.
37 "would have power": Quoted in Parks, *Joseph E. Brown*, 296–97.
38 "may stand": OR 39/2:412.
38 "why will it not do"/"It will be": OR 39/3:3, 162.
40 "We were as brothers": Sherman, "Grand Strategy of the War," 593.
40 "He stood by me": Quoted in Glatthaar, *Partners in Command*, 135.
40 "This may not be war": Quoted in Davis, *Sherman's March*, 25.
40 "Hood may turn"/"If there is any way"/"feels much solicitude": OR 39/3:202, 222.
41 "On mature reflection": OR 39/3:239–40.
41 "Your friends": Quoted in Kennett, *Sherman*, 259.
41 "You may count": OR 39/3:240.
42 "I want the first positive": OR 39/3:311, 333, 324–25, 357–8.
42 "Damn Hood!": Quoted in Hirshson, *White Tecumseh*, 246.
43 "1,500,000 rations"/"If you can defend"/"By this I propose": OR 39/3:370, 365, 377–78.
43 "I feel perfectly master"/"Go on": OR 39/3:395, 406, 408.
44 "All Georgia is now open"/"I must leave it to you"/"will enable him to hold": OR 39/3:408, 449, 661.
44 "Do you not think": OR 39/3:576, 581, 594.

45   "With the force"/"you may look"/"Sherman's army": OR 39/3:594, 596, 727.

46   "I hope we shall be ready"/"I have made great": OR 39/3:600, 613–14, 618, 740, 756.

46   "I answered": Sherman, *Memoirs*, 2:169.

46   "Free and glorious": Quoted in Miers, *General Who Marched*, 218.

47   "The expedition": Quoted in Hart, *Sherman*, 225.

47   "I have no hesitation"/"When the provisions": Quoted in Marszalek, *Sherman*, 254, 251.

47   "The enemy cannot use": OR 32/1:176.

48   Special Field Orders No. 120: OR 39/3:713.

48   "looked to personal fame": Sherman, *Memoirs*, 2:171.

49   "needed commanders": Sherman, *Memoirs*, 2:86.

50   "I know [that] Kilpatrick": Quoted in Martin, *Kill-Cavalry*, 193, 185.

51   "reduced to a minimum": Oakey, "Marching through Georgia," 672.

52   "I had wagons": Howe, *Home Letters*, 321.

52   "little loose": OR 44:14.

53   "Evidently it is": Howe, *Marching with Sherman*, 125.

53   "Of course you cannot": Simpson and Berlin, *Sherman's Civil War*, 820, 598–602.

54   "Now it is clearly": Ibid., 818.

54   "domestic slavery": Sherman, "Old Shady," 4.

54   "The U.S. has its hands"/"Now you Know": Simpson and Berlin, *Sherman's Civil War*, 574, 794.

55   "That was his conception": Quoted in *Army Reunion*, 102–3.

56   "I have enough": OR 39/3:577.

57   "I would be lost": OR 44:833.

58   "The rains": Howe, *Marching with Sherman*, 42.

58   "This is the rain"/"is now raining": OR 39/3:700, 697.

CHAPTER 5. "PARADISE OF FOOLS"

59   "It would astonish": Bachelder, *Bachelder Family Letters*, 50.

59   "several trains of cattle": Pendergast, Family Papers, MHS.

59   "The Railroad Depots": Platter, "Civil War Diary," UGA.

59   "The light of the conflagration": *Cincinnati Daily Commercial*, 11/19/1864.

60   "passed Cartersville": Miller, Diary, IHS.

60   "railroads, depots": OR 44:59–60.

60   "detail of men": Cruikshank, "Civil War Letters."

60   "knocking things": Byrne, Diary and Journal, RU.

60   "opened with a grand": Widney, Diary and Letters, KNP.

60   "Perhaps I may prove": Bachelder, *Bachelder Family Letters*, 50.

60   "It is very evident": Bradley, *Star Corps*, 180.

61   "Events are shaping": Ray, Diary, GSA.

61   "I remember seeing": Taylor, *Lights and Shadows*, 19.

61   "many officers": Hedley, *Marching through Georgia*, 254.

61   "slowly but majestically": Strong, Papers, ALL.

61   "in good spirits": Howe, *Marching with Sherman*, 51.

61   "will live long": Quoted in Merrill, *William Tecumseh Sherman*, 268.

62   "I may be in error": Quoted in Hirshson, *White Tecumseh*, 250.
62   "I will not attempt": Simpson and Berlin, *Sherman's Civil War*, 752.
62   "Our men": Cate, *"If I Live,"* 258.
62   "fire suddenly burst": Byrne, *Uncommon Soldiers*, 201.
62   "A cable was attached": Fleharty, *Our Regiment*, 108.
62   "It is evident": Quoted in Miles, *To the Sea*, 18.
63   "very quick": Quoted in Dyer, *From Shiloh to San Juan*, 5.
63   "were convinced": Lafferty, "Civil War Reminiscences," 14.
64   "There are the men": Howe, *Marching with Sherman*, 52–53.
64   "was greeted": Ward, Diary, IHS.
64   "a beautiful sight": *Lancaster Daily Evening Express*, 1/3/1865.
64   "superb for picture": Howe, *Marching with Sherman*, 54.
64   "The railroad": *Philadelphia Inquirer*, 1/2/1865.
65   "Sherman will move forward": OR 44:857.
66   "carried out": Roman, *Military Operations*, 287.
67   "big Yankee lie": Quoted in *Philadelphia Inquirer*, 11/17/1864.
67   "We burn all": Inskeep, Diary, OHS.
67   "Today we are": Roseberry, Diary, UMB.
67   "was a fine building": Storrow, Papers, MAS.
67   "I saw that": Carr Diary, KNP.
67   "see the smoke": Hubert, *Fiftieth Regiment*, 321.
67   "Tremendous fires": Kellogg, *Army Life of an Illinois Soldier*, 319.
68   "the flames mount": Trowbridge, Papers, UMC.
68   "vast waves": Hopkins, "March to the Sea," 47.
68   "They came burning": Quoted in Carter, *Siege of Atlanta*, 372.
68   "We already had marched": Rosenow, *Pen Pictures*, 100.
68   "there was swearing": Parker, Papers, HL.
68   "overhauled our knapsacks": Christie Family Papers, MHS.
68   "a feeling of loneliness": Fleharty, *Our Regiment*, 102.
69   "the earth seems": Dunbar, Diary, BHS.
69   "came uncomfortably near": Sherman, *Memoirs*, 2:177.
69   "the prospect": Quaife, *From the Cannon's Mouth*, 351.
69   "Straggling and pillaging": OR 44:463.
69   "the greatest": OR 44:452.
70   "the flanks of the army": OR 44:458.
70   "Was there no enemy": *New York Times*, 2/16/1876.
70   "signal that a great": *Lancaster Daily Evening Express*, 1/3/1865.
70   "position of the cavalry": Hamilton, *Recollections*, 153.
70   "via McDonough": OR 44:451.
70   "opposition at these great rivers": *New York Times*, 1/29/1876.
71   "The general commanding": Sherman, *Memoirs*, 2:174.

CHAPTER 6. "DIES IRAE FILLED THE AIR"

75   "waiting and working": Byrne, Diary and Journal, RU.
75   "They had just been paid": Federico, *Civil War Letters*, 163–64.
76   "Here we saw": Bauer, *Soldiering*, 175.

76   "I beheld": Benton, *As Seen*, 211.
76   "fearful sight": Byrne, Diary and Journal, RU.
76   "as we left": Michael, Diary, IHS.
77   "with a [supply] train": *New York Herald*, 12/28/1864.
77   "found every street": Angle, *Three Years*, 300.
77   "battering down": OR 44:60.
77   "First, there was": Hight and Stormont, *Fifty-eighth Regiment*, 409.
78   "which could be converted": Sherman, *Memoirs*, 2:178.
78   "We have been fighting": Howe, *Marching with Sherman*, 58.
79   "Exciting time": Carter, *Story*, 304.
79   "We were cheery": Saunier, *History*, 351.
79   "Started early": Clark, *Downing's Civil War*, 229.
79   "on our strength": Scheel, *Rain, Mud & Swamps*, 455.
79   "It took some time": *National Tribune*, 4/16/1903.
79   "We . . . made slow": Brown, *Fourth Regiment*, 339.
80   "We found some Rebel": Sherlock, *Memorabilia*, 143.
80   "if she was in good voice": Joyce, "From Infantry to Cavalry," 253–54.
81   "The session": *Augusta Daily Chronicle & Sentinel*, 11/19/1864.
81   "Nearly one thousand": Barber, *Army Memoirs*, 178.
81   "slaughtered thirty-five": Davidson, *Fourteen Months*, 337.
81   "We have found": Hinkley, Papers, WHS.
82   "a small": Chapman, *Civil War Diary*, 99.
82   "its Court House": Byrne, Diary and Journal, RU.
82   "As our advances": Grunert, *History*, 123.
82   "many of the buildings": OR 44:339.
82   "I remember": Storrs, *Twentieth Connecticut*, 149.
82   "a vast body": McCreary, Papers, DU.
82   "Standing thus": Benton, *As Seen*, 213.
82   "surprise and wonder": Bauer, *Soldiering*, 177.
82   "the western sky": Fleharty, *Our Regiment*, 109.
83   "I suppose": Russell, Letter, OHS.
83   "Dies irae": Merrill, *Seventieth Indiana*, 524.
83   "I saw 4 or 5": Daniels, Diary, HL.
83   "The wagons": Bargus, Diary, MHI.
83   "a disagreeable task": Sharland, *Knapsack Notes*, 10.
83   "advanced with infantry": Quoted in Dodson, *Campaigns of Wheeler*, 285.
84   "We charged them": Ward, Diary, IHS.
84   "I deemed it best": OR 44:381.
84   "were hitting": Joyce, "From Infantry to Cavalry," 254.
84   "We made lots of noise": Rogers, *Great Civil War*, 13.
84   "We had a very hard": Patchin, *Letters of Jonathan Bridges*, 57.
85   "where re-enforcements": OR 44:858.
85   "destroy everything": Quoted in Dyer, *From Shiloh to San Juan*, 159.
85   "The whole region": Pepper, *Personal Recollections*, 240.
85   "Atlanta on fire": Pittenger, Diary, OHS.
86   "soldiers to go in": Angle, *Three Years*, 301.
86   "As we left the town": Burton, Diary, EU.
86   "It must have been a weird": Moffatt, *Union Soldier's Civil War*, 134–35.

86   "military purposes"/"lawless persons": OR 44:56, 60.

86   "great scandal": Poe, Papers and Letters, LOC.

86   "smoke, dust": Tourgee, *Story of a Thousand*, 335.

86   "This has been": Berry, Diary, AHC.

86   "Every instant": Rogers, *125th Regiment*, 108.

87   "probably . . . visible": Howe, *Marching with Sherman*, 57.

87   "I saw Gen. Sherman": Kellogg, *Army Life of an Illinois Soldier*, 25.

87   "The [blazing]": Westervelt, *Lights and Shadows*, 84.

87   "was truly superb": Storrow, Papers, MAS.

87   "strange light": Underwood, *Three Years' Service*, 240.

88   "always will . . . carry me back": Howe, *Marching with Sherman*, 59.

88   "I have never heard": Nichols, *Great March*, 41.

88   "Nero made music": Hunter, *Eighty-Second Indiana*, 136.

88   "only danger yet": Howe, *Marching with Sherman*, 59.

88   "it looked like": Berry Diary, AHC.

CHAPTER 7. "LURID FLAMES LIT UP THE HEAVENS"

89   "The air was resonant": Kerr, "From Atlanta to Raleigh," 208.

89   "The roaring": Althouse and Hughes, *Civil War Letters*, 120.

89   "Who set it afire?": *National Tribune*, 6/28/1900.

89   "A last look": Ege, Papers, WHS.

89   "Country sandy": Porter, Diary, OHS.

89   "men were cheering": Kerr, "From Atlanta to Raleigh," 208.

89   "The Corps": Floyd, *History of the Seventy-fifth*, 344.

90   "All believed": Kerr, "From Atlanta to Raleigh," 208.

90   "What doubts": Ladd, "From Atlanta to the Sea," 6.

91   "General rode quietly": Howe, *Marching with Sherman*, 60.

91   "Behind us": Sherman, *Memoirs*, 2:178–79.

91   "Felt a little sore": *National Tribune*, 2/26/1925.

91   "tired and sleepy": Buckingham, Papers, AAS.

91   "We know not": Wheeler, Letters and Journal, ALL.

91   "picked up": Byrne, Diary and Journal, RU.

91   "The marching to-day": OR 44:269.

91   "We marched": *National Tribune*, 2/26/1925.

92   "train of freight cars": Storrow, Papers, MAS.

92   "The modus operandi": *National Tribune*, 2/26/1925.

92   "destroyed two miles": OR 44:216.

92   "only partially": *Augusta Daily Chronicle & Sentinel*, 12/24/1864.

92   "Piled all surplus": Sligh, *History of the Services*, 26.

92   "perfect ruin": Howland, Papers, MHS.

92   "Mr. Soldier": Campbell, Civil War Experiences, MCA.

93   "Enemy advancing": OR 44:859.

93   "The temptation": Fultz, "History of Company D," 73.

93   "enjoyed a good rest": Duke, *Fifty-third*, 161.

94   "The shells whistled": Eisenhower, Diary, MHI.

94   "route was blocked": OR 44:374.

94 "We were so completely": Quoted in Miles, *To the Sea*, 142.

94 "a six-gun battery": *National Tribune*, 3/23/1922.

94 "nonsensical": Quoted in *Cincinnati Daily Commercial*, 11/23/1864.

95 "that a [Confederate] force": Ibid.

95 "with unsparing vehemence": *Augusta Daily Chronicle & Sentinel*, 11/22/1864.

95 "one of the boldest": *Cincinnati Daily Commercial*, 11/16/1864.

95 "An officer of Sherman's staff": *Chicago Tribune*, 11/16/1864.

95 "no shelter was provided": Davidson, *Fourteen Months*, 332–3.

96 "Old worn-out": Rosenow, *Pen Pictures*, 101.

96 "Foragers were sent out": Otto, *Civil War Memoirs*, WHS.

96 "No one knew": Miller, Diary, IHS.

96 "tenderly laid": Floyd, *History of the Seventy-fifth*, 346.

96 "a seedy Southern village": Rosenow, *Pen Pictures*, 101.

96 "a small place": Wilcox, Diary, MHI.

96 "old, weather-beaten": Angle, *Three Years*, 304.

96 "dilapidated": Clark, Diaries, LHS.

97 "a desolate looking town": Widney, Diary and Letters, KNP.

97 "Saw good looking girl": Edmonds, Papers, MHI.

97 "the old man": Angle, *Three Years*, 307.

97 "Marched slow": Omvig, Diaries, 114.

97 "Roads bad": Byrne, Diary and Journal, RU.

97 "a good bridge": *New York Herald*, 12/28/1864.

97 "east of the Yellow River": OR 44:270.

98 "Forage is very plentiful": Hoerner, *Chattanooga, Savannah and Alexandria*, 41.

98 "got plenty": Harper, Diary, MHI.

98 "the crowing": *Paterson Daily Register*, 1/3/1865.

98 "I find [it] very hard": Storrs, *Twentieth Connecticut*, 150.

98 "I ate some hard tack": Lathrop, *John Smethurst*, 59.

98 "some of the 3rd": Byrne, Diary and Journal, RU.

98 "burnt a cotton mill": Ostrum Diary, MHI.

98 "isolated houses": McBride, *Thirty-third Indiana*, 151.

99 "the lurid flames": Davis-Quillin, Papers, AHC.

99 "Absorbed in thought": Howe, *Marching with Sherman*, 60.

99 "either Savannah": Sherman, *Memoirs*, 2:179.

99 "sitting on the porch"/"sitting in the passageway": Calkins, *One Hundred and Fourth Regiment*, 257.

99 "no fear"/"intelligent fellow"/"Line of fires": Howe, *Marching with Sherman*, 60–61.

100 "Three days more": Ibid., 63.

100 "to assist": OR 44:475–76.

101 "Begin to-day": Force, Papers, UWA.

101 "it very hard": Platter, "Civil War Diary," UGA.

101 "The boys went out": Saunier, *History*, 352.

101 "I was detailed this day": Lyftogt, *Left for Dixie*, 61.

101 "foragers got lots": Unknown Diarist, SHI.

101 "Some skirmishing": Scheel, *Rain, Mud & Swamps*, 456.

101 "a brigade of rebel cavalry": OR 44:96.

101 "We entered the town": Duke, *Fifty-third Regiment*, 161.

101 "a lot of cotton": Judkins, Diary, ISL.
101 "large Confederate mail": Trimble, *Ninety-third Regiment*, 145.
101 "We buried him": Christie, Family Papers, MHS.
102 "It is perfectly"/"take such steps": OR 44:472.
102 "carried through": Carter, *Story*, 304.
102 "Forage of all kinds": Tomlinson, *"Dear Friends,"* 172.
103 "most unmilitary": OR 44:485.
103 "Augusta or Macon": OR 44:859.
103 "You will cut": OR 45/1:1213.
104 "There was nothing": Taylor, *Destruction and Reconstruction*, 246.
104 "safety of prisoners"/"no serious fears": Quoted in Iobst, *Civil War Macon*, 339–40.
104 "If Sherman advances": OR 44:860.

CHAPTER 8. "FORAGE OF ALL KINDS ABOUNDS"

105 Buttrills of Sylvan Grove: Buttrill, "Experience in the War," GSA.
107 "a byroad": Cryder and Stanley, *"War for the Union,"* 457.
107 "Orders to be ready": McMillan, Papers, WHS.
107 "to help": Force, Papers, UWA.
107 "Advance ordered to kill": Jamison, *Recollections*, 280.
107 "The wagon trains": Hubert, *Fiftieth Regiment*, 322.
107 "We are flankers": Dunbar, Diary, BHS.
107 "fine lot of Hogs": Black, *"Marching with Sherman,"* 454.
108 "The poor people": Pepper, *Personal Recollections*, 240.
108 "Now I reckon": Berry, Letter, EU.
108 "Country beautiful": Berkenes, *Private William Boddy*, 151.
108 "Have had": Ward, Diary, IHS.
108 "had to stop": Brockman, "John Van Duser Diary," 221–22.
109 "standing on the R.R.": Angle, *Three Years*, 307.
109 "I attached much": Sherman, *Memoirs*, 2:180.
109 "fine dwelling": Fahnestock, Diary, KNP.
109 "The picture": Widney, Diary and Letters, KNP.
109 "full of women": Edmonds, Papers, MHI.
109 "flocked in large numbers": *New York Herald*, 12/22/64.
109 "Pretty foot and ankle": Edmonds, Papers, MHI.
109 "she reckoned": Calkins, *One Hundred and Fourth Regiment*, 257.
110 "We left them": Angle, *Three Years*, 308–9.
110 "sandy & timber stands": Reed, "Civil War Diaries," MHS.
110 "Forage of all kinds": Clark, Diaries, LHS.
110 "All kind of forage": Bruce, "Daniel E. Bruce," 195.
110 "Our course": Storrow, Papers, MAS.
110 "My duties were defined": Baldwin, Papers, HL.
111 "From the calves": Grunert, *History*, 124.
111 "carrying an armful": Reed, "Civil War Diaries," MHS.
111 "huge on catching fowls": Failing-Knight, Papers, MHS.
111 "[Cotton] Gin house": Maguire, Papers, AHC.

111 "The trains moved": Padgett, "With Sherman through Georgia," 57.
111 "Short marches": Storrow, Papers, MAS.
111 "Standing still": Morgan, Diary, MHI.
111 "waited till heartily tired": Hinkley, Papers, WHS.
112 "Please give me": Drake, *Army of Tennessee*, 355.
112 "shortest road": OR 44:863.
112 "we shall have lively times": Cobb, Papers, UGA.
112 "the most dangerous": OR 44:861–62.
112 "Things are very bad": OR 44:862.
112 "Macon is to be defended": Quoted in *Augusta Daily Chronicle & Sentinel*, 11/22/1864.
112 "with such things": Chapman, *Civil War Diary*, 100.
113 "When General Sherman left": Quoted in Stewart, *Reward of Patriotism*, 198.
113 "the passage": Chandler, *Confederate Records*, 791.
113 "do all I can"/"we have not force": Quoted in Iobst, *Civil War Macon*, 340–41.
113 "The prisoners": OR 44:862.
114 "found plenty": *Downing's Civil War*, 229.
114 "A plenty": House, "Civil War Diary," MHS.
114 "Our men are clear discouraged"/"The men detailed": *Reminiscences of the Civil War*, 149.
114 "Along our route": Platter, "Civil War Diary," UGA.
114 "We . . . obtained a number": Cryder and Stanley, *"War for the Union,"* 457.
114 "Fire is doing its work": Pittenger, Diary, OHS.
114 "[Rebel] cutthroats": Unknown Diarist, SHI.
114 "a troop of Confederate": *Fifty-fifth Regiment*, 392-93.
114 "A couple of orderlies": Daniels, Diary, HL.
114 "They retreated": McMichael, "Burning of the Courthouse," UDC.
115 "think we are making": OR 44:485.
115 "Great excite[ment]": Ray, Diary, GSA.
116 "If this war": Buttrill story in Buttrill, "Experience in the War," GSA.
117 "no one to fall behind": OR 44:481–82.
117 "It has been": Johnson, " 'Make a Preacher Swear,' " 33.
117 "Moving very slow": Michael, Diary, IHS.
117 "there was but little": OR 44:339.
117 "we had slow": Byrne, Diary and Journal, RU.
117 "Some wagon": Wagoner, "From Wauhatchie," 118.
117 "The niggers flock": McLean, Family Papers, NYL.
117 "Massa, I'se gwine": Otto, "Civil War Memoirs," WHS.
118 "got into conversation": Storrs, *Twentieth Connecticut*, 150.
118 "shot, burned and drowned": Howe, *Marching with Sherman*, 64.
118 "Don't want white man": Howe, *Marching with Sherman*, 66–67.
119 "I have seen no enemy": OR 44:482.
119 "We pry some of the rails": Parker, Papers, HL.
119 "The ties were all burned": Hapeman, Diary, ALL.
119 "we arrived at the": Rosenow, *Pen Pictures*, 102.
119 "I shut my eyes": Widney, Diary and Letters, KNP.
120 "dashed into Social Circle": *New York Herald*, 12/28/1864.
120 "attempted to sham": Rosenow, *Pen Pictures*, 102.

120 "He is dressed": Litton, *Union Soldier Returns South,* 26.
120 "tried to get away": Parker, Papers, HL.
120 "He still tells": Litton, *Union Soldier Returns South,* 26.
121 "Brigade commanders"/"use of cartridges": OR 44:483–84.

CHAPTER 9. "ARISE FOR THE DEFENSE OF YOUR NATIVE SOIL!"

123 "an old fe[r]ry": Moses, "Civil War Diary."
123 "about 30 men": Glossbrenner, Diary, MHI.
123 "As the enemy": Brown, *Fourth Regiment,* 340.
124 "We lived": Platter, "Civil War Diary," UGA.
124 "abundance of sweet": Force, Papers, UWA.
124 "About a hundred": Cryder and Stanley, *"War for the Union,"* 457.
124 "he took a frantic spill": Macy, Papers, SHI.
124 "all put their": Stauffer, *Civil War Diary,* n.p.
124 "There was a grist mill": Keyes, Diary, MHI.
124 "2 splendid buildings": Christie, Family Papers, MHS.
124 "lots of women": Girdner, Letters, EU.
124 "The most majestic": Anderson, *Civil War Diary,* 177.
125 "convinced that the impression": OR 44:363.
125 "bridges on the road": *Augusta Daily Chronicle & Sentinel,* 11/19/1864.
125 "On the 18th": Drake, *Army of Tennessee,* 356.
125 "reached Forsythe": Smith, "Georgia Militia," 667.
125 "long before chicks": Omvig, Diaries, 115.
125 "Some of the 85th boys": Herron, *Reminiscences,* 22.
126 "I thought this": Garrett, "Uninvited Guests," UDC.
126 "Citizens don't like the 'Yanks' ": Morrow, Diary, MHI.
126 "good looking girls": McLean, Family Papers, NYL.
126 "no evidence": Bauer, *Soldiering,* 183.
126 "In less than ten minutes": Angle, *Three Years,* 309.
127 "cloudy and threatening rain": Howe, *Marching with Sherman,* 67–68.
127 "fordable": Ibid., 68.
127 "not anxious to witness": Brockman, "John Van Duser Diary," 222.
127 "there is a mighty": Howe, *Marching with Sherman,* 68.
127 This was all intended": Brockman, "John Van Duser Diary," 223.
128 "To the People of Georgia": Beauregard/Hill proclamations in OR 44:867.
129 "In addition": OR 44:865.
129 "that the military authorities": Quoted in Iobst, *Civil War Macon,* 342.
129 "in the fortifications": OR 44:868.
129 "Employ your cavalry": OR 44:867.
129 "should not allow": OR 44:868.
129 "Enemy pressing": OR 44:868.
130 "rendered valueless": *Acts of the General Assembly,* 16–24.
130 "Some members"/"Everything in the Executive": McAdoo, Diary, LOC.
130 "A heavy force": OR 44:865.
130 "By paying": Barber, *Army Memoirs,* 179.
131 "Here many of our boys": Saunier, *History,* 352.

131 "The Confederate officials": Sherlock, *Memorabilia*, 145.
131 "entered into interesting": Wright, *Sixth Iowa*, 360.
131 "But the tears": Ibid., 360–61.
132 "Drove in the enemy's pickets": McClintock, Papers, HL.
132 "in this way": Christie, Family Papers, MHS.
132 "This looked hard": Baker, *Soldier's Experience*, 40.
132 "At the eastern end": Harwell and Racine, *Fiery Trail*, 55.
132 "The crossing of the Ocmulgee": Howard, "Sherman's Advance from Atlanta," 664.
133 "a considerable amount": Hoerner, *Chattanooga, Savannah and Alexandria*, 41.
133 "along the R.R.": Parmater, Diary, OHS.
133 "Men feel a little jaded": Ames, Diary, MHI.
133 "Forage abundant": Brant, *History of the Eighty-fifth*, 76.
133 "Sent out two": OR 44:245.
133 "proceed along": OR 44:233.
134 "whiskey uppermost": Kendall, Diary and Letters, CHS.
134 "After a run": Scott, " 'With Tears in Their Eyes,' " 28.
134 "were angry": Parker, Papers, HL.
134 "On the 18th": Floyd, *History of the Seventy-fifth*, 348.
134 "a crippled Confederate": McNeil, *Personal Recollections*, 59.
134 "Every window and door": *New York Herald*, 12/22/1864.
135 "attempted to": Jones, *When Sherman Came*, 6–7.
135 "Negroes all want": Emmons, Diaries, UIA.
135 "saw several darkey women": Kellogg, *Illinois Soldier*, 28.
135 "Some of the boys": Otto, *Civil War Memoirs*, WHS.
135 "Your soldiers": Jones, *When Sherman Came*, 6–7.
136 "a deep, sluggish stream": Hight and Stormont, *Fifty-eighth Regiment*, 416–18.
136 "village of negro huts": *New York Herald*, 12/22/1864.
136 "I was bound to come": Howe, *Marching with Sherman*, 70.
136 "supposed that slavery"/"with a ham on his musket": Sherman, *Memoirs*, 2:180–81.
137 "a number of soldiers": *New York Herald*, 12/22/1864.
137 "I don't mean to hurt her": Howe, *Marching with Sherman*, 72–73.
137 "Oh, how I trust": Lunt, *Woman's Wartime Journal*, 17–20.

CHAPTER 10. "WHITES LOOK SOUR & SAD"

138 "We got up": Roe, Papers, KNX.
138 "roads today": Clark, *Downing's Civil War*, 230.
138 "On both sides": Hedley, *Marching through Georgia*, 310.
138 "blankets are so wet": Brown, *Fourth Regiment*, 340.
139 "source of anxiety": Howard, "Sherman's Advance," 664.
139 "as soon as over": Howard, *Autobiography*, 2:71.
139 "Great fires were kept": *92nd Illinois Volunteers*, 175.
139 "The cavalry cross two by two": Ibid., 176.
140 "The weather is wet": Hoerner, *Chattanooga, Savannah and Alexandria*, 41.
140 "Colored people": Ames, Diary, MHI.
140 "A wag in Company A": Boyle, *Soldiers True*, 258.

140 "our men ransacked": Wheeler, Letters and Journal, ALL.

140 "It is the finest": Trego, Diary, CHI.

140 "the town looked": *New York Herald*, 12/28/864.

140 "The men have obtained": Fleharty, *Our Regiment*, 111.

140 "Cotton stored": Osborn, *Trials and Triumphs*, 177.

140 "The Calaboos[e]": Kittinger, Diary, MHI.

141 "But it was of no use": Chapman, *Civil War Diary*, 100.

141 "stripped of all": Jones, *When Sherman Came*, 15.

141 "fine style": Short, Diary, WHS.

141 "with handsomely aligned": Byrne, *Uncommon Soldiers*, 258.

141 "We spent the whole forenoon": Herron, *Reminiscences*, 23.

142 "the roads were found": *New York Herald*, 12/22/1864.

142 "ahead in a heavy rain": McAdams, *Every-day Soldier Life*, 117.

142 "You awake in the morning": Parker, Papers, HL.

142 "the General explained": Howe, *Marching with Sherman*, 74.

142 "The enemy": Hardee messages in OR 44:870.

143 "divide [his force]": Ibid.

143 "After a careful survey": Quoted in *Philadelphia Inquirer*, 12/5/1864.

143 "country cannot support": Ibid., 11/23/1864.

143 "would have turned": Barber, *Army Memoirs*, 179–80.

144 "Burned many cotton mills": Parmater, Diary, OHS.

144 "the water-tank": OR 44:270.

144 "several thousand": Hoerner, *Chattanooga, Savannah and Alexandria*, 42.

144 "a first rate time": Harper, Diary, MHI.

144 "tearing up": *Paterson Daily Register*, 1/3/1865.

144 "a considerable distance": OR 44:283.

144 "Our Division started": Quoted in Schmidt, *Civil War History*, 1036.

144 "thoroughly destroyed": OR 44:270.

145 "The roads are rather": McLean, Family Papers, NYL.

145 "loaded down": Grunert, *History*, 126.

145 "There were old Pomps": Wagoner, "From Wauhatchie," 119.

145 "You Yankees did it": Fleharty, *Our Regiment*, 112.

145 "I don't know": Bradley, *Star Corps*, 187.

145 "Why ma'am": Byrne, *Uncommon Soldiers*, 260.

145 "Like demons": Lunt, *Woman's Wartime Journal*, 20–32.

146 "Troops have plenty": Burkhalter, Diary, ALL.

146 "Plenty of corn": Ege, Papers, WHS.

146 "There was sport": Otto, *Civil War Memoirs*, WHS.

146 "Several . . . men wounded": Ege, Papers, WHS.

146 "were accidentally shot": Ladd, "From Atlanta to the Sea," 7.

146 "accidentally wounded": Payne, *Thirty-fourth Regiment*, 164.

146 "Provost guards": Emmons, Diaries, UIA.

146 "Negroes by the hundred": Essington, Diary, ISL.

147 "the negroes": Angle, *Three Years*, 311.

147 "queer old cock"/"Confederates were a great deal"/"I have been three years": Howe, *Marching with Sherman*, 750.

147 "Gen. Sherman sitting": Ross, Diary, ALL.

147 "The country was sparsely settled": Sherman, *Memoirs*, 2:183.

147 "rapidly disappearing": Howe, *Marching with Sherman*, 75–76.
148 "beautiful town": Hedley, *Marching through Georgia*, 311.
148 "colors flying": McMillan, Papers, WHS.
148 "any amount of fine looking"/"a pretty little village"/"it was reduced": Christie, Family Papers, MHS.
149 "the point of it": Harwell and Racine, *Fiery Trail*, 56.
149 "the men floundering": Wright, *Sixth Iowa*, 361.
149 "We took the wrong road": Brown, *Fourth Regiment*, 341.
149 "every man": Dunbar, Diary, BHS.
149 "Gen. Howard sat": Jones, *When Sherman Came*, 20.
149 "divided amongst": Gay, Diary, SHI.
150 "Roads very slippery": Tomlinson, *"Dear Friends,"* 172.
150 "a hard day's travel": Berkenes, *Private William Boddy*, 152.
150 "General Kilpatrick": *New York Herald*, 12/28/1864.
150 "valuable information": OR 44:369.
150 "learned that part": Moore, *Kilpatrick and Our Cavalry*, 178.
151 "ordered Wheeler": OR 44:870.

CHAPTER 11. "UGLY WEATHER"

152 "push on toward": OR 44:496.
153 "ugly weather": Howe, *Marching with Sherman*, 76.
153 "the plantation": *New York Herald*, 12/22/1864.
153 "We are told": Howe, *Marching with Sherman*, 78.
153 "The brigade band": Owens, *Greene County*, 100.
154 "that she had heard": Sawyer, Letters, WHS.
154 "the weather rainy": OR 44:270.
154 "was thick": Chapman, *Civil War Diary*, 101.
154 "the clayey roads": Trowbridge, Papers, UMC.
154 "The roads were in a bad": Cruikshank, "Civil War Letters."
154 "The Yankees left us": Massey, "Recollections," UDC.
154 "The inhabitants seemed": Boies, *Record*, 104.
154 "While passing": Fleharty, *Our Regiment*, 113.
155 "We must go": Halsey, *Yankee Private's Civil War*, 113–14.
156 "The animals": Baker, *Soldier's Experience*, 40.
156 "supposed [it] to be": Platter, "Civil War Diary," UGA.
156 "A colored gal": Cryder and Stanley, *"War for the Union,"* 458.
156 "It excited many a pun": Sharland, *Knapsack Notes*, 17–18.
156 "muddy & very foggy": Unknown Diarist, SHI.
156 "The roads were so": Saunier, *History*, 353.
156 "nearly every man": Grecian, *History*, 61.
157 "Push on active": Beauregard messages in OR 44:872–74.
157 "Let not this stirring": *Augusta Daily Chronicle & Sentinel*, 11/20/1864.
157 "I think Sherman": Miers, *Rebel War Clerk's Diary*, 450.
158 "We were free": Barber, *Army Memoirs*, 180.
159 "The arsenal was guarded": *National Tribune*, 6/9/1887.
159 "After this work": OR 44:390.

160 "given orders to search": *Augusta Daily Chronicle & Sentinel,* 12/1/1864.

160 "numbering from": Ibid.

160 "convinced the inhabitants": OR 44:270–71.

160 "The shoes were given": Hoerner, *Chattanooga, Savannah and Alexandria,* 42.

160 "Every house": Noble, Papers, UMB.

160 "the reg't passed": Storrow, Papers, MAS.

160 "Every cotton shed": Trowbridge, Papers, UMC.

161 "I believe": Byrne, Diary and Journal, RU.

161 "We would hear": Jones, *When Sherman Came,* 29.

161 "factory was burnt": Poe, Papers and Letters, LOC.

161 "a large cotton factory": Ladd, "From Atlanta to the Sea," 7.

162 "Plenty of forage": Ege, Papers, WHS.

162 "The foragers brought in": McAdams, *Every-day Soldier Life,* 117.

162 "We have marched": Pendergast, Family Papers, MHS.

162 "Here the colored peoples": Essington, Diary, ISL.

162 "dancing and bobbing": Kellogg, *Army Life of an Illinois Soldier,* 28.

162 "formed into a ring": Girardi and Cheairs, *Memoirs,* 149.

162 "In moving to Milledgeville": OR 44:501.

162 "The discharge": Orders in OR 44:502–3.

163 "I don't think": Howe, *Marching with Sherman,* 79.

163 "It has commenced to rain": Bargus, Diary, MHI.

163 "awful for man": McMillan, Papers, WHS.

163 "mud is deep": Anderson, *Civil War Diary,* 177.

163 "the roads have become": Clark, *Downing's Civil War,* 230.

163 "during the day": *National Tribune,* 6/6/1901.

163 "outrages committed": OR 44:505.

164 "Lots of rain": Keyes, Diary, MHI.

164 "In the mud": Scheel, *Rain, Mud & Swamps,* 462.

164 "All quiet": Engerud, *1864 Diary,* 48.

164 "This evening the cavalry": Moses, "Civil War Diary."

164 "a second demonstration": Howard, "Sherman's Advance from Atlanta," 664.

164 "but not sacrifice": *New York Herald,* 12/22/1864.

164 "There was a rebel force": *New York Times,* 2/26/1876.

164 "They made a stubborn resistance": Ward, Diary, IHS.

165 "Do you recollect": Swedberg, *Three Years,* 233.

165 "For God's sake": Kilpatrick telegraph incident in *New York Times,* 12/28/1864; *New York Herald,* 12/28/1864.

165 "Our fun was over": *New York Times,* 2/26/1876.

166 "It was quite a descent": *National Tribune,* 5/10/1883.

166 "Seeing that the [captured] guns": OR 44:404.

168 "until the trains": OR 44:498.

168 "Some of our troops": *Augusta Daily Chronicle & Sentinel,* 11/30/1864.

CHAPTER 12. "BUT BLESS GOD, HE DIED FREE!"

169 "Burned Denham's Factory": OR 44:306.

169 "When we left": Failing-Knight, Papers, MHS.

169 "were burning": OR 44:320.

169 "roads were perfectly horrid": Failing-Knight, Papers, MHS.

170 "very deep": OR 44:271.

170 "The skies were heavy": Harris, *On the Plantation*, 227–28.

170 "morning dawned dark": OR 44:252.

170 "Men under difficulty": Byrne, Diary and Journal, RU.

170 "Ground very soft": Trego, Diary, CHI.

170 "The roads were so bad": Lathrop, *John Smethurst*, 60.

171 "Genl Slocum cussed": Trego, Diary, CHI.

171 "yelled [until] their throats": Duncan, Papers, NJH.

171 "looked like": Michael, Diary, IHS.

171 "quite a ridiculous": Byrne, Diary and Journal, RU.

171 "Burnt 3 large": Kittinger, Diary, MHI.

171 "a very shammy": *New York Herald*, 12/28/1864.

171 "You never saw": Quoted in Walters, *Oconee River*, 298. 171

171 "passed through Eatonton": Adams, Diary, n.p.

171 "At Eatonton": Hurst, *Journal-History*, 156.

171 "the darkies there": Howe, *Marching with Sherman*, 78.

171 "I never saw": McDonnell, "Reminiscences," UDC.

172 "What is the matter": Harris, *On the Plantation*, 227–28.

172 "soil here": Gould and Kennedy, *Memoirs*, 296.

172 "The mud was ankle deep": Pendergast, Family Papers, MHS.

172 "The difficulties": Widney, Diary and Letters, KNP.

172 "Every body": Ege, Papers, WHS.

173 "Dismal day"/"a very smart negro": Howe, *Marching with Sherman*, 80.

173 "Dar's de man": Ibid., 81–82.

174 "might . . . catch": Howard, *Autobiography*, 2:71.

174 "Weather wet": McKee, Diary, SHI.

174 "The roads": Cluett, *History of the 57th*, 90.

174 "mud in places": Hubert, *Fiftieth Regiment*, 324.

174 "continuous wet": OR 44:125.

175 "They drove off": Jones, *When Sherman Came*, 20.

175 "in some places": Grunert, *History*, 128.

175 "I went to a farm house": Noble, Papers, UMB.

175 "living bully": Pierce, Diary, MHI.

175 "captured thirty mules": Hoerner, *Chattanooga, Savannah and Alexandria*, 42.

175 "I . . . was compelled": Storrow, Papers, MAS.

176 "about sixty wagons": OR 44:253–54.

176 "The rest of my vigil": *National Tribune*, 1/25/1923.

176 "tore down": Sheahan, Diary, ALL.

176 "Men are foraging": Orr, "Civil War Diary."

176 "Plenty of forage": Fahnestock, Diary, KNP.

176 "Many of the female slaves": Pendergast, Family Papers, MHS.

177 "not heartless": Howe, *Marching with Sherman*, 82–83.

179 "Satisfied": Beauregard, Papers, DU.

179 "Rebs attacked": Keyes, Diary, MHI.

179 "This evening the rebel cavalry": Bush, "Civil War Letters and Diary," ISL.

179 "tried to cut off": Corbin, *Star for Patriotism*, 159.

179 "went off in a bigger": Gay, Diary, SHI.
179 "The rebels attacked": Schweitzer, Diary, MHI.
179 "Met the rebel cavalry": Unknown diarist, in Sherman Papers, LOC.
179 "corralled the wagons": Clark, *Downing's Civil War*, 230.
180 "General, what": Rufus Kelly incident in OR 53:32; Tinsley, "Kelly's Defense of Gordon," 335.
181 "General Sherman": *Chicago Evening Journal*, 1/10/1865.

CHAPTER 13. "WE 'SHOT LOW AND TO KILL'"

182 "Very cold last night": Parker, Papers, HL.
183 "the cold wind": Pendergast, Family Papers, MHS.
183 "men really suffered": Wilcox, Diary, MHI.
183 "Nearly every man": Widney, Diary and Letters, KNP.
183 "foraged sweet potatoes": Chamberlain, Papers, IHS.
183 "help feeling pity": Reeve, Papers, WHS.
183 "Miserable, cloudy": Byrne, Diary and Journal, RU.
183 "blankets were wet": Failing-Knight, Papers, MHS.
184 "It told heavily": Bryant, *History*, 278.
184 "extensive gardens": Byrne, Diary and Journal, RU.
184 "lives like a *prince*": Ames, Diary, MHI.
184 "the good people": Short, Diary, WHS.
184 "him out of everything": Morrow, Diary, MHI.
184 "I immediately": Moore, *Rebellion Record*, 9:147.
185 "we were escorted": Bartlett, *"Dutchess County Regiment,"* 139.
185 "a blank-looking set": Potter, *Reminiscences*, 112.
185 "old negroes": Byrne, Diary and Journal, RU.
185 "God bless you!"/"Why-why": Merrill, *Seventieth Indiana*, 225, 220.
185 "To-day we followed": Scott, " 'With Tears in Their Eyes,' " 28.
186 "We had time": Brockman, "John Van Duser Diary," 224.
186 "Not so much shooting": Howe, *Marching with Sherman*, 83.
186 "Sherman was in fine": OR 44:183.
186 "pick out the place": Sherman, *Memoirs*, 2:185.
186 "I sent word back": Ibid.
187 "He's got the Linkum head": Angle, *Three Years*, 317.
187 "Dis Mr. Sharman?": Sherman and slave story in Howe, *Marching with Sherman*, 84; Brockman, "John Van Duser Diary," 224; Sherman, *Memoirs*, 2:186.
188 "uncle was not cordial": Ibid., 2:187.
188 "greatest general": Howe, *Marching with Sherman*, 85.
188 "making further orders": OR 44:519.
188 "All supplies": OR 44:880.
188 "to direct efforts": OR 44:881.
189 "every other consideration": OR 44:883.
189 "I have assumed": Ibid.
189 "I need scarcely": McAdoo, Diary, LOC.
189 "lengthened": Chandler, *Confederate Records*, 676–771.
189 "was at Macon": OR 44:884.

190 "Georgia's hour of trial": *Augusta Daily Chronicle & Sentinel*, 11/22/1864.
190 "a few shoemakers": Quoted in Hillhouse, *History of Burke County*, 134–35.
190 "Cold and snowflakes": Daniels, Diary, HL.
190 "ground froze": McMillan, Papers, WHS.
190 "roasted Chicken": Grender, *Civil War Diary*, 48.
190 "We have just left": Sharland, *Knapsack Notes*, 21.
190 "The citizens somewhat": Lybarger, *Leaves*, 2.
191 "This was a very nice": Daniels, Diary, HL.
191 "If we started south": Fultz, "History of Company D," 74.
191 "First, and all-important": Hedley, *Marching through Georgia*, 314–18.
191 "all . . . crowded": Rood, "Sketches," 366.
191 "Very heavy cannonading": Bargus, Diary, MHI.
192 "twenty miles": OR 55:33.
192 "Heavy cannonading": OR 44:882.
192 "marched about a mile": Dunbar, Diary, BHS.
192 "through the woods": Trimble, *Ninety-third Regiment*, 146.
192 "The rails are laid": Kinley, Diary, SHI.
192 "the plan adopted": *National Tribune*, 4/23/1903.
193 "We enjoyed a snow": Platter, "Civil War Diary," UGA.
193 "cleared up": Gore, Diary, MHI.
193 "Yankee picnic": Unknown Diarist, in Sherman, Papers, LOC.
193 "Roads very bad": Smith, *Seventh Iowa*, 199.
193 "As the mules drop": Hubert, *Fiftieth Regiment*, 324.
193 "Every one": Gore, Diary, LOC.
193 "hard pulling": Chamberlin, *History*, 150.
193 "wagons broke": Roe, Papers, KNX.
193 "and after robbing": Castel, *Tom Taylor's Civil War*, 199.
194 "It was the bitterest": Account in Taylor, *Destruction and Reconstruction*, 250.
197 "All the fire": King, Letter, GSA.
197 "to halt before reaching": Smith, "Georgia Militia," 667.
198 "fugitives . . . dashing"/"for the double purpose": OR 44:382.
198 "severe skirmishing": *Lancaster Daily Evening Express*, 1/3/1865.
198 "Cobb was delighted": Taylor, *Destruction and Reconstruction*, 250.
198 "General Walcutt": OR 44:82.
198 "Found Rebel Cav'y": *Reminiscences of the Civil War*, 151.
199 "east toward Savannah": Taylor, *Destruction and Reconstruction*, 250.
199 "was instructed": Smith, "Georgia Militia," 667.
199 "We drove back": Kirwan, *Johnny Green*, 175.
199 "We . . . drove them back": *Reminiscences of the Civil War*, 153–54.
200 "After finding": Wheeler, Letter, UGA.
200 "an open prairie": OR 44:83.
201 "at 12 or 1 o'clock": OR 53:41.
202 "We gathered rails": *National Tribune*, 2/17/1887.
203 "We were getting dinner": *Reminiscences of the Civil War*, 151.
203 "We used everything": Anderson, *We Are Sherman's Men*, 118.
203 "the enemy posted": OR 53:41.
204 "an eligible site": OR 53:42.
204 "avoid a fight"/"If pressed"/"General: the whole division": OR 53:40.

205 "lying behind a [tree] stump": Arndt, "Reminiscences of an Artillery Officer," 288.

206 "jeers and sneers": Quoted in Bragg, "Little Battle," 49.

206 "an advance": OR 53:42.

206 "The enemy's forces": Wright, *Sixth Iowa*, 366.

206 "The enemy advanced": *National Tribune*, 2/17/1887.

207 "after the sponge and rammer": Arndt, "Report of Griswoldville," 523.

207 "made the rails": *National Tribune*, 9/25/1890.

207 "The enemy's well served": Wright, *Sixth Iowa*, 368.

208 "The rebel infantry approached": *National Tribune*, 9/25/1890.

208 "We charged them": Jackson, Diary, KNP.

208 "The music of shot": *National Tribune*, 9/1/1910.

208 "As soon as": OR 44:107.

208 "was most terrible": *Reminiscences of the Civil War*, 155.

208 "enabled us to keep": Winther, *With Sherman to the Sea*, 137.

208 "we 'shot low' ": *National Tribune*, 2/17/1887.

208 "in fine style": OR 53:42.

209 "quite a hard fight": Anderson, *We Are Sherman's Men*, 117.

209 "came at us with force": Bush, "Civil War Letters and Diary," ISL.

209 "charged us": Carr, Diary, KNP.

209 "We kept on loading": *National Tribune*, 9/1/1910.

210 "As I had already": OR 44:105.

210 "The firing was incessant": OR 53:44.

210 "the boys fell": Quoted in Bragg, *Griswoldville*, 126.

210 "(from some cause": OR 53:42.

212 "My neighborhood": Wright, *Sixth Iowa*, 368.

212 "I never saw our boys fight": Winther, *With Sherman to the Sea*, 136.

212 "At one time": OR 44:107.

212 "a rather severe": Osterhaus, "U.S. Army Generals' Report," NA.

212 "Just about half way across": Langford, "William Bedford Langford," UDC.

212 "and, ammunition": OR 53:44.

213 "leaving some of our killed": Quoted in Livingston, *Fields of Gray*, 151.

213 "The scenes of death": Wright, *Sixth Iowa*, 368.

213 "It was a harvest": Winther, *With Sherman to the Sea*, 138.

213 "I was never so affected": *Reminiscences of the Civil War*, 153.

213 "I could not help but pity": Bush, "Civil War Letters and Diary," ISL.

213 "The field was almost covered": *National Tribune*, 9/1/1910.

213 "We took all inside": *Reminiscences of the Civil War*, 153.

214 "They were badly mixed up": *National Tribune*, 2/17/1887.

214 "mournful sighing": Wright, *Sixth Iowa*, 371.

214 "The Militia has been": Quoted in Livingston, *Fields of Gray*, 159.

214 "distinguished gallantry": Text contained on Georgia State Historical Marker 084-21.

215 "and supposed killed": *Macon Daily Telegraph*, 11/24/1864.

215 "it would have resulted": OR 53:42.

215 "success in driving": OR 53:40.

215 "to avoid an engagement": OR 44:414.

215 "From all the information": King, Letter, GSA.

CHAPTER 14. "THE FIRST ACT IS WELL PLAYED"

216 "the now important": OR 44:878.
217 "The cadets": Joyce, "From Infantry to Cavalry," 300.
218 "I am expecting": OR 44:878.
218 "The first stage": Sherman, *Memoirs*, 2:187.
218 "not used": Howe, *Marching with Sherman*, 86.
218 "First act": Ibid., 85.
219 "looked . . . like a person": McKinley, "Memories," UDC.
219 "Captured wagons": *Philadelphia Weekly Times*, 1/17/1880.
219 "The bravery of the school boys": Joyce, "From Infantry to Cavalry," 300.
220 "completely destroyed": Cruikshank, "Civil War Letters."
220 "It was really amusing": Scofield, Papers, GHS.
220 "all public buildings": Collins, *Memoirs*, 294.
220 "The State House": Byrne, Diary and Journal, RU.
220 "All polite and intelligent": Trego, Diary, CHI.
221 "Stayed in the city": Chapman, "Civil War Diary," 102.
221 "very curious way": Storrow, Papers, MAS.
221 "valuable things": Grunert, *History*, 123.
221 "many a poor soldier": Wallace, *Sixty-First Ohio*, 29.
221 "purchasing power": Wagoner, "From Wauhatchie," 120.
221 "them happy": Bryant, *History*, 284.
221 "Settlement was made": Baldwin, Papers, HL.
222 "miserable weapons": Ames, Diary, MHI.
222 "if they intended to fight": Short, Diary, WHS.
222 "formidable looking": Fleharty, *Our Regiment*, 114.
222 "a pretty fair sample": Byrne, Diary and Journal, RU.
222 "Choice literary"/"Public libraries": Angle, *Three Years*, 408.
222 "He looked": Trego, Diary, CHI.
222 "Motions were made": Boies, *Record*, 101.
222 "Gen. Kilpatrick": Bryant, *History*, 285.
222 "In a moment": Boies, *Record*, 101.
223 "not present": Sherman, *Memoirs*, 2:190.
223 "How my blood boiled": Harris, Papers, DU.
223 "We got plenty": Abernethy, Diary, SHI.
223 a flurry of orders: Hazen, *Narrative*, 315–17.
224 "We sent a few bullets": Joyce, "From Infantry to Cavalry," 300.
224 "We kept down": Cryder and Stanley, *"War for the Union,"* 457.
224 "the enemy": OR 44:154.
224 "carpets, curtains": Sherman, *Memoirs*, 2:188.
225 "It would have been wrong": Howe, *Marching with Sherman*, 86.
225 "Augusta [was not]": *New York Times*, 1/29/1876.
226 Special Field Orders No. 127: OR 44:527.
226 "These were, substantially": Sherman, *Memoirs*, 2:190.
226 "I want you": *New York Times*, 2/26/1876.
227 "I advanced": Quoted in Jones, *Siege of Savannah*, 48.
227 "became panic stricken": *Augusta Daily Chronicle & Sentinel*, 11/29/1864.
228 "Send me 5,000": OR 44:887.

228 "found about": Christie, Family Papers, MHS.

228 "I heard a loud explosion": Bradley, *Star Corps*, 191.

228 "in well-informed circles"/"Milledgeville": Quoted in *Philadelphia Inquirer*, 11/28/1864.

229 "General Sherman is not": *Richmond Examiner*, 9/24/64.

229 "that SHERMAN'S march": Quoted in *Philadelphia Inquirer*, 11/28/1864.

229 "every effort": OR 44:891.

229 "might have to ask him": Howard, *Autobiography*, 2:79.

230 "3,000 men": OR 44:891–93.

230 "more than 800": OR 53:34.

231 "positive information": OR 44:536.

231 "a long and important": Roman, *Military Operations*, 2:302.

231 "the most direct route": OR 44:890.

232 "I will be obliged": OR 44:536.

233 "an intelligent gentleman": *Augusta Daily Chronicle & Sentinel*, 11/24/1864.

233 "had enjoyed a fine march": Howard, "Sherman's Advance from Atlanta," 664.

233 "dense, penetrating": Storrow, Papers, MAS.

234 "The roads are frozen": Wagoner, "From Wauhatchie," 121.

234 "a continuous medley": Byrne, *Uncommon Soldiers*, 201.

234 "Each regiment": *National Tribune*, 10/21/1937.

234 "We had pancakes": Lathrop, *John Smethurst*, 61.

234 "a grand scene": Underwood, *Three Years' Service*, 248.

234 "saw no signs": Westervelt, *Lights and Shadows*, 85.

235 "a woman on horseback": Girardi and Cheairs, *Memoirs*, 152.

235 "were quite numerous": Ladd, "From Atlanta to the Sea," 8.

235 "In passing through": Hapeman, Diary, ALL.

235 "a soldier asked a woman": McAdams, *Every-day Soldier Life*, 118.

235 "duly confiscated": Johnson, "March to the Sea," 321.

235 "The morning was quite frosty"/"Two of our boys": Rosenow, *Pen Pictures*, 105.

236 "A very unfortunate": Floyd, *History of the Seventy-fifth*, 351.

236 "God hasten the day": Howe, *Marching with Sherman*, 88.

236 "If they die": *Sunny South*, 11/30/1901.

236 "General Sherman passed": Hoerner, *Chattanooga, Savannah and Alexandria*, 42.

236 "General Sherman rode": Bryant, *History*, 286.

236 "We are now": Howe, *Marching with Sherman*, 90.

237 "Rascals *borrowed*": Ibid., 89.

CHAPTER 15. "WE WENT FOR THEM ON THE RUN"

241 "rang out beautifully": *92nd Illinois Volunteers*, 180–81.

242 "Morning cold": Trego, Diary, CHI.

242 "doubtless breathe": Johnson, "March to the Sea," 321.

242 "two explosions": Parker, Papers, HL.

242 "Blew up": Levey, Diary, MHI.

243 "Our cavalry": Jones, *When Sherman Came*, 30–31.

243 "mere boys": Ibid., 32.

243 "very ragged": McKinley, "Memories," UDC.

243 "women ran out": Heyward-Ferguson, Papers, SHC.

243 "told him": McKinley, "Memories," UDC.

243 "plundering band": Quoted in Bonner, *Milledgeville*, 290.

244 "Then you have done": Howe, *Marching with Sherman*, 92.

244 "a few houses": Sheahan, Diary, ALL.

244 "the usual amount": Byrne, Diary and Journal, RU.

244 "This Creek of itself": Brockman, "John Van Duser Diary," 226.

244 "The stream or swamp": OR 44:272.

245 "The first thing": Lockhart, "Civil War Memoir," WHS.

245 "using timber": OR 44:272.

245 "People are silly": Byrne, Diary and Journal, RU.

245 "While waiting here": Parmater, Diary, OHS.

246 "In war everything": Howe, *Marching with Sherman*, 92–93.

246 "Long Bridge": *Philadelphia Inquirer*, 12/23/1864.

247 "We went double quick": Lathrop, *John Smethurst*, 62.

247 "From this on": Howe, *Marching with Sherman*, 91.

247 "Forage plenty": Brant, *History of the Eighty-Fifth*, 80.

248 "Among the variety": Marvin, *Fifth Regiment*, 356.

248 "The rebel bushwhackers": Payne, *Thirty-Fourth Regiment*, 165.

248 "The foragers": Hapeman, Diary, ALL.

248 "We get meat fresh": Daniels, Diary, UMB.

248 "The d——d old rebel": Ross, Diary, ALL.

248 "little girl [who] said": Hickman, Diary and Letters, UMB.

248 "had left them": Trego, Diary, CHI.

248 "kept up a continual": Sheahan, Diary, ALL.

249 "Here we destroyed": *Lancaster Daily Evening Express*, 1/3/1865.

249 "May all the names": Quoted in Shivers, *Land Between*, 163.

249 "The 1st and 3rd": Federico, *Civil War Letters*, 166.

249 "to have your picketing": OR 44:546.

249 "I got on a post": Omvig, Diaries, 114.

250 "If Georgia is saved": Quoted in Hallock, *Braxton Bragg*, 226.

250 "a great nuisance": McAdoo, Diary, LOC.

250 "Now is the time": *Augusta Daily Chronicle & Sentinel*, 11/25/1864.

250 "seems to be tending"/"will determine": OR 44:895.

251 "thick haze": Sharland, *Knapsack Notes*, 23.

251 "Countermarched": Jamison, *Recollections*, 281.

251 "had to cut two roads": Force, Papers, UWA.

252 "had to tare up": Pratt Diary, WHS.

252 "General Howard": Howard and Osterhaus exchange in *National Tribune*, 1/23/1896; Howard, *Autobiography*, 2:80.

253 "burning the Court House": Chamberlin, *History*, 151.

253 "mostly burned": Burton, Diary, EU.

253 "now in ruins": Hubert, *Fiftieth Regiment*, 325.

253 "We . . . carried out the goods": Gore, Diary, MHI.

253 "I then instructed": Howard, *Autobiography*, 2:80.

254 "I think": OR 44:897.

254 "a ladies handsome": Heyward-Ferguson Papers, SHC.

CHAPTER 16. "POOR FOOLISH SIMPLETONS"

255 "less than 1,000": OR 53:34.
256 "to send off all movable": OR 44:407.
256 "a very small": Quoted in Davis, *Sherman's March*, 74.
256 "There was not an adult": *Atlanta Journal*, 6/14/1902.
257 "was well named": Benton, *As Seen*, 234.
257 "and with shouts"/"the sound of horses": Toombs, *Reminiscences*, 179.
257 "Presently, the pop-pop-pop": Bryant, *History*, 286.
257 "all the mounted officers": Byrne, Diary and Journal, RU.
257 "warm work": Ladd, "From Atlanta to the Sea," 9.
257 "I myself saw": Sherman, *Memoirs*, 2:191.
257 "not a battle": Howe, *Marching with Sherman*, 95.
258 "L.F.J.": Incident recounted in Jones, *When Sherman Came*, 41; *National Tribune*, 3/31/1910.
258 "There was a wild chase": Duncan, Papers, NJH.
258 "women were in great": Storrow, Papers, MAS.
259 "Saw the 20th [Corps]": Fultz, "History of Company D," 5.
259 "and went to [a] large": Howe, *Marching with Sherman*, 96.
259 "We immediately commenced": Short, Diary, WHS.
259 "This evening we got chickens": Saylor, Letter, WHS.
260 "transfixed with terror": Benton, *As Seen*, 236–37.
260 "very angry": Howe, *Marching with Sherman*, 96.
260 "The co[u]rt house"/"went into a large drug store": Johnson, " 'Make a Preacher Swear,' " 33.
261 "He was a happy man": Ibid.
261 "had made odd fellows"/"Should judge the poor fellow": Byrne, Diary and Journal, RU.
261 "one of Co. C": Storrow, Papers, MAS.
261 "putting him into a rough coffin": Bradley, *Star Corps*, 196.
261 "So sudden an advent": Champlin, Diary, WRS.
261 "strong secesh": McLean, Family Papers, NYL.
261 "an intelligent half blood": Trowbridge, Papers, UMC.
262 "I don't war on women": Howe, *Marching with Sherman*, 97.
262 "that, if the enemy"/"heard that the right wing": Sherman, *Memoirs*, 2:191.
262 "it may give the whole army": Angle, *Three Years*, 324.
262 "We marched at 7 A.M.": *Philadelphia Inquirer*, 12/24/1864.
263 "forced march to rescue"/"The roads were dry": *National Tribune*, 5/17/1883.
263 "How our hearts leaped": Ibid.
264 "destroyed a portion of the track": OR 44:363.
264 "had lit out": Lybarger, *Leaves*, 2.
264 "to wash their clothing": *Fifty-Fifth Regiment*, 394.
264 "busy chucklucking": Schweitzer, Diary, MHI.
265 "Officers from other commands": *Reminiscences of the Civil War*, 159.
265 "Old man to right of road": Jamison, *Recollections*, 281.
265 "would settle the frail": Wright, *Sixth Iowa*, 374.
265 "to take in all horses": Schweitzer, Diary, MHI.
265 "We . . . went to the river": Black, "Marching with Sherman," 456.

265 "immense cavalcade": Strong, Papers, ALL.

266 " 'Bummers' are entitled": OR 44:597.

266 "He was a logical product"/"The typical military bummer": Taylor, *Lights and Shadows*, 21.

266 "The Georgia forager": Merrill, *Seventieth Indiana*, 223.

266 "To provision his army": *Springfield Daily Republican*, 4/25/1887.

267 "It was an almost": Fultz, "History of Company D," 75.

267 "Georgia now seems": Saunier, *History*, 357.

267 "obliged to wade": Osborn, Diary, MHI.

267 "Here we had plenty": Hubert, *Fiftieth Regiment*, 325.

267 "a lot of chairs": Girdner, Letters, EU.

267 "have a skirmish nearly every day": Roe, Papers, KNX.

267 "It is reported": Clark, *Downing's Civil War*, 232.

267 " 'out let,' and if 10,000": Platter, "Civil War Diary," UGA.

CHAPTER 17. "I NEVER WAS SO FRIGHTENED IN ALL MY LIFE"

268 "all combinations"/"In assuming it": OR 44:901.

268 "Here, then, will be war": Miers, *Rebel War Clerk's Diary*, 452-3.

270 "Here tearing the track": Schwab, "Civil War Letters," CIN.

270 "Good work": Sherwood, Journal, MHI.

270 "Soldier, will you work": Hubert, *Fiftieth Regiment*, 325.

270 "This is the Sabbath": Roe, Papers, KNX.

270 "a great deal of cotton": Quint, *Record*, 251.

270 "large buildings": Pendergast, Family Papers, MHS.

270 "As the dense columns": Fleharty, *Our Regiment*, 117.

271 "Country very level": Inskeep, Diary, OHS.

271 "There is strict orders": Allspaugh, Diaries, UIA.

271 "Country good": Wheeler, Letters and Journal, ALL.

271 "I think we destroy": Parker, Papers, HL.

271 "I think a katydid": *National Tribune*, 4/2/1903.

271 "These animals were": *National Tribune*, 4/30/1903.

271 "sot fire to the well": Sherman, *Memoirs*, 2:192.

272 "great crowd of miserable": Reeve, Papers, WHS.

272 "Women came with large": Bradley, *Star Corps*, 196.

272 "They would not leave us": Otto, *Civil War Memoirs*, HS.

272 "It makes but little difference": Wagoner, "From Wauhatchie," 121–22.

272 "If ever Old Smith": Brown, *Fourth Regiment*, 343.

272 "About noon Slocum": Sheahan Diary, ALL.

272 "Had quite an exhibition": Bohrnstedt, *Soldiering with Sherman*, 145.

272 "Gen. Slocum": Trego, Diary, CHI.

273 "asking God's blessing": Jones, *When Sherman Came*, 41; *National Tribune*, 3/31/1910; [footnote] *National Tribune*, 2/9/1911.

273 "If she spoke": Howe, *Marching with Sherman*, 99.

274 "it's impossible": Ibid., 101.

274 "Being as full of curiosity": Angle, *Three Years*, 326.

274 "not a plank disturbed": Ibid., 326–27.

275 "an old wooden bridge": Essington, Diary, ISL.
275 "tomorrow the second Act": Howe, *Marching with Sherman*, 106.
276 "unexpected, and in the darkness": *National Tribune*, 9/10/1903.
276 "fell back": Ward, Diary, IHS.
276 "we could hear": *National Tribune*, 9/10/1903.
276 "Being mindful": OR 44:408.
277 "A company of fifty men": *92nd Illinois Volunteers*, 183.
277 "Marched thirty miles": Carter, *Story*, 307.
277 "The rebels followed close": Berkenes, *Private William Boddy*, 154.
277 "It was evident": *Lancaster Daily Evening Express*, 1/3/1865.
278 "certainly the vilest": Harper, *Second Georgia Infantry*, 66.
278 "It is needless to say": OR 44:363.
278 "sadly in need": OR 44:375.
278 "The town was in flames": OR 44:408.
278 "I deemed it prudent": OR 44:363.
279 "The enemy's position": Quoted in *Philadelphia Inquirer*, 12/5/1864.
280 "I cannot too strongly": Jones-Seddon exchange in OR 44:903.
280 "The time has come": Quoted in *Philadelphia Inquirer*, 12/7/1864.
280 "Thus we approached": Howe, *Marching with Sherman*, 107.
280 "on sandy roads": Ibid., 107.
281 "one of the most": Ibid., 109–10.
281 "runs through a dismal": Marvin, *Fifth Regiment*, 356.
281 "We tried various modes": Storrow, Papers, MAS.
281 "The troops moved": Byrne, *Uncommon Soldiers*, 270.
281 "I think the Div[ision]": *Reminiscences of the Civil War*, 166.
282 "wilderness. It is all": Glossbrenner, Diary, MHI.
282 "In making the order": Harwell and Racine, *Fiery Trail*, 61.
282 "Colonel Adams": Chamberlin, *History*, 151.
282 "These roads are generally": Harwell and Racine, *Fiery Trail*, 61.
282 "men immediately fell in": OR 44:317.
282 "Hang onto it": Lockhart, "Civil War Memoir," WHS.
283 "Large quantities of stores": Duncan, Papers, NJH.
283 "foragers got lots of stuff": Saylor, Letter, WHS.
283 "must have lived": Byrne, Diary and Journal, RU.
283 "Here we had to lay": Buckingham, Papers, AAS.
283 "pontoniers and pioneers": OR 44:326.
284 "The facility in crossing": Brant, *History of the Eighty-fifth*, 81.
284 "I . . . was probably": Angle, *Three Years*, 329.
284 "crossed the river": Johnson, "March to the Sea," 322.
284 "a deep stream": Woodard, *Civil War Letters*, 20.
284 "It was a very long": Emmons, Diaries, UIA.
284 "The boys made quite": Brower, *Foragin'*, 28.
284 "Books, clothing, cutlery": Pendergast, Family Papers, MHS.
284 "One fellow played": Porter, Diary, OHS.
285 "We burnt some": Essington, Diary, ISL.
285 "I never can sanction": Emmons, Diaries, UIA.
285 "I [am] getting ashamed": Quoted in DeLaubenfels, "Where Sherman Passed," 297.
285 "before night": OR 44:164.

285 "old general": Williams, Diary, IU.

285 "General Davis then summoned": Widney, Diary and Letters, KNP.

286 "so much so": *New York Herald*, 12/9/1864.

286 "seeing that he was cut off": *National Tribune*, 5/17/1883.

286 "not twenty-five yards": *Philadelphia Inquirer*, 12/23/1864.

286 "only hard fighting": *New York Herald*, 12/9/1864.

287 "I have to this day": *National Tribune*, 9/10/1903.

288 "As company after company": *National Tribune*, 9/20/1903.

288 "Is this the rear guard": Ibid.

288 "boys, make you some coffee": Ward, Diary, IHS.

288 "I . . . took up": OR 44:364.

288 "put about 100": *National Tribune*, 11/26/1903.

288 "By the side": *92nd Illinois Volunteers*, 186–87.

289 "Colonel, you are disgracing": Ibid.

289 "night was fast": OR 44:409.

289 "Reaching the open": *Confederate Veteran*, 11:354.

289 "with great fierceness": Miller, "We Scattered," 45.

290 "they made charge": *National Tribune*, 2/25/1904.

290 "shot in seven": Berkenes, *Private William Boddy*, 155.

290 "The rebels seemed": *National Tribune*, 11/26/1903.

290 "We fought General Kilpatrick": OR 44:910.

291 "It was a night": *National Tribune*, 5/17/1883.

291 "We are very tired": Ward, Diary, IHS.

291 "It proved to be": Angle, *Three Years*, 331.

292 "saw the line of blue": Ibid., 332.

292 "This is one of the times": Johnson, "March to the Sea," 324.

292 "I can assure you": *National Tribune*, 11/26/1903.

293 "about one day's march": OR 44:9.

293 "learn definitely": OR 44:572.

293 "pacing to and fro": Cryder and Stanley, *"War for the Union,"* 460.

294 "Yes, it is very good land": Christie, Family Papers, MHS.

294 "been brought up"/"Please, Sir": Howe, *Marching with Sherman*, 114–15.

295 "bare feet in slippers": Howe, *Marching with Sherman*, 112–13.

295 "The country from Atlanta": Belknap, *Fifteenth Regiment*, 413.

295 "All day in an awful": *Reminiscences of the Civil War*, 160.

296 "Trees tall and stately": Hubert, *Fiftieth Regiment*, 326.

296 "Only saw three houses": Platter, "Civil War Diary," UGA.

296 "Poor people live here": Scheel, *Rain, Mud & Swamps*, 469.

296 "found the refugees' ": Corbin, *Star for Patriotism*, 160.

296 "got 60 horses": Unknown Diarist, SHI.

296 "It was more of a shock": Hubert, *History of the Fiftieth Regiment*, 326.

296 "Had to make right angle": Burton, Diary, EU.

296 "Our course is marked": Dunkelman and Winey, *Hardtack Regiment*, 127.

296 "The marching by the side": Storrow, Papers, MAS.

297 "Burned it": Morgan, Diary, MHI.

297 "Hung an old man": Trego, Diary, CHI.

297 "It is really heart-rending": Winkler, Letters, 10.

297 "But as we were filling": Ladd, "From Atlanta to the Sea," 9.

297 "Col. [James W.] Langley": Ross, Diary, ALL.

298 "is just now playing": Porter, Diary, OHS.

298 "about December 1": OR 39/3:740.

302 "Every place we come to": Brockman, "John Van Duser Diary," 229–30.

302 "There are not many rebels": Rosenow, *Pen Pictures*, 107.

303 "As we filed up the road"/"all shot through the head": Ross, Diary, ALL.

303 "foragers are circumscribed": OR 44:582.

303 "Any quantity of forage": Hapeman, Diary, ALL.

303 "The negroes had a grand jubilee": Calkins, *One Hundred and Fourth Regiment*, 265.

304 "Thousands of colored people": Morhous, *Reminiscences*, 141.

304 "Supposed to be": Morrow, Diary, MHI.

304 "roads a complete wilderness": Scheel, *Rain, Mud & Swamps*, 469.

304 "during that whole distance": Platter, "Civil War Diary," UGA.

304 "This is the first music": *Reminiscences of the Civil War*, 161.

304 "Have to make our roads": Keyes, Diary, MHI.

304 "The sloughs are called creeks": Jackson, *Colonel's Diary*, 167.

304 "The roads are desperate": Ambrose, *Seventh Regiment*, 281.

305 "Listen Miss Sue": Sample plantation incident in Jones, *When Sherman Came*, 46–47.

305 "The railroad bridge": Hickenlooper, Collection, CIN.

305 "wagons, footmen and horsemen": Howe, *Marching with Sherman*, 117.

305 Johnny Wells: Ibid., 119; Nichols, *Story of the Great March*, 74–75; Brockman, "John Van Duser Diary," 229.

306 "in case you hear": OR 44:581.

306 "within three miles of Millen": OR 44:578.

306 "crossing by light of fires": Howe, *Marching with Sherman*, 118.

306 "A novel and vivid sight": Quoted in *New York Times*, 12/23/1864.

CHAPTER 18. "GIVE THOSE FELLOWS A START"

307 "in the direction of Augusta": OR 44:9.

307 "to cover the movements": OR 44:364.

308 "The General pointed": Angle, *Three Years*, 333–34.

309 "Sherman didn't know": Ibid., 334.

309 "fought us": Ward, Diary, IHS.

309 "nothing save bulldog fighting": OR 44:385.

309 "We then moved rapidly": OR 44:598.

310 "Here, I'll give this to you": Quoted in Durden, *History*, 77.

310 "What kind of folks": Jones, *When Sherman Came*, 49–59.

310 "Broke camp at 7": Jamison, *Recollections*, 282.

310 "The rail was of": Hedley, *Marching through Georgia*, 320.

310 "heated in the middle": Fultz, "History of Company D," 76.

310 "The practice of indiscriminate": OR 44:596.

311 "On the 1st": Canfield, *21st Regiment*, 176.

311 "Rebels . . . captured": Clark Diaries, LHS.

311 "numbering thirty-two": OR 44:172.

311 "said to be": Lybarger, *Leaves*, 2.

312 "Come, Come, Come": Morrow, Diary, MHI.

312 "This was a busy day": Trimble, *Ninety-Third Regiment*, 148.

312 "We . . . have to wade": Schaum, Diary, DU.

312 "substantially parallel to": OR 44:84.

312 "American scorpions": Saunier, *History*, 358.

312 "the foragers coming in": Unknown Diarist, in Sherman Papers, LOC.

312 "The beds were torn": Sample plantation incidents in Jones, *When Sherman Came*, 46–47.

313 "with great caution": OR 44:593.

313 "cover the enemy's front": OR 44:916.

313 "took the trouble": Brockman, "John Van Duser Diary," 229.

314 "sick in bed"/"rather hang-dog": Howe, *Marching with Sherman*, 124–25.

314 "have been entirely satisfactory": OR 44:601.

316 "well together": Jackson, *Colonel's Diary*, 167.

316 "men across the creek"/"We would set a hive": Jackson, *Colonel's Diary*, 168.

316 "Some of the boys": Cryder and Stanley, "*War for the Union*," 460.

316 "The railroad": Lybarger, *Leaves*, 2.

317 "We had to wade": Schweitzer, Diary, MHI.

317 "The roads very bad": Osborn, Diary, MHI.

317 "What is the news?": Lonergan telegraph incident in OR 44:604.

318 "While soul stirring music": Burton, Diary, EU.

318 "We now considered": Widney foraging incident in *National Tribune*, 3/20/1902.

319 "Commenced skirmishing"/"our movement was slow": Angle, *Three Years*, 336, 337.

319 "We have had sharp": Ward Diary, IHS.

319 "a lively, rollicking": Angle, *Three Years*, 339.

320 "We made them fly": Eisenhower, Diary, MHI.

320 "He also told us": Angle, *Three Years*, 339.

320 "If we get any communication": Angle, *Three Years*, 339.

321 "No, Sir": Howe, *Marching with Sherman*, 128.

321 "continue to march": OR 44:609.

322 "The fewer the men": OR 44:602.

323 "would cut my rear": OR 53:35.

323 "There we must cross": Howe, *Marching with Sherman*, 136.

323 "the whole army": Sherman, *Memoirs*, 2:193.

323 "There was a forage party": Glossbrenner, Diary, MHI.

324 "He was buried": Duke, *Fifty-third Regiment*, 166.

324 "how terrible the sweep": Ambrose, *Seventh Regiment*, 282.

324 "At Millen": Wescott, Papers, WHS.

324 "Broke camp at daylight": Jamison, *Recollections*, 284.

324 "Having stacked arms": Grunert, *History*, 139.

325 "Visited the Stockades": Storrow, Papers, MAS.

325 "The prisoners were compelled": Potter, *Reminiscences*, 114.

325 "The huts were built": Bradley, *Star Corps*, 203.

325 "There was not a soul": Bauer, *Soldiering*, 193–94.

326 "We saw one": Hoerner, *Chattanooga, Savannah and Alexandria*, 41.

326 "We found the bodies": Anderson, *They Died*, 238–39.

326 "was to make the": Jackson, *Colonel's Diary*, 169.

327 "Got lost": Emmons, Diaries, UIA.

327 "Moved at 6 A.M.": Reeve, Papers, WHS.

327 "In a raw state": Otto, "Civil War Memoirs," WHS.

327 "While crossing the pontoon": McAdams, *Every-day Soldier Life*, 121.

327 "can do nothing": Quoted in Hughes and Whitney, *Jefferson Davis in Blue*, 157.

327 "Nothing could induce": *Quincy Daily Whig & Republican*, 1/6/1865.

328 "were left on the wrong side": OR 44:184.

328 "very plain": Jackson, *Colonel's Diary*, 169.

328 "most incomprehensible": Pittenger, Diary, OHS.

328 "At Millen I learned": Sherman, *Memoirs*, 2:193.

328 "are to move up": Angle, *Three Years*, 343.

328 "to send surplus": OR 44:364.

329 "Roads good generally": Howe, *Marching with Sherman*, 137.

330 "passed 'Uncle Billy' ": Jamison, *Recollections*, 285.

330 "was fordable above us"/"Skirmishing began": OR 53:35–36.

331 "must have seen": Sherman, *Memoirs*, 2:193.

331 "exhausted but lively": Force, Papers, UWA.

331 "on a large plantation": *National Tribune*, 6/6/1901.

332 "We could see the smoke": Roe, Papers, KNX.

332 "Almost all of the people": Kellogg, *Army Life*, 331.

332 "Went into camp": Gay, Diary, SHI.

332 "kept wrathfully blackguarding": *Fifty-fifth Regiment*, 395.

332 "They loaded their wagons": Quoted in Brannen, *Life in Old Bulloch*, 51–52.

332 "bought used coffee": Ibid., 51.

333 "swamp, swampy, swampier": Parmater, Diary, OHS.

333 "found roads or ground": Byrne, Diary and Journal, RU.

333 "teams at bad holes"/"The crackers": Byrne, *Uncommon Soldiers*, 279.

333 "overflowed the road": Kittinger, Diary, MHI.

333 "swelling at so rapid": Grunert, *History*, 141.

333 "Everyone wet": Byrne Diary and Journal, RU.

334 "We have not": Bradley, *Star Corps*, 204.

334 "A large number present": Ames, Diary, MHI.

334 "burning the ties"/"a very poor country": OR 44:172.

334 "No forage": Holmes, *52d O.V.I.*, 18.

334 "Rebs make their appearance": Clark, Diaries, LHS.

334 "too much demoralized": OR 44:409.

335 "After some parleying:" Angle, *Three Years*, 345.

335 "General Kilpatrick": Hunter, *Eighty-second Indiana*, 140.

335 "to prepare for a fight": *National Tribune*, 12/8/1887.

335 "So many cavalry in line": Angle, *Three Years*, 345.

336 "in order to accomplish": OR 44:618.

336 "a splendid defensive position": *New York Herald*, 12/22/1864.

336 "Come on now": Ibid.

336 "We moved up": Tomlinson, *"Dear Friends,"* 174.

338 "grinding out the shot": Swedberg, *Three Years*, 234–35.

338 "I ordered my bugler": Hamilton, *Recollections*, 163.

338 "Away we went": McKeever, "Atlanta to the Sea," WRS.

338 "landed lengthwise": *National Tribune*, 4/9/1891.

338 "At the word of command": *National Tribune*, 2/12/1891.

338 "We could see an officer": *National Tribune*, 5/17/1883.

338 "Now for a name": OR 44:392.

338 "had to form": Robertson, *Michigan in the War*, 712.

338 "fog and smoke": *National Tribune*, 11/17/1887.

338 "was knocked from his horse": OR 44:397.

339 "I was glad I did not kill him": Quoted in Lee, "Tangling with Kilcavalry," 175.

339 "and pumped their Spencers": *92nd Illinois Volunteers*, 191.

339 "I'm shot": *Toledo Daily Blade*, 1/24/1865.

339 "He never spoke": More, *Soldier Boy*, 308.

339 "made several counter-charges": OR 44:365.

339 "Col. Heath": *National Tribune*, 9/20/1893.

339 "They rode over": *New York Herald*, 12/28/1864.

339 "The charge by our cavalry": Johnson, "March to the Sea," 327.

339 "had to retreat": Miller, Diary, IHS.

340 "Between us and Waynesboro": *National Tribune*, Nov. 26, 1903.

340 "flanks [were] so far extended": OR 44:365.

340 "No body of men": OR 44:380.

340 "moved rapidly": *National Tribune*, Nov. 26, 1903.

340 "our whole line": Miller, "We Scattered," 48.

341 "enjoyed the sweetest draught": Jordan, "Civil War Letters," PAH.

341 "whipped": *Lancaster Daily Evening Express*, 1/3/1865.

341 "Through the streets": *National Tribune*, 11/26/1903.

341 "were so warmly pressed": OR 44:410.

341 "Kilpatrick stopped": *National Tribune*, 4/15/1920.

341 "rushing around like a child": *National Tribune*, 11/26/1903.

341 "I seen one old Reb": Miller, Diary, IHS.

342 "woman [who] was kneeling": McNeil, *Personal Recollections*, 62.

342 "amused themselves": *Lancaster Daily Evening Express*, 1/3/1865.

342 "They made me play": Quoted in Lee, "Tangling with Kilcavalry," 175.

342 "alive with women": Miller, Diary, IHS.

342 "as there was no minister": *Atlanta Constitution*, 5/16/1926.

342 "For the memory": OR 44:627.

343 "upwards of 200": OR 44:635.

343 "the rebel cavalry": Woodard, *Civil War Letters*, 24.

343 "A cavalry fight": Angle, *Three Years*, 345.

CHAPTER 19. "SPLENDID SIGHT TO SEE COTTON GINS BURN"

347 "No trouble": Carter, *Story*, 309.

347 "entering the swampy country": *Lancaster Daily Evening Express*, 1/3/1865.

347 "Good water": Berkenes, *Private William Boddy*, 157.

347 "receive every attention": OR 44:635.

348 "Kilpatrick is the most vain": Angle, *Three Years*, 348.

348 "Two or three plantations": Emmons, Diaries, UIA.

349 "All our bed clothes": Rosenow, *Pen Pictures*, 110.

349 "The number of negroes": Emmons, Diaries, UIA.
349 "They were a motley crowd": McCain, *Soldier's Diary*, 43.
349 "However they do not": Emmons, Diaries, UIA.
349 "Streams or water swamps": Trego, Diary, CHI.
349 "much of the road": Boyle, *Soldiers True*, 267.
349 "The wagons often get stuck": Wagoner, "From Wauhatchie," 123.
349 "scarce": Johnson, " 'Make a Preacher Swear, ' " 35.
349 "sweet potatoes": Chapman, "Civil War Diary," 105.
349 "Stop at house": Morrow, Diary, MHI.
350 "three foraging teams": OR 44:323.
350 "Uncultivated land": Trowbridge, Papers, UMC.
350 "such fires": OR 44:633.
350 "Seen far in advance": Fleharty, *Our Regiment*, 121.
350 "Trampled by day": Byrne, Diary and Journal, RU.
350 "After considerable maneuvering": Jackson, *Colonel's Diary*, 170.
350 "of course was pleasant": Brockman, "John Van Duser Diary," 232.
351 "concluded that they": Clark, *Downing's Civil War*, 234.
351 "We got a number": Christie, Family Papers, MHS.
351 "tied by thumbs": Jamison, *Recollections*, 285.
351 "splendid sight": McMillan, Papers, WHS.
351 "Sat waiting": Howe, *Marching with Sherman*, 144–45.
352 "we must move in concert": OR 44:628.
352 "seemed to favor us": Sherman, *Memoirs*, 2:193.
352 "Negroes swarmed to us": Kellogg, *Army Life*, 332.
352 "a negro on the place": Trimble, *Ninety-third Regiment*, 149.
352 "gentle Milly": Kellogg, *Army Life*, 332.
353 "have kept the enemy": *Augusta Daily Chronicle & Sentinel*, 12/7/1864.
353 "Sherman's campaign": Quoted in *Philadelphia Inquirer*, 12/9/1864.
353 "We are . . . hopeful": Miers, *Rebel War Clerk's Diary*, 456.
355 "Before going into camp"/"There is nothing new": Byrne, Diary and Journal, RU.
355 "Were delayed much": OR 44:318.
355 "Stopped at the home": Noble, Papers, UMB.
355 "woman under such a trying ordeal": Ross, Diary, ALL.
355 "Yam, yam, yam": Emmons, Diaries, UIA.
355 "the worst of swamp water": Fahnestock, Diary, KNP.
356 "waiting for a long swamp": OR 44:275.
356 "We are on what": Wagoner, "From Wauhatchie," 123.
356 "I got a rebel paper": Miller, Diary, IHS.
356 "make a good deal of smoke": OR 44:647.
356 "covered with blood": *National Tribune*, 5/24/1883.
356 "that her children could say": Kellogg, *Army Life*, 25.
357 "There is a considerable": Daniels, Diary, HL.
357 "As we are performing": Sharland, *Knapsack Notes*, 41.
357 "plenty of sweet potatoes": Clark, *Downing's Civil War*, 235.
357 "danger of having": Cryder and Stanley, *"War for the Union,"* 61.
357 "the inevitable Yankee": Pittenger, Diary, OHS.
357 "I have been dividing": Howe, *Marching with Sherman*, 148.

358 "100 horses": OR 44:638.

358 "in order to keep you": OR 44:647.

358 "I used to be": Howe, *Marching with Sherman*, 150.

358 "When we got there": Corbin, *Star for Patriotism*, 160.

358 "While they were out": Utterback, Diary, SHI.

359 "Upon arriving at the river": OR 44:120.

359 "press well on the enemy's left": OR 44:934.

359 "all that could be": OR 44:931.

360 "Since the last annual message": Quoted in Basler, *Collected Works*, 8:148, 154.

360 "Well I'll be hanged": Quoted in Marszalek, *Sherman's March*, 102–3.

360 "I have no good news": Quoted in Basler, *Collected Works*, 8:148, 154.

362 "Draw saber": McKeever, "Atlanta to the Sea," WRS.

362 "He is very proud": Sloan, Diary, TSL.

362 "bespattered with mud": Otto, "Civil War Memoirs," WHS.

362 "badly obstructed": OR 44:181.

363 "We were aroused at 11:30": Hight and Stormont, *Fifty-eighth Regiment*, 430.

363 "He said he was too weak": Overmyer, *Stupendous Effort*, 158.

363 "in places": Noble, Papers, UMB.

363 "distributed along": OR 44:284.

363 "quicksand": Schwab, "Civil War Letters," CIN.

363 "we had to pry": Short, Diary, WHS.

363 "looking like so many stranded": Byrne, Diary and Journal, RU.

363 "a poor looking": Wheeler, Letters and Journal, ALL.

363 "white flags flying": Trego, Diary, CHI.

364 "An almost endless variety": Fleharty, *Our Regiment*, 122.

364 "All were in a wild state": Darnell, "Reminiscences," UDC.

364 "a very wet swampy": Daniels, Diary, HL.

364 "had to build four or five": Clark, *Downing's Civil War*, 235.

364 "Stopped often": Anderson, *Civil War Diary*, 181.

364 "about 2,000": Bargus, Diary, MHI.

365 "some poor fellow's": Howe, *Marching with Sherman*, 153–54.

365 "McLaws' division": Sherman, *Memoirs*, 2:194.

365 "We hear that the enemy": OR 44:652.

365 "indications now point": Brockman, "John Van Duser Diary," 233.

365 "All the way": Arbuckle, *Civil War Experiences*, 112.

366 "about ½ mile": McKee, Diary, SHI.

366 "charge over an open": *National Tribune*, 6/19/1919.

366 "They took the cars": Gore, Diary, MHI.

367 "At Black Creek": OR 44:121.

367 "There they come": Grecian, *History*, 64–65.

368 "An apparently small trifle": *Augusta Daily Chronicle & Sentinel*, 12/11/1864.

368 "We are camped here": Prior, Letters, GSA.

369 "small road branching off": OR 44:276.

370 "the lusty black": Bryant, *History*, 289.

370 "the worst roads": Saylor, Letter, WHS.

370 "cussing mad": Trego, Diary, CHI.

370 "Captain, corduroy it good": Brant, *History of the Eighty-fifth*, 83–84.

370 "had raised 'Hail Columbia' ": Otto, "Civil War Memoirs," WHS.

371   "Like a flash of lightning": Hight and Stormont, *Fifty-eighth Regiment*, 431.
371   "Our Brigade just got over": Porter, Diary, OHS.
371   "The curiosity of all": Widney, Diary and Letters, KNP.
371   "I dare say the captain": Miller, Diary, IHS.
371   "We had our dinner ready": Dresbach, Letters and Reminiscence, MHS.
372   "The Rebels said"/"The negroes come into our lines": *92nd Illinois Volunteers*, 196.
372   "Up to this time": Miller, Diary, IHS.
372   "The groups gathered": ORS, 7:636.
372   "Trees had been felled": *National Tribune*, 6/13/1901.
372   "A good deal of corduroy": Force, Papers, UWA.
373   "The army has been advancing": Nichols, *Great March*, 59.
373   "We don't draw ours": Howe, *Marching with Sherman*, 156–58.
373   "General very much provoked": Ibid.
373   "had washing done": Engerud, *1864 Diary*, 51.
373   "We sent our forage": Glossbrenner, Diary, MHI.
374   "Our camp was in a pine woods": Saunier, *History*, 360.
374   "built works": Corbin, *Star for Patriotism*, 160–61.
374   "moved without supply trains": Chamberlin, *History*, 152.
374   "not sufficiently serious": OR 44:126.
374   "Around us are magnificent": Burton, Diary, EU.
374   "Went in swimming": Roe, Papers, KNX.
374   "This is an important point": Howe, *Marching with Sherman*, 159.
374   "inform the naval commander": OR 44:658.
375   "two days [before]": OR 44:160.
375   "against the destructive": Quoted in Stewart, *Reward of Patriotism*, 195.
375   "injury to the service": Beauregard, Papers, DU.
375   "Having no army of relief": OR 44:940.
377   "thirty-two days": Jones, *Siege of Savannah*, 107.
377   "Detached field works": Ibid., 78.
377   "overflow": OR 53:381.
377   "consisted of detached works": Jones, *Siege of Savannah*, 80.
378   "The boys were marching along": Morhous, *Reminiscences*, 145.
378   "occupy the attention": OR 44:218.
378   "with instructions to advance": OR 44:218.
378   "swamp just at the left": Wagoner, "From Wauhatchie," 124.
378   "After plunging around": Duncan, Papers, NJH.
378   "obliged at one time": Funk, Diary, MHI.
379   "We waded through a": Rattenbury, *From Wisconsin to the Sea*, 79.
379   "not . . . to fight the enemy": Clark, *Histories*, 2:634.
379   "Advanced as skirmishers": Rugg, Papers, CSL.
379   "most magnificent view": Short, Diary, WHS.
379   "The enemy kept blazing": Bryant, *History*, 290.
380   "the Johnnies break": Storrow, Papers, MAS.
380   "three or four": Clark, *Histories*, 4:334.
380   "As I came splashing": *National Tribune*, 1/29/1891.
380   "the swamp was so deep": OR 44:250.
381   "Useless negroes": OR 44:502.

382 "I . . . knew [this] must result": Angle, *Three Years*, 354.

382 "Some hid in the wagons": Bruce, Personal Memorandum, ISL.

382 "As soon as the army": Pendergast, Family Papers, MHS.

382 "It was really pitiful": Miller, Diary, IHS.

382 "The Negro men constructed": Reed, "Civil War Diaries," MHS.

382 "the raft would carry only": Rosenow, *Pen Pictures*, 112.

383 "As soon as we were over": Kerr, "From Atlanta to Raleigh," 215–16.

383 "a great many negroes": OR 44:410.

384 "opened upon us": McAdams, *Every-day Soldier Life*, 123.

384 "his usual rashness": Rogers, *125th Regiment*, 109.

384 "He was literally torn": Woodruff, *Fifteen Years Ago*, 434.

384 "order was for": Saunier, *History*, 361.

385 "magnificent . . . railroad": OR 44:121.

385 "soon encountered": OR 44:138.

385 "breast-works": OR 44:141.

385 "The rebels open fire": Kimmell, Journal-Report, NYH.

385 "to fire altogether": OR 44:127.

386 "The Brigade was too far": Chamberlin, *History*, 153.

386 "Strong sea breeze": Jamison, *Recollections*, 286.

386 "We found the enemy": OR 44:149.

387 "subterra shells": Sherman and the torpedoes in Howe, *Marching with Sherman*, 161–62: Sherman, *Memoirs*, 2:194.

387 "These torpedoes": *National Tribune*, 2/19/1925.

388 "In the entrance": Nichols, *Great March*, 86.

388 "Torpedoes at the entrance": Howe, *Marching with Sherman*, 161.

388 "This was not war": Sherman, *Memoirs*, 2:194.

388 "One of the Rebels": Cryder and Stanley, *"War for the Union,"* 462.

388 "A Rebel major": Christie, Family Papers, MHS.

389 "This is a new mode": Hunter, Diary, MHI.

389 "disappeared like a covey": Jamison, *Recollections*, 286.

389 "was on his horse": *Cincinnati Daily Commercial*, 1/2/1865.

389 "The event distributed": Pittenger, Diary, OHS.

389 "simply a small neat station": Howe, *Marching with Sherman*, 165.

389 "To-morrow we may expect": Nichols, *Great March*, 86–87.

390 "dressed in what may be considered": *Cincinnati Daily Commercial*, 12/21/1864.

390 "I don't think": Duncan expedition in Howard, "Incidents and Operations," 433–34; *National Tribune*, 4/2/1925.

391 "to defend the city": OR 53:382.

392 "The outlook": Roman, *Military Operations*, 2:313-4.

392 "The battery that annoyed": *Quincy Daily Whig & Republican*, 1/6/1865.

392 "a splendid plantation": Ladd, "From Atlanta to the Sea," 11.

393 "What have you got": Bircher incident in Bircher, *Drummer-Boy's Diary*, 147–48.

394 "We tore up the track"/"made it 'red hot' ": Miller, Diary, IHS.

394 "certain what was firing": Kellogg, *Army Life of an Illinois Soldier*, 37.

394 "through thick underbrush": Grunert, *History*, 147.

394 "for he knows": Storrs, *Twentieth Connecticut*, 155.

395 "I have the honor": Gildersleeve report in Carmen, Papers, NJH.

396 "Confederate trash": Ross, Diary, ALL.

396 "The weather is cold": Brown, *History of the Fourth Regiment*, 346.
396 "We then commenced"/"was not hurt": Glossbrenner, Diary, MHI.
396 "Every thing is a black muck": Winther, *With Sherman to the Sea*, 139–40.
397 "The rebels shelled us": Fultz, "History of Company D," 77.
397 "pell mell through": Hawley, Diary, WHS.
397 "In our front": *National Tribune*, 6/13/1901.
398 "He had dismounted": Hedley, *Marching through Georgia*, 324.
398 "The boys thought": Fultz, "History of Company D," 77.
398 "loud *rush*": Howe, *Marching with Sherman*, 170.
399 "I could see": Sherman, *Memoirs*, 2:195.
399 "may be considered": Howe, *Marching with Sherman*, 166.
399 "I was driving out": *Philadelphia Weekly Times*, 11/21/1885.
400 "enemy is in heavy force": Hardee statements in Beauregard, Papers, DU.
400 "some roast pig": Duncan expedition in Howard, "Incidents and Operations," 433–44; *National Tribune*, 4/2/1925.

CHAPTER 20. "I WAS SOON COVERED WITH BLOOD FROM HEAD TO FOOT"

405 "It was supposed": *New York Herald*, 1/7/1865.
405 "We found by trial": Widney, Diary and Letters, KNP.
405 "noise enough to wake"/"Better keep quiet": Andrews, *Footprints*, 152.
405 "One man had": Jackson, *Colonel's Diary*, 172.
406 "lustily": Brown, *Signal Corps*, 347.
406 "Rations are very": McLean, Family Papers, NYL.
406 "All that was issued": Cruikshank, "Civil War Letters."
406 "Our infantry came round": Christie, Family Papers, MHS.
406 "Foraging is played out": Wilcox, Diary, MHI.
406 "found the enemy": Sloan, Diary, TSL.
406 "As we filed": Storrow, Papers, MAS.
406 "found the rebels": Quint, *Record*, 253.
407 "crossing was slow": Bryant, *History*, 293.
407 "General . . . gave him"/"very quiet": Howe, *Marching with Sherman*, 173–75.
408 "every inquiry": Howe, *Marching with Sherman*, 177.
408 "a plan of Fort McAllister": OR 44:61.
408 "about 200 men": OR 44:690.
409 "I was thus thrown": Quoted in Jones, *Siege of Savannah*, 123.
409 "I have been obliged": Beauregard, Papers, DU.
409 "It was a bitter pill": Heyward-Ferguson, Papers, SHC.
409 "Sherman was in no condition": *New York Herald*, 1/7/1865.
409 "battle must certainly occur": Miers, *Rebel War Clerk's Diary*, 458.
410 "Our situation": Duncan expedition in Howard, "Incidents and Operations," 433–34; *National Tribune*, 4/2/1925.
411 "Sir: It is my happiness": Dahlgren message in ORN, 16:127–28.
412 "The excitement": Quoted in Lawrence, *Present for Mr. Lincoln*, 181–82.
412 "and the vessels": *Philadelphia Inquirer*, 12/16/1864.
412 "the Corps and Division": Howe, *Marching with Sherman*, 176.
412 "Ambitious Geary": Parmater, Diary, OHS.

413 *"dried beef"*: Brant, *History of the Eighty-fifth*, 85.

413 "one of our boys": Strickling, Memoir, OHS.

414 "As soon as it was": Cryder and Stanley, *"War for the Union,"* 463.

414 "You may judge": Gross, Journal and Letters, MHI.

414 "spied a light": *National Tribune*, 3/4/1920.

414 "As we went along": ORN, 16:486.

415 "falling short": Bradley, *Star Corps*, 210.

415 "terrific fire": Text on Georgia State Historical Marker 025-79.

415 "was struck three times": ORN, 16:486.

416 "Turn back, Cap": Bryant, *History*, 293–94.

416 "the first *naval* engagement": Howe, *Marching with Sherman*, 176–77.

417 "We were hotly pursued": Quoted in Jones, *Siege of Savannah*, 123.

417 "a beautiful place": Eisenhower, Diary, MHI.

417 "too salty": Ward, Diary, IHS.

418 "I determined": Quoted in Jones, *Siege of Savannah*, 123.

418 "We wanted": OR 44:10.

418 "gave me a little map": Hazen, *Narrative*, 330.

418 "I gave General Hazen": Sherman, *Memoirs*, 2:196.

419 "not to find myself": Hazen, *Narrative*, 332.

419 "some time must elapse": *Augusta Daily Chronicle & Sentinel*, 12/13/1864.

419 "rice-mills to their full capacity": *National Tribune*, 1/29/1891.

420 "We drove them off": Hinkley, Papers, WHS.

420 "covered with mud": Glossbrenner, Diary, MHI.

421 "will be found": OR 44:704.

422 "There was a general notion": *Philadelphia Weekly Times*, 2/6/1886.

422 "about two miles": Hazen, *Narrative*, 331.

422 "While we were going": *Philadelphia Weekly Times*, 2/6/1886.

423 "The day was bright": Hazen, *Narrative*, 331.

424 "looking closely": OR 44:751.

424 "had reconnoitered the fort": *Philadelphia Weekly Times*, 2/6/1886.

425 "Have you seen": Brown, *Signal Corps*, 562.

425 "plainly seen": Sherman, *Memoirs*, 2:196.

425 "the use of the glass": Brockman, "John Van Duser Diary," 236.

425 "timber in rear": Harwell and Racine, *Fiery Trail*, 71.

425 "the place looked": Sherman, *Memoirs*, 2:196.

426 "a careful and close": OR 44:751.

426 "This humane and proper act": *Philadelphia Weekly Times*, 2/6/1886.

426 "and large, black, ugly-looking": *National Tribune*, 2/20/1896.

427 "believing that it would": Hazen, *Narrative*, 332.

427 "the feebleness": Quoted in Jones, *Siege of Savannah*, 124–25.

427 "observed signs": Sherman, *Memoirs*, 2:197.

427 "by the little round puffs": Strong, Papers, ALL.

427 "I . . . saw": OR 44:752.

429 "watch me make": Saunier, *History*, 367.

429 "out of a detachment": Quoted in Jones, *Siege of Savannah*, 124.

429 "position on the left": Hazen, *Narrative*, 332.

429 "To make the chance": Ibid., 332–33.

430 "On being assured": Sherman, *Memoirs*, 2:197.

430 "south and east": *National Tribune*, 6/14/1900.

430 "I and others": *National Tribune*, 9/12/1901.

431 "Keep them down": Shuttinger incident in Saunier, *History*, 366.

431 "cautioned his men": Ibid., 372.

431 "My comrades": *National Tribune*, 2/20/1913.

431 "Colonel, you know": Connelly, *History*, 137.

431 "found itself behind": Quoted in Christman, *Undaunted*, 65.

432 "Look! Howard": *New York Herald*, 12/22/1864.

432 "Who are you?": Fisher-McClintock exchange in OR 44:752.

432 "a big [tree] stump": *National Tribune*, 6/28/1906.

433 "Is Fort McAllister taken?": Fisher-Sherman exchange in Sherman, *Memoirs*, 2:197.

433 "To my great surprise": Hazen, *Narrative*, 332.

433 "The forward movement"/"they all started off": Saunier, *History*, 372.

434 "There was no firing": *Philadelphia Weekly Times*, 2/6/1886.

434 "out of the dark fringe": Sherman, *Memoirs*, 2:197.

434 "a long line": Nichols, *Great March*, 90.

434 "a single line": *National Tribune*, 2/20/1896.

434 "The musketry": Harwell and Racine, *Fiery Trail*, 71.

434 "seemed alive with flame": Connelly, *History*, 137.

434 "This was the moment": Brockman, "John Van Duser Diary," 237.

434 "When we got up close": *National Tribune*, 3/14/1907.

434 "One of my company": *National Tribune*, 6/19/1913.

435 "I had arrived": Quoted in Christman, *Undaunted*, 68.

435 "Some 50 yards out": *National Tribune*, 2/20/1913.

435 "I was knocked down": *National Tribune*, 9/12/1901.

435 "I remember very distinctly": *National Tribune*, 7/11/1907.

435 "the netted abatis": Connelly, *History*, 138.

435 "crawling under": Burt, Diary.

435 "to charge with a rush": Quoted in Christman, *Undaunted*, 67.

435 "tangle of buckhorns": *National Tribune*, 2/20/1913.

436 "that it would take four": Quoted in Livingston, *"Among the Best Men,"* 104.

436 "Some got through": *National Tribune*, 6/20/1907.

436 "from the bullets": *National Tribune*, 1/29/1914.

436 "There they go": *New York Herald*, 12/22/1864.

436 "the most difficult part": *National Tribune*, 6/14/1900.

436 "They crossed the ditch": Howard, *Autobiography*, 2:91.

437 "The wind lifted the smoke": Nichols, *Great March*, 90.

437 "were all engaged": Saunier, *History*, 364.

437 "we had to bayonet": Dye, Letter, MCA.

437 "I would . . . most respectfully": Quoted in Jones, *Siege of Savannah*, 127.

438 "Get to the rear, George": Gordon, Letter, HFL.

438 "recognized and spoke": Quoted in Christman, *Undaunted*, 71.

438 "the parapets were blue": Sherman, *Memoirs*, 2:198.

438 "Then all of us": Nichols, *Great March*, 91.

438 "so wild and boisterous": Brown, *Signal Corps*, 564.

438 "Fort McAllister is ours": OR 44:753.

439 "held out your hand": Anderson, Papers, GHS.

439 "Take a good big drink": OR 44:704.

440 "they were good oarsmen": Sherman, *Memoirs*, 2:198.

440 "even Generals Sherman": Strong, "Account," LOC.

440 "he invited us to join them": Sherman, *Memoirs*, 2:199.

440 "I'se workin' ": Hazen, *Narrative*, 334.

441 "When the news was received": Cryder and Stanley, *"War for the Union,"* 464.

441 "I would the world": Pittenger, Diary, OHS.

441 "I hear the troops": Vail, Diary, OHS.

441 "Fort McAllister is taken": Owens, *Greene County*, 105.

441 "a great load": Quoted in Schmidt, *Civil War History*, 1065.

441 "Hardtack!": Taylor, *Lights and Shadows*, 22.

441 "some news": Sherman, *Memoirs*, 2:199.

441 "an ambulance": Howard, *Autobiography*, 2:92.

442 "an unwarrantable": Quoted in Jones, *Siege of Savannah*, 126.

442 "reporting the loss": OR 44:955.

442 "What boat": OR 44:753.

442 "succeeded in avoiding": Howard, *Autobiography*, 2:92.

442 Sherman's dispatches: OR 44:701–2.

443 "shared my blankets": Hazen, *Narrative*, 334.

443 "Signals, shots and fires": *National Tribune*, 1/30/1902.

444 "The officers and sailors": Ibid.

444 "I was extremely weary": Sherman, *Memoirs*, 2:202.

444 "He may have been a lion": Hight and Stormont, *Fifty-eighth Regiment*, 442.

445 "the most American looking": Gray and Ropes, *War Letters*, 427.

445 "strongly intrenched": Sherman, *Memoirs*, 2:202.

445 "ample supplies": OR 44:708.

445 "perfectly sure of capturing": OR 44:713.

445 "says the city is his sure game": Gray and Ropes, *War Letters*, 427.

445 "indispensable": Sherman, *Memoirs*, 2:202.

446 "Anchored immediately": ORN, 16:361.

446 "I was not personally acquainted": Sherman, *Memoirs*, 2:203.

447 "that navy officers": Howe, *Marching with Sherman*, 188.

447 "Not liking to rejoice": OR 44:611–12.

447 "News came about 10 o'clock": Hickman, Diary and Letters, UMB.

447 "have been cheering": Angle, *Three Years*, 363.

447 "Now we are knocking": Jones, "For My Country," 173.

448 "They would make a mark": *National Tribune*, 3/7/1907.

448 "to be employed": Beauregard clipping, in Sherman, Papers, LOC.

448 "We will soon have rations": Cruikshank, "Civil War Letters."

448 "must soon end our season": Champlin, Diary, WRS.

448 "Our food line": Buerstatte, "Civil War Diary."

448 "Almost every tree": Parker, Papers, HL.

448 "We captured a yawl": Kittinger, Diary, MHI.

449 "If Hood's Battalion": Quoted in Rogers and Saunders, "Scourge of Sherman's Men," 358.

449 Mary Jones Jones: Incident recounted in Jones and Mallard, *Yankees A'Coming*, 33–37.

451 "No change from yesterday": Morrow, Diary, MHI.

451 "The frogs are peeping": Boies, *Record*, 104.

451 "This morning": Hancock, Diary.

451 "We were stationed": Allspaugh, Diaries, UIA.

452 "a heavy detail": *National Tribune*, 6/13/1901.

452 "lost three men": Bush, "Civil War Letters and Diary," ISL.

452 "Rations getting scarce": Armstrong, Diary, IHS.

452 "Living on rice": Burt, Diary.

452 "We are now living": Bircher, *Drummer-Boy's Diary*, 152.

452 "The story they tell": *Lancaster Daily Evening Express*, 1/3/1865.

452 "There is much diversity": Reeve, Papers, WHS.

453 "The boys waded": Calkins, *One Hundred and Fourth Regiment*, 270.

453 "boats enough": Carmen, "General Hardee's Escape," 194.

453 "Damn it!": Ibid.

454 "seal up that side": OR 44:719–20.

454 "The citizens of Savannah": *Augusta Daily Chronicle & Sentinel*, 12/15/1864.

454 "I desire being informed"/"I shall be compelled": OR 44:959–60.

455 "I feel uneasy": OR 44:962.

455 "come here": Quoted in Lawrence, *Present for Mr. Lincoln*, 192.

455 "services [were] not being longer needed": Quoted in Hallock, *Braxton Bragg*, 227.

455 "the part of chronicler": Miers, *Rebel War Clerk's Diary*, 474.

455 "a truly formidable work"/"still there cooking": ORN, 16:361.

455 "How on earth": Howe, *Marching with Sherman*, 189.

455 "very busy pulling": ORN, 16:362.

456 "about noon": Sherman, *Memoirs*, 2:203.

456 "group of twenty-five": Howe, *Marching with Sherman*, 193.

456 "For the present": OR 44:720–21.

456 "thinking of various things": Woodhull, "Glimpse of Sherman," 457–58.

457 "the most important operation": OR 44:636.

457 "The contents": Sherman, *Memoirs*, 2:206.

457 "He now stood": Woodhull, "Glimpse of Sherman," 458.

CHAPTER 21. "I BEG TO PRESENT YOU AS A CHRISTMAS GIFT THE CITY OF SAVANNAH"

459 "initiated measures": Sherman-Grant message in OR 44:726–28; Sherman, *Memoirs*, 2:207.

460 "I had no idea": Grant-Sherman message in Grant, *Personal Memoirs*, 2:401; OR 44:728–29.

461 "Attack Hood at once": Quoted in Sword, *Embrace an Angry Wind*, 291.

462 "They all scampered": Ibid., 387.

462 "the worst broke": Ibid., 406.

463 "was slow, deliberate": Quoted in Hirshson, *White Tecumseh*, 357.

463 "Our company": Lovrien, Diary, KNP.

463 "hereby placed in charge": OR 44:732.

463 "a total force": Hickenlooper, Collection, CIN.

465 "Johnnies have thrown": Parmater, Diary, OHS.

465 "make us lay": Brown, Papers, DU.

465 "Now thinks I": Fisher, Letters, NYL.

465 "Rations are getting shorter": Cruikshank, "Civil War Letters."

465 "I manage to get": Armstrong, Diary, IHS.

465 "Received a large mail": Johnson, "March to the Sea," 333.

466 "This last trip": Putney, Papers, WHS.

466 "three hundred dollars'"/"Some of us": Calkins, *One Hundred and Fourth Regiment*, 272–73.

466 "the highest honor": in Simpson and Berlin, *Sherman's Civil War*, 767–68.

467 "I've brought you": Quoted in Davis, *Sherman's March*, 107–8.

467 "thankful for his": Simpson and Berlin, *Sherman's Civil War*, 777.

467 "A rice field": Morgan, Diary, MHI.

467 "any quantity of rice": *Historical Sketch of Co. D*, 37.

467 "knew enough": Toombs, *Reminiscences*, 182.

467 "annoying, stopping": Quint, *Record*, 253.

467 "They made excellent practice": Storrow, Papers, MAS.

467 "Even while lying": Byrne, Diary and Journal, RU.

468 "I was sent with my Company": Hinkley, *Narrative of Service*, 161.

468 "lads of the company": Bryant, *History*, 295.

468 "We blazed away": Storrow, Papers, MAS.

468 "Gen. Sherman does not seem": Duncan, Papers, NJH.

468 "only about one-third": Chisolm, "Failure to Capture Hardee," 680.

469 "attack is of no importance": OR 44:963.

469 "and all persons": Quoted in *New York Herald*, 12/22/1864.

469 "My time": OR 44:150.

469 "Broke camp": Jamison, *Recollections*, 289.

469 "Saw Men": Pratt, Diary, WHS.

469 "We got some sweet": McConnell, *John D. Martin's Journal*, 26.

470 "Leaving camp": *Fifty-fifth Regiment*, 399–400.

470 "man in Company B": Saunier, *History*, 373.

470 "a low level": Champlin, Diary, WRS.

470 "I shot a hog": Miller, Diary, IHS.

470 "there was plenty": Parker, Papers, HL.

470 "Card-playing": Charlton, "From Atlanta to the Sea," MHI.

470 "the hearts of the men": Aten, *History*, 254.

470 "how glad we were": Quoted in Schmidt, *Civil War History*, 1067.

470 "The 29th presents": Parmater, Diary, OHS.

470 "Rebels shell": McMillan, Papers, WHS.

470 "We lie in a swampy": Henney, Letters, MHI.

471 "Our pickets are so close": Cutter, Letters, MHS.

471 "One of ours": Storrow, Papers, MAS.

471 "I rode from my headquarters": Sherman, *Memoirs*, 2:210.

471 Sherman surrender demand: OR 44:737.

473 "My rank": Carmen, "General Hardee's Escape," 210.

473 "was suddenly surrounded": Jones, *Siege of Savannah*, 138.

473 "the fullest possible defense": OR 44:963.

473 "make the dispositions": OR 44:964.

474 "after full consultation": Roman, *Military Operations*, 2:316.

474 "I have to acknowledge": Hardee surrender response in OR 44:736–37.

475 "both": Harwell and Racine, *Fiery Trail*, 72.

475 "on the successful": OR 44:741.

475 "more delay": OR 44:741–43.

475 "I . . . resolved": Sherman, *Memoirs*, 2:210.

476 "Of course I must fight": Quoted in Marszalek, *Sherman*, 309.

476 "It is all important": OR 44:750.

476 "the enemy held the river": OR 44:11.

476 "to make a mistake": Sherman, *Memoirs*, 2:216.

477 "commenced taring up": Sebring, Diary, ISL.

477 "went to work": Saunier, *History*, 374.

477 "a small aristocratic": Jamison, *Recollections*, 289.

477 "There we got some": McConnell, *John D. Martin's Journal*, 26.

477 "found plenty of sweet": Reed, "Civil War Diaries," MHS.

477 "glad after all to know": Essington, Diary, ISL.

478 "whether the joke": Patrick and Willey, " 'We Have Surely,' " 234.

478 "bombs, shells, and balls": *National Tribune*, 6/17/1926.

478 "It looks very romantic": Hight and Stormont, *Fifty-eighth Regiment*, 436–37.

478 "Our Division was drawn up": Quoted in Schmidt, *Civil War History*, 1068.

479 "informed me": Carmen, "General Hardee's Escape," 198.

479 "Active, urgent preparations": Roman, *Military Operations*, 2:317.

479 "prosecuted with . . . vigor": Chisolm, "Failure to Capture Hardee," 680.

480 "If Hoke and Johnson": OR 44:966.

480 "Of our weakness": Graves, Letters, UDC.

480 "Our works are very": Swiggart, *Shades of Gray*, 77.

481 "to push the preparations": OR 44:756, 761.

482 "great disappointment": ORN, 16:362.

482 "Still taring up": Sebring, Diary, ISL.

482 "loaded the [wagon]": Judkins, Diary, ISL.

482 "Moved out": Pratt, Diary, WHS.

482 "our teams all loaded": Reed, "Civil War Diaries," MHS.

482 "would sing hymns": Cryder and Stanley, *"War for the Union,"* 465.

483 "It was a strange": Angle, *Three Years*, 367–68.

483 "and the men": Cryder and Stanley, *"War for the Union,"* 465.

483 "with view to the adoption": OR 44:279.

483 "make thorough": OR 44:761.

483 "the opposite shore": Parrott, Letters, SHI.

483 "some heavy cannonading": Clark, *Downing's Civil War*, 239.

483 "We lay within 100 yds": Noble, Papers, UMB.

484 "upon one of the thread-like": Force, Papers, UWA.

484 "He was a fine officer": Rood, *Story of the Service*, 376.

484 "without opposition": Bryant, *History*, 297.

484 "If they had had their guns": Storrow, Papers, MAS.

484 "The rebs made but little": Hinkley, Papers, WHS.

484 "exceeded . . . [my] instructions"/"the contest became severe": Carmen, "General Hardee's Escape," 202.

484 "It was known": Toombs, *Reminiscences*, 185.

484 "We came right across": Storrow, Papers, MAS.

485 "had some severe work": Kendall, Diary and Letters, CHS.

485 "line nearly two": OR 44:762.

485 "I had not reached": Carmen, "General Hardee's Escape," 203.

486 "Gentlemen, this is not": Quoted in Lawrence, *Present for Mr. Lincoln*, 198–99.

486 "a general rush": *Milwaukee Daily Sentinel*, 1/5/1906.

487 "represented the matter": Sherman, *Memoirs*, 2:216–17.

487 "off the only": Howe, *Marching with Sherman*, 198.

487 "lines of army wagons": Summerell, "General Hardee Evacuates Savannah," 5.

487 "Very few of the citizens": Quoted in *New York Herald*, 1/7/1865.

487 "became quite incensed": *Philadelphia Weekly Times*, 11/21/1885.

488 "Our batteries were awake": Roe, Papers, KNX.

488 "have kept up": Unknown Diarist, SHI.

488 "On account of getting so many": Parmater, Diary, OHS.

488 "Heavy cannonading": Dunbar, Diary, BHS.

488 "This intimation": Kurtz, "War Diary," 83–84.

489 "opened on our positions": Carmen, Papers, NJH.

489 "From one portion of our line": Hinkley, Papers, WHS.

489 "could see wagons": Carmen, "General Hardee's Escape," 205.

489 "crowd of women": *Philadelphia Weekly Times*, 11/21/1885.

489 "busy burning": Jones, *When Sherman Came*, 86.

489 "Sherman had burned Atlanta": Summerell, "General Hardee Evacuates Savannah," 5.

489 "Sick of war": Anderson, *Civil War Diary*, 184.

489 "There has been a rumor": Bradley, *Star Corps*, 213–14.

490 "that the enemy had completed": OR 44:279.

490 "lost considerable time": Howe, *Marching with Sherman*, 198.

490 "light batteries will . . . be withdrawn": OR 44:967.

490 "It is feared": McAdams, *Every-day Soldier Life*, 126–27.

491 "I feel a cold shiver": Otto, *Civil War Memoirs*, WHS.

491 "When we came to think": Rood, *Story of the Service*, 378.

491 "I have no words": Graves, Letters, UDC.

492 "Men, women and children": *Savannah Morning News*, 12/25/1932.

492 "The shelling to-night": Wagoner, "From Wauhatchie," 125.

492 "opened their batteries": *National Tribune*, 2/11/1915.

492 "a severe artillery fire": Quoted in Schmidt, *Civil War History*, 1069.

492 "By reason of the lack": Jones, *Siege of Savannah*, 162.

493 "Our camp fires": Fort, "History," MHI.

493 "Since my father": Mendel, "Sketch," UDC.

493 "lined by the great live oak": Clark, *Histories*, 4:322.

494 "I can't describe": Quoted in Lawrence, *Present for Mr. Lincoln*, 201.

494 "The scene of our army": Fort, "History," MHI.

494 "As we passed through": *Atlanta Journal*, 8/16/1902.

494 "night was exceedingly dark": Kurtz, "War Diary," 84.

494 "the curses and yells": Carmen, Papers, NJH.

495 "to parts unknown": Quoted in Lawrence, *Present for Mr. Lincoln*, 199–200.

495 "fell into the long line": Graves, Letters, UDC.

495 "constant tread": Elliott, Letters, SHC.

495 "after getting something to eat": *National Tribune*, 7/18/1883.

495 "answered their calls": *National Tribune*, 7/8/1915.

496 "crawled up to their works": *National Tribune*, 7/21/1892.

496 "forward rapidly": OR 44:279.

496 "Soon we met": *National Tribune*, 7/21/1892.

496 "Just outside": OR 44:280.

497 "Sir: The city of Savannah": OR 44:772.

498 "some were still linked": Summerell, "General Hardee Evacuates Savannah," 7.

498 "We rushed": *National Tribune*, 7/21/1892.

498 "We entered the city": Engle, Letters.

498 "he took formal possession": OR 44:319.

498 "every flag": Rey, Letters, NYH.

499 "We passed through": Parmater Diary, OHS.

499 "Oh, Miss!"/"three very orderly": King, "Fanny Cohen's Journal," 410.

499 "By the fortunes of war": Quoted in Lawrence, *Present for Mr. Lincoln*, 208.

499 "the old flag": *National Tribune*, 10/25/1900.

500 "took position": OR 44:355.

500 "tried to behave ourselves": Levings, Papers, WHS.

500 "the white women": McKee, Diary, SHI.

500 "The people of Savannah seemed": *Lancaster Daily Evening Express*, 1/3/1865.

501 "the channel was so narrow": ORN, 16:362.

501 "My eventful career": Blair, *Politician Goes to War*, 219.

501 "protect all peaceable persons": OR 44:782.

501 "I saw some": Merrill, *Seventieth Indiana*, 232.

502 "Dear General": OR 44:771.

502 "A great danger": Kaminsky, *War to Petrify*, 275.

503 "the last man": Carmen, Papers, NJH.

503 "It lit the heavens": Quoted in Smith, *Civil War Savannah*, 196.

503 "it made a fearful": Platter, "Civil War Diary," UGA.

504 "grocery cellars": Wheeler, Letters and Journal, ALL.

504 "The boys got plenty": Stauffer, "Civil War Diary," n.p.

504 "The rebels left everything": *Chicago Evening Journal*, 1/10/1865.

504 "Took dinner": McLean, Family Papers, NYL.

504 "heartily sick of the war": Padgett, "With Sherman through Georgia," 62.

504 "There are eight": Frances Howard incident in Jones, *When Sherman Came*, 87.

504 "The navy-yard": Sherman, *Memoirs*, 2:217.

505 "As I feared": Lamar, Papers, GSA.

505 "You can form no": Anderson, Letter, EU.

505 "When the morning light": Quoted in Drago, "How Sherman's March," 364.

506 "so the rising and falling": Hight and Stormont, *Fifty-eighth Regiment*, 442.

506 "The amount of property": Mead Papers, LOC.

506 "depots of the Savannah and Gulf": *New York Herald*, 12/30/1864.

506 "They looked tired": Frances Howard incident in Jones, *When Sherman Came*, 87–88.

507 "General Sherman, the bravest": *Chicago Evening Journal*, 1/10/1865.

507 "I . . . feel as if": Roe, Papers, KNX.

507 "Savannah has fallen!": Hurlbut, Letters, KNP.

508 "I beg to present you": Sherman, *Memoirs*, 2:231.

CHAPTER 22. "BUT WHAT NEXT?"

509 "All hands are working": Hinkley, Papers, WHS.
509 "Nails had been collected": Grunert, *History*, 160.
509 "The lovely square"/"noble Geary": Quoted in Lawrence, *Present for Mr. Lincoln*, 213–14.
509 "All of our Squares": Quoted in Smith, *Civil War Savannah*, 219.
509 "activated by no motives": Quoted in Lawrence, *Present for Mr. Lincoln*, 213–14.
509 "spectacle of humbled": Blair, *Politician Goes to War*, 220.
510 "In fact, 24 hours": *National Tribune*, 9/12/1901.
510 "On the street": *Cincinnati Daily Commercial*, 1/1/1865.
510 "things that seemed hard for us": Quoted in Lawrence, *Present for Mr. Lincoln*, 224.
510 "They are all astonished": Hutchinson, Papers, LSU.
510 "Where resistance is hopeless": Quoted in Dyer, "Northern Relief for Savannah," 460–61.
510 "Do you think": Quoted in Lawrence, *Present for Mr. Lincoln*, 229.
511 "Oh it is a crying shame": Ibid., 219.
511 "The proceedings will be used": Miers, *Rebel War Clerk's Diary*, 476.
511 "If there is one sink lower": Quoted in Lawrence, *Present for Mr. Lincoln*, 219.
511 "No provision has been made": OR 44:800.
512 "The city is beautifully laid out": *National Tribune*, 9/12/1901.
512 "Many of the parks": *National Tribune*, 6/20/1901.
512 "Every alternate square": Baker, Memoir, ALL.
512 "a place of somber beauty": Willison, *Reminiscences*, 105.
512 "wonderful spring": Stelle, *1861 to 1865*, 22.
512 "The guns, the shot": Hight and Stormont, *Fifty-eighth Regiment*, 446.
512 "have been exposing": Quoted in Lawrence, *Present for Mr. Lincoln*, 231.
512 "one of the theaters": Tallman, Memoir, MHI.
512 "One thing I must mention": Stelle, *1861 to 1865*, 22.
513 "Oh the wickedness": Dillon, Letters, ALL.
513 "Thousands of soldiers": Floyd, *History of the Seventy-fifth*, 360.
513 "Our squad was well provided": Bean, Diary, SHC.
513 "There is a hundred and twenty men": Rattenbury, *From Wisconsin to the Sea*, 81.
513 "Listen to the *menu*": Kerr, "From Atlanta to Raleigh," 217.
513 "There was quite a lot of citizens": Dunbar, Diary, BHS.
513 "delightful entente cordiale"/"the tastiest Secesh": Quoted in Smith, *Civil War Savannah*, 224–25.
513 "Each little knot": Quoted in Wheeler, *Sherman's March*, 142.
513 "There is the most hoars": Quoted in Lawrence, *Present for Mr. Lincoln*, 214.
513 "the best joke": *Lancaster Daily Evening Express*, 1/3/1865.
513 "a rebel blockade runner": Quoted in Wheeler, *Sherman's March*, 144.
513 "They did not find out": Grunert, *History*, 163.
513 "She was a long": Hubert, *Fiftieth Regiment*, 348.
514 "While I am writing this": Stone, "Civil War Letter," 66.
514 "Quite a joke": Emmons, Diaries, UIA.
514 "cleaned our quarters": Buerstatte, "Civil War Diary."
514 "I saw one hundred dollar": Brant, *History of the Eighty-fifth*, 88–89.

514 "It did not seem": Farwell, Papers, SHI.

514 "witnessed the imposing": Quoted in Schmidt, *Civil War History*, 1078.

514 "rice boiled in water": Glossbrenner, Diary, MHI.

514 "most awful lonesome": Utterback, Diary, SHI.

514 "rather a dull Christmas": Engerud, *1864 Diary*, 53.

514 "Had a Review today": Gore, Diary, MHI.

514 "The arms glistened": Brown, *Fourth Regiment*, 354.

515 "The troops made": Inskeep, Diary, OHS.

515 "Uncle Billy's dolled": Quoted in Lawrence, *Present for Mr. Lincoln*, 230.

515 "is a keen looking man": Corbin, Letters, MHI.

515 "The Generals looked well": Daniels, Diary, HL.

515 " 'Uncle Billy' is the pet": Marvin, *Fifth Regiment*, 364.

515 "Gen. Sherman was very much": Duncan, Papers, NJH.

515 "Gen'l Sherman himself": Harwell and Racine, *Fiery Trail*, 185.

515 "They call us": Quaife, *From the Cannon's Mouth*, 355.

515 "We went to the sity": Rowell, *Yankee Cavalrymen*, 218.

515 "did very well": McLean, Family Papers, NYL.

515 "a splendid sight": Dunbar, Diary, BHS.

516 "Such a march": Andrews, *Footprints*, 155.

516 "up a tale of disaster": Younger, *Inside the Confederate Government*, 181.

517 "Therefore it struck me": Sherman, *Memoirs*, 2:236.

517 "but when I ask"/"I treat an English subject": Simpson and Berlin, *Sherman's Civil War*, 778.

517 "was not a man in his army": Hodgson, Journal, UGA.

517 "I would not be surprised": Howe, *Home Letters*, 330.

517 "A single mistake" (footnote): Ibid., 329.

518 "elegant & splendidly furnished": Simpson and Berlin, *Sherman's Civil War*, 778.

518 "gone to join Willy": Quoted in Hirshson, *White Tecumseh*, 268.

518 "It would amuse you to see": Simpson and Berlin, *Sherman's Civil War*, 778.

518 "Frequently they come in": Howe, *Marching with Sherman*, 202.

518 "manifested an almost *criminal* dislike": Sherman, *Memoirs*, 2:247–48.

518 "You are understood": Quoted in Fellman, *Citizen Sherman*, 163.

518 "approaching Savannah I had": Simpson and Berlin, *Sherman's Civil War*, 794–95.

519 "But the nigger?": Ibid.

519 "many interesting incidents": Sherman, *Memoirs*, 2:244.

519 "was an excellent soldier"/"I had heard"/"old and young": Ibid., 2:244–45.

520 "a friend and gentleman"/"hundreds or thousands". Ibid., 2:245–47.

520 "As they marched": *New York Herald*, 1/5/1865.

520 "I am right" (footnote): Howe, *Home Letters*, 328.

521 "temporary provisions": Sherman, *Memoirs*, 2:245–47.

521 "My Dear General Sherman": OR 44:809.

CHAPTER 23. "THE BLOW WAS STRUCK AT THE RIGHT MOMENT AND IN THE RIGHT DIRECTION"

525 "the active campaign": Sherman, *Memoirs*, 2:268.

526 "Oh, proud": quoted in Wheeler, *Sherman's March*, 231.

526 "soon reached": Byers, "Some Personal Recollections," 214.

526 "You hit it splendidly": Ibid.

526 "The importance of the march": *New York Times*, 2/26/1876.

526 "will go down in history": Essington, Diary, ISL.

526 "march has been": Capron, "War Diary," 397.

526 "This part of Georgia": Risedorph, Papers, MHS.

526 "It is terrible to think of": Buckingham, Papers, AAS.

526 "As you are aware": Levings, Papers, WHS.

527 "Georgia [is] in a helpless": *National Tribune*, 1/29/1891.

527 "looks hard to see"/"On the entire route": Elseffer, Papers, LOC.

527 "On our march": *Lancaster Daily Evening Express*, 1/3/1865.

527 "The Union army": Taylor, *Lights and Shadows*, 20.

527 "most fortunate": Howe, *Marching with Sherman*, 167–68.

528 "gentlemen of singular": OR 44:14.

528 "I beg to assure": Moore, *Kilpatrick and Our Cavalry*, 194.

528 "I am nervous": Coker, Letters, UGA.

528 "The people of Georgia": McWhorter, Letter, UGA.

528 "Even Georgian soldiers": *Athens (Georgia) Southern Banner*, 1/11/1865.

528 "I feel very little inclined": Quoted in Kennett, *Marching through Georgia*, 312.

528 "because her people": Ibid.

529 "what in the hell": Ibid.

529 "All around the grove": Jones, Family Papers, UGA.

529 "killed, mules taken": Clark, Papers, EU.

529 "Where there were no houses": Quoted in Brannen, *Life in Old Bulloch*, 55.

529 "Many of us": Quoted in Bryan, *Confederate Georgia*, 169.

529 "What the people": Hoyle letter, Bomar-Killian Family Papers, AHC.

529 "was now winter": Jones, *When Sherman Came*, 44.

529 "kind relatives": Buttrill, "Experience in the War", GSA.

529 "Now I reckon": Berry, Letter, EU.

529 "There was a great crop": Quoted in Brannen, *Life in Old Bulloch*, 56.

530 "time has come": Quoted in Parks, *Joseph E. Brown*, 315.

530 "I hope that S.C.": Maguire, Papers, AHC.

530 "I would rather": Cunningham, Family Papers, UGA.

530 "real Union sentiment": Gatell, "Yankee Views," 430.

530 "We fear the negroes": Hoyle letter, Bomar-Killian Family Papers, AHC.

531 "When Sherman's army": Quoted in Drago, "How Sherman's March," 367.

531 "They thronged the line": Boyle, *Soldiers True*, 262.

531 "It was very amusing": Howland, Letters, NYH.

531 "useless creatures": Girardi and Cheairs, *Memoirs*, 145.

531 "unadulterated miserable": Edmonds, Papers, MHI.

531 "The soldiers had no little fun": *American Tribune*, 2/11/1892.

531 "The poor Darkies": Winther, *With Sherman to the Sea*, 136.

531 "We find the colored": Taylor, Diary, EU.

531 "When, as often happened": *Fifty-fifth Regiment*, 401.

532 "that a large Rebel force": Storrs, *Twentieth Connecticut*, 150–51.

532 "Two Sergeants": Morhous, *Reminiscences*, 135–36.

532 "New negro pioneer squads": Champlin, Diary, WRS.

532 "Pioneer Corps": Christie, Family Papers, MHS.

532 "Rebels have blockaded": Reed, "Civil War Diaries," MHS.

532 "The roads were nothing": Sherlock, *Memorabilia*, 170.

533 "I attached much": Sherman, *Memoirs*, 2:180.

533 "cars now run": OR 44:1013.

535 "I only regarded": Sherman, *Memoirs*, 2:220.

535 "The romantic character": Badeau, "Sherman's March to the Sea," 543.

535 "We had a gay trip": Naylor, Letters, OHS.

536 "this traveling picnic": Quoted in Stern, *Soldier Life*, 172.

536 "bitter feeling toward the North": Eaton, *A History*, 284–58.

536 "by acts of cruelty": *New York Herald*, 5/21/1875.

536 "If W. T. Sherman's face": *Confederate Veteran*, 19:272.

537 "I wish I had a dollar": Quoted in Royster, *Destructive War*, 364–65.

537 "I did that": *Confederate Veteran*, 10:291.

537 "against the use": *Confederate Veteran*, 25:392.

537 "probably its worst devastation"/"the most disliked person": Quoted in Henken, "Taming the Enemy," 291, 293.

538 "rash in cutting loose": Howe, *Home Letters*, 320–21.

539 "with grim despair": Potter, *Reminiscences*, 108.

539 "We were the first": Howland, Letters, NYH.

539 "some few," Brush, Letters, ALL.

542 "I cannot withhold": Brown, Papers, DU.

543 "They would kill": Quoted in Kennett, *Marching through Georgia*, 301.

544 "in favor of Sherman's plan": Grant, *Personal Memoirs*, 2:376.

544 "I will accept no": Thorndike, *Sherman Letters*, 245.

544 "How few there are": Simon, *Papers of Ulysses S. Grant*, 13:203.

544 "the singular friendship": Howe, *Home Letters*, 323.

547 "The 'March to the Sea' ": *New York Times*, 10/5/1875.

Bibliography

Hewett, Janet B., Noah Andre Trudeau, and Bryce A. Suderow, eds. *Supplement to the Official Records of the Union and Confederate Armies*. Vol. 7. Wilmington, N.C.: Broadfoot, 1997.

Ingersoll, Lurton Dunham, ed. *Iowa and the Rebellion*. Philadelphia: J. B. Lippincott, 1866.

Moore, Frank, ed. *The Rebellion Record: A Diary of American Events*. New York: D. Van Nostrand, 1866.

Official Records of the Union and Confederate Navies in the War of the Rebellion. 30 vols. Washington, D.C.: Government Printing Office, 1894–1922.

Reece, J. N., ed. *Report of the Adjutant General of the State of Illinois Containing Reports for the Years 1861–66*. 8 vols. Springfield, Ill.: Phillips Bros., 1900–1902.

Robertson, Jonathan, ed. *Michigan in the War*. Lansing, Mich.: W. S. George, 1882.

Report of the Adjutant General and Acting Quartermaster General of the State of Iowa, January 1, 1865, to January 1, 1866. Des Moines, Iowa: F. W. Palmer, 1866.

Report of the Adjutant General of the State of Indiana, 1861–1865. 8 vols. Indianapolis: Samuel M. Douglass, 1865–1869.

Report of the Adjutant General of the State of Kentucky. Vol. 2, *1861–1866*. Frankfort, Ky.: John H. Harney, 1867.

The War of the Rebellion: A Compilation of the Official Records of the Union and Confederate Armies. 127 vols. Washington, D.C.: Government Printing Office, 1880–1901.

UNION LEADERSHIP

Ambrose, Stephen E. *Halleck: Lincoln's Chief of Staff*. Baton Rouge: Louisiana State University Press, 1962.

Basler, Roy P. *The Collected Works of Abraham Lincoln*. 9 vols. New Brunswick, N.J.: Rutgers University Press, 1953.

Catton, Bruce. *Grant Takes Command*. Boston: Little, Brown, 1968.

Donald, David Herbert. *Lincoln*. London: Jonathan Cape, 1995.

Grant, Ulysses S. *Personal Memoirs of U. S. Grant*. 2 vols. New York: Charles L. Webster, 1885.

Macartney, Clarence Edward. *Grant and His Generals*. New York: McBride, 1953.

McFeely, William S. *Grant: A Biography*. New York: W. W. Norton, 1981.

Oates, Stephen B. *With Malice toward None: The Life of Abraham Lincoln*. New York: Harper & Row, 1977.

Perret, Geoffrey. *Ulysses S. Grant: Soldier & President*. New York: Random House, 1997.

Simon, John Y., ed. *The Papers of Ulysses S. Grant*. Vol. 12, *August 16–November 15, 1864*. Carbondale: Southern Illinois University Press, 1984.

———. *The Papers of Ulysses S. Grant*. Vol. 13. *November 16, 1864–February 20, 1865*. Carbondale: Southern Illinois University Press, 1985.

Simpson, Brooks D. *Ulysses S. Grant: Triumph over Adversity, 1822–1865*. New York: Houghton Mifflin, 2000.

Smith, Jean Edward. *Grant*. New York: Simon & Schuster, 2001.

Temple, Wayne C., ed. *Campaigning with Grant*. 1897. Reprint, New York: Bonanza, 1961.

UNION FORCES (SAVANNAH CAMPAIGN)
Headquarters: Maj. Gen. William T. Sherman

Bower, Stephen E. "The Theology of the Battlefield: William Tecumseh Sherman and the U.S. Civil War." *Journal of Military History* 64, no. 4 (October 2000).

Bowman, S. M., and R. B. Irwin. *Sherman and His Campaigns: A Military Biography*. New York: Charles P. Richardson, 1865.

Boyd, James P. *The Life of General William T. Sherman*. Philadelphia: Publishers' Union, 1891.

Brinsfield, John W. "The Military Ethics of General William T. Sherman." *Parameters: Journal of the U.S. Army War College* 12, no. 2 (June 1982).

Brockman, Charles J., ed. "The John Van Duser Diary of Sherman's March from Atlanta to Hilton Head." *Georgia Historical Quarterly* 53, no. 2 (June 1969).

Byers, S. H. M. "Some Personal Recollections of General Sherman." *McClure's Magazine* 3, no. 3 (August 1894).

Coulter, E. Merton. "Sherman and the South." *North Carolina Historical Review* 8, no. 1 (January 1931).

Cunningham, S. A. "Things Pertinent to War Times." *Confederate Veteran* 1, no. 2 (February 1893).

Disbrow, Donald W., ed. "Vett Noble of Ypsilanti: A Clerk for General Sherman." *Civil War History* 14, no. 1 (March 1968).

Fellman, Michael. *Citizen Sherman: A Life of William Tecumseh Sherman*. New York: Random House, 1995.

———, ed. *Memoirs of General W. T. Sherman*. New York: Penguin, 2000.

Force, Manning F. *General Sherman*. New York: D. Appleton, 1899.

Hart, B. H. Liddell. *Sherman: Soldier, Realist, American*. New York: Da Capo Press, 1993.

Hitchcock, Henry. "General William T. Sherman." In *Sketches of War History 1861–1865*, vol. 1. St. Louis: Becktold, 1892.

Howe, M. A. DeWolfe, ed. *Home Letters of General Sherman*. New York: Charles Scribner's Sons, 1909.

———. *Marching with Sherman*. Lincoln: University of Nebraska Press, 1995.

Hirshson, Stanley P. *The White Tecumseh: A Biography of William T. Sherman*. New York: John Wiley & Sons, 1997.

Kennett, Lee. *Sherman: A Soldier's Life*. New York: HarperCollins, 2001.

Lewis, Lloyd. *Sherman: Fighting Prophet*. New York: Harcourt, Brace, 1932.

"Major-General William T. Sherman." *Hours at Home: A Popular Monthly of Instruction and Recreation* 2, no. 1 (November 1865).

Markland, Absalom H., Papers. Manuscripts Division. Library of Congress.

Marszalek, John F. *Sherman: A Soldier's Passion for Order*. New York: Vintage Books, 1994.

———. *Sherman's Other War: The General and the Civil War Press*. Kent, Ohio: Kent State University Press, 1999.

Merrill, James M. *William Tecumseh Sherman*. New York: Rand McNally, 1971.

Miers, Earl Schenck. *The General Who Marched to Hell*. New York: Dorset, 1990.

Nichols, George Ward. *The Story of the Great March*. New York: Harper & Brothers, 1865.

Noble, Sylvester C. Papers, Vett Noble letters. Ypsilanti Historical Society, Ypsilanti, Mich.

Poe, Orlando M. Papers and Letters. Manuscripts Division. Library of Congress.

Report of the Proceedings of the Society of the Army of the Tennessee at the Twenty-Ninth Meeting, Held at Milwaukee, Wisconsin, October 27–28, 1897. Cincinnati: F. W. Freeman, 1898.

Sherman, William T. *Memoirs of General William T. Sherman*. New York: D. Appleton, 1886.

———. "The Grand Strategy of the War of the Rebellion." *Century Magazine* 35, no. 4 (February 1888).

———. "Old Shady, with a Moral." *North American Review* 147, no. 383 (October 1888).

———. "Sherman Reveals Something about His Strategy." *Civil War Times Illustrated* 33, no. 76 (July/August 1994).

———. Papers. Manuscripts Division. Library of Congress.

———. Papers. Manuscripts Collection. Chicago Historical Society.

Simpson, Brooks D., and Jean V. Berlin, eds. *Sherman's Civil War: Selected Correspondence of William T. Sherman*. Chapel Hill: University of North Carolina Press, 1999.

Smalley, E. V. "General Sherman." *Century Magazine* 27, no. 3 (January 1884).

Spore, John B. "Sherman and the Press, Part One." *Infantry Journal* 63, no. 4 (October 1948).

———. "Sherman and the Press, Part Two." *Infantry Journal* 63, no. 5 (November 1948).

———. "Sherman and the Press, Part Three." *Infantry Journal* 63, no. 6 (December 1948).

Stiles, John C. "Sherman in War and Peace." *Confederate Veteran* 24, no. 7 (July 1916).

Thorndike, Rachel Sherman, ed. *The Sherman Letters: Correspondence between General and Senator Sherman from 1837 to 1891*. New York: Da Capo Press, 1969.

Walters, John Bennett. "General William T. Sherman and Total War." *Journal of Southern History* 14, no. 4 (November 1948).

Wheeler, Richard, ed. *We Knew William Tecumseh Sherman*. New York: Thomas Y. Crowell, 1977.

ENGINEER/SIGNAL CORPS UNITS

Athearn, Robert G., ed. "An Indiana Doctor Marches with Sherman." *Indiana Magazine of History* 49, no. 4 (December 1953).

Baker, Daniel B. *A Soldier's Experience in the Civil War*. Long Beach, Calif.: Graves & Hersey, 1914.

Brown, J. Willard. *The Signal Corps, U.S.A. in the War of the Rebellion*. Boston: U.S. Veteran Signal Corps Association, 1896.

Campbell Family. Papers. Michigan State University, East Lansing.

Hight, John J., and Gilbert R. Stormont. *History of the Fifty-Eighth Regiment of Indiana Volunteer Infantry*. Princeton, Ind.: Press of the Clarion, 1895.

Lovrien, Charles. Diary. Kennesaw Mountain National Battlefield Park, Kennesaw, Ga.

Mellon Jr., Knox, ed. "Letters of James Greenalch." *Michigan History* 44, no. 2 (June 1960).

Neal, William A. *An Illustrated History of the Missouri Engineer and the 25th Infantry Regiments*. Chicago: Donohue & Henneberry, 1889.

Plum, William R. *The Military Telegraph during the Civil War in the United States*. Chicago: Jansen, McClurg, 1882.

Roseberry, Isaac. Diary. Bentley Historical Library, University of Michigan; Robert W. Woodruff Library, Emory University.

Sligh, Charles R. *History of the Services of the First Regiment Michigan Engineers and Mechanics*. Grand Rapids, Mich: White, 1921.

Williams, Joshua W. Diary. Lilly Library, Indiana University, Bloomington.

RIGHT WING: MAJ. GEN. OLIVER OTIS HOWARD

Bedford, Wimer. Papers. Manuscripts Division. Library of Congress.

Harwell, Richard, and Philip N. Racine, eds. *The Fiery Trail*. Knoxville: University of Tennessee Press, 1986.

Howard, Charles H. "Incidents and Operations Connected with the Capture of Savannah." In *Military Essays and Recollections*, vol. 4. Chicago: Cozzens Beaton, 1907.

Howard, Francis Thomas. *In and Out of the Lines*. New York: Neale, 1905.

Howard, Oliver Otis. *Autobiography of Oliver Otis Howard*. 2 vols. New York: Baker & Taylor, 1907.

——. "Sherman's Advance from Atlanta." In *Battles and Leaders of the Civil War*, edited by Robert Underwood Johnson and Clarence Clough Buel, 4 vols. New York: Century Company, 1887–1888.

McClintock, James M. Papers. 1861–1909. Manuscripts Collection. Huntington Library, San Marino, Calif.

Reese, Chauncey B. "Military Messages, 1864." Civil War Miscellaneous Collection, United States Army Military History Institute, Carlisle, Pa.

Sladen Family Papers. "Diary of Operations of the Army of the Tennessee." United States Army Military History Institute, Carlisle, Pa.

Strong, William E. Papers. Abraham Lincoln Presidential Library, Springfield, Ill.
————. "An Account of the Capture of Fort McAllister." William T. Sherman Papers. Manuscripts Division, Library of Congress.
Warnock, William R. "Oration." In *Proceedings of the Annual Meeting of the Society of the Army of the Cumberland*. Cincinnati: Robert Clark, 1892.
Woodhull, Maxwell Van Zandt. "A Glimpse of Sherman Fifty Years Ago." In *War Papers* (District of Columbia Loyal Legion of the United States), vol. 4. Wilmington, N.C.: Broadfoot, 1993.

15TH CORPS: MAJ. GEN. PETER J. OSTERHAUS

Abernethy, Alonzo. Diary, 1864–1865. State Historical Society of Iowa, Des Moines.
————. "Incidents of an Iowa Soldier's Life; or, Four Years in Dixie." *Annals of Iowa*, ser. 3, vol. 12, pp. 401–428 (1920).
Albertson Family Papers. Georgia Historical Society.
Alley, John Marshall. Memoirs. United States Civil War Center. www.cwc.lsu.edu/cwc/projects/alley/alley.htm.
Ambrose, Daniel L. *History of the Seventh Regiment Illinois Volunteer Infantry*. Springfield: Illinois Journal Company, 1868.
Anderson, William M., ed. *We Are Sherman's Men: The Civil War Letters of Henry Orendorff*. Macomb: Western Illinois University, 1986.
Arbuckle, John C. *Civil War Experiences*. Columbus: n.p., 1930.
Armstrong, Robert. Diary. Indiana Historical Society.
Arndt, Albert F. R. "Report of Griswoldville." In *Michigan in the War*, compiled by John Robertson. Lansing, Mich.: W. S. George, 1882.
————. "Reminiscences of an Artillery Officer." In *War Papers*, vol. 1. N.p.: Michigan Military Order of the Loyal Legion of the United States, 1890.
Barker, Lorenzo A. *Military History (Michigan Boys) Company D, 66th Illinois*. Reed City, Mich.: n.p., 1905. Reprint, Huntington, W.Va.: Blue Acorn Press, 1994.
Baugh, William G. Letters. Robert W. Woodruff Library, Emory University.
Bean, Jesse S. Diary. Southern Historical Collection. University of North Carolina, Chapel Hill.
Bell, John T. *Tramps and Triumphs of the Second Iowa Infantry*. Omaha: n.p., 1886.
Black, Wilfred W., ed. "Marching with Sherman through Georgia and the Carolinas." *Georgia Historical Quarterly* 52, no. 4 (December 1968).
Brown, Alonzo L. *History of the Fourth Regiment of Minnesota Infantry Volunteers*. St. Paul: Pioneer Press, 1892.
Brumgardt, John R., ed. *A Scottish Printer "at Johnson's Heels": The Civil War Letters of Colonel Owen Stuart*. N.p., 1976.
Burt, Richard W. Diary, 1864. www.my.oh.voyager.net/C8/D7/Istevens/burt/burintro.html.
Burton, E. P. Diary. Bell I. Wiley Collection. Robert W. Woodruff Library, Emory University.
Burton, William L. *Remember My Children*. Iowa City, Iowa: n.p., 1973.
Bush, Andrew. "Civil War Letters and Diary." Indiana State Library.
Campbell, Walter John. "Civil War Experiences." Fort McAllister Historic Park.
Capron, Thaddeus Hurlbut. "War Diary." *Journal of the Illinois State Historical Society* 12, no. 3 (October 1919).

Carr, John M. Diary. Kennesaw Mountain National Battlefield Park, Kennesaw, Ga.

Case, Isaac. Journal, 1864–1865. State Historical Society of Iowa, Des Moines.

Castel, Albert, ed. " 'Had a Pleasant Time': Excerpts from the Diary of a Yankee in Dixie." *Blue & Gray Magazine* 3 (February/March 1986).

———. *Tom Taylor's Civil War.* Lawrence: University Press of Kansas, 2000.

Chamberlin, William Henry. *History of the Eighty-first Regiment Ohio Infantry Volunteers.* Cincinnati: Gazette Steam, Printing House, 1865.

Cluett, William W. *History of the 57th Regiment Illinois Volunteer Infantry.* Princeton, Ill.: T. P. Streeter, 1886.

Compton, George N. "The March from Atlanta to Savannah." Abraham Lincoln Presidential Library, Springfield, Ill.

Connelly, Thomas W. *History of the Seventieth Ohio Regiment.* Cincinnati: Peak Brothers, 1902.

Cooper, Edward S. *William Babcock Hazen: The Best Hated Man.* Madison, N.J.: Fairleigh Dickinson University Press, 2005.

Corbin, William E. *A Star for Patriotism.* Monticello, Iowa: Privately printed, 1972.

Dillon, Isiah T. and William. Letters, 1861–1865. Abraham Lincoln Presidential Library, Springfield, Ill.

Duke, John K. *History of the Fifty-third Regiment of Ohio Volunteer Infantry.* Portsmouth, Ohio: Blade, 1900.

Dunbar, Aaron. Diary, 1864–1865. Manuscripts Collection. Bureau County Historical Society, Princeton, Ill.

Dye, Isaac. Letter, 1864. Fort McAllister Historic Park.

Eisendrath, Joseph L., Jr., ed. *The Story of Sergeant Robert G. Ardrey.* Collinsville, Ill.: n.p., 1961.

Engerud, H., ed. *The 1864 Diary of Lieutenant Colonel Jefferson K. Scott.* Bloomington, Ind.: Monroe County Civil War Centennial Commission and Monroe County Historical Society, 1962.

Farr, Henry M. "The Career of Henry M. Farr, Civil War Surgeon." *Annals of Iowa* 44 (Winter 1978): 191–211.

Farwell, Sewall S. Papers. State Historical Society of Iowa, Iowa City.

Fryer, David F. *History of the Eightieth Ohio Veteran Volunteer Infantry.* Newcomerstown, Ohio: n.p., 1904.

Gage, Moses D. *From Vicksburg to Raleigh; or, A Complete History of the Twelfth Regiment Indiana Volunteer Infantry.* Chicago: Clarke, 1865.

Gay, John. Diary. State Historical Society of Iowa, Iowa City.

Girdner, Ephraim L. Letters. Union Microfilm Miscellany. Robert W. Woodruff Library, Emory University.

Glossbrenner, George F. Diary, 1864–1865. Civil War Miscellaneous Collection. United States Army Military History Institute, Carlisle, Pa.

Gore, Abijah F. Diary, 1864–1865. Civil War Miscellaneous Collection. United States Army Military History Institute, Carlisle, Pa.

Grecian, Joseph. *History of the Eighty-third Regiment, Indiana Volunteer Infantry.* Cincinnati: John F. Ulhorn, 1865.

Green, Levi N. Diary, 1865. State Historical Society of Iowa, Des Moines.

Hackett, Roger C., ed. "Civil War Diary of Sergeant James Louis Matthews," *Indiana Magazine of History* 24, no. 4 (December 1928).

Hancock, John J. Diary, 1864–1865. www.hson.info/Youelhtm.

Harford, John. Letters, 1864–1865. Manuscripts Collection. Bureau County Historical Society, Princeton, Ill.

Hazen, William B. *A Narrative of Military Service.* Boston: Ticknor, 1885.

———. Papers. United States Army Military History Institute, Carlisle, Pa.

Higby, Charles D. Letters, 1864–1865. Higby Family Papers. Library Division. Ohio
Historical Society, Columbus.

Hoadley, Robert Bruce. Papers, 1861–1866. William R. Perkins Library, Duke University, Durham, N.C.

House, Henry A. "Civil War Diary, 1862–1865." Minnesota Historical Society,
St. Paul.

Hubert, Charles F. *History of the Fiftieth Regiment Illinois Volunteer Infantry.* Kansas
City, Mo.: Western Veteran, 1894.

Johnson, William Benjamin. *Union to the Hub and Twice around the Tire.* Balboa,
Calif.: n.p., 1950.

Jones, Gordon C., ed. *"For My Country": The Richardson Letters, 1861–1865.*
Wendell, N.C.: Broadfoot, 1984.

Judkins, William H. Diary. Indiana State Library, Indianapolis.

Kellogg, Mary E., ed. *Army Life of an Illinois Soldier: Letters and Diary of Charles W.
Wills.* 1906. Reprint, Carbondale: Southern Illinois University Press, 1996.

Keyes, Harrison M. Diary, 1864–1865. Harrisburg Civil War Roundtable Collection.
United States Army Military History Institute, Carlisle, Pa.

Kinley, Oliver. Diary, 1864–1865. State Historical Society of Iowa, Des Moines.

Lair, John A. Papers. Manuscripts Division. Library of Congress.

Lambert, Louis E. "From Atlanta to the Sea." In *Ninth Reunion of the 37th Regiment
O.V.V.I.* Toledo, Ohio: Montgomery & Vrooman, 1890.

Larimer, Charles F., ed. *Love and Valor: The Intimate Civil War Letters between Captain Jacob and Emeline Ritner.* Western Springs, Ill.: Sigourney Press, 2000.

Lyftogt, Kenneth, ed. *Left for Dixie: The Civil War Diary of John Rath.* Parkersburg,
Iowa: Mid-Prairie Books, 1991.

Macy, Jesse. Papers. State Historical Society of Iowa, Iowa City.

Mahon, John K., ed. "The Civil War Letters of Samuel Mahon." *Iowa Journal of History* 51, no. 3 (July 1953).

McKee, John. Diary. State Historical Society of Iowa, Iowa City.

Moffatt, Thomas William. *A Union Soldier's Civil War.* N.p., 1962.

Morrill, Ira N. Diary, 1864–1865. Minnesota Historical Society, St. Paul.

Moses, Thomas Jefferson. "Civil War Diary." 1864. www.ioweb.com/civilwar/html/
marchtothesea.htm.

Muzzy, Isaac W. Papers, 1856–1866. Minnesota Historical Society, St. Paul.

Naylor, James M. Letters, 1864. Library Division. Ohio Historical Society,
Columbus.

Noyes, Katharine Macy, ed. *Jesse Macy: An Autobiography.* Springfield, Ill.,: Charles
C. Thomas, 1933.

Osborn, William W. Diary, 1864–1865. Civil War Miscellaneous Collection. United
States Army Military History Institute, Carlisle, Pa.

Osterhaus, Peter. "U.S. Army Generals' Report of Civil War Service, 1864–1887."
National Archives, Washington, D.C.

Parkinson, Joseph. Diary, 1864. Civil War Times Illustrated Collection. United
States Army Military History Institute, Carlisle, Pa.

Parrott, James C. Letters. State Historical Society of Iowa, Iowa City.

Pepper, George W. *Personal Recollections of Sherman's Campaigns in Georgia and Carolinas.* Zanesville, Ohio: Hugh Dunne, 1866.

Peterson, Ralph C. E., ed. *Marching Barefoot: A Collection of Civil War Letters Written by Peter Daniel Anderson to His Wife and Children in Scandia, Minnesota.* Minneapolis: Bind-a-Book, 1991.

Platter, Cornelius C. "Civil War Diary, 1864–1865." Hargrett Rare Book and Manuscript Library, University of Georgia, Athens.

Preece, Timothy F. *From Iowa to the Sea.* Danville, Calif.: Essex-Overland, 1999.

Reeves, Richard S. Papers, 1861–1865. Minnesota Historical Society, St. Paul.

Reminiscences of the Civil War from Diaries of Members of the 103d Illinois Volunteer Infantry. Chicago: J. F. Leaming, 1904.

Risedorph, John E. Papers, 1862–1911. Minnesota Historical Society, St. Paul.

Roe, Lewis F. Papers. Seymour Library, Knox College, Galesburg, Ill.

Rogers, William H. *The Great Civil War: William H. Rogers's Personal Experience.* N.p., n.d.

Sabin, Marden. "Memoirs of Dr. Marden Sabin. " Indiana State Library, Indianapolis.

Saunier, Joseph A. *A History of the Forty-seventh Ohio Veteran Volunteer Infantry.* Hillsboro, Ohio: Lyle, 1903.

Scheel, Gary L. *Rain, Mud & Swamps.* Pacific, Mo.: Privately printed, 1998.

Schweitzer, Edward E. Diary, 1864–1865. Civil War Times Illustrated Collection. United States Army Military History Institute, Carlisle, Pa.

———. Papers, 1861–1916. Manuscripts Collection. Huntington Library, San Marino, Calif.

Sebring, Ferdinand. Diary. Ripley County Civil War Papers. Indiana State Library, Indianapolis.

Sherlock, Eli J. *Memorabilia of the Marches and Battles in Which the One Hundredth Regiment of Indiana Infantry Volunteers Took an Active Part.* Kansas City, Mo.: Gerard-Woody, 1896.

Sherwood, Frederick. Journal, 1864. Earl M. Hess Collection. United States Army Military History Institute, Carlisle, Pa.

Smith, Henry I. *History of the Seventh Iowa Veteran Volunteer Infantry.* Mason City, Iowa: E. Hitchcock, 1903.

Spencer, Charles H. "Civil War Letters, 1864–1865." Wisconsin Historical Society, Madison.

Stauffer, Nelson. *Civil War Diary.* Northridge, Calif.: State University, Northridge Libraries, 1976.

Story of the Fifty-fifth Regiment Illinois Volunteer Infantry in the Civil War, 1861–1865. Clinton, Mass.: W. J. Coulter, 1887.

Sylvis, G. W. Letter, 1890. Georgia Historical Society, Savannah.

Taylor, Thomas T. Diary. Robert W. Woodruff Library, Emory University.

———. Letters, 1864. Library Division. Ohio Historical Society, Columbus.

Throne, Mildred, ed. "A Commissary in the Union Army." *Iowa Journal of History* 53, no. 1 (January 1955).

Trimble, Harvey Marion. *History of the Ninety-third Regiment Illinois Volunteer Infantry.* Chicago: Blakely, 1898.

Twombly, Voltaire. Letters and Papers, 1864–1865. State Historical Society of Iowa, Des Moines.

Unknown Diarist of the 9th Iowa. Diary. State Historical Society of Iowa, Iowa City.

Utterback, Albert. Diary, 1864–1865. State Historical Society of Iowa, Des Moines.

Willison, Charles A. *Reminiscences of a Boy's Service with the 76th Ohio*. Menasha, Wisc.: George Banta, 1908.

Winther, Oscar Osburn, ed. *With Sherman to the Sea: The Civil War Letters, Diaries & Reminiscences of Theodore F. Upson*. 1943. Reprint, Millwood, N.Y.: Kraus, 1985.

Wright, Charles. *A Corporal's Story: Experiences in the Ranks of Company G*. Philadelphia: James Beale, 1887.

Wright, Henry Haviland. *A History of the Sixth Iowa Infantry*. Iowa City: State Historical Society of Iowa, 1923.

Wylie, E. Burke. Letters. State Historical Society of Iowa, Iowa City.

17TH CORPS: MAJ. GEN. FRANK P. BLAIR JR.

Anders, Leslie. *The Eighteenth Missouri*. New York: Bobbs-Merrill, 1968.

Anderson, Mary Ann, ed. *The Civil War Diary of Allen Morgan Geer*. Tappan, N.Y.: R. C. Appleman, 1977.

Baker, Francis R. Memoir. Abraham Lincoln Presidential Library, Springfield, Ill.

Bargus, George. Diary, 1864. Civil War Times Illustrated Collection. United States Army Military History Institute, Carlisle, Pa.

Bashford, Jared. Letter, 1865. Manuscripts Collection. Georgia State Archives, Atlanta.

Bates, John W. Diary, 1864–1865. Civil War Miscellaneous Collection. United States Army Military History Institute, Carlisle, Pa.

Belknap, William W. Letter, 1864. State Historical Society of Iowa, Des Moines.

———. *History of the Fifteenth Regiment, Iowa Veteran Volunteer Infantry*. Keokuk, Iowa: R. B. Ogden & Son, 1887.

Blair, Frank P., Jr. "U.S. Army Generals' Report of Civil War Service, 1864–1887." National Archives, Washington, D.C.

Brush, Charles H. Letters, 1864. Abraham Lincoln Presidential Library, Springfield, Ill.

Brye, Peter Knudson. Letters, 1862–1865. Wisconsin Historical Society, Madison.

Burge, William. *Through the Civil War and Western Adventures*. Lisbon, Iowa: n.p., n.d.

Cadle, Cornelius. "An Adjutant's Recollections." In *Sketches of War History, 1861–1865*, vol. 5. Ohio Military Order of the Loyal Legion of the United States. Cincinnati: Robert Clarke, 1903.

Clark, Olynthus B., ed. *Downing's Civil War Diary*. Des Moines: Historical Department of Iowa, 1916.

Cheatham, Winston W. Family Papers, 1830–1905. Minnesota Historical Society, St. Paul.

Christie, James C. Family Papers, 1835–1949. Minnesota Historical Society, St. Paul.

Cooke, Fred G., ed. *Georgia and Beyond: The Life and Times of Civil War Brevet Captain David G. James*. Madison: F. G. Cook, 1996.

Cryder, George R., and Stanley R. Miller, eds. *The American "War for the Union": A View from the Ranks*. Delaware, Ohio: Delaware County Historical Society, 1999.

Cullen, John Paul, and Clarence J. Stolt, eds. *Diaries and Letters Written by Pvt. Alonzo Miller, Co. A, 12th Wisconsin Infantry.* Marietta, Ga.: n.p., 1958.

Daniels, Sylvester. Diary, 1864–1865. Theophilus M. Magaw Papers. Manuscripts Collection. Huntington Library, San Marino, Calif.

Dow, G. Wayne, ed. *Civil War Diaries of Wentworth Dow.* N.p., 1991.

Downing, Alexander. Journal, 1864. State Historical Society of Iowa, Des Moines.

Elseffer, Harry S. Papers. Manuscripts Division. Library of Congress.

Eyestone, John Wesley. *Our Family History and Father's War Experiences.* Mount Vernon, Iowa: n.p., 1910.

Farnum, Reuben. Civil War Letters, 1864–1865. Minnesota Historical Society, St. Paul.

Force, Manning F. Papers, 1835–1885. Manuscripts. Special Collections. University Archives. University of Washington Libraries.

———. "The Army of the Tennessee and Georgia, and 'Sherman's March to the Sea.' " In *Proceedings of the Annual Meeting of the Society of the Army of the Cumberland.* Cincinnati, Ohio: Robert Clark, 1872.

———. "U.S. Army Generals' Report of Civil War Service, 1864–1887." National Archives, Washington, D.C.

Foster, Brigham. Diary and Letters, 1864. Civil War Miscellaneous Collection. United States Army Military History Institute, Carlisle, Pa.

Fultz, William Stroup. "A History of Company D, Eleventh Iowa Infantry, 1861–1865." *Iowa Journal of History* 55, no. 1 (January 1957).

Grinder, Albert O., ed. *Civil War Diary of Hans Olson Grinder.* Privately printed, 1997.

Gross, Albion. Journal and Letters, 1864. Civil War Miscellaneous Collection. United States Army Military History Institute, Carlisle, Pa.

Guernsey, Francis M. Letters. Private collection.

Haskell, Orson S. *Memorandum of the Fifty-Third Regiment Illinois Veteran Volunteer Infantry.* Louisville, Ky.: Hanna & Duncan, 1865.

Hawley, Miles L. Diary, 1864–1865. Wisconsin Historical Society, Madison.

Hays, Ebenezer Z. *History of the Thirty-second Regiment Ohio Veteran Volunteer Infantry.* Columbus, Ohio: Cott & Evans, 1896.

Hedley, Fenwick Y. *Marching through Georgia.* Chicago: Donohue & Henneberry, 1890.

Hickenlooper, Andrew. Collection. Cincinnati Historical Society.

Hickenlooper, Gordon, ed. *The Reminiscences of General Andrew Hickenlooper.* N.p., 1984.

Humphrey, Arch K. Letter, 1864. Civil War Miscellaneous Collection. United States Army Military History Institute, Carlisle, Pa.

Hunter, Henry. Diary, 1864–1865. Civil War Times Illustrated Collection. United States Army Military History Institute, Carlisle, Pa.

Hurlbut, George. Letters. Kennesaw Mountain National Battlefield Park, Kennesaw, Ga.

Jackson, Oscar L. *The Colonel's Diary.* Sharon, Pa.: n.p., 1922.

Jamison, Matthew H. *Recollections of Pioneer and Army Life.* Kansas City, Mo.: Hudson Press, 1911.

Jennings, Mifflin. Diary, 1864. State Historical Society of Iowa, Des Moines.

Joyner, F. B., ed. "With Sherman in Georgia—A Letter from the Coast." *Georgia Historical Quarterly* 42, no. 4 (December 1958).

Levings, Edwin D. Papers, 1857–1866. Wisconsin Historical Society, River Falls.

Long, Richard K., ed. *Memorandum of Philip Roesch, Co. H., 25th Regiment Wisconsin Volunteers.* Midland, Mich.: n.p., 1979.

Lybarger, Edwin L. *Leaves from My Diary.* Warsaw, Ohio: n.p., 1910.

McDonald, Granville B. *A History of the 30th Illinois Volunteer Regiment of Infantry.* Sparta, Ill.: Sparta News, 1916.

McMillan, George B. Papers, 1838–1865. Wisconsin Historical Society, Madison.

Michaels, Edward Rynearson, ed. *The Civil War Letters of Sylvester Rynearson.* San Rafael, Calif.: E. R. Michaels, 1981.

Morris, W. S., L. D. Hartwell, and J. B. Kuykendall, eds. *History: 31st Illinois Volunteers.* 1902. Reprint, Herrin, Ill.: Crossfire Press, 1991.

Parrish, William E. *Frank Blair: Lincoln's Conservative.* Columbia: University of Missouri Press, 1998.

Pittenger, William H. Diary, 1864. Library Division. Ohio Historical Society, Columbus.

Poak, David. Papers. Abraham Lincoln Presidential Library, Springfield, Ill.

Pratt, George E. Diary, 1864. Wisconsin Historical Society, River Falls.

Putney, Frank H. Papers, 1859–1865. Wisconsin Historical Society, Madison.

Ranstead, Herbert E. *A True Story and History of the Fifty-third Regiment Illinois Veteran Volunteer Infantry.* N.p., 1910.

Reynolds, Charles. Papers. Manuscripts Division. Library of Congress.

Rood, Henry H. "Sketches of the Thirteenth Iowa." In *War Sketches and Incidents as Related by the Companions of the Iowa Military Order of the Loyal Legion of the United States*, vol. 1. Des Moines: P. C. Kenyon, 1889.

———. *History of Company A, Thirteenth Iowa Veteran Infantry.* Cedar Rapids, Iowa: Daily Republican, 1889.

Rood, Hosea W. *Story of the Service of Company E, and of the Twelfth Wisconsin Regiment.* Milwaukee: Swain & Tait, 1893.

Roesch, Philip. Diary. Wisconsin History Commission Papers, 1861–1865. Wisconsin Historical Society, Madison.

Roster of the 78th O.V.V.I. Regimental Association. N.p., 1901.

Sample, Alvan E. *A History of Company A, 30th Illinois Infantry.* Lyons, Kans.: n.p., 1907.

Sargeant, Charles S. *Personal Recollections of the 18th Missouri Infantry.* Unionville, Mo.: Stille & Lincoln, 1891.

Satterlee, Richard Baxter. Letters, 1864–1865. Wisconsin Historical Society, Madison.

Sharland, George. *Knapsack Notes of Gen. Sherman's Grand Campaign through the Empire State of the South.* Springfield, Ill.: Johnson & Bradford, 1865.

Shepherd, George F. Papers, 1857–1901. Wisconsin Historical Society, Madison.

Sketch of the Forty-first Illinois Veteran Volunteer Infantry. Monticello, Ill.: Piatt, 1888.

Smith, Charles M. Papers, 1864–1865. Wisconsin Historical Society, Madison; Kennesaw Mountain National Battlefield Park, Kennesaw, Ga.

Stevenson, Thomas M. *History of the 78th Regiment O.V.V.I.* Zanesville, Ohio: Hugh Dunne, 1865.

Strickling, Joseph M. Memoir. Library Division. Ohio Historical Society, Columbus.
Throne, Mildred, ed. "An Iowa Doctor in Blue." *Iowa Journal of History* 58, no. 2 (April 1960).
Tillson, John. *The March to the Sea.* Quincy, Ill.: Press of the Daily Whig, 1875.
Tyler, Loren. Diary, 1864–1865. State Historical Society of Iowa, Des Moines.
Wescott, M. Ebenezer. Papers, 1862–1865. Wisconsin Historical Society, River Falls.
———. *Civil War Letters, 1861 to 1865.* Mora, Minn.: n.p., 1909.
Wood, Alanson. *History of the 32nd Regiment Wisconsin Infantry.* Ripon, Wisc.: n.p., 1888.
Wood, David W. *History of the 20th O.V.V.I. Regiment.* Columbus, Ohio: Paul & Thrall, 1876.
Woodruff, George H. *Fifteen Years Ago; or, The Patriotism of Will County.* Joliet, Ill.: Joliet Republican Book and Job Steam, 1876.

LEFT WING: MAJ. GEN. HENRY W. SLOCUM

Foraker, Joseph B. *Notes of a Busy Life.* Cincinnati, Ohio: Stewart & Kidd, 1916.
Howland, Joseph. Letters, 1862–1866. New-York Historical Society.
Melton, Brian Christopher. " 'Stay and Fight It Out': Henry W. Slocum and America's Civil War." Ph.D. diss., Texas Christian University, 2003.
Slocum, Henry W. "U.S. Army Generals' Report of Civil War Service, 1864–1887." National Archives, Washington, D.C.

14TH CORPS: BVT. MAJ. GEN. JEFFERSON C. DAVIS

Abrahams, John H., Jr., ed. "Twenty-first Wisconsin Infantry in the Civil War: Service of John W. Abrahams." *Cump and Company: A Newsletter for Friends and Fanciers of General William T. Sherman* 6, no. 5 (May/June 2000).
Adams, Jacob. *Diary of Jacob Adams.* Columbus, Ohio: F. J. Herr, 1930.
Adams, Kelsey M. Letters, 1859–1871. Wisconsin Historical Society, Madison.
Allspaugh, Harrison. Diaries, 1861–1865. University of Iowa, Iowa City.
Althouse, Jerry A., and Ruth Lauer Hughes, eds. *The Civil War Letters of John A. Boon.* Lincoln, Neb.: Richard C. Ludden, 1994.
Anderson, David, L., ed. "The Life of 'Wilhelm Yank': Letters from a German Soldier in the Civil War." *Michigan Historical Review* 16 (Spring 1990).
Anderson, Godfrey T., ed. " 'My Darling Emeline': The Civil War Letters of Daniel Titus." *Yankee Magazine,* October 1972.
Angle, Paul, ed. *Three Years in the Army of the Cumberland.* Bloomington: Indiana University Press, 1959.
Aten, Henry J. *History of the Eighty-fifth Regiment Illinois Volunteer Infantry.* Hiawatha, Kans.: n.p., 1901.
Bachelder, Glen L., ed. *Bachelder Family Letters.* East Lansing, Mich.: privately printed, 1989.
Barnes, Philander Y. *War Reminiscences.* Shiloh, Ohio: S. F. Rose, 1925.
Belknap, Charles E. "Christmas Day Near Savannah in Wartime." *Michigan History Magazine* 6, no. 4 (1922).
Benedict, William N. Letters, 1865. Harrisburg Civil War Roundtable Collection. United States Army Military History Institute, Carlisle, Pa.

Bircher, William. *A Drummer-Boy's Diary*. St. Paul, Minn.: St. Paul Book and Stationery, 1889.

Bishop, Judson W. *The Story of a Regiment*. St. Paul: n.p., 1890.

———. Family Papers, 1855–1917. Minnesota Historical Society, St. Paul.

Blackburn, Theodore W. *Letters from the Front*. Dayton, Ohio: Morningside, 1981.

Branum, John M. *Letters of Lieut. J. M. Branum from the 98th Ohio Volunteer Infantry*. New Castle, Pa.: Warnock Brothers, 1897.

Brower, William L., and Freeda Craig Brower, eds. *Foragin' with Sherman*. N.p., 1982.

Brown, Charles S. Papers, 1864–1865. William R. Perkins Library, Duke University, Durham, N.C.

Brown, Thaddeus C. S. *Behind the Guns: The History of Battery I, 2nd Regiment Illinois Light Artillery*. Carbondale: Southern Illinois University Press, 1965.

Bruce, Daniel E. Personal Memorandum. Indiana State Library, Indianapolis.

Bruce, Foster. "Daniel E. Bruce, Civil War Teamster." *Indiana Magazine of History* 33, no. 2 (June 1937).

Burkhalter, James. Diary, 1864–1865. Abraham Lincoln Presidential Library, Springfield, Ill.

Calkins, William Wirt. *The History of the One Hundred and Fourth Regiment of Illinois Volunteer Infantry*. Chicago: Donohue & Henneberry, 1895.

Canfield, Silas S. *History of the 21st Regiment Ohio Volunteer Infantry*. Toledo: Vrooman, Anderson & Bateman, 1893.

Chamberlain, Joseph, and Orville Chamberlain. Papers. Indiana Historical Society, Indianapolis.

Champlin, Albert A. Diary. Alfred Mewett Papers. Western Reserve Historical Society, Cleveland, Ohio.

Chase, John A. *History of the Fourteenth Ohio Regiment*. Toledo: St. John, 1881.

Clark, William T. Diaries. Lancaster County Historical Society, Lancaster, Pa.

Corbin, William Z. Letters, 1865. Civil War Times Illustrated Collection. United States Army Military History Institute, Carlisle, Pa.

Daniels, John W. Diary. Bentley Historical Library, University of Michigan.

Develling, Charles Theodore. *History of the Seventeenth Regiment*. Zanesville, Ohio: E. R. Sullivan, 1889.

Drake, Julia A., ed. *The Mail Goes Through; or, The Civil War Letters of George Drake*. San Angelo, Tex.: Anchor, 1964.

Dresbach, Michael R. Letters and Reminiscence, 1864–1865. Minnesota Historical Society, St. Paul.

Dunkel, O. G. Papers. Michigan State University, East Lansing.

Edmonds, James E. Papers. United States Army Military History Institute, Carlisle, Pa.

Ege, Peter. Papers, 1836–1920. Wisconsin Historical Society, Madison.

Eicker, John. Memoir. Harrisburg Civil War Roundtable Collection. United States Army Military History Institute, Carlisle, Pa.

Emmons, W. B. Diaries, 1864–1865. University of Iowa, Iowa City.

Essington, James G. Diary. Indiana State Library.

Fahnestock, Allen L. Diary. Kennesaw Mountain National Battlefield Park, Kennesaw, Ga.

Ferguson, Frank L. Memoir. Civil War Miscellaneous Collection. United States Army Military History Institute, Carlisle, Pa.

Fisher, William E. Letters, 1865. New York State Library, Albany.

Floyd, David Bittle. *History of the Seventy-fifth Regiment of Indiana Infantry Volunteers.* Philadelphia: Lutheran Publishing Society, 1893.

Fulton, William P. Diary. Kennesaw Mountain National Battlefield Park, Kennesaw, Ga.

Funk, Arville Lynn. *A Hoosier Regiment in Dixie.* Chicago: Adams Press, 1978.

Girardi, Robert I., and Nathaniel Cheairs Hughes Jr., eds. *The Memoirs of Brigadier General William Passmore Carlin, U.S.A.* Lincoln: University of Nebraska Press, 1999.

Gould, David, and James B. Kennedy, eds. *Memoirs of a Dutch Mudsill: The "War Memories" of John Henry Otto.* Kent, Ohio: Kent State University Press, 2004.

Grubb, Perry D. Memoir. Abraham Lincoln Presidential Library, Springfield, Ill.

Hapeman, Douglas. Diary, 1864–1865. Abraham Lincoln Presidential Library, Springfield, Ill.

Hickman, John E. Diary and Letters. Squier Family Papers, 1843–1859. Bentley Historical Library, University of Michigan.

Hoffhines, Joseph. Letters, 1864–1865. Library Division, Ohio Historical Society, Columbus.

Holmes, James Taylor. *52d O.V.I. Then and Now.* Columbus, Ohio: Berlin, 1898.

Hormel, Olive D., ed. *With Sherman to the Sea.* New York: John Day, 1960.

Horrall, Spillard F. *History of the Forty-second Indiana Volunteers.* Chicago: Donohue & Henneberry, 1892.

Hughes Jr., Nathaniel Cheairs, and Gordon D. Whitney. *Jefferson Davis in Blue: The Life of Sherman's Relentless Warrior.* Baton Rouge: Louisiana State University Press, 2002.

Hunter, Alfred G. *History of the Eighty-second Indiana Volunteer Infantry.* Indianapolis: William B. Burford, 1893.

Inskeep, John. Diary, 1864–1865. Library Division. Ohio Historical Society, Columbus.

Johnson, William C. "The March to the Sea." In *G.A.R. War Papers.* Papers Read Before Fred C. Jones Post, No. 401. Cincinnati: Fred C. Jones Post, 1891.

Jones, James P. "General Jeff Davis, U.S.A., and Sherman's Georgia Campaign." *Georgia Historical Quarterly* 47, no. 3 (September 1963).

Kemp, Dennis L. Letters, 1864. Civil War Miscellaneous Collection. United States Army Military History Institute, Carlisle, Pa.

Kerr, Charles D. "From Atlanta to Raleigh." In *Glimpses of the Nation's Struggle* (Minnesota Military Order of the Loyal Legion), vol. 1. St. Paul: St. Paul Book and Stationery, 1887.

Kinnear, John R. *History of the Eighty-sixth Regiment Illinois Volunteer Infantry.* Chicago: Tribune, 1866.

Kitts, Susanne B., ed. *The Benedict Schmid Civil War Diary,* Excelsior, Minn.: Excelsior-Lake Minnetonka Historical Society, 1976.

Knapp, Charles W. Letters, 1864–1865. Wisconsin Historical Society, Madison.

Kuntz, John. Diary, 1864–1865. Civil War Miscellaneous Collection. United States Army Military History Institute, Carlisle, Pa.

Ladd, James Royal. "From Atlanta to the Sea." *American Heritage* 30, no.1 (December 1978).

Levey, Samuel. Diary, 1864. Civil War Miscellaneous Collection. United States Army Military History Institute, Carlisle, Pa.

Litton, Mary Ann, ed. *A Union Soldier Returns South: The Civil War Letters and Diary of Alfred C. Willett*. Johnson City, Tenn.: Overmountain Press, 1994.

Marion, Frederick. Letters, 1864–1865. Abraham Lincoln Presidential Library, Springfield, Ill.

McAdams, Francis Marion. *Every-day Soldier Life; or, A History of the One Hundred and Thirteenth Ohio Volunteer Infantry*. East Columbus, Ohio: Charles M. Cott, 1884.

McCaskey, William S. Letters. Lancaster Country Historical Society, Lancaster, Pa.

McNeil, Samuel A. *Personal Recollections of Service in the Army of the Cumberland and Sherman's Army*. Richwood, Ohio: Privately printed, 1910.

Miller, William B. Diary. Gibson County Civil War Papers. Indiana Historical Society, Indianapolis.

Morse, Loren J., ed. *Civil War Diaries and Letters of Bliss Morse*. Wagoner, Okla.: Privately printed, 1985.

Nurse, Henry H. Letters, 1864–1865. Abraham Lincoln Presidential Library, Springfield, Ill.

Orr, James Laughlin. "Civil War Diary." 1864. www.crossmyt.com/hc/gen/civwdiar.html.

Otto, John Henry. "Civil War Memoirs." Wisconsin Historical Society, Madison.

Overmyer, Jack K. *A Stupendious Effort: The 87th Indiana in the War of the Rebellion*. Bloomington: Indiana University Press, 1997.

Owens, Ira S. *Greene County in the War*. Xenia, Ohio: Torchlight, 1872.

Parker, Lovel Newton. Papers, 1794–1917. Manuscripts Collection. Huntington Library, San Marino, Calif.

Patrick, Jeffrey L., and Robert Willey. " 'We Have Surely Done a Big Work': The Diary of a Hoosier Soldier on Sherman's 'March to the Sea,' " *Indiana Magazine of History* 94, no. 3 (September 1998).

Payne, Edwin Waters. *History of the Thirty-fourth Regiment of Illinois Infantry*. Clinton, Iowa: Allen, 1902.

Pendergast, William W. Family Papers, 1833–1903. Minnesota Historical Society, St. Paul.

Perry, Henry Fales. *History of the Thirty-eighth Regiment Indiana Volunteer Infantry*. Palo Alto, Calif.: F. A. Stuart, 1906.

Porter, Styles W. Diary, 1864–1865. Library Division. Ohio Historical Society, Columbus.

Povenmire, H. M., ed. "Diary of Jacob Adams, Private in Company F, 21st O.V.V.I." *Ohio Archaeological and Historical Quarterly* 38, no. 4 (October 1929).

Proceedings of the Twenty-first Wisconsin Regiment Association at Its Fifth Annual Reunion. N.p., 1891.

Proceedings of the Twenty-first Wisconsin Regiment Association at Its Sixth Annual Reunion. N.p., 1892.

Rawdon, Horace Jr. "A Sketchbook through the South." *Civil War Times Illustrated* 12 (November 1973).

Record of the Ninety-fourth Regiment Ohio Volunteer Infantry. Cincinnati: Valley Press, 189[?].

Reed, Axel H. "Civil War Diaries, 1861–1865." Minnesota Historical Society, St. Paul.

Reeve, James T. Papers, 1747–1951. Wisconsin Historical Society, Madison.

Robbins, Edward Mott. *Civil War Experiences, 1862–1865.* Carthage, Ill.: n.p., 1919.

Rogers, Robert M. *The 125th Regiment Illinois Volunteer Infantry.* Champaign, Ill.: Gazette Steam, 1882.

Rosenow, Diane, ed. *Pen Pictures from the Second Minnesota.* Roseville, Minn.: Park Genealogical Books, 1998.

Ross, Levi. Diary, 1864–1865. Abraham Lincoln Presidential Library, Springfield, Ill.

Roth, Nathan. *Farm Boys and Artillery Men.* Monroe, Wisc.: Privately printed, 1997.

Rusk, J. M. *Address to the Survivors of the Twenty-fifth Regiment of Wisconsin Volunteers.* N.p., 1887.

Sawyer, James F. Letters, 1864–1865. Wisconsin Historical Society, Madison.

Smith, Joseph Taylor. Letters. Indiana Historical Society, Indianapolis.

Stone, Sylvanus Whipple. "Civil War Letter to Mrs. Elizabeth Knight Stone." *North Dakota Historical Quarterly* 1, no. 2 (January 1927).

Sutton, Verle Procter. *Benjamin Benn Mabrey, Yankee Soldier.* San Bernardino, Calif.: Crown, 1978.

Taylor, John C. *Lights and Shadows in the Recollections of a Youthful Volunteer in the Civil War.* Ionia, Mich.: Sentinel-Standard, n.d.

Taylor, Lester D. Diary, 1864–1865. Civil War Miscellaneous Collection. United States Army Military History Institute, Carlisle, Pa.

Tourgee, Albion Winegar. *The Story of a Thousand, Being a History of the Service of the 105th Ohio Volunteer Infantry.* Buffalo, Ohio: S. McGerald & Son, 1896.

Vail, John. Diary, 1864–1865. Library Division. Ohio Historical Society, Columbus.

Westervelt, William B. Diary-Journal. Civil War Miscellaneous Collection. United States Army Military History Institute, Carlisle, Pa.

———. *Lights and Shadows of Army Life, as Seen by a Private Soldier.* Marlboro, N.Y.: C. H. Cocrane, 1886.

Widney, Lyman S. Diary and Letters. Kennesaw Mountain National Battlefield Park, Kennesaw, Ga.

———. "Campaigning with 'Uncle Billy,'" *Neale's Monthly* 2, no. 2 (August 1913).

Wilcox, Alfred G. Diary, 1864–1865. Civil War Miscellaneous Collection. United States Army Military History Institute, Carlisle, Pa.

Wilde, Hiram. Reminiscences. New York State Library, Albany.

Williams, Harrison C. "Regimental History of the 79th Pennsylvania Volunteers of the Civil War: The Lancaster County Regiment." *Journal: A Quarterly Publication of the Lancaster County Historical Society* 84, no. 1 (1980).

Woodard, Donald S., ed. *The Civil War Letters of Dwight H. Woodard to His Wife Amelia Martindale Woodard.* Mentor, Ohio: n.p., 1988.

Woodman, Edson. Letter. Charles Butler Correspondence, 1862–1864. Bentley Historical Library, University of Michigan, Ann Arbor.

20TH CORPS: MAJ. GEN. ALPHEUS S. WILLIAMS

Adams, Samuel E. Diary, 1864. Civil War Miscellaneous Collection. United States Army Military History Institute, Carlisle, Pa.

Allen, E. Livington. *Both Sides of Army Life: The Grave and the Gay.* Poughkeepsie, N.Y.: n.p., 1885.

Ames, Lyman D. Diary, 1864. Civil War Times Illustrated Collection. United States Army Military History Institute, Carlisle, Pa.

Anderson, John E. Memoir. Manuscripts Division. Library of Congress.

Anderson, William Martin. *They Died to Make Men Free: A History of the 19th Michigan Infantry in the Civil War.* Berrian Springs, Mich.: Hardscrabble Books, 1980.

Antrim-Erickson, Jean, ed. *Letters of a Civil War Soldier.* Pittsburgh: Dorrance, 1997.

The Army Reunion: With Reports of the Meetings of the Societies of the Army of the Cumberland; the Army of the Tennessee; the Army of the Ohio; and the Army of Georgia. Chicago: S. C. Griggs, 1869.

Baldwin, Frank D. Papers, 1807–1923. Manuscripts Collection. Huntington Library, San Marino, Calif.

Barnum, Henry A. "Oration." In *Proceedings of the Annual Meeting of the Society of the Army of the Cumberland.* Cincinnati: Robert Clark, 1872.

Bartlett, Edward O. *The "Dutchess County Regiment" in the Civil War.* Danbury, Conn.: Danbury Medical Printing, 1907.

Bauer, Jack, ed. *Soldiering: The Civil War Diary of Rice C. Bull.* San Rafael, Calif.: Presidio, 1977.

Baughman, Theodore. *Baughman, the Oklahoma Scout: Personal Reminiscences.* Chicago: Belford, Clarke, 1886.

Bence, Robert F. Papers. Indiana Historical Society, Indianapolis.

Benton, Charles Edward. *As Seen from the Ranks: A Boy in the Civil War.* New York: G. P. Putnam's Sons, 1902.

Blair, William Alan, ed. *A Politician Goes to War: The Civil War Letters of John White Geary.* University Park: Pennsylvania State University Press, 1995.

Bohrnstedt, Jennifer Cain, ed. *Soldiering with Sherman: Civil War Letters of George F. Cram.* DeKalb: Northern Illinois University Press, 2000.

Boies, Andrew J. *Record of the Thirty-third Massachusetts Volunteer Infantry.* Fitchburg, Mass.: Sentinel, 1880.

Boyle, John Richards. *Soldiers True: The Story of the One Hundred and Eleventh Regiment Pennsylvania Veteran Volunteers.* New York: Eaton & Mains, 1903.

Bradley, George S. *The Star Corps.* Milwaukee: Jermain & Brightman, 1865.

Brant, Jefferson E. *History of the Eighty-fifth Indiana Volunteer Infantry.* Bloomington, Ind.: Cravens Brothers, 1902.

Bryant, Edwin E. *History of the Third Regiment of Wisconsin Veteran Volunteer Infantry.* Madison, Wisc.: Veteran Association of the Regiment, 1891.

Buckingham, Philo B. Papers, 1862–1892. American Antiquarian Society, Worcester, Mass.

Buerstatte, Frederick Charles. "Civil War Diary." 1864. www.russcott.com/%7 Erscott/26thwis/fredbdia.htm.

Butterfield, Dexter. *A Brief History of the "Abbott Grays": Co. A, 2nd Massachusetts Volunteer Infantry.* Lowell, Mass.: n.p., 1911.

Byrne, Frank L., ed. *Uncommon Soldiers: Harvey Reid and the 22nd Wisconsin March with Sherman.* Knoxville: University of Tennessee Press, 2001.

Byrne, Garrett S. "Diary and Journal of Military Service." Alexander Library, Rutgers University.

Carmen, Ezra A. Papers, 1861–1903. New Jersey Historical Society, Newark.

————. "General Hardee's Escape from Savannah." In *War Papers* (District of Columbia Loyal Legion of the United States), vol. 1. N.p., 1893.

Carroon, Robert G., ed. *From Freeman's Ford to Bentonville.* Shippensburg, Pa.: Burd Street Press, 1998.

Cate, Jean M., ed. *"If I Live to Come Home": The Civil War Letters of Sergeant John March Cate.* Rancho Santa Fe, Calif.: Privately printed, 1995.

Chapman, Horatio Dana. *Civil War Diary: Diary of a Forty-Niner.* Hartford, Conn.: Allis, 1929.

Charlton, Thomas J. "From Atlanta to the Sea." James J. Garver Collection Scrapbook. United States Army Military History Institute, Carlisle, Pa.

Coble, Samuel. "Civil War Diary." Indiana Historical Society, Indianapolis.

Cogswell, William. Papers. Phillips Library, Peabody Essex Museum, Salem, Mass.

Collins, George Knapp. *Memoirs of the 149th Regiment New York Volunteer Infantry.* Syracuse, N.Y.: n.p., 1891.

Congleton, James A. "Reminiscences of the Civil War." Manuscripts Division. Library of Congress.

Conklin, George W. *Under the Crescent and Star.* Port Reading, N.J.: Axworthy, 1999.

Cosgrove, Charles H. *A History of the 134th New York Volunteer Infantry Regiment.* Lewiston, N.Y.: Edwin Mellen Press, 1997.

Cruikshank, Robert. "Civil War Letters." 1864. www.ehistory.com/usew/library/letters/cruikshank.

Cutter, John. Letters, 1861–1865. Minnesota Historical Society, St. Paul.

"Cy." Letters, 1864. Blanche Spurlock Bentley Papers, 1761–1942. Tennessee State Library, Nashville.

Davenport, Horace W., ed. "Such Is Military: Dr. George Martin Trowbridge's Letters from Sherman's Army, 1863–1865." *Bulletin of the New York Academy of Medicine* 63, no. 9, 2d ser. (November 1987).

Duncan, Sebastian Cabot, Jr. Papers. New Jersey Historical Society, Newark.

Dunkelman, Mark H., and Michael J. Winey. *The Hardtack Regiment: An Illustrated History of the 154th Regiment, New York State Infantry Volunteers.* East Brunswick, N.J.: Associated University Presses, 1981.

————. "Through White Eyes: The 154th New York Volunteers and African-Americans in the Civil War." *Journal of Negro History* 85, no. 3 (Summer 2000).

Eaton, Levi. Family Papers. New York State Library, Albany.

Elliott, Fergus. Diary and Letters, 1864. Civil War Times Illustrated Collection. United States Army Military History Institute, Carlisle, Pa.

————. "Fergus Elliott's Savannah." *Civil War Times Illustrated* 14 (June 1975).

Elmore, Bruce. Diary, 1864–1865. Special Collections and Archives. Auburn University.

Engle, Charles. Letters, 1864. http://members.aol.com/jcoy13/index.html.

Everett, J. H. Papers. Georgia Historical Society, Savannah.

Failing-Knight. Papers. Massachusetts Historical Society, Boston.

Fleharty, Stephen F. *Our Regiment: A History of the 102d Illinois Infantry Volunteers.* Chicago: Brewster & Hanscom, 1865.

Federico, Bianca Morse, ed. *Civil War Letters of John Holbrook Morse.* Washington, D.C.: Privately printed, 1975.

Funk, Peter W. F. Diary, 1864–1865. Civil War Miscellaneous Collection. United States Army Military History Institute, Carlisle, Pa.

Geary, John W. "U.S. Army Generals' Report of Civil War Service, 1864–1887." National Archives, Washington, D.C.

Gorham, J. Martin. Papers, 1864–1865. Schoff Civil War Collection. William L. Clements Library, University of Michigan.

Gourlie, John. Letters, 1864. Civil War Miscellaneous Collection. United States Army Military History Institute, Carlisle, Pa.

Grunert, William. *History of the One Hundred and Twenty-Ninth Regiment Illinois Volunteer Infantry*. Winchester, Ill.: R. B. Dedman, 1866.

Guyer, Henry. "Civil War Letters." Beinecke Library, Yale University.

Halsey, Ashley, ed. *A Yankee Private's Civil War*. Chicago: Henry Regnery, 1961.

Harmon, George D. "The Military Experiences of James A. Peifer, 1861–1865." *North Carolina Historical Review* 32, no. 4 (October 1955).

Harper, William D. Diary, 1864–1865. Mike Winey Collection. United States Army Military History Institute, Carlisle, Pa.

Harryman, Samuel K. Letters. Indiana State Library, Indianapolis.

Henney, Henry. Letters, 1864. Civil War Times Illustrated Collection. United States Army Military History Institute, Carlisle, Pa.

Herron, William. *Reminiscences of the Eighty-fifth Regiment of Indiana Volunteer Infantry*. Sullivan, Ind.: Sullivan Union Office, 1875.

Hinkley, Julian W. *A Narrative of Service with the Third Wisconsin Infantry*. Madison: Wisconsin History Commission, 1912.

———. Papers, 1861–1922. Wisconsin Historical Society, Madison.

Historical Sketch of Co. D, 13th Regiment, N.J. Volunteers. New York: D. H. Gildersleeve, 1875.

History of the 134th Regiment, N.Y.S. Volunteers. Schenectady, N.Y.: J. J. Marlett, n.d.

Hoerner, George M., Jr., ed. *Chattanooga, Savannah and Alexandria: The Diary of One of Sherman's Soldiers*. Easton,: n.p., 1988.

Holzhueter, John O., ed. "William Wallace's Civil War Letters: The Atlanta Campaign." *Wisconsin Magazine of History* 57, no. 2 (Winter 1973–1974).

Hopkins, Charles A. Letters. Alexander Library, Rutgers University.

———. "The March to the Sea." In *Personal Narratives of Events in the War of the Rebellion, Being Papers Read before the Rhode Island Soldiers and Sailors Historical Society*. Vol. 5. N.p., 1885.

Hopper, Hassell. Diary, 1863–1865. www.brainmist.com/civilwar/pt6.htm.

Howland, Thomas S. Papers. Massachusetts Historical Society, Boston.

Huntley, Alden B. Diary. Glover Shoudy Collection. Western Michigan University, Kalamazoo.

Hurst, Samuel H. *Journal-History of the Seventy-third Ohio Volunteer Infantry*. Chillicothe: n.p., 1866.

Hutchinson, Edwin. Papers, 1861–1866. Special Collections—Louisiana & Lower Mississippi Valley Collections. Hill Memorial Library, Louisiana State University, Baton Rouge.

Johnson, W. R., ed. " 'Enough to Make a Preacher Swear': A Union Mule Driver's Diary of Sherman's March." *Atlanta History* 33, no. 3 (Fall 1989).

Kaminsky, Virginia H., ed. *A War to Petrify the Heart*. Hensonville, N.Y.: Black Dome Press, 1997.

Kendall, Edward. Diary and Letters. Chemung County Historical Society, Elmira, N.Y.

Kimmell, Charles F. Journal-Report. Papers of the 66th Illinois. New-York Historical Society.

Kittinger, Isaac. Diary, 1864–1865. Earl M. Hess Collection. United States Army Military History Institute, Carlisle, Pa.

Lake, Delos W. Papers, 1862–1855. Manuscripts Collection, Huntington Library, San Marino, Calif.

Lathrop, Dorothy, and LeRoy Lathrop, eds. *John Smethurst Civil War Diaries*. N.p., 2001.

Lockhart, James W. "Civil War Memoir." Wisconsin Historical Society, Madison.

Lockwood, Dunning K. Diary, 1864. Harrisburg Civil War Roundtable Collection. United States Army Military History Institute, Carlisle, Pa.

Longhons, John. Letter, 1864. Michael Winey Collection. United States Army Military History Institute, Carlisle, Pa.

Marvin, Edwin E. *The Fifth Regiment, Connecticut Volunteers*. Hartford, Conn.: Wiley, Waterman & Eaton, 1889.

McBride, John Randolph. *History of the Thirty-third Indiana Veteran Volunteer Infantry*. Indianapolis: William B. Burford, 1900.

McConnell, Darlene, ed. *John D. Martin's Journal*. Evansville, Ind.: Evansville Bindery, 1999.

McCormick, Thomas. Letter. Jane Stoddard Hagle Collection, Margaret Stanford Papers. Western Michigan University, Kalamazoo.

McCreary, William G. Papers, 1864–1865. William R. Perkins Library, Duke University.

McKay, Charles W. " 'Three Years or During the War,' with the Crescent and Star." N.d. Mike Winey Collection. United States Army Military History Institute, Carlisle, Pa.

McLean, William Clark. McLean Family Papers. New York State Library, Albany.

Mead, Rufus, Jr. Papers. Manuscripts Division. Library of Congress.

Merrill, Samuel. Letters. Indiana State Library, Indianapolis.

———. *The Seventieth Indiana Volunteer Infantry in the War of the Rebellion*. Indianapolis: Bowen-Merrill, 1900.

Michael, Charles Gottlieb. Diary. Indiana Historical Society, Indianapolis.

Morgan, Ambrose B. Diary, 1864. Civil War Miscellaneous Collection. United States Army Military History Institute, Carlisle, Pa.

Morhous, Henry C. *Reminiscences of the 123rd Regiment*. Greenwich, N.Y.: People's Journal, 1879.

Morrow, James E. Diary, 1864. Civil War Times Illustrated Collection. United States Army Military History Institute, Carlisle, Pa.

Morse, Charles F. *Letters Written during the Civil War, 1861–1865*. Boston: T. R. Marvin & Son, 1898.

Nettleton, Elliot. "Civil War Letter." Beinecke Library, Yale University.

Niesen, W. C., ed. *The Artillery Man*. N.p., 1990.

Noble, Henry G. Papers, 1862–1865. Bentley Historical Library, University of Michigan.

Oakey, Daniel. "Marching through Georgia and the Carolinas." *Century Magazine* 34, no. 6 (October 1887).

———. "Marching through Georgia and the Carolinas." In *Battles and Leaders of the Civil War,* edited by Robert Underwood Johnson and Clarence Clough Buel, 4 vols. New York: Century, 1887–88.

Osborn, Hartwell. *Trials and Triumphs, The Record of the Fifty-fifth Ohio Volunteer Infantry.* Chicago: A. C. McClurg, 1904.

Ostrum, Andrew J. Diary, 1864–1865. Civil War Miscellaneous Collection. United States Army Military History Institute, Carlisle, Pa.

Omvig, Glen, and Mark Omvig, eds. *Diaries of Pvt. John W. Houtz, 66th Ohio Volunteer Infantry, 1863–1864.* Homer, N.Y.: Robert T. Pennoyer, 1995.

Padgett, James A., ed. "With Sherman through Georgia and the Carolinas: Letters of a Federal Soldier." *Georgia Historical Quarterly* 33, no. 1 (March 1949).

Parmater, N. L. Diary, 1864–1865. Library Division. Ohio Historical Society, Columbus.

Patton, James H. Memoir. Civil War Miscellaneous Collection. United States Army Military History Institute, Carlisle, Pa.

Perry, Kenneth A., ed. *"We Are in a Fight Today": The Civil War Diaries of Horace P. Matthews & King S. Hammond.* Bowie, Md.: Heritage, 2000.

Pierce, Thomas E. Diary, 1864–1865. Civil War Times Illustrated Collection. United States Army Military History Institute, Carlisle, Pa.

Potter, John. *Reminiscences of the Civil War.* Oskaloosa, Iowa: Globe, 1897.

Pratt, Lorenzo N. Letters, 1864–1865. Civil War Miscellaneous Collection. United States Army Military History Institute, Carlisle, Pa.

Pula, James S. *The Sigel Regiment: A History of the Twenty-sixth Wisconsin.* Campbell, Calif.: Savas, 1998.

Quaife, Milo M., ed. *From the Cannon's Mouth: The Civil War Letters of General Alpheus S. Williams.* Detroit: Wayne State University Press, 1959.

Quint, Alonzo H. *The Record of the Second Massachusetts Infantry, 1861–1865.* Boston: James P. Walker, 1867.

Rattenbury, Richard C., ed. *From Wisconsin to the Sea: The Civil War Letters of Sergeant John V. Richards.* Houston, Tex.: D. Armstrong, 1986.

Remington, Cyrus Kingsbury. *A Record of Battery I, First N.Y. Light Artillery Volunteers.* Buffalo, N.Y.: Courier, 1891.

Rey, Rudolph. Letters. New York Historical Society.

Rilea, Joshua D. Diary, 1864–1865. Abraham Lincoln Presidential Library, Springfield, Ill.

Roberts, John H. "Civil War Letters, 1862–1865." Wisconsin Historical Society, Madison.

Roller, John G. Diary, 1864–1865. Civil War Miscellaneous Collection. United States Army Military History Institute, Carlisle, Pa.

Rosenberger, H. E., ed. "Ohiowa Soldier." *Annals of Iowa* 36, no. 2 (Fall 1961).

Rugg, Harlan P. Papers. Connecticut State Library, Hartford.

Russell, Robert H. Letter, 1864. Library Division, Ohio Historical Society, Columbus.

Saylor, William F. Letter, 1864. Wisconsin Historical Society, Madison.

Schaum, William R. Diary, 1865. William R. Perkins Library, Duke University, Durham, N.C.

Schmidt, Lewis G. *A Civil War History of the 147th Pennsylvania Regiment*. Allentown, Pa.: Privately printed, 2000.

Schroyer, M. S. *The History of Company G, 147th Regiment, Pennsylvania Volunteer Infantry*. N.p., 1994.

Schwab, Mathias. "Civil War Letters." Cincinnati Historical Society.

Scofield, William H. Papers. Georgia Historical Society, Savannah.

SeCheverall, John Hamilton. *Journal History of the Twenty-ninth Ohio Veteran Volunteers*. Cleveland: n.p., 1883.

Sheahan, Daniel W. Diary, 1864. Abraham Lincoln Presidential Library, Springfield, Ill.

Short, Martin C. Diary, 1864–1898. Wisconsin Historical Society, Madison.

Shroyer, Michael Simon. Diary, 1864–1865. Fredericksburg National Military Park, Fredericksburg, Va.

Smith, Abner C. Papers. Connecticut State Library, Hartford.

Society of the Army of the Cumberland Sixteenth Reunion, Rochester, New York, 1884. Cincinnati: Robert Clarke, 1885.

Stelle, Abel Clarkson. *1861 to 1865, Memoirs of the Civil War*. New Albany, Ind.: n.p., 1904.

Storrow, Samuel. Papers. Massachusetts Historical Society, Boston.

Storrs, John Whiting. *The Twentieth Connecticut*. Naugatuck, Conn.: Press of the Naugatuck Valley Sentinel, 1886.

Tallman, William H. H. Memoir, 1864–1865. Charles Rhodes II Collection. United States Army Military History Institute, Carlisle, Pa.

Thackery, David T. *A Light and Uncertain Hold: A History of the Sixty-sixth Ohio Volunteer Infantry*. Kent, Ohio: Kent State University Press, 1999.

Toombs, Samuel. *Reminiscences of the War*. Orange, N.J.: Journal, 1878.

Trego, Alfred H. Diary, 1864. Manuscripts Collection. Chicago Historical Society.

Trowbridge, George M. Papers, 1863–1865. Schoff Civil War Collection. William L. Clements Library, University of Michigan.

Underwood, Adin B. *The Three Years' Service of the Thirty-third Mass. Infantry Regiment, 1862–1865*. Boston: A. Williams, 1881.

Volwiler, A. T., ed. "Letters from a Civil War Officer." *Mississippi Valley Historical Review* 14, no. 4 (March 1928).

Wagoner, Charles Van. Diary, 1864. New York State Library, Albany.

———. "From Wauhatchie to the Capture of Savannah." In *Third Annual Report of the State Historian of the State of New York, 1897*. New York: Wynkoop Hallenbeck Crawford, 1898.

———. "The March to the Sea." N.d. GAR Collection. New York State Library, Albany.

Wallace, Frederick Stephen. *The Sixty-first Ohio Volunteers, 1861–1865*. Marysville, Ohio: Theodore Mullen, 1902.

Wallace, William. Papers, 1861–1864. Wisconsin Historical Society, Madison.

Walton, William, ed. *A Civil War Courtship: The Letters of Edwin Weller from Antietam to Atlanta*. Garden City, N.Y.: Doubleday, 1980.

Ward, William T. "U.S. Army Generals' Report of Civil War Service, 1864–1887." National Archives, Washington, D.C.

Wheeler, Lysander. Letters and Journal, 1864–1865. Abraham Lincoln Presidential Library, Springfield, Ill.

Williams, Alpheus S. "U.S. Army Generals' Report of Civil War Service, 1864–1887." National Archives, Washington, D.C.

Winkler, Frederick C. *Letters of Frederick C. Winkler, 1862 to 1865*. N.p.: William K. Winkler, 1963.

Young, Moses G., ed. *A Condensed History of the 143rd Regiment New York Volunteer Infantry of the Civil War*. Newburgh, N.Y.: Newburgh Journal, 1909.

3RD CAVALRY DIVISION: MAJ. GEN. JUDSON KILPATRICK

Barbour, J., and David M. Dougherty, eds. *The Civil War Diary of William H. Harding*. N.p., 1996.

Berkenes, Robert E., ed. *Private William Boddy's Civil War Journal*. Altoona, Iowa: TiffCor, 1996.

Carmony, Donald F., ed. "Jacob W. Bartmess Civil War Letters." *Indiana Magazine of History* 52, no. 2 (June 1956).

Carter, George E., ed. *The Story of Joshua D. Breyfogle*. Lewiston, N.Y.: Edward Mellen Press, 2001.

Eisenhower, Abner. Diary, 1864–1865. Civil War Miscellaneous Collection. United States Army Military History Institute, Carlisle, Pa.

Hamilton, William D. *Recollections of a Cavalryman of the Civil War*. Columbus, Ohio: F. J. Herr, 1915.

Hinman, Wilbur F. *The Story of the Sherman Brigade*. Alliance, Ohio: Press of Daily Review, 1897.

Hoole, William S. *Alabama Tories: The First Alabama Cavalry, U.S.A., 1862–1865*. Confederate Centennial Studies No. 16. Tuscaloosa, Ala.: Confederate, 1960.

Jordan, Thomas J. Civil War Letters, 1864. Historical Society of Pennsylvania, Philadelphia.

King, G. Wayne. "General Judson Kilpatrick." *New Jersey History* 91, no. 1 (Spring 1973).

Martin, Samuel J. *Kill-Cavalry: The Life of Union General Hugh Judson Kilpatrick*. Mechanicsburg, Pa.: Stackpole, 2000.

McCain, Warren. *A Soldier's Diary; or, The History of Co. L, Third Indiana Cavalry*. Indianapolis: William A. Patton, 1885.

McKeever, Elliott B. "Atlanta to the Sea" (Memoir) 1911. Western Reserve Historical Society, Cleveland, Ohio.

Miller, James Cooper. "We Scattered the Rebels." *Civil War Times Illustrated* 8 (August 1969): 42–48.

———. "With Sherman through the Carolinas." *Civil War Times Illustrated* 8 (October 1969): 34–44.

Moore, James. *Kilpatrick and Our Cavalry: Comprising a Sketch of the Life of General Kilpatrick*. New York: International, 1865.

More, Betty E., ed. *Soldier Boy*. Bowie, Md.: Heritage Books, 2000.

92nd Illinois Volunteers. Freeport, Ill.: Journal, 1875.

Palmore, John S. *Riding with Sherman: The Civil War Travels of the Fifth Kentucky Cavalry*. Frankfort, Ky: J. S. Palmore, 2000.

Pickerill, William N. *History of the Third Indiana Cavalry*. Indianapolis: Aetna, 1906.

Rowell, John William. *Yankee Cavalrymen: Through the Civil War with the Ninth Pennsylvania Cavalry*. Knoxville: University of Tennessee Press, 1971.

Smith, Frank. "A Maine Boy in the Tenth Ohio Cavalry." *Maine Bugle,* campaign 4, call 1 (January 1897).

Swedberg, Clare E., ed. *Three Years with the 92nd Illinois: The Civil War Diary of John M. King.* Mechanicsburg, Pa.: Stackpole, 1999.

Thompson, James M. Journal. Indiana Historical Society, Indianapolis.

Tomlinson, Helyn W., ed. *"Dear Friends": The Civil War Letters and Diary of Charles Edwin Cort.* Minneapolis: n.p., 1962.

Ward, Williamson D. Diary. Indiana Historical Society, Indianapolis.

UNION FORCES (MISCELLANEOUS)

Gray, John Chipman, and John Codman Ropes. *War Letters, 1862–1865.* Cambridge, Mass.: Riverside Press, 1927.

PRISONS/PRISONERS

Barber, Lucius W. *Army Memoirs.* Chicago: J. M. W. Jones, 1894.

Davidson, Henry M. *Fourteen Months in Southern Prisons.* Milwaukee: Daily Wisconsin Printing House, 1865.

Isham, Asa B., Henry M. Davison, and Henry B. Furness. *Prisoners of War and Military Prisons.* Cincinnati: Lyman & Cushing, 1890.

Lyon, W. F. *In and Out of Andersonville Prison.* Detroit: George Harland, 1905.

NEWSPAPERS/REPORTING

Andrews, J. Cutler. *The North Reports the Civil War.* Pittsburgh: University of Pittsburgh Press, 1955.

———. *The South Reports the Civil War.* Pittsburgh: University of Pittsburgh Press, 1985.

"Atlanta as Sherman Left It: Atlanta Then and Now: Correspondence Chronicle and Sentinel, of Augusta, Ga." *Atlanta Historical Bulletin,* no. 3 (May 1930).

Beckett, Ian F. W. *The War Correspondents: The American Civil War.* Dover, N.H.: Alan Sutton, 1993.

Brogan, Hugh, ed. *The Times Reports the American Civil War.* London: Times Books, 1975.

Albany (Georgia) Patriot
American Tribune
Athens (Georgia) Southern Banner
Athens (Georgia) Southern Watchman
Atlanta Daily Intelligencer
Atlanta Journal
Augusta Daily Chronicle & Sentinel
Augusta Daily Constitutionalist
Boston Evening Journal
Boston Post
Broome (New York) Republican

Charleston Daily Courier
Charleston Mercury
Chicago Evening Journal
Chicago Tribune
Cincinnati Daily Commercial
Cincinnati Gazette
Columbus Daily Sun
Galesville (Wisconsin) Transcript
Harper's Weekly
Indianapolis Journal
Jones County (Georgia) News
Lancaster (Pennsylvania) Daily Evening Express
Leavenworth (Kansas) Daily Times
Macon Daily Telegraph
Milwaukee Daily Sentinel
National Tribune (Washington, D.C.)
New Haven Daily Morning Journal
New York Herald
New York Post
New York Times
New York World
Paterson (New Jersey) Daily Register
Philadelphia Inquirer
Philadelphia Weekly Times
Quincy (Illinois) Daily Whig and Republican
Savannah Morning News
Savannah Republican
Springfield (Illinois) Republican
Sullivan County Union
The Sunny South
Troy (Ohio) Times
Washington Post
Weekly Missouri Democrat

CONFEDERATE LEADERSHIP
Primary Sources

Beauregard, Pierre Gustave Toutant. Papers, 1844–1893. William R. Perkins Library, Duke University, Durham, N.C.

Brown, Joseph Emerson. Papers, 1859–1889. William R. Perkins Library, Duke University, Durham, N.C.

Chandler, Allen D., comp. *The Confederate Records of the State of Georgia*. 5 vols. Atlanta: Charles P. Byrd, 1910–1941.

Chisolm, Alexander R. "The Failure to Capture Hardee." In *Battles and Leaders of the Civil War*, edited by Robert Underwood Johnson and Clarence Clough Buel, 4 vols. New York: Century, 1887–1888.

Cobb, Howell. Papers: Correspondence. Hargrett Rare Book and Manuscript Library, University of Georgia, Athens.

Davis, Jefferson. *The Rise and Fall of the Confederate Government, 1881*. Reprint, New York: Da Capo Press, 1990.

Georgia, General Assembly. *Acts of the General Assembly of the State of Georgia Passed in Milledgeville at the Annual Session in November 1864; also, Extra Session of 1865*. Milledgeville, Ga.: Boughton, Nisbet, Barnes & Moore, 1865.

Hood, John Bell. *Advance and Retreat, 1880*. Reprint, Secaucus, N.J.: Blue and Grey Press, 1985.

Miers, Earl Schenck, ed. *A Rebel War Clerk's Diary*. New York: A. S. Barnes, 1961.

Phillips, Ulrich, ed. *Annual Report of the American Historical Association for the Year 1911: The Correspondence of Robert Toombs, Alexander H. Stephens, and Howell Cobb*. Washington, D.C.: American Historical Association, 1913.

Richardson, James D., comp. *The Messages and Papers of Jefferson Davis and the Confederacy*. 2 vols. Washington, D.C.: n.p., 1905.

Roman, Alfred. The Military Operations of General Beauregard. 2 vols. 1884. Reprint, New York: Da Capo Press, 1994.

————. Papers. Manuscripts Division. Library of Congress.

Raines, C. W., ed. *Six Decades in Texas; or, Memoirs of Francis Richard Lubbock*. Austin, Tex.: Ben C. Jones, 1900.

Rowland, Dunbar, ed. *Jefferson Davis, Constitutionalist: His Letters, Papers and Speeches*. Jackson: Mississippi Department of Archives and History, 1923.

Taylor, Richard. *Destruction and Reconstruction*. 1879. Reprint, New York: Bantam Books, 1992.

Tower, R. Lockwood, ed. *A Carolinian Goes to War: The Civil War Narrative of Arthur Middleton Manigault*. Charleston: University of South Carolina Press, 1983.

Younger, Edward, ed. *Inside the Confederate Government: The Diary of Robert Garlick Hill Kean*. 1957. Reprint, Westport, Conn.: Greenwood Press, 1973.

Secondary Sources

Ballard, Michael B. "Breakdown in Macon." *Civil War Times Illustrated* 19, no. 6 (October 1980).

Bragg, William Harris. "Joe Brown vs. the Confederacy." *Civil War Times Illustrated* 26 (November 1987): 40–43.

Cooper, William J., Jr. *Jefferson Davis, American*. New York: Vintage Books, 2000.

————. "A Reassessment of Jefferson Davis as War Leader: The Case from Atlanta to Nashville." *Journal of Southern History* 36, no. 2 (May 1970).

Cunningham, S. A. "Why General Sherman's Name Is Detested." *Confederate Veteran* 14, no. 7 (July 1906).

Davis, William C. *Jefferson Davis: The Man and His Hour*. New York: HarperCollins, 1991.

Ellis, Robert R. "From Atlanta to the Sea." *Military Engineer* 51, no. 344 (November–December 1959); 52, no. 345 (January–February 1960).

Hallock, Judith Lee. *Braxton Bragg and Confederate Defeat*. Tuscaloosa: University of Alabama Press, 1991.

Hill, Louise Biles. *Joseph E. Brown and the Confederacy*. Chapel Hill: University of North Carolina Press, 1939.

Hughes, Nathaniel Cheairs, Jr. *General William J. Hardee: Old Reliable*. Baton Rouge: Louisiana State University Press, 1965.

Martin, Thomas H. *Atlanta and Its Builders: A Comprehensive History of the Gate City of the South*. Atlanta: Century Memorial, 1902.

McMurry, Richard M. *John Bell Hood and the War for Southern Independence*. Lexington: University Press of Kentucky, 1982.

Overley, Milton. "Sherman Helped Starve Union Prisoners." *Confederate Veteran* 14, no. 11 (November 1906).

Parks, J. H. *Joseph E. Brown of Georgia*. Baton Rouge: Louisiana State University Press, 1977.

Parrish, T. Michael. *Richard Taylor: Soldier Prince of Dixie*. Chapel Hill: University of North Carolina Press, 1992.

Pickett, W. D. "Why General Sherman's Name Is Detested." *Confederate Veteran* 14, no. 9 (September 1906).

Reid, Randy L. "Howell Cobb of Georgia: A Biography." Ph.D. diss. Louisiana State University, 1995.

Wiley, Bell Irvin, ed. *Letters of Warren Akin, Confederate Congressman*. Athens: University of Georgia Press, 1959.

Williams, T. Harry. *Beauregard: Napoleon in Gray*. New York: Collier Books, 1962.

CONFEDERATE FORCES (MISCELLANEOUS)

Primary Sources

Anderson, Edward C. Papers. Southern Historical Collection. Wilson Library, University of North Carolina, Chapel Hill.

Anderson, George W. Papers. Georgia Historical Society, Savannah.

Andrews, W. H. *Footprints of a Regiment: A Recollection of the 1st Georgia Regulars, 1861–1865*. Atlanta: Longstreet Press, 1992.

Clark, Walter. *Histories of the Several Regiments and Battalions from North Carolina in the Great War 1861–65*. 5 vols. Goldsboro, N.C.: Nash Brothers, 1901. Reprint: Wendell, N.C.: Avera Press, 1982.

Coker, Francis Marion. Letters. Hargrett Rare Book and Manuscript Library, University of Georgia, Athens.

Elliott, Habersham. Letters. Southern Historical Collection. Wilson Library, University of North Carolina, Chapel Hill.

Fort, John Porter. "History of the Last Campaign of the First Georgia Regulars of the Confederate States Army in the Civil War." Civil War Times Illustrated Collection. United States Army Military History Institute, Carlisle, Pa.

Gordon Family Papers. Southern Historical Collection. Wilson Library, University of North Carolina, Chapel Hill.

Gordon, Arthur. Letter, 2/23/1938. Henry Ford Library, Dearborn, Mich.

Graves, Henry. Letters, 1864–1865. United Daughters of the Confederacy Georgia Division Collection. Georgia State Archives, Atlanta.

Harris, G. B. "The Enemy Had Horns." *Confederate Veteran* 26, no. 7 (July 1918).

Hawley, F. O. "Sherman's Love (?) for the South." *Confederate Veteran* 19, no. 5 (May 1911).

Heyward-Ferguson, S. W. Papers. Reminiscences. Southern Historical Collection. Wilson Library, University of North Carolina, Chapel Hill.

Jackson, Alphonzo J. Diary. 2nd Regiment Infantry Georgia State Line Papers. Georgia State Archives. Kennesaw Mountain National Battlefield Park, Kennesaw, Ga.

Jones, Charles Colcock. Family Papers. Charles Colcock Jones, Jr., Letters. Hargrett Rare Book and Manuscript Library, University of Georgia, Athens.

King, Jack H. Letter, 1864. Georgia State Archives, Atlanta.

Kurtz, Elma S., ed. "War Diary of Cornelius R. Hanleiter." *Atlanta Historical Bulletin* 44 (1970).

Lawson, A. "Sherman's Devastation in Georgia." *Confederate Veteran* 19, no. 2 (February 1911).

Mason, B. F. Letter, 1865. Manuscripts Collection. Georgia State Archives, Atlanta.

McLaws, Lafayette. Papers. Southern Historical Collection. Wilson Library, University of North Carolina, Chapel Hill.

McWhorter Family Papers. Letter. Hargrett Rare book and Manuscript Library, University of Georgia, Athens.

Mercer, George Anderson. Papers, 1851–1889. Southern Historical Collection. Wilson Library, University of North Carolina, Chapel Hill.

Patchin, Richard M, and Deborah Jean Patchin, eds. *Letters of Jonathan Bridges, a Confederate Soldier of Stewart County, Georgia.* N.p.: R & D Patchin, 1985.

Prior, Felix W. Letters, 1864. Manuscripts Collection. Georgia State Archives, Atlanta.

Skinner, Arthur N., and James L. Skinner, eds. *The Death of a Confederate.* Athens: University of Georgia Press, 1996.

Swiggart, Carolyn Clay, ed. *Shades of Gray: The Clay & McAllister Families of Bryan County, Georgia, during the Plantation Years.* Darien, Conn.: Two Bytes, 1999.

Tomb, James H. "Why the Bridge Wasn't Destroyed." *Confederate Veteran* 31, no. 7 (July 1923).

Secondary Sources

Adamson, Augustus P. *Brief History of the Thirtieth Georgia Regiment.* 1912. Reprint, Jonesboro, Ga.: Freedom Hill Press, 1987.

Conrad, James Lee. *The Young Lions: Confederate Cadets at War.* Mechanicsburg, Pa,: Stackpole, 1997.

Latty, John W. *The Gallant Little 7th.* Wilmington, N.C.: Broadfoot, 2004.

Sullivan, David M. "The Confederate States Marine Corps in Georgia, 1861–1865." *Atlanta Historical Journal* 29, no. 4 (Winter 1985–1986).

WHEELER'S CAVALRY

Barnett, T. S. "The Eleventh Texas Cavalry." *Confederate Veteran* 19, no. 9 (September 1911).

Beasley, John F. "3rd Georgia Cavalry and the Role of John F. Beasley." N.d., http://home.earthlink.net/~larsbl/CW/3GACavpage.htm.

Collier, Calvin L. *The War Child's Children: The Story of the Third Regiment Arkansas Cavalry.* Little Rock, Ark.: Pioneer Press, 1965.

Cook, Gustave. Letter, 1864. Gilder Lehrman Collection. New-York Historical Society.

Cunningham, S. A. "Terry's Texas Rangers." *Confederate Veteran* 15, no. 11 (November 1907).

Daiss, Timothy. *In the Saddle: Exploits of the 5th Georgia Cavalry.* Atglen, Pa.: Schiffer Military History, 1999.

Davis, W. H. "Cavalry Service under Gen. Wheeler." *Confederate Veteran* 11, no. 8 (August 1903).

Davis, William C., ed. *Diary of a Confederate Soldier.* Columbia: University of South Carolina Press, 1997.

Dodson, William C., ed. *Campaigns of Wheeler and His Cavalry, 1862–1865.* Atlanta: Hudgins, 1899.

———. "Wheeler on Sherman's Flanks in Georgia." *Confederate Veteran* 12, no. 12 (December 1904).

DuBose, John Witherspoon. *General Joseph Wheeler and the Army of the Tennessee.* New York: Neale, 1912.

———. "Maj. Gen. Joseph Wheeler." *Confederate Veteran* 25, no. 10 (October 1917).

Dyer, John P. *From Shiloh to San Juan: The Life of "Fightin' Joe" Wheeler.* 1961. Reprint, Baton Rouge: Louisiana State University Press, 1989.

Dyer, John Will. *Reminiscences; or, Four Years in the Confederate Army.* Evansville, Ind.: Keller, 1898.

Evans, Clement A. "Gen. Clement A. Evans's [Memorial] Address." *Confederate Veteran* 14, no. 6 (June 1906).

Fleming, William Augustus. "Reminiscences of the Liberty Independent Troop." Midway Georgia Museum Collection; also in Civil War Times Illustrated Collection, United States Army Military History Institute, Carlisle, Pa.

Giles, Leonidas B. *Terry's Texas Rangers.* Austin, Tex.: Von Boeckmann-Jones, 1911.

Graber, Henry William. *The Life Record of H. W. Graber.* Austin, Tex.: State House Press, 1987.

Guild, George B. *A Brief Narrative of the Fourth Tennessee Cavalry Regiment.* Nashville: n.p., 1913.

Hargis, O. P. *Thrilling Experiences of a First Georgia Cavalryman.* Atlanta: n.p., n.d.

———. "We Kept Fighting and Falling Back." *Civil War Times Illustrated* 7, no. 8 (December 1968).

Henderson, William Michael. "War Record and Letters." N.d. www.5thgacavalry.info/5thcav/famhistory/2nd_lieutenant_william_michael-h.htm.

Joyce, Fred. "From Infantry to Cavalry." *Southern Bivouac* 3, nos. 6–7 (February–March 1885).

Kirwan, A. D., ed. *Johnny Green of the Orphan Brigade.* Lexington: University of Kentucky Press, 1956.

Lafferty, W. T., ed. "Civil War Reminiscences of John Aker Lafferty." *Register of the Kentucky Historical Society* 59, no. 1 (January 1961).

Lambright, James T. *History of the Liberty Independent Troop during the Civil War.* Brunswick, Ga.: Press of Glover Brothers, 1910.

Miller, Rex. *Wheeler's Favorites, 51st Alabama Cavalry.* Depew, N.Y.: Patrex Press, 1991.

Mims, Wilbur F. *War History of the Prattville Dragoons.* Thurber, Tex.: Journal Printery, n.d.

Moor, James A. Letter, 1864. Georgia State Archives, Atlanta.

Overley, Milford. " 'Williams's Kentucky Brigade,' C.S.A." *Confederate Veteran* 13, no. 10 (October 1905).

Poole, John Randolph. *Cracker Cavaliers: The 2nd Georgia under Wheeler and Forrest.* Macon, Ga.: Mercer University Press, 2000.

Ray, Lavender R. Diary, 1864. Georgia State Archives, Atlanta.

———. Letters. Robert W. Woodruff Library, Emory University.

Scott, Paul, ed. " 'With Tears in Their Eyes': On the Road to the Sea: Shannon's Scouts." *Civil War Times Illustrated* 21 (January 1983).

Sloan, William E. Diary, 1864–1865. Civil War Collection: Confederate and Federal. Tennessee State Library, Nashville.

Thompson, Edwin Porter. *History of the Orphan Brigade.* Louisville, Ky.: Lewis N. Thompson, 1898.

Walden, Geoffrey R. "Opposing Sherman's March to the Sea." 1996. www.rootsweb .com/~orphanhm.

Wheeler, Joseph. Letter, 1864. Hargrett Rare Book and Manuscript Library, University of Georgia, Athens.

GEORGIA MILITIA

Accounts in *Confederate Reminiscences and Letters, 1861–1865* (Atlanta: United Daughters of the Confederacy, 1995–1999):
- Cochrane, Anne Cleveland. "Demetrius A. Cochrane." Vol. 1, 1995.
- Unknown. "The Services of James L. Heard in the Confederate Army." Vol. 3, 1997.
- Wade, Milton C., Sr. "Military Record of Milton C. Wade, Sr." Vol. 5, 1997.

Smith, Gustavus W. "The Georgia Militia during Sherman's March to the Sea." In *Battles and Leaders of the Civil War,* edited by Robert Underwood Johnson and Clarence Clough Buel, 4 vols. New York: Century, 1887–1888.

———Smith, Gustavus W., and Henry C. Wayne. *Reports of the Operations of the Militia, from October 13, 1864, to February 11, 1865, Together with Memoranda by Gen. Smith, for the Improvement of the State Military Organization.* Macon, Ga.: Boughton, Nisbet, Barnes & Moore, 1865.

Tinsley, T. D. "Kelly's Defense of Gordon." *Confederate Veteran* 35, no. 9 (September 1927).

CIVILIAN ACCOUNTS

Accounts in *Confederate Reminiscences and Letters, 1861–1865* (Atlanta: United Daughters of the Confederacy, 1995–1999):
- Adams, James Monroe. "James Monroe Adams." Vol. 8, 1998.
- Anderson, Frances B. "A True Reminiscence of the Confederate Era." Vol. 2, 1996.

- Baldwin, Lucile McDaniel. "Reminiscing." Vol. 1, 1995.
- Blount, Louise Anderson. "A Reminiscence of the War between the States." Vol. 2, 1996.
- Burden, Jane Symons. "Reminiscences." Vol. 2, 1996.
- Curry, Ella Mae Garrett. "Sherman's March through Emanuel County, Georgia." Vol. 8, 1998.
- Drake, Mary. "The Drake Plantation on the Ogeechee River." Vol. 4, 1996.
- Darnell, Jennie Ihly. "Reminiscences of the War between the States." Vol. 3, 1997.
- Drew, Frances K. "A Savannah Reminiscence." Vol. 8, 1998.
- Everett, Emma Borders. "Reminiscence of the War between the States." Vol. 3, 1997.
- Fields, Flossie B. "A Reminiscence." Vol. 1, 1995.
- Frye, Kate D. "Reminiscences of the Sixties." Vol. 4, 1996.
- Glenn, Layona. "Scilla's Return: A Reminiscence." Vol. 6, 1997.
- Garrett, Maggie. "Uninvited Guests Enjoy Turkey Dinner at Social Circle, Georgia." Vol. 5, 1997.
- Graham, Omye Howard. "Reminiscence of the Civil War." Vol. 5, 1997.
- Griswold, Samuel. "Aunt Peny." Vol. 7, 1998.
- Hanson, Mary Jewell Travis. "Reminiscence." Vol. 3, 1997.
- Harbuck, Angela Chambers. "Reminiscences." Vol. 9, 1999.
- Hughes, Rufus Paul. "My Great-Grandmother, Minerva Moore Hughes." Vol. 9, 1999.
- Johnson, Martha Arnall. "Page Memoirs." Vol. 2, 1996.
- Kauffman, Louisa White. "Fleeing from Sherman and a Consequent Romance." Vol. 7, 1998.
- Langford, Willam Bedford (daughters and granddaughters of). "William Bedford Langford." Vol. 7, 1998.
- Lockridge, Dora Jeanne Smith. "A Reminiscence of Sherman's March through Georgia and the Burning of Cassville, Georgia." Vol. 2, 1996.
- Maddox, Eliza Frances Weaver. "A Reminiscence of the Sixties." Vol. 6, 1997.
- Martin, Gussie Rustin. "Reminiscence of the War between the States." Vol. 4, 1997.
- Massey, Nathan. "Recollections of the Late War between the States and the Incidents as They Transpired under My Own Observation and from Reliable Sources." Vol. 1, 1995.
- McDonell, Mrs. Alan M. "Reminiscences." Vol. 2, 1996.
- McKinley, G. C. "Memories of My Youth." Vol. 2, 1996.
- McMichael, Areetas. "Burning of the Courthouse at Jackson, Georgia." Vol. 6, 1997.
- McRae, Colon. "Reminiscence." Vol. 5, 1997.
- McSwain, Eleanor Davis. "Reminiscences." Vol. 3, 1997.
- Mendel, W. H. "A Sketch of My Activities during the War between the States." Vol. 8, 1998.
- Miller, Sarah Rudolph. "Reminiscences of the Sixties." Vol. 4, 1996.
- Moore, Lula Gunn. "Reminiscence." Vol. 6, 1997.
- Moore, Susan Catharine Juhan. "A Collection of Incidents and Experiences during the Civil War, 1861–1865." Vol. 1, 1995.

- Reeves, Lillian Clyde Wallace. "Another Side to General William T. Sherman's Nature." Vol. 4, 1996.
- Roberts, Mattie. "History of Milledgeville, Georgia." Vol. 7, 1998.
- Tyler, Dora Hunt. "Reminiscence." Vol. 6, 1997.
- Tucker, Opal. "Interesting True Story of Civil War Days." Vol. 8, 1998.
- Unknown: "Sherman 'Visited' Mable Home." Vol. 7, 1998.
- Unknown: "Refugee: Stories from a Young Girl of the Sixties." Vol. 5, 1997.
- Watson, Mrs. Larkin D. "The Confederacy's Best-Dressed Mule." Vol. 4, 1996.
- Wilson, Ena Mann. "Miss Gay and the Yankees." Vol. 8, 1998.

Accounts in *Recollections and Reminiscences, 1861–1865*, II vols. [S.C.]: (South Carolina Division, United Daughters of the Confederacy, 1990):

- Lott, Mrs. T. W. "Fleeing before Sherman." Vol. 1, 1990.
- Stribling, E. R. "Letter from E. R. Stribling to Her Husband, Warren[,] Walnut Hill, Richland, South Carolina, November 28, 1864." Vol. 2, 1991.

"A.E.D." Letter. Confederate Miscellany. Series Ie. Robert W. Woodruff Library, Emory University.

Anderson, Mrs. G. W. Letter. Confederate Miscellany. Series Ie. Robert W. Woodruff Library, Emory University.

Baber-Blackshear Collection. Letters. Hargrett Rare Book and Manuscript Library, University of Georgia, Athens.

Banks, John. Journal. Hargrett Rare Book and Manuscript Library, University of Georgia, Athens.

Barnett, May A. "Great State Seal of Georgia." *Confederate Veteran* 7, no. 8 (August 1899).

Berry, Carrie. Diary, 1864–1865. Atlanta History Center.

Berry, Peggy Mira (Cox). Letter. Confederate Miscellany. Series Ie. Robert W. Woodruff Library, Emory University.

Blanton Family Papers. Mary E. Hopkins and Carrie V. Timberlake letters. Virginia Historical Society, Richmond.

Bomar-Killian Family Papers. Imogene Hoye letter. Atlanta History Center.

Bratton, J. R. "Letter of a Confederate Surgeon on Sherman's Occupation of Milledgeville." *Georgia Historical Quarterly* 32, no. 3 (September 1948).

Bryan, T. Conn, ed. "A Georgia Woman's Civil War Diary: The Journal of Minerva Leah Rowles McClatchey, 1864–65." *Georgia Historical Quarterly* 51, no. 2 (June 1967).

Burr, Virginia Ingraham, ed. *The Secret Eye: The Journal of Ella Gertrude Clanton Thomas.* Chapel Hill: University of North Carolina Press, 1990.

Buttrill, Mary. *Experience in the War of the Sixties.* Georgia State Archives, Atlanta.

Clack, Louise. *Our Refugee Household.* New York: Blelock, 1866.

Clark, John Osgood Andrew. Papers. "Ella Anderson Clark Reminiscence." Robert W. Woodruff Library, Emory University.

Cornwell, Bessie Reese. "Stoneman's and Sherman's Visit to Jasper County." Confederate Miscellany. Series Ie. Robert W. Woodruff Library, Emory University.

Cunningham, George A. Family Papers. Hargrett Rare Book and Manuscript Library, University of Georgia, Athens.

Davis-Quillin Papers. Amanda Quillin letter. Atlanta History Center.

Felton, Rebeca Latimer. *County Life in Georgia in the Days of My Youth.* Atlanta: Index Printing, 1919.

Gatell, Frank Otto, ed. "A Yankee Views the Agony of Savannah." *Georgia Historical Quarterly* 43, no. 4 (December 1959).

Gay, Mary A. H. *Life in Dixie during the War, 1861–1862–1863–1864–1865*. Atlanta: Constitution Job Office, 1892.

Harper, F. Mikell, ed. *The Second Georgia Infantry Regiment: As Told through the Unit History of Company D, Burke Sharpshooters*. Macon, Ga.: Indigo, 2005. [Catharine Whitehead Rowland diary.]

Harris, Iverson Louis. Papers, 1827–1878. William R. Perkins Library, Duke University.

Harris, Joel Chandler. *On the Plantation: A Story of a Georgia Boy's Adventures during the War*. Athens: University of Georgia Press, 1980.

Harwell, Richard Barksdale, ed. *Kate: The Journal of a Confederate Nurse*. Baton Rouge: Louisiana State University Press, 1959.

Hodgson Journal. Charles Colcock Jones Jr. Collection. Hargrett Rare Book and Manuscript Library, University of Georgia, Athens.

Jones, Katharine M. *When Sherman Came: Southern Women and the "Great March."* New York: Bobbs-Merrill, 1964.

Jones, Mary Sharpe, and Mary Jones Mallard. *Yankees A'Coming: One Month's Experience during the Invasion of Liberty County, Georgia, 1864–1865*. Tuscaloosa, Ala.: Confederate Publishing, 1959.

King, Spencer B., Jr., ed. "Fanny Cohen's Journal of Sherman's Occupation of Savannah." *Georgia Historical Quarterly* 41, no. 4 (December 1957).

Lamar, Charles. Papers. Georgia State Archives, Atlanta.

LeConte, Joseph. *'Ware Sherman: A Journal of Three Months Personal Experience in the Last Days of the Confederacy*. Berkeley and Los Angeles: University of California Press, 1937.

Lovett, Howard Meriwether. "Airy Mount—In Sherman's Track." *Confederate Veteran* 26, no. 5 (May 1918).

Lunt, Dolly Sumner. *A Woman's Wartime Journal*. New York: Century, 1918.

Maguire, Thomas. Papers. Atlanta History Center.

McAdoo, William G. Diary. Manuscripts Division. Library of Congress.

McKinley, Guy Cummins. Memoirs. Special Collections. Georgia College & State University, Milledgeville.

Morgan, Mrs. Irby. *How It Was: Four Years among the Rebels*. Nashville: Publishing House Methodist Episcopal Church, South, 1892.

Noble, Mary. Papers. Southern Historical Collection. Wilson Library, University of North Carolina, Chapel Hill.

Overley, Milford. "What 'Marching through Georgia' Means." *Confederate Veteran* 12, no. 9 (September 1904).

Stephenson, Eudora Weaver. "Refugeeing in War Time." *Confederate Veteran* 39, no. 4 (April 1931).

Stevens, John. "Personal Narrative of Sherman's Raid in Liberty County, Ga." Civil War Times Illustrated Collection. United States Army Military History Institute, Carlisle, Pa.

Stewart, Lucy S. *The Reward of Patriotism*. New York: Walter Neale, 1930.

Sutherland, Daniel E., ed. *A Very Violent Rebel: The Civil War Diary of Ellen Renshaw House*. Knoxville: University of Tennessee Press, 1996.

Walraven Family Papers. Matt Carolina Marshall letter. Atlanta History Center.

Watson, W. M. "Old Midway Church." *Confederate Veteran* 36, no. 8 (August 1928).

Williams, Ben Ames, ed. *A Diary from Dixie.* 1905. Revised reissue, Boston: Houghton Mifflin, 1949. [Mary Boykin Chesnut diary.]

Zettler, Berrien McPherson. *War Stories and School-Day Incidents for the Children.* New York: Neale, 1912.

AFRICAN-AMERICANS

Drago, Edmund L. "How Sherman's March through Georgia Affected the Slaves." *Georgia Historical Quarterly* 57, no. 3 (Fall 1973).

Escott, Paul D. "The Context of Freedom: Georgia's Slaves during the Civil War." *Georgia Historical Quarterly* 58, no. 1 (Spring 1974).

Georgia Narratives. Vol. 4, pts. 2 and 4. Federal Writers' Project of the Works Progress Administration for the State of Georgia, 1937.

Johnson, Whittington B. *Black Savannah, 1788–1864.* Fayetteville: University of Arkansas Press, 1996.

Mohr, Clarence L. "Before Sherman: Georgia Blacks and the Union Civil War Effort, 1861–1864." *Journal of Southern History* 45, no. 3 (August 1979).

———. *On the Threshold of Freedom: Masters and Slaves in Civil War Georgia.* Athens: University of Georgia Press, 1986.

Rawick, George P., ed. *The American Slave: A Composite Autobiography.* Vols. 12 and 13, *Georgia Narratives.* Westport, Conn.: Greenwood, 1972–1978.

Simms, James M. *The First Colored Baptist Church in North America.* Philadelphia: n.p., 1888.

Stampp, Kenneth M. *The Peculiar Institution.* New York: Vintage Books, 1956.

CAMPAIGN AND BATTLE STUDIES

Andrews, E., and J. M. Woodworth. "The Primary Surgery of Gen. Sherman's Campaigns." *Chicago Medical Examiner* 7, no. 6 (June 1866).

Andrews, Matthew Page. "Marching with Sherman." *Confederate Veteran* 36, no. 4 (April 1928).

Badeau, Adam. "Sherman's March to the Sea." *St. Nicholas: An Illustrated Magazine for Young Folks* 14, no. 7 (May 1887).

Bailey, Anne J. *The Chessboard of War.* Lincoln: University of Nebraska Press, 2000.

———. *War and Ruin: William T. Sherman and the Savannah Campaign.* Wilmington, Del.: SR Books, 2003.

Bonner, James C. "Sherman at Milledgeville in 1864." *Journal of Southern History* 22, no. 3 (August 1956).

Bowman, Samuel Millard. *Sherman and His Campaigns.* New York: C. B. Richardson, 1868.

Boynton, Henry Van Ness. *Sherman's Historical Raid: The Memoirs in Light of the Record.* Cincinnati: Wilstach, Baldwin, 1875.

Bragg, William Harris. *Griswoldville.* Macon, Ga.: Mercer University Press, 2000.

———. "A Little Battle at Griswoldville." *Civil War Times Illustrated* 19, no. 7 (November 1980).

Burke, Sadie C. "Sherman's Raid through Georgia." *Confederate Veteran* 12, no. 3 (March 1904).

" 'Bummers' in Sherman's Army." *Beadle's Monthly* 1 (May 1866).

Castel, Albert. *Decision in the West*. Lawrence: University Press of Kansas, 1992.

Christman, William E. *Undaunted: The History of Fort McAllister, Georgia*. Darien, Ga.: Darien Printing & Graphics, 1996.

Conyngham, David P. *Sherman's March through the South*. New York: Sheldon, 1865.

Cox, Jacob D. *Sherman's March to the Sea*. 1882. Reprint, New York: Da Capo Press, 1994.

Cubbison, Douglas. *A Pretty Rough Time and One of the Hardest Battles of the War: The Battle of Griswoldville*. Saline, Mich.: McNaughton and Gunn for the Blue and Gray Education Society, 1997.

Cunningham, S. A. "Why Sherman Snubbed Augusta." *Confederate Veteran* 22, no. 8 (August 1914).

Davis, Burke. *Sherman's March*. New York: Random House, 1980.

DeLaubenfels, D. J. "Where Sherman Passed By." *Geographical Review* 47 (July 1957).

Durham, Roger S. *Images of America: Fort McAllister*. Charleston, S.C.: Arcadia, 2004.

Dyer, John P. "Northern Relief for Savannah during Sherman's Occupation." *Journal of Southern History* 19, no. 4 (November 1953).

Gatell, Frank Otto, ed. "A Yankee Views the Agony of Savannah." *Georgia Historical Quarterly* 43, no. 4 (December 1959).

Gibson, John M. *Those 163 Days: A Southern Account of Sherman's March from Atlanta to Raleigh*. New York: Brahmall House, 1961.

Glatthaar, Joseph T. *The March to the Sea and Beyond: Sherman's Troops in the Savannah and Carolinas Campaigns*. New York: New York University Press, 1985.

———. "Sherman's Army and Total War." *Atlanta Historical Journal* 29 (Spring 1986): 41–52.

Graber, H. W. "Why Sherman Did Not Go to Augusta." *Confederate Veteran* 22, no. 7 (July 1914).

Gray, Tom S., Jr. "The March to the Sea." *Georgia Historical Quarterly* 14, no. 2 (June 1930).

Jones, Charles Colcock. *The Siege of Savannah in December, 1864, and the Confederate Operations in Georgia and the Third Military District of South Carolina during General Sherman's March from Atlanta to the Sea*. Albany, N.Y.: Joel Munsell, 1874.

Kennett, Lee. *Marching through Georgia: The Story of Soldiers & Civilians during Sherman's Campaign*. New York: HarperCollins, 1995.

Klingberg, Elizabeth Wysor. "Campaigns of Lee and Sherman." *Confederate Veteran* 24, no. 8 (August 1916).

Lee, Angela. "Tangling with Kilcavalry." *Civil War Times Illustrated* 38, no. 3 (June 1998).

Livingston, Gary. *Fields of Gray: The Battle of Griswoldville*. Cooperstown, N.Y.: Caisson Press, 1996.

———. *"Among the Best Men the South Could Boast": The Fall of Fort McAllister*. Cooperstown, N.Y.: Caisson Press, 1997.

Marszalek, John F. *Sherman's March to the Sea*. Abilene, Tex.: McWhiney Foundation Press, 2005.

McInvale, Morton R. " 'All That Devils Could Wish For': The Griswoldville Campaign." *Georgia Historical Quarterly* 60, no. 2 (Summer 1976).

McMurry, Richard M. "Sherman's Savannah Campaign." *Civil War Times Illustrated* 21, no. 9 (January 1983).

McNeill, William J. "A Survey of Confederate Soldier Morale during Sherman's Campaign through Georgia and the Carolinas." *Georgia Historical Quarterly* 55, no. 1 (Spring 1971).

Miles, Jim. *To the Sea: A History and Tour Guide of Sherman's March.* Nashville: Rutledge Hill Press, 1989.

Monroe, Haskell. "Men without Law: Federal Raiding in Liberty County, Georgia." *Georgia Historical Quarterly* 44, no. 2 (June 1960).

Mosser, Jeffrey. "Gateway to the Atlantic." *Civil War Times Illustrated* 33, no. 5 (November–December 1994).

Nevin, David. *Sherman's March.* Alexandria, Va.: Time-Life Books, 1986.

Pfadenhauer, Ruby McCrary. "Why Sherman By-passed Augusta." *Richmond County History* 15, no. 2 (Summer 1983).

Rhodes, James Ford. "Sherman's March to the Sea." *American Historical Review* 6, no. 3 (April 1901).

Righton, Ralph V. "Fort McAllister: Her Flags Never Furled." *Atlanta Historical Journal* 24, no. 3 (Fall 1980).

Robertson, Felix H. "Sherman and Augusta." *Confederate Veteran* 22, no. 9 (September 1914).

Rogers, George A., and R. Frank Saunders Jr. "The Scourge of Sherman's Men in Liberty County, Georgia." *Georgia Historical Quarterly* 60, no. 4 (Winter 1976).

Scaife, William R. *The March to the Sea.* Atlanta: McNaughton & Gunn, 1993.

Schwabe, Edward, Jr. "Sherman's March through Georgia: A Reappraisal of the Right Wing." *Georgia Historical Quarterly* 69, no. 4 (Winter 1985).

Scruggs, Carroll Proctor, ed. *Georgia Historical Markers.* Helen, Ga.: Bay Tree Grove, 1976.

"Sherman's March to the Sea." *Official Programme and Guide Book, Reunion, Georgia Division, U.C.V.* Savannah, Ga.: Morning News Print, 1899.

Spengler, Bruce G., and Walter W. Spengler. *Griswoldville: A Collection of Maps, Pictures, Stories and Personal Comments about the Man, the Town, the Battle.* 4 vols. Sherman Oaks, Calif.: Heritage Research, 1992–1994.

Star, Stephen Z. *The Union Cavalry in the Civil War: The War in the West, 1861–1865.* Baton Rouge: Louisiana State University Press, 1985.

Summerell, M. L. "General Hardee Evacuates Savannah." *Confederate Veteran,* November–December 1990.

Sword, Wiley. *Embrace an Angry Wind: The Confederacy's Last Hurrah: Spring Hill, Franklin, and Nashville.* New York: HarperCollins, 1992.

Teague, B. H. "Why Gen. Sherman Did Not Come to Augusta." *Confederate Veteran* 22, no. 5 (May 1914).

Wheeler, Richard, ed. *Sherman's March.* New York: Thomas Y. Crowell, 1978.

Wells, Charles. *The Battle of Griswoldville.* Macon, Ga.: Privately printed, 1961.

GENERAL SECONDARY SOURCES

"American Medical Association: Seventeenth Annual Session—Report of the Medical Jurisprudence, Physiology, and Hygene Section." *Medical and Surgical Magazine* 14, no. 22 (June 2, 1866).

Andrews, J. Cutler. "The Confederate Press and Public Morale." *Journal of Southern History* 32, no. 4 (November 1966).

———. "The Southern Telegraph Company, 1861–1865: A Chapter in the History of Wartime Communication." *Journal of Southern History* 30, no. 3 (August 1964).

Ash, Stephen V. "Poor Whites in the Occupied South, 1861–1865." *Journal of Southern History* 57, no. 1 (February 1991).

Ashe, S. A. "The Treatment of Prisoners in 1864–65." *Confederate Veteran* 35, no. 5 (May 1927).

Bigelow, John. "Did Grant, Sherman and Sheridan Teach Militarism to Germany?" *William and Mary College Quarterly Historical Magazine* 24, no. 1 (July 1915).

Black, Robert C., III. *The Railroads of the Confederacy.* 1952. Reprint, Chapel Hill: University of North Carolina Press, 1998.

Bonner, James C. *Milledgeville: Georgia's Antebellum Capital.* 1978. Reprint, Macon, Ga.: Mercer University Press, 1985.

Boritt, Gabor S., ed. *Jefferson Davis's Generals.* New York: Oxford University Press, 1999.

Bragg, C. L., Charles D. Ross, Gordon A. Blaker, Stephanie A. T. Jacobe, and Theodore P. Savas, eds. *Never for Want of Powder: The Confederate Powder Works in Augusta, Georgia.* Columbia: University of South Carolina Press, 2007.

Brannen, Dorothy. *Life in Old Bulloch: The Story of a Wiregrass County in Georgia.* Gainesville, Ga.: Magnolia Press, 1987.

Bryan, T. Conn. *Confederate Georgia.* Athens: University of Georgia Press, 1953.

Carnes, Marcia Hayes, John P. Harvey, and Irene Roberts Malon, eds. *History of Jasper County, Georgia.* Roswell, Ga.: W. H. Wolfe, 1976.

Carter, Samuel, III. *The Siege of Atlanta, 1864.* New York: Ballantine Books, 1973.

Cobb, Angela W., ed. *Roster of the Confederate Soldiers of Burke County, Georgia, 1861–1865.* Baltimore, Md.: Gateway Press, 1998.

Cook, Anna Maria. *History of Baldwin County, Georgia.* Spartanburg, S.C.: Reprint Company, 1978.

Cunningham, S. A. "Sherman's Picture on U.S. Postage Stamps." *Confederate Veteran* 19, no. 6 (June 1911).

———. "Marching through Georgia." *Confederate Veteran* 25, no. 9 (September 1917).

Daiss, Timothy. *Rebels, Saints & Sinners: Savannah's Rich History and Colorful Personalities.* Gretna, La.: Pelican, 2002.

Davidson, Victor. *History of Wilkinson County.* Macon, Ga.: J. W. Burke, 1930.

Drake, Edwin L., ed. *The Annals of the Army of Tennessee and Early Western History.* Nashville: A. D. Haynes, 1878.

Durden, Marion Little. *A History of Saint George Parish, Colony of Georgia, Jefferson County, State of Georgia.* Swainsboro, Ga.: Magnolia Press, 1983.

Dyer, Thomas G. *Secret Yankees: The Union Circle in Confederate Atlanta.* Baltimore: Johns Hopkins University Press, 1999.

Eaton, Clement. *A History of the Southern Confederacy*. New York: Collier Books, 1954.

Faust, Drew Gilpin. "Altars of Sacrifice: Confederate Women and the Narratives of War." *Journal of American History* 76, no. 4 (March 1990).

Figg, Laurann, and Jane Farrell-Beck. "Amputation in the Civil War: Physical and Social Dimensions." *Journal of the History of Medicine and Allied Sciences* 48, no. 4 (October 1993).

Flanigan, James C. *History of Gwinnett County, Georgia: Volume 1, 1818–1943*. Hapeville, Ga.: Privately printed, 1943.

Fleming, Berry. "Autobiography of a City in Arms: Augusta, Georgia, 1861–1865." *Richmond County History* 7, no. 1 (Winter 1975).

Fornell, Earl W. "The Civil War Comes to Savannah." *Georgia Historical Quarterly* 43, no. 3 (September 1959).

Glatthaar, Joseph T. *Partners in Command: The Relationships between Leaders in the Civil War*. New York: Free Press, 1994.

Graham, Stephen. "Marching through Georgia: Following Sherman's Footsteps Today." *Harper's Magazine* 140 (1920).

Granger, Mary, ed. *Savannah River Plantations*. Savannah: Georgia Historical Society, 1947.

Grimsley, Mark. *The Hard Hand of War: Union Military Policy toward Southern Civilians, 1861–1865*. New York: Cambridge University Press, 1995.

Henken, Elissa R. "Taming the Enemy: Georgian Narratives about the Civil War." *Journal of Folklore Research* 40, no. 3 (2003).

Hillhouse, Albert M. *A History of Burke County, Georgia, 1777–1950*. Swainsboro, Ga.: Magnolia Press, 1985.

Huxford, Folks. *The History of Brooks County Georgia*. Quitman, Ga.: Daughters of the American Revolution, 1948.

Iobst, Richard W. *Civil War Macon: The History of a Confederate City*. Macon, Ga.: Mercer University Press, 1999.

Janda, Lance. "Shutting the Gates of Mercy: The American Origins of Total War, 1860–1880." *Journal of Military History* 59, no. 1 (January 1995).

Jones, Mary G., and Lilly Reynolds. *Cowety County Chronicles*. Atlanta: Stein, 1928.

Julian, Allen Phelps. "Atlanta's Last Days in the Confederacy." *Atlanta Historical Bulletin* 11, no. 2 (June 1966).

Lawrence, Alexander A. *A Present for Mr. Lincoln: The Story of Savannah from Secession to Sherman*. 1961. Reprint, Savannah, Ga.: Oglethorpe Press, 1997.

Lee, F. D., and J. L. Agnew, *Historical Record of the City of Savannah*. Savannah, Ga.: J. H. Estill, 1869.

McCaskey, Glen. *The View from Sterling Bluff*. Atlanta: Longstreet Press 1989.

McMichael, Lois, ed. *History of Butts County, Georgia, 1825–1976*. Atlanta: Cherokee, 1978.

Moore, John G. "Mobility and Strategy in the Civil War." *Military Affairs* 24, no. 2 (Summer 1960).

Moore, John Hammond. "In Sherman's Wake: Atlanta and the Southern Claims Commission, 1871–1880." *Atlanta Historical Journal* 29, no. 2 (Summer 1985).

Olson, Myke Eric Scott. "Greensboro." N.d. http://myke.olson.name/papers/sherman/page 10.html.

Perkerson, Medora Field. *White Columns in Georgia*. New York: Bonanza Books, 1952.

Rable, George C. *The Confederate Republic: A Revolution against Politics*. Chapel Hill: University of North Carolina Press, 1994.

———. *Civil Wars: Women and the Crisis of Southern Nationalism*. Chicago: University of Illinois Press, 1989.

Rice, Thaddeus Brockett, and Carolyn White Williams. *History of Greene County, Georgia*. Macon, Ga.: J. W. Burke, 1961.

Royster, Charles. *The Destructive War: William Tecumseh Sherman, Stonewall Jackson, and the Americans*. New York: Alfred A. Knopf, 1991.

Russell, Preston, and Barbara Hines. *Savannah: A History of Her People since 1733*. Savannah, Ga.: Frederic C. Beil, 1992.

Shivers, Forrest. *The Land Between: A History of Hancock County, Georgia to 1940*. Spartanburg, S.C.: Reprint Company, 1990.

Silver, James W. "Propaganda in the Confederacy." *Journal of Southern History* 11, no. 4 (November 1945).

Smith, Derek. *Civil War Savannah*. Savannah, Ga.: Frederic C. Beil, 1997.

Speer, Lonnie R. *Portals to Hell: Military Prisons of the Civil War*. Mechanicsburg, Pa.: Stackpole, 1997.

Stern, Philip van Doren, ed. *Soldier Life in the Union and Confederate Armies*. Greenwich, Conn.: Fawcett, 1961.

Sullivan, Buddy. *From Beautiful Zion to Red Bird Creek: A History of Bryan County, Georgia*. Pembroke, Ga.: Bryan County Board of Commissioners, 2000.

Walters, Katherine Bowman. *Oconee River: Tales to Tell*. 1995. Reprint, Spartanburg, S.C.: Reprint Company, 2000.

Warlick, Roger K. *As Grain Once Scattered: The History of Christ Church Savannah, Georgia*. Columbia, S.C.: State Printing Company, 1987.

Williams, Carolyn White. *History of Jones County, Georgia*. Macon, Ga.: J. W. Burke, 1957.

Williams, Noble C. *Echoes from the Battlefield; or, Southern Life during the War*. Atlanta: Franklin, 1902.

Williams, T. Harry. *Lincoln and His Generals*. New York: Vintage Books, 1952.

Woodworth, Steven E. *Jefferson Davis and His Generals: The Failure of Confederate Command in the West*. Lawrence: University of Kansas Press, 1990.

Acknowledgments

The men who marched with Sherman from Atlanta to the sea hailed from some fifteen different states, with the preponderance representing the Midwest. Finding their words about and memories of this operation necessitated visits to nearly every one, with stops at numerous state libraries and historical societies. While my encounters were invariably helpful and professional, I did come away from the experience sobered by witnessing firsthand the difficult limitations under which some were forced to operate. Part of the challenge in undertaking research of this kind is adjusting travel schedules to match with important repositories that operate on limited schedules because of budget restrictions. Then there are limitations of space, parking, or equipment. At one state library (which will not be named) I came upon a useful microfiche collection that was utterly unusable because the machines needed to read the microcards had died and not been replaced. Yet throughout, I was struck by the dedication to their craft shown by the often unsung guardians of America's historical legacy.

Several went above and beyond the call. For putting up with my numerous requests during a weeklong sojourn, a tip of the hat to the staff at the United States Army Military History Institute in their fancy new digs in Carlisle, Pennsylvania. For kindly helping me with access to material at their respective facilities, I'm grateful to Kimberly Richards of the Chemung Valley Museum and Matthew D. Norman of Knox College. Glen L. Bachelder kindly provided copies of an ancestor's Civil War diary by making copies from the limited-edition book he had prepared for his family. The Richmond Battlefield National Park's Robert E. L. Krick dipped into his archive on my behalf to come up with some key letters from Georgia soldiers. A big thanks to Pam Knox, Georgia assistant state climatologist, University of Georgia, who helped me make sense out of the weather observations I had compiled.

Even with the miles that I racked up on my car's odometer, I needed extra hands in many places. Yet again, Bryce Suderow was my principal researcher in the Washington, D.C., area. He not only located what I asked him to find but also uncovered material not on my search list, which often proved quite helpful. Outside of D.C. I called upon a small squad of researchers to cover places I couldn't reach, or revisit an archive on my behalf to retrieve something I had missed in my stop there. With fingers crossed that I haven't forgotten anyone, let me here express my grateful thanks to: David Cleutz, Mary Kathleen Clucas, Carolyn L. Garner-Reagan, Robert I. Girardi, Angie Hogencamp, David Hudson, Evan Jurkovich, Hannah Lee, Brian McGowan, Patrick Pospisek, Alan Rockman, Vincent W. Slaugh, Susan H. Truax, Eric J. Wittenberg, Peter Wyant, and Steve L. Zerbe.

An intense but relatively short-term immersion in a subject always benefits from the counsel of those who have lived with it for many years longer. In that regard, thanks to Roger S. Durham, expert on Fort McAllister, and William Harris Bragg, all-knowing about Griswold-ville and pretty smart about the campaign in general. Another able Georgia historian, W. Todd Groce, gave me much to ponder regarding Ebenezer Creek, while Barry Sheehy guided me to many of Savannah's extant 1864 earthworks. Daniel Brown, superintendent for Fort McAllister Park, shared research and information with me during my visits there.

Finally, thanks to my literary agent, Raphael Sagalyn, who knew when to check in and when not to; and to my editor at HarperCollins, Tim Duggan, supportive and blessed with a keen editor's eye. HarperCollins editorial assistant Allison Lorentzen helped me bridge my twentieth-century computer knowledge with twenty-first-century devices, and copyeditor Miranda Ottewell helped keep me in line with the *Chicago Manual of Style*.

As I learned long ago, the "facts" of history aren't always as hard and fast as we would like them to be. At various points in the narrative I had to choose among conflicting recollections and local lore; and while I always treasured the advice of individuals with knowledge of the subject, ultimately I had to decide among them. For those decisions, the buck stopped here.

Index

Acworth, Ga., 62

Adams, Robert N., 282, 386

African-Americans, aid Sherman's men, 147, 531–32; Buckhead Creek incident, 327–28, 381–82; Confederate soldier treatment, 185; desire for freedom, 21, 47–48, 117–18, 136, 146–47, 154–55, 172, 176, 272, 304, 505–6, 530–31; Ebenezer/Lockner creeks incident, 372, 380–83; effects of campaign, 519–21; Georgians, 20–22; join Meridian Campaign columns, 47–48; mistreatment, 135, 261, 352; Sherman prejudices, 54, 518–19; transported to Hilton Head, 482–83; Union soldier reactions, 54–5, 117–18, 135, 176, 349, 422; Union soldier treatment, 135, 272, 310, 531–32; vignettes, 124, 145, 153–54, 156, 173, 185, 187, 191, 271, 352, 372, 467–68, 477–78, 482

Aiken, Francis B., 16

Alabama troops (U.S.): cavalry (1st Regiment, 116, 163–64, 218, 316, 387)

Alcovy River, 135, 142

Alexander, Ga., 342

Alexander, James, 221

Allatoona Pass, 38

Allen, Julian, 511

Allen, William Wirt, 336

Altamaha River, 449, 463

Ames, Lyman, 333–34

Amick, Myron J., 442; mission to contact fleet, 390–91, 401–2, 410–12

Anderson, Charles, wounded, 211

Anderson, David, 326

Anderson, George W., 376, 409, 417–18; Fort McAllister assault, 422–40

Anderson, Mrs. George W., 505

Anderson, Ruel W., Griwsoldville, 203–5

Andersonville, Ga., 18

Apalachee River, 144

Appel, Charles A., 196

Arcadia plantation, 449

Argyle Island, Union operations, 406–7, 414–16, 419, 453, 467, 469, 471–73, 476, 478–79, 481, 484–85, 488–89, 502–3

Army of Georgia, 48n

Army of Tennessee, 5, 12, 462; reviewed by Davis, 7–8

Army of the Tennessee, 48n, 547

Arndt, Albert F.R., 202, 204–5, 206–7

Arnold, Peter K., 326

Arnold, Richard D., 280, 490, 509; Savannah occupation, 510; Savannah surrender, 496–97

Atkins, Smith D., 159, 288, 336

Atlanta Campaign, 34

Atlanta Medical Collage, 87

Atlanta, Ga., civilians expelled, 35; destruction, 60, 62, 67, 77–8, 85–8, 89; entertainments, 60

Audenreid, Joseph C., 440

Augusta and Savannah Railroad, 533

Augusta Daily Chronicle & Sentinel,
81, 95, 157, 168, 233, 353, 419, 454

Augusta Daily Constitutionalist, 95, 143,
511

Augusta Register, 279

Augusta Road, 355, 380, 383

Augusta, Ga., 9–10, 16, 416;
considered a target, 70, 188, 225;
defenses, 249–50

Babcock, Orville, 456–7

Baird, Absalom, 126, 292, 307–9, 319–20;
Waynesboro, 335–36, 342

Baker, Daniel B., 155–56

Baldwin, Frank D., 110–11

Baldwin, Oliver L., 196

Ball's Ferry, Ga., 218, 232, 255;
November 23 fight, 227–28;
November 25 fight, 251–54

Barber, Lucius W., 158

Barnard, George N., 358

Barnett, Nathan C., 17, 221

Barnum, Henry A., 495–96, 498, 499

Barr, Robert, 495

Basinger, Elizabeth, 499

Bay Street, 490, 504

Bear Creek Station, Ga., November 16
fight, 102

Beauregard, Pierre Gustave Toutant, 6,
113, 268–69, 479–80; coordinates
Sherman response, 103–4, 128–9,
143, 157, 231, 255–56, 301–2,
352–53, 359, 392–93, 419, 468–69;
considers Savannah expendable,
375–76, 391–92, 454, 468–69,
485–86; Davis meeting, 10–11;
described, 10; Hood relationship,
65–66, 143, 231; placed in overall
command of region, 11, 353;
post-Savannah strategy, 516;
proclamation, 128; reacts to Hood
plan, 11; reacts to Sherman torpedo
removal policy, 448; Savannah
visits, 468–69, 479–80, 485;
seeks reinforcements, 480; Wheeler
replacement considered, 256

Beaverdam Creek, 349

Beecher, Henry Ward, 220–21

Bennefield, Willis, 21–2

Berry, Carrie, 68, 86, 88

Bethany, Ga., 297

Beulah plantation, 184, 219

Big Sandy Creek, 205, 209

Billings, John D., 536

Bircher, William, 393–94

Birdsville, Ga., 309, 311

Black Creek, 366–67

Black, William, 289

Blair Jr., Frank P., 69, 148, 163, 231,
251, 280–81, 481–82

Bloodgood, Edward, 111

bloodhounds. *See* dogs

Blue Springs, Ga., 144

Booth, John, 435

Boston Post, 516

Boyd's Neck, 298

Boynton, Henry Van Ness, 33

Bradley, George S., 325

Bragg, Braxton, 6, 188–89, 455;
Augusta defense, 249–50, 268, 359;
regional defense, 228–9

bridges, destroyed/repaired, 93, 107,
144, 263, 277, 305, 312, 316, 342,
349, 350, 358; taken intact, 97.
See also pontoons

Brier Creek Bridge, 263, 342

Broad River, 298, 445

Brown, A. G., 507–8

Brown, Captain, 356

Brown, J. H., 431, 433

Brown, Joseph E, 510; abandons
Milledgeville, 150–51; addresses
Georgia legislature, 17, 113, 528–29;
claims is not incapacitated, 189;
disputes Confederate policies, 4;
rejects Sherman overtures, 37;
seeks furnishings returned, 368;
seeks reinforcements, 130

Brunner, John F., 417n

Bryan County Court House, 367, 374

Buck, Wilson S., 379

Buckhead Church, 287, 288, 319

Buckhead Creek, 287, 309, 316, 320,
322, 327; December 3 incident, 327

Buckhead, Ga., 144

Buell, George P., 448–49, 478

Buffalo Creek, 241, 244–45, 246, 248

Bull Street, 504

Bull, Rice C., 325

bummers, 188, 233, 265–6, 531, 536.
  See also foragers

Burge, Dolly Sumner Lunt, 15, 145–6

Burge, Sarah (Sadai), 15

Burton, Ga. (CRR No. 9 1/2), 293

Bussey, Jack, 215

Buttrill Family, 105–6, 115–17

Byers, Samuel H. M., 525–26

Byrne, Edmund, 347

Byrne, Garrett S., 220, 222, 261

Cameron, Ga., 332

Camp Lawton, Ga., 18–90, 81, 95–96,
  113, 130–31, 143–44, 158, 190,
  276, 358; liberation mission, 262–64;
  Union soldier impressions, 325–26

Camp Sumter, Ga., 18

Canoochee River, 358–59, 366–67

Carlin, William P., 162, 235, 531

Carmen, Ezra A., 133, 486; Argyle
  Island operations, 467–68, 471–73,
  478–79, 484–85, 488–89, 494, 502–3;
  Monteith Swamp fight, 377–80

Carswell, John W., 19, 287

Carswell, Reuben W., 178

Carswell, Sarah Ann Devine, 19, 287

Cartersville, Ga., 46, 59

Castle, George E., 439

casualties, Bear Creek Station, 102;
  December 7 action, 362; Fort
  McAllister, 439; Franklin, 300;
  Griswoldville, 214–5; Honey Hill,
  299; Nashville, 463; Reynolds
  plantation, 291; Sandersville, 258n;
  Savannah Campaign, 542–43;
  Waynesboro, 343

Catterson, Robert F., 210, 212

Cedar Creek, 182

Central of Georgia Railroad, 3, 14, 17–19,
  130, 158, 171, 190, 204, 223, 224,
  232–3, 250, 255, 259, 266, 293,
  296, 302, 309, 313, 317, 331, 405,
  407, 506, 533

Charleston and Savannah Railroad, 392,
  414

Charleston, S.C., 9, 189, 225, 280, 359,
  375, 391, 454, 485

Chatfield, Harvey S., 495

Chesnut, James, 12

Chesnut, Mary, 12–13

Cheves' Rice Mill, 408, 423, 425, 427,
  432, 434, 436–7, 438, 439–40, 447,
  455, 502, 503

Cheves, Langdon, 408

Chicago Tribune, 95, 516

Church of the Immaculate Conception, 87

Cincinnati Daily Commercial, 60, 95

City Exchange, 490, 492

Clarke, John G., 391, 451

Clay, Thomas Carolin, 480

Clifton Ferry, 317

Clinch, Duncan L., 395, 407

Clinch, Nicholas B., 437–38

Clinton, Ga., 21, 150, 151, 152, 156, 529;
  November 20 fight, 156–57

Cobb, Howell, 113, 128–9, 231;
  addresses Augusta audience, 11n;
  Davis meeting, 3–4; Macon defense,
  112, 194; plantation wrecked
  by Sherman, 186–7;
  seeks reinforcements, 84–5, 112

Coe, Albert L., 384

Cohen, Fanny, 20, 499

Cohen, Octavus, 20

Colerain plantation, 415

Colt, Mrs. Mary, 160

Columbia, S.C., 12

Columbus, Ga., 36

Combahee River, 516

Compton, John, 431, 435

Confederate Powder Magazine
  (Savannah), 497

Confederate Powder Works (Augusta),
  250, 545–56

Connolly, James A., 126, 146–7, 274–75,
  284, 291–92, 308–9, 319–20,
  328–29, 335–36, 344, 348, 447,
  482–83; Ebenezer Creek, 382;
  Waynesboro, 334–36, 344

Conyers, Ga., 109–10, 118, 126

Cook and Brother Armory, 195

Cook, Ferdinand W.C., 195, 200, 202, 203, 210, 454

Cook, William C., 338

Cooper, John, 235

Corse, John M., 156, 174, 282, 366, 374

Costley's Mill, Ga., 109

Covington, Ga., 14, 127, 134

Cowart's Bridge, 303

Crew, Charles C., 165

Cuyler plantation, December 9 fight, 384

Cuyler, Richard R., 386, 407, 417

Dahlgren, John A., 411–12, 432, 442, 443, 490, 493, 498, 500–501; Sherman relationship, 446–47, 455–56, 482

D'Alvigny, Peter Paul, 87

Dandelion (tugboat), 410, 423–4, 427, 430, 432, 438, 442, 455, 459

Darien Road, 385

Davies, Y. R., 435

Davis, Jefferson (Confederate president), 156, 466, 473; advises Georgians, 128–29, 188–89, 229; Augusta visit, 10–11; Beauregard appointment, 10–11; Bragg temporary appointment, 188–89, 249, 268; Cobb meeting, 3–4; Columbia visit, 11–2; Confederate Congress address, 13; defensive scheme failure, 540–2; effigy hung, 156; Hardee meetings, 8, 9–10; Hood meeting, 5–8, Macon visit, 3–5; Montgomery visit, 8–9; opinions of Beauregard, 10; Palmetto visit, 5–8; reacts to Hood's plans, 6, 7, 65; reassigns Hardee, 8; relaxes militia laws, 249–50; reviews Army of Tennessee, 7–8; Taylor meeting, 9

Davis, Jefferson C. (Union general), 142, 186, 285, 292, 303, 383; defends actions, 519–20; racial incidents, 163, 327, 380–3; racial prejudice, 327, 381

Davis, Mrs. William D., 160

Davisboro, Ga. (CRR No. 12), 251, 270, 280, 283

Dayton, Lewis F., 373, 439, 502

Decatur Road, 75, 89

Decatur, Ga., 82, 96–97

DeGress, Francis, 417n

Denham's Tanyard and Leather Factory, 160, 169

Dennis Station, Ga., 176, 184

Dillon's Bridge, 374, 389

dogs, 20, 98, 107

Downey, William A., 284

Downs, George "Wait," 339

Drake, Milly, 352

Dublin, Ga., 232, 247

Duncan, William, 306, 442; mission to contact fleet, 390–91, 401–2, 410–12

Dunlap's Hill. *See* Macon, Ga.

Dunwoody, H. H. C., 58

Early, Jubal, 293

East Point, Ga., November 15 fight, 79

Eatonton Factory, 152, 161

Eatonton, Ga., 18, 20, 21, 171, 381

Ebenezer Church, 370

Ebenezer Creek, 363, 370; December 8 fight, 361–62; December 9 incident, 380–83

Eden, Ga. (Bryan County Court House), 367

Eden, Ga. (CRR No. 2), 323, 359, 367, 372

Elkins, Mrs., 365

Engle, Charles, 498

Este, George P., 275

Estes, Llewellyn G., 263–4, 278, 443

Evans, Beverly D., 201, wounded, 212

Evans, William, 215

Ewing, Charles, 127, 246, 471

Ewing, Thomas, 24

Fair, Azora (Zora) M., 15, 137

Fallis, Leroy S., 276, 287, 288, 290, 292

Farrar farm, 20, 171

fascines, 478

Felton, Rebeca, 16

Fenn's Bridge, 270, 274–75

Ferguson, Samuel W., 243, 254, 409, 491

Fernandina, U.S.S., 443

Firefly (steamer), 496

Fisher, George A., 423–24, 424, 425–26, 430, 432, 438, 442–43

Fisher, William E., 465

Flag, U.S.S., 410

foragers, ammunition abuse, 103, 121, 162–3, 310–11; casualties, 91, 98, 114, 133–4, 146, 175, 235–6, 248, 303, 311, 543; civilian abuse, 126, 193, 277–8, 283, 297, 310; Confederate accounts, 85, 243–4, 294, 375; confiscation, 132; importance, 539; Liberty County, 449–51, 482; payment in Confederate script, 221; regular details, 101, 110–11, 234; Union accounts, 98, 101, 107–8, 110–11, 114, 124, 126, 133, 141, 145, 146, 160, 162, 171–72, 174–75, 176, 183, 219, 234, 247–48, 259, 271, 284, 297, 310–11, 312–13, 318–19, 332, 349, 355–56, 364, 373, 392–94, 470, 477, 500. *See also* bummers

Force, Manning F., 79, 107, 331

Forrest, Nathan Bedford, 38, 461, 462

Forsyth Park, 19

Forsyth, Ga., 115, 125

Fort Argyle, 374

Fort Jackson, 496, 499–500, 513

Fort McAllister, 376–77, 390, 397, 402, 408, 445, 455, 471, 502; December 13 assault, 421–39; torpedo removal, 448

Foster, John G., Sherman relationship, 444–47, 476, 480–81, 486–87

Franklin, Benjamin, 57

Franklin, Tenn., November 30 battle, 300–301

Frobel, B.W., 451

Fultz, William S., 93

Galt, Laura Talbot, 537

galvanized Confederates/Rebels, 19, 250

Garrett family, 126

Gaylesville, Ala., 41

Geary, John W., 125, 133, 140, 144, 154, 159–60, 169, 270, 412, 420, 490, 494, 496, 498; accepts Savannah surrender, 496–97; Savannah occupation, 501, 509–10

Genesis Point, 376, 418, 424

Georgia State Legislature, 81, 95, 129–30

Georgia Military Institute, 151, 217

Georgia Railroad, 14–16, 133, 144, 232–33, 533

Georgia State troops, Home Guard/Local Defense (Athens and Augusta Battalions, 195, 473), (Ashley Dragoons, 241), (Hazzard's Scouts, 353), (Foreign Battalion, 452–53, 469, 473), (Penal Battalion, 130, 151, 219); Militia (7th Regiment, 214–15), (29th Battalion Cavalry, 449); Reserves (1st Regiment, 493); State Line (1st and 2nd Regiments, 197, 201, 208, 209, 210)

Georgia troops, artillery (14th Light, 197); infantry (3rd Regiment, 528), (55th Regiment, 473)

Georgia, C.S.S., 480, 496

Gilberg, Jacob A., 288

Gildersleeve, Henry A., 394–5

Gilmer, J. F., 533

Goodman, Wiley, 115

Gordon, Ga. (CRR No. 17), 155, 156, 161, 165, 171, 173, 174, 178, 179, 190, 191, 196, 201

Grant, Ulysses S., 23, 34; considers Sherman proposals, 40–46; Nashville battle management, 461–63, 475; Sherman relationship, 40, 475, 544; strategic thinking, 457, 459–61

Gray, Reverend, 127

Greaves, Henry, 203

Grecian, Joseph, 367

Green, Anna Maria, 17, 161, 243

Green, Charles, 505

Green, Thomas F., 17

Greensboro, Ga., 160

Griffin, Ga., 83, 84, 87, 104, 112–13, 115

Griswold, Samuel, 158, 202

Griswoldville, Ga. (CRR No. 18), described, 158–9; destruction, 159; November 22 battle, 193–215

Groce, John H., 429
Gumm Creek, 237, 245
Guyton, Ga. (CRR No. 3), 358, 365

Halleck, Henry W., 41, 44, 46, 269,
    298, 460–61, 518
Hamilton, William D., 338
Hamrick, W. F., 389
Hanleiter, Cornelius R., 488
Hardee, William J., 6, 128, 165, 247,
    273, 279, 353; command decisions,
    178–79; Davis meetings, 6, 9–10;
    fails to burn Savannah cotton, 506;
    Macon defense, 142–43, 151, 168,
    174, 178–79; opinion of Hood, 6–7;
    Savannah defense, 143, 231–32,
    250–51, 253–54, 255, 302, 323,
    368, 371, 375–77, 391–92, 409, 414,
    419, 451, 454, 468–69, 473–75,
    485–86, 487; Savannah evacuation,
    492; seeks Sherman protection for
    family, 517
Hardman, Lyman, 435
Harpath River, 300
Harris, Joel Chandler, 21, 170, 171–72
Harris, Judge, 136
Harrison, Thomas H., 94
Hartridge, Alfred L., 192, 216–17, 227,
    229–30, 241
Harvest Moon, U.S.S., 446, 447, 455,
    482, 486, 493, 498, 500–501
Harvey's Creek, 424
Hatch, John P., 444
Haughawut, Wilbur F., 380
Hawley, William, 184, 406–7, 448–49,
    453
Hayes, Edward M., 263–64
Hazen, William B., 58, 193, 223–24,
    373–74, 463; Fort McAllister
    operation, 418–9, 421–43
Hazzard, Richard C., 437
Hebron, Ga., 244
Heidt, Reverend, 373
Hell Gate, 430
Henly, D. H., 215
Henry, Joseph, 57
Hickenlooper, Andrew, 463
High, Emma, 15, 141, 154

Hill, Benjamin H., proclamation, 128
Hill, Joshua, 145
Hillsboro, Ga., 16–17, 139, 148, 149,
    151, 155, 156, 174
Hilton Head, S.C., 269, 481, 482, 490
Hinesville, Ga., 465, 477
Hinkley, Julian, 468
Hitchcock, Henry M., 58, 63–64,
    87–88, 90–91, 99–100, 118, 127,
    136–37, 142, 147–48, 162–63, 171,
    173, 176–77, 186, 187–88, 218,
    225, 236–37, 244, 247, 260, 275,
    280–81, 293, 294–95, 305–6, 314,
    320–21, 323, 326, 329–30, 351,
    357–58, 365, 372–73, 374–75, 387,
    407–8, 412, 416, 456, 487, 490, 504;
    campaign assessment, 527; considers
    Sherman's point of view, 63–4,
    78, 153, 237, 246, 273–74;
    December 10 incident, 398–99;
    Millen, 350–51; misses observing
    Fort McAllister attack, 423, 447, 455;
    Sandersville, 257–58, 259, 261;
    Sherman and African-Americans, 518;
    torpedoes, 387–89
Hoke, Robert F., 480
Holt family, 310
Honey Hill, S.C., November 30 battle,
    298–300, 302, 444
Hood, Arthur, 449
Hood, John B., 94, 460; advises
    Wheeler, 104, 129; argues with
    Sherman, 35–6; Beauregard
    relationship, 10–11, 63, 65–66, 143,
    231, 256; Davis meeting, 5–8;
    described, 5; Franklin battle, 300;
    Nashville battle, 461–63; opinion
    of Hardee, 6; plan to combat
    Sherman, 7; post-Atlanta campaign,
    41–45, 66, 300–301
Horner, J. H., 435
Horse Creek, 333
hounds. *See* dogs
Houtz, John W., 249
Howard, Charles H., 229, 248
Howard, Frances Thomas, 20, 504, 506–7
Howard, Oliver Otis, 48–49, 69, 101,
    149, 175, 188, 212, 225, 233, 264,

282, 293, 306, 321–22, 352, 366, 374, 443, 463, 502, 520, 528; command decisions, 115, 121, 125, 132–33, 138–39, 155, 164, 174, 177, 181, 196, 229, 230–31, 232, 251, 252, 358, 408
Hubert, Charles F., 270
Huffine, L. C., 434
Hughes, Samuel T., 119
Humes, William Y. C., 340
Hunt, Alexander, 496, 498
Hunter, Morton C., 292, 335
Hurricane plantation, 186–87
Hutchings, Richard, 152
Hutchinson Island, 420, 476, 485, 506

Ida (steamer), December 10 capture, 394–95
Ihly, Jennie, 19
Illinois troops: artillery (1st Artillery, Battery H, 417n), (2nd Artillery, Battery I, 384); cavalry (10th Regiment, 390); infantry (10th Regiment, 324, 351), (12th Regiment, 253), (20th Regiment, 124, 163), (32nd Regiment, 138), (34th Regiment, 146, 248, 285), (40th Regiment, 202), (48th Regiment, 429, 434, 439), (50th Regiment, 174, 193, 253, 267, 270, 296, 332, 488, 512, 514), (55th Regiment, 114, 264, 332, 432, 470), (63rd Regiment, 123, 124, 324, 396, 514), (64th Regiment, 83, 156, 441, 482), (66th Regiment, 312, 385), (83rd Regiment, 367), (85th Regiment, 470), (86th Regiment, 176, 248, 302–3, 395), (90th Regiment, 429, 437), (93rd Regiment, 101, 107, 123, 192, 488), (101st Regiment, 245, 325), (102nd Regiment, 140, 145, 176, 242, 272), (103rd Regiment, 198, 202–3, 208, 209, 212, 213, 304, 332, 352), (104th Regiment, 235, 303, 453), (105th Regiment, 91, 272), (111th Regiment, 426, 430, 436, 437, 439), (116th Regiment, 252, 429, 430, 435, 436),

(129th Regiment, 221, 311, 349, 394, 451); mounted infantry (7th Regiment, 386), (9th Regiment, 119, 257, 394–95), (16th Regiment, 257, 383), (92nd Regiment, 102, 150, 165–67, 277, 288–89, 335–39)
Indian Springs, Ga., 107, 125, 131
Indiana troops: cavalry (8th Regiment, 84, 94, 108, 276, 287, 288, 290, 292, 340–41, 417); engineers (58th Regiment, 56, 77, 120–21, 127, 135–36, 245, 246, 283–84, 327, 349, 363, 370–71, 448, 478, 502, 506); infantry (22nd Regiment, 470), (25th Regiment, 469), (48th Regiment, 101, 179, 304), (59th Regiment, 107, 179, 373); (66th Indiana, 267), (70th Regiment, 171), (74th Regiment, 320), (75th Regiment, 96, 134, 183, 236, 356, 470, 477–78), (83rd Regiment, 482), (85th Regiment, 141, 370), (87th Regiment, 363), (88th Regiment, 311), (97th Regiment, 179, 198, 202, 209), (100th Regiment, 80, 131, 202, 209, 212–14, 396, 531), (101st Regiment, 120, 371)
Indianapolis Journal, 45
Ingraham, David P., 335
Iowa troops: infantry (2nd Regiment, 366), (4th Regiment, 365), (5th Regiment, 525), (6th Regiment, 202, 207, 495), (7th Regiment, 365, 483), (9th Regiment, 179, 374, 488), (10th Regiment, 124, 192), (11th Regiment, 93, 113–14, 179–80, 190, 267), (25th Regiment, 179, 469), (31st Regiment, 79)
Irwinton, Ga., 223, 252–53
Isondiga, C.S.S., 496
Izard's plantation, 420, 484, 486

Jackson's Ferry, Ga., 229, 230–31, 232
Jackson, Ga., 105; November 17 fight, 114–15
Jackson, Nathaniel J., 377–9
Jackson, Oscar L., 315–16
Jacksonboro, Ga., 349

Jasper County, Ga., 16, 115
Jasper Springs, 512
Jenks' Bridge, 359, 365–66, 373, 374
Jerry (slave), 319
Johnson, Bushrod R., 480
Johnson, Herschel V., 283
Johnston, Joseph E., 5, 34, 181
Jones Sr., Charles Colcock, 449
Jones, Joseph B. (plantation), 311, 314
Jones, Mary Jones, 449–50
Jones, Samuel, 280, 391, 454, 468
Jones, Theodore, 429, 430, 433
Jones, Wells S., 426, 429–30
Jonesboro, Ga., 63–64, 94; November 15 fight, 83–84
Jordan, Lee, 144, 154
Jordan, Reverend, 184
Jordan, Thomas J., 341

Kelly, Rufus, 180
Kentucky troops (C.S.): mounted infantry (Orphan Brigade, 80, 84, 93, 101, 217), (4th Regiment, 217)
Kentucky troops (U.S.): cavalry (2nd Regiment, 94, 248–49, 276, 340–41), (3rd Regiment, 94, 164, 340), (5th Regiment, 84, 108, 196, 198, 309, 340, 342)
Kerr, Charles D., 383
Kilbourne, Julius B., 263
Kilkenny Bluff, 443
Kilpatrick, Hugh Judson, 63, 165, 222, 249, 346, 356–57, 421; ambushed, 150, 286–87; campaign thoughts, 70, 164, 526; cavalry reviewed by Sherman, 64, 218, 515; command decisions, 152, 177, 286, 320; described, 348; discipline, 103; diversionary operations, 115, 125, 164, 226–27, 307–9, 356; Fort McAllister, 408–9, 418, 424, 443–44; Griswoldville, 177–78; Liberty County, 449–51; loses hat to enemy, 286–87, 291; Lovejoy's Station fight, 94; Macon attack, 166–68; Millen rescue mission, 226–27, 262–63, 278; personal combat, 286, 339; picked by

Sherman, 50; praised by Sherman, 314, 528; Reynolds's plantation fight, 287–91; seeks permission for terror retaliation, 226, 314–15; Waynesboro fight, 314, 334–44
King's Bridge, 376, 384–85, 390, 397, 408, 417, 421–22, 445, 446, 463, 465, 470, 481–82
King, Davis (Spence), 101
King, T. G., 215
Kingston, Ga., 59
Kirby, Colonel, 253

"L.F.J.," 258, 261, 273
Ladd, Frederick S., 159, 362
Lamar, Caro, 20, 505
Langford, William Bedford, 212
Langley, James W., 297
Lawson, P. A., 112
Le Sage, John B., 245
Ledyard, Edwin, 399–400
Lee's Mill, Ga., 100
Lee, Custis, 12–13
Lee, Robert E., 3, 10, 95, 189, 330, 443, 457, 480, 528
Liberty County, Union foraging, 449–51, 482
Lincoln, Abraham, 40–41, 140, 359–60, 467, 508, 521
Lithonia, Ga., 21, 96, 97, 99–100, 108, 109
Little Ogeechee River, 423–24, 430, 480
Little Ohoopee River, 282
Little River, 161n, 184
live oaks, 374, 423, 448, 493
Lockhart, William James, 282
Lockner Creek, 372; December 9 incident, 380–83
Locust Grove, Ga., 107
Logan, John A., 462
Lonergan, Jonathan, 317
Long Bridge, 246
Louisiana Military Seminary, 25
Louisiana troops: band (20th Regiment, 7).
Louisville, Ga., 270, 273, 275, 280, 283, 291, 302, 303, 529, 539; destruction of, 284–85, 297

Lovejoy's Station, Ga., 6, 84; November 16 fight, 94
Lufburrow, Matthew, 351
Lumpkin's Station, Ga., 334
Lunt, Dolly Sumner. *See* Burge, Dolly Sumner Lunt

Macon and Western Railroad, 14, 16, 80, 84, 108
Macon Daily Telegraph, 112, 129, 215
Macon, C.S.S., 371, 414–16
Macon, Ga., 3–5, 9, 16, 95, 103, 112, 142, 157, 188; Cobb defense, 84–85, 112, 194; Hardee defense, 142–43, 178–79; November 20 fight (Dunlap's Hill), 164–68; Sherman bypasses, 70; Taylor defense, 193–94, 198, 199
Madison, Ga., 15–16, 112, 140–41, 144, 145, 154–55
Maguire, Thomas, 111
Mallard, Robert Quarterman, 450
Mallory, Mr., 314
Mallory, Rollin, 158
Manley, Emma, 105
Mann, James N., wounded, 211
March to the Sea, Altamaha River operation, 463, 469–70, 477, 482; animal incidents, 132, 155–56, 271, 327, 356, 364; animal requisition, 54, 357–58; authorized destruction, 53, 85, 92, 136–37, 144, 154, 155, 157, 160–61, 169, 186, 220, 253, 260, 271, 349–50, 385, 529–30, 532–33, 539–40; campaign assessments, 526–28; cattle herd, 51–52, 111, 127, 156, 267, 297, 412–13; civilian experiences, 82, 97, 99, 105–6, 109, 115–17, 126, 131, 140, 141, 145, 149, 171, 219, 243, 248, 258–60, 273, 287, 294, 304–5, 310, 312, 355, 365; communication by rocket, 149; cotton destroyed, 101, 108, 110, 114, 140, 145, 154, 160–61, 174, 219, 253, 270; cotton not destroyed, 225; forage liberally, 52–53, 108, 136–37; grass fires, 350;
Hinesville operation, 465, 470, 477; maps, 56, 149, 229, 272, 418; march discipline, 79, 131, 351; marching orders, 50–52, 100, 102, 117, 163, 223–24; marching pace, 79, 82, 83, 91–92, 97, 101, 111, 117, 132–33, 138, 154, 156, 163, 169–71, 172, 174, 175, 251, 267, 282, 295–96, 312, 327, 333, 348–50, 363–64, 369–70; morale/mail, 465–66, 470; obstructed roads, 349, 355, 362, 364, 367, 372; oysters, 513; popular impressions, 535–38; pioneers, 55–56, 120, 223, 226, 283, 295, 312, 333, 349, 351, 355, 367, 370, 371, 374, 421, 481, 532; plan precedents and orders, 47–57; rape, 243; ration scarcity, 406, 412–13, 441, 448, 452, 465; rice making by soldiers, 452; straggling/stragglers, 82, 88, 117, 142, 147, 159–60, 173, 186, 254, 283, 334; swamps, 154, 190, 217, 224, 244, 246, 249, 251, 267, 283, 284, 285, 295, 296, 304, 312, 317, 333, 339, 347, 349, 355–56, 363, 364, 366, 378–80, 386, 394, 397–98; torpedoes, 129, 387–88, 426, 428, 434–35, 448, 456; total war designation, 534–38; unauthorized destruction, 82, 98–99, 109, 140, 176, 310, 364; use of African-Americans, 54–55, 531–32; wagon train, 50–51, 77, 79, 83, 90, 91, 97, 100–102, 107, 117, 121, 138–39, 149, 154, 170–71, 173, 174, 175, 176, 179–80, 193, 219, 226, 234, 270, 332–33, 349, 358, 363, 373; weather planning, 57–58; wing commanders, 48–49
"Marching Through Georgia" (song), 536–38
Marietta, Ga., 60
Markland, A. H., 467
Marshall, Matt, 171
Martin, James, 79
Martin, James S., 430, 438

Massachusetts troops: band (33rd
Regiment, 88); infantry (2nd
Regiment, 92, 261, 325, 380, 406,
453, 468, 484–85), (33rd Regiment,
92), (54th Colored Regiment, 299)

Massey, R. J., 178, 236

Maybank plantation, 449

McAdoo, William G., 130

McAllister, Joseph L., 417, 423

McCaskey, William S., 500

McCauley, C. M. T., 380

McClintock, James M., 132, 425, 432, 438

McClure, A. K., 360

McCoy, James, 118

McDonough, Ga., 100

McKinley, Guy, 219

McKinley, William, 184, 219

McLaws, Lafayette, 143, 328, 330–31,
365, 400, 493

McLeans, J. C., 215

McSweeny, Captain, 358

Meade, George Gordon, 49

Medway River, 443

Mendel, W. H., 493

Mercer, Hugh W., 400

Merritt, Nehemiah, 440

Michigan troops: artillery (1st Artillery,
Battery B, 202, 204–5); cavalry (9th
Regiment, 159, 286, 335, 336–37,
362); engineers and mechanics (1st
Regiment, 56, 92, 108, 246, 316, 420,
463); infantry (19th Regiment, 110,
175, 326, 350), (21st Regiment, 441)

Middleton house, 426, 429, 440, 443

Midway Church, 469, 477

Mill Creek, 332, 367

Milledgeville, Ga., 17–18, 112, 113, 228,
161; destruction of, 219, 220–23,
235, 242; Confederate reoccupation,
243–44, 254; evacuation, 129–30;
mock legislative session, 222–23;
Union occupation, 181–85, 220–23,
224–27, 233–36

Milledgeville Hotel, 184

Millen, Ga. (CRR No. 8), 18–19, 251,
275, 293; destruction, 326; Union
occupation, 315–16

Miller, Jerry J., 93

Miller, John A., 160

Mills, Thomas J., 426

Minnesota troops: artillery (Light
Artillery, 1st Battery, 68, 101, 224,
351, 414, 417n); infantry (2nd
Regiment, 111, 183, 235, 382),
(4th Regiment, 123, 138, 405–6)

Missouri troops: artillery (1st Artillery,
385); engineers (1st Regiment, 56,
79–80, 123, 131, 155–56, 253, 264,
317, 366, 408, 421); infantry (6th
Regiment, 429), (23rd Regiment,
284), mounted infantry (29th
Regiment, 84, 115, 122)

Mobile, Ala., 34, 191, 301

Monteith Swamp, December 9 fight,
377–80

Montevideo plantation, 449

Montgomery, Ala., 8–9, 352

Monticello, Ga., 132, 139, 148–49

Moore, John, 100

Moore, Joseph, 245, 283

Morgan, James D., 186, 285

Morse, W. H., 414–15

Mountain Springs Church, 196

Mower, Joseph A., 386, 463, 469

Moye, J. C., 281

Murder Creek, 172, 176–77

Murray, Eli H., 288, 340–42

National Tribune, 273n

Nashville, Tenn., December 15–16 battle,
461–63

Neal, John, 69

Nelson, George, 439

Nemaha (revenue cutter), 444

Nesbit, Dr., 176

New Hope Church, 280

New Jersey troops: infantry (13th
Regiment, 98, 171, 220, 257, 484),
(35th Regiment, 350)

New York Herald, 33, 76–77, 109, 134,
136, 140, 142, 150, 153, 164, 171,
286, 336, 339

New York Post, 306

New York Times, 34, 45

New York troops: artillery (1st Artillery,
415–16, 479); infantry (17th Regiment,

234–15, 257, 465), (102nd Regiment, 495, 496, 498), (107th Regiment, 133–34, 184, 485), (123rd Regiment, 325, 377–78, 406, 532), (134th Regiment, 159–60, 420), (137th Regiment, 282, 498), (149th Regiment, 111, 183–84), (150th Regiment, 133, 394–95, 485)

Newborn, Ga., 142, 147, 152

Nichols, George, 305, 306, 439, 440; torpedoes, 388

North Carolina troops, infantry (Baker's Brigade, 493), (10th Battalion, 380)

Norton, Samuel E., 338, 342, 347

Oakey, Daniel, 51

Ocmulgee River, 115, 116, 122, 129, 131, 132, 138–39, 142, 148–49, 155–56, 164

Oconee, Ga. (CRR No. 14), 267

Oconee River, 140, 144, 154, 159–60, 184, 189, 219, 233, 235, 254, 267; defense, 143, 165, 180, 191–92, 216–18, 219–20, 224, 227–28, 229–32, 241, 251–55, 255–56, 264–65

Ogeechee Creek, 323, 330, 350–52

Ogeechee River, 273, 309, 312, 313, 315, 316, 317, 318, 322, 323, 324, 331–2, 347, 352, 354, 358–59, 364, 365, 374, 376, 384, 389, 390, 397, 401–2, 408, 417, 418, 445, 455, 465, 475, 482, 501. *See also* Fort McAllister, December 13 assault

Ogeechee Shoals, 248–49

Ohio troops: cavalry (5th Regiment, 288, 339, 342), (9th Regiment, 336–37, 362), (10th Regiment, 79, 102, 165–68, 336–38, 342); infantry (5th Regiment, 75, 176), (21st Regiment, 311), (29th Regiment, 133, 245, 334, 470, 488, 499), (30th Regiment, 179, 264, 429, 434, 435), (31st Regiment, 134), (32nd Regiment, 219, 224, 316), (38th Regiment, 441), (39th Regiment, 413, 441), (43rd Regiment, 316), (46th Regiment, 198, 202), (47th Regiment, 193, 267, 317, 385, 426, 431, 436, 437, 439, 470), (52nd Regiment, 298), (53rd Regiment, 324), (54th Regiment, 426), (57th Regiment, 252), (61st Regiment, 175, 379), (63rd Regiment, 315–16, 326, 405), (66th Regiment, 512), (68th Regiment, 331, 452), (70th Regiment, 332, 429, 431, 435, 436, 437, 439), (74th Regiment, 441), (81st Regiment, 253, 267, 385), (89th Regiment, 284), (94th Regiment, 97), (105th Regiment, 134, 135, 284, 448, 470, 532), (113th Regiment, 146, 235, 257)

Old Bay, 332

Old Savannah Road, 316

Oliver, Ga. (CRR No. 4 1/2), 323; December 4 probe, 330–31

Oliver, John M., 366–67, 384–85, 429

Olmsted, Frederick Law, 21

Opelika, Ga., 8

O'Reilly, Thomas, 86

Orme, Mrs. Richard McAllister, 18, 220–21

Ossabaw Sound, 423, 442, 444, 445, 446, 455, 471, 498, 501

Osterhaus, Peter J., 69, 102, 115, 157; Ball's Ferry fight, 252–53; described, 195–96; Griswoldville fight, 195–201, 212

Oxford, Ga., 15, 134, 137

Palmetto, Ga., 5–8

Parks Mill, 154, 159–60

Parry, Augustus C., 436

Pennsylvania troops: artillery (Battery E, 500); cavalry (9th Regiment, 94, 150, 196, 198, 249, 340–41, 449); infantry (28th Regiment, 133, 326), (79th Regiment, 311, 452), (111th Regiment, 92, 140), (147th Regiment, 441, 470, 470, 514)

Pennyworth Island, 485

Philadelphia Inquirer, 262, 286, 517

Philadelphia, U.S.S., 411

Philips, Henry L., 431

Philips, Pleasant J., 197, 199, 200, 202–3, 203–4, 205–6, 208–9, 210–11, 213–15

Phillips Academy, 221

pioneers. *See* March to the Sea

Pitts Chapel, 179

Pitts, John W., 147

Planter's Factory, 115, 122, 129; described, 124–25; destroyed, 149–50, 155

Plumb, William, 207

Poe, Orlando M., 511, 538; Atlanta destruction, 60, 62, 67, 77, 86; Buffalo Creek, 244–47; described, 55–57; Eatonton Factory destruction, 161

pontoons, 43, 55–56, 120–21, 123, 127, 131, 135–36, 139, 184, 193, 245–47, 264–65, 283, 303, 305, 317, 327, 365–66, 370–71, 383–84, 417, 468–69, 479–80, 485–86, 497; described, 120–21; importance, 538. See also *bridges*

Pooler, Ga. (CRR No. 1), 331, 389

Port Royal, S.C., 231, 410–11, 466

Post, S. V. W., 88

Potter, John, 325

Potts, Benjamin F., 219, 481

Price, John M., 483–84

Prior, Felix W., 368

prisoners, 35–36, 148–49, 157, 236, 395–96, 489–90

Puckett, Aunt Winnie, 109

Pulaski House, 504

Pulaski Monument, 512

Quillin, Martha Amada, 98–99

Quimby, George W., 442; mission to contact fleet, 390–91, 401–2, 410–12

Quincy Daily Whig & Republican, 516

railroads, destruction, 92, 100, 108, 119, 125, 133, 141, 144, 168, 171, 191, 192, 220, 223, 251–52, 259, 264, 270, 271, 278, 281, 296–97, 303, 310, 316, 324, 384–85, 394, 449, 463, 469–70, 477, 482, 532–33; intelligence gathering, 232–33;

Sherman's orders, 226; trains captured, 385–86, 506

Rains, George Washington, 250

rape. *See* March to the Sea

Red Legs (tugboat), 501–3

Reese, Chauncey B., 397, 417

Reese, Louise, 17, 149, 174–75

Reese, Tabitha, 17

Reid, George W., 133–34

Resolute, C.S.S., 414–16, 448–49, 476, 479

Reynolds plantation, November 28 fight, 287–91

Reynolds, J. A., 500

Rice, Elliott W., 365–66

Riceboro, Ga., 477

Richmond, Va., 3, 5, 13, 67, 94–95, 228–29, 268, 353–54

Richmond Dispatch, 94

Richmond Examiner, 67, 228–29

Richmond Sentinel, 228, 353

Richmond Whig, 229

Robertson, Felix H., 288

Robinson, James S., 378

Robinson, Mrs. Philip, 160

Rocky Comfort Creek, 284

Rocky Creek, 294, 309, 313; December 2 fight, 319–20

Roe, Lewis F., 270

Rome, Ga., 59

Romney Marsh, 501

Rose Dhu Island Battery, 424, 442

Rosemary Creek, 327

Ross, Levi, 302–3

Rough and Ready, Ga., November 15 fight, 80

Rutledge, Ga., 133

Salkehatchie River, 516

Sample, Sue, 304–5, 312–13

Sampson, C.S.S., 414–16

Sandersville, Ga., 241, 259–62, 529, 539; November 25 fight, 247; November 26 fight, 256–59

Savannah and Gulf Railroad, 384–5, 449, 463, 482, 506, 533

Savannah Campaign, development and evolution, 33–58

Savannah, C.S.S., 480, 496, 500, 503
Savannah Morning News, 499
Savannah-Ogeechee Canal, 385, 390;
    December 9 fight, 374
Savannah Republican, 499
Savannah River, 16, 354–55, 356, 359,
    361, 370, 371, 374, 391–92, 394–95,
    400, 406, 407, 419, 441, 453–54, 476
Savannah, Ga., 19–20, 280, 351, 353,
    409; Beauregard considers
    expendable, 375, 454–55;
    defenses, 65, 143, 365, 377, 400, 409;
    evacuation, 487–97; evacuation
    planning, 468–69, 479–80, 485–86;
    evacuation pontoon, 486, 494, 497–8;
    Hardee surrender response, 473–75;
    material captured, 506; Sherman
    surrender demand, 471–72; siege
    conditions, 405, 478, 489–90;
    Southern response to surrender, 511;
    surrendered, 496–7; threatened, 65;
    Union occupation, 498–521; Union
    siege operations, 405–7, 412–14,
    420–21, 448–49, 452–53, 463–65,
    470–71, 478, 483–84, 490–91
Savannah River Squadron, 480, 491, 496
Scarboro (CRR No. 7), 313, 317, 322,
    323, 324, 331
Schofield, John M., 300
Scott, Mrs., 118
Screven's Ferry, 503
Scudder, Jotham, 282
Scull's Creek, 317
Sebastopol, Ga. (CRR No. 10), 255,
    302, 303
Seddon, James, 280
Selfridge, James L., 378–80
Shady Dale, Ga., 142, 153, 162
Sherfy, William H., 426
Sherman, Charles Celestine, 518
Sherman, Ellen Ewing, 24, 25, 466, 518
Sherman, William Ewing (Willy), 23–24,
    518
Sherman, William Tecumseh: African-
    American interaction, 99–100, 118,
    136, 173, 186–7, 320–21, 518–21;
    antipathy toward England, 517–18;
    Atlanta, 69, 77–8, 87–8, 90–91;

briefs soldiers on campaign, 71; called
    insane, 25; campaign assessment,
    547–8; campaign planning, 538–40;
    cavalry management, 275–76;
    civilian interaction, 147–78, 176–77,
    237, 248, 261–62, 373; collective
    responsibility, 29, 226, 246;
    command decisions, 186, 225–26,
    262, 292–93, 307–9, 314–15, 321–22,
    323, 330, 351–52, 357–58, 365,
    408, 418–19, 442–43, 445–47, 456,
    466, 471, 475–77, 480–85, 544–46;
    command style, 118–19; considers
    options, 99, 142, 185–86, 225–26;
    Dahlgren relationship, 446–47,
    455–56, 482; death of sons, 23–24,
    518; December 10 incident, 398–99;
    described, 25–26, 295, 328; destiny,
    31; expels Atlanta civilians, 35;
    fears social disruption, 29–30;
    forage liberally incident, 136–37;
    foraging (approves), 41, 43, 147;
    foraging (disapproves), 27; Fort
    McAllister, 397, 407, 417, 421–39;
    Foster relationship, 444–47, 476,
    480–81, 486–87; free press, 30,
    274, 373; Georgia political
    machinations, 37; Grant relationship,
    40, 447, 456–61, 475, 544; hard war,
    31; idealized vision of America,
    28–29; Kilpatrick relationship,
    226–27, 314, 358, 528; leadership
    qualities, 26–27; learns of Savannah
    surrender, 502; limits POW
    exchange, 35–36; Louisiana Military
    Seminary, 25; march orders, 48–55,
    77–8, 225–6; March to the Sea
    authorship, 33–34; *Memoirs*, 33, 87,
    99, 188n, 223, 272, 331, 460, 463,
    475, 487, 536, 546; Meridian
    Campaign, 47; military expertise,
    26–28; Milledgeville occupation,
    218, 224–27, 236; newspaper praise,
    516–17; perpetual motion, 26;
    personality, 24–32, 90–91, 273–74,
    466; philosophy of war, 27–8;
    political generals, 48; postage stamp,
    536; proposes to capture Augusta, 37;

Sherman, William Tecumseh *(cont.)*:
    proposes to capture Columbus, 36;
    proposes to capture Macon, 37;
    proposes Savannah campaign, 38–46;
    racial prejudices, 30–31, 518–21;
    removes Augusta from target list,
    225–26; removes Macon from target
    list, 70; reviews troops, 514–15;
    Sandersville, 257–8, 261–62;
    Savannah occupation, 504–5, 507–8,
    511, 514–15; soldier sightings, 87,
    99, 109, 137, 222, 259, 293–94,
    328, 330, 388, 514–15; southern
    animosity, 536–37; southern guilt,
    29, 32; Special Field Orders No. 15,
    521; Special Field Orders No. 120,
    48–55, 373; storm metaphors,
    31–32; supremacy of law, 29–30;
    terror retaliation, 226, 245–46,
    314–15; Thomas relationship, 38,
    43–46, 460, 463; torpedoes, 387–89,
    441, 448; views Atlanta destruction,
    69, 87, 91; weather acumen, 57–58,
    127
Sherwood, Frederick, 270
Shull, John S., 96
Shuttinger, Louis, 431
Sloan, Thomas S., 500
Slocum, Henry W., 42–43, 48–49, 62,
    69, 78, 119, 140, 141, 162, 171, 184,
    272, 373, 407, 453, 467, 472–73,
    481, 501, 528, 531, 539
Smethurst, John, 247
Smith, Giles A., 219, 224, 230–31
Smith, Gustavus W., 125, 129, 197, 199,
    204, 215, 368, 400, 451, 493–94;
    seeks Sherman protection for family,
    517
Smith, John E., 192, 272, 313
Smith, Milo, 196
Smith, Robert F., 257
Snelling, David R., 187–88
Social Circle, Ga., 120, 125–26, 142
Southern Telegraph Company, 419, 533
Spanish moss, 267, 374, 448
Spencer, George, 116, 163
Spier's Turnout (CRR No. 11), 281
Spring Hill, Tenn., 300

Springfield, Ga., 363–64
Stanley, T. N., 434
Stanton, Edwin, 41; Savannah visit,
    519–21
Statesboro, Ga., December 4 fight, 332
Stiles, Robert M., 485–86
Stockbridge, Ga., 100, 101; November
    15 fight, 84; November 16 fight, 93
Stoneman, George, 150, 165
Stone Mountain, Ga., 82, 91, 92, 96
Storrow, Samuel, 325
Strathy Hall, 423
Strong, William E., 61, 265–66, 440
Stubbs family, 80
Swan (steamer), 492, 497
Sylvan Grove, Ga., 105, 117
Sylvania, Ga., 330, 349

Tarver, Judge, 294
Tattnall, Josiah, 491–2
Taylor, Richard, 128, 231; appointed to
    Macon defense, 103–4; Davis
    meeting, 9; declines to provide
    Georgia support, 9; Macon defense,
    193–3, 198, 199; reacts to
    Beauregard appointment, 9;
    reacts to Hood plan, 9
Taylor, Thomas, 193
Taylor, Zachary, 9
Tennessee troops (C.S.): infantry (24th
    Regiment, 167)
Tennille, Ga. (CRR No. 13), 247, 250,
    254, 255, 259, 270, 271, 273, 280
Texas troops: cavalry (8th Regiment,
    134, 185)
Thackeray, William, 19
Thomas Station, 328, 334, 528
Thomas, George H., 38, 41, 281,
    300–301, 447, 460–61, 475, 521,
    547; Nashville battle, 461–63;
    Sherman relationship, 38, 43–46,
    460, 463; worries about Tennessee
    defense, 42–46
Toombs, Robert A., 95, 112, 199, 323
Toomsboro, Ga. (CRR No. 15), 228
Towaliga River, 108
Travis, Tillie, 14–5, 134–5
Trego, Alfred, 220, 272

Il Trovatore, 88
Turkey Roost Swamp, 377. *See also* Monteith Swamp
Turnwold plantation, 170. *See also* Harris, Joel Chandler
Tybee Roads, 490

Union Causeway, 453, 473, 485, 487, 489, 503
United States Customs House, 498, 504

Vaughan, J. A., 432
Vaun, Mr., 176–77
Verdi, Giuseppe, 88
Vernon River, 423–24, 430

Walcutt, Charles C., 196, 198, 201, 202, 204–5, 209; wounded, 210
Walker, Edmund B., 15–16, 141
Wallace, William, 120
Walnut Creek, 165–8
Walthourville, Ga., 477
Ward, William T., "Old Shaky," 370
Ware, V. Thornton, 495
Wayne, Henry C., 150, 178n, 180, 191–92, 216–18, 227–28, 229–30, 251, 253–54, 313, 323, 330
Waynesboro, Ga., 19, 22, 278, 347; December 4 battle, 334–44
weather, 57–58, 127
Weller, John, 80, 84, 217, 218, 219, 224
Wellman, D. L., 406
Wells, Johnny, 305–6, 313
Wentz, F. J., 338
Wheeler, Joseph, 39, 125, 129, 276, 347, 375, 486, 540–41; Beauregard considers replacing, 256; combat, 102, 157, 285–91, 361–62; command decisions, 63, 174, 195, 200, 232, 247, 264, 276–77; described, 63, 256; Ebenezer Creek incident, 383; foraging excesses, 112–13, 294, 375, 541–42; foraging policy, 85; Griswoldville actions, 195–200;

Macon defense, 151, 157, 168; ordered into South Carolina, 419; reports on Federal advance, 64–65, 83, 93, 111–12, 129, 312; Reynolds plantation fight, 288–89; Rocky Creek fight, 319–20; Sandersville fight, 256–59, 260; seeks guidance, 112; Waynesboro, 278, 334–44
Whitehead, Catherine, 277–78
Whitfield, Matthew, 153
Widney, Lyman, 318–19
Wilcox, M. K., 215
William (slave), 20, 505
Williams, Alpheus S., 69, 453, 479, 515
Williams, William F., 215
Williamson, James A., 365
Wilson, Kline, 363
Winder, John H., 448
Winegar, Charles E., 415–16, 479
Wisconsin troops: artillery (10th Battery, 288, 336, 340–1), (12th Battery, 452); infantry (3rd Regiment, 98, 184, 380, 406–7, 414, 416, 419, 448, 453, 468, 484–85, 489), (12th Regiment, 364, 483), (16th Regiment, 364, 470), (21st Regiment, 135, 146, 452–53), (22nd Regiment, 282, 325, 414, 448), (26th Regiment, 514), (31st Regiment, 98, 247, 379–80), (32nd Regiment, 390)
Womble, George, 21
Woodhull, Maxwell Van Zandt, 456–58
Woods, Charles R., 196
Work, Henry Clay, 536–8
Wright's Bridge, 358, 365–6
Wright, Ambrose Ransom, 189, 400, 491
Wright, Oscar, 176
Wrightsville, Ga., 282
W. W. Coit (steamer), 509

Yellow River, 97, 110, 118, 120, 127, 135

Zachry family, 126